POWERING TO THE RESCUE

A history of the Royal National Lifeboat Institution's steam and motor lifeboats

Nicholas Leach

LIFEBOAT LISTS

	Steam lifeboats	11
	Motor lifeboat conversions	15
1	Self-righting motor	20
2	Norfolk & Suffolk motor	22
3	Watson motor 38ft-43ft	25
4	Self-righting motor 40ft	29
5	Watson motor 45ft	34
6	Self-righting motor 35ft	48
7	Barnett 60ft twin screw	50
8	Ramsgate	54
9	Watson cabin motor 45ft 6in	56
10	Barnett 'Stromness' motor 51ft	60
11	Fast lifeboat 64ft	64
12	Self-righting motor 35ft 6in	66
13	Liverpool motor single-engined	72
14	Beach 'Aldeburgh' motor 41ft	78
15	Watson motor 41ft	80
16	Surf motor 32ft	84
17	Watson cabin motor 46ft	88
18	Harbour 28ft	95
19	Liverpool motor twin-engined	96
20	46ft 9in Watson cabin motor	106
21	52ft Barnett	112
22	42ft Watson motor	118
23	47ft Watson cabin motor	122
24	37ft Oakley	128
25	37ft 6in Rother	128
26	48ft 6in Oakley	138
27	48ft 6in Solent	141
28	Clyde cruising	144
29	44ft Waveney	152
30	Keith Nelson	157
31	50ft Thames	158
32	52ft Arun	160
33	33ft Brede	168
34	Medina	172
35	47ft Tyne	180
36	12m Mersey	190
37	17m Severn	198
38	14m Trent	208
39	16m Tamar	214
40	13m Shannon	220
	A class	234
	B class	238
	C class	244
	D class	248
	E class	254

Contents

	Introduction	5
1	Steam power	7
2	The first steps to motorisation	13
3	Twin engines and diesels	39
4	Rebuilding after 1945	101
5	The quest for speed	147
6	Into the twenty-first century	175
7	Inshore Lifeboats	231
	Lifeboats on display	260
	Index	262
	Bibliography	264

ISBN 978191177579

© Nicholas Leach 2019

The rights of Nicholas Leach to be identified as the Author of this work have been asserted in accordance with the Copyrights, Designs and Patents Act 1988. All rights reserved. No part of this book may be reprinted or reproduced or utilised in any form or by any electronic, mechanical or other means, now known or hereafter invented, including photocopying and recording, or in any information storage or retrieval system, without permission in writing from the publishers.

This is a non-official RNLI publication. Any views or opinions expressed in this publication are solely those of the author and do not necessarily represent those of the RNLI.

Published by Lily Publications Ltd, PO Box 33, Ramsey, Isle of Man; tel +44 (0) 1624 898446
www: lilypublications.co.uk

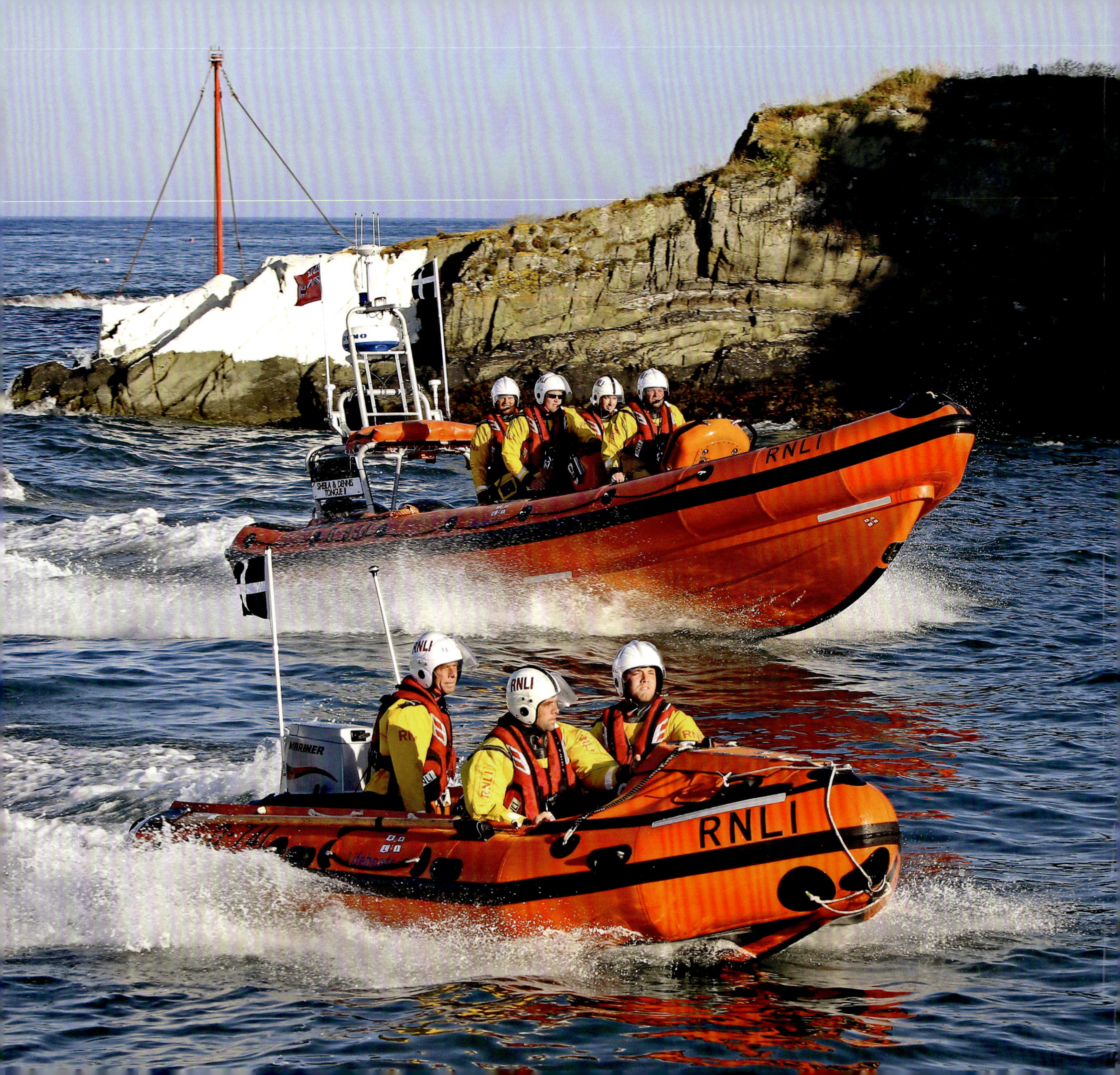
RNLI
MARINER
RNLI

Introduction

The Royal National Lifeboat Institution's (RNLI) most sophisticated all-weather class of lifeboat, the 13m Shannon, powering along at twenty-five knots, is an extremely impressive sight. The modern technology employed throughout the lifeboat's advanced design provides its volunteer crew with a safe and sophisticated tool to face the worst of weathers and deal with the wide range of casualties at sea typical of the modern era. The advanced technology used in the Shannon makes rescue at sea safer than ever, and it is hard to compare such a rescue craft with its predecessors when recalling how, more than a century ago, the RNLI tentatively began the first experiments to provide power for lifeboats.

Indeed, comparing the Shannon, or its bigger fleetmates, the 16m Tamar and 17m Severn, with the early motor lifeboats might lead to the conclusion that they have little or nothing in common. But in fact, the lifeboat designs of the twenty-first century are the culmination not only of more than two centuries of lifeboat development, as designers have sought to find a coastal lifeboat that best fits the purpose of saving 'those in peril on the sea', but also of more than a century of motor lifeboat development. In the twenty-first century technology has been harnessed to provide rescue craft for Britain's lifeboat crews that are second to none, and ensure that the volunteers around the RNLI's network of more than 230 lifeboat stations can respond to incidents quickly, safely and efficiently. And it is testament to the advances in design, construction and capability of lifeboats, as well as the high standard of training, that it is almost forty years since any lifeboat crew member was lost on service.

This book traces the developments in powered lifeboat design that have taken place since the 1890s, when the first steam lifeboats entered service, and lists in chronological order all of the RNLI's motor lifeboats by type. It describes how the first motor lifeboats, which were essentially pulling and sailing craft fitted with rather basic and often unreliable engines, were developed, built and trialled, and examines the first purpose-designed and -built motor lifeboats, all of which were single-engined, which entered service just before the outbreak of war in 1914.

During the inter-war period came the first the twin-engined craft, with twin propellers and rudimentary crew shelters. The story then moves to the post-war era and the RNLI's efforts to rebuild the fleet, through to the introduction of faster lifeboats in the 1960s and the subsequent provision of an all-weather fleet of twenty-five-knot lifeboats in the twenty-first century. The volume ends with a chapter on inshore lifeboats, which are often widely regarded as the workhorses of the fleet.

The sections detailing individual motor lifeboat classes include representative photographs of members of each class, together with diagrams and listings of boats; in the lists, ON stands for Official Number, a consecutive number given to every lifeboat since 1886, and Op No for Operational Number, which can be seen on the bow of modern lifeboats.

▲ The 16m Tamar Diamond Jubilee (ON.1303) on exercise off the Sussex coast in February 2018. Before taking up operational duties at Eastbourne, she took part in the Thames Pageant on 3 June 2012 as part of the celebrations of the Diamond Jubilee of Queen Elizabeth II. (Nicholas Leach)

◀◀ The inshore lifeboats stationed at Looe, Cornwall, the D class inflatable Ollie Naismith (D-741) and the Atlantic 85 Sheila & Dennis Tongue II (B-894), returning to harbour. (Nicholas Leach)

Acknowledgements

May people have assisted with this volume: Hayley Whiting and Joanna Bellis at the RNLI Heritage Trust have facilitated my research at the RNLI's headquarters in Poole on many occasions, and I am grateful for their time and support; the line drawings mostly come from the RNLI's collections. The records of the late Grahame Farr, and his pioneering work to document lifeboat history, proved invaluable in tracing the lineage of motor lifeboat development; as did the work of Jeff Morris, archivist of the Lifeboat Enthusiasts' Society for many years. Martin Fish, Tony Denton and Richie Leonard all offered help and advice during the preparation of this volume, for which I am grateful. Many people contributed photographs and illustrations, and I would like to thank Nathan Williams at the RNLI's Film & Image team for providing suitable images when requested; Hayley Whiting and Joe Williams for supplying images from the historic Beken collection; and John Harrop, Iain Booth and Peter Edey for supplying photographs and postcards. I owe a huge debt of gratitude to the crews and personnel at lifeboat stations around the United Kingdom and Ireland, who have been so hospitable and welcoming during my numerous visits to the coast, and who have enabled me to take many of the photographs contained in this volume.

Nicholas Leach, Lichfield, September 2019

Timeline

1890
The first steam lifeboat, Duke of Northumberland, enters service; five more steam-powered lifeboats are built by the RNLI

1894
First gasoline-powered car in the United Kingdom built by Santler from Malvern heralds the start of the era of the internal combustion engine

1901
Unique steam tug Helen Peele enters service at Padstow, working in tandem with a large sailing lifeboat

1904
First lifeboat to be fitted with a motor, J. McConnel Hussey, undertakes trials

1909
The RNLI's first purpose-built motor lifeboats enter service, making an epic journey north to their respective stations in Orkney

1914
Rohilla rescue off Whitby proves the benefits of motor lifeboats

1920
First experiments with caterpillar tractor for launching lifeboats

1923
First twin-engined motor lifeboat enters service at New Brighton (below)

1930
The fast motor lifeboat Sir William Hillary arrives at the newly reopened Dover station; she was unique and served for just a decade

1936
The last lifeboat launch using horses takes place at Wells; motorised tractors take over from horse for carriage-launching lifeboats

1936
The rescue of the Daunt Rock lightvessel by Ballycotton lifeboat Mary Stanford and her crew earns Coxswain Patrick Sliney a Gold medal after he and his crew spend fifty hours at sea in gale-force winds (above)

1939
Outbreak of Second World War, which sees the almost complete cessation of lifeboat construction due to wartime pressures

1940
On 30 May 1940 two RNLI crews join the little ships for Operation Dynamo at Dunkirk, with nineteen RNLI lifeboat also involved

1958
The 37ft Oakley class is introduced, the first design of lifeboat which has an inherent self-righting capability and yet is also stable when afloat

1963
Inflatable inshore lifeboats introduced; radar is first fitted to offshore lifeboats

1964
The first of a new breed of fast lifeboat, the 44ft Waveney, designed and built in America, arrives for trials around the UK and Ireland

1967
The first British Waveneys enter service, having been built in Lowestoft; a total of twenty-two of the boats are completed

1969
Longhope lifeboat T.G.B. capsizes on service in the Pentland Firth in March, with the loss of eight crew members

1970
Fraserburgh lifeboat Duchess of Kent capsizes on service in January with the loss of five crew members; this, and the Longhope tragedy, results in the RNLI embarking on a programme of building a fleet of self-righting lifeboats

1971
The 52ft Arun class lifeboat, with a top speed of eighteen knots, is introduced; the last of the 46 Aruns is completed in 1990

1972
The rigid-inflatable Atlantic 21 inshore lifeboat is introduced into service

1981
Penlee lifeboat Solomon Browne and her eight crew are lost trying to save those on the coaster Union Star in atrocious conditions off the Cornish coast in December

1982
The 47ft Tyne class lifeboat introduced, designed for slipway launching

1983
After a year of trials, the first Talus MB-H launching tractor enters service at Hoylake

1988
The 12m Mersey class (below) introduced, designed for carriage launching, as the RNLI embarks upon a programme of operating fast all-weather lifeboats at every station

1991-92
The 14m Trent and 17m Severn classes are developed, and introduced a couple of years later, having been designed to lie afloat

2001
The first inland lifeboat station, at Lough Erne in County Fermanagh, Northern Ireland, is established, becoming the RNLI's first non-tidal inshore lifeboat station (above)

2002
The RNLI begin operating lifeboats on the tidal reaches of the River Thames on 2 January from lifeboat stations at Chiswick, Gravesend, Teddington and Tower

2002
Inshore rescue hovercraft joins the RNLI fleet to carry out rescue work in areas inaccessible to conventional lifeboats

2006
The 16m Tamar class is introduced, designed to be launched down slipways; the boats are fitted with a SIMS computer system; a total of twenty-seven of the boats are completed

2013
The 13m Shannon class is introduced; it is the first RNLI all-weather lifeboat type to be propelled by waterjets, and is designed to be launched from a carriage, replacing the Mersey

2014
The first 13m Shannon class lifeboat enters service at Dungeness

2015
The All-weather Lifeboat Centre (ALC) at Poole begins operations, building six new Shannon lifeboats per annum

Chapter 1
Steam power

Steam power

▲ The first steam lifeboat Duke of Northumberland (ON.231), which was built in 1889, on trials in the early 1890s (right). The print depicting the lifeboat (above) was used in many contemporary publications.

▼ Plans of Duke of Northumberland accompanied extensive descriptions which were published in contemporary engineering magazines when the boat was completed. She went on to have a highly successful life-saving career.

Since its foundation in 1824, the RNLI has been continually seeking to design and build the best possible lifeboat for service off the coasts of the United Kingdom and Ireland. For over a century prior to the first powered lifeboats, lifeboatmen using pulling and sailing lifeboats performed remarkable feats of life-saving. Crews would often row quite small lifeboats through heavy seas to reach a casualty. As advances were made in boat design and naval architecture during the nineteenth century, more sophisticated lifeboats were developed, with drop keels, water ballast tanks and sails all being introduced. However, when heading into wind and sea, a pulling and sailing lifeboat struggled. The answer was some form of power, and during the latter years of the century the first mechanical lifeboats, powered by steam engines, were introduced.

Steam had been used to power vessels since the 1820s, and steam packets plying their trade on coastal routes and to the continent became an increasingly common sight in Britain's ports as the century progressed. Although the use of steam power in a lifeboat offered significant advantages over a lifeboat relying on sails, oars, or a combination of the two, it was not until almost the end of the century that a steam lifeboat became a reality for the RNLI. Designing and building a steam-powered lifeboat presented designers with a completely different set of problems to those of pulling lifeboats. Since 1825 the idea of a steam lifeboat had been discussed, but none of the proposals had been deemed suitable.

At a number of ports, notably Ramsgate, Gorleston and Lowestoft on the east coast, pulling and sailing lifeboats often worked in conjunction with local steam tugs. Many coxswains and crews regarded this as an ideal arrangement, as the close-quarter manoeuvrability of a pulling lifeboat when attending a wreck was better, they believed, than that of a larger and more cumbersome steam tug. The benefits of the steam tug and lifeboat combination were clearly demonstrated during the service to the barque Indian Chief, one of the most famous rescues in the RNLI's history.

The barque went aground on the Long Sand at the mouth of the Thames at 2am on 6 January 1881 and slowly began to break up forcing the crew to take to the rigging. Both Harwich and Clacton sailing lifeboats were launched, but neither found the casualty despite many hours searching. Just after midday, Ramsgate's lifeboat Bradford, a large 44ft self-righter intended primarily for sailing, set out. She was towed by the steam-paddler Vulcan for thirty miles until she reached the casualty, by when it was dark.

Throughout the passage, the lifeboat crew faced biting winds and heavy seas as their open lifeboat offered no shelter from the elements. As the steamer and lifeboat cruised between the Sands amid the full fury of the storm, the steamer sustained some damage to her deck housing, but at daybreak, under her own sail, the lifeboat negotiated the seas around the wreck and succeeded in rescuing the remaining survivors. She then sailed back across the Sands to Vulcan and both vessels returned to Ramsgate, having been away for more than twenty-four hours. The Gold medal was awarded to Coxswain Charles Fish and various other awards went to his crew for a remarkable rescue which no pulling and sailing lifeboat could have performed on its own.

But, however good tugs were at getting a lifeboat to the scene of a wreck, they were not widely available and considerable effort was still required on the part of the lifeboat crews to complete a rescue, the outcome of which was not always successful. The inadequacies of the pulling lifeboat were demonstrated in 1883 during a rescue off the coast of Anglesey. On 31 April 1883, the Greenock barque Norman Court went ashore on rocks in a heavy gale and sunk, forcing her crew to take to the rigging. At dawn the following day, the Rhosneigr lifeboat Thomas Lingham, a small 30ft self-

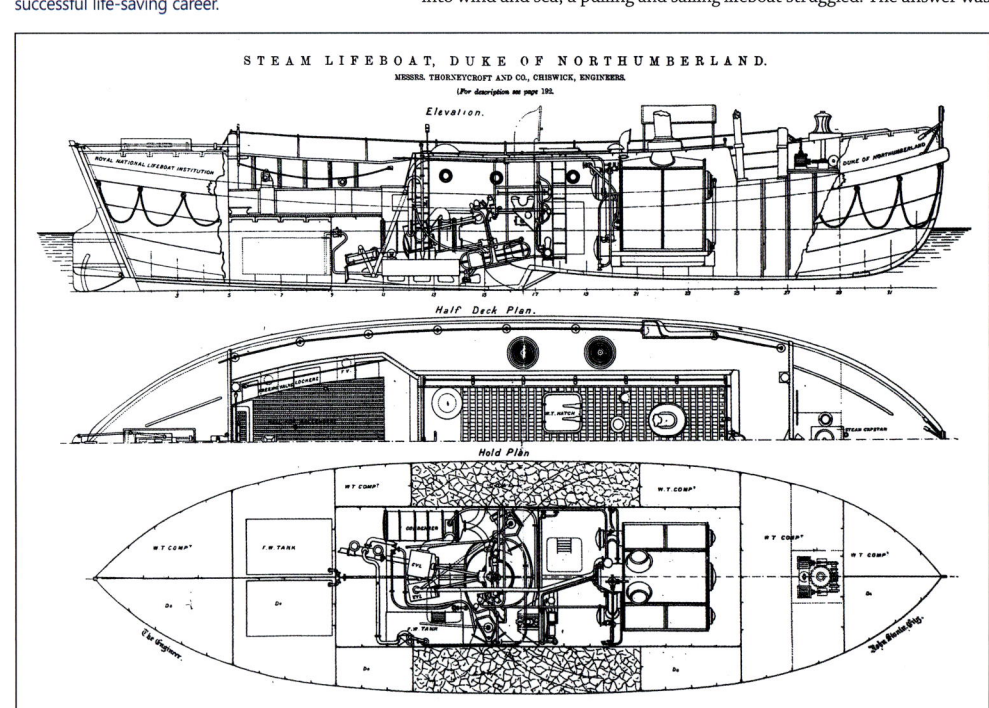

8   MOTOR LIFEBOATS

Steam power

righting type, was launched but failed to effect a rescue after being nearly overwhelmed in terrible conditions and forced to return to station.

Later in the day, a second launch was attempted, but in the heavy breakers the boat could not get to sea. As tugs were on hand at Holyhead, a few miles round the coast, the lifeboat Thomas Fielden, a larger 37ft self-righter stationed at Holyhead, was towed to the scene by the steam tug Challenge. The lifeboat was brought to within a mile of the wreck, at which point she cast off from the tug. But in the severe weather, under oars and sail, the lifeboat could not get close enough to save the stranded men and was forced back. A third attempt was therefore made to launch the Rhosneigr lifeboat. Manned by a Holyhead crew, she finally got away, and succeeded in saving twenty people from the barque after considerable exertion. Following this very arduous rescue, Holyhead Coxswain Thomas Roberts was awarded the Silver medal in recognition of his efforts.

The Norman Court incident showed the difficulties and challenges of using not only pulling lifeboats but also steam tugs for rescue work, and within five years of this rescue the RNLI's Committee of Management was considering steam power for lifeboat use. Although doubts remained about the efficiency of a steam lifeboat, the potential advantages it offered over the pulling and sailing boats convinced the Institution to go ahead with construction. Advances in engineering techniques during the 1880s meant that building a steam-powered lifeboat was feasible and, in June 1888, plans submitted by R. & H. Green, shipbuilders of Blackwall, were taken up, and the RNLI ordered Green to build a steam lifeboat.

The new lifeboat, named Duke of Northumberland (ON.231), was launched from her builder's yard on the Thames on 31 May 1889 to make

▲ The second City of Glasgow (ON.446) moored at Harwich, the station she served from 1901 to 1917. She was the last steam lifeboat to be built by the RNLI. After her life-saving service, she was sold to the Admiralty and, renamed Patrick, was converted into a patrol boat.

Steam power

▶ Generic plans of the three screw-propelled steam lifeboat from the RNLI's Annual Reports, circa 1900-27. The diagrams show the master after the funnel as it appeared on James Stevens No.4 (ON.421), City of Glasgow (ON.362) and James Stevens No.3 (ON.420).

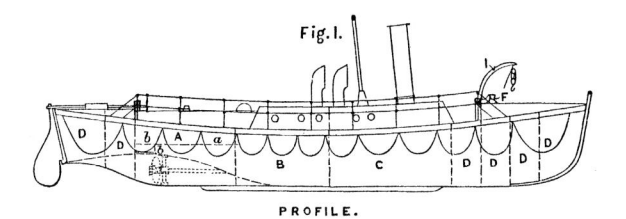

▶ A rare photograph of James Stevens No.4 (ON.421) getting up steam. She was built for Padstow, entering service in February 1899, but was wrecked on service on 11 April 1900 with the loss of eight of her crew; she was later brought ashore and broken up. (By courtesy of Padstow RNLI)

▼ The 1897-built steam lifeboat Queen (ON.404) served the busy New Brighton station on the Mersey, where she is pictured with her crew wearing cork life-jackets. (By courtesy of the RNLI)

her first trial trip. The Thornycroft engine with which she was fitted, with its 'patent tubulous pattern' boiler, produced 170hp and drove hydraulic pumps, which were in effect an early form of water jet. On 4 August 1890 the new lifeboat was taken to the Maplin measured mile for speed trials, during which she averaged more than nine knots. With a full bunker, of three tons of coal, her radius of action was 254 miles at eight and a half knots. She was sent to Harwich in September 1890 and undertook her first service less than a month later, on 8 October, when she towed the station's 38ft self-righting lifeboat Reserve No.3 to the Cork Sand to stand by the brigantine Ada, of Faversham, which had gone aground.

During the next decade, the RNLI had further steam lifeboats built. The next, completed in 1894, was larger than Duke of Northumberland at 53ft in length and was named City of Glasgow (ON.362). A third steam boat, named Queen to mark Queen Victoria's 60th anniversary, was launched in June 1897, and both these new vessels were driven by hydraulic pumps. The RNLI ordered three more steam lifeboats but, having reviewed the method of propulsion, employed screws rather than hydraulic pumps because it was found that the hydraulic propulsion did not give the boats sufficient speed. Screw propulsion had originally been rejected in the late 1880s, because of the possibility of the propeller being damaged, but a tunnel was incorporated into the hull which provided the necessary protection to the propellers.

Two further boats, sisterships and 56ft 6in in length, were ordered in January 1898 from J.S. White of Cowes. Named James Stevens No.3 (ON.420) and James Stevens No.4 (ON.421), having been provided from a large legacy left to the RNLI in 1894 from the estate of an Edgbaston property developer in Birmingham, the first was sent to Grimsby, to cover the Humber estuary, and the other to Padstow for working off the treacherous Cornish coast. A sixth and final steam lifeboat, named City of Glasgow (ON.446) and identical to the other two screw-powered boats, was ordered in 1901 to serve at Harwich, an important station which covered the outlying sandbanks at the north end of the Thames Estuary.

Steam lifeboats offered many benefits. Not only were they able to head into the wind, but they could also tow a pulling lifeboat to the scene of a casualty, stay at sea for longer than a pulling lifeboat and had a far greater range. But they also had their drawbacks. Their size, 50ft in length and more than thirty tons in weight, restricted the number of places where they could be stationed. They had to be kept afloat at a time when lifeboats were operated from moorings only as a last resort, as anti-fouling paints were not as effective as they later became.

Getting the necessary steam up before setting out could take twenty minutes and even then they were comparatively slow, making no more than seven knots in practice, despite achieving higher speeds during trials. Manning was also problematic as they required specialist engineers to service the boiler, while their relatively large draught meant they were not ideal for shallow water operations. Construction costs were higher too,

Steam power

working out more than three times greater than the cost of an average Watson sailing lifeboat. But despite these handicaps, steam lifeboats remained in use for almost three decades, saved more than 600 lives in total and performed some excellent rescues.

At Gorleston, the much-travelled James Stevens No.3, which went to the station in 1903, undertook an outstanding service on 15 January 1905 that proved steam lifeboats could operate in the worst of weathers. She went to a vessel in distress four miles south of Gorleston in a severe south-easterly gale with freezing temperatures. In charge was Coxswain Sydney Harris, who later said that he had never before experienced seas as bad. But in spite of the horrendous conditions, the steam lifeboat battled her way out of harbour, frequently disappearing from view in mountainous seas, and found the brig Celerity, of Lowestoft, dragging her anchors and in danger. With outstanding seamanship, Coxswain Harris manoeuvred the lifeboat up to the brig and, despite their vessel rolling and heaving, the lifeboat crew got a line aboard. The brig's crew of six were then brought to safety, the line was cut and the lifeboat pulled clear.

When the lifeboat arrived at the harbour entrance, extremely heavy seas were breaking across it, so Coxswain Harris dropped anchor in the Roads to await an improvement in conditions. On the lifeboat, rescuers and rescued endured repeated soakings as waves swept over them, with water freezing on the decks. Eventually, shortly after 2am, Harris took the lifeboat into the harbour with tremendous skill. For his outstanding seamanship, he was awarded the Silver medal, but the rescue could not have been achieved without the skill of the boat's engineers and firemen. They had to remain in the engine room throughout and in recognition of his courage, determination and fine leadership, the Chief Engineer, James Sclanders, was awarded the Silver medal.

The first steam lifeboat, Duke of Northumberland, was involved in a Gold medal-winning rescue when she was stationed at Holyhead. On 22 February 1908 she put to sea just after 2pm to go to the aid of the steamship Harold, a small seventy-five-ton vessel, which was being driven towards the shore between the North and South Stacks in atrocious weather, with winds of over eighty miles per hour, conditions in which a pulling and sailing lifeboat would have struggled. But in the mountainous seas, Duke of Northumberland forged ahead, with Coxswain William Owen using all his skill, courage and experience to keep the lifeboat on course as she fought her way through the worst seas he had ever encountered.

In such severe weather the crew who worked the boilers below, battened down in the stoke hold, went through a terrible ordeal during this rescue as, for over two hours, Coxswain Owen fought to get the lifeboat close enough to save the crew of Harold. Eventually, with outstanding skill and courage, he manoeuvred the lifeboat close enough for a line to be thrown across to the steamer and seven men were hauled through the churning water, one at a time, to the safety of the lifeboat.

At this point, a huge wave suddenly caught the lifeboat and swept her towards the steamer, threatening to smash the craft together. Desperately, Coxswain Owen fought to avert a total disaster, but as the two boats were touching the last two men were snatched from Harold. The rope was cut and Owen called for full speed on the speaking tube to the engine room, so the lifeboat could pull away into deeper water. The lifeboat, crew and survivors faced more heavy seas as they negotiated the dark coast before harbour was reached, but Duke of Northumberland got back to port safely.

RNLI STEAM LIFEBOATS

ON	Year Builder	Length Breadth	Name Donor	Engines	Stations (launches/lives saved) Notes/disposal
231	1889 R. & H. Green	50' 14'3"	**Duke of Northumberland** RNLI Funds.	1x170hp water pump single screw	Harwich 1890-92 (15/33); Holyhead 1892-93 (6/9); New Brighton 1893-7 (29/14); Holyhead 1897-1922 (125/239)
362	1894 R. & H. Green	53' 16'	**City of Glasgow** City of Glasgow Lifeboat Fund.	1x200hp scoop single screw	Harwich No.2 1894-97 (23/4) Gorleston 1897-98 (1/0) Harwich 1898-1901 (5/28)
404	1897 J. I. Thornycroft	55' 16'6"	**Queen** RNLI Funds.	1x198hp water pump single screw	New Brighton No.2 1897-1923 (81/196)
420	1898 J. S. White, Cowes	56'6" 15'9"	**James Stevens No.3** Legacy of James Stevens, Birmingham.	1x180hp compound single screw	Grimsby 1898-1903 (6/0); Gorleston 1903-08 (37/30); Angle 1908-15 (12/5); Totland 1915-19 (6/0); Dover 1919-22 (5/1); Holyhead 22-28 (20/18)
421	1899 J. S. White, Cowes	56'6" 15'9"	**James Stevens No.4** Legacy of James Stevens, Birmingham.	1x180hp compound single screw	Padstow 1899-1900 (4/9); Capsized and wrecked on service, 11.4.1900, eight lost
446	1901 J. S. White, Cowes	56'6" 15'9"	**City of Glasgow** City of Glasgow Lifeboat Fund.	1x180hp compound single screw	Harwich 1901-1917 (98/87)
478	1901 Ramage & Ferguson	95'6" 19'6"	**Helen Peele** Legacy of Mr C. J. Peele, Chertsey.	2x331hp compound twin screw	Padstow 1901-29 (steam tug working in conjunction with pulling & sailing lifeboat, 19/10 on own account)

◀ The first screw-propelled steam lifeboat James Stevens No.3 (ON.420) returning to Gorleston from a salvage mission. When built, she had the mast in front of the funnels, but it was later placed abaft the funnel as the steadying sail tended to cause smoke to obstruct the View from the helm.

MOTOR LIFEBOATS

Steam power

▶ The 59ft 10in steam lifeboat-cum-pilot vessel Princess of Wales, pictured on the Thames, was built in 1903 for the Crown Agents at Mauritius by Thornycroft and Co at Chiswick. She was screw-propelled and her 142hp engines gave her a speed of nine and a half knots. (From an old postcard supplied by Iain Booth)

The RNLI account stated that the 'service was attended by the greatest danger, as the lifeboat was at times in imminent peril of being driven against the disabled ship'. The crew's considerable efforts, together with the Coxswain's gallantry and skilful management, resulted in Coxswain Owen being awarded the Gold medal for his truly outstanding courage, skill and seamanship, with each of the eleven engine-room staff and crew members being awarded the Silver medal.

As well as steam lifeboats, a unique steam tug was developed for service at Padstow in the early years of the twentieth century. Named Helen Peele, the craft, which measured 95ft 6in by 19ft, was built in Scotland specifically to deal with the unusual conditions on the North Cornwall coast which had led to the disaster to James Stevens No.4. The RNLI decided not to replace the wrecked steam lifeboat, but to substitute for it a sailing lifeboat towed by a steam tug, which was specially designed for the purpose by George Lennox Watson, the RNLI's Consulting Naval Architect. This move resulted in the creation of a unique set-up at Padstow, with the operation of the only steam tug the RNLI ever built.

The tug was built of steel, fitted with a Scotch boiler and two sets of direct-acting, inverted compound condensing marine engines, indicating collectively 300hp with natural draught, and 400hp collectively with mild forced draught, and these drove twin screws. During her trials, she developed a speed of over ten knots, which was regarded as 'very satisfactory'. Built by Ramage and Ferguson Ltd, of Leith, she was launched from their yard on 28 June 1901, with trials taking place between 2 and 5 September 1901. These proved to be satisfactory, and showed the new tug with her twin screws to be very manoeuvrable when going both ahead and astern, with speed runs also undertaken on the measured mile. Helen Peele arrived at Padstow in September 1901 and operated in conjunction with the 42ft twelve-oared self-righting lifeboat Edmund Harvey (ON.475), serving the station for the best part of thirty years, with the steam tug credited with saving twenty lives on her own account.

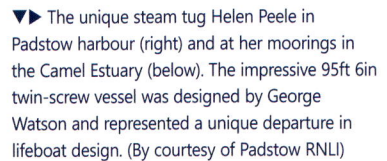

▼▶ The unique steam tug Helen Peele in Padstow harbour (right) and at her moorings in the Camel Estuary (below). The impressive 95ft 6in twin-screw vessel was designed by George Watson and represented a unique departure in lifeboat design. (By courtesy of Padstow RNLI)

MOTOR LIFEBOATS

Chapter 2
The first steps to motorisation

The first steps to motorisation

◀ (chapter frontispiece) The second Norfolk & Suffolk motor lifeboat, H.F. Bailey (ON.670), was built for Cromer but served at Great Yarmouth & Gorleston for most of her career. She measured 46ft 6in in length, making her one of the largest motor lifeboats of her era, and carried a full set of sails. (By courtesy of the RNLI)

▼ The first motor lifeboat, J. McConnell Hussey (ON.343), undergoing her self-righting trials after she had been fitted with an engine in 1904. The box housing the motor can be seen amidships. (From an old photo supplied by Jeff Morris)

As the shortcomings of steam power when applied to lifeboats in operational conditions became evident during the 1890s, the RNLI's designers turned to the newly-invented internal combustion engine, which offered greater promise. Petrol-driven engines, developed during the second half of the nineteenth century, had powered motor vehicles since the 1880s and, by the 1900s, it was inevitable that motor power, in the form of the internal combustion engine, would be applied to sea rescue. The RNLI's Committee of Management, according to The Lifeboat (journal of the RNLI) of 1 August 1904, had been examining 'the successful employment of a motor in a Life-boat, so as to assist by mechanical means, and thus relieve some of the tremendous work entailed by getting a Life-boat to a wreck against wind and sea.'

By this time, the Committee believed that the motor had been developed from a 'more or less unreliable and often capricious machine' to one with 'nearly all its previous faults eliminated, and ready for use afloat'. Preparations were made for its introduction into the lifeboat fleet and, in the autumn of 1903, George Lennox Watson, the RNLI's Consulting Naval Architect, was asked to determine the best way to develop a motor lifeboat. Watson, who had already formulated a successful sailing lifeboat design and produced plans on which several steam lifeboats were based, decided that an existing lifeboat should be motorised.

The conversion project was entrusted to Captain E. du Boulay, of Thellusson & Co, who had experience of fitting engines into yachts. The Folkestone lifeboat J. McConnell Hussey (ON.343), a 38ft self-righting type built in 1893 and pulled by twelve oars, was chosen to be converted and was taken to Guy's yard at Cowes, where the motor was fitted. The work necessitated major alterations to the boat, starting with the fitting of a watertight mahogany box amidships to house the 11hp two-cylinder Fay & Bowen petrol engine and its associated equipment. The motor drove a three-bladed propeller through a long shaft, via a disconnecting clutch. The petrol was contained in a metal tank inside the forward end box and sufficient fuel was carried for over ten hours of continuous running.

The technical problems that had to be overcome to successfully operate an engine on a lifeboat were complex and numerous. The engine had to start easily under any conditions and be capable of surviving severe motion when operating in heavy seas, while the propellers might at times be out of the water. It had to be housed in a casing that was watertight, in case of capsize, but not airtight because the carburettor needed a supply of air. The risk of fire had to be minimised and the engine's lubricating system had to be self-maintaining. The propellers themselves had to be carefully considered so that they were located in a position on the hull which would prevent their damage during launching and when working either in shallow waters or round floating wreckage.

None of these problems proved insurmountable, and once they had been solved, lifeboats powered by the internal combustion engine represented the future for lifeboat design, with powered lifeboats offering considerable advantages over their pulling counterparts. They could sail into the wind, giving them a far greater and more flexible operational scope; approach a casualty from any direction (not just to windward); had considerably better manoeuvrability; and could be operated by fewer crew. Another benefit, albeit achievable in the long term, was the gradual removal of sails, which took up valuable space on board and required considerable expertise to deploy.

Once J. McConnell Hussey had been fitted with an engine, she was subjected to a series of trials during April 1904, including using the engine as auxiliary to the sails. Her speed on the measured mile, with full crew and stores on board, was just over six knots. She underwent four capsize trials, and each time successfully righted herself with the motor stopping automatically after the boat had heeled over just beyond 'her beam ends'.

In November 1904 she was sent to Newhaven for station evaluation, where she spent six months being tested under operational conditions. Although she was not called upon to perform any services, the coxswain and crew were so impressed by her performance that they asked for their own lifeboat, Michael Henry (ON.407), to be converted to motor. The RNLI acceded to the crew's wishes and, on 5 July 1905, ordered an engine from Thornycroft at Chiswick so Michael Henry could be motorised. Two further engines were also ordered so that two other lifeboats could be similarly converted. On 19 July 1905 a 30bhp engine was ordered from Tylor for the 42ft self-righter Bradford, built in 1893, recently replaced

The first steps to motorisation

at Ramsgate and then renamed Reserve No.2, and on 5 August 1905 a 40bhp motor was ordered from Blake for the 43ft Norfolk & Suffolk boat at Walton-on-the-Naze, James Stevens No.14 (ON.432).

The conversion to motor of these four lifeboats during the 1904-06 period proved to be a difficult process. The engines were found to be unreliable at almost every stage and the RNLI's engineers had their work cut out repairing them, finding improvements necessary to make them function properly, as well as contend with working on the engines at sea, often in bad weather. During the trials, the engines frequently broke down, but even before the Walton-on-the-Naze boat's trials began the crank shaft and gear casing were found to be faulty during installation, and this delayed the completion of the conversion.

While she was on trials out of Harwich in November 1906, the Newhaven boat's sparking and air supply went wrong, causing the engine to stop, and the Reserve No.2 boat's first trials in June 1906 proved unsatisfactory when the reversing gear failed and the carburettor was found to be of the wrong type. Worse was to come for this boat after her self-righting trial on 2 August 1906; she righted after being deliberately turned over but when the engine was restarted an explosion ripped through the engine casing and the hatches were blown open. The explosion had been caused by petrol from the carburettor igniting. Fortunately nobody was hurt in the incident.

Although making the engines work reliably and efficiently in the conversions involved considerable effort, the RNLI's engineers and naval architects persevered and the boats were eventually returned to service. J. McConnell Hussey went to Tynemouth after her trials at Newhaven and on the Tyne a new problem had to be faced – crew mistrust of a motorised lifeboat. The Tynemouth crew was made up of local fishermen and pilots, who were very reluctant to man the motor boat and so, for the first eight months of her service in the north-east she was crewed by soldiers stationed at the nearby Clifford Fort in North Shields, commanded by Lieut Herbert Burton, an Officer of the Royal Engineers and an experienced yachtsman. However, gradually, after seeing the motor boat prove herself in action, the local men offered their services, although Burton remained in charge as Superintendent of the lifeboat.

After trials and tests of the converted boats and their engines, and in spite of these proving rather temperamental and unreliable at times, the RNLI's Committee of Management decided to meet the next challenge, that of constructing a purpose-built motor lifeboat. As early as 1905 it had been decided that the lifeboats destined for Fishguard, Stronsay, Stromness and Thurso would be built as motor lifeboats. In the event, the Thurso boat was completed without an engine, and the motor intended for her was placed into the Broughty Ferry boat instead.

In the November 1905 edition of The Lifeboat, it was explained: 'Fitting these lifeboats for motors entails considerable structural alterations, which have occupied a considerable time in carrying out, but as soon as all is completed, and the engines installed, a very interesting series of trials is anticipated.' Protecting the propeller from damage was a major concern for the naval architects, so a protective tunnel was built as far forward along the hull as possible.

The new motor lifeboats, all over 40ft in length, were built to either Watson's plans or the self-righting design with high end boxes and a narrow beam. The work of construction and testing lasted throughout

▲ The Newhaven lifeboat Michael Henry (ON.407), a 37ft self-righter built in 1897, was fitted with a 24hp Thornycroft engine in 1906; she was one of five pulling and sailing lifeboats converted to motor. (From and old photo supplied by Jeff Morris)

MOTOR LIFEBOAT CONVERSIONS

	ON	HP Cyl	RPM Weight	Engine maker Reverse gear	Max speed Fuel	Stations
1	343	11hp 2	500 24cwt	Fay & Bowen Durham Churchill	5.9 knots 12 pints/hour	Tynemouth Sunderland
2	350 (1907)	40hp 4 35hp 4	900 8cwt 900 18.5cwt	Briton Tylor Buffalo	 6.75 knots 18.5 pints/hour	Seaton Snook Teesmouth
3	407 (1913)	24hp 4 20hp 4	1,000 20cwt 1,000 12.25cwt	Thornycroft Thornycroft Gardner Gardner	6.8 knots 15.6 pints/hour	Newhaven Dunmore East
4	432	40hp 4	600 22.5cwt	Blake Caledonia	7.42 knots 20.4 pints	Walton & Frinton
5	463	40hp	700 32cwt	Tylor Gardner No.4	7.63 knots 40 pints/hour	Clacton-on-Sea Arranmore

MOTOR LIFEBOATS

The first steps to motorisation

1908 and not until 1909 did the Fishguard boat, the 40ft self-righter Charterhouse (ON.563), arrive at her station. Following this, the two boats destined for the Orkney stations of Stromness and Stronsay, John A. Hay (ON.561) and John Ryburn (ON.565), were sent north from the Thames in company with the pulling lifeboat for Thurso. The crew at Stromness were keen to have a motor lifeboat because the conditions they faced, in the treacherous Pentland Firth and also when they were just getting out of the harbour at Stromness, could be tackled effectively only by a powered lifeboat. That two motor lifeboats were sent to stations in Orkney suggests a far-sightedness in realising that motor lifeboats would be particularly effective at stations where heavy seas and strong currants were the norm, and often considerable distances – well beyond the range of a pulling lifeboat – had to be travelled to reach casualties.

John Ryburn and John A. Hay, together with the pulling lifeboat Sarah Austin (ON.585), left London Docks on 15 April 1909 and began an epic journey north under their own power. Hitherto, new lifeboats had usually been delivered to their station by steamship or railway, and so a sea voyage as far as Orkney was a major undertaking and a very challenging test for the new motor lifeboats. Although the boats eventually reached their stations safely, the passage had not been without incident, with the motors breaking down on several occasions and at one port of call, Aberdeen, the boats needing assistance from the local steam tug to reach harbour. The RNLI published a positive account of the journey, in spite of the difficulties, as part of the Institution's campaign to promote motor lifeboats around the coasts where their acceptance could not be taken for granted. However, over the next few years, as more motor craft were built and entered service, local opposition diminished considerably and soon many crews were requesting a motor lifeboat.

In 1910 motor lifeboats had been ordered for a new station at Donaghadee, at the entrance to Belfast Lough, and Wicklow, an important station on Ireland's east coast to the south of Dublin. In 1911 three 43ft Watson type motor boats were ordered, being allocated to Campbeltown, Beaumaris and Peterhead; they were among the largest motor lifeboats built hitherto and, fitted with a 60hp engine, the most powerful.

Two years after the motor lifeboats had gone to Orkney in convoy, a similar passage was undertaken in April 1911 by three motor lifeboats travelling together up the east coast. The boats were destined for Tynemouth, Seaham Harbour and St Abbs, with the motor boat being used to establish a new station at St Abbs. The passage up the east coast represented another long journey for such small boats and, as with the earlier convoy, the engines proved a little unreliable; about half way through, a day had to be spent at Gorleston after one of the motors failed to start.

Although the new boats reached their respective stations safely, doubts about motor power remained and, throughout the initial stages of providing motor power to the lifeboat fleet, the RNLI's Committee of Management found it necessary to constantly restate the advantages of

▲ The early motor lifeboat John A. Hay (ON.561) alongside the slipway at Stromness, possibly just after she had first arrived. This view shows the boat's open layout which provided virtually no shelter for her crew who, on many occasions, performed long and arduous services in dreadful weather. (Orkney Photographic Archives)

▶ The flotilla of lifeboats at Thurso nearing the end of their epic journey north from London. The Stromness lifeboat John A. Hay (ON.561) is on the left, nearest the quayside, with the Stronsay boat John Ryburn (ON.565) in the middle. On the outside is the Thurso boat Sarah Austin (ON.585), a twelve-oared Watson sailing type. (RNLI)

The first steps to motorisation

▲ The 38ft Watson motor Elliot Galer (ON.602) at Seaham Harbour in April 1911; she served the station for more than twenty-five years.

◀ Helen Smitton (ON.603), pictured at St Abbs, was the second of the two 38ft Watsons completed by Thames Ironworks in 1911, along with Elliot Galer, both of which undertook the long passage to station with the Tynemouth motor lifeboat in April 1911.

▼ The 38ft self-righter Sir Fitzroy Clayton (ON.628) being launched down the slipway at Fleetwood into the River Wyre. She spent most of her life-saving career at Newhaven. (From an old postcard supplied by John Harrop)

the motor lifeboat, while also pointing out that the motor was in fact an auxiliary to sails and oars. The Lifeboat, of February 1913, stated that, 'should the motor in a Life-boat break down, the boat, with her masts, sails, and oars is really no worse than if she had gone to sea without a motor. This is an important point which should always be brought to the notice of local committees and crews at those stations where a question of supplying a motor Life-boat has come to the front.'

However, by 1914 the number of motor lifeboats in service was well into double figures, despite the fact that the engines had still not reached the degree of reliability required, and, up to 1918, non-motorised lifeboats were still being built. But if doubts about the motor lifeboat's capabilities remained at the outbreak of war in 1914, the events of the war involving, most notably, the motor lifeboats on the east coast proved beyond doubt that motor-powered lifeboats could outperform pulling boats every time and accomplish feats hitherto unachievable.

Perhaps the most noteworthy of all rescues was undertaken by the 40ft self-righter Henry Vernon (ON.613) at Tynemouth, which performed many rescues and in less than seven years of service on the Tyne is credited with saving over 200 lives. With a dedicated crew, her greatest achievement came during one of the most famous rescues in the history of the RNLI, the wreck of the hospital ship Rohilla in 1914. According to

MOTOR LIFEBOATS

The first steps to motorisation

▲ Dramatic photos of the hospital ship Rohilla wrecked at Saltwick Nab on 30 October 1914; the upper left photo was taken early in the afternoon of the day the ship went aground; right, Whitby's No.2 lifeboat John Fielden is dragged across the beach by hundreds of helpers to launch to the stranded hospital ship; above the Tynemouth lifeboat crew involved in the Rohilla rescue were led by Coxswain Robert Smith and Captain Herbert Burton. (By courtesy of the RNLI)

▼ The purpose-built motor lifeboat Henry Vernon (ON.613) pictured on the Tyne; a 40ft self-righter, she was powered by a single 40bhp Tylor engine.

James Barnett, the Consulting Naval Architect who played a major role in motor lifeboat development, the Rohilla rescue 'cannot be recalled too often, for that rescue clearly demonstrated that what is impossible for a pulling and sailing boat can be accomplished by a motor-lifeboat'.

The rescue took place shortly after the outbreak of War after the hospital ship Rohilla, with 229 people on board, was wrecked near Whitby on 30 October 1914. Huge waves broke over the vessel, and many of those on board were washed overboard and drowned. Frantic efforts were made to help, and the Whitby's No.2 lifeboat John Fielden (ON.379), a 34ft self-righter pulled by ten oars, was launched, with considerable difficulty. In two trips, she saved thirty-five lives, but was so badly damaged as a result that she could not go to sea again. The pulling lifeboat from the neighbouring station at Upgang was brought through the town and lowered down the steep cliffs opposite the wreck but, in the terrible seas breaking on the cliffs, it was impossible to launch her until the following morning. After many attempts, she was taken to within fifty yards of the wreck by her brave crew, only to be swept back by the heavy seas.

The Teesmouth motor lifeboat Reserve No.2B (ON.350) was then summoned, but got badly damaged attempting to cross the Tees Bar in mountainous seas, and a tug had to help her. The Scarborough lifeboat, and another from Whitby, were also towed out by tugs, but neither could get close to the wrecked hospital ship. The only hope was the motor lifeboat Henry Vernon (ON.613) at Tynemouth and so an urgent telegram was sent north requesting assistance. As soon as the message was received, she left the Tyne at 4.30pm, as darkness was falling, under Coxswain Robert Smith and arrived in Whitby harbour after midnight having travelled over forty miles contending with horrendous weather and, because of the war, navigating without any lights to guide her southwards. She was met at Whitby by Lieut Basil Hall, the Inspector of Lifeboats, who had several barrels of oil loaded on board ready to calm the seas.

At daybreak on 1 November Henry Vernon set out from Whitby harbour, made to windward of the wreck, and got within 200 yards before discharging the oil to smooth the breaking waves. Coxswain Smith then swung the lifeboat round and made straight for the wreck, heading past the stern of Rohilla at full speed to reach the lee side of the vessel, below the bridge. Ropes were lowered and all fifty people were taken off. Perhaps the most dangerous part of the rescue was getting away from the wreck. As the lifeboat cleared the casualty, she was struck by a huge wave that threatened to upset her, but she withstood this and battled through the tremendous waves to reach the open sea. She then made for the harbour,

The first steps to motorisation

where she landed the survivors, being greeted by tumultuous cheers from the thousands of people who lined the quays and cliffs.

This prolonged and difficult rescue, which lasted for two and a half days and involved lifeboatmen and helpers from several stations, is one of the most famous in the history of the RNLI. Gold medals were awarded to Coxswain Robert Smith and Captain Burton of Tynemouth, as well as to Whitby's Coxswain Thomas Langlands, while the Second Coxswain of the Tynemouth lifeboat, James Brownlee, received the Silver medal, and additional monetary awards were made to the rest of the intrepid Tynemouth volunteers, and various other awards were also made. The delay in sending for the motor lifeboat from the Tyne had not, in the end, proved fatal, but it highlighted the continuing mistrust at lifeboat stations of the motor craft despite their becoming increasingly numerous.

The rescue, though, did prove that even the most basic early motor lifeboats, that had relatively low-powered engines, could work in worse weathers than pulling boats, and provide lifeboat crews with a far better means to effect rescues than they had hitherto. As Captain Basil Hall stated afterwards, the rescue showed, 'the inestimable importance of the Motor Life-boat, for not only could no other kind of boat have come forty-four miles, as this one did, . . . but owing to the tortuous nature of the passage between the rocks, no other than a Motor Life-boat could have safely reached the vessel at all'. Notwithstanding the incredible Rohilla rescue and its significance in advancing the cause of the motor lifeboat, the challenges of war saw lifeboat development effectively put on hold, and delayed further advances in motor lifeboats.

War also affected the service in various other ways, the most serious of which was a significant loss of revenue. Lifeboat operations themselves were made more difficult by the removal of aids to navigation. On a positive note, on 4 August 1915, a year to the day after war broke out, a new motor lifeboat, Lady Rothes (ON.641), was named at Fraserburgh. This 42ft self-righter powered by a single 40bhp Tylor engine was christened by Lady Rothes, having been provided as a 'thank offering' from the donor for the survival of his daughter, the Countess of Rothes, a passenger when the famous liner Titanic had sunk in 1912.

But more than three years passed before another new lifeboat was completed and christened, as new lifeboat construction was halted. When peace came in 1918 the next challenge faced by the RNLI was to rebuild the fleet, continue with advances to the motor lifeboat and introduce motor power around the entire coast, a task not achieved until another World War had started and ended. In 1920 the 'present scheme of the Institution [was] to build a fleet of Motor Life-boats and station them at salient points around the coast, not, if possible, more than fifty miles apart'.

▲ The 40ft self-righter Ethel Day Cardwell (ON.647), built in 1917 for service at Teesmouth, being launched at Port Erin, the Isle of Man station she served for fourteen years.

▼ Herbert Joy (ON.683) at Scarborough, where she served for eight years. She was one of only three 35ft self-righting motor lifeboats, developed for carriage launching; her double fender was unusual and not repeated on any other British-built motor lifeboat. (RNLI, by courtesy of Jeff Morris)

◄ The 1911-built self-righter General Farrell (ON.614) being launched down the slipway at St Davids. She was one of the few lifeboats to enter service before the outbreak of the First World War.

MOTOR LIFEBOATS

1 • Self-righting motor

KEY DATA
- Introduced 1904
- Last built 1920
- 7 built, including three conversions

The RNLI's first experiments with motor power took place in 1904, when the Folkestone lifeboat J. McConnell Hussey (ON.343) was taken out of service and fitted with a petrol engine at Guy's Yard, Cowes, IOW. The success of this conversion, and the other subsequent conversions, pointed the way to future motor lifeboat development. The first three lifeboats to be fitted with motors, ON.343, ON.350 and ON.407, were all self-righters, and were essentially similar in design and layout to, although slightly larger than, the pulling and sailing self-righters that had been given widespread service during the nineteenth century. The pulling self-righters, mostly 34ft or 35ft in length, had been built in large numbers since their introduction in the 1850s.

While the dimensions of the early motor self-righters varied, their hull design and deck layout were based on the ideas of the nineteenth century, with any design advances confined solely to the operation of the petrol engines. The challenge was to make the motor lifeboat a reality, and the problems faced by the engineers in getting a powered lifeboat to be reliable and efficient, took precedence over altering or improving the basic hull design. The motor self-righters were therefore open boats, as their pulling predecessors had been, and carried sails which would be used in the event of engine failure. They had heavy keels and were also fitted with drop keels, making them in effect motor sailers.

The early motor self-righters were essentially one-off designs with little or no standardisation, something attempted in most subsequent motor lifeboat designs. The First World War interrupted development of the motor lifeboat, but during the inter-war years a standard motor 40ft self-righter was developed (see table 4), superseding the 38ft and 42ft boats which can thus be regarded as essentially experimental. During trials of the converted boats, all self-righted as intended after the fitting of an engine, and this capability was never in doubt. The problems almost always centred around the reliability and performance of the engine.

During the construction of the boat for Stromness, *John A. Hay* (ON.561), the first purpose-built motor self-righter, much use was made of experience gained from the screw-driven steam lifeboats. As with these craft, the propeller for the new motor lifeboat was housed in a protective shaft tunnel made from wood with a bronze frame inside. A single drop keel replaced the two which were usual in sailing lifeboats of this type. A system was devised so that the propeller was accessible from inside the boat and could thus be cleared if fouled. The boats were equipped with both sails and oars, but these were specific to each, so at Fraserburgh, *Lady Rothes* (ON.641) carried a modified No.1 rig as well as ten oars, while at Lizard, *Frederick H. Pilley* (ON.657) had a No.1 special rig without mizen.

Lady Rothes (ON.641) capsized on service at Fraserburgh with tragic consequences, despite righting as designed. On 28 April 1919 she was launched to help the Admiralty drifter *Eminent* in a north-easterly gale and heavy seas. As she headed into the Bay, she was struck by very heavy seas; she was hit on her port bow by two huge waves, which threw her on her beam ends, and all the crew, except for three, were washed out. The boat righted immediately, and four of the crew managed to get back on board, while two hung on to the lifelines. The boat and men were swept helplessly towards the beach and went ashore. Unfortunately, Coxswain Andrew Noble and Second Coxswain Andrew Farquhar were unable to regain the lifeboat and were so badly injured that they never recovered.

▲ John A. Hay (ON.561) launching on exercise at Stromness in 1909. One of the first purpose-built motor lifeboats, she had the external appearance of a sailing lifeboat. (Orkney Photographic Archives)

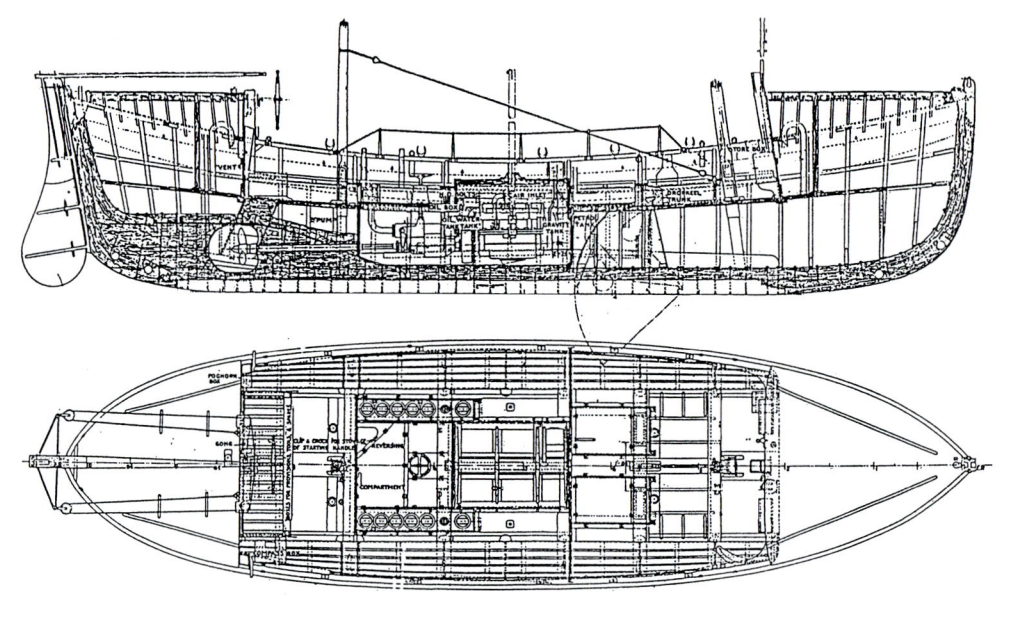

▶ 38ft motor self-righter Sir Fitzroy Clayton (ON.628) which served at Newhaven, Lizard and Fleetwood. The high end boxes and narrow beam were typical features of the self-righting design, first developed in the 1850s.

20　　　MOTOR LIFEBOATS

1 • Self-righting motor

	Year* (Yd No) Builder Place	Length Breadth Crew	Name Donor	ON Cost Weight	Engines	Stations (launches/lives saved)	Notes Disposal
1	1893/1904 (E6) W. T. Ellis Lowestoft	38' 8' 14	**J. McConnell Hussey**/ 1905- **Reserve 2a** Gift Miss Curling, London.	343 £418 5t9	1x11bhp (p) Fay & Bowen 2-cyl (originally 12 oars)	Folkestone 4.12.1893-3.1903 (5/10) Newhaven 16.11.1904-4.1905 (0/0) Tynemouth 1.5.1905-1911 (9/8) Sunderland 1911-1914 (6/3)	Sold 1914
2	1893/1906 (W253) Woolfe Shadwell	42' 11' 15	**Bradford**/ 1905- **Reserve No. 2** Bradford Lifeboat Fund.	350 £896 9t	1x40bhp Briton (p)/ 1907- 1x30bhp Tylor 4-cyl (p) (originally 12 oars)	Ramsgate 9.4.1893-1905 (121/53) Harwich 1907 (0/0), Seaton Snook 9.1907-1909 (0/0) Seaham Harbour No.2 1909-1911 (1/0) Teesmouth 16.6.1911-11.1917 (10/12)	Sold 1918
3	1897/1906 (TI15) Thames IW Blackwall	37' 9'3" 9	**Michael Henry**/ **Reserve 2b** Jewish Scholars Lifeboat Fund.	407 £728 5t19	1x24bhp 4-cyl (p) Thornycroft/ 1913- 1x20hp Gardner (originally 12 oars)	Newhaven 7.12.1897-1905 (16/16) Newhaven 1.1908-30.11.1912 (23/89) Dunmore East 12.2.1914-12.1919 (3/4)	Sold 1919
4	1908 (TK99) Thames IW Blackwall	42' 11'6" 12	**John A. Hay** Legacy Mr John A. Hay, Cheltenham.	561 £2,995 11t5	1x30bhp (p) Tylor 4-cyl model A	Stromness 15.4.1909-15.2.1928 (32/90) Fenit 4.7.1928-8.9.1932 (3/0)	Sold 1932
5	1912 (TL77) Thames IW Blackwall	38' 9'9" 11/8	**Sir Fitzroy Clayton** RNLI Funds.	628 £3080.19.0 8t15	1x35bhp (p) Tylor 4-cyl model B	Newhaven 11.1912-5.18 and 1.1919-8.1930 (66/108) Lizard 4.5.1918-1.1919 (2/0) Fleetwood 1.1933-1935 (4/4)	Sold 8.1935
6	1915 (TL92) Thames IW/ Saunders (S6)	42' 11'6" 12/9	**Lady Rothes** Gift of T. Dyer Edwardes, London.	641 £3,714.10.5 11t6	1x40bhp (p) Tylor 4-cyl model C1	Fraserburgh 13.7.1915-9.3.1937 (66/65)	Capsized on service 28.4.1919, two lost Sold 2.1937
7	1920 (SP72C) Summers & Payne/ Saunders (S31)	38' 9'9" 8	**Frederick H. Pilley** Gift of Frederick Hounslow Pilley, Norwood, London.	657 £5,592.0.8 9t11	1x45bhp (p) Tylor 4-cyl model JB4	Lizard 12.11.1920-2.1934 (19/130) Port Askaig 21.3.1934-6.1935 (2/0) Fleetwood 8.1935-16.2.1939 (12/19)	Sold 3.1939

* The second date, where applicable, indicates the year the boat was converted to motor.

▲ One of the few lifeboats built during the First World War, 42ft self-righter motor Lady Rothes (ON.641) served at Fraserburgh, being slipway launched. (From an old postcard in the author's collection)

▲ 38ft motor self-righter Frederick H. Pilley (ON.657) was completed in 1920 by Saunders at Cowes; on trials, she reached a maximum speed of 7.49 knots and consumed thirty-five pints of petrol an hour.

MOTOR LIFEBOATS

2 • Norfolk & Suffolk motor

KEY DATA
- Introduced 1906
- Last built 1925
- 4 built, including one conversion

The non-self-righting Norfolk & Suffolk sailing lifeboat was first developed during the early nineteenth century and was similar in many respects to the large sailing yawls, upon which it was based, that operated throughout East Anglia. As a sailing lifeboat it had a far greater range than the small rowing lifeboats, and was intended for service in and around the extensive sandbanks off the coasts of Norfolk and Suffolk, many of which were some distance from the shore. These heavily-built sailing lifeboats, which had an almost flat bottom, were regarded as ideal for the conditions in the North Sea and were well suited to working in shallow waters close to the outlying sandbanks.

Of the four lifeboats selected to be converted for motor operation during the early experiments with motor power, three were self-righting types and the other, James Stevens No.14 (ON.432), was a Norfolk & Suffolk type. This boat was fitted at Thames Ironworks, Blackwall with an early design of engine, a 32hp Blake four-cylinder, which ran at 550rpm and weighed approximately sixteen hundredweight. The conversion work took place during 1905-06, and on 13 June 1906 she undertook trials on the Thames out of West India Docks before returning to service. On the Maplin measured mile she reached 9.2 knots under motor and sail.

She served the Walton & Frinton station with distinction, often going out to the Longsand and Kentish Knock sandbanks, proving that a motor was well suited to powering large lifeboats, although the sails, consisting of a special rig with dipping fore lug and standing mizen, were retained as auxiliary. In 1913 James Stevens No.14 was fitted with another engine, a 40bhp Brook four-cylinder petrol engine, along with a Caledonian reverse gear, but this proved troublesome and was deemed so unreliable that it was replaced in 1922 by a Clyde reverse gear model PK.

The other three Norfolk & Suffolk types were purpose-built as motor lifeboats, and intended for specific stations for which no other motor type was deemed suitable. The advantage of the design was its shallow draught, which, in the third boat, John and Mary Meiklam of Gladswood (ON.670), was 3ft 5.75in, and just 3ft 2.5in in the fourth boat, Mary Scott (ON.691). The engines, housed amidships, were different types in each of the boats. In none of Norfolk & Suffolk boats was the propeller housed in a tunnel, a feature regarded as necessary by the RNLI's pioneering motor lifeboat designers, but was instead protected by the deadwood at the stern. The boats had a maximum speed of approximately eight knots. The last of the type, Mary Scott (ON.691), had a range of 117 miles at her 7.3-knot cruising speed, much greater than the similar-sized Watson types. The boats carried a crew of thirteen.

The Norfolk & Suffolk motor type something of an anomaly in terms of lifeboat design, with only four being built. They were completed as essentially open boats, very similar to their sailing predecessors, but in the course of their careers rudimentary shelters were added as crew protection became an issue when the boats undertook services that were far longer than those performed by sailing lifeboats. Although built for service in East Anglia, the boats enjoyed long careers, spending many years as Reserve boats and serving at stations throughout the UK and Ireland.

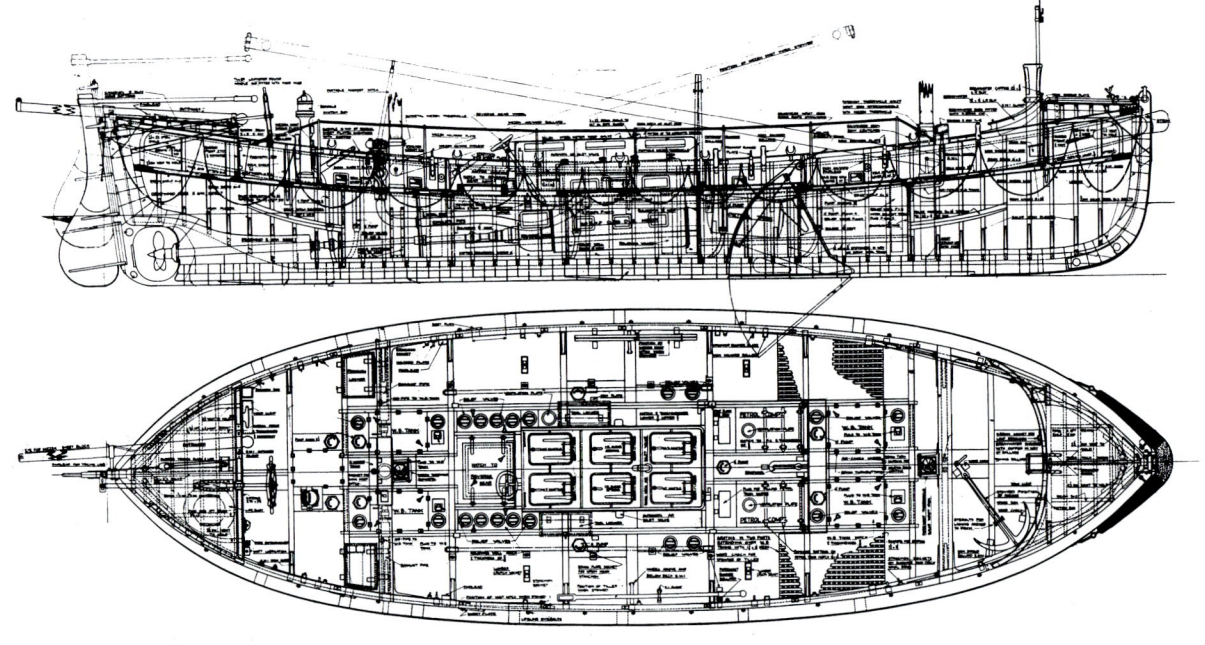

▲ The Norfolk & Suffolk sailing lifeboat James Stevens No.14 (ON.670) was fitted with a 32hp Blake petrol engine in 1906; she served at Walton and Frinton throughout her twenty-eight year operational career. In the late 1990s work started on restoring her to her original appearance. (By courtesy of John Steer)

▲ The second Norfolk & Suffolk motor, H.F. Bailey (ON.670); built for Cromer, she was stationed at Great Yarmouth & Gorleston for most of her life-saving career. (By courtesy of the RNLI)

▶ General profile of 46ft 6in Norfolk & Suffolk motor John and Mary Meiklam of Gladswood (ON.670), which served at Great Yarmouth & Gorleston for most of her career. This type was basically an open boat fitted with an engine, similar in almost every respect to the sailing Norfolk & Suffolk lifeboats used extensively but not exclusively in the counties after which the type was named. (By courtesy of the RNLI)

2 • Norfolk & Suffolk motor

	Year* (Yd No) Builder Place	Length Breadth Crew	Name Donor	ON Cost Weight	Engines	Stations (launches/lives saved)	Notes Disposal
1	1900/1906 (TI32) Thames IW Blackwall	43' 12'6" 13	**James Stevens No.14** Legacy of James Stevens, Birmingham.	432 £1,420 10t16	1906- 1x32bhp Blake 4SA 4-cyl (p)/ 1913- 40 bhp 4-cyl Brook (p)	Walton-on-the-Naze 5.7.1900-4.7.1928 (126/227)	Originally 12 oars Sold 6.1928- £180
2	1921 (S26) S.E. Saunders Cowes	46'6" 12'9" 15	**John and Mary Meiklam of Gladswood**/ 1921- **Agnes Cross** Legacies of Miss J. A. Meiklam, Mrs May, and gift of Mrs Moysey/ 1921- Gift of Miss Agnes Cross.	663 £8,620 14t2	1x60hp 4-cyl Tylor D.1 No tunnel	Gorleston 9.2-21.3.1921 (0/0) Lowestoft 31.3.1921-19.10.39 (124/209) Dover 24.10.1940-41 (11/65) Reserve 1939-52 (28/62)	Sold 10.1952- £900
3	1923 (W1566) J.S. White Cowes	46'6" 12'9" 13	**H. F. Bailey**/ 1924- **John and Mary Meiklam of Gladswood** Legacy of H. F. Bailey/ 1924- Legacies of Miss J. A. Meiklam, Mrs May, and gift Mrs Moysey.	670 £10,993.6.0 14t10	1x80bhp 6-cyl Weyburn DE6 (p) No tunnel	Cromer No.1 5.1923-4.5.1924 (3/12) Gorleston 5.5.1924-5.1939 (155/211) Reserve 1939-1952 (49/62)	Sold 10.1952- £950
4	1925 (W1608) J.S. White Cowes	46'6" 12'9" 13	**Mary Scott** Legacy of Miss M. A. J. Scott, Wanstead.	691 £7,827 17t	1x80bhp 6-cyl White DE6 (p) No tunnel	Southwold 19.6.1925-29.5.1940 (30/23) Reserve 5.1940-1953 (52/24)	Sold 3.1953- £611

* The second date, where applicable, indicates the year the boat was converted to motor.

▲ The last Norfolk & Suffolk motor lifeboat to be built was Mary Scott (ON.691), which served at Southwold until that station was closed in 1940. Built as an open lifeboat, she was later fitted with a shelter. After the closure of Southwold station in 1940, Mary Scott was used as a Reserve lifeboat for a number of years, covering at stations throughout the country, including Weymouth, where she is pictured at moorings in the harbour. (From an old photo from David Hancox, by courtesy of Jeff Morris)

◀ John and Mary Meiklam of Gladswood (ON.670) leaving Gorleston harbour. In this photograph the lack of protection for the crew of early motor lifeboats is evident; the small cover for the motor can just be seen amidships. The large number of crew was needed to operate the sails, if they were needed, carried as auxiliary to the single engine. A canvas canopy was fitted in about 1927.

MOTOR LIFEBOATS

2 • Norfolk & Suffolk motor

▲ John and Mary Meiklam of Gladswood (ON.670) with her sails set and after the canopy had been fitted to provide a degree of crew protection. At the time of their construction, the Norfolk & Suffolk lifeboats were the largest motor craft in the RNLI's fleet. Sent to Cromer under the name H.F. Bailey on 23 May 1923, this lifeboat had her stern frame damaged when she bumped on the slipway in 1923 and was damaged on service in January 1924. She was not liked at the station and was replaced after less than a year, being transferred to Gorleston in May 1924 after being repaired. (By courtesy of the RNLI)

3 • Watson motor 38ft-43ft

The early lifeboat designs were based on standard pulling and sailing lifeboat hulls, and the first motorised Watsons were no different. The basic hull shape laid down by George Lennox Watson towards the end of the nineteenth century remained more or less the same in the motor lifeboats which took his name, although the hulls gradually became larger and heavier as motors were so much more powerful than oars or sail.

In the early Watson motor lifeboats efforts were concentrated on ensuring that the engine worked reliably, so the boats remained essentially open. The necessary alterations to incorporate a petrol engine, housed in a watertight mahogany box, together with the additions of a propeller protected by a tunnel built into the hull, were the main differences between these boats and their sailing predecessors. Apart from the group of four boats built towards the end of the 1920s, the early Watson motor boats were fitted with Tylor petrol engines, the RNLI' standard engine of this era. As all were single-screwed, auxiliary sails were carried, usually in the form of jib, lug and mizzen sails, and oars were also provided.

Of these early Watson motor types, six were 43ft in length and two were just 38ft; four built after 1918 were 40ft, and this size was developed into the 40ft 6in version, of which four were built in 1929. The two smallest Watsons were sister vessels, Elliot Galer (ON.602) and Helen Smitton (ON.602), for Seaham Harbour and St Abbs respectively; the type and size of these 38ft by 10ft boats, powered by 34hp Wolseley engines running at 700rpm at full speed, as well their equipment, were selected by the crews, as the RNLI 'consider[ed] that the men who man the boats should always have this choice.'

The first Watsons, Maria (ON.560) and John Ryburn (ON.565), were two of the RNLI's earliest purpose-built motor lifeboats. Both were powered by single 40bhp Tylor engines, which gave them a maximum speed of just over seven knots, and they carried fifty and sixty gallons of fuel respectively. The three 43ft Watsons, built just before the First World War, were fitted with single 60hp Tylor four-cylinder engines, which was considered ample to give ample power and speed for service conditions.

Just after the war the 40ft type was developed, and in the late 1920s further advances saw the 40ft 6in type, the first of which, Lady Kylsant (ON.721), went to Weymouth. This improved design was six inches longer and had eight inches broader than the 40ft Watsons, which meant it was more stable. The freeboard of 8.75 inches, an increase of over five inches, and higher ends made the boats much drier. The hull was divided into six watertight compartments, and was fitted with 160 air cases. The increased stability and buoyancy meant that, compared with the 40ft boat which could take fifty-six people, the new type could carry up to 160 people; forty people could be carried in rough weather.

KEY DATA
▶ Introduced 1908
▶ Last built 1930
▶ 15 built

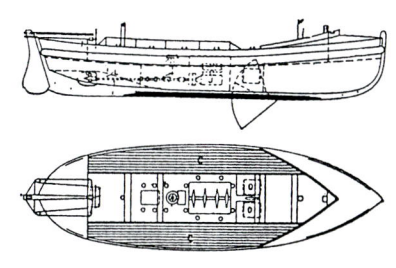

▲ Generic profile drawing of the 43ft by 12ft 6in Watson motor lifeboat, fitted with a 40bhp engine, of which only five were built, published in the RNLI's Annual Reports during the 1910s. (RNLI)

◀ Profile drawing of the 40ft 6in Watson, of which four were built; fitted with a single 50hp engine, they had a speed of seven and a half knots and enough fuel to travel 115 miles. (RNLI)

▼ 40ft Watson Prince David (ON.677) moored at Barry Dock, the station she served for fourteen years. As well as her 40hp engine, she carried eight oars and a no.1 sailing rig. (RNLI)

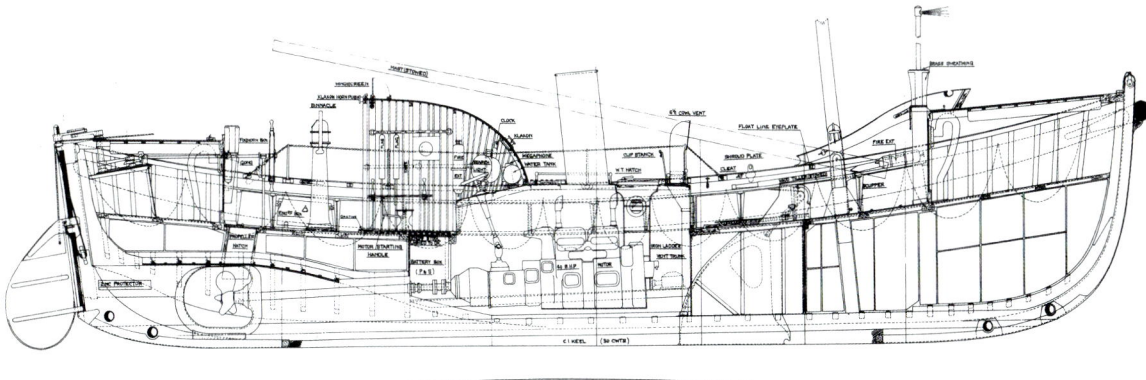

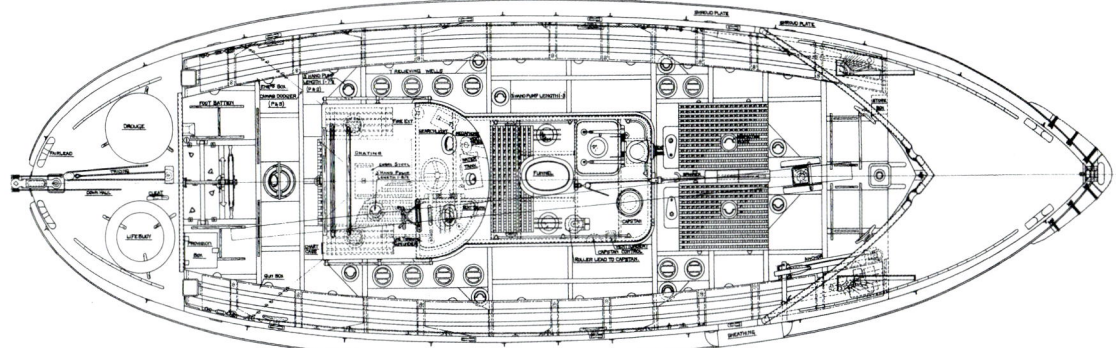

MOTOR LIFEBOATS

3 • Watson motor 38ft-43ft

#	Year* (Yd No) Builder Place	Length Breadth Crew	Name Donor	ON Cost Weight	Engines	Stations (launches/lives saved)	Notes Disposal
1	1908 (TK98) Thames IW Blackwall	40' 11' 12/9	**Maria** Gift of Miss Maria Clarke, Balham, London.	560 £2,344.11.11 10t11	1x40bhp Tylor C 4-cyl (p)	Broughty Ferry 11.10.1910-7.1921 (21/14), Portpatrick 8.4.1922-3.12.29 (10/6), Pwllheli 3.3.1930-4.5.31 (0/0), Shoreham Harbour 11.8-13.10.1931 (1/1)	Sold 1932
2	1908 (TL.3) Thames IW Blackwall	43' 12'6" 12/9	**John Ryburn** Legacy of Mr William McCunn, Largs.	565 £3,431.4.5 14t2	1x40bhp Blake 4-cyl (p)/ 1914- 1x40bhp Tylor C.1	Stronsay 14.4.1909-1915 (11/4) Peterhead No.2 6.10.1915-6.1920 (21/158) Broughty Ferry 6.1921-2.1935 (15/6)	Sold 2.1935
3	1910 (TL.38) Thames IW Blackwall	43' 12'6" 12/9	**William and Laura** Legacy of Miss A. W. Clark Hall, Bournemouth.	595 £4,507.14.0 13t6	1x40bhp Blake 4-cyl (p)/ 1914- 1x40bhp Tylor C.1	Donaghadee 1.7.1910-4.6.1932 (61/65) Arranmore 7.1932-17.4.1935 (2/0)	Sold 1935
4	1910 (TL.46) Thames IW Blackwall	38' 10' 10/8	**Elliot Galer** Legacy of E.J.N. Galer, Walton-on-Thames.	602 £2,607.3.8 7t17	1x34hp Wolseley model 4 (p)	Seaham Harbour 22.4.1911-5.12.1936 (26/59)	Sold 1936
5	1910 (TL.47) Thames IW Blackwall	38' 10' 10/8	**Helen Smitton** Legacy of Mr James Hodge, Greenhays, Manchester.	603 £2,615.4.9 7t17	1x34hp Wolseley model 4 (p)	St Abbs 22.4.1911-5.12.1936 (27/37)	Sold 1936
6	1912 (TL.68) Thames IW Blackwall	43' 12'6" 12/9	**William MacPherson** Gift of Mrs William MacPherson, Helensburgh.	620 £3,423.4.10 14t5	1x60bhp Tylor 4cyl model D (p)	Campbeltown 4.7.1912-4.9.1929 (12/29) Aldeburgh 10.2-23.10.1930 (0/0) Pwllheli 4.5.1931-8.1940 (16/4)	Sold 9.1940
7	1913 (TL.69) Thames IW Blackwall	43' 12'6" 12/9	**Frederick Kitchen** Legacy of Mr Frederick Kitchen, Carnarvon.	621 £3,726.15.4 14t5	1x60bhp Tylor 4cyl model D (p)	Beaumaris 9.7.1914-9.1945 (38/46) Reserve 1945-1948 (3/0)	Shelter fitted 1928 Sold 1948
8	1912 (TL.70) Thames IW Blackwall	43' 12'6" 12/9	**Alexander Tulloch** Legacy of Miss Jane Tulloch, Bayswater, London.	622 £3,436.12.5 14t4	1x60bhp Tylor 4cyl model D (p)	Peterhead No.2 11.12.1912-1914 (11/28)	Wrecked on service 26.12.1914, three lost
9	1918 (S16) Smrs & Payne; S. E. Saunders	40' 11' 12/8	**Samuel Oakes** Legacy of Mrs E. M. Laing, Barnes.	651 £7,155.10.5 10t4	1x40bhp Tylor C2 4-cyl (p)	Spurn Point 11.11.1919-4.11.1923 (33/25) Weymouth 14.5.1924-27.7.1929 (16/9) Shoreham 8.10.1929-1.1933 (11/7)	Sold 1.1933
10	1922 (W1571) J. S. White Cowes	40' 11' 9	**Prince David** Welsh Lifeboat Fund.	677 £8,018.10.8 11t6	1x45bhp Tylor JB4 4-cyl (p)	Barry Dock 5.9.1922-9.12.1937 (29/43)	Sold 12.1937
11	1922 (W1572) J. S. White Cowes	40' 11' 9	**K. B. M.** Legacies of William Kirkhope, Charles Baily and Miss Charlotte McInroy.	681 £8,179.5.0 11t6	1x45bhp Tylor JB4 4-cyl (p)	Buckie 1.8.1922-25.11.1949 (62/12) Reserve 1949-52 (1/0)	Sold 9.1952
12	1929 (W1673) J. S. White Cowes	40'6" 11'8" 9/8	**Lady Kylsant** Gift of Royal Mail and Union Castle Steamship Co.	721 £5,864.14.3 12t	1x50bhp Weyburn CE4 4-cyl (p)	Weymouth 27.7.1929-6.11.1930 (8/9) Howth 8.11.1930-17.1.1937 (6/2) Wicklow 27.5.1937-7.6.1956 (47/61)	Sold 1956
13	1929 (W1674) J. S. White Cowes	40'6" 11'8" 9/8	**J. and W.** Legacies Mrs A. Calquhoun and Mrs E. Ashton.	722 £6,052.6.0 12t10	1x50bhp Weyburn CE4 4-cyl (p)	Portpatrick 3.12.1929-20.3.37 (14/27) Reserve 1937-1940 (6/2) Berwick 2.1940-9.5.1957 (50/46)	Sold 5.1957
14	1929 (W1675) J. S. White Cowes	40'6" 11'8" 9/8	**Sir David Richmond of Glasgow** Legacy of Lady Richmond, and gift from Mrs Fairlie.	723 £5,877.16.0 12t10	1x50bhp Weyburn CE4 4-cyl (p)	Troon 4.12.1929-19.2.1955 (71/101)	Sold 6.1956
15	1930 (W1676) J. S. White Cowes	40'6" 11'8" 9/8	**G. W.** Legacies of Dr T. W. Richards and Mrs E. H. Scott, and the Northampton Lifeboat Fund.	724 £5,886.9.0 12t10	1x50bhp Weyburn CE4 4-cyl (p)	Moelfre 15.1.1930-18.4.1956 (71/147)	Sold 5.1956

3 • Watson motor 38ft-43ft

▶ The 40ft Watson Maria (ON.560) on the slipway at Broughty Ferry, the first station she served. She was the first Watson motor lifeboat to be built, and was fitted with a 4ft 6in sliding steel keel and 20ft bilge keels. Her 40bhp Tylor model C petrol engine gave her a top speed of 7.22 knots and she carried fifty gallons of fuel.

▲ Helen Smitton (ON.603) was one of the a pair of 38ft Watson motor lifeboats built in 1910-11 by Thames Ironworks; pictured at St Abbs, she served the station for twenty-five years. At first glance it is difficult to tell that she is a motor lifeboat. (From an old postcard supplied by John Harrop)

▲ Frederick Kitchen (ON.621) launching down the slipway at Beaumaris, where she was stationed for over thirty years. Built as an open boat, she had a shelter fitted in 1928. She was fitted with a 10ft iron keel and a 5ft 6in steel drop keel, and carried a No.1 modified rig. (From an old postcard supplied by John Harrop)

MOTOR LIFEBOATS

3 • Watson motor 38ft-43ft

▲ The 40ft by 11ft Watson K.B.M. (ON.681) was fitted with a 45hp Tylor engine and also carried sails. (By courtesy of the RNLI)

▶ The first of the four 40ft 6in Watsons was Lady Kylsant (ON.721), which served at Weymouth, Howth and Wicklow.

▲ The last 40ft 6in Watson motor to be built, G.W. (ON.724), served at Moelfre in Anglesey for more than a quarter of a century. (By courtesy of the RNLI)

◀ A fine photograph of Sir David Richmond of Glasgow (ON.723), one of four 40ft 6in Watson motor lifeboats built in 1929 by J.S. White at Cowes. Powered by a single 50hp Weyburn CE.4 engine, she also carried four oars as well as a forelug and staysail. She had a 4ft steel drop keel, fourteen relieving tubes and 18ft bilge keels. Taken into service on 26 October 1929, she undertook on trials out of Cowes until being sent to Troon on 23 November 1929. (By courtesy of the RNLI)

MOTOR LIFEBOATS

4 • Self-righting motor 40ft

The 40ft motor self-righter, one of the earliest standard motor designs, was conceived as a medium-sized lifeboat primarily for launching down a slipway, with the propeller recessed in a protective tunnel. Almost all were operated from slipways or, in one or two instances, from trolleys that ran down slipways. The first 40ft motor self-righter was the first motor lifeboat in Wales, and the 40ft boats were among the earliest motor craft to see service.

The hull shape was more or less identical to that of the pulling and sailing self-righters, with high end boxes at bow and stern, and a narrow beam, which combined to provide the self-righting ability. Air cases were also fitted at the sides and in the hold area. The single engine was housed in a watertight box amidships and, because the boats were single-engined, auxiliary sails were carried. The mast was hinged so that it could fold flat when the boats were housed. An iron keel was fitted, as was a drop keel for use when the boat was being sailed.

The first of the type, Charterhouse (ON.563), completed in 1908, was powered by a 24bhp Tyler four-cylinder engine, which developed 650rpm and gave a speed of 6.79 knots, and she carried fifty gallons of fuel. She served at Fishguard for twenty-one years and was involved in the Gold medal-winning service on 2 December 1920 to the Dutch motor schooner Hermina from which the Fishguard crew saved seven people. Between 1910 and 1918, a further seven 40ft boats were built but a slightly more powerful 40bhp four-cylinder Tylor engine was installed and these boats had a slightly greater speed of approximately seven and a half knots, and could carry could carry more than sixty survivors, in addition to the crew and gear. One of these, Henry Vernon (ON.613) from Tynemouth, was involved in the rescue from the hospital ship Rohilla.

In the early 1920s the design was further modified and five 40ft boats were completed in 1922. These with more powerful 45hp engines, and, during the course of their service careers, had a small canopy fitted aft of the engine which contained the engine controls. The engines for these five boats were supplied by Tylor, but the reverse gears fitted came from various different manufacturers. The Tylor four-cyilinder petrol engine, model JB.4, operated at 950rpm and consumed 34.5 pints of fuel an hour.

The last of the 40ft motor self-righters, Thomas Markby (ON.706), was something of an anomaly as she used the same type of engine – the 40hp four-cylinder Weyburn – then being fitted in the larger 45ft 6in Watsons, making her a one-off. She was built because other slipway-launched types were too large for its intended station, Swanage. She had a maximum speed of 7.53 knots and carried sixty gallons of fuel.

KEY DATA
▶ Introduced 1908
▶ Last built 1928
▶ 14 built

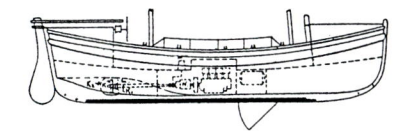

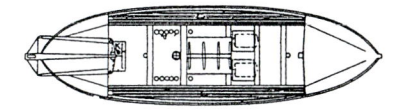

▲ Generic profile drawing published in the RNLI's Annual Reports in the 1910s showing the 40ft by 10ft 6in self-righting motor lifeboat. The boats were all fitted with 40hp four-cylinder engines.

◀ Charterhouse (ON.563), the first motor lifeboat in Wales, pictured in Fishguard harbour, with her crew and station officials on board. She had a 4ft 6in sliding drop keel and carried a modified no.1 rig, with the sails to be used in the event of engine failure. She served Fishguard for more than twenty years, and was launched down a slipway. (By courtesy of the RNLI)

MOTOR LIFEBOATS

4 • Self-righting motor 40ft

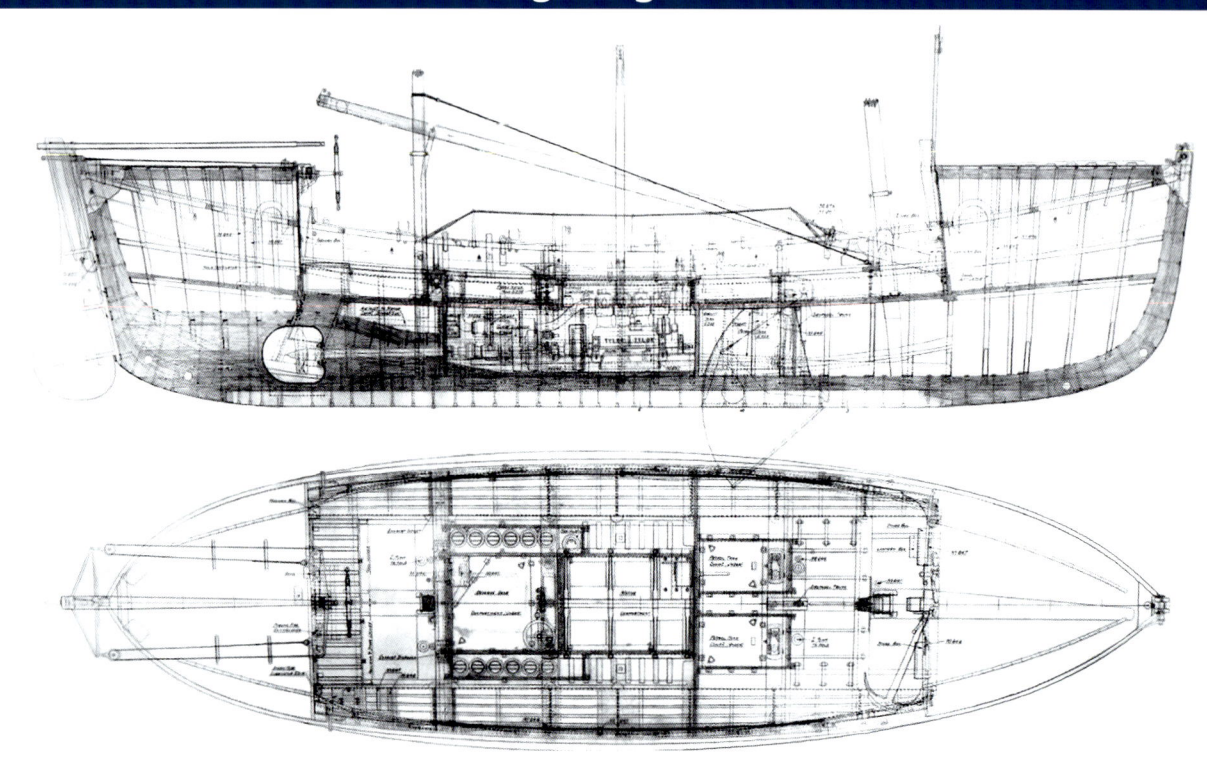

◀ Deck plan and profile of Henry Frederick Swan (ON.646), which served at Tynemouth throughout the inter-war years. She was launched from a trolley down a slipway. This line drawing shows how similar the motor self-righters were to their pulling and sailing predecessors, with their large end boxes and open deck layout. Her propeller was 22 inches in diameter and she was manned by a crew of nine, including the motor mechanic. (By courtesy of the RNLI)

▶ Deck plan and profile of Thomas Markby (ON.706), which served at Swanage, and later Whitehills, and was the last 40ft motor self-righter to be built; she was the only 40ft self-righter one fitted with a Weyburn engine. The steel drop keel was 4ft 6in, and she carried ten round oars, and a No.1 modified rig without mizzen. (By courtesy of the RNLI)

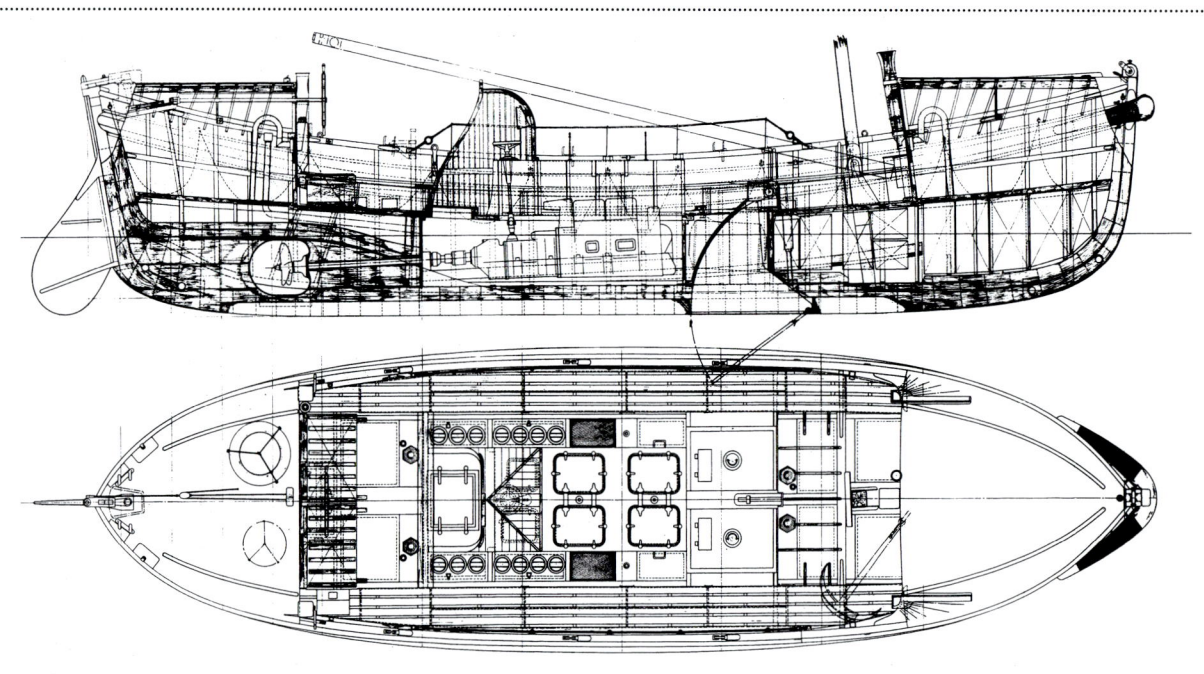

MOTOR LIFEBOATS

4 • Self-righting motor 40ft

	Year (Yd No) Builder Place	Length Breadth Crew	Name Donor	ON Cost Weight	Engines	Stations (launches/lives saved)	Notes Disposal
1	1908 (TL1) Thames IW Blackwall	40' 10'6" 12/9	**Charterhouse** Old and present Carthusians.	563 £2,946 10t17	1x24hp Tylor 4-cyl model A (p)	Fishguard 14.10.1909-8.1930 (20/47)	Sold 1931
2	1910 (TL54) Thames IW Blackwall	40' 10'6" 12/9	**Robert Theophilus Garden** Legacy of Mr R. J. Garden, London and Co Clare.	609 £4,015 10t11	1x40hp Tylor 4-cyl model C (p)	Wicklow 24.2.1911-27.5.1937 (42/31)	Sold 1937
3	1911 (TL58) Thames IW Blackwall	40' 10'6" 12/9	**Henry Vernon** Legacy of Mrs A. Vernon, Weston-super-Mare.	613 £3,664 10t18	1x40hp Tylor 4-cyl model C (p)	Tynemouth 1911-10.2.1918 (26/206) Sunderland 16.2.1918-11.1935 (28/64)	Sold 1936
4	1911 (TL59) Thames IW Blackwall	40' 10'6" 12/9	**General Farrell** Legacy of Mrs C. M. Leckie, Walton-on-Thames.	614 £3,003 10t19	1x40hp Tylor 4-cyl model C (p)	St Davids 24.9.1912-3.4.1936 (26/17)	Sold 1936
5	1914 (TL93/S7) Thames IW/ S. E. Saunders	40' 10'6" 12/9	**John Taylor Cardwell** Legacy of Mr John T. Cardwell, Ilkley, Yorkshire.	642 £3,599 10t19	1x40hp Tylor 4-cyl model C.1 (p)	Arklow 2.2.1915-14.7.1938 (20/20)	Sold 1938
6	1917 (S11) S. E. Saunders Cowes	40' 10'6" 12/9	**Henry Federick Swann** Gift of Mrs Lowe, Bath.	646 £6,901 10t18	1x40hp Tylor 4-cyl model C.2 (p)	Tynemouth 10.2.1918-10.1939 (28/8) Reserve 1939-1941 (0/0) Tynemouth 22.10.1941-11.1947 (4/0)	Sold 1947
7	1917 (S12) S. E. Saunders Cowes	40' 10'6" 12/9	**Ethel Day Cardwell** Legacy of Mr John T. Cardwell, Ilkley, Yorkshire.	647 £4,746 10t18	1x40hp Tylor 4-cyl model C.2 (p)	Teesmouth 22.11.1917-12.1924 (8/29) Port Erin 12.8.1925-17.10.1939 (19/4) Reserve 1939-1942 (7/0)	Sold 1942
8	1918 (S23) S. E. Saunders Cowes	40' 10'6" 12/9	**Margaret Harker-Smith** Legacy of Miss M. Harker Smith, Sheffield.	667 £5,023 10t18	1x40hp Tylor 4-cyl model C.2 (p)	Whitby 31.5.1919-12.4.1938 (117/86)	Sold 4.1938
9	1922 (W1574) J. S. White Cowes	40' 10'6" 12/9	**Alfred and Clara Heath** Legacy of Mr Alfred J. Heath, Putney, London.	672 £8,302 11t6	1x45hp Tylor 4-cyl model JB (p)	Torbay 18.3.1922-23.9.1930 (39/37) Salcombe 6.12.1930-5.1938 (22/73) Reserve 1938-1945 (6/20) Guernsey 6.4.1940-29.8.1945	Taken over by enemy forces while on reserve duty at St Peter Port Sold 2.10.1945
10	1922 (W1575) J. S. White Cowes	40' 10'6" 12/9	**Jane Holland** Legacy of Mr W. H. Clarke, London.	673 £8,202 11t14	1x45hp Tylor 4-cyl model JB (p)	Selsey 20.5.1922-1929 (15/11) Eastbourne 27.7.1929-6.1949 (55/65) Reserve 1949-1953 (11/14)	Sold 3.1953
11	1922 (W1576) J. S. White Cowes	40' 10'6" 12/9	**The Newbons** Legacy of Mr R. A. Newbon, Islington, London.	674 £8,622 11t16	1x45hp Tylor 4-cyl model JB (p)	Sennen Cove 1.5.1922-7.1948 (54/36) Port St Mary 11.11.1949-9.1950 (1/0)	Sold 7.3.1951
12	1922 (W1577) J. S. White Cowes	40' 10'6" 12/9	**V. C. S.** Legacies of H. J. Vagg, Alfred Sleemin, and Miss L. A. Marshall.	675 £8,162 11t13	1x45hp Tylor 4-cyl model JB (p)	Appledore 2.5.1922-14.8.38 (40/41) Reserve 1938-45 (3/3)	Sold 16.9.1945
13	1922 (W1573) J. S. White Cowes	40' 10'6" 12/9	**Langham** Legacy of Mr T. G. Langham, Maida Vale; gift from his executors.	676 £7,781 11t13	1x45hp Tylor 4-cyl model JB (p)	Bembridge 4.9.1922-24.5.1939 (61/62) Reserve 5.1939-11.1950 (35/38)	Sold 11.1950
14	1928 (S46) S. E. Saunders Cowes	40' 10'6" 12/9	**Thomas Markby** Legacy of Mrs Gertrude H. Markby, Willesden.	706 £6,559 11t14	1x40hp Weyburn 4-cyl model CE.4 (p)	Swanage 14.6.1928-26.2.1949 (67/27) Whitehills 22.5.1949-9.3.1952 (5/0) Reserve 3.1952-1957 (16/14)	Sold 5.1957

MOTOR LIFEBOATS

4 • Self-righting motor 40ft

▲ (left) General Farrell (ON.614), built in 1911, on the slipway at St Davids. The tunnel in which the propeller was protected can be seen clearly, while the drogue is hanging over the port side. General Farrell was one of two 40ft motor self-righters built in 1911, which were fitted with a single 40hp Tylor model C engine; she reached a top speed of 7.29 knots during her trials. (From an old postcard supplied by John Harrop)

▲ (right) Henry Frederick Swann (ON.646) on the purpose-designed launching trolley outside the lifeboat house at Tynemouth. She was one of two 40ft motor self-righters to be launched from a trolley which ran down the slipway on rails.

▶ Ethel Day Cardwell (ON.647) was stationed initially at Teesmouth, and then transferred to Port Erin in August 1925, where she served for a further fourteen years. She is pictured moored at the quayside in West India Dock in June 1925 during her trials after being reconditioned at the RNLI's storeyard on the Thames prior to going to Port Erin. She left he Thames on 1 August 1925 and arrived at Port Erin on 10 August 1925. (By courtesy of the RNLI)

4 • Self-righting motor 40ft

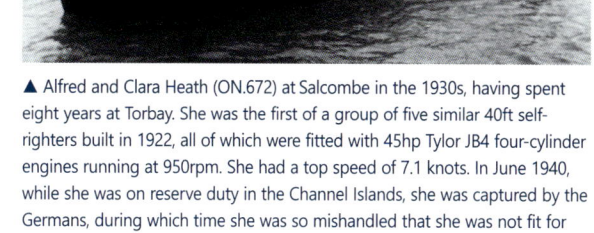

▲ Alfred and Clara Heath (ON.672) at Salcombe in the 1930s, having spent eight years at Torbay. She was the first of a group of five similar 40ft self-righters built in 1922, all of which were fitted with 45hp Tylor JB4 four-cylinder engines running at 950rpm. She had a top speed of 7.1 knots. In June 1940, while she was on reserve duty in the Channel Islands, she was captured by the Germans, during which time she was so mishandled that she was not fit for service afterwards and when the war ended she was sold.

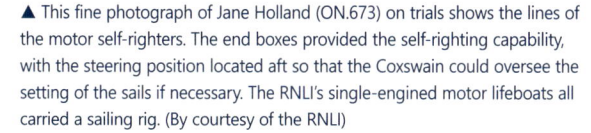

▼ Thomas Markby (ON.706) on trials prior to going on station at Swanage in June 1928. She carried sails and oars, and her Weyburn engine gave her a speed of 7.53 knots. She was transferred to Whitehills in Scotland in May 1949 and had an RNLI career lasting almost thirty years. (By courtesy of the RNLI)

▲ This fine photograph of Jane Holland (ON.673) on trials shows the lines of the motor self-righters. The end boxes provided the self-righting capability, with the steering position located aft so that the Coxswain could oversee the setting of the sails if necessary. The RNLI's single-engined motor lifeboats all carried a sailing rig. (By courtesy of the RNLI)

▼ The Newbons (ON.674) approaches the slipway at Sennen Cove to be rehoused. This photo shows clearly the deck layout and engine compartment, and the high end boxes typical of the self-righters, as well as the small shelter aft of amidships which was an addition during the boat's service career. (By courtesy of the RNLI)

MOTOR LIFEBOATS

5 • Watson motor 45ft

KEY DATA
- Introduced 1912
- Last built 1928
- 22 built
- Crew 8

▲ Mumbles lifeboat Edward Prince of Wales (ON.678) undergoing a refit in Bristol in 1936. She was involved in a Gold medal rescue in 1944, but tragically capsized with the loss of her entire crew three years later. (Grahame Farr, courtesy of RNLI)

▼ (left) The first 45ft Watson Albert Edward (ON.463), which served at Clacton for almost twenty-eight years. She is pictured on Clacton pier after she had been converted to motor, with the propeller clearly visible. She carried twelve oars as well as a full sailing rig.

▼ (right) William Evans (ON.653), with her masts raised, was one of the first 45ft Watsons. The hull shape and design were almost identical to the Watson sailing lifeboats of the 1890s.

The 45ft Watsons were the largest motor lifeboats built during the 1920s with the exception of the 60ft Barnetts. As with all the Watsons, they were non-self-righting, having a hull similar in shape to that of the Watson sailing and pulling lifeboats. The early boats in the class were ordered just before the outbreak of the First World War in 1914, but, because of the difficulty in obtaining the necessary materials during the conflict period, the boats were not completed until 1919.

The first 45ft Watson was Albert Edward (ON.463), which was built in 1902 as a sailing lifeboat and fitted with an engine in 1912. Her conversion to motor proved to be successful, and she enjoyed a long RNLI career, although, being a conversion, she was rather different from the 45ft Watsons built after the First World War. Her success undoubtedly proved to the RNLI the viability of motor power in larger boats, having also gained experience of operational conditions with the 43ft Watsons.

A total of eleven 45ft boats were built to the open deck design, all of which were single-engined, carried a full set of sails and were fitted with a drop keel. The boats had a flush deck, except for the end boxes and cockpit aft protected by the engine canopy. Although good sea boats, they gained a reputation for being very wet, and so rudimentary deck shelters were fitted between 1927 and 1929 to provide some protection for the crews.

The programme of retrospectively fitting shleters was authorised by the RNLI's Construction Sub-committee in May 1927, which gave authority to the Chief Inspector to provide canopies and binnacles for eighteen non-self-righting, non cabin motor lifeboats, at an estimated cost of £60 for the canopy and £25 for the binnacle. As well as canopies being fitted to the 45ft Watsons, they were also added to 43ft Watsons and the three 46ft 6in Norfolk & Suffolk motor lifeboats.

Adding canopies to previously open motor lifeboats came after the RNLI designers and engineers, gaining operational experience with motor lifeboats, realised that, as the December 1923 edition of The Lifeboat stated, 'the value of cabins is very great, and the need for them is greater now that we have powerful Motor Life-baots with a radius of action of anything from fifty to 100 miles'. Crew protection on motor lifeboats had become essential – the boats could remain at sea far longer than sailing lifeboats, and travel considerably further.

The 60ft Barnett lifeboat was the first design to be built with a cabin, and in 1923 the 45ft Watson design was modified to incorporate greater protection for crews. The 45ft Watsons from John R. Webb (ON.684) onwards were built with a self-draining cockpit aft, protected by the cabin, and a small cabin forward of the engine room, which was equipped with bench-type seats and could accommodate up to twenty survivors. A total of ten boats were built in this cabin series. John R. Webb was completed in June 1923 and before going on station visited the Thames to give a display to the British Motor Boat Club on the Chelsea Reach.

The hulls of the 45ft Watsons were built of Honduras mahogany on English oak framing, and the outer planking was of double diagonal construction. The open 45ft Watsons had endboxes at bow and stern, and a self-draining deck which had little freeboard. The front endbox had a breakwater built of two-inch thick English elm to deflect spray from the decks. The rear endbox had a watertight hatch allowing access into the endbox, inside which were two wells which allowed the crew to access the propeller and shaft should they become fouled. The engine room floor and sides were covered in copper sheeting so as to make this compartment flame proof. In case of fire the hatches would be closed and the air intakes blocked, thus restricting the fire to this one compartment.

The first 45ft Watsons were fitted with single 60bhp Tyler petrol engines, while later boats had single 80bhp DE engines designed by the RNLI and built either by the Weyburn Engineering Company or the J.S.

5 • Watson motor 45ft

#	Year* (Yd No) Builder Place	Length Breadth Crew	Name Donor	ON Cost Weight	Engines	Stations (launches/lives saved)	Notes Disposal
1	1902/1912 (TI70) Thames IW Blackwall	45' 12'6" 12/9	**Albert Edward** Grand Lodge of Freemasons.	463 £1,890 14t3	(Originally 12 oars) 1x40bhp Tylor 4-cyl C (p)	Clacton 13.12.1901-3.29 (160/277) Arranmore 19.6.1929-7.32 (1/0)	Sold 10.1932- £100
2	1919 (S13) S. E. Saunders Cowes	45' 12'6" 12/9	**Elsie** Gift of Rt Hon Arnold Morley, London.	648 £6,295 15t	1x60bhp Tylor D.1 4-cyl (p)	St Mary's 16.10.1919-27.3.30 (24/88) Helvick Head 31.3.1930-1.7.46 (16/9) Reserve 1946-51 (12/5)	Sold 1.1.1951- £425
3	1919 (S14) S. E. Saunders Cowes	45' 12'6" 12/9	**Duke of Connaught/ 1920- Shamrock** RNLI Funds.	649 £6,013 15t	1x60bhp Tylor D.1 4-cyl (p)	Baltimore 20.8.1919-14.5.50 (43/34) Reserve 5.1950-2.52 (1/0)	Sold 2.1952
4	1921 (S30) Smrs & Payne/ S. E. Saunders	45' 12'6" 12/9	**William Evans** Legacy of Mr William Evans, Wolverhampton.	653 £7,730 15t	1x60bhp Tylor D.1 4-cyl (p)	Wexford 14.8.1921-1.25 (1921-27: 33/80) Rosslare Harbour 1.1925-25.6.27 Galway Bay 2.7.1927-3.39 (24/29)	Sold 11.1940- £90
5	1921 (S27) S. E. Saunders Cowes	45' 12'6" 12/9vw	**Joseph Adlam** Legacy of Mr Joseph Adlam, Worcester.	654 £7,020 15t	1x60bhp Tylor D.1 4-cyl (p)	Blyth 4.10.1921-16.3.48 (82/74) Reserve 1948-51 (8/0)	Sold 2.1952- £400
6	1919 (S17) S. E. Saunders Cowes	45' 12'6" 12/9	**Dunleary (Civil Service No.7)** Civil Service Lifeboat Fund.	658 £6,074 15t	1x60bhp Tylor D.1 4-cyl (p)	Dun Laoghaire 22.12.1919-21.7.38 (23/55) Lytham 1.1939-19.4.51 (58/30)	Sold 5.1951- £500
7	1921 (S25) S. E. Saunders Cowes	45' 12'6" 12/9	**Frederick and Emma** Legacy of Miss E. M. Beer, Selly Park, Birmingham.	659 £7,141 15t	1x60bhp Tylor D.1 4-cyl (p)	Wick 22.6.1921-4.10.38 (19/37) Amble 13.1.1939-8.6.50 (34/57)	Sold 8.1950- £750
8	1921 (S24) S. E. Saunders Cowes	45' 12'6" 12/9	**Duke of Connaught** Gift of United Grand Lodge of Freemasons, England.	668 £6,889 15t	1x60bhp Tylor D.1 4-cyl (p)	Peterhead No.2 21.6.1921-15.6.39 (45/107) Reserve 6.1939-51 (30/97)	Sold 10.1951- £750
9	1922 (W1567) J. S. White Cowes	45' 12'6" 8	**The Brothers** Gift of the Misses H. A. A. and C. M. Eddy.	671 £13,214 16t15	1x80bhp Weyburn 6-cyl DE.6 (p)	Penlee 6.12.1922-22.6.31 (19/12) Falmouth 14.4.1931-3.11.34 (2/0) Reserve 1934-48 (45/27) Selsey 18.6.1937-26.8.38 (2/0) Workington 9.11.1948-3.2.52 (7/0)	Sold 8.1952- £800
10	1924 (W1568) J. S. White Cowes	45' 12'6" 8	**Edward, Prince of Wales** The Welsh Lifeboat Fund.	678 £12,811 16t18	1x80bhp Weyburn 6-cyl DE.6 (p)	Mumbles 18.5.1924-23.4.47 (64/129)	Capsized on service 23.4.1947, eight lost, later burnt in situ
11	1923 (W1569) J. S. White Cowes	45' 12'6" 8	**Elizabeth Newton** Legacy of Mr R. Newton.	679 £12,724 16t19	1x80bhp Weyburn 6-cyl DE.6 (p)	Hartlepool 10.1.1924-19.10.39 (23/16) Reserve 10.1939-53 (23/11)	Sold 5.1953- £400
12	1923 (W1570) J. S. White Cowes	45' 12'6" 8	**City of Bradford/ 1929- City of Bradford I** City of Bradford Lifeboat Fund.	680 £12,758 16t19	1x80bhp Weyburn 6-cyl DE.6 (p)	Humber 14.11.1923-11.3.29 (29/37) Humber Emergency 9.1.1930-2.32 (7/0) Reserve 1932-52 (43/55)	Sold 10.1952
13	1923 (W1594) J. S. White Cowes	45' 12'6" 8	**John R. Webb/ 1931- 684 RM/ 1934- Hearts of Oak** Legacy of J. Russell Webb, Leicester/ 1934- Hearts of Oak Benefit Society.	684 £8,747 17t8	1x80bhp Weyburn DE.6 6-cyl (p)/ 1934- 85hp Ferry (d)/ 1945- 80bhp Weyburn-White DE.6 (d)	Tenby 11.8.1923-11.4.30 (16/32) Barra Island 2.9.1931-28.7.32 (1/0) Yarmouth 7.1.1934-8.36 (15/7) and 18.6.1937-4.1938 (3/2) Reserve 1938-55 (46/13)	Cabin series Sold 2.1955- £753

MOTOR LIFEBOATS

5 • Watson motor 45ft

	Year* (Yd No) Builder Place	Length Breadth Crew	Name Donor	ON Cost Weight	Engines	Stations (launches/lives saved)	Notes Disposal
14	1924 (W1601) J. S. White Cowes	45' 12'6" 8	**J. W. Archer** Gift of J. W. Archer.	685 £7,515 17t9	1x80bhp White 6-cyl DE.6 (p)	Teesmouth 13.12.1924-22.2.50 (37/120) Amble 8.6.1950-9.54 (8/0) Reserve 1954-56 (6/0)	Cabin series Sold 7.1956
15	1924 (W1602) J. S. White Cowes	45' 12'6" 8	**T. B. B. H.** Legacies of Mrs Thornton, Mr Bartlett, Miss Boustred and Miss Hooper.	686 £7,435 17t6	1x80bhp White 6-cyl DE.6 (p)	Portrush 16.7.1924-18.7.49 (75/17) Reserve 1949-53 (10/0)	Cabin series Sold 1.1953- £305
16	1924 (W1610) J. S. White Cowes	45' 12'6" 8	**B. A. S. P.** Legacies of Mr Blackburn, Mrs Armstrong, Mrs Smart and Mrs Price.	687 £7,519 17t17	1x80bhp White 6-cyl DE.6 (p)	Yarmouth 31.10.1924-7.11.34 (42/30) Falmouth 3.11.1934-7.1.1940 (8/0) Reserve 1.1940-47 (12/5) and 1951-55 (5/0) Valentia 17.5.1947-2.5.51 (14/2)	Cabin series Sold 2.1955
17	1924 (S36) S. E. Saunders Cowes	45' 12'6" 8	**The Lord Southborough (Civil Service No.1)** Civil Service Lifeboat Fund.	688 £8,997 17t2	1x80bhp Weyburn 6-cyl DE.6 (p)	Margate 27.3.1925-18.3.51 (278/269) Reserve 3.1951-55 (14/17)	Cabin series Named Grace Darling for Wembley Exhibition, 1924 Sold 1.1955
18	1924 (S37) S. E. Saunders Cowes	45' 12'6" 8	**Manchester and Salford** Manchester and Salford Lifeboat Fund.	689 £8,456 17t10	1x80bhp Weyburn 6-cyl DE.6 (p)	Douglas 20.11.1924-18.7.46 (27/8) Reserve 7.1946-54 (13/5)	Cabin series Sold 10.1954- £750
19	1925 (S38) S. E. Saunders Cowes	45' 12'6" 8	**C. and S.** Legacy of Miss Emily Smart, Dublin; gift from executors of Peter Coates.	690 £8,424 17t6	1x80bhp Weyburn 6-cyl DE.6 (p)	Dunmore East 24.3.1925-19.3.40 (12/31) Pwllheli 26.4.1940-5.11.43 (12/7) Reserve 1943-46 (6/0) Valentia 18.11.1946-17.5.47 (2/0)	Cabin series Sold 11.1947- £250
20	1925 (S39) S. E. Saunders Cowes	45' 12'6" 8	**Milburn** Legacy of Sir Charles Stamp Milburn, gift of Frederick Milburn, Newcastle.	692 £8,449 17t8	1x80bhp Weyburn 6-cyl DE.6 (p)	Holy Island 1.6.1925-4.11.46 (57/81) Reserve 1946-55 (32/13)	Cabin series Sold 9.1955- £350
21	1924 (W1603) J. S. White Cowes	45' 12'6" 8	**H. F. Bailey/ 1936- J. B. Proudfoot** Legacy of Henry F. Bailey/ 1936- Legacy of Miss F. Proudfoot.	694 £7,530 17t9	1x80bhp White 6-cyl DE.6 (p)	Cromer No.1 15.8.1924-5.12.28 and 14.5.1929-12.12.35 (67/160) Reserve 1935-47 and 1949-56 (107/190) Southend-on-Sea 2.12.1941-2.45 (23/136) Dover 28.5.1947-11.3.49 (19/6)	Cabin series Sold 9.1956- £350
22	1925 (W1611) J. S. White Cowes	45' 12'6" 8	**M. O. Y. E.** Legacies of Miss Manby, the Misses J. L. and J. C. Owen, Mr Yates and Mr Lloyd.	695 £7,614 18t15	1x80bhp White 6-cyl DE.6 (p)	Porthdinllaen 24.2.1926-11.3.49 (56/16) Reserve 1949-56 (17/7)	Cabin series Named Grace Darling for Wembley Exhibition, 1925 Sold 4.1956- £350

▶ Two photographs of the 45ft Watson motor for Blyth, Joseph Adlam (ON.654). She was built as an open boat and is pictured (left) on trials with her sails raised. As with all of the early 45ft Watsons, she had a canopy added during the late 1920s (right). (By courtesy of the RNLI)

5 • Watson motor 45ft

◀ The 1923-built 45ft Watson City of Bradford I (ON.680) at Spurn Point; she was the last of the 45ft Watsons built without a canopy, and this photo, taken at her naming ceremony on 25 May 1924, shows the engine casing and her open deck layout.

▶ City of Bradford I at Southend with the canopy, fitted retrospectively during the late 1920s.

▲ (left) John R. Webb (ON.684) was the first 45ft Watson to be built with a cabin, but it was somewhat rudimentary as seen her; she was also fitted with Marconi radio telegraphy. (RNLI)

▲ (right) J.W. Archer (ON.685) on the Thames in July 1924 during a fund-raising trip. She is pictured at Oxford, the furthest she went, having stopped at various places on the way to promote the work of the RNLI. (RNLI)

White boatyard, with a self-contained reverse gear. The engine, housed in a watertight compartment, gave the boats a speed of just over eight knots and a range of about 125 miles. A full set of sails was carried and the dropkeel was fitted at the after end of the cabin. Buoyancy was provided by ninety-one air cases which would keep the boat afloat even if every compartment was flooded. In terms of performance of specific boats, Elsie (ON.648) had a maximum speed of 7.75 knots, while William Evans (ON.653) reached eight knots during her trials. The Brothers (ON.671), the first boat fitted with a Weyburn engine, reached a speed of 8.4 knots, and the other Weyburn-engined boats achieved a similar speed.

The first of the cabin boats was renamed Hearts of Oak (ON.684) and was re-engined in 1934 with an 85hp Ferry diesel engine, thus becoming the first RNLI lifeboat powered by diesel. The engine was of the same output as the petrol unit that it replaced, and drove the propeller through a two-to-one reduction gear, with the engine running at 1,600rpm. The engine was built by the Ferry Engine Co, Southampton, and, once it had been fitted in the lifeboat, extensive trials were undertaken. One of the benefits of diesel as a fuel was that it was less flammable than petrol, which lessened the risk of fire, while diesel-powered lifeboats also had a far greater range than petrol-engined ones.

MOTOR LIFEBOATS

5 • Watson motor 45ft

▶ Lord Southborough (Civil Service No.1) (ON.688) at moorings when she was being used as a reserve lifeboat. She was on station at Margate for twenty-six years, during which time she was involved in the Dunkirk evacuation in 1940. She was sold out of service in 1955 to the Provincial Government of Cyrenaica, a district of Libya once under British administration.

▼ (left) C. and S. (ON.690) on trials, with her sails raised, prior to going on station at Dubmore East. She carried a standing lug and jib for use in case of engine failure. (By courtesy of the RNLI)

▼ (right) The last 45ft Watson cabin motor to be built, M. O. Y. E. (ON.695), on trials prior to taking up duties at Porthdinllaen. This fine photograph shows her deck layout, with cabin and low endboxes, to good effect. (By courtesy of the RNLI)

38   MOTOR LIFEBOATS

Chapter 3
Twin engines and diesels

Twin engines and diesels

◀ (chapter frontispiece) William and Kate Johnston approaching New Brighton pier in a heavy swell on the Mersey after rescuing the crews of the casualties Progress and Loch Ranza Castle, 23 November 1938. (By courtesy of the RNLI)

▶ The 60ft twin-screw Barnett Robert and Marcella Beck (ON.696) was one of the four such boats to be built. (Beken, by courtesy of the RNLI)

▲ James Rennie Barnett (1864-1965) was appointed Consulting Naval Architect to the RNLI in 1904, as the first experiments with motor lifeboats were taking place. On his retirement, in 1947, he had been engaged in the work of designing lifeboats for sixty years. Of the many contributions he made to lifeboat design that of twin engines, as used first in the 60ft class, was probably the most significant. He also first thought of fitting shelters and cabins for crews and survivors, a feature that has since been taken for granted. Midship steering was another of his ideas, although it was only being fully utilised by the time of his retirement.

▶ An impressive gathering of lifeboats at Douglas, Isle of Man on 11 May 1932, when every IOM lifeboat came to the island's capital for a ceremony to mark the centenary of the building of the Tower of Refuge. On the slipway is the 45ft Watson motor Manchester and Salford (ON.689), while moored alongside are two motor lifeboats and two pulling and sailing lifeboats from the other IOM stations. During this era the RNLI's fleet was a mix of powered and pulling lifeboats.

Following the cessation of hostilities in 1918, the RNLI soon adopted a policy of renewal, building many new motor lifeboats to modernise the fleet and replace the pulling, sailing and steam lifeboats from the previous century. An ambitious building programme for fifty new motor lifeboats was announced and, as motor lifeboats became operational at more and more stations, they had a significant impact on the overall number of lifeboats in operation. Motor lifeboats had a greater range than pulling boats, so could effectively serve a coastline that, during the nineteenth century, had been covered by several pulling lifeboats. At their peak, more than 300 pulling lifeboats were in service, with some stations, mainly on the east coast, operating two or, in some cases, more boats to cover specific danger spots and be in the optimal location to sail downwind to a casualty. The motorisation of the fleet, therefore, resulted in a significant reduction in the number of stations. When a motor lifeboat was sent to a station, it was often found that a neighbouring station could be closed, yet rescue coverage of the area was actually improved.

Another significant advance during the inter-war years was the development of lifeboats which took advantage of the specific benefits motor power offered, with boats being larger and providing protection for the crew. Hitherto, motor lifeboats had been based on pulling and sailing designs but fitted with a single engine, driving a single propeller. But as the RNLI gained greater experience in the operation of motor craft, and more reliable and powerful engines were developed, so larger boats with a greater range could be built. The largest of the early motor lifeboats was the 45ft Watson which weighed about fifteen tons, and was powered by a single 60bhp engine. The prototype of the class, Elsie (ON.648), was launched in 1919 and placed on station at St Mary's (Isles of Scilly). Between 1919 and 1925, more than twenty 45ft Watsons were completed and it proved to be a first step towards building some kind of standard motor type. Another early motor lifeboat was the Norfolk & Suffolk, which at 46ft 6in in length was large for the time, with three being built.

Twin engines and diesels

While these first motor boats proved very capable and were clearly better than their pulling and sailing counterparts, motor lifeboat design took a significant step forward in 1922 when James Barnett, the RNLI's Consulting Naval Engineer, designed a 60ft lifeboat that employed twin engines, in separate watertight engine rooms, driving twin propellers. This new boat, which heralded the introduction of twin engines to lifeboat design, was one of the most significant developments of the inter-war era.

The impressive 60ft lifeboat was a ground-breaking design in many other ways and it represented the first of many significant contributions Barnett made to motor lifeboat design during more than half a century as the Consulting Naval Architect to the Institution. His pioneering ideas moved lifeboat design forward, with the twin engine arrangement eliminating the need for auxiliary sails necessary in single-engined motor lifeboats. Several other advances incorporated in the 60ft boat included, for the first time in a lifeboat, shelters for crew and survivors, a feature taken for granted on modern lifeboats. Displacing over forty tons, a lifeboat of such size had never been seen before. The design reflected a new era as the RNLI, preparing to celebrate its centenary, entered the second century of its existence with confidence and assurance after the difficulties of operating during the First World War.

The first of the new 60ft type, William and Kate Johnston (ON.682), was allocated to the New Brighton station at the mouth of the River Mersey, guarding one of the busiest shipping lanes in the country. During a career of more than twenty-five years, she saved almost 250 lives and performed several outstanding rescues, perhaps the most notable of which began in the early hours of 24 November 1928, when she went to the aid of the French steamer Emile Delmas, of La Rochelle. The steamer had been dragging her anchors in violent seas and strong gale-force winds four miles west-north-west of the Bar Lightvessel while she was making for Holyhead. The lifeboat put to sea at 7.45am with a crew of eight. It proved to be a particularly difficult rescue carried out in a strong gale, high seas, blinding rain squalls and 100 mile per hour winds.

Once the lifeboat reached the casualty, Coxswain George Robinson had difficulty in getting her alongside due to the steamer's violent motion. However, with outstanding seamanship, courage and teamwork among the lifeboat's crew, he succeeded in bringing William and Kate Johnston close enough for twenty-three of the steamer's crew to jump to safety. Although the lifeboat was damaged during this manoeuvre, Coxswain Robinson brought her safely clear and then set course for New Brighton.

During the return journey, extreme seas were encountered and one huge wave, which swept over the lifeboat, washed two of the lifeboat crew overboard, as well as the Chief Engineer from the steamer. The wave flooded the engine rooms and, only with great difficulty, was Robinson able to bring the lifeboat round so that the two lifeboatmen could be picked up; unfortunately, however, the lifeboat was unable to reach the Chief Engineer, who drowned. After more than six hours at sea in the worst conditions imaginable, William and Kate Johnston arrived back at her station. For this outstanding service, Robinson was awarded the Silver medal and Bronze medals went to the rest of the lifeboat crew. The French Government awarded Gold medals to Coxswain Robinson and to the two men who had been washed overboard, George Carmody and Samuel Jones.

Rescues such as this helped to overcome any lingering doubts shown by lifeboat crews about the capabilities of motor lifeboats. Many who had been sceptical about the powered boats, and suspicious of the benefits an engine provided, were soon won over and, by the 1920s, most crews, such as at Sennen Cove in Cornwall for example, expressed a desire for a new motor lifeboat, with the Sennen Coxswain, writing in 1921, stating 'don't delay the new boat'. His new boat, a 40ft self-righter named The Newbons (ON.674), arrived on 1 May 1922 after a three-day journey from Cowes, in company with another 40ft motor self-righter, the new Appledore lifeboat V.C.S. (ON.675). A number of boats of these 40ft self-righting type boats were built during the 1920s and gave good service at their stations.

The 40ft self-righters were among the smaller motor types planned during the 1920s, as the inter-war years saw a series of ever larger motor lifeboats being built. The debate over whether self-righting or non-self-righting craft was preferable had been ongoing since the end of the nineteenth century, when Watson had first introduced his non-self-righting sailing design. This was more stable than the self-righters with

▲ The 48ft Ramsgate motor lifeboat Prudential (ON.697) on trials. (Beken, by courtesy of the RNLI)

▼ The 48ft Ramsgate motor lifeboat Greater London (Civil Service No.3) (ON.704) at sea off Southend pier. (By courtesy of the RNLI)

MOTOR LIFEBOATS

Twin engines and diesels

45ft 6in Watson motor K.E.C.F. (ON.700) served at Rosslare Harbour and was powered by two 40hp Weyburn CE.4 petrol engines. She was the first Watson with twin 40hp engines and the first lifeboat to be fitted with a wireless with which the crew could communicate with the shore. (By courtesy of the RNLI)

their narrow beam, but of course if turned over would not come upright. Following the introduction of Watson's design in the 1890s, the RNLI built lifeboats to the two basic designs, the self-righter and Watson's non-self-righter, deployed according to local conditions and local preferences. Designers had been unable to produce a lifeboat which was self-righting and yet retained the same lateral stability as Watson's non-self-righting designs. Barnett also favoured the non-self-righting principle, with his designs for large twin-engined non-self-righting boats becoming the mainstay of the lifeboat fleet; these 'deepwater boats', as he termed them, served at stations where a greater range was needed, notably on west coasts of Scotland and Ireland and England's south coast.

The deepwater boats that were built from his plans, of which the 60ft Barnett was the first example, were all over 45ft in length, and had ample beam, large cockpits and rudimentary crew shelters. They were kept afloat or launched from a slipway. However, for stations where carriage launching was practised, a lighter type was necessary. Getting an engine small enough to fit into a boat that was easily manhandled across a beach and hauled onto a carriage was the next challenge for the RNLI's engineers. Plans for such a design had first been drawn up before 1914, and in 1915 a small 15hp engine was being developed by Tylor & Sons for a light motor lifeboat. However, it was not until 1921 that a carriage-launched motor boat entered service, when a 35ft self-righter was built, Priscilla MacBean (ON.655), fitted with a 15hp Gardner engine. She was initially used as an experimental craft, and was the first of three.

Although they were small, carriage-launched motor boats were effective rescue tools, and their development meant that all stations, no matter which method of launching they employed, could now operate a motor lifeboat. After the three 35ft motor self-righters lifeboats had entered service, the type was subsequently enlarged by six inches and improved, and then entered service on a widespread basis. A non-self-righting carriage-launched type was also developed, the Liverpool class, for crews preferring a more stable boat, albeit one that was not self-righting.

The last of the small experimental 35ft motor self-righters, L.P. and St Helen (ON.703), remained in service for the longest of the three, operating during the Second World War from the Newcastle station in County Down, and being involved in one of the most famous services of the war. On 21 January 1942 she was launched to the aid of the steamship Browning, of Liverpool, which had gone ashore off Ballyquinton Point, twenty miles from Newcastle. She launched just after 5am into gale force winds and, after overcoming confused seas off Strangford Bar, forced her way against the weather until, at 10.30am, she reached the scene to find seven ships from the convoy ashore with Browning stern first on the rocks.

Trying to take the lifeboat alongside the casualty proved to be impossible, and at one point she was almost flung onto the steamer's deck by the seas. So Coxswain Pat Murphy went to the lee side of the vessel and steered between the casualty and rocks, through a channel only

Twin engines and diesels

20ft wide. In the relative lee of the ship, it was a straightforward task to rescue the steamer's crew. The small self-righter could carry a maximum of twenty-eight in rough weather, but thirty-nine men had to be saved. After assessing the situation, the Coxswain decided there was no choice but to take them all, as returning to the steamer would not be possible.

Once the men were all aboard the lifeboat, getting away was a major problem, as the channel was too narrow for the lifeboat to turn round. So Coxswain Murphy decided to cross the reef on which the steamer had been wrecked, but any mistake in doing so would have capsized the lifeboat with tragic consequences. But, as three big seas washed over the reef, the lifeboat was successfully taken across it, with the Coxswain driving her at full speed to the open sea. The lifeboat was still twenty miles from her station, but, as it was impossible to return against the gale, she was taken north and, nine hours after setting out, reached the safety of the small harbour at Portavogie to land the survivors. For this outstanding rescue, which consisted of several episodes of superb seamanship, Coxswain Murphy was awarded the Gold medal, while Silver and Bronze medals went to the other members of the gallant crew.

Although the carriage-launched self-righters were built to what was basically a standard design, standardisation was not the rule at the time, and a number of unusual types were developed with only a few examples, and sometimes only one, being built of each. These one-off boats were

▲ Old and new lifeboats at Stromness in 1928: the new 51ft Barnett J.J.K.S.W. (ON.702) on the slipway dwarfs the station's first motor lifeboat, John A. Hay (ON .561). J.J.K.S.W. left Cowes on 15 February 1928 and reached Stromness on 3 March, covering 1,007 miles in eighteen days, five of which were spent at Guernsey. She was at sea for 125 hours and averaged eight and a half knots during this epic journey. (Orkney Photographic Archive)

◀ Peter and Sarah Blake (ON.755) on trials; she was one of a pair of 51ft Barnetts built in 1932. Stationed at Fenit from 1932 to 1958, she also served for fourteen years in the Reserve Fleet, and this, making a total of forty years of service, made her one of the longest-ever serving lifeboats in the RNLI fleet. She was sold out of service in 1972. (Beken, by courtesy of the RNLI)

MOTOR LIFEBOATS

Twin engines and diesels

built as a result of the RNLI's policy of consulting coxswains and crews about their preferences, and the result was a fleet of motor lifeboats that had considerable variations. Lifeboats were thus built for the specific conditions of a particular station, where it was deemed local conditions justified the building of a new and different class.

These one-off types included a special design for working in estuaries, known as the Ramsgate class; a motorised version of the Norfolk & Suffolk sailing lifeboat for service at Gorleston and Lowestoft; variations of the 41ft Watson lifeboat with a broader beam than the standard, and a strengthened hull, for launching over skids laid on a beach; a fast 64ft vessel for air-sea rescue in the English Channel which operated from Dover; and in the mid-1930s, a light Surf lifeboat intended for carriage launching and working close inshore. With the latter design, the RNLI ventured into new territory as several of the boats, which were just 32ft in length, were driven by an early form of water jet; however, this did not prove particularly successful and only nine Surf lifeboats were built.

At the opposite end of the scale from the small Surf boats were the 60ft Barnetts, of which four were built during the 1920s. But these large lifeboats proved a little too big and were impractical for operations at many stations. As they had to be kept afloat, they were restricted to where a sheltered mooring could be found. Consequently, a smaller Barnett, 51ft in length, was introduced in 1928, known as the 'Stromness' class after the station at which the first one served. Like the larger 60ft type, it had twin engines and twin screws incorporated into the design but, being smaller and lighter, proved to be was more practical and served at a wider range of stations. Able to be slipway launched, the 51ft Barnett became one of the RNLI's standard heavy weather lifeboats during the 1930s and 1940s, usually operating from stations where a large sea area had to be covered.

While the power and range of the motor lifeboat had resulted in the closure of stations which were located close to each other, particularly down England's east coast, lifeboats such as the 51ft Barnett type could be operated effectively at more remote places, where rescue work usually involved covering distances that were far beyond the capabilities of the pulling and sailing lifeboat, even when the pulling boats were operated by a skilled and strong crew. Notably, rescue coverage in the Channel Islands and Orkney was greatly improved as motor lifeboats could cope effectively in the heavy seas often found around these islands.

In Guernsey, for almost fifty years down to 1929 the pulling lifeboats operated from the station at St Peter Port performed just thirteen effective services. In eleven years of service by 51ft Barnett Queen Victoria (ON.719), from her arrival in 1929 until 1940, she completed no fewer than forty-five rescue missions – more than three times as many as the various pulling boats had managed in total. On the west coast of Ireland, at Valentia, Galway Bay and Baltimore, new stations were established with motor lifeboats where lifeboat operations had not hitherto been possible due to the nature of the seas on the country's Atlantic seaboard and the distances involved in reaching casualties. Meanwhile, two new stations were established in Shetland in the 1930s, at Lerwick and Aith, where operating a pulling and sailing lifeboat would not have been possible.

Before the Shetland stations had been established, a challenging service took place involving the 51ft Barnett at Stromness, J.J.K.S.W. (ON.702). This long service, during which the boat's range and the endurance of her crew were tested to the extreme, was one of the most tragic incidents to take place in the Northern Isles. On the night of 28 March 1930 the Aberdeen trawler Ben Doran ran aground off Shetland. But in the gale force winds and heavy seas, nothing could be done to assist those on board. The nearest lifeboat was in Orkney at Stromness and so, late on the afternoon of 30 March, J.J.K.S.W. was called to help. She fought her way north through the heavy seas and gale force winds until she reached Scalloway, 134 miles from Stromness, to where a telegram was sent asking for food, fuel and a local pilot to be ready.

She arrived at Scalloway at 7.30am on 31 March after completing a passage of almost fifteen hours, during which she and her crew battled atrocious conditions. After being refuelled, the boat set out, with the pilot on board. On reaching the scene of the casualty, only the upper part of the trawler's mast could be seen above the waves and, despite a thorough search of the area, no survivors were found. The lifeboat

▼ The twin-engined Watson motor Mona (ON.775) at Groves & Guttridge, where she was completed in the spring of 1935. This fine photograph shows clearly the deck layout and cockpit arrangements of the 45ft 6in Watson. Mona served at Broughty Ferry for almost a quarter of a century, but tragically capsized on service to the North Carr lightvessel, which had broken adrift from its moorings on 8 December 1959, with the loss of her entire crew of eight; she was subsequently dismantled and burnt on the beach. (Beken, by courtesy of the RNLI)

Twin engines and diesels

returned to Scalloway, where the crew managed a few hours sleep. Early on 1 April they headed south, but the journey back to Orkney took over sixteen hours and J.J.K.S.W. reached Stromness after more than fifty-five hours away having travelled nearly 260 miles. This, according to the RNLI account, was 'the longest journey on service which has been made by any Motor Lifeboat', and proof if it were needed of the capabilities of Barnett's design. Coincidentally, the RNLI had announced plans in March 1930 for establishing a lifeboat station at Lerwick, and if Ben Doran had been wrecked a year later her crew would most probably have been saved.

The 51ft Barnett design proved itself on many other occasions and some amazing rescues carried out during the inter-war years enabled lifeboat crews to demonstrate that their bravery, skill and stamina, allied to a powered rescue craft, was a formidable combination. One of the most extraordinary rescues of all, which would have been inconceivable in lifeboats operated just two decades earlier, took place off the coast of County Cork in 1936 when the Ballycotton lifeboat went to aid the Daunt Rock Lightvessel. The Lightvessel, with eight men on board and usually anchored twelve miles off the coast in Ballycotton Bay, broke her moorings on 11 February and began to drift during a severe gale, which had been blowing for several days. Conditions were so bad that it was not thought possible to launch the lifeboat.

However, Ballycotton Coxswain Patrick Sliney managed to board the 51ft Barnett Mary Stanford (ON.733), which was kept at moorings in the harbour, and with a full crew succeeded in taking her through the narrow harbour entrance. The station's watching Honorary Secretary, Robert Mahony, later wrote in his account: 'I did not believe it was possible for the coxswain to even get aboard the lifeboat. . . [but] to my amazement the lifeboat headed out between the piers. . . As I watched the lifeboat, I thought every minute she must turn back. At one moment a sea crashed on her; the next she was standing on her heel. But she went on.'

Despite mountainous seas, the lifeboat cleared the harbour and set course for the drifting vessel, reaching her at noon, a quarter of a mile south-west of the Daunt Rock, and only half a mile from the shore. The crew remained standing by the lightvessel, knowing the danger to shipping of an abandoned lightvessel out of position. As towing the lightvessel was impossible, the lifeboat stood by until darkness and then made for Queenstown to refuel. On 12 February, Mary Stanford returned to the casualty and stood by throughout the day, battling horrendous conditions throughout. At daylight on 13 February, Coxswain Sliney again went to Queenstown to refuel. Despite being swept constantly by breaking seas for over twenty-five hours and having had no food, the lifeboat crew set out again as soon as the lifeboat was refuelled. But that evening, as the weather worsened, the lightvessel's situation became increasingly perilous. She was in serious danger of striking the Daunt Rock with potentially fatal consequences, so Coxswain Sliney decided to take the lightvessel's crew off. In a dangerous manoeuvre that risked the lifeboat

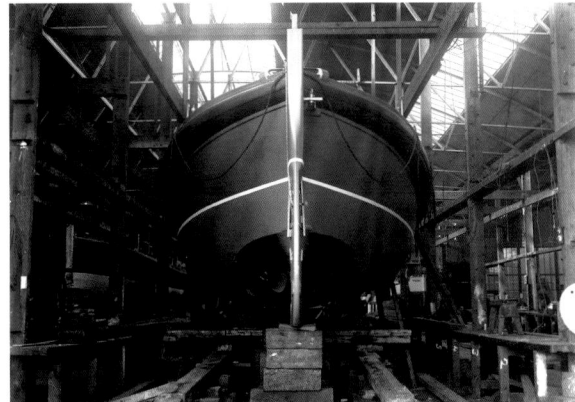

◀ The single-engined 35ft 6in Liverpool Harriot Dixon (ON.770) at sea off Cromer pier, with Coxswain Jimmy Davies at the helm. With her arrival as the No.2 lifeboat, Cromer become one of only a handful of stations that operated two motor lifeboats at the same time. She served the Norfolk station for thirty years. (By courtesy of Port of Lowestoft Research Society)

◀ The 45ft 6in Mona (ON.775) nearing completion at Groves and Guttridge's boatyard, Cowes. This fine photograph clearly shows the propellers and tunnel arrangement which was a feature common to all Watson and Barnett motor lifeboats. (Beken, by courtesy of the RNLI)

▼ The 45ft 6in Watson motor S.G.E. (ON.804) was built by J.S. White at Cowes. Unusually, she was named at White's yard, Cowes, on 12 April 1938 by Lady Baring, rather than at her station, and was one of four 46ft Watsons built at White's during 1938. (Beken, by courtesy of the RNLI)

MOTOR LIFEBOATS

Twin engines and diesels

▶ Ballycotton lifeboat Mary Stanford (ON.733) on exercise in July 1956, with on board, from left to right, Second Coxswain James McLeod, Coxswain Michael Lane Walsh, Honorary Secretary Robert H. Mahony, Richard Fitzgerald, Joseph McNamara, Bobby Blake and Bowman Maurice Connolly Walsh. This 51ft Barnett was the lifeboat involved in the epic rescue of crew of the Daunt Rock lightvessel in February 1936. (By courtesy of Ballycotton RNLI)

▼ The twin-engined 46ft Watson motor Jeanie Speirs (ON.788) moored in the small harbour at Portpatrick. (By courtesy of Portpatrick RNLI)

itself, he took Mary Stanford alongside the drifting vessel several times.

With seas sweeping over the wildly plunging lightvessel, the lifeboat had to make numerous passes to take off the eight men, with the last two being dragged to safety by the lifeboat's crew. Some suffered injuries during their ordeal, while the lifeboat crew also endured extreme hardship throughout the rescue. Mary Stanford had been away from station for seventy-six hours, at sea for forty-nine and the crew had been without food for twenty-five by the time they returned; all were suffering from the cold, and had salt water burns. For what was a truly remarkable rescue, the Gold medal was awarded to Coxswain Sliney; Silver medals went to Second Coxswain John Lane Walsh and Motor Mechanic Thomas Sliney; and Bronze medals to the rest of the crew. The motor lifeboat proved its worth during this gruelling service, and the extra power and endurance it offered enabled the successful completion of an extraordinary rescue, one of the most outstanding ever performed by an RNLI lifeboat crew.

At the time of the Daunt Rock rescue, attempts were under way to improve motor lifeboats' endurance through the use of diesel engines; the rescue highlighted the relative lack of range afforded by petrol engines, as the lifeboat had to return to harbour to refuel. Although petrol engines had been refined and developed since being first used, the introduction of diesel engines during the 1930s was a significant step forward. The former Tenby and Barra Island lifeboat John R. Webb (ON.684, later renamed 684RM) was the first lifeboat to be fitted with a diesel engine. In 1932 she was taken off station and, in September 1934, fitted with a single six-cylinder 85hp diesel built to a design by the Ferry Engine Co.

684RM was then put through a series of trials, during which she was compared with the Portpatrick boat, the CE.4 petrol-engined Jeanie Speirs (ON.788), a 46ft Watson built in 1936. The trials soon proved that diesel engines outperformed their petrol counterparts. 684RM could travel at full speed for 118 miles using just under thirty pints of fuel an hour, whereas the Portpatrick boat travelled just fifty-seven miles at full speed, yet consumed almost sixty-five pints an hour. The difference in consumption at cruising speed was even greater. The trials concluded by the summer of 1936 as the first lifeboat built with a diesel engine, S.G.E. (ON.787) destined for Yarmouth, was completed. Unfortunately, S.G.E. was destroyed by fire at Groves & Guttridge boatyard at Cowes in June 1937 after less than a year of service, but in that time she had proved that diesel engines represented the future for lifeboat power.

Twin engines and diesels

Both Jeanie Speirs and S.G.E. were 46ft Watsons, a design introduced in the mid-1930s and the latest incarnation of the Watson motor lifeboat to enter service. During the inter-war years, Watsons of varying lengths had been built as standard types. The 45ft version was the first, and this was superseded by the 45ft 6in version, which in turn was replaced by the 46ft boats. The new designs each incorporated various advances, usually in the form of better equipment, better engines and improved deck layouts. The first of the 46ft Watsons was H.F. Bailey (ON.777), and she went on to become one of the most famous in the history of the lifeboat service.

By the outbreak of the Second World War, almost the whole of the fleet had been motorised, with just fifteen pulling and sailing boats remaining in service. But even with motor lifeboats, lifeboat crews were severely tested by the events of the conflict. They were forced to operate in conditions more hazardous than ever and even routine services were more difficult. But during the course of the war, some of the most outstanding rescues and courageous acts in RNLI history were performed by lifeboat crews, and nobody was more courageous than Henry Blogg, the renowned Coxswain of the Cromer lifeboat. In the Cromer lifeboat H.F. Bailey, he helped to save many lives on numerous occasions, undertaking some daring rescues.

One of the most extraordinary was that to six vessels forming part of Convoy 559, which went ashore on the Haisborough Sands on 5 August 1941 in a severe gale and heavy seas. The Cromer lifeboat launched at 8am on 6 August with Blogg at the helm and the Cromer crew found the vessels close together but rapidly breaking up. In a series of daring manoeuvres, the lifeboat was taken alongside or, in some cases, driven over the decks of the ships to save those on board. In total eighty-eight lives were rescued during what was later described as 'one of the finest feats of seamanship . . . ever seen'. When H.F. Bailey and her crew returned to their station, the lifeboat was found to be severely damaged, having been driven over sunken decks, bumped severely on the sands, and at one point run aground, with three holes punched in her bow. Much of her port fender had been torn off and her stem was damaged, but she survived as the strength of the Watson motor lifeboat contributed to the rescue's successful outcome. Blogg was awarded the Gold medal for this service, his third such award, with Silver and Bronze medals going to the rest of the crew.

As well as Blogg, many other lifeboat men carried out remarkable rescues during the war, including Robert Cross, the full-time Coxswain of the Humber lifeboat station at Spurn Point at the mouth of the Humber. On 7 January 1943 he was in command of the lifeboat City of Bradford II (ON.709), a 45ft 6in Watson motor, when she went to HM trawler Almondine, which was stranded on a sandbank, lying on her side, and being swept by heavy seas. The lifeboat was taken alongside the casualty twelve times and nineteen men were rescued. Several times the lifeboat was smashed against the hull of the trawler, causing her stem to be splintered and some planking to be holed. But she survived her ordeal and made it back to station to land the survivors. For this service, made possible only by fine seamanship and great determination, the Gold medal was awarded to Cross, the Silver medal to Reserve Mechanic George Richards and Bronze medals to five other members of the crew.

The years of the Second World War had tested the lifeboat service and lifeboat crews to the limit. But the volunteers had risen to the challenges and, exclusive of Dunkirk, 6,376 lives had been saved. On many occasions lifeboats had been manned by older crews than had been usual, as the regular volunteers were serving in the forces, and shortage of suitable men had been an issue on occasions. But the lifeboats, more powerful and better equipped than those in service during the First World War, and their crews had more than contributed to Britain's war effort.

◀ 41ft Watson Edmund and Mary Robinson (ON.812) was built in 1938 as the New Brighton No.2 lifeboat, serving on the Mersey for fourteen years; she was one of nine 41ft Watson lifeboats built during the 1930s by Groves & Guttridge, the Cowes boatyard where many RNLI lifeboats were constructed. She was powered by twin 35hp Weyburn AE.6 petrol engines, which gave her a top speed of 7.89 knots. (By courtesy of the RNLI)

▼ The twin-engined 35ft 6in Liverpool motor St Albans (ON.863) on trials, prior to going on station at New Quay in Wales. One of the first of the twin-engined Liverpools, she replaced the 35ft Liverpool sailing lifeboat William Cantrell Ashley (ON.578), which had the distinction of being the last sailing lifeboat in RNLI service. (By courtesy of the RNLI)

MOTOR LIFEBOATS

6 • Self-righting motor 35ft

KEY DATA
- Introduced 1921
- Last built 1927
- 3 built

The early motor lifeboats were built for stations where they could be launched down a slipway or operate from a mooring. However, a motor-powered lifeboat which could be launched by carriage off an open beach, and was light enough to be manhandled ashore, was also needed. Such a motor lifeboat had to be light enough so that it could be dragged across a beach at a time when motor tractors were not yet in widespread use, and it also had to be strong enough to withstand heavy seas.

In July 1921 a light experimental prototype self-righter, Priscilla Macbean (ON.655), was sent for trials at Eastbourne. Built specially for launching from the beach, she was powered by a 15hp engine and weighed just over six tons, compared to the nine tons of the next lightest lifeboat. She had a speed of six knots and a radius of action of just thirty-four miles. She was followed two years later by another experimental 35ft boat, Herbert Joy (ON.683), which was sent to Scarborough, where she was carriage launched, and was fitted with a more powerful 35hp engine.

A third boat, L.P. and St Helen (ON.703), was built in 1927, and this went to Eastbourne to replace Priscilla Macbean, which was transferred to Kirkcudbright and later served at Maryport. L.P. and St Helen was powered by a different engine, which gave her a top speed of 7.43 knots.

Following re-engining in 1930, her speed increased slightly, to 7.66 knots, and she had a radius of action of thirty-nine miles. At her cruising speed of 6.26 knots she had a radius of action of fifty-five miles.

These three boats were all different, having different engines, and can be regarded as essentially experimental designs, based largely on the standard pulling self-righters that were in widespread use during the second half of the nineteenth century, but fitted with a single engine driving a single propeller, which was housed in a tunnel and protected by part of the keel. All carried sails and the RNLI emphasised that the motor was regarded as auxiliary to the sails rather than their replacement. In the event of the engine not working, the boats would be almost as effective being sailed as an ordinary pulling lifeboat without an engine.

The third of the 35ft self-righters, L.P. and St Helen, had the longest and most distinguished career of the three experimental boats, being involved in a Gold medal-winning rescue in January 1942 while she was stationed at Newcastle (Co Down). She was also closer in design to the 35ft 6in self-righters that had become the standard type at the end of the decade, and was regarded by the Institution's engineers as a satisfactory design for stations operating lifeboats which were launched over a beach.

▶ The first 35ft self-righting motor lifeboat, Priscilla Macbean (ON.655) ashore at Maryport, where she served for over three years. At her first station, Eastbourne, she was launched across the beach, and at both Kirkcudbright and Maryport down a slipway. (From an old postcard supplied by Iain Booth)

▶▶ The third of the small 35ft self-righting motor lifeboats, L.P. and St Helen (ON.703), under sail. The engine casing is the only indication that she is a motor lifeboat. (By courtesy of the RNLI)

	Year* (Yd No) Builder Place	Length Breadth Crew	Name Donor	ON Cost Weight	Engines	Stations (launches/lives saved)	Notes Disposal
1	1921 (W1578) J. S. White Cowes	35' 8'6" 10/7	**Priscilla Macbean** Legacy of Edward Macbean, Helensburgh and Glasgow.	655 £6,622.13.10 6t7	1x15hp Miller E4 4-cyl (p)	Eastbourne 29.7.1921-4.11.1927 (11/6) Kirkcudbright 3.3.1928-8.4.1931 (5/1) Maryport 19.4.1931-28.8.1934 (5/18)	Shelter fitted 1928 Sold 5.9.1934
2	1923 (S35) S. E. Saunders Cowes	35' 8'10" 10/7	**Herbert Joy** Gift of Alexander O. Joy, London, in memory of his brother.	683 £3,691.5.0 5t4	1x35hp Sage 6A 4-cyl (p)	Scarborough 28.5.1923-4.6.1931 (49/9) Reserve 1931-1937 (0/0)	Sold 4.3.1937
3	1927 (S45) S. E. Saunders, Cowes	35' 8'10" 10/7	**L. P. and St Helen** Legacies of Miss Ann Lovelock, Alfred Henry Pett and Miss H. Maynard Turner.	703 £4,960.10.10 5t16	1x30hp Halford (p)/ 1930- 1x35hp Weyburn AE6 (p)	Eastbourne 4.11.1927-14.1.1929 (2/0) Boulmer 28.2.1931-11.2.1937 (17/3) Newcastle 6.9.1937-17.7.1949 (26/63)	Sold 11.11.1949

6 • Self-righting motor 35ft

▶ Herbert Joy (ON.683) on her launching carriage at Scarborough, the station she served for eight years. Her double fender was unusual and not repeated on any other British-built motor lifeboat. (By courtesy of the RNLI)

▼ (left) Launch of Herbert Joy (ON.683) at Scarborough, with the propeller tunnel, visible at the stern, housing the single screw. (RNLI, by courtesy of Jeff Morris)

▼ (right) Herbert Joy (ON.683) in the harbour at Scarborough. The engine housing is amidships, and the steering wheel can be seen at the stern mounted on the aft end box. (By courtesy of the RNLI)

MOTOR LIFEBOATS 49

7 • Barnett 60ft twin screw

KEY DATA
- Introduced 1923
- Last built 1929
- 4 built

The 60ft Barnett was the first twin-engined and twin-screw motor lifeboat built by the RNLI. Designed by and named after James Barnett, the Consulting Naval Architect of the RNLI, the design was ground-breaking in many ways and, when the prototype William and Kate Johnston (ON.682) was launched in 1923, she was the largest lifeboat that had ever been built in Britain. Not only was she twin-engined, but she also had cabins to protect the rescuers and rescued, something hitherto considered unnecessary, but as motor lifeboats could undertake far longer services crew comfort became an issue. William and Kate Johnston entered service at New Brighton in August 1923, covering the entrance to the busy River Mersey. She was exhibited on the Thames at the first International Lifeboat Conference in 1924, which was held to mark the centenary of the RNLI.

The 60ft Barnett design was regarded as a 'deepwater' boat, suitable for travelling long distances in the worst of weathers. The hull, of teak, was double-skinned, and had eleven transverse and three longitudinal steel bulkheads, forming fifteen main watertight compartments. The twin 80hp engines were housed in separate watertight engine-room compartments so that, even if the compartments were flooded, the engines would continue to operate as long as the air intakes remained above water. The engines themselves were designed by the RNLI and built by Weyburn Engineering Co, Godalming, or at J.S. White's yard in Cowes. The twin propellers were arranged in protective tunnels on each side of the after end of the boat, minimising the risk of damage should the boat come into contact with another vessel or be grounded on a sandbank.

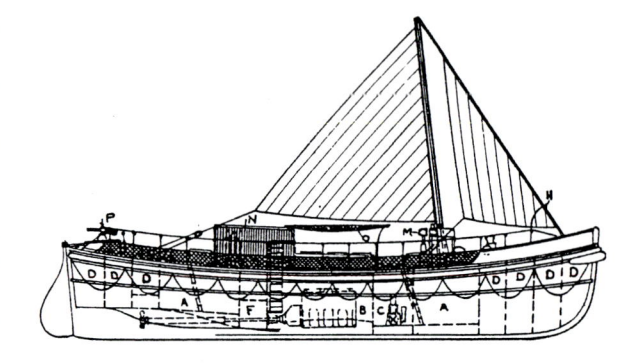

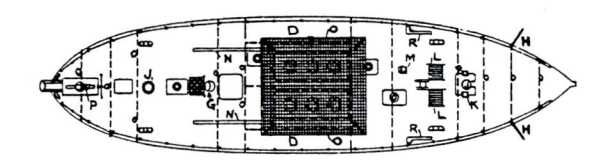

▼ The prototype 60ft Barnett lifeboat William and Kate Johnston (ON.682) on trials. The jumping net was subsequently removed while the boat was in service. The boat had flush decks, without sunken wells or cockpits, and was fitted with a stove and lavatory so that, as The Lifeboat for May 1922 explained: 'For the first time, it will be possible to give at once to the rescued . . . shelter, warmth and warm food', clearly something of a novelty. (By courtesy of the RNLI)

▲ A basic line drawing of the prototype 60ft Barnett published in The Lifeboat journal when the design was first announced. (By courtesy of the RNLI)

With two engines, only a jury rig, consisting of a small triangular fore-lug and jib which could be set on a single mast, was provided. A searchlight, sited by the boat's mast, was fitted and a life-saving net was suspended by four corner stanchions amidships over the engine room casing, although this was later removed during the boats' service careers. A line-throwing gun was provided to assist in getting a line across to wrecked ships. The class had flush decks, without sunken well or cockpits, with the shelters for the crew and mechanics also protecting the entrance to the engine room hatches, which were mounted at deck level, and a rudimentary windscreen was fitted to protect the man at the helm. For the first time in a lifeboat, two cabins were provided, one fore and one aft, to hold about fifty people in total. The boat could take 130 persons on board in rough weather and 200 persons in fine weather.

In October 1924, by when the first 60ft boat (ON.682) had been in service for more than a year, two more boats to the design were ordered; these second and third boats incorporated several modifications, based on the experience of operating the first boat. The engine rooms were enlarged, as were the two cabins, so that between fifty and sixty people could be accommodated. Fuel capacity was increased by 100 gallons, so the boats had a radius of action of 250 miles at a cruising speed of eight knots, approximately 100 miles more than that of the first boat.

Two funnels were added amidships for the exhaust so that, instead of having exhaust outlets on the side of the boat, as with the prototype, the outlets were now located above deck. This was beneficial because the side

MOTOR LIFEBOATS

7 • Barnett 60ft twin screw

Year* (Yd No) Builder Place	Length Breadth Crew	Name Donor	ON Cost Weight	Engines	Stations (launches/lives saved)	Notes Disposal
1923 (W1586) J. S. White Cowes	60' 15' 8	**William and Kate Johnston** Gifts of Stewart Johnston and his sister, W.H. Kendall; Liverpool Lifeboat Fund.	682 £16,084.8.10 41t5	2x80bhp Weyburn DE 6-cyl (p)	New Brighton 13.8.1923-23.9.1950 (94/248)	Sold 12.12.1950
1926 (S40) S. E. Saunders Cowes	60' 15' 8	**Emma Constance** Legacy of Mr John Mackie, York.	693 £15,821.7.3 41t18	2x80bhp Weyburn DE 6-cyl (p)	Aberdeen No.1 27.10.1926-30.8.1951 (92/95)	Sold 11.1951
1926 (W1626) J. S. White Cowes	60' 15' 8	**Robert and Marcella Beck** Legacy Mr R.A. Beck, Worthing.	696 £14,535.16.3 41t18	2x80bhp White DE 6-cyl (p)	Plymouth 1.7.1926-3.1943 (36/70) and 2.1947-30.3.1952 (14/2)	Used by the Royal Navy 21.3.1943-4.1946 Sold 6.1952
1929 (S50) S. E. Saunders Cowes	61' 15' 8	**Princess Mary** Gift of the P&O Group of shipping companies.	715 £14,602.3.0 43t10	2x80bhp Weyburn DE 6-cyl (p)	Padstow 25.5.1929-1.12.1952 (63/48)	Sold 6.1952

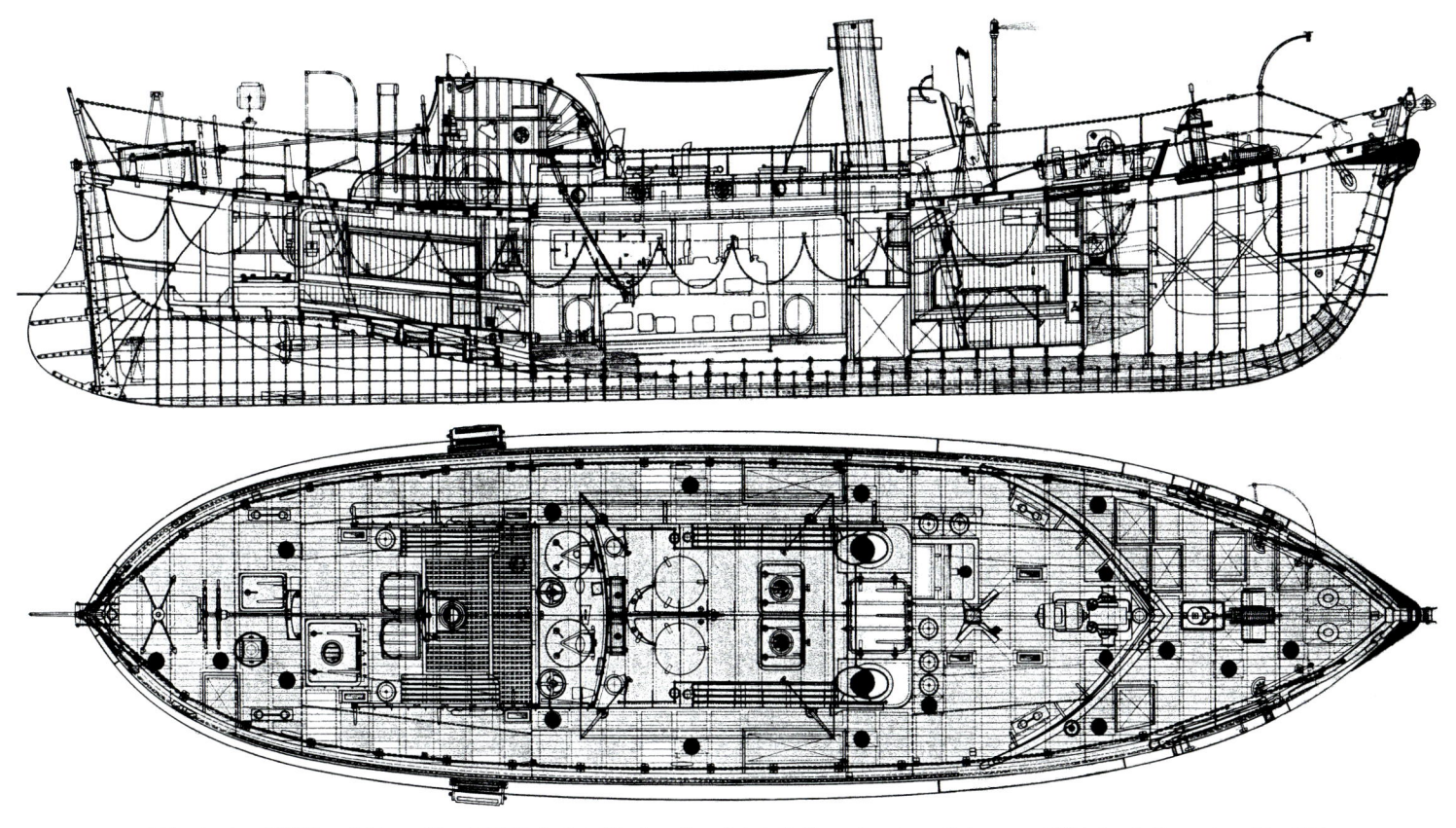

▲ Line drawing of 61ft Barnett Princess Mary (ON.715), the last of the large Barnetts to be built and the only one that measured 61ft in length. (By courtesy of the RNLI)

MOTOR LIFEBOATS

7 • Barnett 60ft twin screw

outlet occasionally allowed water into the engines. The fourth and last of the large Barnetts (ON.715) was completed in 1929 and sent to Padstow in May 1929. At 61ft, she was longer than her three sister vessels due to her bow being raked forward, but in other respects was similar to the second and third boats. The boats had a draught of 4ft 6in, were usually manned by a crew of eight, and all were kept moored afloat.

Although their size was of great benefit when they were working in severe weather, it limited the stations from which they could be operated. They had to be kept permanently afloat at a relatively deep-water and sheltered mooring, which the crew could reach using a small boarding boat. At the time, the RNLI favoured keeping lifeboats out of the water, in lifeboat houses, from which they would be launched via a slipway or, with the lighter lifeboats, from a carriage. Berths able to accommodate a lifeboat of 60ft in length were not widespread. The limitation imposed by the design's size therefore meant that only four of the class were built.

Following the introduction of the 60ft Barnetts in the 1920s, several other lifeboat classes were developed by Barnett which utilised the design ideas first seen in the 60ft boats. A smaller Barnett type, 51ft in length and known as the 'Stromness' class after the station at which the first one served, was built, incorporating twin engines and twin screws. Being smaller and lighter than the 60ft Barnett, the 51ft boats were more practical and better suited to serve at a wider range of stations, as they could be slipway launched. Although only four lifeboats were built to Barnett's 60ft design, they embodied ideas and technology that pointed the way ahead for motor lifeboat design, with twin engines, twin screws, cabins, shelters and other equipment, which could only be accommodated in a motor lifeboat, becoming the norm in all future lifeboat designs.

▲ William and Kate Johnston (ON.682) moored in the Mersey at New Brighton. Twin funnels, located aft of the mast, were additions for the exhaust.

◀ A cutaway drawing of William and Kate Johnston (ON.682) which appeared in the May 1922 edition of The Lifeboat. It was taken from a painting by S.W. Clatworthy and provides an idea of the deck layout of the boat. Among the new features incorporated in the boat, as well as twin engines, were a searchlight, a life-saving net and a line-throwing gun. (RNLI)

MOTOR LIFEBOATS

7 • Barnett 60ft twin screw

◀ 61ft Barnett Princess Mary (ON.715), the last of the large Barnetts to be built and the only one which was 61ft in length, moored at Padstow. This fine photograph gives a good idea of the boat's deck layout and cabin. She served at Padstow for more than twenty-three years. (By courtesy of the RNLI)

▼ (left) The second 61ft Barnett, Emma Constance (ON.693), pictured on the day of her arrival at Aberdeen in October 1926. She had a range of 250 miles at her cruising speed of eight knots, and had a top speed of over nine knots. (By courtesy of the RNLI)

▼ (right) The third 61ft Barnett, Robert and Marcella Beck (ON.696), was stationed at Plymouth where moorings for her were found in the port's large harbour. (Grahame Farr, by courtesy of the RNLI)

MOTOR LIFEBOATS

8 • Ramsgate

KEY DATA
- Introduced 1925
- Last built 1928
- 3 built

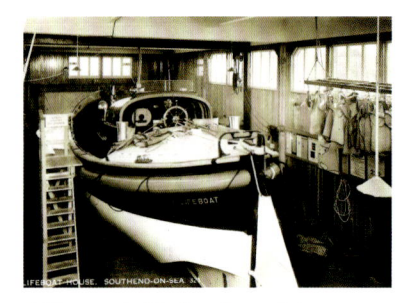

In the early 1920s, the RNLI turned its attention to the development of a motor lifeboat which could operate in shallow waters, and this culminated in the introduction of a new type in 1925. Designed specifically for the challenging waters of the Goodwin Sands, the new type was known as the Ramsgate class after the station at which the first was operated. The RNLI designers combined various elements of the Watson motor lifeboat with those of the Norfolk & Suffolk type in the new type, which was larger than either of the designs it was based on, at 48ft 6in in length. However, despite their size, the boats had a very shallow draught, and this, in conjunction with the line-throwing gun which had a range of eighty yards, made it possible, according to the RNLI's statement, for any vessel likely to get upon the Goodwin Sands to be reached.

The boats were of a low, squat, open design, with no cockpits and long low end boxes. The long straight iron keel weighed 2.6 tons. The wooden hull was subdivided into nine watertight compartments and 217 air cases. The boats were built of East India teak, instead of mahogany. Although mahogany was usually used for building lifeboats during this era, teak was chosen as it was seen as being better able to last in a boat which had to lie afloat, as the first of the class had to. The boats weighed over twenty tons, and could take on board up to 195 persons if weather conditions allowed.

The first boat, ON.697, was powered by a single engine developing 80bhp, which drove a single screw, and gave a top speed of 8.25 knots. The other two boats of the class had twin screws and twin engines, each of 40bhp, giving the same power output as the single-engined prototype, and a maximum speed of 8.3 knots. The boats carried 114 gallons of petrol, and had a radius of action of just over seventy nautical miles at the cruising speed of 7.5 knots. In addition to the engines, six oars were carried, as were sails; ON.697 carried standing lug, mizzen and jib sails as auxiliary to the engine. In the event of the engine room being completely submerged, the engines themselves were designed to continue operating.

The shallow draught made the boat ideal for working in the shallow waters, and after the first boat had gone to Ramsgate, the station she was designed for, two further boats were built to cover the Thames Estuary, operating from Walton and Frinton on the north side, and Southend-on-Sea on the south side. The three Rasgate type lifeboats gave outstanding service, giving a quarter of a centruy and more to their respective stations, and all three played their part in sea rescue during the Second World War. Indeed, all three went aross the Channel to Dunkirk in 1940 to assist with the evacuation, with Prudential credited with off from the beaches some 2,800 men of the British Expeditionary Force

▲ The second of the three Ramsgate type lifeboats, Greater London (Civil Service No.3) (ON.704), served for most of her career at Southend-on-Sea, and is pictured inside the boathouse there. (Author's collection)

▶ The first Ramsgate class lifeboat, Prudential (ON.697), during her naming ceremony at Ramsgate, 14 April 1926. (By courtesy of the RNLI)

▼ The last of the Ramsgate lifeboats, E.M.E.D. (ON.705), off Walton. (By courtesy of the RNLI)

MOTOR LIFEBOATS

8 • Ramsgate

	Year* (Yd No) Builder Place	Length Breadth Crew	Name Donor	ON Cost Weight	Engines	Stations (launches/lives saved)	Notes Disposal
1	1925 (S41) S. E. Saunders Cowes	48' 13' 9	**Prudential** Gift from the Prudential Assurance Company, London.	697 £8,417.8.6 20t16	1x80bhp (ss) Weyburn 6-cyl DE6 (p)	Ramsgate 30.12.1925-25.9.53 (276/330)	Sold 11.1953
2	1928 (W1648) J. S. White Cowes	48'6" 13' 9	**Greater London (Civil Service No.3)** Civil Service Lifeboat Fund.	704 £8,668.0.1 22t10	2x40bhp (ts) Weyburn 4-cyl CE4 (p)	Southend-on-Sea 5.1928-12.41 & 2.1945-4.55 (253/218) Reserve 1941-45 & 1955-57 (22/22)	Sold 9.1957 to ADES (Uruguay lifeboat service)
3	1928 (W1649) J. S. White Cowes	48'6" 13' 9	**E.M.E.D.** Legacies of Mr I. Dewhirst, Miss H. Yates, Mr R. Barnes and Miss J. E. Watkins.	705 £8,699.13.5 22t10	2x40bhp (ts) Weyburn 4-cyl CE4 (p)	Walton & Frinton 4.7.1928-2.11.53 (177/217) Reserve 1953-55 (8/26)	Sold 1.1956 to Valparaiso Lifeboat Institution, Chile

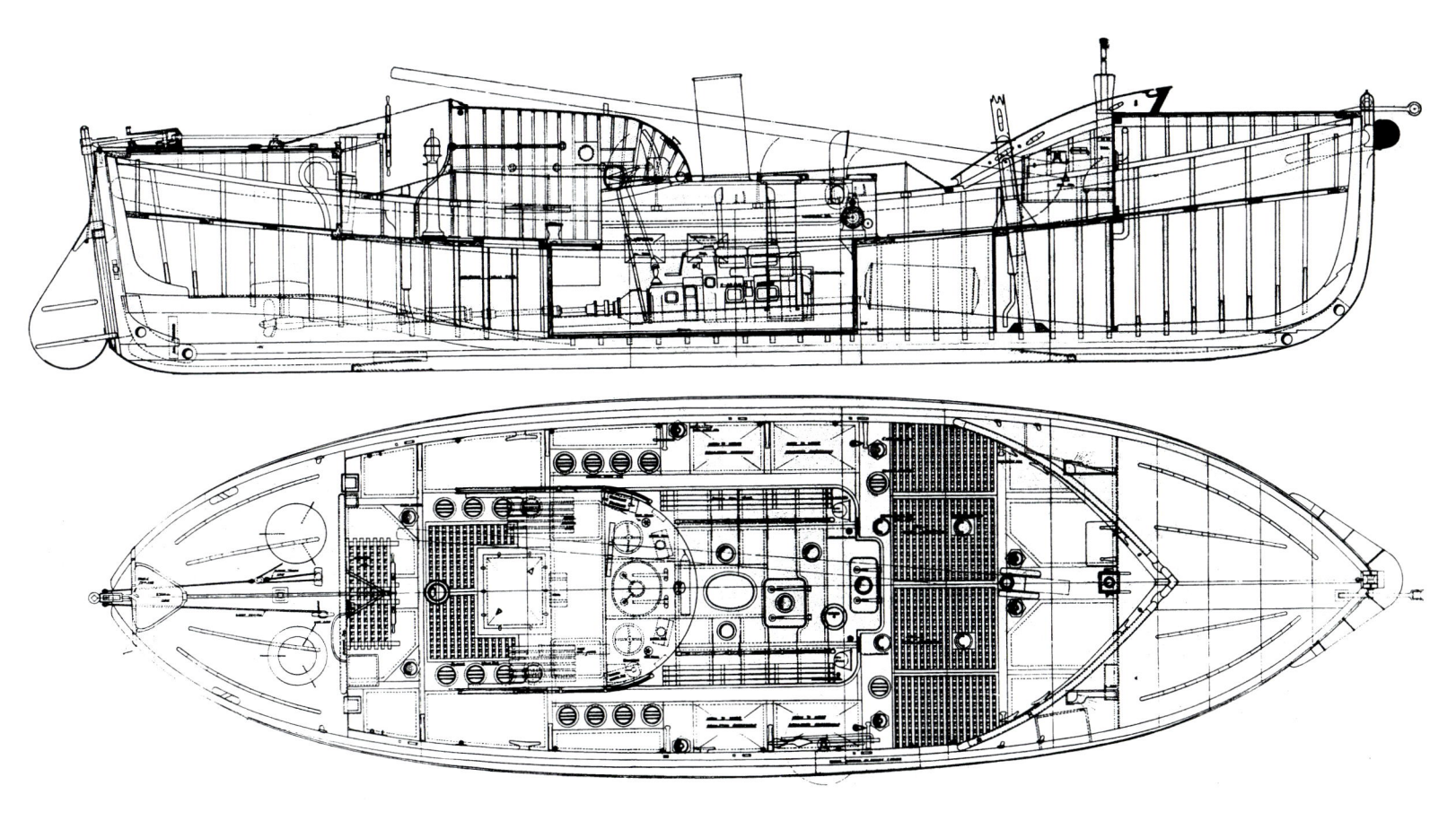

▲ General deck arrangement of the last Ramsgate type lifeboat, E.M.E.D. (ON.705), which served the Walton & Frinton station in Essex, covering the northern waters of the Thames Estuary. (RNLI)

MOTOR LIFEBOATS

9 • Watson cabin motor 45ft 6in

KEY DATA
- Introduced 1926
- Last built 1935
- 23 built

▶ The first 45ft 6in Watson class to be built, K.T.J.S. (ON.698), with her sails set during her time on station at Longhope, in Orkney; she later served at Aith and Arranmore. She was one of only two 45ft 6in Watsons built with a single engine. (RNLI)

▼ General deck arrangement of the 45ft 6in Watson motor Thomas McCunn (ON.759), which served for almost thirty years at Longhope and was one of many Watsons to be launched down a slipway. (By courtesy of the RNLI)

The 45ft 6in Watson, a non-self-righting type designed around the traditional Watson hull shape by James Barnett, was essentially a development of the earlier 45ft Watson. It was 6in longer as a result of a more raked bow, while the end box layout was replaced by a through deck, flush with the gunwales. The steering position was located aft, while a turtle-shell shaped shelter was introduced, incorporating an aft cockpit with a one-piece central windscreen. At the forward end of the aft shelter was the engine room access hatch. The exhaust funnel was positioned forward of this shelter, while a small shelter was located towards the bow. In rough weather, ninety-five people could be taken on board. The hull, with a displacement of 20.5 tons, was divided into eight watertight compartments and fitted with 142 air cases and ten relieving scuppers. The range of stability was 100 degrees.

In total twenty-three boats were built to this design, which proved well suited to a variety of stations. The first two were single-engined, being powered by a single 80bhp Weyburn motor, giving a similar speed and

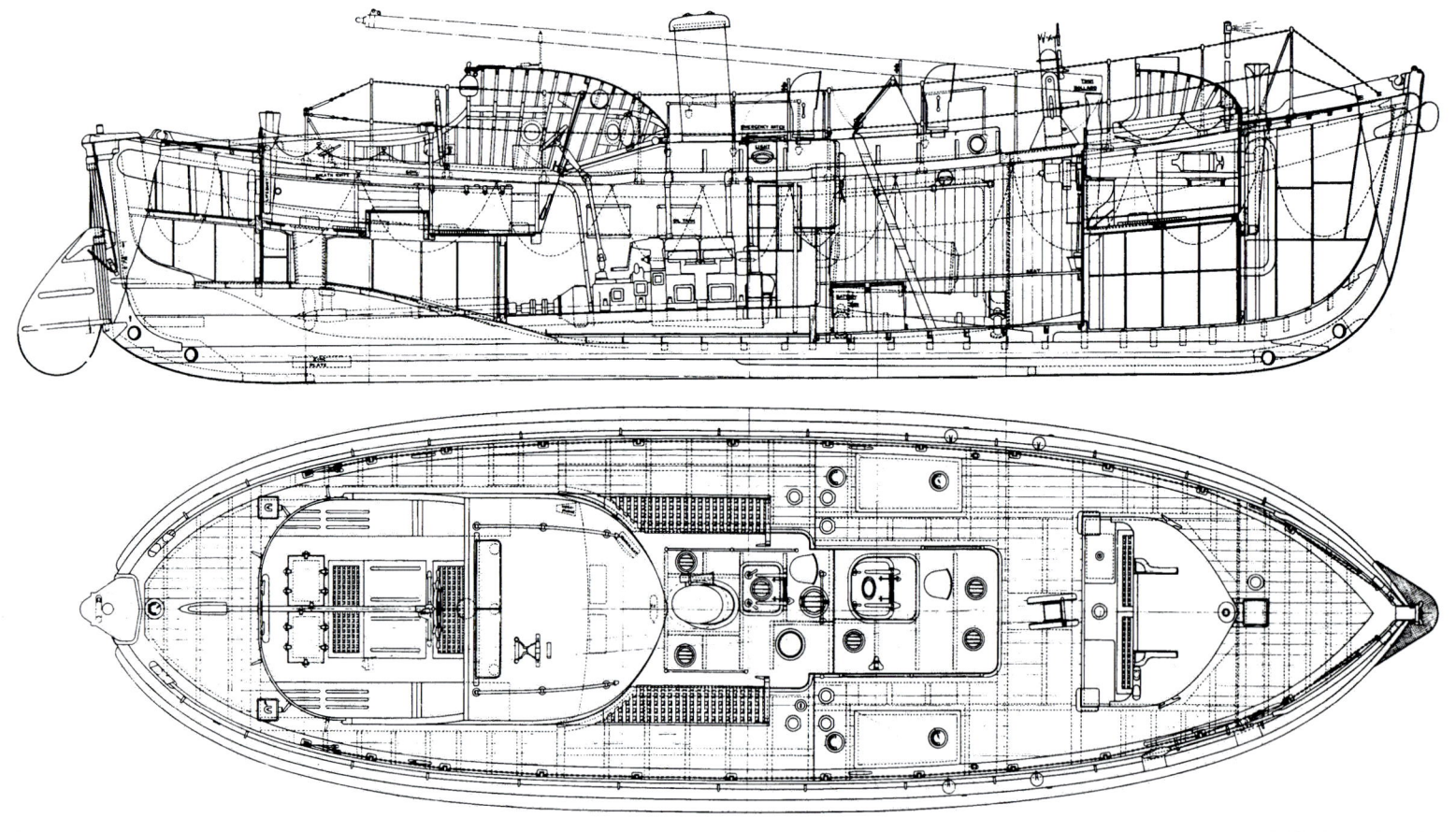

MOTOR LIFEBOATS

9 • Watson cabin motor 45ft 6in

	Year* (Yd No) Builder Place	Length Breadth Crew	Name Donor	ON Cost Weight	Engines	Stations (launches/lives saved)	Notes Disposal
1	1926 (S42) S. E. Saunders Cowes	45'6" 12'6" 8	**K. T. J. S.** Legacies of William G. King, J. Turnbull, M. Jesset and Mrs S. H. Sandford.	698 £8,330.1.1 18t13	1x80bhp (ss) Weyburn DE.6 (p)	Longhope 1.9.1926-4.1.1933 (24/25) Aith 2.5.1933-12.5.1935 (3/0) Arranmore 17.8.1935-9.5.1950 (37/29) Reserve 1950-52 (7/2)	Sold 5.1952
2	1926 (S43) S. E. Saunders Cowes	45'6" 12'6" 8	**John Russell** Legacy of Miss Ann Russell.	699 £8,272.10.3 18t14	1x80bhp (ss) Weyburn DE.6 (p)	Montrose No.1 1.9.1926-9.10.1939 (32/26) Reserve 1939-1955 (30/49)	Sold 7.1956
3	1927 (W1630) J. S. White Cowes	45'6" 12'6" 8	**K. E. C. F.** Legacies of Mrs E. Kirby, Mrs E. Dudley, Mr E. Kleeman and Miss M. Potton.	700 £11,116.0.5 19t5	2x40bhp (ts) Weyburn CE.4 (p)	Rosslare Harbour 7.4.1927-2.3.1939 (63/127) Galway Bay 16.3.1939-3.1952 (37/48) Reserve 1952-1956 (11/8)	Sold 12.1956
4	1927 (W1629) J. S. White Cowes	45'6" 12'6" 8	**N. T.** Legacy of Mrs Maria C. Myers and gift from Mr StephenThompson, Birmingham.	701 £10,826.18.1 19t6	2x40bhp (ss) Weyburn CE.4 (p)	Barrow 19.8.1927-11.1951 (68/64) Workington 2.3.1952-3.1953 (10/11) Reserve 1953-1956 (8/0)	Sold 12.1956
5	1929 (S47) S. E. Saunders Cowes	45'6" 12'6" 8	**Edward Z. Dresden** Legacy of Edward Dresden, London.	707 £8,496 20t7	2x40bhp (ts) Weyburn CE.4 (p)	Clacton-on-Sea 20.3.1929-14.1.1952 (181/112) Stronsay 23.10.1952-27.2.1955 (8/0) Reserve 1955-1968 (49/37)	Sold 12.1968
6	1928 (W1656) J. S. White Cowes	45'6" 12'6" 8	**H. C. J.** Legacies of H. T. Richardson, S. Stephens, and gift from John A. Fielden.	708 £8,390 18t5	2x40bhp (ts) Weyburn CE.4 (p)	Fowey 11.8-6.12.1928 (0/0) Holyhead 7.12.1928-17.5.1929 (3/0) Thurso 25.6.1929-1.1956 (102/138) Reserve 1956-1962 (11/8)	Sold 1962
7	1929 (S48) S. E. Saunders Cowes	45'6" 12'6" 8	**City of Bradford II** City of Bradford Lifeboat Fund and legacy of Mr J. M. Howson, Harrogate.	709 £8,662.11.2 18t10	2x40bhp (ts) Weyburn CE.4 (p)	Humber 13.2.1929-27.1.1954 (228/305) Amble 9.1954-1.1957 (7/0) Broughty Ferry 23.12.1959-11.1960 (6/0) Reserve 1956-1968 (30/4)	Sold 12.1968
8	1930 (W1657) J. S. White Cowes	45'6" 12'6" 8	**White Star** Oceanic Steam Navigation Company (White Star Line).	710 £7,877.18.7 18t14	2x40bhp (ts) Weyburn CE.4 (p)	Fishguard 28.5.1930-20.2.1956 (56/66) Reserve 1956-1968 (52/13)	Sold 10.6.1968
9	1929 (W1662) J. S. White Cowes	45'6" 12'6" 8	**James Macfee** Legacy of Dr J. Macfee, Auchterarder.	711 £8,205.2.11 18t10	2x40bhp (ts) Weyburn CE.4 (p)	Cromarty 20.10.1928-9.1955 (51/17) Thurso 11.12.1956-7.12.1957 (1/0) Reserve 1955-59 (7/3)	Sold 1959
10	1928 (W1663) J. S. White Cowes	45'6" 12'6" 8	**C. D. E. C.** Legacies C. C. Nottage, Miss G. Moss, Mrs J. Liddell and Mrs A. S. Picking.	712 £8,309.6.3 18t10	2x40bhp (ts) Weyburn CE.4 (p)	Fowey 6.12.1928-21.11.1954 (65/49) Reserve 1954-1959 (19/2)	Sold 1959
11	1929 (W1664) J. S. White Cowes	45'6" 12'6" 8	**Elizabeth Elson** Legacy of Mr B. Elson.	713 £8,253.6.1 18t14	2x40bhp (ts) Weyburn CE.4 (p)	Angle 10.1.1929-19.2.1957 (58/144) Reserve 1957-1968 (108/67)	Sold 12.1968
12	1928 (S49) S. E. Saunders Cowes	45'6" 12'6" 8	**H.F. Bailey II**/1929- **Canadian Pacific** Legacy of Henry F. Bailey, Brokenhurst/ 1929-Canadian Pacific Steamship Co.	714 £8,470.5.9 18t4	2x40bhp (ts) Weyburn CE.4 (p)	Cromer No.1 1928-14.5.1929 (3/5) Selsey 29.7.1929-6.1937 (35/30)	Burnt in fire at Groves & Guttridge, 18.6.1937
13	1929 (W1666) J. S. White Cowes	45'6" 12'6" 8	**Sarah Ward and William David Crossweller** Legacy of William T. Crossweller, Sidcup.	716 £8,453.14.6 18t14	2x40bhp (ts) Weyburn CE.4 (p)	Courtmacsherry Harbour 3.3.1929-1958 (47/63) Reserve 1958-1959 (11/0) Whitehills 11.1959-61 (1/0)	Sold 1961
14	1930 (S53) Saunders-Roe Cowes	45'6" 12'6" 8	**Cunard** Gift of Cunard Steamship Company.	728 £8,324.4.10 18t14	2x40bhp (ts) Weyburn CE.4 (p)	St Mary's 27.5.1930-12.12.1955 (71/104) Reserve 1955-1969 (70/26)	Sold 1969

9 • Watson cabin motor 45ft 6in

	Year* (Yd No) Builder Place	Length Breadth Crew	Name Donor	ON Cost Weight	Engines	Stations (launches/lives saved)	Notes Disposal
15	1930 (S54) Saunders-Roe Cowes	45'6" 12'6" 8	**John R. Webb** Legacy of Mr J. R. Webb, Belgrave, London.	729 £8,318.11.9 18t14	2x40bhp (ts) Weyburn CE.4 (p)	Tenby 11.4.1930-20.9.1955 (91/53) Reserve 1955-1969 (76/49)	Sold 9.1969
16	1930 (W1694) J. S. White Cowes	45'6" 12'6" 8	**Cecil and Lilian Philpott** Gift of Mrs L. Philpott, London.	730 £7,982.15.2 18t14	2x40bhp (ts) Weyburn CE.4 (p)	Newhaven 8.1.1930-11.7.1959 (156/99) Reserve 1959-1969 (48/56)	Sold 10.1969
17	1930 (W1696) J. S. White Cowes	45'6" 12'6" 8	**Catherine** —	732 — 18t14	2x40bhp (ts) Weyburn CE.4 (p)	Built for Bombay Port Trust in 1930	Sold 1935
18	1931 (W1705) J. S. White Cowes	45'6" 12'6" 8	**W. and S.** Legacies of Miss E. Young and Miss W. A. Coode.	736 £7,684.7.2 18t10	2x40bhp (ts) Weyburn CE.4 (p)	Penlee 26.6.1931-4.7.1960 (94/83) Buckie 9.1960-6.1961 Reserve 1960-1969 (15/10)	Sold 1970
19	1931 (W1718) J. S. White Cowes	45'6" 12'6" 8	**George and Sarah Strachan** Legacy of George Strachan, Glasgow.	749 £7,680.1.10 18t10	2x40bhp (ts) Weyburn CE.4 (p)	Dunbar 28.6.1931-4.2.1959 (74/16) Exmouth 29.2.1961-1.11.1963 (2/0) Reserve 1959-1961 & 1964-1969 (20/9)	Sold 3.1969
20	1932 (W1732) J. S. White Cowes	45'6" 12'6" 8	**Civil Service No.5** Civil Service Lifeboat Fund.	753 £7,293.15.9 19t10	2x40bhp (ts) Weyburn CE.4 (p)	Donaghadee 4.6.1932-6.1950 (80/56) Port St Mary 19.9.1950-7.1956 (7/0) Reserve 1956-1958 (7/2)	Sold 2.1958
21	1933 (182) Groves & Guttridge Cowes	45'6" 12'6" 8	**Thomas McCunn** Legacy of Mr William McCunn, Largs.	759 £7,120.18.5 18t16	2x40bhp (ts) Weyburn CE.4 (p)	Longhope 4.1.1933-4.1962 (101/308) Reserve 1962-1972 (26/12)	Sold 8.1972
22	1935 (201) Alex Robertson Sandbank	45'6" 12'6" 8	**Charlotte Elizabeth** Gift of Miss E. Sinclair.	774 £8,380.15.3 18t16	2x40bhp (ts) Weyburn CE.4 (p) [Internal rudder]	Islay 26.6.1935-11.7.1959 (101/162) Reserve 1959-1961 (8/7)	Sold 1961
23	1935 (196) Groves & Guttridge Cowes	45'6" 12'6" 8	**Mona** Gift from an anonymous lady in the west of Scotland.	775 £6,802.15.10 18t16	2x40bhp (ts) Weyburn CE.4 (p)	Broughty Ferry 6.5.1935-12.1959 (72/118)	Capsized on service 8.12.1959, burnt on beach after capsize

▶ K.E.C.F. (ON.700) was the first twin-engined and twin-screw Watson class lifeboat. She carried a sharp-headed mainsail and foresail but, once the reliability of the twin engines had been proved in service conditions, the sails were removed. She was also the first lifeboat to be fitted with a short-range wireless, which had a range of over eighty miles, and was housed in a watertight case in the cabin, and meant the lifeboat had to carry a fully-certified wireless operator. During her service at Rosslare Harbour, she was often at sea for prolonged periods, usually escorting the local fishing fleet, and would 'cruise outside the bar until the fleet [was] safely in harbour'. The need to maintain contact with the shore was thus particularly important. (By courtesy of the RNLI)

range to that of the 45ft Watsons. The third boat (ON.700) had twin engines and twin screws, while the fourth boat (ON.701) was built as a twin-engined, single-screwed craft, the only RNLI lifeboat completed with such an arrangement. In this boat, the two engines were coupled to a gearbox through which the single propeller was driven.

Before further boats were ordered, ON.700 and ON.701 were sent to Wexford in Ireland for comparative trials, to assess the seakeeping qualities of the variations in design and motor installation. These proved that twin engines driving twin screws was the optimum arrangement, so the remaining boats all had twin engines and twin screws. The installation consisted of two 40bhp Weyburn CE4 petrol engines, which gave the boats a speed of about 8.25 knots, and a fuel capacity of 100 gallons, which provided a range of about 120 miles. The boats also carried a sailing rig consisting of staysail, trysail and auxiliary, although on the twin-engined boats the drop keel was dispensed with and a reduced sail plan was carried.

9 • Watson cabin motor 45ft 6in

▲ Typical of the standard 45ft 6in Watson class was C.D.E.C. (ON.712), which served at Fowey for more than twenty-five years. She is pictured after her cabin had been extended aft. (RNLI)

◄ City of Bradford II (ON.709) being launched down the slipway at Spurn Point, Humber, the station she served for twenty-four years. This photo shows the boat's propeller tunnel and the rudder is in the raised position for launching.

▼ (left) Cunard (ON.728) in the waters off St Mary's, Isles of Scilly. She had a life-saving career lasting almost forty years. (C. McCutcheon)

▼ (right) Charlotte Elizabeth (ON.774), with her sails set, off Port Askaig, Islay, was one of the last two 45ft 6in Watson to be built.

MOTOR LIFEBOATS 59

10 • Barnett 'Stromness' motor 51ft

KEY DATA
- Introduced 1928
- Last built 1949
- 13 built

▶ Generic profile and deck plan of 51ft Barnett published in the RNLI's Annual Report of 1928. The 51ft Barnett was fitted with small cabins and shelters, which had space for twelve survivors. (By courtesy of the RNLI)

▼ (left) The first 51ft Barnett J.J.K.S.W. (ON.702) launching down the slipway at Stromness. The aft cabin housed the engine controls, the shelter forward was for survivors and crew, and the tunnels at the stern protected the propellers. (Orkney Photographic Archive)

▼ (right) Lady Jane and Martha Ryland (ON.731) served at Lerwick, Shetland for almost thirty years. This profile shows the deck layout with the exhaust funnel amidships. She carried a staysail in addition to the engines. (From an old postcard supplied by John Harrop)

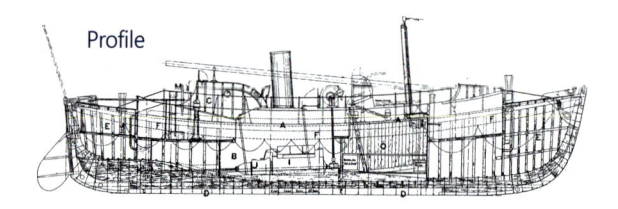

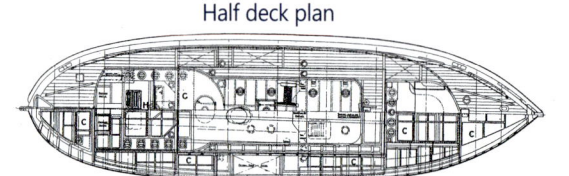

Profile

Half deck plan

Half plan showing air cases

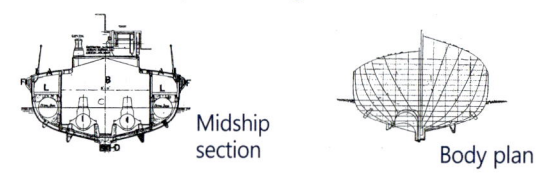

Midship section

Body plan

The 51ft Barnett was developed from the earlier and larger 60-61ft type and, designed by James Barnett, had a hull shape similar to its larger sister. However, the 51ft version, with a draught of 4ft 1in, was smaller and lighter, being just over twenty-six tons in weight as opposed to forty-four tons, and was thus more practical as it could be launched from a slipway, unlike the 60ft Barnett, or kept afloat at moorings. The design initially became known as the 'Stromness' class after the station where the first of the type was stationed as the crew there had specifically requested a larger lifeboat that could be slipway launched.

The hull of the 51ft Barnett, divided into eight watertight compartments and fitted with 160 air cases, was constructed from mahogany with a keel of teak and ribs of Canadian rock-elm and stem and stern post of English oak. The heavy keel, which weighed 2.8 tons, gave her a greater range of stability, ninety degrees as opposed to eight-seven, than that of the 60ft Barnett. The layout incorporated a single cabin, with a single funnel amidships for the exhaust, and an aft cockpit. In rough weather the boats could carry up to 100 survivors, and more in fine weather.

The two 60hp Weyburn CE6 six-cylinder petrol engines, running at 1,200rpm, were housed in a watertight compartment with the air-intakes well above the waterline, so the engines would continue to operate even if the engine room was flooded. At the maximum speed of nine knots, the petrol-engined versions had a range of approximately 120 miles and carried 160 gallons. On trials, the first 51ft Barnetts, J.J.K.S.W. (ON.702), achieved 8.69 knots. Two of the boats, Lloyd's (ON.754) and Peter and Sarah Blake (ON.755), built for the Barra Island and Fenit stations respectively, had enlarged fuel tanks to increase their cruising range to 184 miles. Among the equipment carried were a line-throwing gun, a searchlight, a mechanical capstan and a powered fire-fighting system. The cabin had seating for ten people and cockpits forward and aft.

Twelve of the 51ft boats were built during the initial construction programme, with one further boat completed after the Second World War. This last boat, Southern Africa (ON.860), had a different cabin arrangement, being similar in shape to that on the 41ft Watsons of the same era. Two of the boats, Peter and Sarah Blake (ON.755), as well as Southern Africa (ON.860), were both re-engined, being fitted with 75hp Parsons Barracuda diesels, at a time when such engines were becoming the norm.

10 • Barnett 'Stromness' motor 51ft

	Year* (Yd No) Builder Place	Length Breadth Crew	Name Donor	ON Cost Weight	Engines	Stations (launches/lives saved)	Notes Disposal
1	1928 (S44) S. E. Saunders Cowes	51' 13'6" 8	**J. J. K. S. W.** Legacies of Miss J. Moody, J. P. Traill, W. Aitken, E. J. Hanson and W. Notting.	702 £13,642.9.11 25t18	2x60bhp Weyburn 6-cyl CE6 (p)	Stromness 15.2.1928-21.5.1955 (92/139) Reserve 1955-64 (24/19)	Sold 1965
2	1929 (W1669) J. S. White Cowes	51' 13'6" 8	**A. E. D.** Legacy of Captain William A. Dobie, Ryde, IOW; and gift of G.W. Hayer, Basingstoke.	717 £10,118.18.0 27t	2x60bhp Weyburn 6-cyl CE6 (p)	Holyhead 17.5.1929-21.9.1950 (84/156) Valentia 2.1951-18.9.1957 (57/83)	Sold 1957
3	1929 (W1670) J. S. White Cowes	51' 13'6" 8	**William and Harriot** Legacy of Mrs Harriot Richardson, Greenwich, London.	718 £10,469.1.1 27t2	2x60bhp Weyburn 6-cyl CE6 (p)	Stornoway 12.7.1929-27.9.1954 (77/130) Reserve 1954-1959 (8/2)	Sold 1959
4	1929 (W1671) J. S. White Cowes	51' 13'6" 8	**Queen Victoria** RNLI Funds.	719 £10,480.13.5 27t	2x60bhp Weyburn 6-cyl CE6 (p)	St Peter Port 10.1929-6.1940 (45/53) Killybegs 24.8.1941-8.1945 (14/4) St Peter Pt 29.8.1945-5.1954 (78/71) Reserve 1954-1958 (24/2)	Sold 5.1958
5	1929 (W1672) J. S. White Cowes	51' 13'6" 8	**City of Glasgow** RNLI Funds.	720 £10,197.9.6 26t18	2x60bhp Weyburn 6-cyl CE6 (p)	Campbeltown 4.9.1929-24.6.1953 (91/173) Reserve 1953-1958 (10/12)	Sold 1959
6	1930 (W1695) J. S. White Cowes	51' 13'6" 8	**Lady Jane and Martha Ryland** Legacy of Mr William Ryland.	731 £10,414.1.6 26t10	2x60bhp Weyburn 6-cyl CE6 (p)	Lerwick 9.7.1930-2.8.1958 (79/80) Reserve 1958-1969 (29/10)	Sold 1969
7	1930 (S55) Saunders-Roe Cowes	51' 13'6" 8	**Mary Stanford** Legacy of Mr J. F. Stanford, London.	733 £9,402.15.11 26t6	2x60bhp Weyburn 6-cyl CE6 (p)	Ballycotton 4.9.1930-27.7.1959 (83/101) Reserve 1959-1968 (47/22)	Sold 2.1968
8	1930 (S56) Saunders-Roe Cowes	51' 13'6" 8	**George Shee** RNLI Funds.	734 £9,613.4.4 27t	2x60bhp Weyburn 6-cyl CE6 (p)	Torbay 23.9.1930-7.1958 (245/190) Reserve 1958 (1/1)	Sold 12.1958
9	1930 (S57) Saunders-Roe Cowes	51' 13'6" 8	**William and Clara Ryland** Legacy of the late William Ryland, Mether Edge, Sheffield.	735 £9,412.11.11 26t13	2x60bhp Weyburn 6-cyl CE6 (p)	Weymouth 6.11.1930-30.10.1957 (156/135)	Sold 1958
10	1932 (180) Groves & Guttridge Cowes	51' 13'6" 8	**Lloyd's** Gift of Members of Lloyd's.	754 £9,443.5.8 26t2	2x60bhp Weyburn 6-cyl CE6 (p)	Barra Island 28.7.1932-27.7.1957 (110/270) Reserve 1957-1969 (101/80)	Sold 1.1970
11	1932 (W1732) J. S. White Cowes	51' 13'6" 8	**Peter and Sarah Blake** Legacy of Miss Sarah Bloomfield Blake, Streatham.	755 £8,978.2.4 26t4	2x60bhp Weyburn 6-cyl CE6 (p)/1965- 2x65hp Parsons Barracuda	Fenit 8.9.1932-12.1958 (38/12) Reserve 12.1958-1972 (93/66)	Sold 10.1972
12	1935 (197) Groves & Guttridge Cowes	51' 13'6" 8	**The Rankin** Gift of Miss Maggie D. Rankin, Glasgow, in memory of her brothers.	776 £9,122.1.4 26t2	2x60bhp Weyburn 6-cyl CE6 (p)	Aith 12.5.1935-28.1.1961 (52/61) Reserve 1961-1969 (47/22)	Sold 1970
13	1949 (S681) Rowhedge IW Rowhedge	51' 13'6" 8	**Southern Africa** Southern Africa Branch of the RNLI.	860 £20,592.11.1 26t10	2x60bhp Ferry VE 6-cyl/ 1976- 2x65hp Parsons Barracuda	Dover 18.6.1949-7.1967 (263/186) Reserve 1967-1981 (39/10)	Sold 7.1981

MOTOR LIFEBOATS

10 • Barnett 'Stromness' motor 51ft

▶ General profile and deck arrangement of the 51ft Barnett Mary Stanford (ON.733). Stationed at Ballycotton, she was involved in the dramatic rescue of the eight crew of the Daunt Rock lightship in February 1936, during which her volunteer crew endured forty-nine hours at sea; Coxswain Patrick Sliney was awarded the Gold medal, Second Coxswain John Lane Walsh and Motor Mechanic Thomas Sliney Silver medals, and Bronze Medals went to the rest of the crew for their extraordinary efforts.

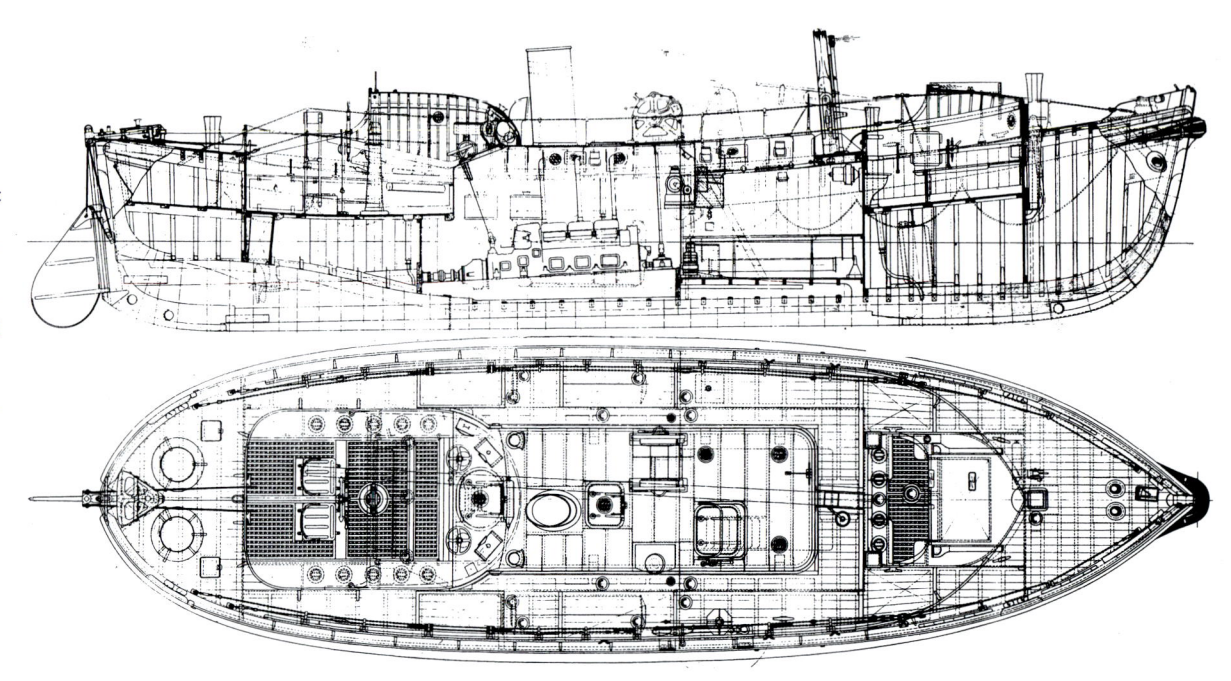

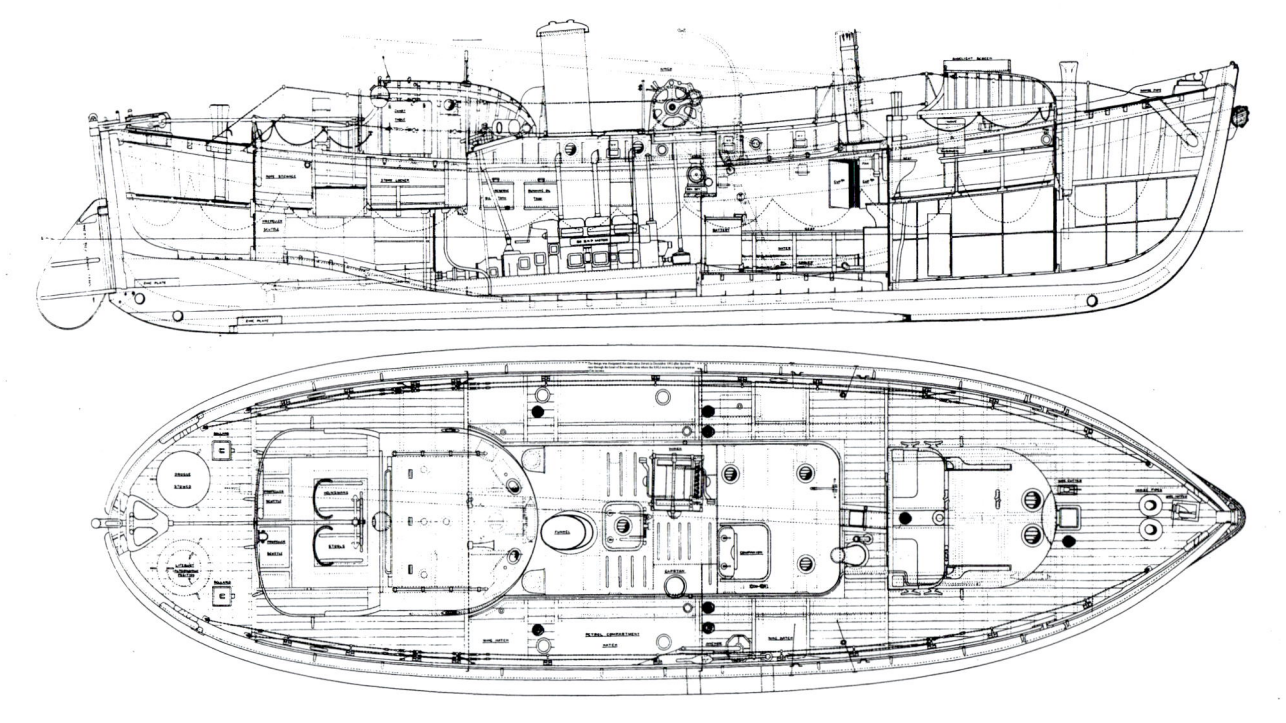

◀ General profile and deck arrangement of the 51ft Barnett Lloyds (ON.754), built two years after ON.733. ON.754 had an RNLI career lasting more than thirty-five years. (By courtesy of the RNLI)

10 • Barnett 'Stromness' motor 51ft

▲ George Shee (ON.734), one of four 51ft Barnetts built in 1930, was named after the Secretary of the RNLI and served for almost thirty years at Torbay before being sold out of service to Guatemala, where she continued in her role as a lifeboat. (By courtesy of the RNLI)

▲ The Rankin (ON.776) was the last 51ft Barnett built before the Second World War; she was the first lifeboat built for Aith, the RNLI's most northerly station.

▼ The last 51ft Barnett Southern Africa (ON.860); built after Second World War, she was different in layout to the earlier boats. (MPL)

▲ Lloyd's (ON.754), pictured on trials, was one of two 51ft Barnetts built in 1932. (RNLI)

▼ Peter and Sarah Blake (ON.755) under sail. Despite being fitted with twin engines, the 51ft Barnetts also carried auxiliary sails. (RNLI)

MOTOR LIFEBOATS

63

11 • Fast lifeboat 64ft

KEY DATA
- Introduced 1929
- Last built 1929
- 1 built

In 1929 a special 64ft high-speed lifeboat was built for service at Dover. According to The Lifeboat of September 1930, 'the conditions of cross-Channel traffic made it desirable to provide a special and faster type of Motor Life-boat [for] Dover. In addition to the very heavy passenger-steamer traffic across the Straits, there is now a considerable daily traffic by aeroplane, maintained in all but the worst weather'. The new design was primarily intended for rescuing airmen who had ditched in the English Channel, and on such rescues speed was crucial. To achieve the desired speed, a unique lifeboat was constructed to a specification different from that of any other contemporary motor lifeboat.

The new boat was designed by James Barnett, of Messrs G.L. Watson & Co, of Glasgow, the Consulting Naval Architect of the RNLI, and John Thornycroft & Co. The hull was built of lighter timber than on traditional motor lifeboats, and the beam was smaller in proportion to the length, sacrificing some stability. It was divided into eight watertight compartments with steel bulkheads, and fitted with eighty-two air cases, which gave the boat an excess of buoyancy of fifty per cent of her weight. The skin of the hull consisted of double planking of mahogany, and her timbers, or ribs, were placed much closer together than on other lifeboats.

Whereas engines installed in most motor lifeboats of the inter-war era were of between 60bhp and 80bhp, this fast lifeboat had two 375hp units. The RNLI deemed that 'the only well-tried engine suitable' was the Thornycroft Y.12 engine, used mainly in naval launches, and subsequently adopted by the Royal Air Force for its fast launches during the war. The twin engines driving twin screws gave the boat a maximum speed of 17.5 knots. She carried 350 gallons of petrol in four tanks, and had a range of 156 miles at full speed, or 198 miles at twelve knots. She was provided with two cabins, and could carry a maximum of 200 persons.

The keel was laid down in September 1928, and the boat was completed in November 1929. Early in December 1929 she ran her trials at the mouth of the Thames, and on her way down paid a visit to Chelsea, where she was welcomed by the Mayor of Chelsea. After returning to Hampton for some minor modifications, she went to Dover on 21 January 1930.

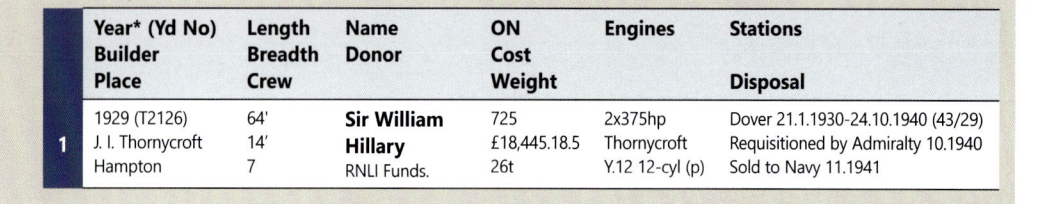

	Year* (Yd No) Builder Place	Length Breadth Crew	Name Donor	ON Cost Weight	Engines	Stations Disposal
1	1929 (T2126) J. I. Thornycroft Hampton	64' 14' 7	**Sir William Hillary** RNLI Funds.	725 £18,445.18.5 26t	2x375hp Thornycroft Y.12 12-cyl (p)	Dover 21.1.1930-24.10.1940 (43/29) Requisitioned by Admiralty 10.1940 Sold to Navy 11.1941

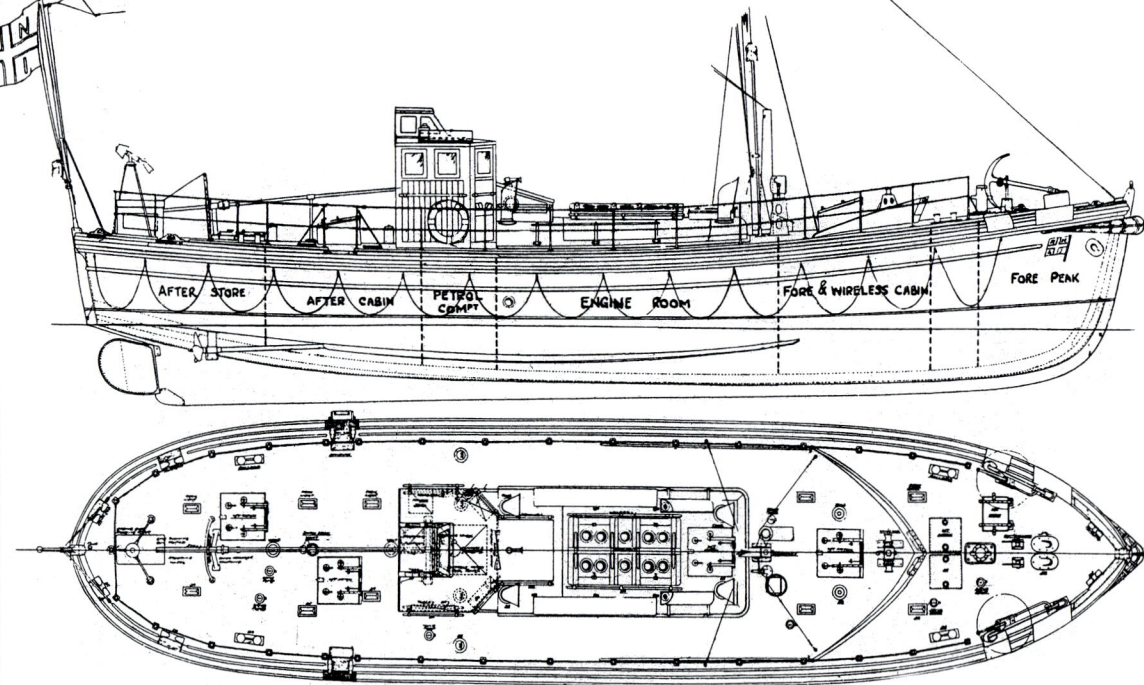

▶ Profile and deck arrangement of ON.725, the unique 64ft fast lifeboat, which was completed in November 1929 and entered service in January 1930. (By courtesy of the RNLI)

▼ The unique 64ft lifeboat Sir William Hillary (ON.725) on trials, during which she achieved a speed of seventeen knots. She was fitted with a Marconi receiving and transmitting wireless telephony set, which had an operating range of over fifty miles. Operated by a crew of seven, of whom four were full-time paid employees of the RNLI, she was kept afloat in Dover harbour during her operational career. (RNLI)

MOTOR LIFEBOATS

11 • Fast lifeboat 64ft

▲ Naming ceremony of Sir William Hillary (ON.725) at Wellington Docks, Dover on 10 July 1930. She was the only lifeboat built to this design and served the RNLI for just a decade. Soon after the war broke out, the Admiralty had the Dover station closed but, because of the boat's design, she was of limited use at any other RNLI stations. The problem was solved in October 1940 when the Admiralty requisitioned her for air-sea rescue work and she was sold outright to the Navy a year later. (By courtesy of the RNLI)

MOTOR LIFEBOATS

12 • Self-righting motor 35ft 6in

KEY DATA
- Introduced 1929
- Last built 1951
- 27 built

Development of a design a motor lifeboat that could be carriage-launched took place during the early 1920s and resulted in the 35ft self-righting type, of which three were built (see List 6). These three boats were essentially experimental, but all saw operational service. The design was subsequently modified and improved, with the hull being slightly lengthened, to make it more suitable for service. At 35ft 6in in length and 8ft 10in in beam, the new design was slightly larger than the experimental boats, and became the first motor lifeboat in production specifically designed for launching off a carriage. Its introduction was an important step forward as it meant that the RNLI then had suitable designs for stations where large motor lifeboats could not be operated.

The first 35ft 6in boat, City of Nottingham (ON.726), weighed only five tons nine cwt with crew and gear on board, and was thus well suited to being manhandled taken across a beach for launching and transported on a carriage. The 35bhp Weyburn AE6 petrol engine, running at 3,000rpm, was designed by the RNLI and built by Weyburn. This newly-designed power unit was intended specifically for the small motor self-righter. It had been developed from the Halford engine of the same power and size used in L.P. and St Helen (ON.703), one of the 35ft experimental boats that were the forerunners of the 35ft 6in self-righter, and which had been fitted in ON.703 in 1930. Carrying fifty gallons, she could reach a top speed of 7.5 knots and could travel 116 miles at this speed without refuelling.

The small shelter in the self-righters provided only enough space for the mechanic, who operated the engine controls while the boat was at sea. Access to the engine was through large doors set at an angle to the deck. The hull incorporated large end boxes, which were kept to the minimum height required to provide the self-righting capability, and was divided into eight watertight compartments with 115 air cases. A water ballast tank was incorporated to improve stability at sea, while the boats' waterline length was 32ft 1in and the draught was shallow at 2ft 8in. ON.726 was fitted with vertical scuppers, instead of relieving valves in the deck, the first such motor lifeboat to carry these fittings. If a wave broke over the boat, she could free herself of water in about twelve seconds, and, even with a hole in the bottom would right in about four seconds. Sails were carried as auxiliary to the engine, and a single drop keel was fitted.

After the Second World War the design was improved and refined, and the last five boats were built with twin Ferry FKR3 diesel engines driving twin screws of eighteen inches in diameter. The beam on the boats was also increased to give better stability, and the shelter was enlarged. The five twin-engined boats had whaleback shelters, giving them an appearance similar to that of the Liverpool class. City of Nottingham (ON.726) was originally allocated to Eastbourne, but was sent to Hythe in January 1930, while the second boat was to go to Scarborough, but instead was stationed at Berwick-upon-Tweed; at both Hythe and Berwick, the boats were launched across beaches on rudimentary slipways, rollers or skids and not from carriages. Subsequent boats were mostly carriage launched.

The 35ft 6in self-righters were relatively small lifeboats, and offered little in the way of protection for their crews. Five of the twenty-seven boats suffered accidents, either being capsized or wrecked while on service, with loss of life on three occasions. However, at Bridlington and Scarborough, in 1952 and 1954 respectively, the lifeboats self-righted as designed and this undoubtedly saved the lives of most of the crews.

▲ Westmorland (ON.727) on trials. She was the second of two boats built in 1930, and a further twelve 35ft 6in self-righters were completed in 1931, all of which were built by boatyards at Cowes. (By courtesy of the RNLI)

▲ The first of the 35ft 6in motor self-righters City of Nottingham (ON.726) being launched at Hythe. Note the pushing pole at the stern, used to get the boat through the surf on the beach. (RNLI)

▲ The second 35ft 6in motor self-righter Westmorland (ON.727) launching at Berwick-upon-Tweed after her naming ceremony on 12 June 1930. Her narrow beam is evident in this photograph.

12 • Self-righting motor 35ft 6in

	Year* (Yd No) Builder Place	Length Breadth Crew	Name Donor	ON Cost Weight	Engines (screws)	Stations (launches/lives saved)	Notes Disposal
1	1929 (S51) Saunders-Roe Cowes	35'6" 8'10" 7/8	**City of Nottingham** City of Nottingham Lifeboat Fund.	726 £4,596 5t9	1x35hp (ss) Weyburn 6-cyl AE.6 (p)	Hythe 17.1.1930-24.2.1936 (17/16) Clovelly 6.1936-7.9.1949 (46/27)	Sold 1950
2	1930 (S52) Saunders-Roe Cowes	35'6" 8'10" 7/8	**Westmorland** Westmorland Lifeboat Fund.	727 £4,597 5t10	1x35hp (ss) Weyburn 6-cyl AE.6 (p)	Berwick-on-Tweed 21.2.1930-2.1940 (16/10) Cullercoats 21.2.1940-3.1951 (26/101)	Sold 14.6.1951
3	1931 (S58) Saunders-Roe Cowes	35'6" 8'10" 7/8	**Louisa Polden** Gift of Mr J. J. Polden, Grove Park, Kent, augmented by his family.	737 £3,758 5t4	1x35hp (ss) Weyburn 6-cyl AE.6 (p)	Redcar 13.5.1931-12.5.1951 (36/76)	Sold 1951
4	1931 (W1708) J. S. White Cowes	35'6" 8'10" 7/8	**J. H. W.** Legacies of C. May, G. H. B. Haworth, S. Sackville and W. Johnson.	738 £3,821 5t13	1x35hp (ss) Weyburn 6-cyl AE.6 (p)	Lytham St Annes 4.4.1931-1.1939 (11/1) Padstow No.2 25.1.1939-31.11.1947 (4/0)	Sold 6.4.1948
5	1931 (S59) Saunders-Roe Cowes	35'6" 8'10" 7/8	**Lily Glen – Glasgow** Gift of Mrs Laurence Glen, Glasgow.	739 £3,742 5t9	1x35hp (ss) Weyburn 6-cyl AE.6 (p)	Girvan 11.3.1931-2.4.1952 (50/18)	Sold 5.1952
6	1931 (W1709) J. S. White Cowes	35'6" 8'10" 7/8	**Cyril and Lilian Bishop** Gift of Mrs Lilian Philpott.	740 £3,810 5t12	1x35hp (ss) Weyburn 6-cyl AE.6 (p)	Hastings 31.4.1931-18.3.1950 (99/34)	Sold 17.11.1950
7	1931 (S60) Saunders-Roe Cowes	35'6" 8'10" 7/8	**Morison Watson** Legacy of Mrs E. H. Watson, Bridge of Allan.	741 £3,718 5t12	1x35hp (ss) Weyburn 6-cyl AE.6 (p)	Kirkcudbright 8.4.1931-1953 (30/15)	Sold 1953
8	1931 (W1710) J. S. White Cowes	35'6" 8'10" 7/8	**Herbert Joy II** Gift of Mr Alexander O. Joy, London.	742 £3,791 5t11	1x35hp (ss) Weyburn 6-cyl AE.6 (p)	Scarborough 4.6.1931-10.1.1951 (114/22)	Sold 1951
9	1931 (S61) Saunders-Roe Cowes	35'6" 8'10" 7/8	**John and Sarah Eliza Stych** Legacies of Mr and Mrs Stych.	743 £3,754 5t10	1x35hp (ss) Weyburn 6-cyl AE.6 (p)	Padstow No.1 28.5.1931-8.2.1938 (7/8) St Ives 8.2.1938-23.1.1939 (2/1)	Wrecked on service 23.1.1939, seven lost
10	1931 (W1711) J. S. White Cowes	35'6" 8'10" 7/8	**Laurana Sarah Blunt** Legacy of Dr G. V. Blunt, Birmingham.	744 £3,812 5t10	1x35hp (ss) Weyburn 6-cyl AE.6 (p)	Youghal 20.6.1931-2.8.1952 (18/21)	Sold 1952
11	1931 (S62) Saunders-Roe Cowes	35'6" 8'10" 7/8	**Lady Harrison** Gift of Sir Heath Harrison, Bt.	745 £3,754 5t10	1x35hp (ss) Weyburn 6-cyl AE.6 (p)	Ramsey 31.6.1931-24.9.1948 (43/93) Aberystwyth 3.3.1949-25.10.1951 (4/0)	Sold 1952
12	1931 (W1712) J. S. White Cowes	35'6" 8'10" 7/8	**William Maynard** Legacy of Rev W. S. F. Maynard, Gressingham, Lancs.	746 £3,804 5t10	1x35hp (ss) Weyburn 6-cyl AE.6 (p)	Cloughey 19.1.1931-15.7.1939 (13/36) Reserve 1939-1941 and 1949-1953 (0/0) Ferryside 12.7.1941-1948 (5/2) Whitehills 2.7.1948-22.5.1949 (3/0)	Sold 2.1953
13	1931 (S63) Saunders-Roe Cowes	35'6" 8'10" 7/8	**Stanhope Smart** Legacy of Mr Stanhope Smart, Huddersfield.	747 £3,742 5t8	1x35hp (ss) Weyburn 6-cyl AE.6 (p)	Bridlington 8.6.1931-16.11.1947 (60/53) Padstow No.2 31.1.1947-30.7.1951 (0/0)	Sold 1951
14	1931 (W1713) J. S. White Cowes	35'6" 8'10" 7/8	**Mary Ann Blunt** Legacy of Dr G. V. Blunt, Birmingham.	748 £3,791 5t10	1x35hp (ss) Weyburn 6-cyl AE.6 (p)	Clougher Head 4.7.1931-7.7.1950 (20/9)	Sold 1951

12 • Self-righting motor 35ft 6in

	Year* (Yd No) Builder Place	Length Breadth Crew	Name Donor	ON Cost Weight	Engines (screws)	Stations (launches/lives saved)	Notes Disposal
15	1932 J. Thornycroft Chiswick	35'6" 8'10" 7/8	**John and William Mudie** Legacies of Miss I. and Miss E. Mudie.	752 £3,233 6t15	1x35hp (ss) Weyburn 6-cyl AE.6 (p)	Arbroath 7.1.1932-12.7.1950 (45/27)	Sold 14.6.1951
16	1932 (W1734) J. S. White Cowes	35'6" 8'10" 7/8	**Civil Service No.4** Civil Service Lifeboat Fund.	756 £3,342 6t6	1x35hp (ss) Weyburn 6-cyl AE.6 (p)	Whitehills 10.8.1932-4.1948 (26/9)	Damaged on service, 8.4.1948, none lost Sold 16.6.1948
17	1932 (W1735) J. S. White Cowes	35'6" 8'10" 7/8	**Frederick Angus** Legacy of Mr F. Angus, Poole.	757 £3,326 6t5	1x35hp (ss) Weyburn 6-cyl AE.6 (p)	Aberystwyth 23.9.1932-3.3.1949 (25/25)	Sold 17.8.1949
18	1933 (W1745) J. S. White Cowes	35'6" 9'3" 7/8	**Caroline Parsons** Legacies of Miss Caroline Parsons and Mrs E. Noy.	763 £3,213 6t	1x35hp (ss) Weyburn 6-cyl AE.6 (p)	St Ives 18.3.1933-1.1.1938 (7/73)	Wrecked on service 31.1.1938, none lost
19	1933 (W1749) J. S. White Cowes	35'6" 9'3" 7/8	**Catherine Harriet Eaton** Legacy of Rev Charles P. Eaton, Milford Haven.	767 £3,009 6t	1x35hp (ss) Weyburn 6-cyl AE.6 (p)	Exmouth 18.8.1933-9.10.1953 (34/31)	Sold 1953
20	1933 (W1750) J. S. White Cowes	35'6" 9'3" 7/8	**Thomas and Annie Wade Richards** Legacy of Dr Thomas Richards, Llangadoch, augmented by Miss Sarah Lewis, Aberystwyth.	768 £3,010 5t16	1x35hp (ss) Weyburn 6-cyl AE.6 (p)	Llandudno 15.9.1933-6.1953 (57/38)	Sold 1953
21	1936 (W1810) J. S. White Cowes	35'6" 9'6" 7/8	**Sir Heath Harrison** Gift of Mary, Lady Harrison, Le Court, Liss, Hampshire.	785 £3,279 6t1	1x35hp (ss) Weyburn 6-cyl AE.6 (p)	Port St Mary 18.4.1936-11.11.1949 (36/31) Reserve 1949-1955 (0/0)	Sold 1.1956
22	1940 (S570) Rowhedge IW Rowhedge	35'6" 9'10" 7/8	**Guide of Dunkirk** Girl Guides of the Empire.	826 £5,523 6t8	1x35hp (ss) Weyburn 6-cyl AE.6 (p)	Cadgwith 10.5.1941-31.5.1963 (15/17)	Sold 1963
23	1947 (W5381) J. S. White Cowes	35'6" 10' 7/8	**Tillie Morrison, Sheffield** Gift from James and David Morrison, of Sheffield	851 £10,573 7t15	2x18hp (ts) Weyburn 4-cyl AE.4 (p)	Bridlington 16.11.1947-1953 (23/0) Llandudno 1953-1959 (17/8)	Capsized on service 19.8.1952, one lost Sold 11.1959
24	1950 (506) Groves & Guttridge Cowes	35'6" 10' 7/8	**M. T. C.** Trained Women Drivers' Association.	878 £11,283 8t12	2x18hp (ts) Weyburn 4-cyl AE.4 (p)	Hastings 18.3.1950-11.1963 (107/28)	Sold 1964
25	1950 (507) Groves & Guttridge Cowes	35'6" 10' 7/8	**E. C. J. R.** Legacies of A. E. Wildish, R. Mundy, L. Crichton and P. E. Wood.	879 £12,095 8t8	2x20hp (ts) Ferry FKR.3 3-cyl (d)	Scarborough 1.1951-10.1956 (31/15) Reserve 1956-1963 (1/0)	Capsized on service 8.12.1954, three lost Sold 3.1963
26	1950 (508) Groves & Guttridge Cowes	35'6" 10' 7/8	**Isaac and Mary Bolton** Legacy of Miss Bolton and Northumberland War Distress Relief Fund.	880 £12,548 8t15	2x20hp (ts) Ferry FKR.3 3-cyl (d)	Cullercoats 15.3.1951-21.11.1963 (29/31)	Sold 1964
27	1950 (510) Groves & Guttridge Cowes	35'6" 10' 7/8	**City of Leeds** City of Leeds Lifeboat Fund.	881 £13,939 8t16	2x20hp (ts) Ferry FKR.3 3-cyl (d)	Redcar 15.5.1951-2.1965 (52/31)	Sold 3.1965

12 • Self-righting motor 35ft 6in

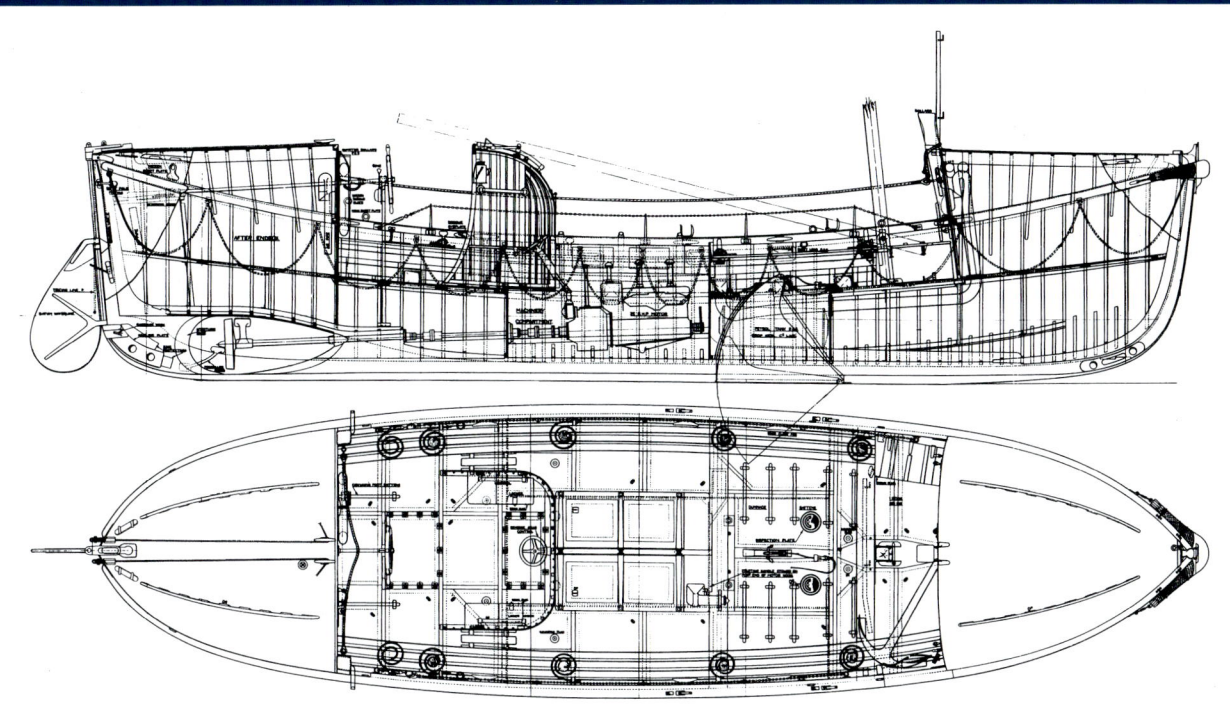

◀ General profile and deck arrangement of the 35ft 6in motor self-righter Caroline Parsons (ON.763) with a small shelter for the engine and a tunnel to protect the single screw. This lifeboat served at St Ives until 1938, when she was wrecked on service while on service on 31 January to the steamer Alba. This was the first time a motor lifeboat capsized. None of the lifeboat crew were lost, but five of the crew of Alba were lost. (By courtesy of the RNLI)

▶ General profile and deck arrangement of the 35ft 6in self-righting motor City of Leeds (ON.881), one of the five twin-engined boats of the class fitted with an engine shelter, which gave them an appearance similar to that of the non-self-righting Liverpool motor lifeboats (see page 96). (By courtesy of the RNLI)

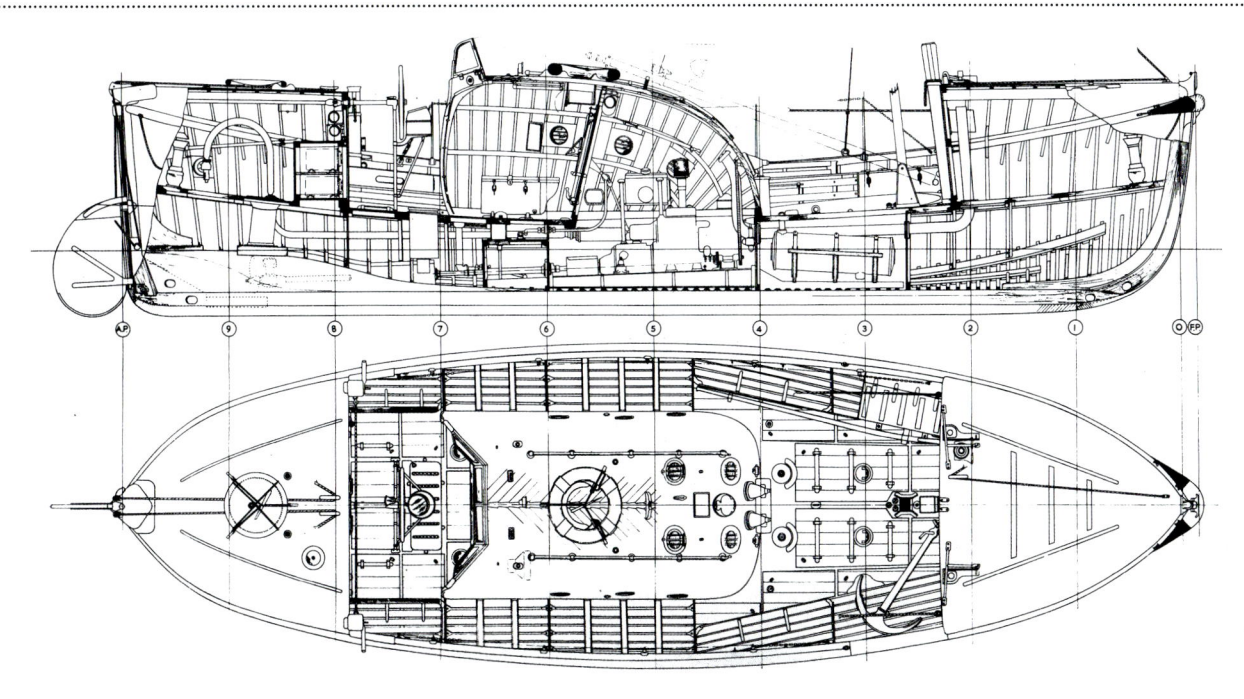

MOTOR LIFEBOATS 69

12 • Self-righting motor 35ft 6in

◀ Cyril and Lilian Bishop (ON.740) on the beach at Hastings with her crew. The 35ft 6in motor self-righting lifeboats were intended for carriage launching, being light enough to be manhandled across a beach before launching tractors had been introduced across the country, and so at some stations the boats were often hauled by large numbers of shore helpers when being launched.

▶ One of a dozen 35ft 6in self-righters built in 1931, Mary Ann Blunt (ON.748) served at Clogher Hed for nineteen years, and is pictured on trials in the Solent. (By courtesy of the RNLI)

▲ The St Ives lifeboat John and Sarah Eliza Stych (ON.743) ashore near Godrevy of the Cornish coast on 23 January 1939 after she had capsized three times while searching for a vessel reported to be in distress, with the loss of seven St Ives lifeboat crew. During each capsize, crew were lost overboard, and when the boat was eventually thrown onto the rocks, having had its propeller fouled and engine failed, only one man remained, William Freeman, who was injured and exhausted from his ordeal, but still alive.

70 MOTOR LIFEBOATS

12 • Self-righting motor 35ft 6in

▲ (left) The scene at Whitehills during the naming ceremony of the 35ft 6in motor self-righting lifeboat Civil Service No.4 (ON.756) on 5 October 1932. She was the twenty-first lifeboat provided by the Civil Service Lifeboat Fund, despite her name, and was christened by the Duchess of Fife. (By courtesy of the RNLI)

▲ (right) Guide of Dunkirk (ON.826) on trials. She was the last single-engined self-righter, and served at Cadgwith for more than twenty years. Funded from an appeal by the Girl Guides during Empire Week in 1940, she was completed in April 1940, just before a call came for boats to help evacuate the British Expeditionary Force from Dunkirk. She was the only self-righter to be built at Rowhedge, and was sent from there straight to Dunkirk, afterwards returning to her building yard for repairs, before being sent to Cadgwith and being given a name to reflect her wartime exploits across the Channel. (By courtesy of the RNLI)

▶ City of Leeds (ON.881) on her carriage at Redcar. Built in 1951, she was one of five self-righters built after Second World War which were twin-engined and had distinctive engine shelters that gave the boats an appearance similar to that of the 35ft 6in Liverpools. (By courtesy of the RNLI)

MOTOR LIFEBOATS

13 • Liverpool motor single-engined

KEY DATA
- Introduced 1931
- Last built 1941
- 28 built

▲ Anne Allen (ON.760) served at Skegness for more than twenty years. This photograph shows the deck layout of the Liverpool motor. (RNLI)

The Liverpool motor lifeboat, designed by James Barnett, was developed from the 35ft 6in self-righting type and the two classes shared many features, while the main difference was that the Liverpool class boats were not self-righting. However, but it was light enough to be suitable for carriage launching, having been designed in response to requests from crews at carriage stations who preferred non-self-righting boats because of their greater initial stability. The Liverpool was designed with a beam of 10ft, as opposed to 8ft 10in in the self-righters. The first of the Liverpool class, Oldham (ON.750), was, appropriately enough, sent to Hoylake. She arrived in October 1931 and her remit was to cover the port of Liverpool and the busy Mersey estuary.

The hull of the Liverpool was built with a double skin of mahogany, keel of teak, ribs of Canadian rock elm, stem and stern posts of English oak, and air cases of Columbian red cedar. It was divided into six watertight compartments, with 129 air cases fitted into the hold, wing compartments and end boxes. Although end boxes were incorporated into the hull, these were less tall than those on the self-righting type, on which they were needed to aid righting. There were eighteen relieving scuppers, which would free the boats entirely of water in about twenty seconds. Being single-engined, the Liverpool carried auxiliary sails, consisting of jib, fore-lug and jib-headed mizzen, in accordance with RNLI policy, and could be accurately described as a motor sailer. A drop keel was housed in a casing beneath the well deck, just forward of the engine-room canopy, and the rudder could be triced up as required.

Power came from an RNLI-designed six-cylinder Weyburn AE6 petrol engine, which developed 35bhp at 3,300rpm and drove a shrouded single screw through a four to one reduction gear. The engine was watertight and able to continue running even if submerged, provided the air intake remained above water level, and was housed in a cuddy amidships that formed a watertight compartment. The protective tunnel for the propeller was formed by increasing the height of the deadwood, the external top of which formed the top of the tunnel, with the propeller shaft running through the reinforced deadwood.

Oldham (ON.750) carried a total of fifty gallons of fuel, stored in two twenty-five gallon petrol tanks located below the deck, one on either side of the centre-plate. Fuel consumption was just over three gallons an hour at full speed. She had a range of about fifty-two nautical miles at her maximum speed of 7.26 knots, with the propeller running at 865rpm, and this increased to sixty-five nautical miles at the cruising speed of 6.5 knots, with the propeller running at 710rpm. With a displacement of 6.75 tons and a stability range of ninety-three degrees, the Liverpools could accommodate up to forty-five survivors, in addition to a crew of between seven and ten, in rough weather.

The boats had a shallow draft, making them eminently suitable for launching off flat beaches, and their designer James Barnett regarded the type as 'shallow-water boats'. Of the twenty-eight single-engined Liverpools built between 1931 and 1941, the majority were launched by carriage, while those stationed at Weston-super-Mare, Coverack, Flamborough, Maryport, Seaham Harbour and St Abbs were slipway launched. They were well liked by the crews and gave good service, operating through the challenges of the Second World War. Only one 35ft 6in Liverpool motor capsized, Richard Silver Oliver (ON.794), on exercise at Cullercoats in 1939.

▲ The first 35ft 6in Liverpool motor lifeboat, Oldham (ON.750), on trials; she served at Hoylake for just over twenty years, was fitted with a single drop-keel and carried a reduced yawl rig. (RNLI)

▲ Fifi and Charles (ON.765) was the fourth 35ft 6in Liverpool motor lifeboat to enter RNLI service, and the first to operate from a slipway; the slipway at Weston was 368ft in length, one of the longest in use.

13 • Liverpool motor single-engined

	Year* (Yd No) Builder Place	Length Breadth Crew	Name Donor	ON Cost Weight	Engines	Stations (launches/lives saved)	Notes Disposal
1	1931 (175) Groves & Guttridge Cowes	35'6" 10' 8/7	**Oldham** Gift from the inhabitants of the town of Oldham.	750 £3,995 5t16	1x35hp Weyburn 6-cyl AE6	Hoylake 1.10.1931-14.2.1952 (43/20)	Sold 1952
2	1932 (T2255) Thornycroft Chiswick	35'6" 10' 8/7	**Anne Allen** Legacy of Mrs Anne Allen, Spalding, Lincs.	760 £3,340 6t8	1x35hp Weyburn 6-cyl AE6	Skegness 10.12.1932-8.12.1953 (120/43)	Sold 1953
3	1933 (W1746) J. S. White Cowes	35'6" 10' 8/7	**Nellie and Charlie** Legacy of Neil Robinson, Pitlochry.	764 £3,416 6t	1x35hp Weyburn 6-cyl AE6	Anstruther 18.3.1933-18.6.1950 (54/72)	Sold 4.1951
4	1933 (W1747) J. S. White Cowes	35'6" 10' 8/7	**Fifi and Charles** Legacy of Mr Charles C. Ashley, Mentone, France.	765 £3,297 6t	1x35hp Weyburn 6-cyl AE6	Weston-super-Mare 7.9.1933-17.3.1962 (68/83)	Sold 10.1962
5	1933 (W1748) J. S. White Cowes	35'6" 10' 8/7	**The Always Ready/** 1934- **Robert Paton – The Always Ready** Legacy of Mrs E. B. Browne, renamed after Runswick Coxswain.	766 £3,187 6t	1x35hp Weyburn 6-cyl AE6	Runswick 1.10.1933-14.1.1954 (51/17)	Sold 5.1954
6	1934 (194) Groves & Guttridge Cowes	35'6" 10'3" 8/7	**Harriot Dixon** Legacy of Mr W. E. Dixon.	770 £3,317 6t	1x35hp Weyburn 6-cyl AE6	Cromer No.2 8.1934-28.10.1964 (55/20)	Sold 12.1964
7	1934 (W1771) J. S. White Cowes	35'6" 10' 8/7	**The Three Sisters** Legacy of Miss Margaret Quiller Couch.	771 £3,248 6t	1x35hp Weyburn 6-cyl AE6	Coverack 14.8.1934-24.7.1954 (26/61)	Sold 1954
8	1934 (195) Groves & Guttridge Cowes	35'6" 10' 8/7	**Elizabeth and Albina Whitley** Legacy of Mr Whitley.	772 £3295 6t	1x35hp Weyburn 6-cyl AE6	Flamborough 31.8.1934-7.12.1948 (56/63) Reserve 1948-1952 (0/0)	Sold 1.1953
9	1934 (W1772) J. S. White Cowes	35'6" 10' 8/7	**Joseph Braithwaite** Legacy of Mr Joseph Braithwaite.	773 £3,210 6t	1x35hp Weyburn 6-cyl AE6	Maryport 28.8.1934-31.12.1949 (35/30) Reserve 1950-1952 (1/0)	Sold 12.1952
10	1936 (W1803) J. S. White Cowes	35'6" 10'3" 8/7	**W. R. A.** Legacies of Mr A. Gardiner, Miss M. B. Savage, and Miss A. Matthews.	781 £3,447 6t1	1x35hp Weyburn 6-cyl AE6	North Sunderland 30.1.1936-8.4.1954 (56/44) Reserve 1954-1958 (6/0)	Sold 1958
11	1936 (W1804) J. S. White Cowes	35'6" 10'3" 8/7	**Margaret Dawson** Legacy of Mrs M. Dawson.	782 £3,437 6t1	1x35hp Weyburn 6-cyl AE6	Gourdon 20.1.1936-26.4.1952 (37/13) Reserve 1952-1955 (0/0)	Sold 1956
12	1936 (210) Groves & Guttridge Cowes	35'6" 10'3" 8/7	**Foresters' Centenary** Ancient Order of Foresters.	786 £3569 6t1	1x35hp Weyburn 6-cyl AE6	Sheringham 25.6.1936-10.7.1961 (129/82)	Sold 1961
13	1936 (W1817) J. S. White Cowes	35'6" 10'3" 8/7	**Elizabeth Wills Allen** Executors of the late Miss E. W. Allen, Northam, Devon.	791 £3776 6t4	1x35hp Weyburn 6-cyl AE6	Seaham Harbour 5.12.1936-12.1.1950 (18/17) Reserve 1950-1953 (0/0)	Sold 2.1953
14	1936 (W1818) J. S. White Cowes	35'6" 10'3" 8/7	**Annie Ronald And Isabella Forrest** Gift from Miss A. Ronald, Paisley; and legacy of Mrs I. Forrest, Glasgow.	792 £3771 6t4	1x35hp Weyburn 6-cyl AE6	St Abbs 5.12.1936-20.10.1949 (28/73) Reserve 1949-1956 (17/7) Bridlington 22.8.1952-17.6.1953 Scarborough 3.1956-21.10.1958 (9/0) Llandudno 10.1959-31.1.1964 (36/21)	Sold 3.1965

MOTOR LIFEBOATS

13 • Liverpool motor single-engined

	Year* (Yd No) Builder Place	Length Breadth Crew	Name Donor	ON Cost Weight	Engines	Stations (launches/lives saved)	Notes Disposal
15	1937 (W1822) J. S. White Cowes	35'6" 10'3" 8/7	**Clarissa Langdon** Legacy of Mr Walter Langdon.	793 £3,669 6t1	1x35hp Weyburn 6-cyl AE6	Boulmer 11.2.1937-9.10.1962 (68/24) Seaham Harbour 13.2-10.9.1963 (1/0) Reserve 1963-65 (2/0)	Sold 3.1965
16	1937 (W1823) J. S. White Cowes	35'6" 10'3" 8/7	**Richard Silver Oliver** Legacy of Mrs I. A. Oliver, Tadcaster.	794 £3,684 6t1	1x35hp Weyburn 6-cyl AE6	Cullercoats 11.2.1937-22.4.1939 (3/0) Newquay 22.3.1940-4.6.1945 (21/11) Ilfracombe 10.1945-9.10.1952 (15/23) Criccieth 1953-1961 (13/0)	Capsized on exercise 22.4.1939, six lost Sold 1963
17	1937 (218) Groves & Guttridge Cowes	35'6" 10'3" 8/7	**Frank and William Oates** Legacy of Mr C. G. Oates.	795 £3,835 6t1	1x35hp Weyburn 6-cyl AE6	Eyemouth 11.3.1937-12.12.1951 (17/9) Girvan 2.4.1952-2.9.1956 (17/0) Reserve 1956-1964 (21/8)	Sold 1964
18	1937 (219) Groves & Guttridge Cowes	35'6" 10'3" 8/7	**[Herbert John]** -	796 £3,838 6t1	1x35hp Weyburn 6-cyl AE6	[Stemmed for Cloughey]	Destroyed by fire at Groves & Guttridge boatyard, 18.6.1937
19	1937 (S64) Saunders-Roe Cowes	35'6" 10'3" 8/7	**Howard D** Gift of Mr T. B. Davis, Jersey.	797 £3,623 6t1	1x35hp Weyburn 6-cyl AE6	St Helier 12.8.1937-14.10.1948 (23/46)* Flamborough 7.12.1948-20.6.1953 (25/16) Arbroath 7.10.1953-26.6.1956 (9/1) Reserve 1956-1964 (13/3) Seaham Harbour 29.11.1962-2.1963 (0/0)	*Under enemy control at Jersey 1.7.1940-9.5.1945 Sold 1964
20	1937 (220) Groves & Guttridge Cowes	35'6" 10'3" 8/7	**Ann Isabella Pyemont** Gift of John Pyemont, Epsom, Surrey.	798 £3,908 6t1	1x35hp Weyburn 6-cyl AE6	Kilmore Quay 12.8.1937-10.1965 (76/44)	Sold 1966
21	1937 (S65) Saunders-Roe Cowes	35'6" 10'3" 8/7	**Helen Sutton** Executors of the late Mrs Helen C. Sutton.	799 £3,637 6t1	1x35hp Weyburn 6-cyl AE6	Peel 17.7.1937-29.7.1952 (38/14) Reserve 1952-1958 (4/2)	Sold 1958
22	1937 (221) Groves & Guttridge Cowes	35'6" 10'3" 8/7	**Sarah Ann Austin** Legacy of Mrs Sarah Ann Walker, Leeds; Governors of the Skelton Bounty.	800 £3,895 6t1	1x35hp Weyburn 6-cyl AE6	Blackpool 12.6.1937-12.1961 (47/30) Reserve 1962-1965 (6/0)	Sold 8.1965
23	1939 (257) Groves & Guttridge Cowes	35'6" 10'3" 8/7	**Herbert John** Legacies of Miss B. A. Athill and Mr S. M. Poland.	825 £4,054 6t15	1x35hp Weyburn 6-cyl AE6	Cloughey 15.7.1939-17.6.1952 (46/67) Youghal 2.8.1952-19.10.1966 (14/30)	Sold 1966
24	1939 Morgan Giles Teignmouth	35'6" 10'3" 8/7	**George and Elizabeth Gow** Legacy of Mrs E. L. Gow, London.	827 £4,709 6t17	1x35hp Weyburn 6-cyl AE6	Aberdeen No.2 19.10.1939-16.10.1943 & 14.4.1947-62 (2/0); taken over by RAF 1943, used for rescue work in Azores, Reserve 1962-64 (15/0)	Sold 1965
25	1939 (262) Groves & Guttridge Cowes	35'6" 10'3" 8/7	**Caroline Oates Aver and William Maine** Legacies of Mrs C. Aver and Miss C. L. Maine.	831 £4,289 6t14	1x35hp Weyburn 6-cyl AE6	St Ives 13.1.1940-11.4.1948 (50/34) Ferryside 4.1948-6.1960 (4/0)	Sold 7.1960
26	1939 (263) Groves & Guttridge Cowes	35'6" 10'3" 8/7	**W. & .B/** 1940- **Lucy Lavers** 1940- Legacy of Mr Lavers and estate of Mr E. J. Williams.	832 £4,455 6t18	1x35hp Weyburn 6-cyl AE6/ 1963- 1x47hp Parsons Porbeagle (d)	[Stemmed- Porthoustock] Aldeburgh 2 5.1940-10.2.1959 (30/7) Reserve 1959-1968 (52/37)	Sold 1968
27	1940 (264) Groves & Guttridge Cowes	35'6" 10'3" 8/7	**The Cuttle** Legacy of Miss F. L. Cuttle, Rotherham.	833 £4,444 6t13	1x35hp Weyburn 6-cyl AE6	Filey 22.5.1940-21.10.1953 (77/28) Skegness 8.12.1953-20.4.1964 (48/11) Reserve 1964-1966 (0/0)	Sold 8.1966
28	1941 (265) Groves & Guttridge Cowes	35'6" 10'3" 8/7	**Jose Neville** Legacy of Mrs E. Neville, Barnes, Surrey.	834 £4,474 6t11	1x35hp Weyburn 6-cyl AE6	Caister 15.5.1941-22.1.1964 (107/75) Reserve 1964-1966 (1/0)	Sold 8.1966

13 • Liverpool motor single-engined

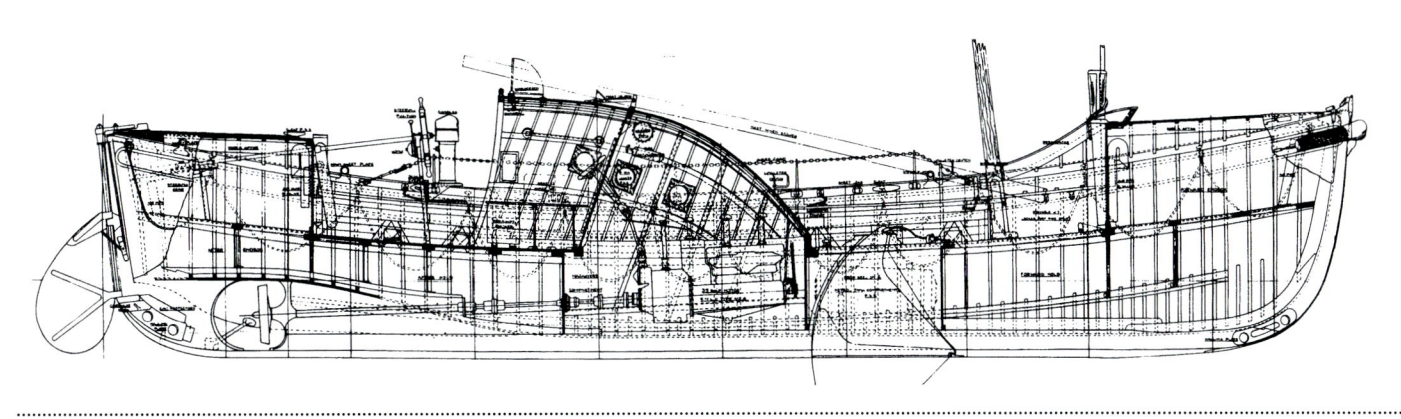

◀ General profile of the non-self-righting 35ft 6in Liverpool motor Robert Paton – The Always Ready (ON.766). The single propeller was protected by the keel, a design feature which made the boat ideal for launching and recovering over a beach.

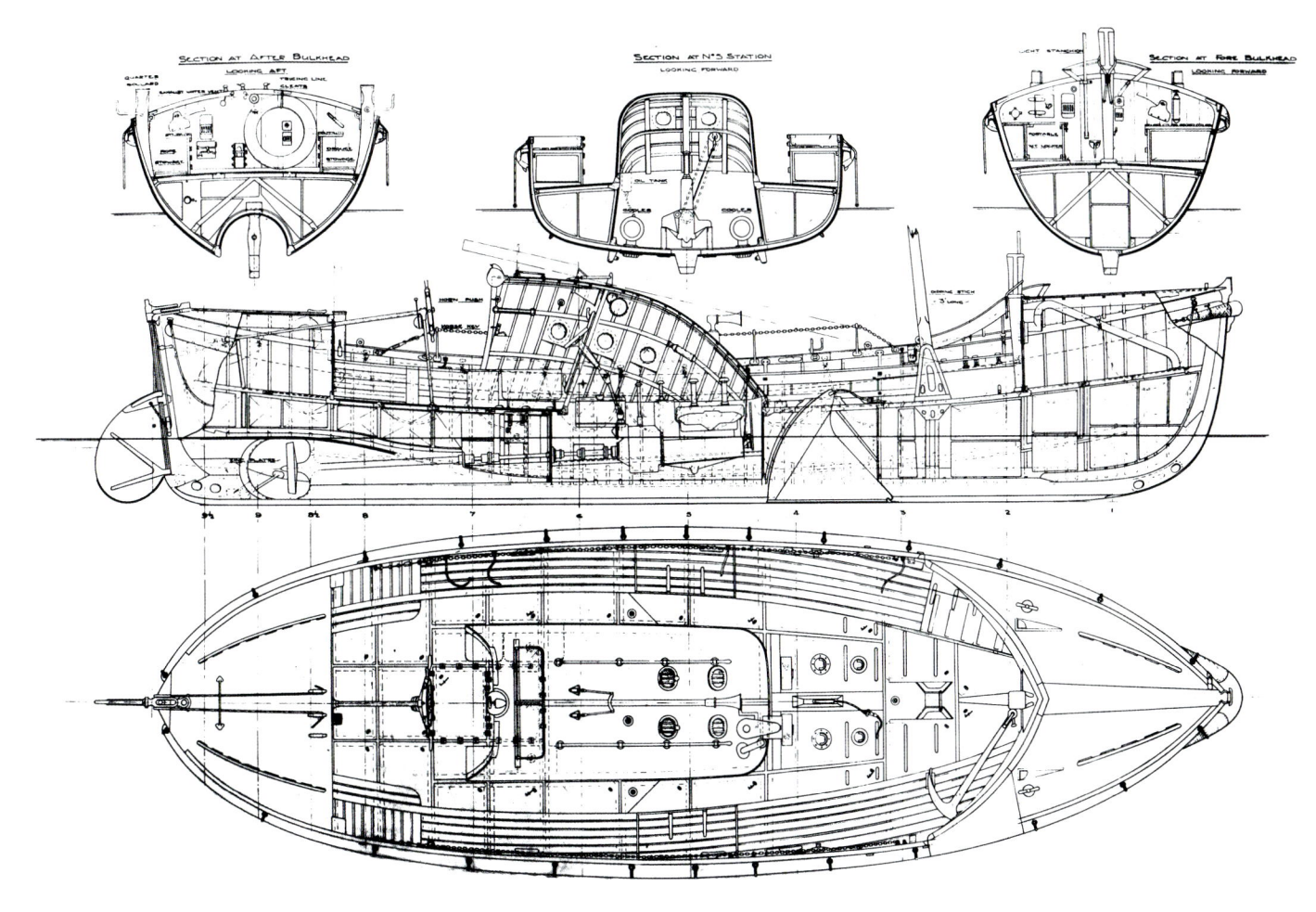

◀ General profile and deck arrangement of Foresters' Centenary (ON.786), which served at Sheringham for a quarter of a century and gained a fine record of service. The boat carried sails and was fitted with a drop keel, which can be seen in the profile diagram, just forward of the engine. (By courtesy of the RNLI)

MOTOR LIFEBOATS

13 • Liverpool motor single-engined

◀ The Aberdeen No.2 lifeboat George and Elizabeth Gow (ON.827) with sails stowed. The sails were auxiliary, and necessary for the single-engined Liverpool lifeboats for use in case of engine failure. (By courtesy of the RNLI)

▲ Sarah Ann Austin (ON.800) under sail. She was one of eight 35ft 6in Liverpools built during 1937, as the RNLI continued to motorise the fleet, with the boats all replacing pulling and sailing craft at their stations. (By courtesy of the RNLI)

▶ Bound for Skegness, The Cuttle (ON.833) on trials in 1940. She was one of the last 35ft 6in Liverpools to be built and one of very few lifeboats completed during the Second World War. (By courtesy of the RNLI)

▲ Elizabeth and Albina Whitley (ON.772) on the tipping cradle at the head of the slipway at North Landing, Flamborough. She served as the station's No.1 lifeboat for fourteen years, and then served in the Reserve Fleet for three years. (From an old postcard supplied by John Harrop)

76 MOTOR LIFEBOATS

13 • Liverpool motor single-engined

14 • Beach 'Aldeburgh' motor 41ft

KEY DATA
- Introduced 1931
- Last built 1949
- 5 built

SPECIFICATIONS
- Length 41ft
- Beam 12ft 3in

▶ Walmer's motor lifeboats were kept on a cradle at the head of the beach, with Charles Dibdin (Civil Service No.2) (ON.762) operating from here for more than twenty-five years.

▼ (left) Charles Cooper Henderson (ON.761) on trials. The hull of the 41ft Beach type was strengthened so that it would withstand the potentially damaging beach launch and recovery procedure. (By courtesy of the RNLI)

▼ (right) Beryl Tollemache (ON.859) served at Eastbourne for twenty-eight years; a turntable at the top of the beach, on which she is pictured, meant she could be recovered bow first up the beach, and then turned through 180 degrees outside the boathouse. (Jeff Morris)

The 41ft Beach motor was designed for stations where conditions at sea require a fairly large and heavy type, but where the Barnett or Watson cabin types were too large as the boat has to be light enough to be launched off the beach, and the smaller 35ft 6in types were deemed too lightweight. The 41ft boat was regarded as a development of the Norfolk & Suffolk type and became known as the 'Aldeburgh' type after the station at which the first boat served. However, it was similar in many respects to the 41ft Watson, notably in its deck layout, but the hull, similar in shape to the Watsons, was strengthened to withstand the extra stresses of being dragged over a beach, as well as being of greater breadth, with good freeboard, a flat floor, stout bilge keels and a heavy iron keel weighing a ton and a half. Launching across a beach involved the use of skids and rollers to get the boats afloat.

The Beach type was non-self-righting, with no end boxes and flush decks fore and aft, carried no water ballast, and the hull, which measured 41ft by 12ft 3in, was divided into seven watertight compartments and 135 air cases. The boat was not self-righting because, according to James Barnett, 'the fishermen never have favoured the self-righting boat'. A large after cockpit provided shelter for crew and engine controls, 110 gallons of fuel was carried, and on service, with crew and gear on board, she weighed 16.25 tons. She carried a line-throwing gun and an electric searchlight, and was lighted by electricity.

The boats were powered by twin 35hp petrol engines, while two of the five were re-engined with more powerful 47hp diesels during their time were in service. The engines were in a watertight compartment and were themselves watertight, so would continue running if the engine room were flooded. The twin propellers were housed in protective tunnels. Maximum speed was just over seven and a half knots, giving a range of 116 miles; at the cruising speed of 6.75 knots, the range increased to 160 miles. In rough weather sixty-five people could be taken on board, and eighty people could be carried in fine weather; the boats carried a crew of ten.

Because only a few stations needed to launch the lifeboat across the beach, only five boats of this type were built, four in the 1930s and the last in 1949. This last boat, Beryl Tollemache (ON.859), had a superstructure and deck layout similar to that of the post-war 41ft Watsons. The Viscountess Wakefield (ON.783), when stationed at Hythe, was taken to Dunkirk on 31 May 1940 but she was lost on the beaches while evacuating troops.

14 • Beach 'Aldeburgh' motor 41ft

	Year* (Yd No) Builder Place	Length Breadth Crew	Name Donor	ON Cost Weight	Engines	Stations (launches/lives saved)	Disposal
1	1931 (W1726) J. S. White Cowes	41' 12'3" 10	**Abdy Beauclerk** Legacy of Mrs Jane E. King, St Leonards-on-Sea.	751 £6,384.6.10 15t12	2x35bhp (ts) Weyburn AE.6 6-cyl (p)	Aldeburgh No.1 11.12.1931-31.12.1958 (118/139)	Sold 1959
2	1933 (183) Groves & Guttridge Cowes	41' 12'3" 10	**Charles Cooper Henderson** Legacy of Henry Cooper Henderson, Ramsgate	761 £5,704.12.6 15t9	2x35bhp (ts) Weyburn AE.6 6-cyl (p)/1963- 2x47hp Parsons Porbeagle (d)	Dungeness 18.7.1933-31.8.1957 (170/63) Reserve 1957-1974 (126/93)	Sold 1.1976
3	1933 (184) Groves & Guttridge Cowes	41' 12'3" 10	**Charles Dibdin (Civil Service No.2)** Civil Service Lifeboat Fund.	762 £5,664.3.7 15t	2x35bhp (ts) Weyburn AE.6 6-cyl (p)	Walmer 28.7.1933-18.3.1959 (241/412)	Sold 1961
4	1936 (207) Groves & Guttridge Cowes	41' 12'3" 10	**The Viscountess Wakefield** Gift of Right Hon The Lord Wakefield of Hythe, CBE.	783 £6,089.3.0 14t8	2x35bhp (ts) Weyburn AE.6 6-cyl (p)	Hythe 24.2.1936-5.1940 (17/9)	Lost on beaches of Dunkirk, 31.5.1940
5	1949 Sussex Yacht Co Shoreham	41' 12'3" 8	**Beryl Tollemache** Gift of Sir Lionel and Lady Tollemache, Richmond.	859 £15,011.12.4 15t2	2x35bhp (ts) Weyburn AE.6 6-cyl (p)/1963- 2x47hp Parsons Porbeagle (d)	Eastbourne 25.6.1949-21.5.1977 (176/154) Reserve 1977-1979 (5/7)	Sold 9.1979

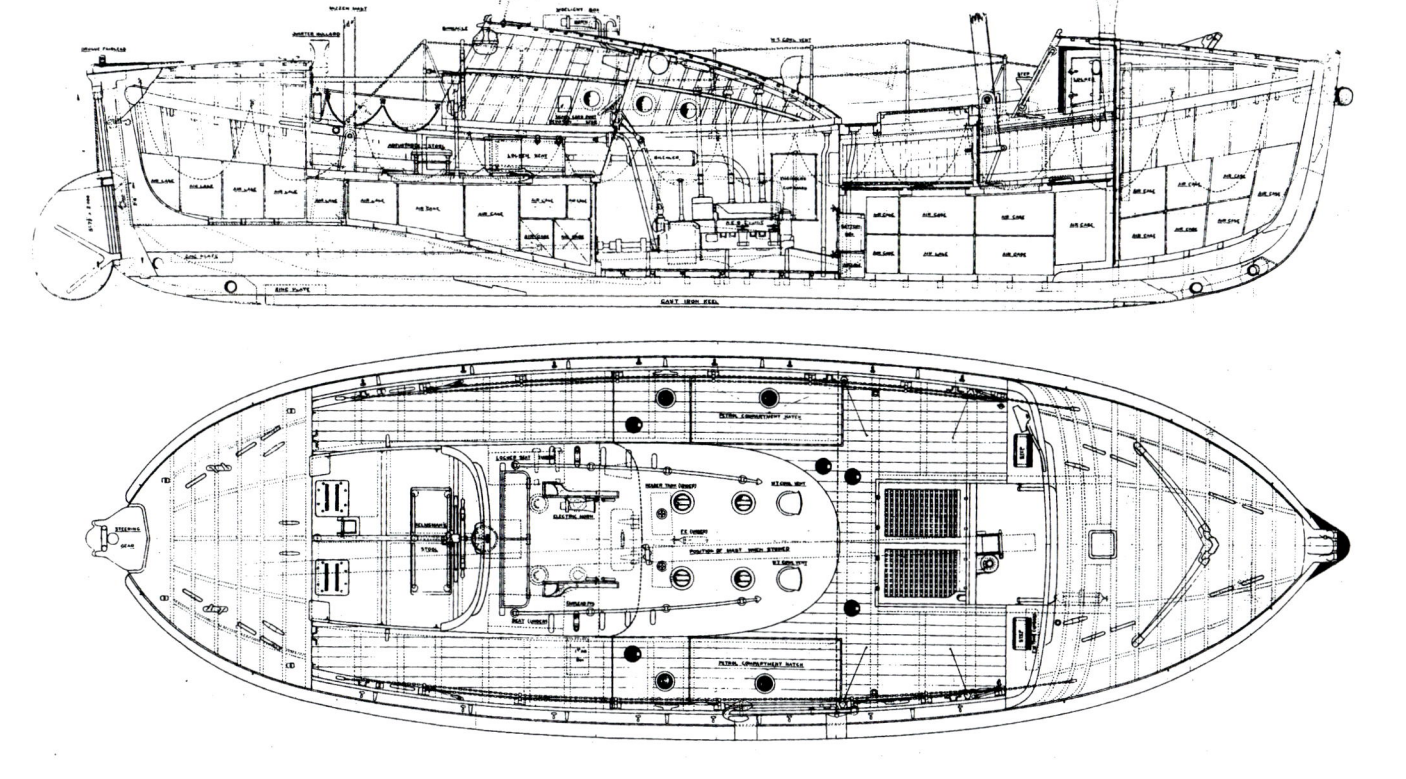

◀ Plans of the second 41ft Beach motor lifeboat, Charles Cooper Henderson (ON.761). The type was similar to the 41ft Watson but was broader and had a strengthened hull so that it could withstand the stresses of launch and recovery across shingle beaches, such as that at Dungeness, where this lifeboat was stationed for more than twenty years.

MOTOR LIFEBOATS

15 • Watson motor 41ft

KEY DATA
- Introduced 1933
- Last built 1952
- 13 built

SPECIFICATIONS
- Length 41ft
- Beam 11ft 8in
- Crew 8

The 41ft Watson was designed for stations at which a powerful lifeboat was deemed necessary but where the larger Barnett or Watson motor lifeboats were not suitable, usually because they were regarded as being too large. This version of the Watson was regarded as an intermediate design intended primarily for launching down slipways, and apart from the New Brighton boat all were slipway launched. The non-self-righting hull was divided into five watertight compartments fitted with 145 air cases, and had sixteen relieving scuppers which could free the boat of water in less than half a minute. The nine 41ft Watsons were built during the 1930s had two cockpits, one forward and the other aft, with room for up to sixteen people. The larger aft cockpit provided shelter for the crew of eight and housed the engine controls; a line-throwing gun and an electric searchlight were also carried

The boats' waterline length was 39ft 6in, draught was 3ft 8in, and power came from twin 35bhp Weyburn AE6 six-cylinder petrol engines, giving a maximum speed of between seven and a half and eight knots, with the propellers housed in separate tunnels. The design had a displacement of approximately fourteen tons. The engine-room was a watertight compartment, and each engine was itself waterproofed so that it would continue running even if the engine room were flooded The first boat, Rosa Woodd and Phyllis Lunn (ON.758), reached a top speed of 8.06 knots on trials, at which speed she had a range of sixty-seven nautical miles; at her cruising speed of seven knots her radius of action increased to 100 nautical miles. The boats carried a total of 112 gallons of fuel.

Several of the 41ft Watsons were re-engined during 1963 and continued in service. They were fitted with new 47hp Parsons Porbeagle four-cylinder diesels, which were more powerful than the original petrol engines, gave the boats an increased range, and also reduced the risk of fire on board. In addition to their engines, the boats carried two sails for use either as a steadying sail or in the event of engine failure. The last four boats, built after the end of the Second World War between 1948 and 1952, were a modified cabin version with a small superstructure offering protection for the mechanics operating the engine controls. Different from the pre-war boats, they were built before the 42ft Watson had been designed.

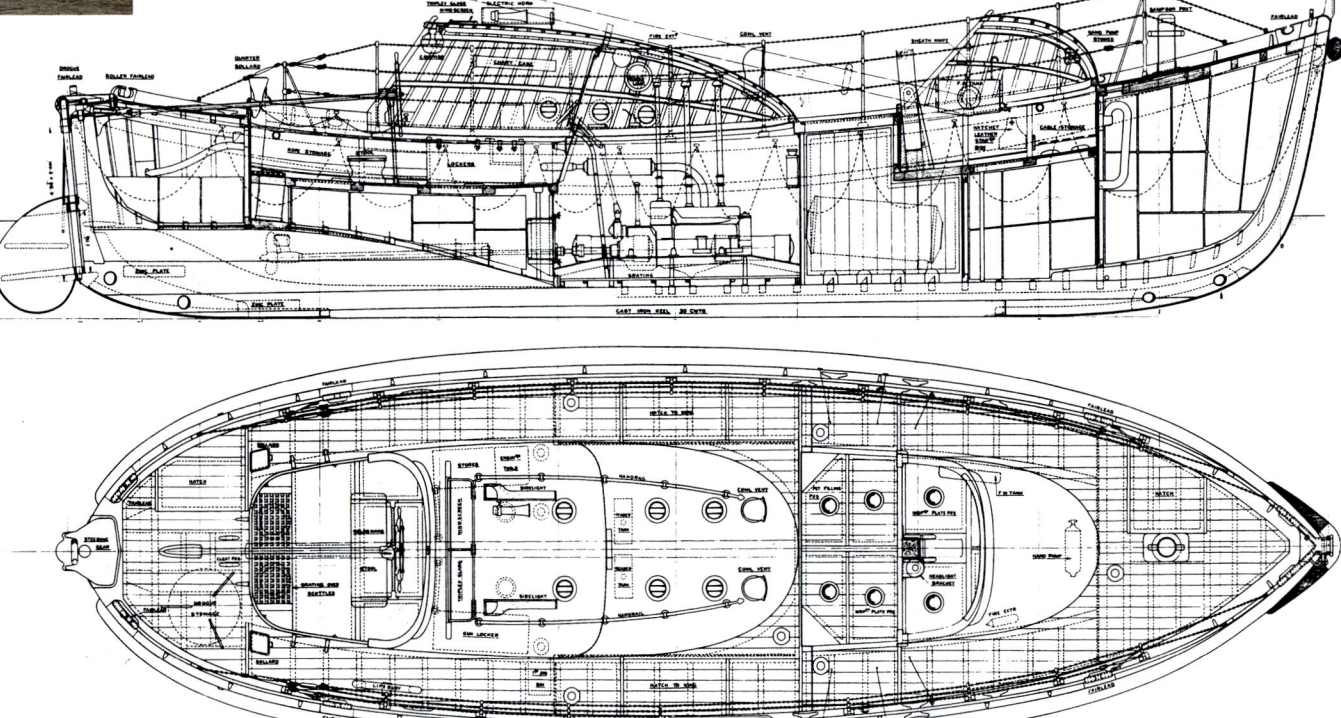

▲ The first 41ft Watson motor Rosa Woodd and Phyllis Lunn (ON.758). (By courtesy of the RNLI)

▶ General arrangement of the first 41ft Watson, Rosa Woodd and Phyllis Lunn (ON.758), which served at Shoreham Harbour. The nine 41ft Watsons built before the Second World War had two cockpits, one forward and one aft. (By courtesy of the RNLI)

80　　　　　　　　　　　　　　　　　　　　　　　　　　　　　　　　　　　　　　MOTOR LIFEBOATS

15 • Watson motor 41ft

	Year* (Yd No) Builder Place	Length Breadth Crew	Name Donor	ON Cost Weight	Engines	Stations (launches/lives saved)	Notes Disposal
1	1933 (181) Groves & Guttridge Cowes	41' 11'8" 8	**Rosa Woodd and Phyllis Lunn** Legacy Mrs Rose Lord and collections by Mr W. Lunn and Mrs Perowne.	758 £6,132 14t10	2x35bhp Weyburn AE.6 6-cyl (p)/1963- 2x47hp Parsons Porbeagle (d)	Shoreham Harbour 4.1.1933-17.1.1963 (244/143) Reserve 1963-1973 (53/19)	Sold 1973
2	1933 (185) Groves & Guttridge Cowes	41' 11'8" 8	**Duke of York** King George's Fund for Sailors.	769 £5,635 14t10	2x35bhp Weyburn AE.6 6-cyl (p)	Lizard 14.2.1934-1961 (58/82)	Sold 1961
3	1936 (226) Groves & Guttridge Cowes	41' 11'8" 8	**Rachel and Mary Evans** Legacy of Mr T. D. Evans, Malpas, Monmouthshire.	806 £6,458 12t4	2x35bhp Weyburn AE.6 6-cyl (p)	Barry Dock 9.12.1937-3.1968 (96/80) Reserve 1968-4.1969 (1/0)	Broke moorings at Weston, wrecked 12.4.1969
4	1938 (227) Groves & Guttridge Cowes	41' 11'8" 8	**Inbhear Môr** RNLI Funds.	807 £6,506 13t18	2x35bhp Weyburn AE.6 6-cyl (d)/1963- 2x47hp Parsons Porbeagle (p)	Arklow 14.7.1938-12.1968 (87/98) Reserve 1968-1973 (23/42)	Sold 1974
5	1938 (228) Groves & Guttridge Cowes	41' 11'8" 8	**Mary Ann Hepworth** Gift of W. W. Hepworth, Hessle, Hull.	808 £6,575 14t2	2x35bhp Weyburn AE.6 6-cyl (p)/1963- 2x47hp Parsons Porbeagle (d)	Whitby 12.4.1938-11.1974 (372/201)	Sold 1975
6	1938 (237) Groves & Guttridge Cowes	41' 11'8" 8	**Edmund and Mary Robinson** Gift of Mrs Mary Robinson, Liverpool.	812 £6,533 14t3	2x35bhp Weyburn AE.6 6-cyl (p)	New Brighton No.2 15.12.1938-23.9.1950 (69/80) Reserve 9.1950-1964 (45/41)	Sold 3.1964
7	1938 (238) Groves & Guttridge Cowes	41' 11'8" 8	**Ann Letitia Russell** Legacy of Miss A. L. Russell, Manchester.	813 £6,634 13t10	2x35bhp Weyburn AE.6 6-cyl (p)/1963- 2x47hp Parsons Porbeagle (d)	Fleetwood 16.2.1939-24.1.1976 (205/158)	Sold 4.1977
8	1939 (255) Groves & Guttridge Cowes	41' 11'8" 8	**Matthew Simpson** Legacy of Miss C. F. Simpson, Lancaster.	823 £7,206 13t10	2x35bhp Weyburn AE.6 6-cyl (p)/1963- 2x47hp Parsons Porbeagle (d)	Port Erin 17.10.1939-1.4.1972 (72/24) Reserve 1972-1976 (21/14)	Sold 1976
9	1939 (256) Groves & Guttridge Cowes	41' 11'8" 8	**John Pyemont** Legacy of Mr John Pyemont, Epsom.	824 £7,357 13t10	2x35bhp Weyburn AE.6 6-cyl (p)	Tynemouth 24.10.1939-4.1941 (20/59)	Destroyed through enemy action, 9.4.1941
10	1948 (481) Groves & Guttridge Cowes	41' 11'8" 8	**Susan Ashley** Legacy of Charles Carr Ashley, Mentone, France.	856 £13,357 14t16	2x35bhp Weyburn AE.6 6-cyl (p)/1963- 2x47hp Parsons Porbeagle (d)	Sennen Cove 25.7.1948-1972 (87/64) Barry Dock No.2 1973-7.1979 (7/3) Tynemouth (BB) 1979-1980 (0/0)	Displayed at Historic Dockyard, Chatham
11	1949 Morgan Giles Teignmouth	41' 11'8" 8	**Glencoe, Glasgow** Legacy of Mrs L. Glen, Glasgow.	857 £11,885 14t	2x35bhp Weyburn AE.6 6-cyl (d)/1963- 2x47hp Parsons Porbeagle (d)	Buckie 25.11.1949-8.1960 (27/9) Reserve 1960-1965 (9/7) Portavogie 26.10.1965-1978 (39/27)	Sold 1979
12	1949 Sussex Yacht Co Shoreham	41' 11'8" 8	**R. L. P.** Legacy of Mrs Alice Pugh, Kensington.	859 £15,584 14t12	2x35bhp Weyburn AE.6 6-cyl (p)	Swanage 26.2.1949-10.1975 (341/242) Reserve 1975-1981 (13/2)	Sold 8.1981
13	1952 (897) William Osborne Littlehampton	41' 11'8" 8	**St Andrew (Civil Service No.10)** Civil Service Lifeboat Fund.	897 £20,700 14t5	2x35bhp Weyburn AE.6 6-cyl (p)/1963- 2x47hp Parsons Porbeagle (d)	Whitehills 9.3.1952-11.1959 (9/0) Girvan 1961-1968 (18/8) Arklow 1968-2.1973 (24/6) Reserve 1959-1961 (5/0) and 1973-1982 (25/7)	Sold 1982

MOTOR LIFEBOATS

15 • Watson motor 41ft

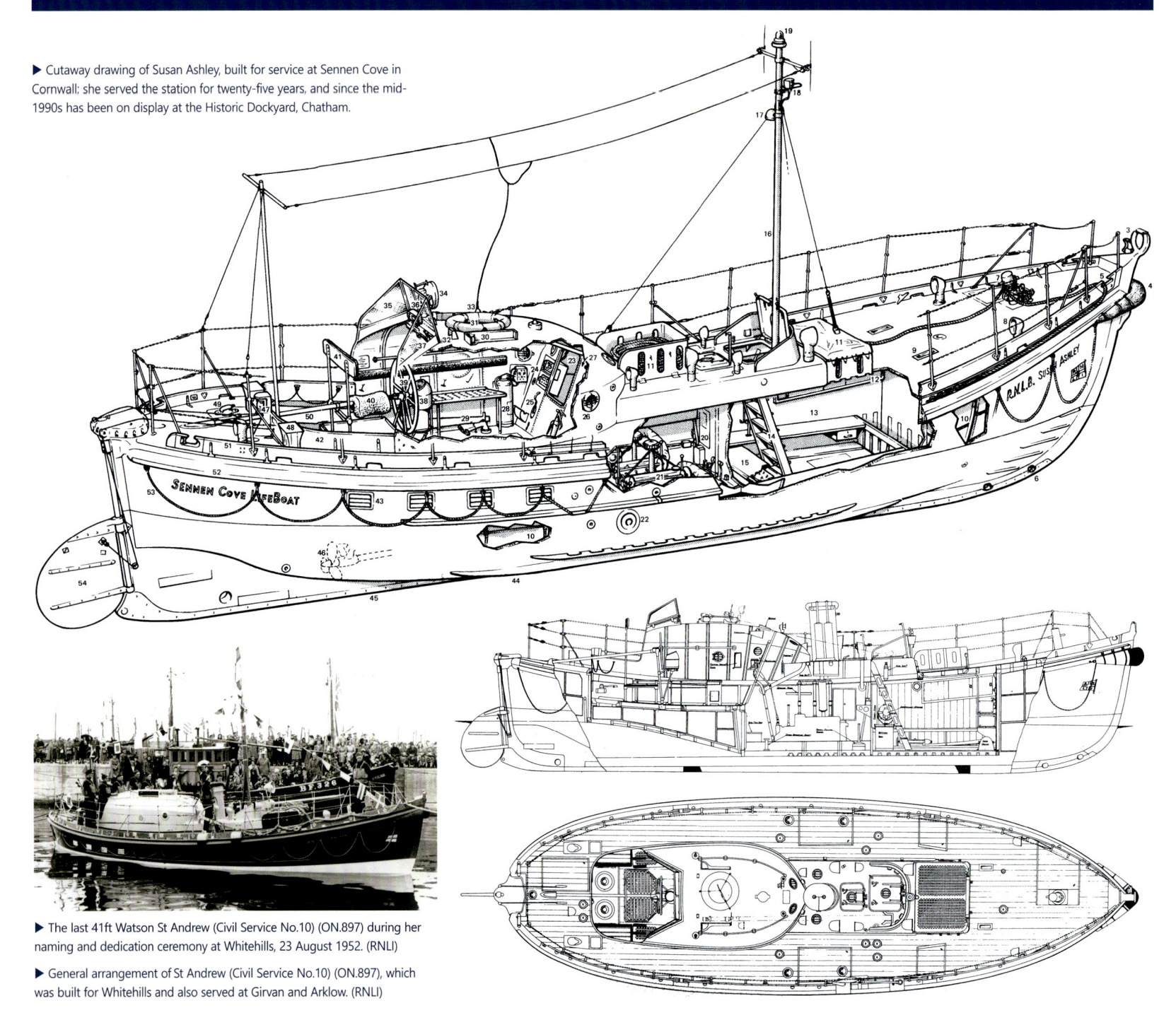

▶ Cutaway drawing of Susan Ashley, built for service at Sennen Cove in Cornwall; she served the station for twenty-five years, and since the mid-1990s has been on display at the Historic Dockyard, Chatham.

▶ The last 41ft Watson St Andrew (Civil Service No.10) (ON.897) during her naming and dedication ceremony at Whitehills, 23 August 1952. (RNLI)

▶ General arrangement of St Andrew (Civil Service No.10) (ON.897), which was built for Whitehills and also served at Girvan and Arklow. (RNLI)

82 MOTOR LIFEBOATS

15 • Watson motor 41ft

▲ The Whitby lifeboat Mary Ann Hepworth (ON.808) heads out through breakers at the entrance to the harbour. She was one of the 41ft Watsons which were kept in a boathouse and slipway launched.

▲ The Tynemouth lifeboat John Pyemont (ON.824) on trials at Cowes. She went to the Tyne in October 1939, but during an air-raid on 10 April 1941 she and her boathouse were totally destroyed by two bombs.

▲ Susan Ashley (ON.856) on display at the Chatham Historic Dockyard. (Nicholas Leach)

▶ R. L. P. (ON.858), one of the four 41ft Watsons built after the Second World War, on trials. She was one of only a handful of lifeboats built by the Sussex Yacht Co. (By courtesy of the RNLI)

▼ Ann Letitia Russell (ON.813), the 41ft Watson that served at Fleetwood for well over thirty years.

MOTOR LIFEBOATS 83

16 • Surf light motor 32ft

KEY DATA
- Introduced 1935
- Last built 1941
- 9 built

The 32ft Surf non-self-righting type, designed by James Barnett, was a small lifeboat which could be launched from a carriage and operate in shallow waters. Intended for stations where launching a heavier type was difficult, the Surf type enabled the RNLI to fulfil its long-term plan to provide motor lifeboats at the few remaining stations which operated pulling and sailing lifeboats, and it filled a gap in motor lifeboat cover at stations where a light boat was deemed most suitable. The first two boats, when carrying crew and gear on board, weighed only 4.25 tons, more than two tons lighter than the 35ft 6in self-righting type, the other carriage-launched design. Their size and weight, however, while making launching easier, limited them to inshore work in relatively moderate conditions. They were fitted with two engines and, when introduced, were the only twin-engined lifeboats capable of being carriage-launched.

The most noteworthy aspect of the design was the innovative means of propulsion, an early type of waterjet, that was employed. While the first boat (ON.779) was powered by conventional screw propellers, the second (ON.780) was fitted with the Hotchkiss Internal Cone, and a later boat (ON.816) had Gill Jet Units. The Hotchkiss Cones were seen as particularly advantageous for boats operating in shallow water, as they were set inside the hull, unlike a propeller, and were thus less susceptible to being damaged. The first boat fitted with the Cones, Royal Silver Jubilee 1910-1935 (ON.780), was stationed at Wells-next-the-Sea in Norfolk.

The Surf boats had twin engines and carried two oars, but no auxiliary sails. Although three different forms of propulsion were used, the engines were all based on the same F.2 model, a special light horizontal design with twin cylinders built by Weyburn Engineering to an RNLI design for full load operation of 3,000rpm, but rated down to 2,400rpm. As the normal arrangement for Hotchkiss Cones was for a pair to be fitted, this dictated the need for twin engines. The performance of the boats differed, with the screw-powered boat having a slight edge over those powered by the Cones. ON.779 achieved a top speed of seven and a half knots and

▲ The first 32ft Surf motor lifeboat Rosabella (ON.779) at Ilfracombe. The only Surf lifeboat to be powered by conventional screw propellers, she was a completely open boat, with the engine housed in a wooden box amidships. Later boats of the class had a rudimentary shelter fitted.

▶ The second 32ft Surf motor lifeboat Royal Silver Jubilee 1910-1935 (ON.780), pictured on trials, was the first Surf lifeboat to be driven by Hotchkiss Cones. She spent less than a decade in RNLI service before being transferred to the Netherlands at the end of the Second World War. (By courtesy of the RNLI)

16 • Surf light motor 32ft

▶ General arrangement and profile drawings of the second Surf lifeboat Royal Silver Jubilee 1910-1935 (ON.780), the first to be fitted with Hotchkiss Cone impellers. (By courtesy of the RNLI)

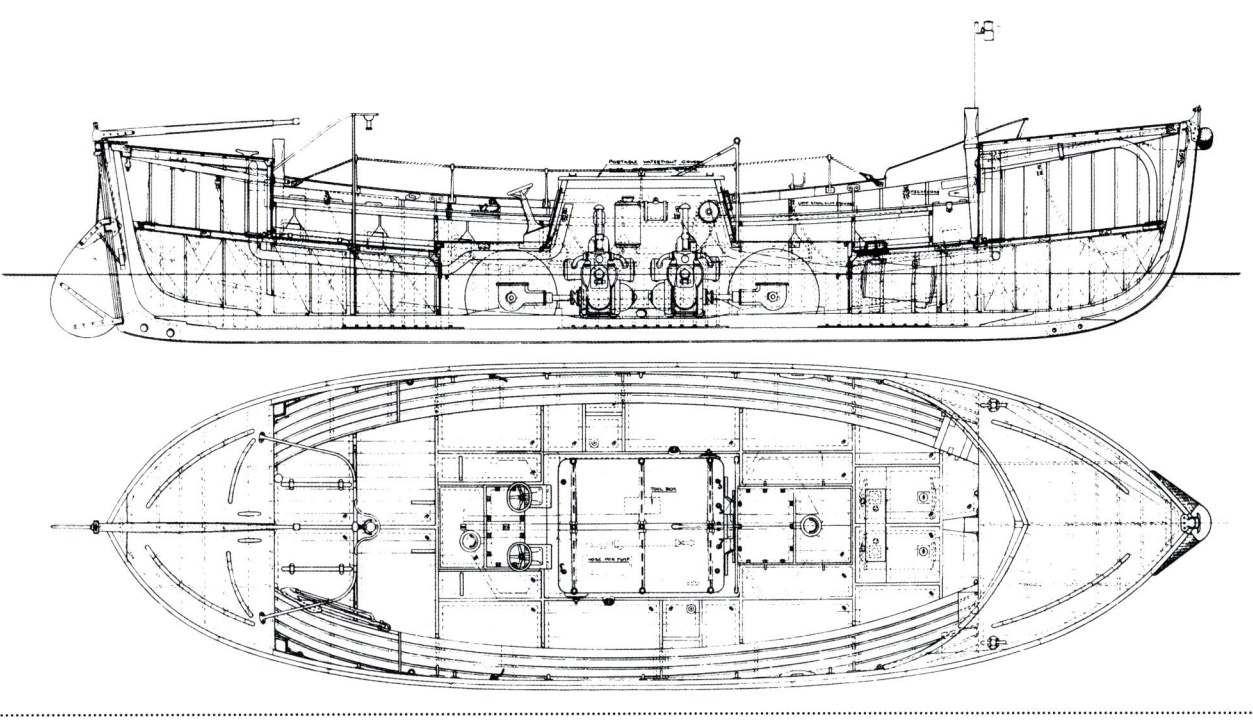

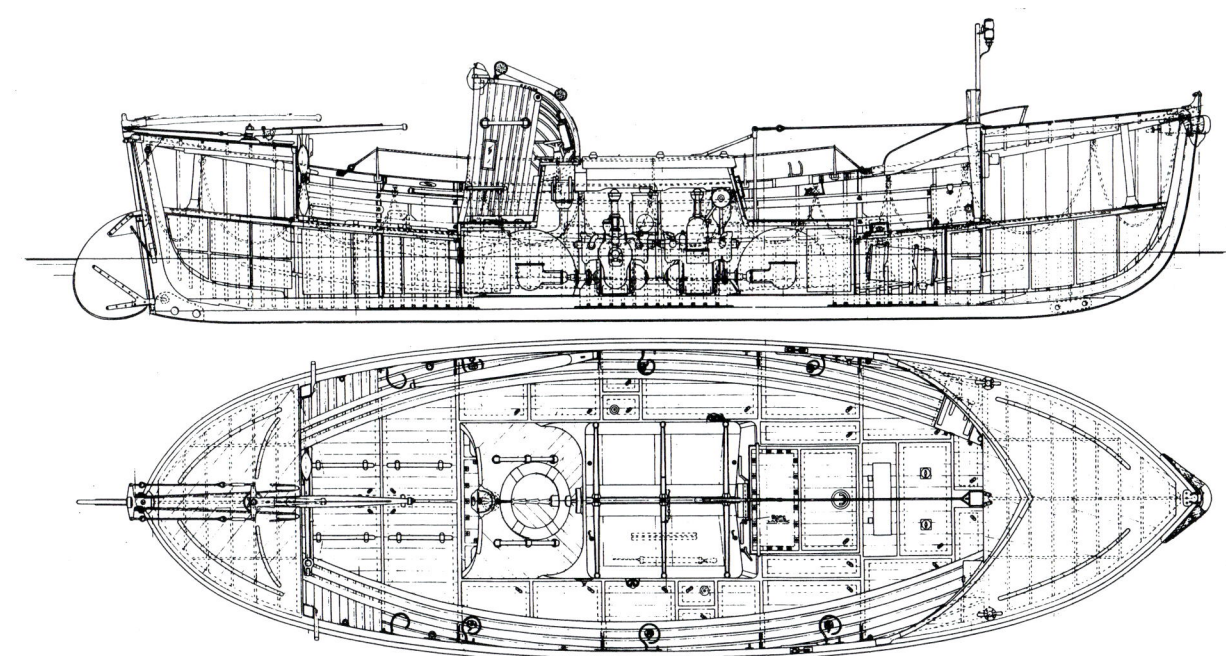

◀ General arrangement and profile drawings of the fourth Surf lifeboat to be built, Thomas Kirk Wright (ON.811), fitted with Hotchkiss Cone impellers. Seven of the nine Surf lifeboats had this method of propulsion installed. (By courtesy of the RNLI)

MOTOR LIFEBOATS

16 • Surf light motor 32ft

▲ Kate Greatorex (ON.816) was the only Surf motor lifeboat to be powered by Gill Jet Units. She served at Minehead in Somerset for twelve years. (By courtesy of the RNLI)

▶ The first of the nine Surf boats to fitted with the Cones, Royal Silver Jubilee 1910-1935 (ON.780), was stationed at Wells on the Norfolk coast, an area characterised by sandbanks and shallow seas, and where at low tide the boat had to travel a considerable distance to be launched. She is pictured during her formal naming and inauguration ceremony at Wells on 13 July 1936; she was christened to commemorate the Silver Jubilee of King George V and Queen Mary.

was able to travel fifty-six miles without refuelling, while ON.780, fitted with Hotchkiss Cones, managed 6.82 knots in calm weather, 6.66 knots in rough conditions, and 4.25 knots on one engine with a radius at cruising speed of forty-three miles. However, the boats were rather underpowered, and this proved to be their undoing, as in some instances they were unable to make headway against strong tides and in heavy seas.

The non-self-righting hull, made of double-skin mahogany, was essentially open with small end boxes fore and aft. The bulkheads surrounding the engines and fuel tanks were also of double mahogany. Between eighty and 100 air cases were fitted throughout the hull. Because the boats were not intended to be at sea for more than a few hours, they were initially open, although small shelters became a feature from the third of the class onwards. Unusually for motor lifeboats, they were steered by tiller, the position of which changed in some of the class. It was placed further forward on some boats by the utilisation of relieving ropes.

MOTOR LIFEBOATS

16 • Surf light motor 32ft

	Year* (Yd No) Builder Place	Length Breadth Crew	Name Donor	ON Cost Weight	Engines	Stations (launches/lives saved)	Notes Disposal
1	1935 (W1790) J. S. White Cowes	32' 9' 7	**Rosabella** Legacy of John Hogg, Boscombe.	779 £3,264.18.0 3t17	2x12hp Weyburn F2 Twin screw	Ilfracombe 9.3.1936-4.6.1945 (24/12)	Sold to KNZHRM 6.1946 (Terschelling 1946-55) Sold 1955
2	1935 (206) Groves & Guttridge Cowes	32' 9' 7	**Royal Silver Jubilee 1910-1935** Gift of Mrs E.W. Montford, JP.	780 £2,918.19.11 3t17	2x12hp Weyburn F2 Hotchkiss cone	Wells 6.2.1936-4.6.1945 (43/23)	Sold to KNZHRM 6.1946 (renamed Rosilee, Vlieland 1946-59) Sold 1959
3	1938 (235) Groves & Guttridge Cowes	32' 9'3" 7	**Augustus and Laura** Legacy Miss E.A. Northey, London.	810 £3,355.15.3 4t16	2x12hp Weyburn F2 Hotchkiss cone	Newbiggin 21.10.1938-3.8.1950 (28/17)	Sold 2.10.1950
4	1938 (236) Groves & Guttridge Cowes	32' 9'3" 7	**Thomas Kirk Wright** Legacy Mr T. Kirk Wright, Bournemouth.	811 £3,337.5.9 4t19	2x12hp Weyburn F2 Hotchkiss cone	Poole 12.1.1939-18.7.1962 (64/15)	Sold 1963
5	1939 (250) Groves & Guttridge Cowes	32' 9'3" 7	**Kate Greatorex** Legacy Mrs K. Greatorex, Mytton Hall, Shrewsbury.	816 £3,478.0.10 5t6	2x12hp Weyburn F2 Gill Jet Units	Minehead 30.5.1939-10.12.1951 (20/7)	Sold 27.3.1952
6	1939 (251) Groves & Guttridge Cowes	32' 9'3" 7	**Laurence Ardern, Stockport** Legacy Mrs M.A. Ardern, Prestbury.	817 £3,492.4.3 5t6	2x12hp Weyburn F2 Hotchkiss cone	Barmouth 22.5.1939-11.3.1949 (35/1) Reserve 1949-1951 (0/0)	Sold 27.12.1951
7	1939 (W5007) J. S. White Cowes	32' 9'3" 7	**Gordon Warren** Legacy of Mr H.B.G. Warren, Liverpool.	835 £3,701.12.0 4t14	2x12hp Weyburn F2 Hotchkiss cone	Rhyl 3.11.1939-15.9.1949 (35/5) Reserve 1949-1951 (0/0)	Sold 10.1.1952
8	1940 (R225) Alexander Robertson Sandbank	32' 9'3" 7	**Norman Nasmyth** Legacy of the late Norman J. Nasmyth, Glenfarg.	836 £3,690.9.7 4t10	2x12hp Weyburn F2 Hotchkiss cone	Montrose No.2 30.6.1940-18.5.1950 (0/0) Reserve 1950-1965 (0/0)	Sold 1966
9	1941 (R224) Alexr. Robertson Sandbank	32' 9'3" 7	**John Ryburn** Legacy of William McCunn, Largs.	837 £3,791.3.7 4t14	2x12hp Weyburn F2 Hotchkiss cone	Newburgh 6.1941-30.9.1965 (11/19)	Capsized on service 26.1.1942, two lost Sold 1966

◀ 32ft Surf lifeboat Augustus and Laura (ON.810), fitted with Hotchkiss cone propulsion units, served at Newbiggin for twelve years. (Beken, by courtesy of the RNLI)

◀ Gordon Warren (ON.835) was one of the last three Surf lifeboats to be built. She served at Rhyl for ten years from where she was launched across a flat, shallow beach. All the Surf lifeboats served through the Second World War. (From an old photo supplied by Jeff Morris)

MOTOR LIFEBOATS

17 • Watson cabin motor 46ft

KEY DATA
▶ Introduced 1936
▶ Last built 1946
▶ 28 built, 2 not finished

SPECIFICATIONS
▶ Length 46ft
▶ Beam 12ft 9in
▶ Crew 7/8

▶ The first 46ft Watson motor, H. F. Bailey (ON.777), was sent to Cromer in Norfolk. Under the command of Coxswain Henry Blogg, one of the best known lifeboatmen of the twentieth century, she was involved during the Second World War in some of the most famous rescues in the history of the RNLI.

▼ (left) The second 46ft Watson motor Edward and Isabella Irwin (ON.778) being recovered at Sunderland. (By courtesy of the RNLI)

▼ (right) Julia Park Barry of Glasgow (ON.819), built in 1939, served at Peterhead for thirty years. In January 1942 she was called out four times in the space of seventy-five hours to save the crews of three steamers in difficulties for which Coxswain John McLean was awarded the Gold medal. (By courtesy of the RNLI)

In 1933-34 a conference was held at Clacton-on-Sea to consider what alterations should be incorporated into a new design of Watson cabin lifeboat. Among those present during the discussions were Consulting Naval Architect James Barnett; Commander E.D. Drury, Chief Inspector of Lifeboats; S.T.C. Bone, Surveyor of Lifeboats; John Lamb, Chairman of the Boat and Construction Committee; and three Coxswains, Henry Blogg from Cromer, Robert Cross from Spurn Point and Ellis from Clacton.

As a result of their deliberations, during which it was agreed that the 45ft 6in Watson was a fine sea boat, a slightly larger Watson was designed by Barnett. The length was increased by six inches and the beam by three inches over the precious version. Although slightly longer and wider, the first few 46ft lifeboats were similar in many respects to the 45ft 6in design. However, on later boats, while the layout of the after end of the boat and engine room remained much the same, the fore shelter was dispensed with to give a clear fore-deck and the anchor cable was stowed in a well at the after end of the cabin. The hull was divided into seven watertight compartments and fitted with 142 air cases. A line-throwing gun and electric searchlight were carried.

The first four 46ft Watsons were powered by twin 40hp Weyburn CE4 four-cylinder petrol engines. The first two boats, H.F. Bailey (ON.777) and Edward and Isabella Irwin (ON.778), achieved a maximum speed of 8.03 knots 8.19 knots respectively, and their radius of action at this speed was seventy-six and fifty-nine nautical miles respectively. However, with the introduction of diesel engines into the lifeboat fleet, the rest of the 46ft boats were fitted with twin 40hp Ferry four-cylinder VE4 diesels, driving twin screws, through a two-to-one reduction gear. This gave the later boats a similar speed of just over eight knots, but the diesel engines offered a much greater range. The second diesel-engined 46ft Watson, R.P.L. (ON.789), had a radius of action of 110 nautical miles at her full speed of 8.08 knots, while at the cruising speed of 7.5 knots this increased to an impressive 152 nautical miles. Several of the boats were re-engined with Parsons Barracuda diesels in the mid-1960s.

The rudder installations on the 46ft Watsons varied: some had internal rudders protected by stern frames, while the stern frames in others were omitted. After crews at two stations complained about the handling of their boats with internal rudders and stern frames, these boats were converted to have outside rudders in an attempt to improve matters, and the rudder on R.P.L. (ON.789) was free of surrounding keel altogether.

A number of variations of the 46ft design were built, as it was gradually improved during the decade it was in production and became one of the mainstays of the RNLI's fleet in the immediate post-1945 era. However,

17 • Watson cabin motor 46ft

	Year* (Yd No) Builder Place	Length Breadth Crew	Name Donor	ON Cost Weight	Engines	Stations (launches/lives saved)	Notes Disposal
1	1935 (204) Groves & Guttridge Cowes	46' 12'9" 8	**H. F. Bailey** Legacy of Henry Francis Bailey, Brockenhurst.	777 £7,308 20t	2x40hp Weyburn CE4 4-cyl (p)	Cromer No.1 15.12.1935-12.1945 (154/448) Helvick Head 15.8.1946-7.60 (24/12) Reserve 1960-72 (21/15)	Internal rudder Sold 1972
2	1935 (205) Groves & Guttridge Cowes	46' 12'9" 8	**Edward and Isabella Irwin** Legacy of Mrs I. Irwin, Morpeth, Northumberland.	778 £7,378 20t	2x40hp Weyburn CE4 4-cyl (p)	Sunderland 8.11.1935-5.1963 (89/88) Reserve 1963-69 (64/29)	External rudder Sold 1971
3	1935 (208) Groves & Guttridge Cowes	46' 12'9" 8	**Civil Service No.6/** 1956- **Swn-Y-Mor (Civil Service No.6)** Civil Service Lifeboat Fund.	784 £7,618 19t9	2x40hp Weyburn CE4 4-cyl (p)	St Davids 3.4.1936-8.1963 (90/108) Eyemouth 17.11.1964-12.1967 (3/0) Reserve 1967-1972 (21/7)	External rudder Sold 2.1973
4	1936 (213) Groves & Guttridge Cowes	46' 12'9" 8	**S. G. E.** Legacies of Mr D. H. Altschul, Mrs J. E. C. Edmunds and Miss H. E. G. Gartside.	787 £8,505 19t13	2x40hp Ferry VE4 4-cyl (d) [first LB built with diesel engines]	Yarmouth 22.8.1936-6.1937 (2/31)	Destroyed by fire at Groves & Guttridge,18.6.1937
5	1937 (R211) Alexr. Robertson Sandbank	46' 12'9" 8	**Jeanie Speirs** Gift of Mrs E. S. Paterson, Paisley.	788 £8,434 21t5	2x40hp Weyburn CE4 4-cyl (p)	Portpatrick 20.3.1937-18.7.1961 (66/18)	Internal rudder Sold 4.1961
6	1936 (215) Groves & Guttridge Cowes	46' 12'9" 8	**R. P. L.** Legacies of Mr L. W. Rignal, Miss M. A. Butterworth, and Miss M. S. Phillips.	789 £8,191 21t2	2x40hp Ferry VE4 4-cyl (d)	Howth 7.5.1937-18.7.1962 (95/62)	Internal rudder Sold 7.9.1962
7	1936 (216) Groves & Guttridge Cowes	46' 12'9" 8	**John and Charles Kennedy** Legacy of Mrs M. Kennedy, Steyning, Sussex.	790 £8,178 21t	2x40hp Ferry VE4 4-cyl (d)	Fraserburgh 9.3.1937-2.1953 (99/199)	External rudder Capsized on service 9.2.1953, six lost, later broken up
8	1938 (R219) Alex Robertson Sandbank	46' 12'9" 8	**Sir Arthur Rose** Gift of Miss Margaret Lithgow, Tobermory.	801 £8,358 22t	2x40hp Ferry VE4 4-cyl (d)	Tobermory 15.11.1938-13.11.1947 (28/20) Mallaig 15.1.1948-27.10.1957 (43/76) Courtmacsherry Harb 2.1958-8.1969 (22/9) Reserve 1969-1972 (7/4)	Internal rudder Sold 2.1973
9	1938 (R218) Alexr. Robertson Sandbank	46' 12'9" 8	**City of Edinburgh** RNLI Funds, in appreciation of Scottish Branches.	802 £8,155 20t18	2x40hp Ferry VE4 4-cyl (d)/ 1966- 2x65hp Parsons Barracuda (d)	Wick 4.10.1938-2.1968 (133/204) Reserve 2.1969-1976 (39/27)	Internal rudder Sold 7.1976
10	1938 (R217) Alex Robertson Sandbank	46' 12'9" 8	**Canadian Pacific** Gift of Canadian Pacific Steamship Company.	803 £8,314 20t5	2x40hp Ferry VE4 4-cyl (d/ 1961- 2x47hp Parsons Marlin/ 1963- 2x65hp Parsons Barracuda	Selsey 26.8.1938-22.1.1969 (286/157) Reserve 1969-1977 (44/35)	Internal rudder Sold 3.2.1978
11	1938 (W1831) J. S. White Cowes	46' 12'9" 8	**S. G. E.** Legacies of Mr D. Altshul, Mrs J. E. C. Edmunds and Miss H. E. Gartside.	804 £8,266 20t5	2x40hp Ferry VE4 4-cyl (d)	Yarmouth 12.4.1938-31.5.1943 and 22.2.1945-9.1963 (139/164) Reserve 5.1943-1945 (2/0)	Internal rudder Sold 4.1964
12	1938 (W1832) J. S. White Cowes	46' 12'9" 8	**Samuel and Marie Parkhouse** Legacy of Mrs Marie Parkhouse, Cricklewood.	805 £8,451 20t5	2x40hp Ferry VE4 4-cyl (d)	Salcombe 12.5.1938-6.1962 (100/126)	Internal rudder Sold 9.1963
13	1938 (W1839) J. S. White Cowes	46' 12'9" 8	**Dunleary II** RNLI Funds.	814 £8,258 20t2	2x40hp Ferry VE4 4-cyl (d)	Dun Laoghaire 21.7.1938-5.1967 (104/136) Lochinver 18.8.1967-7.1969 (9/0) Reserve 1969-1972 (19/11) Dunmore East 6.1972-6.1973 (8/4)	Internal rudder Sold 7.8.1974

MOTOR LIFEBOATS

17 • Watson cabin motor 46ft

	Year* (Yd No) Builder Place	Length Breadth Crew	Name Donor	ON Cost Weight	Engines	Stations (launches/lives saved)	Notes Disposal
14	1938 (W1840) J. S. White Cowes	46' 12'9" 8	**Violet Armstrong** Gift of Gordon Armstrong, Beverley, Yorkshire.	815 £8,833 21t19	2x40hp Ferry VE4 4-cyl (d)	Appledore 14.8.1938-5.1962 (69/62)	Internal rudder Sold 10.1962
15	1939 (W1871) J. S. White Cowes	46' 12'9" 8	**Mabel Marion Thompson** Legacy of Miss M. M. Thompson, Bognor Regis.	818 £9,649 21t1	2x40hp Ferry VE4 4-cyl (d)	Rosslare Harbour 2.3.1939-1.1952 (59/54) Galway Bay 22.3.1952-10.1968 (177/72) Arranmore 10.1968-8.1970 (9/4) Reserve 1970-1974 (11/10)	Internal rudder Sold 4.1975
16	1939 (R222) Alexr. Robertson Sandbank	46' 12'9" 8	**Julia Park Barry, of Glasgow** Gift of Mrs Park Barry, Glasgow.	819 £9,055 20t6	2x40hp Ferry VE4 4-cyl (d)/ 1964- 2x65hp Parsons Barracuda	Peterhead 15.6.1939-10.1969 (162/496) Reserve 10.1969-2.1979 (64/26)	External rudder Sold 3.1979
17	1939 (W1872) J. S. White Cowes	46' 12'9" 8	**Louise Stephens** Legacy of Mrs L. Stephens, Ewhurst, Surrey.	820 £9,351 20t19	2x40hp Ferry VE4 4-cyl (d)	Gt Yarmouth & Gorleston 4.5.1939-19.8.1967 (305/177) Eyemouth 10.1967-7.2.1974 (6/0)	External rudder Sold 8.1974
18	1939 (R223) Alexr. Robertson Sandbank	46' 12'9" 8	**The Good Hope** An anonymous gift.	821 £9,070 20t10	2x40hp Ferry VE4 4-cyl (d)/ 1966- 2x65hp Parsons Barracuda	Montrose No.1 9.10.1939-1972 (77/32) Reserve 1972-1980 (35/26)	External rudder Sold 1981
19	1939 (W1873) J. S. White Cowes	46' 12'9" 8	**Jesse Lumb** Legacy of Miss Annie Lumb, Huddersfield.	822 £9,455 20t10	2x40hp Ferry VE4 4-cyl (d)/ 1965- 2x65hp Parsons Barracuda	Bembridge 24.5.1939-17.1.1970 (294/280) Reserve 1970-1980 (59/19)	External rudder Sold 6.7.1981
20	1939 (W5004) J. S. White Cowes	46' 12'9" 8	**The Princess Royal (Civil Service No.7)** Civil Service Lifeboat Fund.	828 £10,145 20t8	2x40hp Ferry VE4 (d)/ 1965- 2x65hp Parsons Barracuda (d)	Hartlepool 19.10.1939-6.1968 (152/94) Reserve 1968-1976 (41/24)	External rudder Sold 1976
21	1939 (W5005) J. S. White Cowes	46' 12'9" 8	**Crawford and Constance Conybeare** Gift of Mrs Constance Conybeare, London.	829 £10,268 20t14	2x40hp Ferry VE4 4-cyl (d)	Falmouth 17.1.1940-9.1968 (122/126) Reserve 1968-1974 (32/30)	External rudder Sold 8.1974
22	1939 (W5006) J. S. White Cowes	46' 12'9" 8	**Annie Blanche Smith** Legacies Mrs Smith, Mrs Lucas, plus the executors of the late Mr Stephens.	830 £10,279 20t14	2x40hp Ferry VE4 4-cyl (d)	Dunmore East 19.3.1940-9.1970 (88/88) Reserve 10.1970-71 (0/0)	Internal rudder Sold 7.1971
23	1939 (W5015) J. S. White Cowes	46' 12'9" 8	**Michael Stephens** Legacy of Mrs Louise Stephens, Ewhurst, Surrey.	838 £10,104 20t2	2x40hp Ferry VE4 4-cyl (d)	Lowestoft 19.10.1939-7.1963 (134/73) Exmouth 1.11.1963-13.8.1968 (25/11) Reserve 1968-76 (21/9)	External rudder Sold 1.1976
24	1945 Sussex Yacht Co Shoreham	46' 12'9" 8	**Millie Walton/** 1947- **Henry Blogg** Legacy of Mrs M. E. Walton, Derby/ 1947- RNLI Funds.	840 £15,242 21t2	2x40hp Ferry VE4 4-cyl (d)	[Stemmed for Douglas] Cromer No.1 20.12.1945-3.4.1966 (99/149) Reserve 1966-76 (58/65)	Internal rudder Midships steering Sold 4.1977
25	1943 (W5111) J. S. White Cowes	46' 12'9" 8	**Manchester and Salford XXIX** Manchester and Salford Lifeboat Fund.	841 £11,912 20t12	2x40hp Ferry VE4 4-cyl (d)	Pwllheli 5.11.1943-21.1.1953 (21/4) Workington 3.1953-9.1972 (116/67) Reserve 1972-74 (7/0)	External rudder Sold 8.1974
26	1940 (309) Groves & Guttridge Cowes	46' 12'9" 8	**[Millie Walton]** —	842 — —	2x40hp Ferry VE4 4-cyl (d)	[Stemmed for Douglas]	Destroyed in air raid on builder's yard, 4.5.1942
27	1940 (310) Groves & Guttridge Cowes	46' 12'9" 8	**[Charles Henry Ashley]** —	843 — —	2x40hp Ferry VE4 4-cyl (d)	[Stemmed for Porthdinllaen]	Destroyed in air raid on builder's yard, 4.5.1942

17 • Watson cabin motor 46ft

	Year* (Yd No) Builder Place	Length Breadth Crew	Name Donor	ON Cost Weight	Engines	Stations (launches/lives saved)	Notes Disposal
28	1945 (MG456) Morgan Giles Teignmouth	46' 12'9" 8	**Field Marshall and Mrs Smuts** Southern African Branch of the RNLI.	846 £13,865 20t4	2x40hp Ferry VE4 4-cyl (d)	Beaumaris 25.9.1945-2.2.1977 (136/119) Reserve 1977-79 (0/0)	Internal rudder Midships steering Sold 21.8.1979
29	1946 (R622) Rowhedge IW Rowhedge	46' 12'9" 8	**Gertrude** Legacy of Lady Struthers.	847 £17,048 21t	2x40hp Ferry VE4 4-cyl (d)/ 1965- 2x65hp Parsons Barracuda (d)	Holy Island 4.11.1946-31.3.1968 (37/9) Exmouth 13.8.1968-11.2.1970 (11/0) Sheerness 22.4.1971-4.4.1974 (91/61) Fowey 1.5.1980-25.11.1981 (8/2) Reserve 5.1974-1.1982 (42/29)	Internal rudder Sold 2.1982
30	1946 (390) Groves & Guttridge Cowes	46' 12'9" 8	**Millie Walton** Legacy of Mrs Walton.	848 £14,462 20t5	2x40hp Ferry VE4 4-cyl (d)	Douglas 18.7.1946-29.3.1956 (25/17) Amble 4.1.1956-6.1974 (67/12) Reserve 1974-1977 (4/10)	Internal rudder Sold 24.10.1977

Rudder arrangements
Internal rudders: ON.777, ON.788, ON.789, ON.801, ON.802, ON.803, ON.804, ON.805, ON.814, ON.815, ON.818, ON.830, ON.840, ON.846, ON.847, ON.848
External rudders: ON.778, ON.784, ON.790, ON.819, ON.820, ON.821, ON.822, ON.828, ON.829, ON.838, ON.841

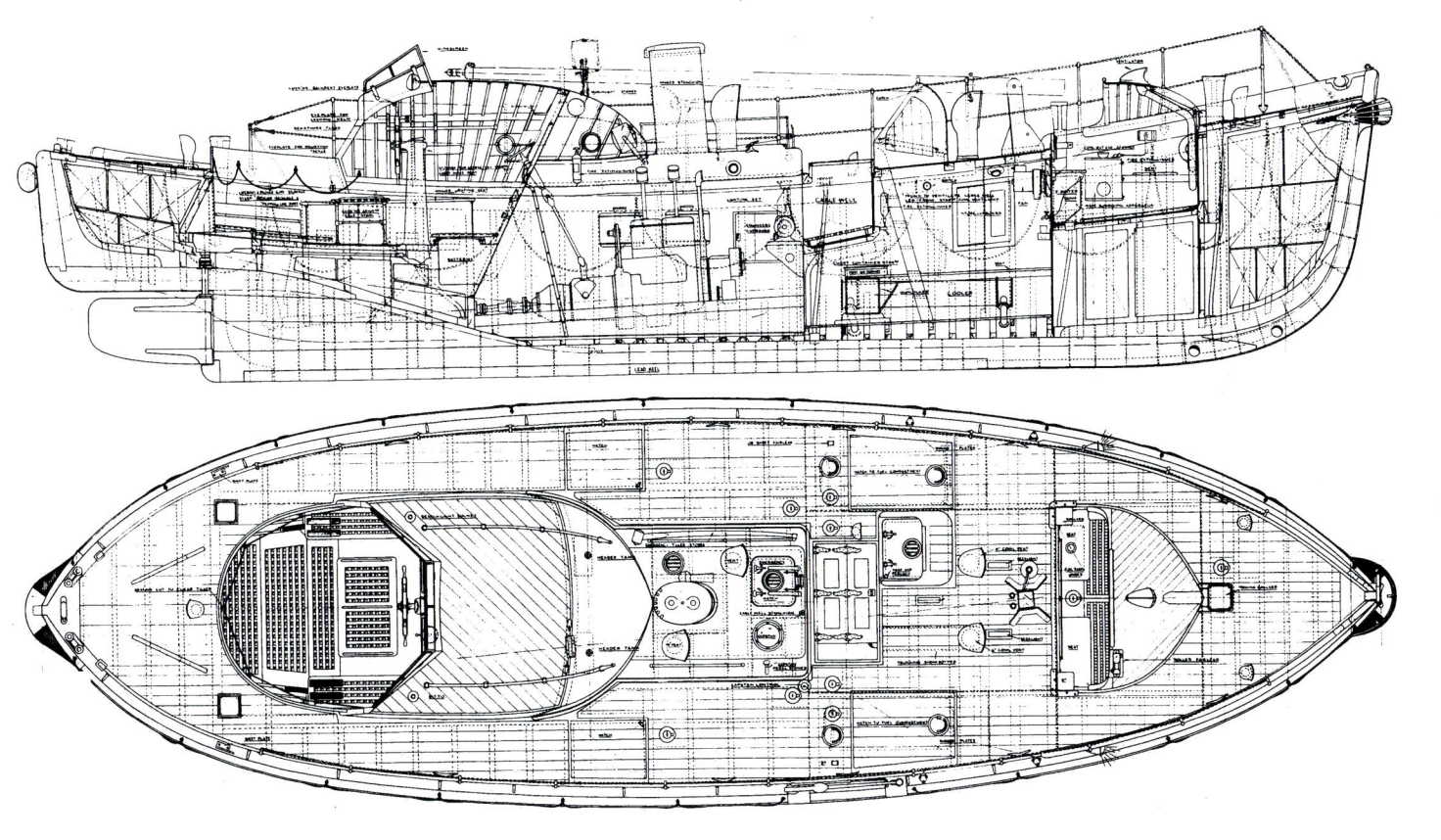

◄ General arrangement of the 1938-built 46ft Watson Dunleary II (ON.814), for Dun Laoghaire, an internal rudder without deadwood and deck layout typical of most 46ft Watsons. She was slipway launched during her service career at Dun Laoghaire, from where she covered Dublin Bay. (By courtesy of the RNLI)

MOTOR LIFEBOATS

17 • Watson cabin motor 46ft

▶ General arrangement of the Great Yarmouth & Gorleston Watson motor Louise Stephens (ON.820), one of several 46ft Watsons built to the requirements of a specific station. Both this boat and Michael Steohens (ON.838), which served at Lowestoft, were of the Gorleston sub-type, which had features such as a shallower draft than standard 46ft Watsons, making them well suited for services on the outlying sandbanks and shallow water found in the North Sea off the Norfolk and Suffolk coasts. (By courtesy of the RNLI)

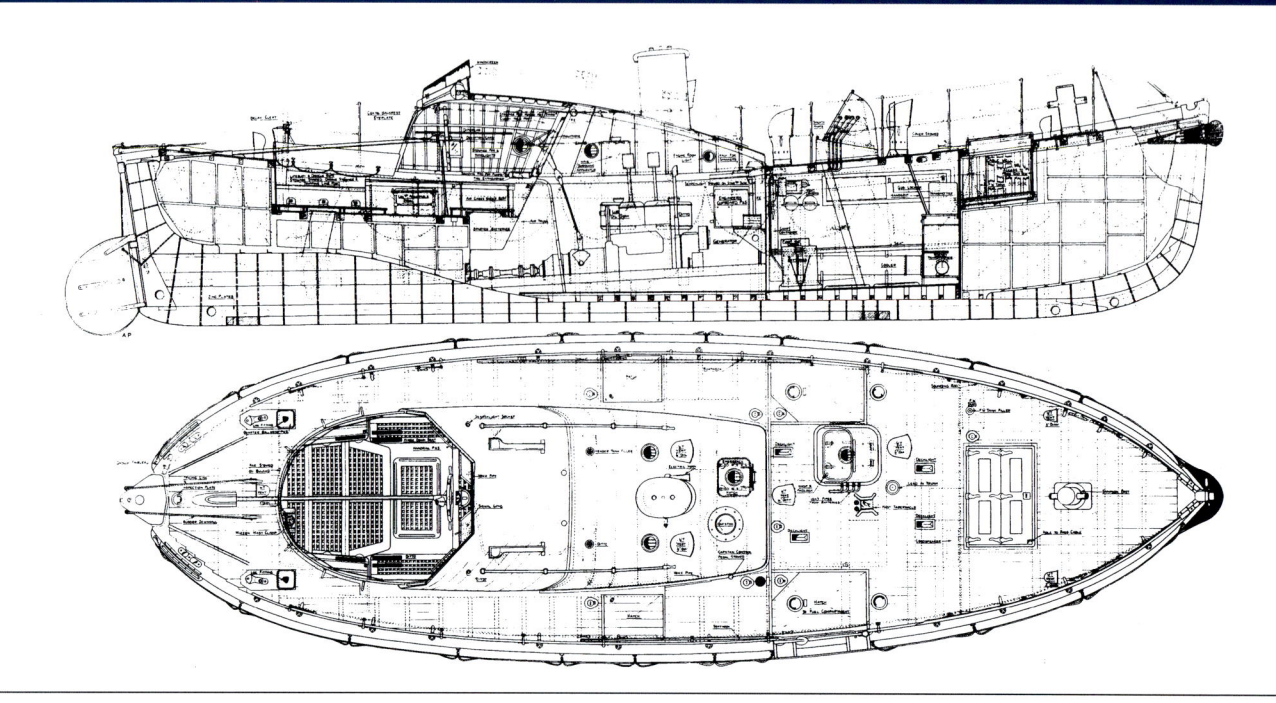

▶ General arrangement of Henry Blogg (ON.840) which, with ON.846, was one of only two 46ft Watsons with a midship steering position. The boats' deck layout incorporated two shelters of similar design but different size, with the exhaust funnel positioned amidships, and an internal rudder. ON.840 was originally allocated to Douglas, but was diverted to Cromer, where she was liked so much by the respected Coxswain Henry Blogg and his crew that she remained on station and was renamed in the Coxswain's honour. (By courtesy of the RNLI)

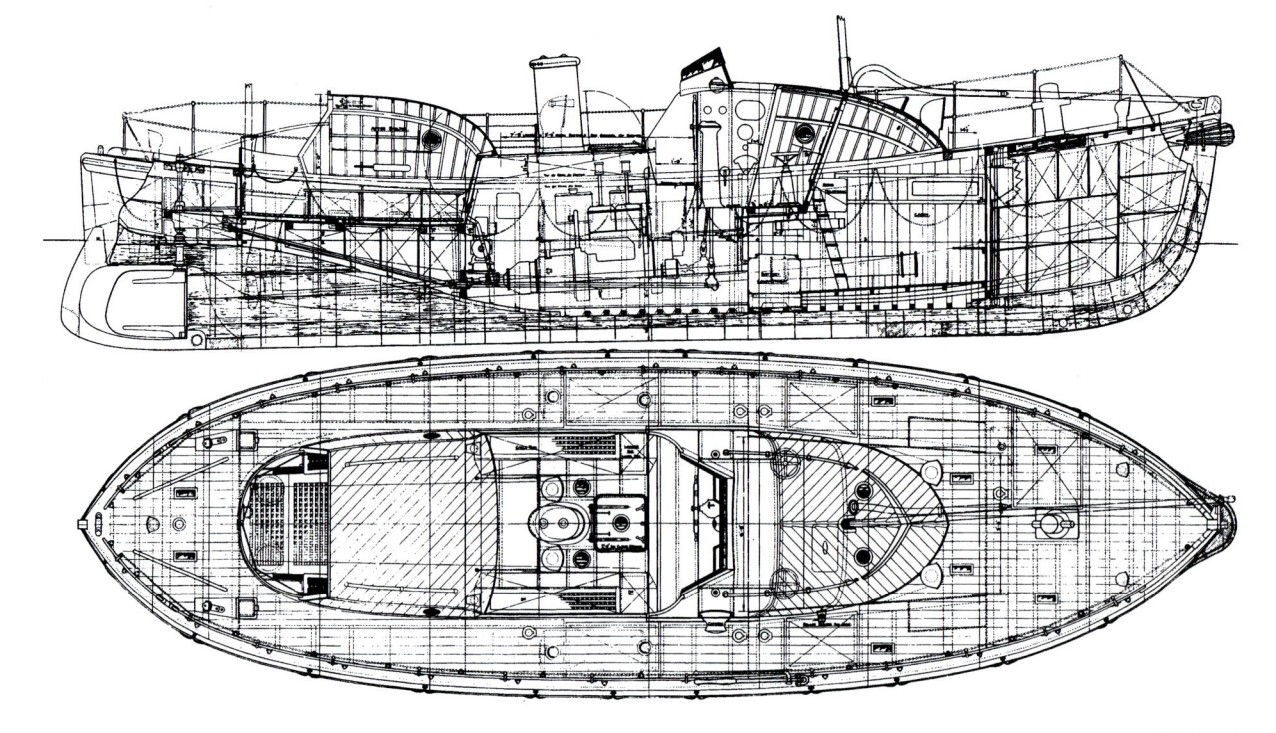

17 • Watson cabin motor 46ft

the boat was far from a standard design and alterations were consistently being made. For example, in some of the later boats, the cable well was omitted and a return made to the stowage of the cable on deck in trays.

The majority of the 46ft Watsons were built with an open aft cockpit, a shelter for the mechanic and a small forward shelter. However, in some boats the deck layout was modified to suit local conditions; Samuel and Marie Parkhouse (ON.805) and Violet Armstrong (ON.815) were designed for the conditions at Salcombe and Appledore respectively, where dangerous bars had to be crossed, and both boats had a much longer deck shelter to assist in the rapid clearance of water.

Louise Stephens (ON.820) and Michael Stephens (ON.838), built for Gorleston and Lowestoft respectively, were also different. The coxswains would not accept the standard Watson design, which they considered to be unsuitable for working near the sandbanks off East Anglia, so the Gorleston sub-type, as the two boats were classified, was developed; this had a slightly different hull shape and a shelter similar to that on ON.805. Further layout modifications were made to ON.840 and ON.846, with the steering position moved amidships, forward of the engine room. The last two 46ft Watsons, completed in 1946, both reverted to the standard deck layout with the cockpit aft.

▲ The Good Hope (ON.821), one of four 46ft Watsons built by Alexander Robertson, served at Montrose. She is pictured towards the latter stages of her career, after being re-engined and having had a fixed shelter added over the aft cockpit to provide protection for the helm and crew. At least one 46ft Watson, Gertrude (ON.847), was fitted with radar. (By courtesy of the RNLI)

MOTOR LIFEBOATS

17 • Watson cabin motor 46ft

▲ (left) The 46ft Watson Louise Stephens (ON.820) for Gorleston was specially designed for working the sandbanks off the coast of Norfolk.

▲ (right) Jesse Lumb (ON.822), stationed at Bembridge, was a typical 46ft Watson with the main cockpit aft and a small shelter forward. She is pictured after a shelter had been fitted over the aft cockpit.

◀ The midship steering 46ft Watson Field Marshall and Mrs Smuts (ON.846) was the first new lifeboat to be completed in the post-war era. She was built by Morgan Giles, one of only a handful of lifeboats ordered from the yard, and served at Beaumaris for twenty-two years. She was one of two midship-steering 46ft Watsons, and the two deck shelters were unlike those on the more standard 46ft Watsons, while the exhaust funnel was just forward of the aft shelter. (By courtesy of the RNLI)

MOTOR LIFEBOATS

18 • Harbour 28ft

The Harbour class was a small motor lifeboat, only one of which was built. Specially designed for the Poolbeg station in Ireland by Richard Oakley, the RNLI's Surveyor and later Consulting Naval Architect, she was just 28ft in length and weighed just over three tons. A series of small self-righting lifeboats had served at Poolbeg until the early years of the twentieth century, when lifeboats to a whale-boat design were purpose-built for the station. When it was decided to provide a motor lifeboat for the area, the Harbour class was developed as no comparable class of motor lifeboat existed which was deemed suitable for the conditions in Dublin Bay. The boat was operated from a boathouse at Poolbeg, in Dublin Docks on the south side of the River Liffey, and was used to cover the comparatively sheltered waters of the river and estuary.

The boat's hull was divided into eight watertight compartments and fitted with twenty-nine air cases; unusually for a lifeboat, she had a transom stern, while there were two whaleback shelters. Her crew numbered five, including a mechanic, and she could take eighteen people in rough weather. The 20hp Hyland engine, which was housed in its own watertight compartment, powered a single screw. At her maximum speed of 7.63 knots, the boat had a range of forty miles; at her cruising speed of seven knots, her range doubled. A total of fifteen gallons of fuel was carried. This design foreshadowed the need for a smaller type of rescue boat that could be used inshore in sheltered waters, and can be regarded as a forerunner of the inshore lifeboat introduced in the 1960s.

A class of ten Harbour lifeboats was planned and, had the Second World War not broken out soon after Helen Blake had been completed, more boats of the class would almost certainly have been built. The sole example of the Harbour class served her station for more than twenty years, before being sold out of service in 1959. By then, more powerful motor lifeboats had been stationed at Howth and Dun Laoghaire, and they could cover Dublin Bay effectively, so the Poolbeg station was closed.

KEY DATA
▶ Introduced 1938
▶ Last built 1938
▶ 1 built

▲ After being owned privately, Helen Blake was restored to her service conditon and has been on display as part of the Lifeboat Collection in Chatham Historic Dockyard since the mid-1990s.

	Year* (Yd No) Builder Place	Length Breadth Crew	Name Donor	ON Cost Weight	Engines	Stations	Disposal
1	1938 (G&G 234) Groves & Guttridge Cowes	28' 8' 5	**Helen Blake** Legacy of Mrs Helen Blake, Handcross.	809 £1893.8.6 3t4	1x20hp Hyland XL 4-cyl (p)	Poolbeg 4.1938-31.10.1959 (13/5)	Sold 11.1959

▲ 28ft Harbour boat Helen Blake (ON.809) served Poolbeg and covered the Liffey estuary and Dublin Bay.

▲ Helen Blake (ON.809) on the river Liffey in the centre of Dublin, probably on a fund-raising trip.

MOTOR LIFEBOATS

19 • Liverpool motor twin-engined 35ft 6in

KEY DATA
- Introduced 1940
- Last built 1954
- 31 (32) built

For stations that employed carriage launching, the RNLI built two types of motor lifeboat: the self-righter and the non-self-righting Liverpool class. Advances in one type mirrored the developments with the other and so, with the introduction of twin engines and twin screws in the post-1945 motor self-righters, the Liverpool class was developed with twin engines and twin screws soon afterwards. The introduction of the motorised tractor to assist beach launching and recovery meant heavier boats could be built for carriage launching as weight was not such a great consideration, so having twin engines and carrying more equipment became possible. The twin-engined Liverpool class weighed approximately 8.5 tons, more than two tons heavier than the original light self-righting motor types of the late 1920s.

The 35ft 6in Liverpool was built with a ballast tank which filled with half a ton of water when the boats went afloat so that, according to James Barnett, 'when launched they are practically on a level keel'. As soon as the boat was clear of the shore, the water-ballast valve was opened and the water ballast bring the boat down at the stern, which was seen as a better trim when at sea. With a heavier iron keel, which weighed just over a ton, than that fitted to the single-engined Liverpools, it was possible to increase the breadth, so the boats had better stability. The hull was divided into six watertight compartments and fitted with 120 air cases. The engine room formed one of the watertight compartments and the engines would continue to run even if the engine room was flooded. Clearing the decks of water took about twelve seconds.

The twin-engined Liverpool was designed just before the outbreak of the Second World War, and the first boat of the class was laid down in 1940 but never completed as it was destroyed in an air raid on Cowes, and the first of the new design did not enter service until 1945. The twin 18hp engines gave the boats a top speed of 7.25 knots and a cruising speed of seven knots. Fuel capacity was fifty-two gallons, and at the cruising speed

▲ The first 35ft 6in twin-engined Liverpool to enter service was Cecil Paine, which served at Wells-next-the-Sea in Norfolk from 1945 to 1965 and later at Kilmore Quay.

▶ General arrangement drawings of Aguila Wren (ON.892) shwing the deck layout and hull shape with the tunnels for the twin propellers. (By courtesy of the RNLI)

▼ Edgar, George, Orlando and Eva Child (ON.861) was the second 35ft 6in twin-engined Liverpool to enter service. She is pictured on her carriage at St Ives, the station for which she was built. (Grahame Farr, by courtesy of the RNLI)

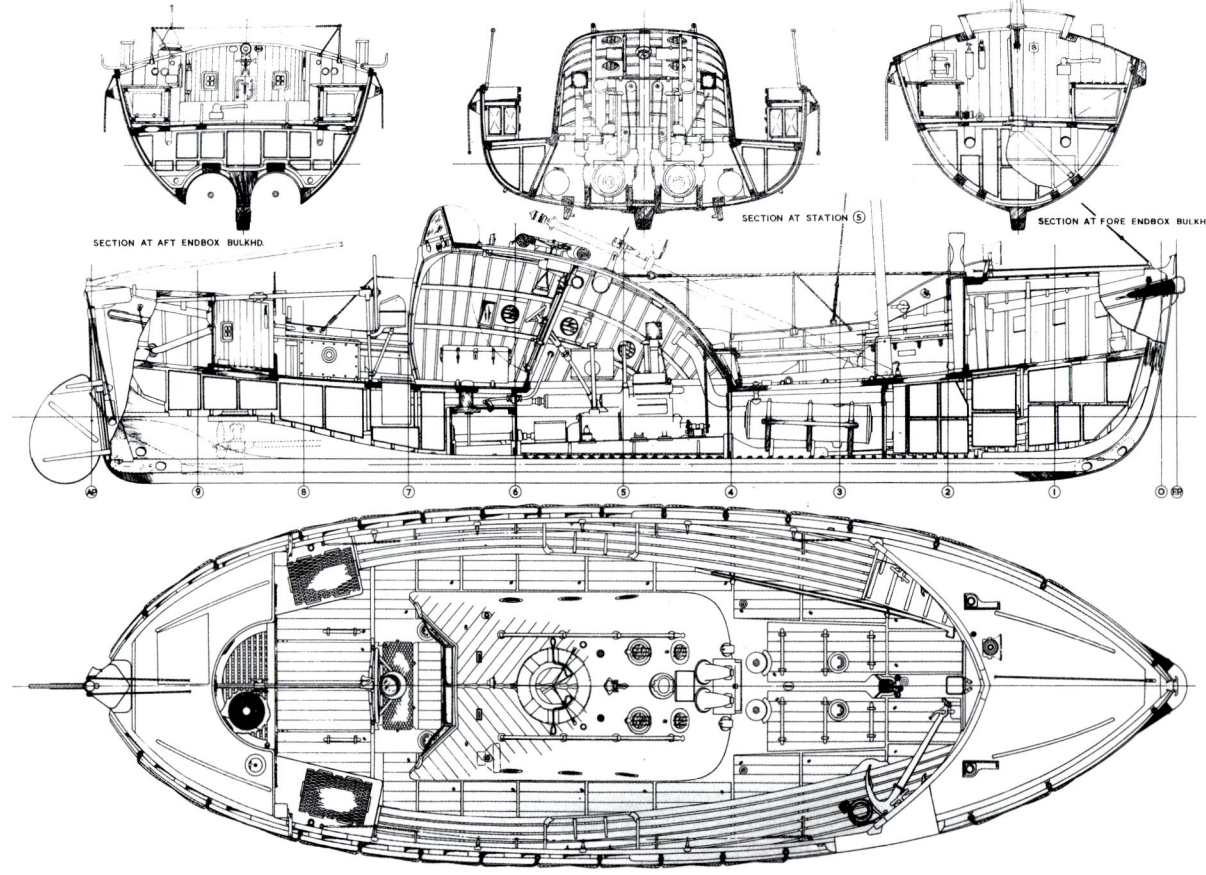

96 MOTOR LIFEBOATS

19 • Liverpool motor twin-engined 35ft 6in

the boats had a radius of action of seventy miles. The diesel-engined version, from Anthony Robert Marshall (ON.869) onwards, had a top speed of 7.5 knots and carried enough fuel to travel 120 miles at full speed. In the 1960s, nearly all of the original twin-screw Liverpools built with petrol engines were re-engined with more powerful diesel engines, which gave the boats a greater range and were more economical to run.

The majority of the twin-engined Liverpool class were built at Cowes by Groves & Guttridge, with the last boat being completed in 1954. Over the course of less than a decade all thirty-one boats of the class were built. Two of the Liverpools (ON.873 and ON.874) suffered tragic capsizes, with crews being drowned after the boats were turned over in heavy seas. Many Liverpools gave over two decades of service, although some, notably those at Barmouth and Newcastle, served more than thirty years. They were mostly phased out during the 1960s and 1970s, by when the Oakleys and Rothers had been introduced for carriage-launching, while some were replaced by Atlantic 21 rigid-inflatables.

▼ (left) Launch of Anthony Robert Marshall (ON.869) at Rhyl, with the crew standing by ready to release the holding chains. (Jeff Morris)

▼ (right) One of five twin-screw Liverpool motor lifeboats completed in 1950, Richard Ashley (ON.875) on trials before going on station at Newbiggin. (By courtesy of the RNLI)

▲ B.H.M.H. (ON.882) at Minehead, the station she served for twenty-two years. (By courtesy of the RNLI)

▲ Recovery of Edith Clauson-Thue (ON.895) at Gourdon on Scotland's east coast. (By courtesy of the RNLI)

MOTOR LIFEBOATS

19 • Liverpool motor twin-engined 35ft 6in

	Year* (Yd No) Builder Place	Length Breadth Crew	Name Donor	ON Cost Weight	Engines	Stations (launches/lives saved)	Notes Disposal
1	1940 (275) Groves & Guttridge Cowes	35'6" 10'8" 7	[W. and B.] —	839 — —	2x18hp Weyburn 6-cyl AE4 (p)	[Prototype - not stemmed] Blitzed at boatyard 4.5.1942	
2	1945 (418) Groves & Guttridge Cowes	35'6" 10'8" 7	Cecil Paine Legacy of Arthur Cecil Paine, of Torquay.	850 £7,462 7t15	2x18hp Weyburn AE4 6-cyl (p)/ 1964- 2x32hp Parsons Penguin (d)	Wells 25.7.1945-1.6.1965 (47/20) Kilmore Quay 10.1965-2.1972 (22/0) Reserve 1972-1973 (0/0)	Sold 1973
3	1945 (485) Groves & Guttridge Cowes	35'6" 10'8" 7	Edgar, George, Orlando and Eva Child Legacies of Mr R. B. Poll, Mr O. E. Child, and Major G. W. Wilson.	861 £9,751 8t14	2x18hp Weyburn AE4 6-cyl (p)/ 1965- 2x32hp Parsons Penguin (d)	St Ives 11.4.1948-4.1968 (116/61) Reserve 7.1968-70 (3/0) and 1975-82 (0/0) Blackpool 6.1970-5.6.1975 (16/3)	Sold 1983
4	1948 (486) Groves & Guttridge Cowes	35'6" 10'8" 7	Thomas Corbett Gift from the Thomas Corbett Charity, London.	862 £9,581 8t10	2x18hp Weyburn AE4 6-cyl (p)/ 1964- 2x32hp Parsons Penguin (d)	Ramsey 24.9.1948-20.2.1970 (60/10) Hoylake 26.9.1970-18.5.1974 (12/6) Clogher Head 11.1974-1981 (12/0)	Sold 1982
5	1948 (487) Groves & Guttridge Cowes	35'6" 10'8" 7	St Albans St Albans Lifeboat Fund.	863 £9,836 7t17	2x18hp Weyburn AE4 6-cyl (p)/ 1964- 2x32hp Parsons Penguin (d)	New Quay 12.12.1948-7.1970 (66/78)	Sold 12.1970
6	1948 (488) Groves & Guttridge Cowes	35'6" 10'8" 7	The Chieftain Legacy of P. C. Peak, Branksome, Dorset.	864 £9,943 7t19	2x18hp Weyburn AE4 6-cyl (p)/ 1964- 2x32hp Parsons Penguin (d)	Barmouth 11.3.1949-27.2.1982 (113/132)	Sold 14.4.82
7	1949 (500) Groves & Guttridge Cowes	35'6" 10'8" 7	Anthony Robert Marshall Legacy of A. R. Marshall, Liverpool.	869 £11,763 8t4	2x20hp Ferry Kadenacy FKR3 3-cyl (d)/ 1965- 2x32hp Parsons Penguin (d)	Rhyl 15.9.1949-26.9.1968 (102/51) Reserve 1968-1972 (3/0) Pwllheli 7.1972-18.5.1979 (20/6)	Sold 1980
8	1949 (501) Groves & Guttridge Cowes	35'6" 10'8" 7	William and Laura Legacy of Miss A. W. Clarke Hall, Bournemouth.	870 £10,843 8t	2x18hp Weyburn AE4 6-cyl (p)/ 1964- 2x32hp Parsons Penguin (d)	Newcastle 17.7.1949-5.1980 (58/54)	Sold 9.1980
9	1949 (502) Groves & Guttridge Cowes	35'6" 10'8" 7	William Cantrell Ashley Legacy of Charles Carr Ashley, Mentone, France.	871 £10,964 8t13	2x18hp Weyburn AE4 6-cyl (p)/ 1964- 2x32hp Parsons Penguin (d)	Clovelly 7.9.1949-3.1967 (38/24)	Sold 1968
10	1949 (503) Groves & Guttridge Cowes	35'6" 10'8" 7	J. B. Couper of Glasgow Legacy of James B. Couper, Argyllshire.	872 £10,899 8t3	2x18hp Weyburn AE4 6-cyl (p)/ 1965- 2x32hp Parsons Penguin (d)	St Abbs 20.10.1949-7.2.1953 (4/1) Kirkcudbright 4.1953-2.5.1965 (35/17) Youghal 1966-1971 (10/3) Poole 1972-17.1.1974 (31/19) Reserve 1974-1975 (2/0)	Sold 2.1976
11	1950 (504) Groves & Guttridge Cowes	35'6" 10'8" 7	George Elmy Legacy of Miss E. Elmy, Stoke Newington.	873 £10,983 8t1	2x18hp Weyburn AE4 6-cyl (p)/ 1963- 2x32hp Parsons Penguin (d)	Seaham Harbour 12.1.1950-11.1962 (26/20) Reserve 1963-1969 (9/2) Poole 11.1969-1972 (12/3)	Capsized on service 17.11.1962, nine crew lost Sold 9.1972
12	1950 (505) Groves & Guttridge Cowes	35'6" 10'8" 7	Robert Lindsay Legacy of Mr R. Lindsay, jnr, Carnoustie.	874 £11,857 8t6	2x20hp Ferry Kadenacy FKR3 3-cyl (d)	Arbroath 12.7.1950-10.1953 (4/0) Girvan 2.9.1955-1960 (13/2) Criccieth 16.11.1961-6.4.1968 (12/0)	Capsized on service 27.10.1953, six crew lost Sold 1968
13	1950 (511) Groves & Guttridge Cowes	35'6" 10'8" 7	Richard Ashley Legacy of Mr Charles Carr Ashley, Mentone, France.	875 £13,154 8t8	2x20hp Ferry Kadenacy FKR3 3-cyl (d)	Newbiggin 3.8.1950-5.9.1966 (44/11)	Sold 1967
14	1950 (512) Groves & Guttridge Cowes	35'6" 10'8" 7	James and Ruby Jackson Legacy of Mr James Jackson, Falkland.	876 £13,231 8t7	2x20hp Ferry Kadenacy FKR3 3-cyl (d)	Anstruther 3.8.1950-5.1965 (63/45) Reserve 1965-1967 (0/0)	Sold 1969

19 • Liverpool motor twin-engined 35ft 6in

	Year* (Yd No) Builder Place	Length Breadth Crew	Name Donor	ON Cost Weight	Engines	Stations (launches/lives saved)	Notes Disposal
15	1950 (W5416) J. S. White Cowes	35'6" 10'8" 7	**George and Caroline Ermen** Legacy of Mr G. H. Ermen, Chester.	877 £14,596 8t8	2x20hp Ferry Kadenacy FKR3 3-cyl (d)	Clogher Head 7.7.1950-11.1974 (50/24)	Sold 7.1974
16	1951 (RIW721) Rowhedge IW Rowhedge	35'6" 10'8" 7	**B. H. M. H.** Legacies of Mr C. H. Bailey and Mrs L. Hall, plus gift of Mr F. H. Heys and anonymous.	882 £13,913 8t8	2x18hp Weyburn AE4 6-cyl (p)/ 1964- 2x32hp Parsons Penguin (d)	Minehead 10.12.1951-5.1973 (46/11) Relief 1973-1981 (16/9) Clogher Head 1981-26.8.1984 (3/0)	Sold 1985
17	1951 (515) Groves & Guttridge Cowes	35'6" 10'8" 7	**Bassett-Green** Gift of Mr W. H. Bassett Green, Winchcombe.	891 £14,038 8t3	2x20hp Ferry Kadenacy FKR3 3-cyl (d)	Padstow No.2 30.7.1951-3.1962 (13/6) Poole 18.7.1962-11.1969 (17/9)	Sold 1969
18	1951 (516) Groves & Guttridge Cowes	35'6" 10'8" 7	**Aguila Wren** Aguila Wren Memorial Fund and legacy of Mr Moorhouse.	892 £14,172 7t19	2x20hp Ferry Kadenacy FKR3 3-cyl (d)	Aberystwyth 10.1951-1964 (21/14) Redcar 2.1965-11.1972 (32/24)	Sold 12.1972
19	1951 (517) Groves & Guttridge Cowes	35'6" 10'8" 7	**Clara and Emily Barwell** Legacies of the Misses C. and E. H. Barwell.	893 £14,008 8t9	2x20hp Ferry Kadenacy FKR3 3-cyl (d)	Eyemouth 12.12.1951-1963 (14/6) Reserve 1963-1968 (11/2)	Sold 2.1969
20	1952 (518) Groves & Guttridge Cowes	35'6" 10'8" 7	**Oldham IV** RNLI General Funds.	894 £14,162 8t4	2x20hp Ferry Kadenacy FKR3 3-cyl (d)	Hoylake 14.2.1952-26.9.1970 (62/45)	Sold 9.10.1970
21	1952 (519) Groves & Guttridge Cowes	35'6" 10'8" 7	**Edith Clauson-Thue** Legacies of Miss E. M. M. Clauson-Thue, Sir Lockhart, Miss Anderson.	895 £14,436 8t18	2x20hp Ferry Kadenacy FKR3 3-cyl (d)	Gourdon 26.4.1952-4.5.1969 (14/0)	Sold 1969
22	1952 (520) Groves & Guttridge Cowes	35'6" 10'8" 7	**Constance Calverley** Legacy of Miss Constance Calverley, Huddersfield.	902 £14,337 8t15	2x20hp Ferry Kadenacy FKR3 3-cyl (d)	Cloughey 17.6.1952-10.1965 (22/21) Reserve 1965-1970 (2/0)	Sold 1970
23	1952 (521) Groves & Guttridge Cowes	35'6" 10'8" 7	**Helena Harris – Manchester & District XXXI** Legacy of Miss Harris, and Manchester and District Branch.	903 £13,764 8t5	2x20hp Ferry Kadenacy FKR3 3-cyl (d)	Peel 29.5.1952-5.1972 (32/15)	Sold 1972
24	1952 (522) Groves & Guttridge Cowes	35'6" 10'8" 7	**Robert and Phemia Brown** Legacy of Captain Robert Brown, Anstruther.	904 £14,200 8t4	2x20hp Ferry Kadenacy FKR3 3-cyl (d)	Ilfracombe 6.10.1952-7.1966 (46/24)	Sold 1967
25	1952 (523) Groves & Guttridge Cowes	35'6" 10'8" 7	**Katherine and Virgoe Buckland** Legacies of Cdr Virgoe Buckland, Mr H. Woodhead, and British Services Charities.	905 £14,395 8t7	2x20hp Ferry Kadenacy FKR3 3-cyl (d)	Pwllheli 21.1.1953-7.1972 (44/11)	Sold 1972
26	1952 (524) Groves & Guttridge Cowes	35'6" 10'8" 7	**W. Ross MacArthur of Glasgow** Legacy of Mr W. Ross MacArthur, Glasgow.	906 £14,398 8t10	2x20hp Ferry Kadenacy FKR3 3-cyl (d)	St Abbs 7.2.1953-11.1964 (32/13) Reserve 1964-1968 (4/0)	Sold 1968
27	1953 (525) Groves & Guttridge Cowes	35'6" 10'8" 7	**Tillie Morrison, Sheffield II** Legacy of Mr Whitaker and RNLI Funds.	914 £14,482 8t6	2x20hp Ferry Kadenacy FKR3 3-cyl (d)	Bridlington 17.6.1953-9.1967 (106/36) Reserve 1967-1968 (0/0)	Sold 1969
28	1953 (526) Groves & Guttridge Cowes	35'6" 10'8" 7	**Friendly Forester** Ancient Order of Foresters.	915 £15,738 8t1	2x20hp Ferry Kadenacy FKR3 3-cyl (d)/ 1969- 2x32hp Parsons Penguin (d)	Flamborough 20.5.1953-18.1.1983 (186/89)	Sold 1984

MOTOR LIFEBOATS

19 • Liverpool motor twin-engined 35ft 6in

	Year* (Yd No) Builder Place	Length Breadth Crew	Name Donor	ON Cost Weight	Engines	Stations (launches/lives saved)	Notes Disposal
29	1953 (527) Groves & Guttridge Cowes	35'6" 10'8" 7	**Maria Noble** Legacies of Mr H. Noble, Mr West, Mrs Andrews and Mr Williams.	916 £14,594 8t6	2x20hp Ferry Kadenacy FKR3 3-cyl (d)	Exmouth 9.10.1953-2.1960 (30/35) Blackpool 12.1961-6.1970 (25/3) Reserve 1970-1973 (0/0)	Sold 1974
30	1954 (528) Groves & Guttridge Cowes	35'6" 10'8" 7	**Isa and Penryn Milsted** Legacy of Mrs A. P. Milsted, London.	917 £14,881 8t4	2x20hp Ferry Kadenacy FKR3 3-cyl (d)	Filey 21.10.1953-18.5.1968 (87/12)	Sold 1969
31	1954 (529) Groves & Guttridge Cowes	35'6" 10'8" 7	**Elliott Gill** Legacy of Miss E. M. Gill, Leicester.	918 £15,254 8t15	2x20hp Ferry Kadenacy FKR3 3-cyl (d)	Runswick 14.1.1954-9.1970 (39/24) Reserve 1970-1974 (1/0)	Sold 8.1974
32	1954 (530) Groves & Guttridge Cowes	35'6" 10'8" 7	**Grace Darling** RNLI General Funds.	927 £15,040 8t10	2x20hp Ferry Kadenacy FKR3 3-cyl (d)/ 1971- 2x32hp Parsons Penguin (d)	North Sunderland 8.4.1954-7.1967 (69/16) Reserve 1967-1971 (6/1) Youghal 1971-23.5.1984 (31/17)	Display from 1985 at Bristol, later Chatham Dockyard

▲ Helena Harris (ON.903) at Peel, Isle of Man, where she was launched from a carriage down a steep slipway. (By courtesy of the RNLI)

▶ Friendly Forester (ON.915) at sea off Flamborough Head. One of the last twin-engined Liverpools to be built, she served the station at Flamborough in Yorkshire for almost thirty years, and was launched down a steep slipway from her boathouse at North Landing.

Chapter 4
Rebuilding after the Second World War

Rebuilding after the Second World War

◀ (chapter frontispiece) The 37ft Oakley William Henry and Mary King (ON.980) on trials off Cowes, October 1964. She was one of twenty-six Oakleys to be built; the design was noteworthy for the water ballast tanks which provided the self-righting capability. (Beken, by courtesy of the RNLI)

▶ The 52ft Barnett St Cybi (Civil Service No.9) (ON.884) on trials in July 1950, shortly after completion by J.S. White, Cowes. She was one of the first two 52ft Barnetts to be built. St Cybi had an illustrious thirty-year career at Holyhead and is now on display at the Historic Dockyard, Chatham. (By courtesy of the RNLI)

▼ The 41ft Watson Matthew Simpson (ON.823) launching down the steep slipway at Port Erin, Isle of Man. Powered initially by twin 35hp Weyburn petrol engines, she was fitted with twin 47hp Parsons Porbeagle diesels in 1961, the first boat to be so re-engined. (From an old postcard supplied by John Harrop)

Although many gallant rescues were performed during the Second World War, lifeboat construction and development effectively ceased. Therefore, after 1945, new lifeboats were needed urgently. Embarking on an ambitious building programme for new boats, all of which had twin engines and twin propellers, the RNLI shared the optimism for a better and brighter future that swept the nation in the immediate post-war years. New motor lifeboats were soon completed as boatyards returned to normal production following the naval demands of wartime. As they entered service, the pulling and sailing lifeboat was phased out completely during the 1950s, with the last leaving Whitby in 1958.

The introduction of midship steering, fully enclosed cockpits and commercial diesel engines were the most significant technical advances. Midship steering was first proposed during the early years of the war. In the April 1940 edition of The Lifeboat, James Barnett announced his ideas for the next stage in lifeboat development by noting that, as future lifeboats would be built with twin engines, sails were no longer necessary. As long as sails were required, the coxswain had to steer from a position located aft so that he could keep an eye on them. However, without sails, Barnett believed, 'the proper place for the steersman in a power vessel . . . is amidships. He would have a much better view not only forward, but all round, and that position is much better for controlling his crew.'

Barnett designed a 46ft lifeboat which embodied this new feature. A cockpit forward of the engines was provided for the wheel, just forward of which sat the mechanic with the instrument panels under a shelter. Instead of a cabin below deck, a large cockpit and shelter was provided aft, with room beneath the shelter for at least two stretchers. Although the design was never built owing to the outbreak of war, Barnett's ideas were not wasted, and were employed in many of the larger boats designed after the war. The 46ft 9in Watson was the first new post-war lifeboat type and, fitted with twin 40bhp four-cylinder diesel engines, was the first to be diesel-powered. The boats of this class built after 1948 all had midship steering. The next Watson, slightly larger at 47ft, also had midship steering, as did the 52ft Barnett, which was first built in 1950.

Rebuilding after the Second World War

Subsequently, the cockpit on these designs was enclosed so as to provide a degree of shelter for crew and survivors.

The use of diesel engines became widespread after the war. Not only were they more economic, but diesel was less flammable than petrol, so its use reduced the risk of fire. The first boats to be diesel-powered before the war were the 46ft Watsons, fitted with twin 40hp Ferry diesels, following after the war by the 46ft 9in Watsons and 52ft Barnetts. These large lifeboats were powered by what were basically modified bus engines, weighing almost a ton. Their size and weight was unsuitable for the smaller classes of lifeboat, for which a lightweight diesel engine was required. Various units were assessed in the late 1940s, including the Admiralty Coventry Kadenacy four-cylinder two-stroke engine, which was made watertight and manufactured in a three-cylinder version to suit RNLI requirements, developing 20hp at 1,600rpm. The Ferry Kadenacy FKR.3 engine was also used, and was first fitted in the Rhyl lifeboat Anthony Robert Marshall (ON.869). It proved to be a reliable engine and more than twenty other lifeboats were subsequently fitted with the unit.

Another advantage of the diesel engine over its petrol counterpart was its relatively low construction cost. The petrol engines had largely been bespoke units specifically designed for use in the lifeboats in which they were fitted. Such specialised manufacturing was, inevitably, extremely expensive, so in 1950 the RNLI considered the use of commercial engines. Adopting an engine in everyday use in the commercial world, which was made in a range of power and cylinders, with standard parts easily obtainable, and proven reliability had considerable appeal. So in 1954, for a commercial diesel engine was first fitted to a lifeboat when the new 42ft Watson for Coverack, William Taylor of Oldham (ON.907), was completed with 48hp Gardner 4LW diesels. A similar boat was later sent to Troon and all 42ft, 47ft and 52ft boats were then fitted with Gardner engines of varying power, and this proved to be ideal for lifeboat work.

The success of the Gardner diesels during the 1950s resulted in a major re-engining programme after it had been determined that re-engining existing petrol-driven lifeboats would be both possible and beneficial. Trials were undertaken with the 1939-built 41ft Watson motor Matthew Simpson (ON.823) from Port Erin, which, in 1961, was fitted with twin 47hp Ford Parsons Porbeagle diesels. These were more powerful than the petrol engines fitted in the boat when she had been built. The diesel engines increased the boat's maximum speed from 8.12 to 8.57 knots and the radius of action from sixty-four miles to ninety-four. The success of Matthew Simpson's trials led the RNLI's Superintendent Engineer, Cmdr R.A. Gould, to conclude, 'There is now no room for doubt that the policy of fitting commercial diesel engines has been a momentous and outstanding success and will result in a marked financial saving in running and upkeep.'

Several other modifications were introduced to new lifeboats during the 1950s which, although relatively minor, were nevertheless important. They included stainless steel propeller shafts and water-cooled side exhausts in place of stern exhausts, while equipment carried on board also became more sophisticated. Wireless had first been introduced in the 1920s and increasingly advanced radio transmitters had been employed ever since. Other electronic equipment, such as an echo sounder, was also used for the first time in the 1950s, and the first radar set was fitted in 1963 to the 48ft Oakley Earl and Countess Howe (ON.968).

The next major advance came in the mid-1950s. Despite the many improvements in design and advances in equipment, lifeboats were still failing to cope in the worst of conditions and, more importantly, lifeboat men were losing their lives as a result. In April 1947 catastrophe overtook the Mumbles lifeboat Edward, Prince of Wales (ON.678), a 45ft Watson type, when she went to the aid of the steamship Samtampa. The ship was on the rocks at Sker Point of the South Wales coast and, in trying to approach the casualty in heavy surf, the lifeboat overturned and her

▲ The 35ft 6in Liverpool motor Grace Darling (ON.927) was built in 1954. The Liverpool was a pre-war design, but a twin-engined version was developed in the 1940s, and thirty-one such boats were built after 1945, of which Grace Darling was the last; she had a thirty-year career, serving at Seahouses and Youghal. (By courtesy of the RNLI)

▼ (left) The 46ft 9in Watson Douglas Hyde (ON.896) on trials shortly after being built. Completed in 1952, she was typical of the midship-steering designs of the 1950s, with her cockpit being enclosed later in her career, which saw her serve two stations in Ireland over the course of two decades. (By courtesy of the RNLI)

▼ (right) The 47ft Watson Helen Wycherley (ON.959) on trials off the Isle of Wight. She served first at Whitehills, and was subsequently fitted with a self-righting air-bag. During the 1950s the Watson type was redesigned and the 47ft version was the end product, with an enclosed midship steering position. (By courtesy of the RNLI)

MOTOR LIFEBOATS

Rebuilding after the Second World War

▶ The 35ft 6in Liverpool Robert Lindsay after she had capsized on service at Arbroath, on 27 October 1953, with the loss of six of the crew of seven. She capsized after being caught in very steep cross seas, which struck the boat as she tried to enter the harbour. This was one of a number of tragic capsizes during the 1950s and 1960s, which eventually led to the introduction of self-righting lifeboats. (By courtesy of the RNLI)

▼ The 48ft Oakley Earl and Countess Howe (ON.968) served at Yarmouth from 1963 to 1976 and Walton and Frinton from 1977 to 1983. Pictured on trials, she was the first large lifeboat with a cabin and shelter for crew and survivors, which incorporated Oakley's self-righting principle. All controls were centralised near the coxswain at the wheel, and for the first time a radar set was fitted into one of the RNLI's lifeboats. She had a water ballast tank beneath the engines, which filled automatically when the boat entered the sea, and, in the event of a capsize, two and three-quarter tons of water would be transferred into a righting tank on the port side to bring the boat upright again. (By courtesy of the RNLI)

entire crew of eight was lost. In February 1953 the lifeboat at Fraserburgh, on Scotland's north-east coast, John and Charles Kennedy (ON.790), was overwhelmed and capsized close to the harbour entrance, with the loss of six of her seven crew. Further capsizes occurred at Bridlington in 1952, Arbroath in 1953 and Scarborough in 1954, all with fatal consequences. And on 17 November 1962, the 35ft 6in Liverpool type non-self-righting lifeboat at Seaham Harbour, George Elmy (ON.873), capsized only thirty feet from the harbour pier, resulting in the loss of five of her crew.

As a result of the tragedies, the RNLI reviewed its policy on self-righting lifeboats and made increased efforts to find a design of lifeboat with a self-righting capability. The situation that existed in the 1950s was the result of a combination of historical preferences and an inability to overcome the problem of designing a self-righting lifeboat that was as stable as a non-self-righting boat. Crews wanted stable, seaworthy lifeboats with a high degree of lateral stability, something provided by the Watson and Barnett motor lifeboats, which were based on Watson's non-self-righting hull design of the 1890s. But designing such a boat that would also self-right if capsized had challenged naval architects for well over a century, and the problem remained unsolved during the post-war era.

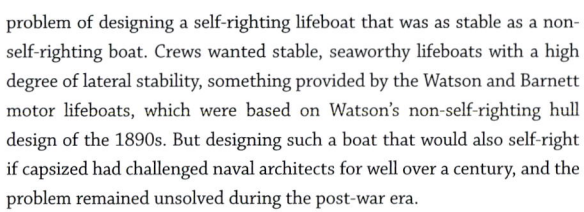

In seeking to overcome the problem, Richard Oakley, the RNLI's Consulting Naval Architect, designed a 37ft lifeboat that employed a system of water ballast transfer, which would right the boat in the event of a capsize. Although the use of water ballast tanks had originally been intended to provide extra ballast for the relatively light carriage-launched type, his design, the 37ft Oakley which entered service in 1958, became the first lifeboat with a high degree of inherent stability which was also self-righting. Oakley had joined the RNLI in the late 1920s and worked his way up to the position of Consulting Naval Architect following Barnett's retirement in the 1960s. His water ballast principal was subsequently applied to a larger 48ft type, which carried two and three-quarter tons of water ballast compared to one and a half tons in the smaller boats.

But although new self-righting designs had been developed, and the water ballast principle had been applied to the larger 48ft type, existing non-self-righting lifeboats remained vulnerable, and, tragically, further capsizes occurred. At Longhope and Fraserburgh, in March 1969 and January 1970 respectively, non-self-righting lifeboats capsized in very heavy seas with heavy loss of life. The entire crew of eight from the Longhope boat was lost, while at Fraserburgh the 1970 capsize was the station's second lifeboat disaster in less than two decades.

The need to deploy lifeboats that were self-righting became more urgent, and the disasters prompted the RNLI to look to provide Watson and Barnett lifeboats with a self-righting capability. An air-bag system was therefore developed by RNLI designers, working in conjunction with technicians from the British Hovercraft Corporation. Fitted on the aft cabin, the air-bag automatically inflated if the boat rolled over more than 100 degrees and acted as a large buoyancy chamber to right the boat in the event of a capsize. Having solved the problem of self-righting, the RNLI declared that the entire fleet of offshore lifeboats would be entirely self-righting by 1980, and air-bags were soon fitted to most of the older types, although the 42ft Watsons and 35ft 6in Liverpools were never able to be converted to be self-righting. However, all subsequent lifeboat designs have been inherently self-righting, and since 1982 no lifeboat crew members have been lost on service.

The new self-righting lifeboats in the fleet proved their worth during the 1970s and 1980s, when several capsized on service but righted successfully. Only once was a volunteer's life lost, when the 37ft Oakley at Kilmore Quay, Lady Murphy (ON.997), capsized and righted twice on service on 24 December 1977 during a search of Bannow Bay. When she

Rebuilding after the Second World War

righted herself after the second capsize, four crew members had been washed overboard. Three were recovered, but the fourth, Finton Sinnott, was not found despite a thorough search. Although one life had tragically been taken, the self-righting system saved the rest of the crew.

The fitting of air-bags to the larger Watsons and Barnetts also saved lives on two other occasions. Firstly in November 1979, when the Barra Island lifeboat R.A. Colby Cubbin No.3 (ON.935) capsized on service and was righted by her air-bag. On the same night and going to the same casualty, the 50ft Thames class lifeboat Helmut Schroder of Dunlossit (ON.1032) from Islay (described in the next chapter) also capsized and righted successfully without any loss of life.

Secondly, less than four years later, on 10 April 1983, when Salcombe lifeboat The Baltic Exchange (ON.964) capsized in heavy seas. She had put out in a force nine southerly gale and battled through extremely heavy seas at the harbour entrance. She cleared these and then set course for the southern end of Start Bay, where it was reported two divers were hanging on to their upturned boat. The gale force nine winds, at times gusting to force eleven, caused the lifeboat to roll very heavily.

The lifeboat crew eventually sighted the casualty, but, as the lifeboat approached, a huge breaking wave, about fifty feet high, hit her port quarter. She rolled heavily to starboard and one crew member, who was attaching his lifeline, was washed overboard. The lifeboat righted herself from that knockdown, but a second enormous wave then struck her and she capsized while travelling at full speed. As the lifeboat heeled beyond the point of no return, the air-bag inflated automatically and righted the boat. The excess water soon drained away and all of the crew, except the one washed overboard, who saw the capsize from the water, were found to be safe. The crewman in the water was recovered and the lifeboat sheltered under the lee of Start Point. The divers were eventually recovered by helicopter and The Baltic Exchange made for Brixham, being escorted part of the way by the Torbay lifeboat. The air-bag system had proved its worth during these two incidents, and, with no lives lost in either, showed the importance of having lifeboats with a self-righting capability.

The next step in self-righting lifeboats was the incorporation of a supestructure which acted as an air chamber large enough to right the boat in the event of a capsize, and the developments of Oakley's two designs were both inherently self-righting using this method: the 37ft 6in Rother and steel-hulled 48ft 6in Solent had superstructures designed to provide sufficient inherent buoyancy so that the water ballast transfer system could be dispensed with. In addition, six 47ft Wtasons were heavily modified with considerable structural changes to make them self-righting without the need for an air-bag as fitted to most boats of the class.

▲ The 48ft 6in Oakley Ruby and Arthur Reed (ON.990) undergoing her self-righting trials at Portsmouth in June 1966. The trial involved turning the boat through 180 degrees, after which she righted herself in six seconds.

▲ Capsize trials of the 47ft Watson Kathleen Mary (ON.950) at Cowes on 16 December 1978 after she had been converted to be inherently self-righting. (By courtesy of the RNLI)

◄ The 52ft Barnett Claude Cecil Staniforth (ON.943) at sea off Lerwick, one of two stations in Shetland. She is pictured having been fitted with a self-righting air-bag, which was kept in a semi-circular container on the aft cabin. (By courtesy of the RNLI)

MOTOR LIFEBOATS

20 • Watson cabin motor 46ft 9in

KEY DATA
- Introduced 1947
- Last built 1956
- 28 built

SPECIFICATIONS
- Length 46ft 9in
- Beam 12ft 9in
- Crew 7/8

The 46ft 9in Watson was the next development of the Watson motor design. Although the first five boats were 9in longer than the 46ft version, the type they superseded, these initial boats had an almost identical deck layout, with turtle-shaped shelters, funnel exhausts and a stern cockpit. Of these five boats, only three were re-engined during their careers, which involved having the funnels removed, and the aft cockpit was fitted with a wheelhouse to give improved crew protection. The last of these five boats, *W. M. Tilson* (ON.855), was sold out of service without being modified.

In 1948 the deck layout was comprehensively redesigned after experience had shown that, with twin screws, auxiliary sails were no longer needed and an aft steering position, from where the coxswain could watch the sails, was unnecessary. In the redesigned version, the wooden turtle shelter was replaced by an aluminium structure which incorporated three sections: a midship steering position in an open cockpit; a small shelter forward of the cockpit, housing the access hatch to the engine room, along with the engine controls and gauges; and a deck cabin behind the cockpit, reached via a sliding door and housing the wireless and other electronic aids. Although the hull was of wooden construction, as with all Watsons, the superstructure was made of aluminium to reduce top weight.

The midship steering position enabled the coxswain to communicate with the mechanic at the engine controls in front of him and the radio operator in the cabin behind him. The boats had an open cockpit when built, but this was enclosed or partially enclosed from the early 1960s onwards. At the aft end of the cabin was a second cockpit, which featured a sliding door into the cabin through which stretchers could be passed; it was also a handy position for crews operating the drogue, and incorporated a second helm position for emergencies. The new deck layout featured an ingenious exhaust system; instead of passing through a funnel sited amidships, fumes were carried up pipes inside the main mast and released above the heads of the crew, eradicating crew nausea, although the mast would get hot after the engine had been running for a few hours.

All the 46ft 9in Watsons were fitted with air-bags to give a once-only self-righting capability, except for those with stern cockpit, ON.849, ON.852 to ON.855, and ON.908; the aft cabin was also made watertight as part of the air-bag installation. The rudder positions on the boats varied: the first nine had internal rudders, but from about 1952 external rudders were fitted to improve the boats' manoeuvrability. Some 46ft 9in Watsons were designed with internal rudders, but these were altered during construction to an external position. Most boats were re-engined with more powerful diesels to extend their service careers, while the others were usually sold out of service earlier than the re-engined boats.

▲ The first 46ft 9in Watson motor *Manchester and District XXX* (ON.849) as built, with an aft steering position and exhaust funnel amidships. She was later named *William Gammon – Manchester and District XXX* after the well-known Mumbles Coxswain who lost his life on service in 1947. (By courtesy of the RNLI)

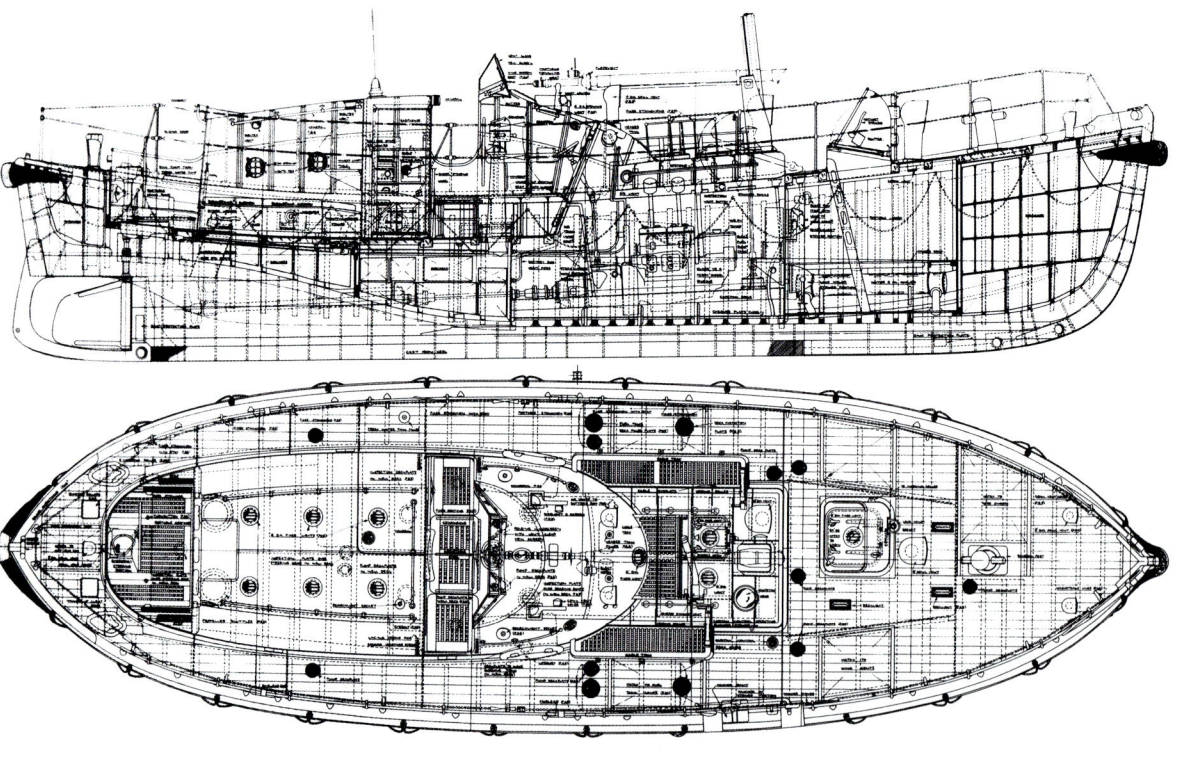

▶ Plans of the 46ft 9in Watson built for Clacton, *Sir Godfrey Baring* (ON.887), showing the rudder arrangement, engine compartments and open steering position. (By courtesy of the RNLI)

▼ *Elizabeth Rippon* (ON.865) was the first 46ft 9in Watson motor built with a midships steering position. This photograph shows the boat after her cockpit had been enclosed and radar had been fitted. (By courtesy of the RNLI)

MOTOR LIFEBOATS

20 • Watson cabin motor 46ft 9in

	Year (Yd No) / Builder / Place	Name / Donor	ON / Cost / Weight	Engines	Stations (launches/lives saved)	Notes / Disposal
1	1947 (391) Groves & Guttridge Cowes	**William Gammon - Manchester and District XXX** Manchester & Salford Lifeboat Fund.	849 £16,962 20t	2x40hp Ferry VE4 (d)/ 1968- 2x65hp Parsons Barracuda (d)	Mumbles 19.7.1947-27.8.1974 (134/74) Relief 1974-1982 (41/10)	Sold 3.1983 and displayed at Maritime and Industrial Museum, Swansea
2	1947 (W5395) J. S. White Cowes	**Tynesider** Tyneside Blitzed Lifeboat Fund.	852 £16,367 21t15	2x40hp Ferry VE4 (d)/ 1965- 2x65hp Parsons Barracuda (d)	Tynemouth 11.1947-4.1979 (153/140) Relief 7.1980-1983 (8/0)	Sold 2.1984
3	1947 (W5399) J. S. White Cowes	**Winston Churchill (Civil Service No.8)** Civil Service Lifeboat Fund.	853 £16,535 21t4	2x40hp Ferry VE4 (d)/ 1966- 2x65hp Parsons Barracuda (d)	Blyth 2.2.1948-18.9.1979 (68/39) Relief 1.1980-11.1982 (22/6)	Sold 7.1983
4	1949 (AR255) Alexr. Robertson Sandbank	**Sarah Tilson** Legacy of W. M. Tilson, Richmond, Surrey.	854 £17,790 20t2	2x40hp Ferry VE4 (d)	Baltimore 15.5.1950-5.1978 (70/21)	Sold 12.1979
5	1949 (AR256) Alex Robertson Sandbank	**W. M. Tilson** Legacy of W. M. Tilson, Richmond, Surrey.	855 £18,057 19t18	2x40hp Ferry VE4 (d)	Arranmore 9.5.1950-31.10.1968 (55/20)	Sold 8.1970
6	1948 (W5405) J. S. White Cowes	**Elizabeth Rippon** Legacy of Mrs Elizabeth Rippon, Hull.	865 £19,094 22t8	2x40hp Ferry VE4 (d)/ 1966- 2x65hp Barracuda (d)	St Helier 14.10.1948-28.2.1975 (141/58) Relief 1975-77 (5/0)	Sold 10.1977
7	1949 (W5406) J. S. White Cowes	**Charles Henry Ashley** Legacy of Charles Carr Ashley, Mentone, France.	866 £19,040 22t	2x40hp Ferry VE4 (d)/ 1969- 2x70hp Watermota Sea Lion (d)	Porthdinllaen 11.3.1949-28.4.1979 (151/89) Relief 5.1979-86 (35/14)	Sold 3.1987
8	1949 (W5407) J. S. White Cowes	**Lady Scott (Civil Service No.4)** Civil Service Lifeboat Fund.	867 £18,972 22t	2x40hp Ferry VE4 (d)/ 1972- 2x70hp Thornycroft 380 (d)	Portrush 18.7.1949-11.3.1981 (148/73) Relief 9.1981-86 (31/0)	Sold 7.1987
9	1950 Sussex Yacht Co Shoreham	**John and Lucy Cordingley** Legacy of Mrs L. J. Cordingley, Bournemouth.	868 £19,816 22t4	2x40hp Ferry VE4 (d)	Teesmouth 22.2.1950-1960 (33/18) Helvick Head 7.1960-25.3.1969 (19/12) Relief 3.1969-81 (44/13)	Sold 11.1981
10	1950 (W5420) J. S. White Cowes	**Sir Samuel Kelly** Gift of Lady Kelly.	885 £25,073 22t6	2x40hp Ferry VE4 (d)/ 1972- 2x70hp Ford Mermaid 595 (d)	Donaghadee 27.5.1950-12.1976 (134/79) Relief 12.1976-12.79 (14/20)	Displayed at Donaghadee Sold 1980
11	1951 (105) Sussex Yt Co Shoreham	**Sarah Townsend Porritt** Legacy of Miss Kate Porritt, Rossendale, Lancashire.	886 £24,427 22t17	2x40hp Ferry VE4 (d)/ 1971- 2x70hp Thornycroft 380 (d)	Lytham St Annes 19.4.1951-3.78 (78/35) Relief 10.1978-82 (16/8)	Sold 10.1982
12	1951 (W5423) J. S. White Cowes	**Sir Godfrey Baring** RNLI Funds.	887 £24,628 21t17	2x40hp Ferry VE4 (d)/ 1972- 2x70hp Ford Mermaid 595 (d)	Clacton-on-Sea 14.1.1952-1.68 (226/106) Wick 2.1968-12.70 (16/25) Workington 6.9.1972-4.2.82 (53/4) Relief 5.1982-7.86 (30/8)	Sold 7.1986
13	1951 (W5424) J. S. White Cowes	**North Foreland (Civil Service No.11)** Civil Service Lifeboat Fund.	888 £24,846 22t	2x40hp Ferry VE4 (d)	Margate 18.3.1951-2.12.78 (389/216) Relief 1978-81 (6/0)	Displayed at Bristol, then Chatham Historic Dockyard
14	1951 Camper & Nicholson Gosport	**Douglas Hyde** RNLI Funds.	896 £33,196 22t19	2x40hp Ferry VE4 (d)/ 1970- 2x70hp Watermota Sea Lion (d)	Rosslare Harbour 1.1952-17.6.69 (75/47) Dunmore East 10.1970-7.72 (11/5)	Sold 2.1973
15	1951 (W5429) J. S. White Cowes	**Herbert Leigh** Gift of Mr Leigh.	900 £25,855 21t13	2x40hp Ferry VE4 (d)/ 1977- 2x70hp Thornycroft 380 (d)	Barrow 15.11.1951-9.82 (136/71) Relief 1983-88 (33/17)	Displayed at Barrow New Dock Museum Sold 1990

MOTOR LIFEBOATS

20 • Watson cabin motor 46ft 9in

	Year (Yd No) Builder Place	Name Donor	ON Cost Weight	Engines	Stations (launches/lives saved)	Notes Disposal
16	1953 (W5430) J. S. White Cowes	**Michael and Lily Davis** Legacies of Mrs L. Davis, Mr Fox, Mrs Halfon and Mr Graystone.	901 £28,811 21t15	2x40hp Ferry VE4 (d)	Ramsgate 25.9.1953-17.6.76 (318/309) Reserve 1976-79 (10/4)	Sold 1979
17	1954 (549) Groves & Guttridge Cowes	**Duchess of Kent** RNLI Funds.	908 £31,773 21t5	2x40hp Ferry VE4 (d)/ 1965- 2x65hp Parsons Barracuda (d)	Fraserburgh 4.6.1954-27.1.1970 (46/11)	Capsized on service 21.1.1970, five lost, broken up 10.1970
18	1953 (W5431) J. S. White Cowes	**Edian Courtauld** Gift of Mr Augustine Courtauld.	910 £29,687 22t	2x40hp Ferry VE4 (d)/ 1967- 2x65hp Parsons Barracuda (d)	Walton-on-Naze 2.11.1953-7.1977 (224/143) Reserve 9.1977-8.1981 (24/1)	Sold 8.1981
19	1954 (W5432) J. S. White Cowes	**City of Bradford III** City of Bradford Lifeboat Fund.	911 £29,593 21t15	2x40hp Ferry VE4 (d)/ 1968- 2x65hp Parsons Barracuda (d)	Humber 27.1.1954-1977 (351/107) Lytham St Annes 4.2.1978-16.3.1985 (26/6)	Sold 8.1985
20	1954 (550) Groves & Guttridge Cowes	**Deneys Reitz** Southern African Branch of the RNLI.	919 £31,922 21t17	2x40hp Ferry VE4 (d)/ 1970- 2x70hp Watermota Sea Lion (d)	Fowey 21.11.1954-5.1980 (155/36)	Sold 9.1980
21	1955 (551) Groves & Guttridge Cowes	**Greater London II (Civil Service No.30)** Civil Service Lifeboat Fund.	921 £32,163 21t7	2x40hp Ferry VE4 (d)/ 1969- 2x70hp Watermota Sea Lion (d)	Southend-on-Sea 3.4.1955-3.1976 (253/139) Beaumaris 2.2.1977-11.4.1989 (38/21)	Sold 1991
22	1955 (W5437) J. S. White Cowes	**Henry Comber Brown** Legacies of Mr H. Comber Brown and Miss A. E. Haldane.	925 £31,674 21t10	2x40hp Ferry VE4 (d)/ 1969- 2x70hp Watermota Sea Lion (d)	Tenby 20.9.1955-6.9.1986 (373/178)	Sold 1987
23	1955 (W5438) J. S. White Cowes	**Guy and Clare Hunter** Legacies of Mrs C. Hunter, Mrs Brown, Mrs Widdrington, and others.	926 £32,103 21t3	2x40hp Ferry VE4 (d)/ 1972- 2x70hp Ford Mermaid 595 (d)	St Mary's 12.1955-7.1981 (177/110) Fowey 11.1981-1.1982 (0/0) Penlee 9.1.1982-8.5.1983 (12/4) Padstow 9.9.1983-2.8.1984 (13/3) Cromer 4.9.1984-12.1985 (9/2) Reserve 8.1984-6.1988 (28/9)	Sold 6.1988
24	1955 (552) Groves & Guttridge Cowes	**Lilla Marras, Douglas and Will** Legacies of Mrs J. L. Marras, London; Mr J. Douglas, Langbank; and Mrs W. Kennedy of Glenbarr; also gift of Miss Robb and RNLI funds.	928 £33,723 21t4	2x40hp Ferry VE4 (d)/ 1978- 2x70hp Thornycroft 380 (d)	Cromarty 2.9.1955-4.1968 (24/10) Falmouth 9.1968-7.71 & 11.1972-10.74 (46/16) Reserve 10.1974-6.1982 (30/11) Donaghadee 7.9.1978-23.8.1979 (4/0)	Sold 10.1982
25	1956 (W5439) J. S. White Cowes	**R. A. Colby Cubbin No.1** Legacy of Mrs Ellen Mary Marsh Gordon Cubbin, Onchan, Douglas, IOM.	929 £32,000 21t15	2x40hp Ferry VE4 (d)/ 1979- 2x70hp Thornycroft 380 (d)	Douglas 29.3.1956-25.11.1988 (113/95)	Sold 1989
26	1956 (W5440) J. S. White Cowes	**R. A. Colby Cubbin No.2** Legacy of Mrs Ellen Mary Marsh Gordon Cubbin, Onchan, Douglas, Isle of Man.	930 £32,829 21t3	2x40hp Ferry VE4 (d)	Port St Mary 5.7.1956-9.1976 (47/39) Reserve 9.1976-10.77 (0/0)	Sold 10.1977
27	1956 (W5441) J. S. White Cowes	**Richard Vernon and Mary Garforth of Leeds** Legacies of Richard Vernon and Isaac Garforth, Leeds, plus RNLI funds.	931 £33,587 21t11	2x40hp Ferry VE4 (d)/ 1980- 2x70hp Thornycroft 380 (d)	Angle 19.2.1957-29.6.1987 (153/71) Wicklow 15.9.1987-10.10.1988 (6/0)	Sold 1989
28	1956 (W5442) J. S. White Cowes	**Howard Marryat** Legacy of Mr H. Marryat and gift from Mr R. Marryat.	932 £33,863 21t11	2x40hp Ferry VE4 (d)/ 1982- 2x70hp Thornycroft 380 (d)	Fishguard 4.9.1957-28.5.1981 (130/73) Barrow 20.9.1982-4.9.1986 (20/11) Moelfre 4.4.1987-22.1.1988 (4/4) Relief 4-12.1988 (0/0)	Sold 9.1989

20 • Watson cabin motor 46ft 9in

◀ John and Lucy Cordingley (ON.868) was one of two 46ft 9in Watsons completed in 1950. She was initially built for service at Teesmouth, but later moved to Helvick Head, by which time the cockpit had been enclosed, as depicted here. She also served as a Relief lifeboat for twelve years. (From an old postcard in the author's collection)

▲ The 1950-built Sir Samuel Kelly (ON.885) in the latter days of her service life, with an enclosed wheelhouse amidships, radar fitted to the wheelhouse roof, and an air-bag mounted on the after cabin. She has also been re-engined with the exhaust trained through the mast. (By courtesy of the RNLI)

▲ North Foreland (Civil Service No.11) (ON.888) at the top of the slipway at Margate, the station was served for twenty-seven years. The 46ft 9in Watsons, as built, had an open midships cockpit as clearly shown in this photograph. (From an old postcard in the author's collection)

MOTOR LIFEBOATS

20 • Watson cabin motor 46ft 9in

Two 46ft 9in Watsons together in Ramsgate harbour. In the foreground is the Margate boat North Foreland (Civil Service No.11) (ON.888), built in 1951, while at moorings is Michael and Lily Davis (ON.901), which was built in 1953 and served at Ramsgate for twenty-three years. Both of these lifeboats were built by J.S. White. (By courtesy of the RNLI)

20 • Watson cabin motor 46ft 9in

▲ Lilla Marras, Douglas and Will (ON.928) on trials prior to going on station at Cromarty. She was one of four Watsons built in 1955 and the last 46ft 9in Watson motor built by Groves & Guttridge, at Cowes. She was also the last lifeboat to serve at Cromarty. (By courtesy of the RNLI)

▲ Launch of Duchess of Kent (ON.908) down the slipway at Fraserburgh. This midship-steering version of the 46ft 9in Watson was built in 1954 and tragically capsized on service in 1970 with the loss of five crew members. (From an old postcard in the author's collection)

◀ The last 46ft 9in Watson to be built, Howard Marryat (ON.932), on trials; this fine photograph clearly shows the deck layout of the Watsons of the 1950s, with midship steering and a small aft cockpit. (By courtesy of the RNLI)

▼ Howard Marryat (ON.932) at Fishguard towards the end of her career after her cockpit had been enclosed and radar had been installed.

MOTOR LIFEBOATS

21 • Barnett 52ft

KEY DATA
▶ Introduced 1950
▶ Last built 1960
▶ 20 built

SPECIFICATIONS
▶ Length 52ft
▶ Length (waterline) 49ft 6in
▶ Beam 13ft 6in and draft 4ft 6in (up to ON.924)
▶ Beam 14ft and draft 4ft 7in (from ON.935)
▶ Crew 8

The 52ft Barnett can be regarded as the culmination of James Barnett's ideas about lifeboat design and development. The class, which was a development of the 51ft version and which it replaced at many stations, had the distinctive deck feature of a midship steering position, as well as twin engines, twin screws and shelter for rescued and rescuers, advances that had first been introduced into lifeboats under Barnett's supervision in the 1920s. Seven years before his retirement in 1947, Barnett had redesigned the 46ft Watson with a midship steering position and thereafter all Watsons and Barnetts followed this practice.

So the deck arrangements on the 52ft Barnett were similar to the post-war Watson cabin types, which had also been designed by Barnett, with midship steering positions and deck cabins. The first boats of the class were designed with a simple open cockpit at the steering position but, from ON.935 onwards, a fully enclosed wheelhouse was incorporated, with all-round windows which could be hinged down if required. Kent clear-view screens were fitted to the front windows. The first ten boats had enclosed wheelhouses fitted over the steering position while in service. The last ten, starting with ON.935 in 1957, all had raised bulwarks at bow and stern, and were similar in appearance to the 47ft Watsons with which they shared a number of design and deck layout features.

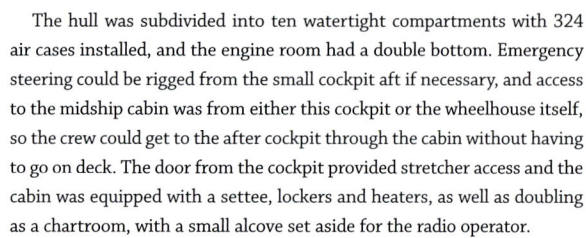

The hull was subdivided into ten watertight compartments with 324 air cases installed, and the engine room had a double bottom. Emergency steering could be rigged from the small cockpit aft if necessary, and access to the midship cabin was from either this cockpit or the wheelhouse itself, so the crew could get to the after cockpit through the cabin without having to go on deck. The door from the cockpit provided stretcher access and the cabin was equipped with a settee, lockers and heaters, as well as doubling as a chartroom, with a small alcove set aside for the radio operator.

As external doors were not watertight on the first ten boats, scuppers were fitted in the side of the boat at cabin-floor level, so that water entering the cabin or wheelhouse flowed under the lockers and overboard. A Coventry Victor generating set in the engine room supplied electrical power, and the deck winch, a feature of most Barnett boats, was mounted on the engine-room casing and driven off the port engine. Instead of the more usual anchor rope, the 52ft Barnetts had wire cables which passed from the winch through a wire-cutter, provided in case the wire had to be cut quickly in an emergency, to a stopper on the foredeck. In addition to the crew, the 52ft Barnett could carry 100 people in rough weather.

The first ten boats were powered by twin 60bhp Ferry VE6 six-cylinder diesels rated at 1,200rpm, while the last ten boats were fitted with more

▼ Joseph Hiram Chadwick (ON.898) at Padstow, with the midship steering position enclosed. (By courtesy of the RNLI)

▼ The second 52ft Barnett St Cybi (Civil Service No.9) (ON.884) pictured after the midship steering position had been enclosed. (By courtesy of RNLI)

▶ The first 52ft Barnett, Norman B. Corlett (ON.883) as built, with the midship steering position open. The forward cabin arrangement on the first ten 52ft Barnetts was similar to that of the 46ft 9in Watsons. (By courtesy of the RNLI)

112

MOTOR LIFEBOATS

21 • Barnett 52ft

	Year* (Yd No) Builder Place	Name Donor	ON Cost Weight	Engines	Stations (launches/lives saved)	Notes Disposal
1	1950 (W5418) J. S. White Cowes	Norman B. Corlett Gift of Mr W. E. Corlett and members of his family.	883 £29,264.9.5 27t18	2x60bhp Ferry VE6 (d)/ 1968- 78hp Ford Thornycroft 360	New Brighton 23.9.1950-4.1973 (215/116) Relief 1973-1981 (72/21)	Sold 2.1982
2	1950 (W5419) J. S. White Cowes	St Cybi (Civil Service No.9) Civil Service Lifeboat Fund.	884 £28,906.0.9 27t18	2x60bhp Ferry VE6 (d)/ 1966- 75hp Parsons Barracuda I (d)	Holyhead 21.9.1950-30.6.1980 (243/152) Relief 1980-1985 (14/9)	Sold 1986
3	1951 (W5425) J. S. White Cowes	Hilton Briggs Legacy of Mrs A. Briggs, Birkdale, Southport.	889 £29,927.16.2 27t19	2x60bhp Ferry VE6 6-cyl (d)	Aberdeen No.1 30.8.1951-25.9.1958 (21/20) Fenit 10.1959- 30.4.1969 (18/11) Longhope 22.5-15.12.1970 (6/0) Relief 1969-1974 (30/17) Invergordon 12.8.1974-11.1975 (0/0)	Sold 7.1976
4	1952 (W5426) J. S. White Cowes	Thomas Forehead and Mary Rowse Gift of Miss A. Charlton Rowse, Birmingham.	890 £30,874.18.0 27t5	2x60bhp Ferry VE6 (d)/ 1972- 78hp Ford Thornycroft 360 (d)	Plymouth 30.3.1952 -22.5.1974 (169/63) Relief 1974-1979 (32/20)	Sold 4.12.1982
5	1952 (W5427) J. S. White Cowes	Joseph Hiram Chadwick Legacy of Miss E. E. Chadwick, Rochdale.	898 £31,583.13.5 27t9	2x60bhp Ferry VE6 (d)/ 1968- 78hp Ford Thornycroft 360 (d)	Padstow No.1 12.1952-11.1967 (91/15) Galway Bay 1968-1977 (194/7) Reserve 1977-1979 (21/9)	Sold 4.1980
6	1953 (W5428) J. S. White Cowes	City of Glasgow II City of Glasgow Lifeboat Fund.	899 £31,628.19.4 27t3	2x60bhp Ferry VE6 (d)/ 1969- 78hp Ford Thornycroft 360 (d)	Campbeltown 24.6.1953-14.10.1979 (110/50)	Sold 4.1980
7	1954 (W5433) J. S. White Cowes	Euphrosyne Kendal Legacy of Mrs E. Kendal.	912 £34,916 27t10	2x60bhp Ferry VE6 (d)/ 1972- 70hp Ford Mermaid 595 (d)	St Peter Port 31.5.1954-10.1972 (158/115) Dunmore East 6.1973-19.3.1975 (10/7) Reserve 1975-1983 (67/48)	Sold 18.5.1983
8	1954 (W5434) J. S. White Cowes	James and Margaret Boyd Legacy of Miss C. Boyd, Mrs C. Grant, Dr J. Tennant.	913 £35,294 27t5	2x60bhp Ferry VE6 (d)/ 1969- 78hp Ford Thornycroft 360 (d)	Stornoway 27.9.1954-7.1973 (143/36) Relief 1973-1974 (8/0) Macduff 1974-1975 (8/6) Invergordon 1975- 16.7.1984 (10/2)	Sold 11.1.1985
9	1955 (W5435) J. S. White Cowes	John Gellatly Hyndman Legacy of Miss Elsie Amelia Hyndman, Greenock.	923 £35,616 27t12	2x60bhp Ferry VE6 (d)/ 1969- 78hp Ford Thornycroft 360 (d)	Stronsay 27.2.1955-30.5.1972 (116/47) Relief 1972-1984 (51/45)	Sold 23.8.1985
10	1957 (W5436) J. S. White Cowes	Archibald and Alexandra M. Paterson Gift of Miss Margaret M. Paterson, Florida, USA.	924 £36,919 27t6	2x60bhp Ferry VE6 (d)/ 1970- 78hp Ford Thornycroft 360 (d)	Stromness 21.5.1955-12.10.1984 (123/52) Arranmore 1.3.1985-5.4.1986 (10/1) Lowestoft 19.10.1986-16.11.1987 (19/0)	Sold 5.1989
11	1957 (W5466) J. S. White Cowes	R. A. Colby Cubbin No.3 Legacy of Mrs Ellen Mary Marsh Gordon Cubbin, Onchan, Douglas, Isle of Man.	935 £38,500 28t6	2x72bhp Gardner 6LW 6-cyl (d)	Barra Island 27.7.1957-16.6.1984 (129/19)	Capsized on service 18.11.1979, none lost Sold 11.1984
12	1957 (W5467) J. S. White Cowes	E. M. M. Gordon Cubbin Legacy of Mrs Ellen Mary Marsh Gordon Cubbin, Onchan, Douglas, Isle of Man.	936 £38,500 27t8	2x72bhp Gardner 6LW 6-cyl (d	Mallaig 27.10.1957-16.7.1982 (142/52) Relief 1982-1985 (5/0)	Sold 1985
13	1957 (568) Groves & Guttridge Cowes	Rowland Watts Legacy of Mr R. Watts, Essex.	938 £38,500 28t3	2x72bhp Gardner 6LW 6-cyl (d)	Valentia 18.9.1957-14.3.1983 (158/132) Relief 1983-1985 (20/6)	Sold 1985
14	1958 (569) Groves & Guttridge Cowes	Frank Spiller Locke Legacy of Dr Frank Spiller Locke, MATD, Tunbridge Wells.	939 £38,500 27t19	2x72bhp Gardner 6LW 6-cyl (d)	Weymouth 30.10.1957-15.3.1976 (249/126) Galway Bay 1977-18.12.1985 (140/8)	Sold 10.10.1986

21 • Barnett 52ft

	Year* (Yd No) Builder Place	Name Donor	ON Cost Weight	Engines	Stations (launches/lives saved)	Notes Disposal
15	1958 (570) Groves & Guttridge Cowes	**Claude Cecil Staniforth** Legacy of Mr C.C. Staniforth, East Molesey, Surrey.	943 £38,500 27t12	2x72bhp Gardner 6LW 6-cyl (d)	Lerwick 21.8.1958-8.6.1978 (94/32) Arranmore 28.10.1978-1.3.1985 (88/10)	Sold 11.1985
16	1959 (591) Groves & Guttridge Cowes	**Ramsay-Dyce** Legacy of Mr William Ramsey, Dyce, Aberdeenshire.	944 £38,232 27t19	2x72bhp Gardner 6LW 6-cyl (d)	Aberdeen 25.9.1958-3.6.1976 (59/30) Reserve 1976-1978 (7/0) Lochinver 3.8.1978-13.2.1985 (21/0)	Sold 8.1985
17	1960 (W5469) J. S. White Cowes	**Princess Alexandra of Kent** RNLI Funds.	945 £38,500 28t7	2x72bhp Gardner 6LW 6-cyl (d)	Torbay 19.7.1958-10.4.1975 (157/69) Reserve 1975-1983 (41/19) Tynemouth 12.1979-28.2.1980	Sold 2.1984
18	1960 (578) Groves & Guttridge Cowes	**Ethel Mary** Trustees of the estate of the late Mrs E.M. Brereton, Hemel Hempstead.	949 £39,900 28t3	2x72bhp Gardner 6LW 6-cyl (d)	Ballycotton 27.7.1959-27.4.1985 (121/70) Reserve 1985-1987 (0/0) Baltimore 3.6.1987-1988 (11/5)	Sold 1.1989
19	1960 (583) Groves & Guttridge Cowes	**Duke of Cornwall (Civil Service No.33)** Civil Service Lifeboat Fund.	952 £39,588.2.5 27t11	2x72bhp Gardner 6LW 6-cyl (d)	Lizard-Cadgwith 31.10.1960-7.1984 (99/85) Padstow 31.7-28.12.1984 (5/6) Reserve 1984-1989 (22/8)	Sold 1989
20	1960 (W5495) J. S. White Cowes	**John and Frances Macfarlane** Gift of Mrs John Ewing Macfarlane and his wife Ann Frances Macfarlane.	956 £39,683.9.4 27t15	2x72bhp Gardner 6LW 6-cyl (d)	Aith 28.1.1961-19.7.1986 (57/28)	Sold 10.1986

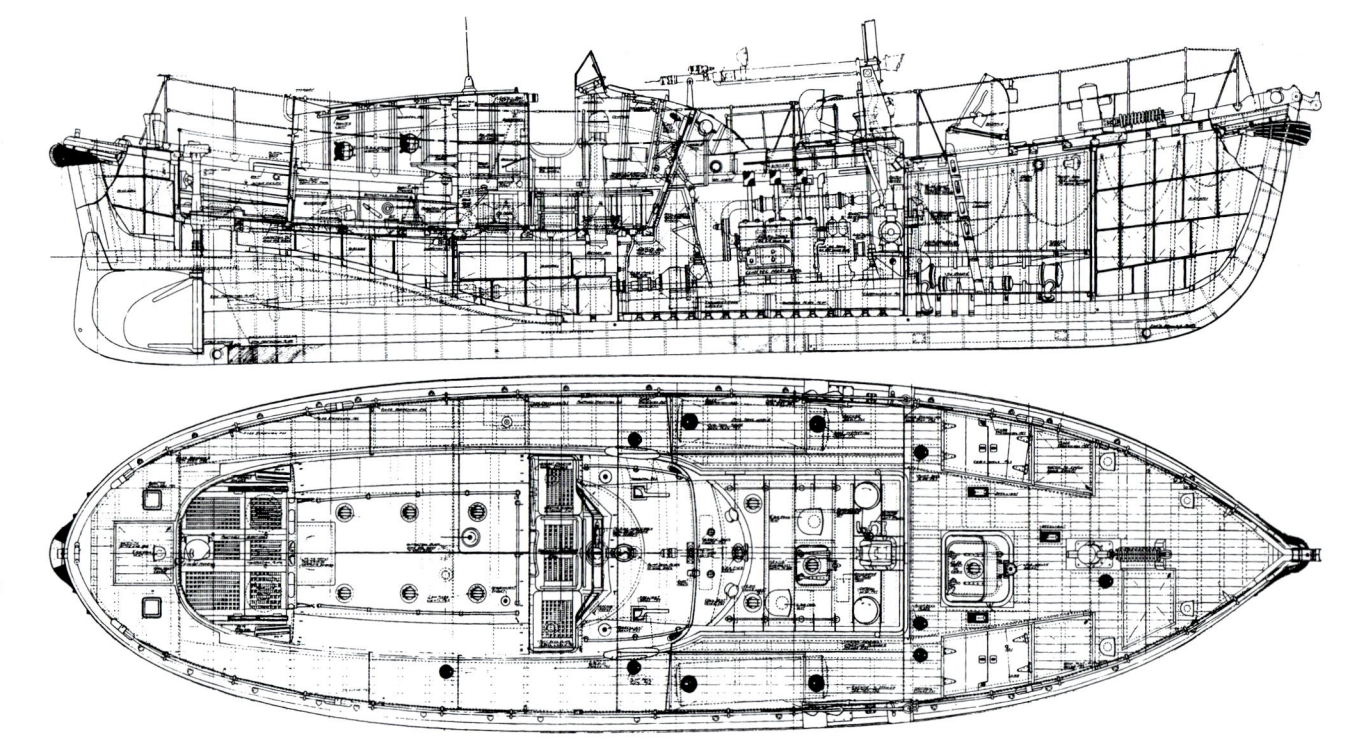

▶ Line drawing and deck plan of Norman B. Corlett (ON.883), the first 52ft Barnett, which replaced the 60ft Barnett William and Kate Johnston (ON.682) at the New Brighton station. The first ten 52ft Barnetts had an open steering position, with an internal rudder protected by an extended keel. (By courtesy of the RNLI)

21 • Barnett 52ft

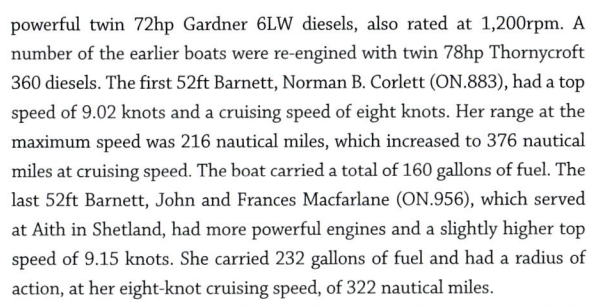

powerful twin 72hp Gardner 6LW diesels, also rated at 1,200rpm. A number of the earlier boats were re-engined with twin 78hp Thornycroft 360 diesels. The first 52ft Barnett, Norman B. Corlett (ON.883), had a top speed of 9.02 knots and a cruising speed of eight knots. Her range at the maximum speed was 216 nautical miles, which increased to 376 nautical miles at cruising speed. The boat carried a total of 160 gallons of fuel. The last 52ft Barnett, John and Frances Macfarlane (ON.956), which served at Aith in Shetland, had more powerful engines and a slightly higher top speed of 9.15 knots. She carried 232 gallons of fuel and had a radius of action, at her eight-knot cruising speed, of 322 nautical miles.

In total, between 1950 and 1960 only twenty 52ft Barnetts were built, sharing a hull shape but half with the old deck layout and the other half with the modified deck layout introduced in the mid-1950s. Following the RNLI's decision to make all lifeboats self-righting, the 52ft Barnetts were all fitted with air-bags in the 1970s to give a once-only self-righting capability. This was used once on service, in November 1979, when the Barra Island boat R. A. Colby Cubbin No.3 ON.935) capsized on service to the 299-ton Danish coaster Lone Dania; the air-bag inflated as intended, the boat righted, and none of the crew were lost.

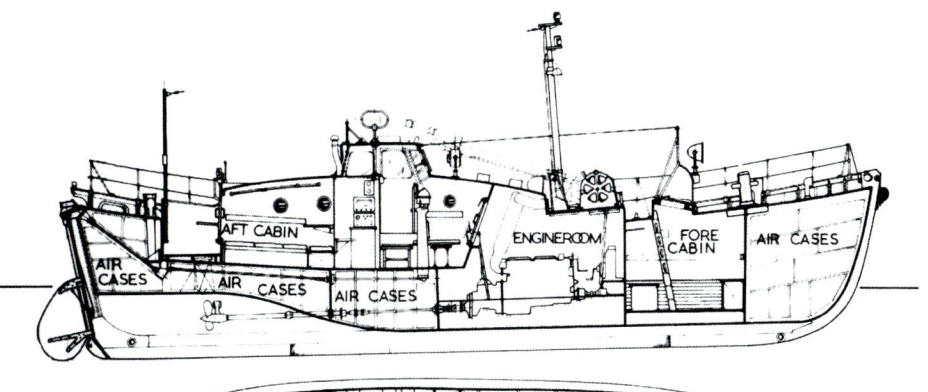

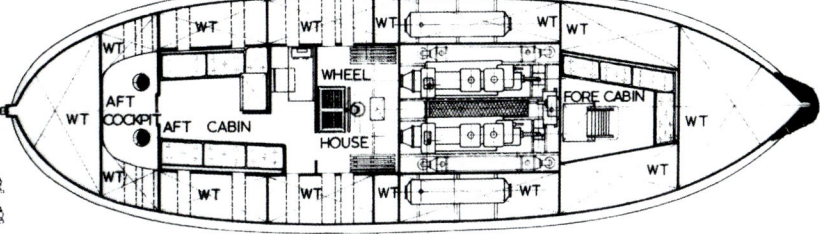

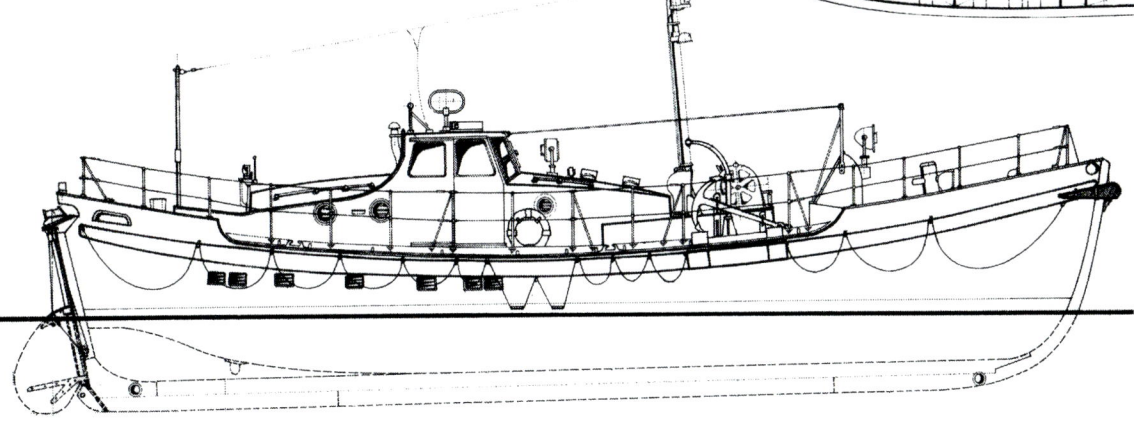

▲ Section and below deck plan of the ten 52ft Barnetts built between 1957 and 1960. The propellers were protected by twin tunnels, while the rudder was external to the hull and could be raised on those boats that were slipway launched. WT indicates watertight compartments.

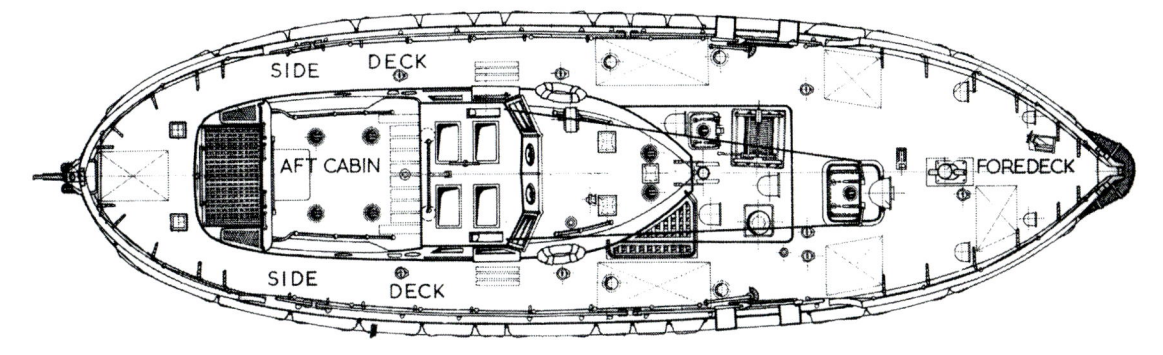

◀ Sheer plan and deck plan of the ten 52ft Barnetts built between 1957 and 1960. The scuppers in the hull below the wheelhouse drained the cockpit, aft canbin and aft cockpit as the sliding door to the wheelhouse was not watertight. On the wheelhouse roof was the D/F loop while the signalling, steaming and deck floodlights were mounted on the mast.

MOTOR LIFEBOATS

21 • Barnett 52ft

◀ 52ft Barnett Hilton Briggs (ON.889) on the River Trent on 23 August 1951 during the passage from her builder's yard at Cowes to Aberdeen; she was in Nottingham for three days for publicity purposes before heading north. (RNLI)

◀ 52ft Barnett James and Margaret Boyd (ON.913) shortly after her completion in 1954 with an open cockpit position and cabin painted light grey. (From an old postcard in the author's collection)

▲ The Stronsay-based John Gellatly Hyndman (ON.923) at Kirkwall pier; this photo shows clearly the cabin and deck layout of the 52ft Barnett. (Orkney Photographic Archives)

▼ Euphrosyne Kendal (ON.912) on relief duty during the latter years of her career, with the housing for the air-bag clearly visible on the aft cabin. (RNLI)

116 MOTOR LIFEBOATS

21 • Barnett 52ft

▲ Frank Spiller Locke (ON.939) at Weymouth; she later served at Galway Bay.

◀ Ethel Mary (ON.939), one of four Barnetts built in 1960, at Ballycotton with her replacement.

▲ Barra Island lifeboat R. A. Colby Cubbin No.3 (ON.935), with her air-bag inflated, being towed by the coaster Sapphire following her capsizing in November 1979. (By courtesy of the RNLI)

▼ The last 52ft Barnett, John and Frances Macfarlane (ON.956), off Shetland, after being fitted with an air-bag. The superstructure and deck layout of the last ten 52ft Barnetts was similar to that of the 47ft Watsons. (By courtesy of the RNLI)

MOTOR LIFEBOATS

117

22 • Watson motor 42ft

KEY DATA
▶ Introduced 1954
▶ Last built 1962
▶ 10 built including three Beach versions

SPECIFICATIONS
▶ Length 42ft
▶ Beam 12ft (12ft 3in Beach version)
▶ Draught 3ft 7in
▶ Crew 7/8

The requirement for a medium-sized motor lifeboat, intended primarily for slipway launching but also to be kept afloat, was fulfilled initially by the 40ft Watson of the 1920s, then by the 41ft Watson during the 1930s, and in the post-1945 era the 42ft version was developed. Although the largest and most advanced of any of the mid-sized Watson designs, the 42ft version in fact differed very little from its predecessors in terms of the hull shape, with the propellers in protective tunnels and the design not self-righting.

Perhaps the most significant aspect of the design was its powerplant. For the first time in a lifeboat, commercially-built diesel engines, in the shape of 48hp Gardner 4LW marine units, housed in a watertight engine room, were used. The first 42ft Watson (ON.907) thus became the first lifeboat to be powered by diesel engines. Installing diesel engines that were widely used in the commercial world meant savings in both running costs and maintenance outlay as spare parts were readily and cheaply available.

The engine controls were initially positioned so that they were operated by the mechanic but, as the boats were updated with new equipment during their service careers, more convenient controls were introduced enabling the coxswain or person at the helm to work the engines directly. The first boat had a top speed of 8.38 knots and carried enough fuel to travel 238 miles at full speed without refuelling.

The 42ft Watsons' wooden hull was divided into nineteen watertight compartments and fitted with 150 air cases. A watertight double bottom below the engine room floor, with watertight bulkheads fore and aft, provided a virtually watertight box within the hull. Other modifications introduced for the first time included a combined mast exhaust, a Kent clear-view screen, a twin R/T aerial, which gave a better range than previous aerials, and wooden bulwarks forward and aft for greater protection from the sea. The superstructure was from aluminium and housed a cabin sited forward of the engine room. Radio telephony equipment and a loudhailer were installed, while a line-throwing pistol and electric searchlight were also carried. In rough weather, up to seventy people could be taken on board.

In May 1954 the prototype, William Taylor of Oldham (ON.907), was taken on a lengthy trials passage up the east coast of Britain, going as far as Inverness, then being taken through the Caledonian Canal and down the west coast back to Littlehampton, visiting lifeboat stations on the way. This not only gave many crews the chance to handle the boat at first hand,

▶ Cutaway drawing of the first 42ft Watson William Taylor of Oldham (ON.907) as she was when built, with an open aft cockpit. (By courtesy of the RNLI)

▼ Charles Dibdin (Civil Service No.32) (ON.948) heading towards the beach at Walmer. In the later stages of her career, she had her aft cockpit enclosed and was fitted with a radar, giving the boat a very different appearance. (Phil Weeks)

22 • Watson motor 42ft

	Year* (Yd No) Builder Place	Name Donor	ON Cost Weight	Engines (Cockpit shelter fitted)	Stations (launches/lives saved)	Notes Disposal
1	1954 (907) William Osborne Littlehampton	**William Taylor of Oldham** Legacy of Miss Clare S. Taylor, Oldham.	907 £29,688 16t5	2x48hp Gardner 4LW (d) (1965)	Coverack 7.1954-5.1972 (49/32) Reserve 1972-1973 (11/10) Arklow 2.1973-7.3.1986 (54/30)	Sold 8.1986
2	1955 (909) William Osborne Littlehampton	**James and Barbara Aitken** Legacies of Miss A. Aitchison and Mrs A. Aitken, and gift of Dr and Mrs Aitken.	909 £25,859 15t18	2x48hp Gardner 4LW (d) (1971)	Troon 19.2.1955-1968 (91/32) Girvan 1968-15.10.1976 (29/26)	Damaged on service 15.10.1976 Sold 4.1977
3	1956 (922) William Osborne Littlehampton	**Watkin Williams** Legacy of Miss Mary Eames Williams, Deganwy, Carnarvonshire.	922 £27,801 16t18	2x48hp Gardner 4LW (d) (1972)	Moelfre 18.4.1956-9.1977 (131/143) Oban 1978-11.1981 (20/0) Reserve 1981-1983 (0/0)	Sold 5.1983
4	1956 (933) William Osborne Littlehampton	**J. W. Archer** Gift of Mr J. W. Archer.	933 £27,871 16t5	2x48hp Gardner 4LW (d) (1971)	Wicklow 7.6.1956-18.9.1987 (166/69)	Sold 31.3.1989
5	1956 (563) Groves & Guttridge Cowes	**Duke of Montrose** RNLI Funds.	934 £28,500 16t9	2x48bhp Gardner 4LW (d) (1971)	Arbroath 26.6.1956-17.12.1982 (64/30) Reserve 1982-1984 (7/0)	Sold 1.1985
6	1957 (937) William Osborne Littlehampton	**Mabel E. Holland** Gift of Miss Maud E. Holland, in memory of her late sister.	937 £30,000 16t17	2x48hp Gardner 4LW (d) (7.1967)	Dungeness 31.8.1957-7.9.1978 (220/74) Reserve 1979-1983 (10/0)	Beach version Sold 1983
7	1957 (941) William Osborne Littlehampton	**William and Mary Durham** Legacies of Mrs M. E. Durham and Mrs M.G. Davenport.	941 £29,500 16t16	2x48bhp Gardner 4LW (d) (1971)	Berwick 9.5.1957-17.9.1976 (55/18) Girvan 1977-16.2.1983 (21/7)	Sold 10.1983
8	1958 (W5470) J. S. White Cowes	**Alfred and Patience Gottwald** Legacy of Mrs P. A. Gottwald.	946 £30,000 17t1	2x48hp Gardner 4LW (d) (not fitted)	Aldeburgh 9.2.1959-4.8.1979 (84/31) Reserve 1979-1980 (0/0)	Beach version Sold 8.1980
9	1958 (948) William Osborne Littlehampton	**Charles Dibdin (Civil Service No.32)** Civil Service Lifeboat Fund.	948 £30,000 17t7	2x48hp Gardner 4LW (d) (1972)	Walmer 18.3.1959-3.2.1975 (143/115) Reserve 1975-1977 Eastbourne 21.5.1977-26.4.1979 (11/13) Aldeburgh 4.8.1979-7.6.1982 (13/5) Reserve 1982-1988 (total Reserve 28/4)	Beach version Sold 1988
10	1962 (600) Groves & Guttridge Cowes	**Dorothy and Philip Constant** Gift of Mr and Mrs Philip Constant, Bexhill-on-Sea.	967 £36,515.10.5 16t10	2x48bhp Gardner 4LW (d)	Shoreham Harbour 17.1.1963-21.8.81 (187/122) Oban 8.11.1981-10.6.1982 (7/1) Reserve 1982-1987 (9/15)	Sold 43.1988

WH indicates the year in which the cockpit was enclosed by a fixed wheelhouse

but also tested the new design as the extended passage was the equivalent of about five years of service.

In 1957 a different version was developed, which was suitable for launching across a beach on skids. The Beach version was constructed with a specially widened and strengthened hull to withstand grounding during the launch and recovery procedure at the few stations where beach launching was employed, such as Dungeness and Aldeburgh. The Beach lifeboats, of which three were built, were in other respects similar to their Watson counterparts, with the hull divided into nineteen watertight compartments and the superstructure of aluminium.

Alfred and Patience Gottwald (ON.946), which served at Aldeburgh, was fitted with a mizzen mast at the request of her crew, for steadying the boat in rough weather. The last 42ft Watson, Dorothy and Philip Constant (ON.967), was the only boat to be built with an enclosed steering position; enclosed wheelhouses were fitted to all but one of the 42ft Watsons while they were in service, to provide improved crew protection. Dorothy and Philip Constant carried 108 gallons of fuel; at full speed, she reached 8.56 knots, consuming 4.55 gallons of diesel per hour, giving a radius of action of 101 miles; she had a cruising speed of 7.5 knots, at which speed she consumed 1.84 gallons per hour giving a radius of action of 220 miles.

MOTOR LIFEBOATS

22 • Watson motor 42ft

▲ During their service careers, most of the 42ft Watsons were fitted with fixed shelters over the aft cockpit to provide improved crew protection, exemplified in this photograph of William Taylor of Oldham (ON.907), the first of the class. (Jeff Morris)

▲ The first 42ft Beach lifeboat Mabel E. Holland (ON.937) being beached at Dungeness. This photograph, which shows the lines and cabin arrangement of the 42ft Beach lifeboats, dates from the 1960s before the aft cockpit had been enclosed by a shelter. (From an old postcard supplied by Paul Russell)

▶ Watkin Williams (ON.922) at sea during the early years of her career at Moelfre, the station in Anglesey she served with distinction for twenty-one years. On 2 December 1966 she was one of two lifeboats which rescued the crew of the motor vessel Nafsiporos, for which her Coxswain, Richard Evans, was awarded the Gold medal by the RNLI. After her RNLI service ended, she was displayed at the Cardiff Industrial Maritime Museum. (By courtesy of the RNLI)

120　　MOTOR LIFEBOATS

22 • Watson motor 42ft

▲ One of the three 42ft Beach lifeboats Alfred and Patience Gottwald (ON.946) launching at Aldeburgh. She was fitted with a mizzen mast at the request of her crew for steadying the boat in rough weather. (Jeff Morris)

▲ William and Mary Durham (ON.941), destined for Berwick-upon-Tweed, on trials off Littlehampton in 1957. (By courtesy of the RNLI)

◀ Charles Dibdin (Civil Service No.32) (ON.948) on the launching cradle at the head of the beach at Walmer. All three of the 42ft Beach lifeboats were launched on skids across open beaches at their respective stations and were kept on some kind of cradle. (Phil Weeks)

MOTOR LIFEBOATS

121

23 • Watson cabin motor 47ft

KEY DATA
- Introduced 1955
- Last built 1963
- 18 built

SPECIFICATIONS
- Length 47ft
- Beam 13ft
- Draught 4ft 5in
- Crew 7/8

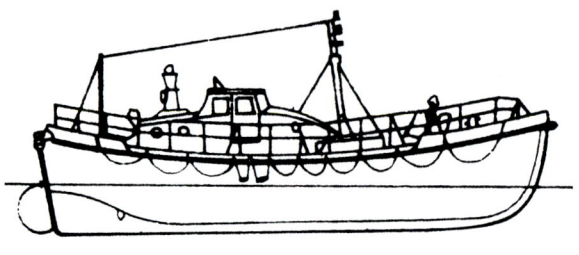

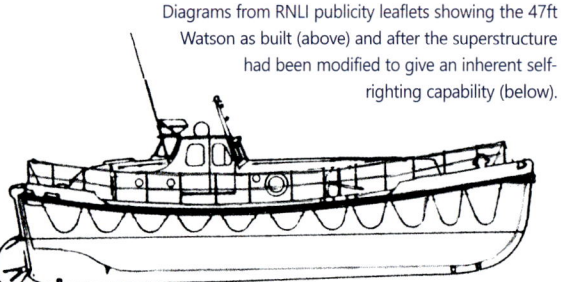

Diagrams from RNLI publicity leaflets showing the 47ft Watson as built (above) and after the superstructure had been modified to give an inherent self-righting capability (below).

▼ The first 47ft Watson Dunnet Head (Civil Service No.31) (ON.920) at Scrabster harbour for her naming ceremony; she served at Thurso for less than a year. (By courtesy of the RNLI)

The 47ft Watson cabin class represented a major revision of the basic Watson design, and proved to be the last Watson type built. It was the result of a design review that came to fruition in 1955 and which resulted in the main features of all three lifeboat types then in production, namely the 46ft 9in Watson, 52ft Barnett and 42ft Watson, being altered. The new 47ft Watson began the process, with deck layout features replicated in the other types, although it was essentially a development of the 46ft 9in Watson rather than a completely new design.

Design work on the Watsons was ongoing and the type was under constant review. So when further development was undertaken during the early 1950s a series of improvements were incorporated on the largest type then in build, the 46ft 9in version. The result was the new 47ft type, in which the main aluminium superstructure was extended forward and the forward shelter, which housed the engine controls and gauges, was more spacious than on previous Watsons. The midship steering position was fully enclosed from the outset, making this the first lifeboat type to have the cockpit covered, and the wheelhouse roof was extended aft so sliding doors could be fitted, port and starboard; the cabin had seats for nineteen persons. The general aesthetic design of the aluminium structure was revised to give the boats a more modern appearance.

The hull was more bulky than that of previous Watsons, with a displacement of approximately twenty-three tons, and it was divided into ten watertight compartments, being fitted with 293 air cases. Substantial bulwarks were fitted above the fenders fore and aft, with a rubber buffer at the bows instead of a separate bow pudding. Worm-drive steering was installed, rather than the self-centring mechanisms used hitherto, and this helped to make the boat more manoeuvrable. The aft cockpit, which had been a feature on the 46ft 9in Watsons, was retained, but there was not a duplication of the helm position in this location.

Power came from twin 60hp Gardner 5LW diesels, installed in an engine room with a watertight inner bottom, and the exhaust being carried up the main mast. The commercially-designed and -built Gardner engines had been used in the 42ft Watsons and were deemed suitable for the larger 47ft type. The first of the type, ON.920, reached a maximum speed was 8.69 knots and had range was 280 nautical miles, compared with 216 nautical miles of the 46ft 9in Watson. The second 47ft Watson, ON.940, had a maximum speed of 8.75 knots and a range of 286 nautical miles. The boats had a carrying capacity of 120 persons in fine weather and ninety-five in rough weather.

Upon completion, the prototype, named Dunnet Head (Civil Service No.31) (ON.920), was allocated to Thurso having been, experimentally, fitted with an echo sounder, among her other equipment. Prior to going to her station, she was taken on extensive trials around the UK and Ireland, and was inspected by deputations from thirty-two lifeboat stations. She became operational at Thurso in January 1956, and was named by HM The Queen Mother in August 1956. However, after less than a year of

MOTOR LIFEBOATS

23 • Watson cabin motor 47ft

	Year* (Yd No) Builder Place	Name Donor	ON Cost Weight	Engines	Stations (launches/lives saved)	Notes Disposal
1	1955 (920) William Osborne Littlehampton	**Dunnet Head (Civil Service No.31)** Civil Service Lifeboat Fund.	920 £35,000 22t9	2x60bhp Gardner 5LW	Thurso 29.1-10.12.1956 (1/4)	Destroyed by fire in boathouse, 10.12.1956
2	1957 (W5468) J. S. White Cowes	**Pentland (Civil Service No.31)** Civil Service Lifeboat Fund (RNLI Funds to replace ON.920).	940 £34,346 22t9	2x60bhp Gardner 5LW/ uprated to 70bhp (CM 1974-5)	Thurso 15.12.1957-15.12.70 (49/15) Reserve 1970-8.1974 (8/0) Mumbles 27.8.1974-3.7.1985 (50/21) Workington 21.2.1986-23.9.1990 (29/4)	Sold 3.1991
3	1958 (576) Groves & Guttridge Cowes	**Margaret** Legacies of Alexander Black, Edinburgh; and John Harold Taylor, Dore, Sheffield.	947 £35,000 22t7	2x60bhp Gardner 5LW (Air-bag)	Dunbar 4.2.1959-24.6.1986 (72/34)	Sold 1987
4	1959 (950) William Osborne Littlehampton	**Kathleen Mary** Anonymous gift (from Miss Joan Kircaldy of Streatham), in memory of Kathleen Mary Haddock.	950 £34,500 22t11	2x60bhp Gardner 5LW (CM 1978-9)	Newhaven 22.7.1959-5.5.1977 (234/123) Porthdinllaen 27.4.1979-27.4.1987 (53/28) Appledore 18.6.1987-7.6.1988 (4/1) Relief 1988-1990 (0/0)	Sold 4.1990
5	1959 (951) William Osborne Littlehampton	**Francis W. Wotherspoon of Paisley** Legacy of Mr F. W. Wotherspoon.	951 £34,432.18.7 22t7	2x60bhp Gardner 5LW (Air-bag)	Islay 11.7.1959-2.5.1979 (93/60) Relief 1979-2.1982 (3/0) Fishguard 2.4-9.1981 (3/1) Workington 2.1982-21.2.1986 (22/3)	Sold 10.1986
6	1960 (584) Groves & Guttridge Cowes	**Sarah Jane and James Season** Legacies of Arthur Season, Ilkley; Frederick Wright, York; Miss Ellen Lax, Leeds; and Mrs Harriet E. Pearson, Sowerby Bridge; and RNLI funds..	953 £34,831.9.1 22t11	2x60bhp Gardner 5LW (Air-bag)	Teesmouth 3.5.1960-22.1.1986 (101/28) Shoreham Harbour 16.7.1986-9.8.1988 (39/27)	Sold 1989
7	1960 (954) William Osborne Littlehampton	**Solomon Browne** Legacies of Miss Lydia Browne, Launceston; Miss Sara Wilhelmina Davies, Timperley, Cheshire; and Miss Blanche Waterhouse, Huddersfield.	954 £34,579.10.5 22t14	2x60bhp Gardner 5LW (Air-bag)	Penlee 4.7.1960-12.1981 (238/91)	Wrecked on service 19.12.1981, eight lost
8	1960 (955) William Osborne Littlehampton	**The Robert** An anonymous gift.	955 £34,826.12.10 22t17	2x60bhp Gardner 5LW/ 1977- uprated to 70bhp (Air-bag, CM 1976-7)	Broughty Ferry 17.11.1960-6.5.1978 (29/3) Baltimore 5.1978-17.7.1984 (44/31) Lytham St Annes 9.3.1985-1.12.1988 (25/11) Beaumaris 11.4.1989-4.7.1991 (2/1)	Sold 2.1992
9	1961 (587) Groves & Guttridge Cowes	**The Jeanie** An anonymous gift.	957 £35,509.1.11 22t13	2x60bhp Gardner 5LW (Air-bag)	Portpatrick 1.3.1961-3.1986 (89/46)	Sold 6.1987
10	1961 (588) Groves & Guttridge Cowes	**Laura Moncur** Legacy of Miss Laura Moncur, Edinburgh; gift from Miss Jessie Mavor, Skelmorlie; and RNLI Funds.	958 £35,636.15.8 22t12	2x60bhp Gardner 5LW/ 1974- uprated to 70bhp (CM 1972-3)	Buckie 6.1961-5.4.1984 (66/39) Relief 1984-1988 (12/8) Appledore 19.10.1986-18.6.1987	Sold 11.1988
11	1961 (589) Groves & Guttridge Cowes	**Helen Wycherley** Legacy of Mr H. Wycherley, gift from Miss Jane W. Robb, RNLI funds.	959 £35,478.19.7 22t5	2x60bhp Gardner 5LW (Air-bag)	Whitehills 6.1961-5.1969 (11/1) Courtmacsherry Harbour 23.8.1969-12.1987 (67/4)	Sold 12.1988
12	1962 (W5520) J. S. White Cowes	**T. G. B.** An anonymous gift.	962 £35,080.1.9 23t16	2x60bhp Gardner 5LW (Air-bag)	Longhope 24.4.1962-3.1969 (34/24) Arranmore 29.9.1970-28.10.1978 (41/31) Relief 1979-1985 (58/24)	Capsized on service 17.3.1969, eight lost Sold 1986
13	1962 (W5521) J. S. White Cowes	**A. M. T.** Legacies of E. A. Austin, New Barnet; Miss J. Mulhauser, Carshalton; A. Toon, Shilton.	963 £36,417.19.1 23t10	2x60bhp Gardner 5LW (Air-bag)	Howth 18.7.1962-23.8.1986 (197/83) Relief 1987-1989 (15/4)	Sold 6.1989

MOTOR LIFEBOATS

23 • Watson cabin motor 47ft

	Year* (Yd No) Builder Place	Name Donor	ON Cost Weight	Engines	Stations (launches/lives saved)	Notes Disposal
14	1962 (W5522) J. S. White Cowes	The Baltic Exchange Contributions from members of The Baltic Exchange.	964 £36,608.9.1 23t10	2x60bhp Gardner 5LW (Air-bag)	Salcombe 6.1962-30.8.1988 (258/76)	Capsized on service 10.4.1983, none lost Sold 1989
15	1962 (594) Groves & Guttridge Cowes	Louisa Anne Hawker Gift of Mr G. P. D. Hawker, Exeter.	965 £37,301.14.2 23t11	2x60bhp Gardner 5LW (Air-bag)	Appledore 5.1962-19.10.1986 (149/52)	Sold 4.8.1987
16	1963 (W5531) J. S. White Cowes	William Myers and Sarah Jane Myers Legacy of Miss E. Myers, Saltburn-on-Sea, Yorkshire, and RNLI funds.	969 £40,626.1.2 23t3	2x60bhp Gardner 5LW (CM 1975-6)	Sunderland 5.1963-17.4.1990 (201/36) Relief 1990-1.2.92 (0/0)	Sold 1992
17	1963 (W5532) J. S. White Cowes	Frederick Edward Crick Legacy of Mrs Florence May Crick, Longfield, Kent.	970 £41,028.4.4 24t3	2x60bhp Gardner 5LW (Air-bag)	Lowestoft 7.1963-19.10.1986 (247/109)	Sold 10.1986
18	1963 (W5533) J. S. White Cowes	Joseph Soar (Civil Service No.34) Civil Service Lifeboat Fund.	971 £41,105.18.3 23t1	2x60bhp Gardner 5LW (CM 1976-7)	St Davids 9.1963-11.12.1985 (99/45) Dunbar 24.6.1986-8.1988 (6/0) Shoreham Harbour 8.9.1988-30.9.1990 (29/8)	Sold 3.8.1992

CM – Cabin modified for self-righting

▼ 47ft Watson motor Kathleen Mary (ON.950) was built in 1959 and served at Newhaven as that station's last slipway-launched lifeboat before going to Porthdinllaen. (By courtesy of the RNLI)

service, she was completely destroyed when the Thurso boathouse caught fire in December 1956. The second 47ft boat, Pentland (Civil Service No.31) (ON.940), replaced her at Thurso in 1957. Owing to the difficulties in fitting the boat with her wheelhouse into the boathouse at Thurso, subsequent 47ft Watsons were offered to crews without the wheelhouse, but in the event all were built with enclosed wheelhouses.

Following the tragic capsizing on service of the 47ft Watson at Longhope, T.G.B. (ON.962), in March 1969 with the loss of eight men, and the capsize at Fraserburgh in December 1970 of the 46ft 9in Watson Duchess of Kent (ON.908), with the loss of five crew, the RNLI adopted a policy of making lifeboats self-righting. Those boats already in service were converted, while all new designs were inherently self-righting. Starting in 1973, most 47ft Watsons were fitted with an air-bag to give a once-only righting ability. This was mounted in a container on the aft cabin, and would inflate if the boat heeled over; other modifications saw replacement of the sliding access doors to the aft deck cabin with watertight doors to enable the sealing of the deck cabin, making it a completely watertight unit. The aft cockpit was also removed on most boats. The 47ft Watson at Salcombe, The Baltic Exchange (ON.964), capsized in April 1983, but righted, thanks to the inflation of her air-bag, and no crew were lost.

Six 47ft Watsons were rebuilt to become inherently self-righting: ON.940, ON.950, ON.955, ON.958, ON.969 and ON.971. The modifications on these involved considerable structural changes, including replacement of the superstructure forward of the wheelhouse with a longer and higher structure, an extension of the aft cabin to include the original after cockpit, and the fitting of a polyurethane foam block covered with glass reinforced plastic to the after cabin top; the top buoyancy was sufficient to give the boats a self-righting capability. During the conversion work, which was undertaken at William Osborne's Arun Shipyard in Littlehampton, the boats' engines were uprated to 70hp and the exhausts on these boats had to be diverted to the waterline, amidships. The 47ft Watsons enjoyed long careers, with almost all being operational for at least twenty-five years.

23 • Watson cabin motor 47ft

◀ 47ft Watson motor Francis W. Wotherspoon of Paisley (ON.951) was built in 1959 and served at Islay for twenty years. She is pictured at Port Askaig, her Islay base, for her naming ceremony on 22 July 1960. (By courtesy of the RNLI)

▲ The Baltic Exchange (ON.964) at her moorings in the estuary at Salcombe; the radar was fitted to the 47ft Watsons mid-life. The casing which houses the self-righting air-bag is fitted to the aft cabin and this inflated successfully when the boat was capsized on service on 10 April 1983. (Paul Russell)

▲ 47ft Watsons Joseph Soar (Civil Service No.34) (ON.971) and Margaret (ON.947, nearest camera) at Dunbar, showing the differences between the original deck layout and the converted layout to provide an inherent self-righting capability, with an enlarged superstructure. ON.971 was the last 47ft Watson built.

MOTOR LIFEBOATS 125

23 • Watson cabin motor 47ft

▲ Laura Moncur (ON.958) during her naming ceremony at Cluny Harbour, Buckie, on 26 August 1961; she was christened by Lady Saltoun. (By courtesy of John Innes)

▲ Laura Moncur (ON.958) leaving Buckie towards the end of her career after having been modified to be inherently self-righting; this photo shows the alterations to good effect. (By courtesy of Buckie RNLI)

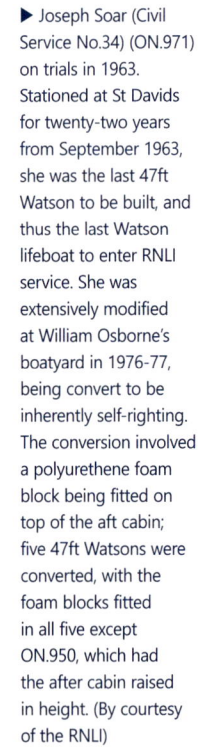

▶ Joseph Soar (Civil Service No.34) (ON.971) on trials in 1963. Stationed at St Davids for twenty-two years from September 1963, she was the last 47ft Watson to be built, and thus the last Watson lifeboat to enter RNLI service. She was extensively modified at William Osborne's boatyard in 1976-77, being convert to be inherently self-righting. The conversion involved a polyurethene foam block being fitted on top of the aft cabin; five 47ft Watsons were converted, with the foam blocks fitted in all five except ON.950, which had the after cabin raised in height. (By courtesy of the RNLI)

126   MOTOR LIFEBOATS

23 • Watson cabin motor 47ft

◀ William Myers and Sarah Jane Myers (ON.969) at Sunderland for her naming ceremony on 4 July 1963, during which she was dedicated by the Lord Bishop of Jarrow and christened by Mrs Marion Dawson. She was one of the last three Watson motor lifeboats to be built, and served at Sunderland for twenty-seven years. (By courtesy of the RNLI)

▼ William Myers and Sarah Jane Myers (ON.969) at Sunderland, where she served as the station's last slipway-launched lifeboat. The superstructure was modified at William Osborne's in the mid-1970s to give the boat an inherent self-righting capability, being extended fore and aft, and having the original aft cockpit position completely enclosed. (H. V. J. Cutter)

▶ T.G.B. (ON.962) on display at the Scottish Maritime Museum, Irvine. She capsized on service at Longhope in March 1969. (N. Leach)

▼ Frederick Edward Crick (ON.970) was the penultimate 47ft Watson and served at Lowestoft.

MOTOR LIFEBOATS

127

24 • 37ft Oakley

KEY DATA
- Introduced 1957
- Last built 1971
- 26 built

SPECIFICATIONS
- Length 37ft
- Beam 11ft 6in
- Draught 3ft 4in
- Crew 7/8

▼ Capsize trials of one of the first 37ft Oakleys; self-righting was achieved using an ingenious water ballast system within the hull. (By courtesy of the RNLI)

▶ The first 37ft Oakley J.G. Graves of Sheffield (ON.942) on trials; the Oakleys were much modified during their service careers.

▼ Launch of J.G. Graves of Sheffield (ON.942) from the beach at Scarborough. The Oakley was designed for carriage launching and many saw service on the east coast of England, where most stations employ this method of launching.

The 37ft Oakley class was designed by and named after Richard Oakley, the RNLI's Consulting Naval Architect. Developed during the mid-1950s, the 37ft Oakley was the first lifeboat design to have a high degree of inherent stability and also be self-righting in the event of a capsize. Previously, self-righting had meant lifeboats having relatively narrow beams, which made them more susceptible to turning over, and they were thus not always popular with crews. In the Oakley, righting was achieved by the use of an ingenious water ballast system, which involved the transfer of 1.54 tons of water ballast into a righting tank on the port side if the boat turned over. During trials, righting took about six seconds from the overturned position to the boat being upright.

The 37ft Oakley was built of wood and, with a displacement of 12.5 tons, was suitable for carriage launching and recovery on a beach. The self-flooding and emptying water ballast tank, fitted into the bottom, added over a ton of ballast in a position within the hull where it would be of most benefit when the boat was afloat. The water ballast taken on once afloat meant the boat had good sea-keeping qualities and provided crews with a solid working platform. The hull was subdivided into eleven watertight compartments and contained 222 air cases. PVC was used to provide buoyancy and blocks were used instead of smaller air cases. Aluminium was used for the double bottom, bulkheads and engine canopy, which helped to reduce the weight of the total machinery installation

In the event of the boat capsizing, provision was made to ensure it could continue to operate: a mechanism to stop the engines was fitted, and non-return valves prevented loss from the water, fuel and oil systems. There were removable independent fuel tanks in separate watertight compartments, and the exhaust and silencers were waterproofed.

The first five Oakleys were fitted with twin Perkins P4M four-cylinder diesel engines which gave a maximum speed of approximately eight knots. The remaining boats were fitted with slightly more powerful Ford Parsons Porbeagle four-cylinder diesels of 52bhp. Two of the Perkins-engined boats were re-engined with the Porbeagle engine during their service career. Those boats fitted with the 52hp Porbeagle diesels had a marginally better performance than the earlier boats powered by Perkins diesels, reaching a maximum speed of approximately 8.2 knots.

Having been built for service at Seaham Harbour, where she was slipway launched, the fifth Oakley, The Will and Fanny Kirby (ON.972), was rebuilt in 1982-83 so that she could handle the unique conditions

MOTOR LIFEBOATS

24 • 37ft Oakley

	Year* (Yd No) Builder Place	Name Donor	ON Cost Weight	Engines	Stations (launches/lives saved)	Notes Disposal
1	1957 (WO942) William Osborne Littlehampton	**J. G. Graves of Sheffield** Gift of the J. G. Graves Charitable Trust.	942 (37-01) £26,700 11t4	2x43hp Perkins P4M	Scarborough 21.10.1958-8.11.1978 (105/9) Relief 1979-1988 (31/9) Clogher Head 9.1988-3.1991 (9/3) Newcastle 1992-1993 (2/0)	Display at Chatham Historic Dockyard
2	1961 (WO960) William Osborne Littlehampton	**Manchester Unity of Oddfellows** Gift Independent Order of Odd Fellows, Manchester Unity Friendly Society.	960 (37-02) £28,215.3.3 11t17	2x43hp Perkins P4M/ 1982- 2x52hp Ford Thornycroft	Sheringham 10.7.1961-10.8.1990 (126/74)	Sold 4.1991 for display at Sheringham
3	1961 (W5496) J. S. White Cowes	**Calouste Gulbenkian** Gift of the Calouste Gulbenkian Foundation.	961 (37-03) £27,536.11.11 11t17	2x43hp Perkins P4M	Weston-super-Mare 17.3.1961-1.3.1969 (33/6) Relief 4.1970-11.1990 (107/15) New Quay 28.1.1990-17.1.1991 (6/6)	Sold 11.1991
4	1962 (595) G & Guttridge Cowes	**Robert and Dorothy Hardcastle** Legacy of Hugh Robert Hardcastle, Boston Spa, Yorkshire.	966 (37-04) £27,538.18.6 11t16	2x43hp Perkins P4M	Boulmer 10.1962-31.3.1968 (30/9) Filey 18.5.1968-2.6.1991 (180/221) Relief 1992-1993 (1/0)	Sold 4.1993
5	1963 (WO972) William Osborne Littlehampton	**Will and Fanny Kirby** The Mr and Mrs W. L. Kirby Benevolent Fund.	972 (37-05) £31,827.1.9 12t1	2x43hp Perkins P4M/ 1982- 2x52hp Ford Thornycroft	Seaham Harbour 10.9.1963-24.2.1979 (46/66) Relief 2.1979-1982 (9/7) Flamborough 18.1.1983-16.8.1993 (142/43)	Display at Chatham Historic Dockyard
6	1964 (WO973) William Osborne Littlehampton	**Fairlight** Legacies of Mrs K.E. Wood and Mrs F.M. Dudman.	973 (37-06) £31,863.13.11 12t8	2x52hp Parsons Porbeagle 4-cyl	Hastings 29.8.1964-15.5.1988 (207/144) Relief 5.1988-9.1989 (5/0) St Ives 9.1989-23.10.1990 (19/11) New Quay 27.1.1991-8.4.1992 (3/0)	Sold 10.1994
7	1964 (WO974) William Osborne Littlehampton	**Jane Hay** Legacies of Mrs M. Erskine, Miss A. Smith, and gift from Miss Gillespie.	974 (37-07) £31,848.9.5 12t4	2x52hp Parsons Porbeagle 4-cyl	St Abbs 3.11.1964-12.7.1974 (20/8) Relief 7.1974-5.1980 (30/12) Newcastle 11.5.1980-3.8.1992 (70/13)	Broken up 1995 at Arklow
8	1964 (G&G604) G & Guttridge Cowes	**Sir James Knott** Sir James Knott Trust, and RNLI General Funds.	975 (37-08) £32,183.0.4 12t4	2x52hp Parsons Porbeagle 4-cyl	Cullercoats 21.11.1963-4.5.1969 (15/14) Relief 5.1969-11.1972 (5/4) Redcar 28.11.1972-13.7.1985 (78/63) Relief 1985-5.1989 (28/0)	Sold 1990 for display at Kirkleatham Old Hall Museum, Redcar
9	1964 (G&G605) G & Guttridge Cowes	**Lilly Wainwright** Legacy of Mr J. H. Wainwright, gift of Arthur Jowett Fund, plus RNLI funds.	976 (37-09) £32,230.11.6 12t8	2x52hp Parsons Porbeagle 4-cyl	Llandudno 30.1.1964-7.8.1990 (124/58) Kilmore Quay 26.1.1991-1.12.1992 (11/2)	Sold 9.1993
10	1964 (G&G606) G & Guttridge Cowes	**Charles Fred Grantham** Legacies of Mrs E. W. Montford, Market Drayton; and Miss E. M. Dearden, Hyde.	977 (37-10) £32,277.12.11 12t4	2x52hp Parsons Porbeagle 4-cyl	Skegness 20.4.1964-7.8.1990 (148/96) Scarborough 10.1990-1991 (5/4) Relief 1.1991-7.1992 (1/0)	Broken up 8.1993 at Ridge, Dorset
11	1964 (W5542) J. S. White Cowes	**The Royal Thames** Legacy of D.A. Forster, gifts from G.J.F. Jackson and Miss Gwladys Ellison and RNLI funds.	978 (37-11) £31,749.0.10 12t5	2x52hp Parsons Porbeagle 4-cyl	Caister 21.2.1964-17.10.69 (30/15) Runswick 20.9.1970-30.6.78 (37/30) Pwllheli 18.5.1979-25.1.91 (32/7) Clogher Head 29.3.1991-3.3.93 (5/0)	Scrapped and sold 10.1994
12	1964 (W5543) J. S. White Cowes	**James and Catherine Macfarlane/ 1967- Amelia** Legacy of Mr R.F. Macfarlane/ 1967- legacy of Mrs A. Borland, RNLI funds.	979 (37-12) £31,858.19.7 12t8	2x52hp Parsons Porbeagle 4-cyl	Relief 23.5.1964-8.11.1978 (43/12) Scarborough 8.11.1978-27.9.1991 (116/18)	Sold 2.1992, display at Charlestown
13	1964 (W5544) J. S. White Cowes	**William Henry and Mary King** Legacy of Miss Jane Graham King and RNLI General Funds.	980 (37-13) £31,913.18.5 12t8	2x52hp Parsons Porbeagle 4-cyl	Cromer No.2 28.10.1964-22.6.1967 (12/1) Bridlington 2.9.1967-15.12.1988 (278/83) North Sunderland 30.3.1989-7.8.1990 (8/0)	Display at Drayton Park School, London, from 1993

24 • 37ft Oakley

	Year* (Yd No) Builder Place	Name Donor	ON Cost Weight	Engines	Stations (launches/lives saved)	Notes Disposal
14	1965 (WO 981) William Osborne Littlehampton	**Mary Pullman** Gift from the late Sir Derek Wheeler, Bt.	981 (37-14) £31,455.17.6 12t6	2x52hp Parsons Porbeagle 4-cyl	Kirkcudbright 2.5.1965-26.4.1989 (89/34)	Display at Baytree Garden Centre, Spalding
15	1965 (WO 982) William Osborne Littlehampton	**Ernest Tom Neathercoat** Legacy Mr E. T. Neathercoat, CBE, and RNLI Funds.	982 (37-15) £31,413.1.1 12t3	2x52hp Parsons Porbeagle 4-cyl	Wells 1.6.1965-3.7.1990 (85/16) North Sunderland 14.8.1990-7.1991 (16/0)	Display at Oulton Broad and Wells
16	1965 (WO 983) William Osborne Littlehampton	**The Doctors** Gift of Dr Nora Allan.	983 (37-16) £31,461.19.7 12t5	2x52hp Parsons Porbeagle 4-cyl	Anstruther 26.5.1965-18.3.1991 (78/22) Relief 1991-1993 (0/0)	Sold 1993 for display at Buckie Drifter Centre
17	1964 Herd & McKenzie Buckie	**Mary Joicey** Donation from the trustees of the late Mrs Mary Joicey, Sunningdale, Berks.	984 (37-17) £33,656.12.3 12t18	2x52hp Parsons Porbeagle 4-cy	Newbiggin 5.9.1966-28.2.81 (52/24) Relief 1981-89 (52/12) [inc Redcar 13.7.1985-22.7.1986 (2/0)] Hastings 15.5.1988-15.3.1989 (9/3) St Ives 29.3-21.9.1989 (5/0)	Display at Child-Beale Trust, Reading; later moved to Newbiggin for display
18	1967 Herd & McKenzie Buckie	**Valentine Wyndham-Quin** Legacy of Mr H. P. Harris and an anonymous gift.	985 (37-18) £33,895.17.4 12t6	2x52hp Parsons Porbeagle 4-cyl	Clacton-on-Sea 19.1.1967-7.1983 (179/61) Clogher Head 26.8.1984-9.9.1988 (9/5)	Display at Cromer, then Harwich Museum
19	1966 Morris & Lorimer Sandbank	**Lloyd's II** Gift from the Corporation of Lloyd's and Lloyd's Brokers.	986 (37-19) £29,133.13.3 12t10	2x52hp Parsons Porbeagle 4-cyl	Ilfracombe 8.7.1966-20.7.1990 (136/116) Sheringham 8.10.1990-18.4.1992 (12/0)	Broken up 1992 at Otterham, Kent
20	1967 (WO 991) William Osborne Littlehampton	**Edward and Mary Lester** Gift and legacy of Miss Mary Lester, Caernarvon.	991 (37-20) £37,102.13.5 11t6	2x52hp Parsons Porbeagle 4-cyl	North Sunderland 18.7.1967-30.3.1989 (109/27)	Broken up 1989 at Southampton
21	1968 (WO 992) William Osborne Littlehampton	**Frank Penfold Marshall** Gift of Mrs Dagmar Marshall.	992 (37-21) £38,207.16.8 12t	2x52hp Parsons Porbeagle 4-cyl	St Ives 7.1968-29.3.1989 (226/85)	Broken up 1989 at Southampton
22	1968 (WO 993) William Osborne Littlehampton	**Har-Lil** Legacy of Miss Jeanie B. Watt, Renfrewshire.	993 (37-22) £38,476.15.6 12t	2x52hp Parsons Porbeagle 4-cyl	Rhyl 26.9.1968-23.12.1990 (109/28)	Sold 12.1991
23	1968 (WO 994) William Osborne Littlehampton	**Vincent Nesfield** Mrs J Giddens' Fund, legacy of Mr Cowls and Mr Ringer.	994 (37-23) £38,879.5.10 12t8	2x52hp Parsons Porbeagle 4-cyl	Relief 1969-1993 (98/39) Port Erin 4.1.1972-1.7.1973 (1/0) Kilmore Quay 25.9.1989-26.1.1991 (12/3)	Broken up 1995 at Dumbarton
24	1970 (WO 995) William Osborne Littlehampton	**James Ball Ritchie** Gift of Mrs Ann A. Ritchie.	995 (37-24) £38,873.9.8 12t2	2x52hp Parsons Porbeagle 4-cyl	Ramsey 20.2.1970-12.7.1991 (144/77)	Broken up 1992 at Arklow
25	1970 (WO 996) William Osborne Littlehampton	**Birds Eye** Birds Eye Foods.	996 (37-25) £44,674.14 12t3	2x52hp Parsons Porbeagle 4-cyl	New Quay 16.7.1970-28.1.1990 (90/42)	Display at Sea Watch Centre, Moelfre
26	1971 (WO 18) William Osborne Littlehampton	**Lady Murphy** Legacy of Lady Frances Murphy, Dun Laoghaire, Co Dublin.	997 (37-26) £46,372.91 12t1	2x52hp Parsons Porbeagle 4-cyl	Kilmore Quay 7.2.1972-25.9.1988 (49/5)	Capsized on service 24.12.1977, one crew member lost Broken up 1995 at Arklow

24 • 37ft Oakley

at Flamborough, where the launchway at North Landing was particularly steep, and at low tide the boat had to be dragged across the beach to get afloat. Between 1982 and 1986 rigid wheelhouses were added to enclose the aft cockpits of all the Oakleys to improve crew protection. As boathouse height was a prime consideration for carriage-launched boats, the wheelhouses were folding as no fixed structure could be added above the casing top. A canvas sheet was also provided to cover the forward well. Radar was installed in the boats during the 1970s, with the equipment being fitted on a tripod mast at the forward end of the engine casing.

Only once was the self-righting ability called upon on service, when *Lady Murphy* (ON.997) was capsized twice off Kilmore Quay on 24 December 1977. On both occasions she righted successfully and the engines were restarted, but, of four crew members washed overboard during the second capsize, one was never recovered. Without the self-righting system, however, it is likely that none would have survived.

During the mid-1980s several of the Oakleys suffered serious problems of hull deterioration, and as a result a number had to be virtually rebuilt. When taken out of service, the boats were deemed unsuitable for private sale and the RNLI adopted a policy whereby a sale would only be agreed if the boat in question was going on static display and not afloat. Where a suitable buyer could not be found, the boats were broken up and a number of boats were completely dismantled as a result.

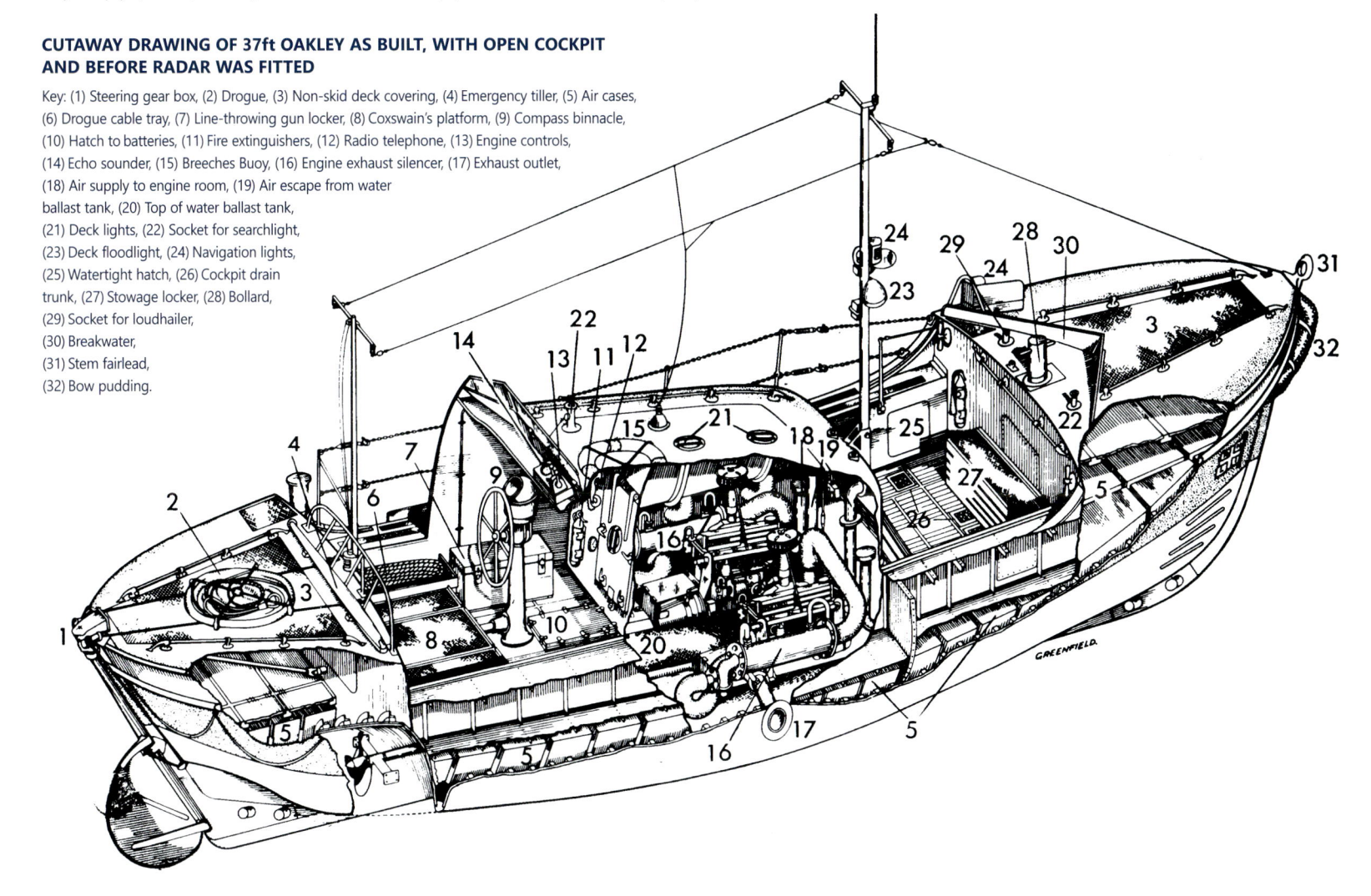

CUTAWAY DRAWING OF 37ft OAKLEY AS BUILT, WITH OPEN COCKPIT AND BEFORE RADAR WAS FITTED

Key: (1) Steering gear box, (2) Drogue, (3) Non-skid deck covering, (4) Emergency tiller, (5) Air cases, (6) Drogue cable tray, (7) Line-throwing gun locker, (8) Coxswain's platform, (9) Compass binnacle, (10) Hatch to batteries, (11) Fire extinguishers, (12) Radio telephone, (13) Engine controls, (14) Echo sounder, (15) Breeches Buoy, (16) Engine exhaust silencer, (17) Exhaust outlet, (18) Air supply to engine room, (19) Air escape from water ballast tank, (20) Top of water ballast tank, (21) Deck lights, (22) Socket for searchlight, (23) Deck floodlight, (24) Navigation lights, (25) Watertight hatch, (26) Cockpit drain trunk, (27) Stowage locker, (28) Bollard, (29) Socket for loudhailer, (30) Breakwater, (31) Stem fairlead, (32) Bow pudding.

MOTOR LIFEBOATS

24 • 37ft Oakley

▲ Launch of the second 37ft Oakley Manchester Unity of Oddfellows (ON.960) from the steeply inclined beach at Sheringham. The boat in pictured in the latter stages of her career having had a radar fitted and the aft cockpit enclosed. (Paul Russell)

▲ The tenth Oakley, Charles Fred Grantham (ON.977), built for Skegness, shortly after her completion, with grey engine casing and her aft cockpit open. (From an old postcard in the author's collection)

◀ 37ft Oakley Jane Hay (ON.974) as built, with an open after cockpit and no radar, on the slipway at St Abbs. After ten years at St Abbs she went to Newcastle for twelve years. (By courtesy of the RNLI)

▲ William Henry and Mary King served at Bridlington from 1967 to 1988 having been built for the Cromer No.2 station. Her operational number, 37-13, was not displayed on the engine canopy as it was considered to be unlucky. (By courtesy of the RNLI)

24 • 37ft Oakley

▲ Valentine Wyndham-Quin (ON.985) being recovered up the slipway at Clacton-on-Sea in the early days of her career, with an open aft cockpit and no radar. She was one of a number of 37ft Oakleys which were slipway launched. (By courtesy of the RNLI)

▶ Har-Lil (ON.985) being recovered on the beach at Rhyl in July 1988 during the latter years of her service career; she was replaced in 1990. (Nicholas Leach)

▲ Ernest Tom Neathercoat (ON.982) being recovered in Seahouses harbour during the boat's brief stint at North Sunderland. She left service in 1992, and has since been restored under private ownership at Wells.

▲ Lady Murphy (ON.997) returning to Kilmore Quay after she had capsized on service on 24 December 1977. Although she self-righted as designed, one of the lifeboatmen on board, Finton Sinnott, was lost.

MOTOR LIFEBOATS 133

25 • 37ft 6in Rother

KEY DATA
- Introduced 1972
- Last built 1982
- 14 built

SPECIFICATIONS
- Length 37ft 6in
- Beam 11ft 6in
- Draught 3ft 6in
- Crew 7/8

The 37ft 6in Rother was a development of the 37ft Oakley. The class was named after the river Rother, a tributary of the river Arun which flows through Littlehampton, where the first of the class was built. This first Rother, ON.998, successfully completed her self-righting trial at Littlehampton on 9 September 1972 watched by Major Osman Gabriel, of Hove, who had funded the boat. Named after the donor, this boat was displayed at the Earl's Court Boat Show in London in January 1973, and entered service at Port Erin in July that year. Over the course of the next ten years the RNLI ordered further Rother lifeboats and, in total, between 1972 and 1982 fourteen of the class were built.

The Rother's hull was basically the same as that of the Oakley, although it was longer at the bow by six inches. However, the superstructure was completely different, having been redesigned so that the self-righting potential was derived from the hull form itself, thus removing the need for the Oakley's water ballast transfer system. The almost full-length watertight casing, stretching from the fore buoyancy chamber to the aft end of the engine room, was the most noticeable difference between this design and the Oakleys. This superstructure, together with the hollow wheelhouse roof, provided the inherent self-righting capability. The space given to the water ballast tank in the Oakleys was taken up by a double-bottom void, so the engine room would not be flooded if the hull was holed.

The layout modifications were based on experience gained through operating the Oakleys. As the RNLI wanted to incorporate radar in new lifeboats built after 1972, the wheelhouse not only provided protection for the crew, but the aft end of the roof supported the radar scanner, which was hinged to swing down into a stowed position beneath the roofline to conform to the restricted headroom of boathouses. The wheelhouse almost fully enclosed the cockpit, which was open only at the rear, although this was eventually closed with a clear plastic screen in most of the boats. The radar control unit and screen, together with other radio equipment, was located in a recess built into the after engine room bulkhead.

The Rothers were powered by twin 52bhp Ford Thornycroft type 250 four-stroke marine diesel engines, driving twin propellers though two-to-one reduction gearboxes at 2,000rpm. The boats had a maximum speed of approximately eight knots and a range at full speed of 180 nautical miles. Of the fourteen Rothers, two, The Hampshire Rose (ON.1024) and James Cable (ON.1068), had strengthened hulls to withstand the rigours of launching over a beach on skids, at Walmer and Aldeburgh respectively, where they were kept outside on cradles. Three of the boats were launched by tractor and carriage, seven went to stations where they were slipway launched, and the other two, at Amble and Barmouth, were kept afloat.

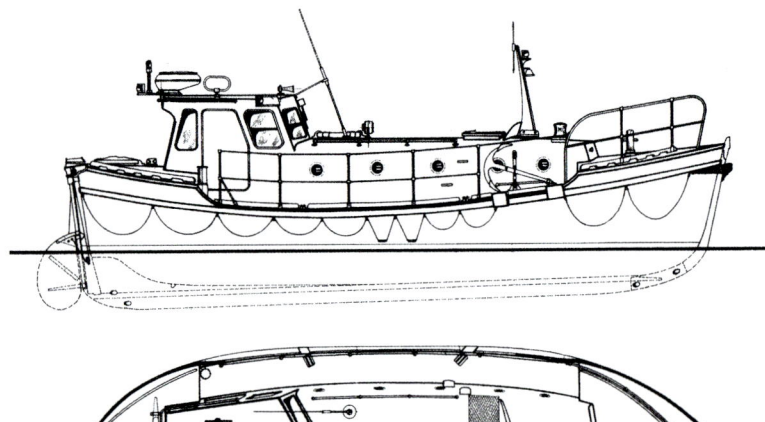

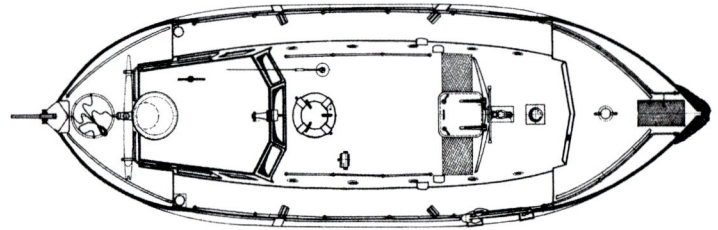

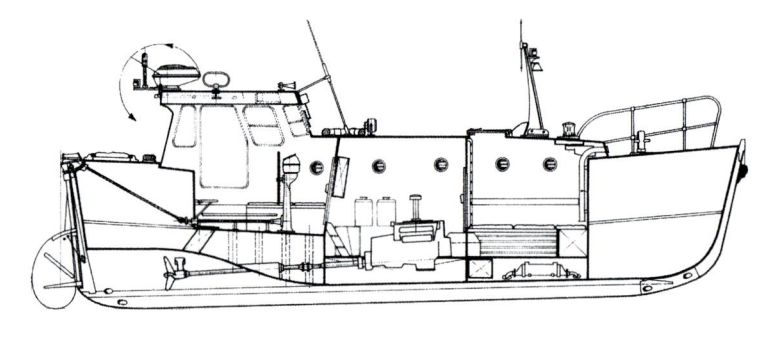

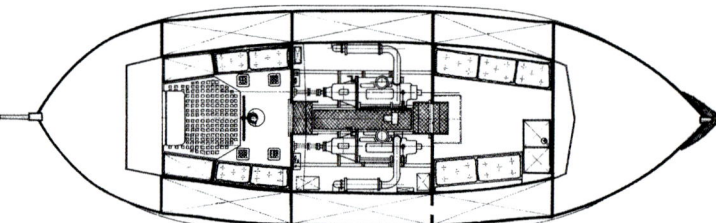

▶ The first 37ft 6in Rother class lifeboat, Osman Gabriel (ON.998), was completed by William Osborne in 1973 and is pictured at Littlehampton shortly after her completion. All but two of the Rothers were built in Littlehampton by Osborne. (By courtesy of the RNLI)

▼ Profile, deck layout and below deck plans of 37ft 6in Rother. The enclosed fore cabin, with access through the engine room and an escape hatch through the roof, provided, for the first time in a small lifeboat, a watertight dry survivor cabin.

MOTOR LIFEBOATS

25 • 37ft 6in Rother

	Year* (Yd No) Builder Place	Name Donor	ON Cost Weight	Engines	Stations (launches/lives saved)	Disposal
1	1972 (WO19) William Osborne Littlehampton	Osman Gabriel Gift of Major Osman B. Gabriel, Hove, Sussex.	998 (37-27) £64,528.69 12t10	2x52hp Ford Thornycroft 250	Port Erin 1.7.1973-22.6.1992 (70/55)	Sold 3.1993
2	1973 (WO20) William Osborne Littlehampton	Diana White An anonymous gift, part of the Cornish Lifeboat Appeal.	999 (37-28) £61,796.43 12t12	2x52hp Ford Thornycroft 250	Sennen Cove 11.1973-12.10.1991 (80/63)	Sold 1992
3	1974 (WO21) William Osborne Littlehampton	Mary Gabriel Gift of Major Osman B. Gabriel, Hove, Sussex.	1000 (37-29) £60,533.29 13t8	2x52hp Ford Thornycroft 250	Hoylake 18.5.1974-12.10.1990 (99/44) Rhyl 23.12.1990-3.4.1992 (6/0)	Sold 10.1992
4	1974 (656) Groves & Guttridge, Cowes	Harold Salvesen Gift of the Salvesen Trust.	1022 (37-30) £74,091.25 13t2	2x52hp Ford Thornycroft 250	Amble 6.1974-6.1986 (61/6) Relief 6.1986-1992 (34/3) Rhyl 3.4-23.6.1992 (1/0)	Sold 10.1992
5	1974 (657) Groves & Guttridge, Cowes	J. Reginald Corah Gift of the J. Reginald Corah Foundation.	1023 (37-31) £72,906.10 13t4	2x52hp Ford Thornycroft 250	Swanage 10.1975-12.6.1992 (411/240)	Sold 6.1995
6	1974 (WO141) William Osborne Littlehampton	The Hampshire Rose The Hampshire Rose Appeal.	1024 (37-32) £59,929.63 12t11	2x52hp Ford Thornycroft 250	Walmer 3.2.1975-5.5.1990 (132/57) Relief 1990-1992 (6/2) Anstruther 18.3-16.10.1991 (8/0)	Sold 10.1992
7	1977 (WO1117) William Osborne Littlehampton	Silver Jubilee (Civil Service No.38) Civil Service and Post Office Lifeboat Fund.	1046 (37-33) £101,715.83 13t7	2x52hp Ford Mermaid 397 4-cyl (d)	Margate 4.10.1977-19.12.1991 (163/76) Relief 1991-1.7.1993 (1/0)	Sold 3.1994
8	1977 (WO1118) William Osborne Littlehampton	Horace Clarkson H. Clarkson & Co Ltd.	1047 (37-34) £105,618.56 12t17	2x52hp Ford Mermaid 397 4-cyl (d)	Moelfre 10.1977-3.11.1986 (55/22) Relief 1987-1993 (49/37)	Sold 5.1993
9	1977 (WO1119) William Osborne Littlehampton	Alice Upjohn Gift of Miss U. M. Upjohn.	1048 (37-35) £101,992.14 12t18	2x52hp Ford Mermaid 397 4-cyl (d)	Dungeness 23.9.1977-24.9.1992 (147/45) Relief 1992-1993	Sold 1995
10	1979 (WO1666) William Osborne Littlehampton	Shoreline Shoreline Appeal.	1054 (37-36) £154,179.05 13t6	2x52hp Ford Mermaid 397 4-cyl (d)	Blyth 18.10.1979-26.10.1982 (9/1) Arbroath 17.12.1982-26.8.1993 (42/5)	Sold 2.1994
11	1979 (WO1667) William Osborne Littlehampton	Duke of Kent Eastbourne Lifeboat Appeal.	1055 (37-37) £157,448.19 12t10	2x52hp Ford Mermaid 397 4-cyl (d)	Eastbourne 26.4.1979-1.8.1993 (353/86)	Sold 6.1995
12	1981 (WO2091) William Osborne Littlehampton	Princess of Wales Welsh Lifeboat Appeal, and other sources.	1063 (37-38) £250,527.67 13t6	2x52hp Ford Mermaid Melody (d)	Barmouth 27.3.1982-7.10.1992 (36/8) Relief 1992-1993 (0/0)	Sold 15.5.1993
13	1981 (WO2092) William Osborne Littlehampton	The Davys Family Gift of Mrs A. E. Mason.	1064 (37-39) £245,515.08 12t18	2x52hp Ford Mermaid Melody (d)	Shoreham Harbour 21.8.1982-16.7.1986 (58/16) Relief 7.1986-1993 (27/6)	Sold 7.1995
14	1982 (WO2222) William Osborne Littlehampton	James Cable Aldeburgh Lifeboat Appeal, and other sources.	1068 (37-40) £277,005.33 13t5	2x52hp Ford Mermaid Melody (d)	Aldeburgh 7.6.1982-19.12.1993 (53/24)	Sold 8.1994

25 • 37ft 6in Rother

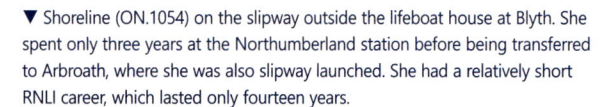

▲ Mary Gabriel (ON.1000) being launched at Hoylake on 20 June 1974 at the end of her service of dedication. The 1954-built Fowler tractor T61, which served at Hoylake from 1969 to 1975, was used prior to the introduction of the more powerful Talus MB-H crawler tractors. (By courtesy of the RNLI)

▼ The RNLI's carriage-launch rig as typified at Rhyl by Harold Salvesen (ON.1022) being pushed into the sea prior to launching. The boat was on relief duty at Rhyl, after twelve years on station at Amble, where she was kept afloat and thus had a red-coloured anti-fouled hull. (Nicholas Leach)

▲ Diana White (ON.999) launching on exercise down the slipway at Sennen Cove. Six of the Rothers were operated from stations where they were slipway launched, rather than carriage launched. (Peter Puddiphatt)

▼ Shoreline (ON.1054) on the slipway outside the lifeboat house at Blyth. She spent only three years at the Northumberland station before being transferred to Arbroath, where she was also slipway launched. She had a relatively short RNLI career, which lasted only fourteen years.

25 • 37ft 6in Rother

◀ The Hampshire Rose (ON.1024) on the slipway at the head of the beach at Walmer. She was one of two Rothers buil with specially strengthened hulls to withstand the rigours of being launched across a beach. (Phil Weeks)

▼ (left) Alice Upjohn (ON.1048) being recovered on the beach at Dungeness. She was the first lifeboat at the station to be launched by tractor and carriage, previous lifeboats having been launched across skids laid on the beach.

▼ (right) Princess of Wales (ON.1063), one of the last three Rothers to be built, served at Barmouth, where she operated from a mooring in the Mawddach estuary, and was one of only two Rothers kept afloat. She was originally allocated to Aldeburgh, but after her trials programme was reallocated to Barmouth (By courtesy of the RNLI)

MOTOR LIFEBOATS

26 • 48ft 6in Oakley

KEY DATA
- Introduced 1963
- Last built 1970
- 5 built

SPECIFICATIONS
- Length 48ft (only ON.968), 48ft 6in
- Length (waterline) 45ft 9in
- Beam 14ft
- Draught 4ft 8in
- Crew 7/8

The 48ft 6in Oakley, designed by Richard Oakley, was a larger lifeboat which incorporated the method self-righting employed on the smaller 37ft Oakley design of the 1950s, whereby the transfer of 2.75 tons of water ballast provided a self-righting capability. The water passed through three trunks or pipes, in each of which was fitted a valve which would open when the boat heeled over to an angle of about 110 degrees. The first boat, Earl and Countess Howe (ON.968), righted herself in five to seven seconds during her capsizing trials. The design also provided cabin accommodation for survivors, and was intended for stations with a slipway or where permanent moorings were used.

The first of the type, which measured 48ft in length, had an aft cockpit which was open towards the stern. The superstructure and deck layout of the other four boats, which were slightly longer at 48ft 6in, consisted of an enclosed steering position located amidships. In these latter four boats, the after cockpit was dispensed with and a cabin formed in its place, extending to the after end of the wheelhouse. This aft cabin could accommodate a loaded stretcher, and also served as the chartroom. Power came from twin Gardner 6LX diesel engines, each developing 110bhp at 1,200rpm, and driving two screws through a two-to-one reduction gearbox. This gave the boats a speed of approximately nine knots, consistent with the other displacement-hulled designs of the time. The air for the engines and ventilation of the boat was delivered by three electric fans. In the event of a capsize, the fans switched off automatically and the ventilation trunks were closed by automatic valves to prevent water from entering. All controls were centralised near the coxswain's position at the wheel.

The first of the class was the first RNLI lifeboat to be fitted with radar, wiht the Decca Type 202 set provided as a memorial to Joseph Conrad, the famous novelist. The wheelhouse shelter had a bulkhead at the fore end, in which was incorporated the instrument panel on the starboard side and the electronic console on the port side. The console also housed the medium wave radio, the VHF radio, the echo sounder recorder, the radar display unit and the radio direction finder. After completing extensive sea trials in the Littlehampton area, ON.968 went to Edinburgh, where she was shown at the ninth International Lifeboat Conference.

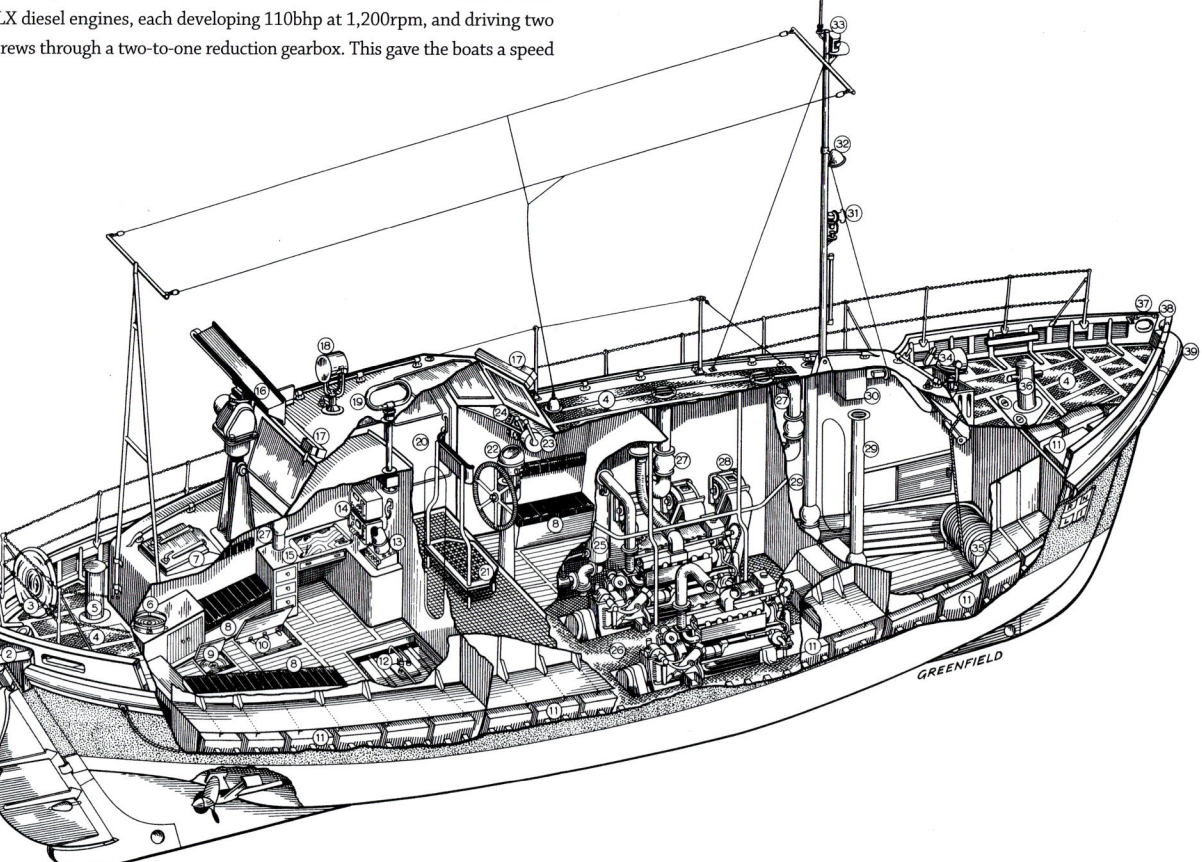

CUTAWAY DRAWING OF 48ft 6in OAKLEY MK.II WITH MIDSHIP STEERING POSITION

Key: (1) Drogue fairlead, (2) Steering gearbox, (3) Drogue, (4) Non-skid deck covering, (5) Quarter bollard, (6) Hot plate, (7) Escape and stretcher case hatch, (8) Locker seat, (9) Propeller scuttle, (10) Battery box compartment, (11) Air cases, (12) Fuel tank compartment, (13) Radar display, (14) R/T set, (15) Chart table, (16) Radar scanner, (17) Straight line windscreen wipers, (18) Searchlight, (19) DF loop, (20) Sliding door, (21) Coxswain's stool and backrest, (22) Compass binnacle, (23) Engine controls, (24) Echo sounder, (25) Engine exhaust silencer, (26) Top of water ballast tank, (27) Righting tank vent valve, (28) Water ballast tank transfer valve, (29) Air escape from water ballast tank, (30) Ventilation valve, (31) Electric horn, (32) Deck floodlight, (33) Masthead light, (34) Loudhailer, (35) Cable reel, (36) Towing bollard, (37) Fairlead, (38) Stemhead roller, (39) Bow pudding.

26 • 48ft 6in Oakley

	Year* (Yd No) Builder Place	Name Donor	ON Cost Weight	Engines	Stations (launches/lives saved)	Notes Disposal
1	1963 (WO968) William Osborne Littlehampton	**Earl and Countess Howe** RNLI General Funds.	968 (48-01) £55,725.3.7 29t2	2x110hp Gardner 6LX	Yarmouth 2.1963-19.2.1977 (168/92) Walton and Frinton 12.7.1977-15.1.1984 (64/21)	Display at RNLI Depot, Poole, 1983 to 2004, broken up 2004 at Portishead
2	1967 (944) Berthon Boat Co Lymington	**James and Catherine MacFarlane** Gift of Mr Robert E. MacFarlane, Glasgow.	989 (48- 02) £61,317.9.1 31t14	2x110hp Gardner 6LX	Padstow 19.7.1967-9.10.1983 (109/63) The Lizard 17.7.1984-20.12.1987 (22/6)	Sold 1988, display at Land's End complex, until 2016
3	1966 (WO990) William Osborne Littlehampton	**Ruby and Arthur Reed** Gift of Mrs R. M. Reed, Eastbourne.	990 (48- 03) £61,595.16.6 30t2	2x110hp Gardner 6LX	Cromer 3.1967-9.1984 (125/58) St Davids 12.1985-5.1988 (10/0)	Sold 9.1988, display at Hythe Marina, Southampton
4	1968 (WO1015) William Osborne Littlehampton	**Charles Henry** Legacy of Mr Charles Henry, Teddington, Middlesex.	1015 (48-12) £73,306.8.3 30t	2x110hp Gardner 6LX	Selsey 22.1.1969-21.11.1983 (176/80) Baltimore 17.7.1984-3.6.1987 (35/33)	Sold 1987, displayed at Merry Hill, near Dudley, until 2000
5	1970 (WO1016) William Osborne Littlehampton	**Princess Marina** Gift of H. M. Thomson Trust and legacy of Mrs D. H. Napier, Dumbarton.	1016 (48-13) £82,807.42 30t8	2x110hp Gardner 6LX	Wick 7.1970-16.9.1988 (70/31)	Display at National Motor Boat Museum fom 1989 to 2003; broken up at Portishead 2004

◀ The prototype 48ft 6in Oakley Earl and Countess Howe (ON.968) on trials. The only boat of the class built with an open stern cockpit, she was stationed at Yarmouth on the Isle of Wight and then Walton and Frinton in Essex. (By courtesy of the RNLI)

▼ Earl and Countess Howe on display at the RNLI Depot, Poole. She was displayed in Poole for a number of years until being broken up in 2004 being beyond economic repair. (Nicholas Leach)

MOTOR LIFEBOATS

26 • 48ft 6in Oakley

▲ Ruby and Arthur Reed (ON.990) served at Cromer for just over seventeen years, and is pictured with her superstructure gray, the livery used by the RNLI during the late 1960s, when the Oakleys first entered service. (RNLI)

▶ The last 48ft 6in Oakley, Princess Marina (ON.1016), served at Wick for her whole career. She was one of four Oakleys built with a midship steering position, and was one of two broken up after service. (By courtesy of Jeff Morris)

Only five 48ft 6in Oakleys were built, with the later four being different to the prototype in a number of respects, and more similar in appearance to the 48ft 6in Solent than to that of the prototype. These four boats were all sent to stations where they were kept in boathouses and launched down slipways. The final boat of the class was built in 1970 and served at Wick in the north of Scotland for eighteen years.

In the late 1980s the Oakleys, both the 48ft 6in version and the smaller 37ft boats, were prone to serious hull deterioration through the effects of electrolysis. This was caused by the water ballast system combining with the aluminium alloy construction of the inner bottom to cause the wooden hulls to rot. As a result, some of the Oakleys were withdrawn from service prematurely, being deemed beyond economic repair. The boats, being unsuitable for private sale due to their condition, were initially placed on display. However, two were later broken up, and the others subsequently entered pleasure ownership, having had the self-righting tanks removed.

27 • 48ft 6in Solent

The 48ft 6in Solent design was based on the 48ft 6in Oakley Mark II and was almost identical in external appearance and internal layout. However, the Solent was constructed with an all-welded steel hull and aluminium alloy upperworks, with the hope that this would reduce building costs when compared to those of the wooden-hulled Oakleys; however, in the event the savings were only about ten per cent. The design was inherently self-righting due to the large watertight superstructure and wheelhouse, which provided sufficient buoyancy in the overturned position to right the boat, so the somewhat complicated system of water ballast transfer used in the 48ft 6in Oakley was eliminated, and the boats were fitted with an iron ballast keel weighing 4.25 tons.

In place of the water ballast tank, a double bottom was formed below the engine room and this, the forepeak, the void under the after cabin and the wing compartments were all filled with rigid foam polyurethane to increase buoyancy and obviate the need for air cases. The hull was divided by four main watertight bulkheads and twenty-five watertight compartments. Cabin arrangements differed, with the first eight boats being fitted with sliding doors and a vertical steering wheel, while the last three had hinged wheelhouse doors and seated steering positions.

Power came from twin Gardner 6LX diesel engines, each of 110hp at 1,300rpm, with Gardner 2UC reverse and two to one reduction gearboxes. More than 200 gallons of fuel was carried; the after tank carried fifty-eight gallons and the fore tank 180 gallons, giving the boats a range of 240 nautical miles at full speed. One of the tanks was an integral part of the double bottom structure forward of the engine room, and the other was a steel tank of sixty gallons in capacity, separate from the hull structure and fitted abaft the engine room. All instruments and gauges were mounted on watertight bulkhead between the wheelhouse and the engine room. The two propellers were twenty-eight-inch aluminium bronze. The steering gear was of Mathway manual type, and twin spade rudders were fitted which gave improved manoeuvrability when compared with the Oakley and Watson designs in service in the 1960s.

The design was designated the Solent class in July 1969 after the river close to the yards at Gosport and Cowes where the boats were built. In total, eleven Solent class boats were built, with the first boat, George Urie Scott (ON.1007) going to Lochinver in the north of Scotland. Some were kept afloat at moorings and others were operated from slipways. The Solent was something of an anomaly in that it was the RNLI's last displacement hulled design, and boats of the class were being built at the same time as the first of the fast semi-planing lifeboats were entering service.

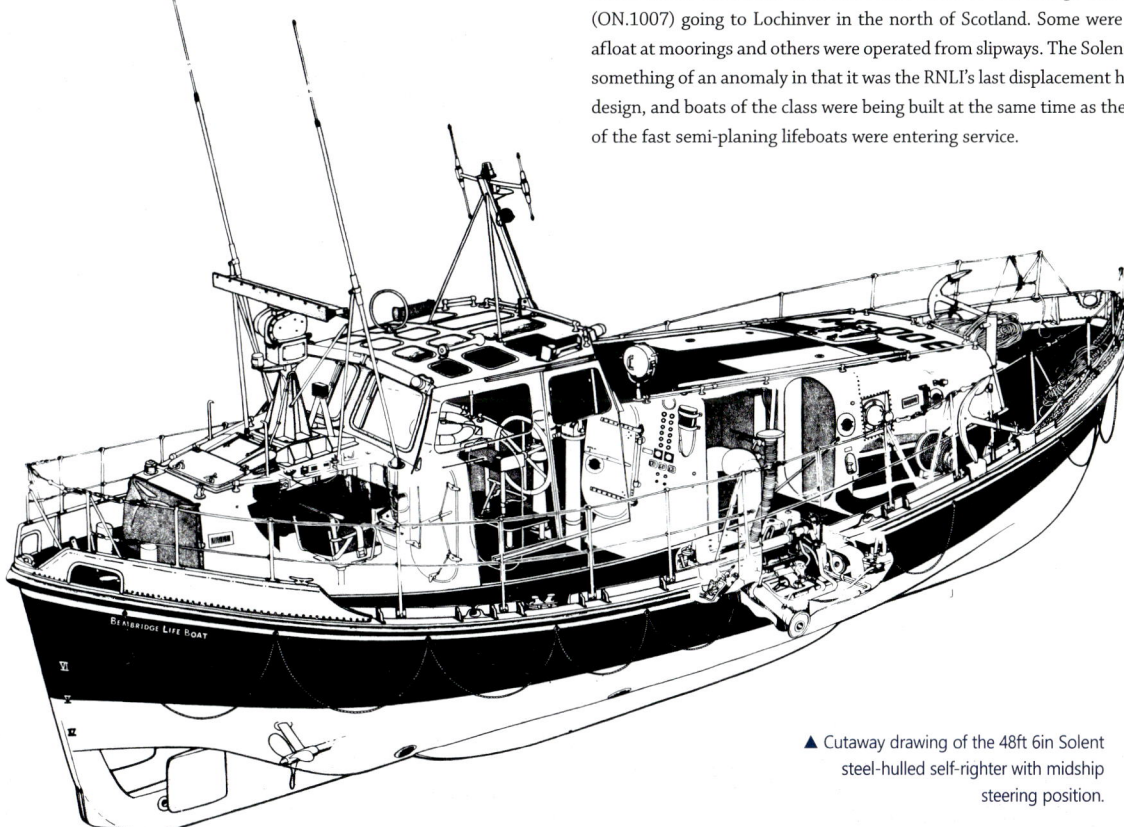

KEY DATA
- Introduced 1969
- Last built 1973
- 11 built

SPECIFICATIONS
- Length 48ft 6in
- Length (waterline) 45ft 9in
- Beam 14ft
- Draught 4ft 8in
- Crew 7/8

▲ George Urie Scott (ON.1007) moored at Rosslare Harbour in 1984. (Nicholas Leach)

▲ James and Mariska Joicey (ON.1008) on trials before being sent to Peterhead. (RNLI)

▲ David and Elizabeth King & E.B. (ON.1010) on trials prior to going to Longhope. (RNLI)

▲ Cutaway drawing of the 48ft 6in Solent steel-hulled self-righter with midship steering position.

MOTOR LIFEBOATS

27 • 48ft 6in Solent

	Year* (Yd No) Builder Place	Name Donor	ON Cost Weight	Engines	Stations (launches/lives saved)	Disposal
1	1969 (625) Groves & Guttridge Cowes	**George Urie Scott** Gift of Mrs Elizabeth Scott, Glasgow, in memory of her late husband.	1007 (48-004) £63,200.15.6 27t	2x110hp Gardner 6LX	Lochinver 27.5.1969-3.8.1978 (25/2) Rosslare Harbour 3.11.1979-1.6.1984 (26/4) Lochinver 13.2.1985-20.7.1989 (27/0)	Sold 1990
2	1969 (626) Groves & Guttridge Cowes	**James and Mariska Joicey** Legacy of Mrs Mariska Joicey, Richmond, Surrey.	1008 (48-005) £62,486 27t10	2x110hp Gardner 6LX	Peterhead 10.1969-7.12.1986 (72/41) Lizard 20.12.1987-17.8.1988 (3/0) Relief 8.1988-4.1989 (10/0)	Sold 1990
3	1969 (627) Groves & Guttridge Cowes	**Jack Shayler and the Lees** Legacies of Miss A. Shayler and Mr A. Lees, and RNLI Funds.	1009 (48-006) £59,323 27t15	2x110hp Gardner 6LX	Bembridge 17.1.1970-24.8.1987 (150/109) Relief 8.1988-5.1993 (15/7)	Sold 6.1994
4	1970 (628) Groves & Guttridge Cowes	**David and Elizabeth King and E.B.** Legacy of Miss C.A. King, plus an anonymous gift.	1010 (48-007) £58,936 27t9	2x110hp Gardner 6LX	Longhope 15.12.1970-26.3.1988 (77/32) Invergordon 7.1988-4.1989 (3/0)	Sold 1990
5	1969 (930) Camper & Nicholson Gosport	**R. Hope Roberts** Legacies of Mrs A. Ronald, Mrs R. Hope and Mrs Roberts, and an anonymous gift.	1011 (48-008) £72,462 27t17	2x110hp Gardner 6LX	Rosslare Harbour 16.7.1969-3.11.1979 (49/28) Fraserburgh 11.1979-5.1985 (28/12) Galway Bay 12.1985-7.1987 (37/5) Courtmacsherry Harbour 12.1987-5.1993 (47/34)	Sold 1993
6	1970 (931) Camper & Nicholson Gosport	**City of Birmingham** City of Birmingham Lifeboat Appeal.	1012 (48-009) £73,407 27t17	2x110hp Gardner 6LX	Exmouth 11.2.1970-4.8.1983 (58/19) Walton & Frinton 15.1.1984-1.8.1993 (186/40)	Sold 7.1995
7	1971 (932) Camper & Nicholson Gosport	**Royal British Legion Jubilee** The Royal British Legion.	1013 (48-010) £73,597 27t11	2x110hp Gardner 6LX	Relief 9.1971-11.1989 (56/50) Fraserburgh 29.4-3.11.1979 (3/11) Peterhead 7.12.1986-14.1.1988 (11/0)	Sold 2.4.1990
8	1970 (933) Camper & Nicholson Gosport	**The Three Sisters** An anonymous gift.	1014 (48-011) £73,260 27t7	2x110hp Gardner 6LX	Thurso 12.1970-3.1988 (97/23) Wicklow 10.10.1988-9.2.1989 (2/0)	Sold 2.4.1990
9	1972 (653) Groves & Guttridge Cowes	**Lady MacRobert** The MacRobert Trust.	1019 (48-014) £93,621 26t12	2x110hp Gardner 6LX	Montrose 12.1972-28.5.1989 (61/17) Relief 10.1989-12.1993 (38/35)	Sold 3.1994
10	1973 (654) Groves & Guttridge Cowes	**Hugh William, Viscount Gough** Gift of The Viscount Gough and Dowager Viscountess Gough.	1020 (48-015) £88,748 27t4	2x110hp Gardner 6LX	Stornoway 7.1973-6.3.1984 (75/49) Barra Island 16.6.1984-22.7.1988 (18/29) Dunbar 28.10.1988-1.8.1993 (33/8)	Sold 9.1993
11	1973 (655) Groves & Guttridge Cowes	**Douglas Currie** Gift from the Douglas Currie Trust; legacy of Mr J.J. Davidson; the Glasgow Ladies Lifeboat Guild; and various other gifts.	1021 (48-016) £95,289 27t5	2x110hp Gardner 6LX	Relief 10.1973-4.1974 (5/0) Kirkwall 6.1974-8.1975 (8/12) Macduff 9.1975-9.1984 (22/6) Fraserburgh 5-11.1985 (3/4) Portpatrick 1.3.1986-3.1989 (22/17) Workington 23.9.1990-8.6.1992 (15/0)	Sold 1992

27 • 48ft 6in Solent

◀ The much-travelled R. Hope Roberts (ON.1011) on exercise at Courtmacsherry Harbour, the last of four stations she served. (By courtesy of the RNLI)

▼ (left) Lady MacRobert (ON.1019) on relief duty at Walton and Frinton. She had previously served Montrose for almost seventeen years. (Paul Russell)

▼ (right) Hugh William, Viscount Gough (ON.1020) moored at Dunbar, where she served during the last years of her lifeboat career. (Phil Weeks)

MOTOR LIFEBOATS 143

28 • Clyde cruising 70ft

KEY DATA
▶ Introduced 1965
▶ Last built 1974
▶ 3 built

SPECIFICATIONS
▶ ON.987 and ON.1030:
Length 71ft (21.64m)
Beam 18ft (5.49m)
Length (waterline) (ON.987) 66ft
▶ ON.988:
Length 70ft (21.44m)
Beam 17ft (5.18m)

▼ The first 70ft Clyde, Charles H. Barrett (Civil Service No.35) (ON.987), served at Clovelly, covering the Bristol Channel, and in the Orkney area before being allocated to the Relief Fleet.

The 70ft Clyde class, the largest rescue vessels ever built by the RNLI, originated in the early 1960s after members of the Institution's Management Committee visited the Netherlands and Germany, where cruising lifeboats were successfully employed. In particular, the German lifeboat society, Deutsche Gesellschaft zur Rettung Schiffbrüchiger (DGzRS), had been using rescue cruisers extensively since the 1950s, with some vessels larger than 40m being operated from key stations and able to cover large areas of the North and Baltic Seas, operated by full-time crews living on board. In 1961, following a review of this visit, the decision was taken by the RNLI to commission the building of two long-range lifeboats. The result was the Clyde class, named after the river on which the first two boats were built, and designed as a cruising rescue craft with a full-time crew who would live on board.

The class was not only the RNLI's largest lifeboat, but was also the first to be constructed of steel. The hull design of the first and third boats, ON.987 and ON.1030, was produced by the RNLI's Naval Architect Richard Oakley, and that of ON.988 by John Tyrrell, FRINA, of Arklow, Ireland. The first two boats, ON.987 and ON.988, were similar in appearance, although dimensions, underwater lines and layout were slightly different. Further changes were made to the layout during annual surveys. The third boat had a superstructure which was much larger than that on the first two boats, giving the boat a completely different appearance and better accommodation. None of the boats was self-righting.

Unlike other lifeboat types, the Clyde had facilities for the crew to live and sleep on board, and the crew's quarters, arranged aft below deck, included four berths, lockers, a lavatory and a shower. At the after end of the wheelhouse was a small messroom and galley, with an electric cooker and refrigerator, and a lavatory attached to the forward cabin. In the forward cabin was stowage for six stretchers, and some of the seats could be converted into berths if needed. Abaft of the steering position in the wheelhouse was a small chart and radio room.

Two additional rescue craft were carried: the duty inflatable inshore rescue boat, stowed on the engine casing forward of the wheelhouse, was powered by a 33hp outboard motor and launched by derricks; a smaller boat of similar type, with an 18hp engine, was stowed in the forward cabin. The boats carried 250 gallons of fresh water, and their electronic equipment included radar, MHF ad VHF radios, a Decca navigator, two echo sounders, a loud hailer and an intercom unit linking the various compartments. Standard items of equipment included a searchlight, a deck floodlight, breeches buoy, parachute flares, hand flares, scrambling nets, a line-throwing pistol, hatchets, axes and knives.

The vessels' hulls were divided by six watertight bulkheads and each engine room was separated from the other by a longitudinal centre line bulkhead which was also watertight. Power was provided by twin Gardner 8L3B diesel engines, each developing 230bhp at 1,150rpm. These engines were the largest Gardners being built at the time. At the maximum speed

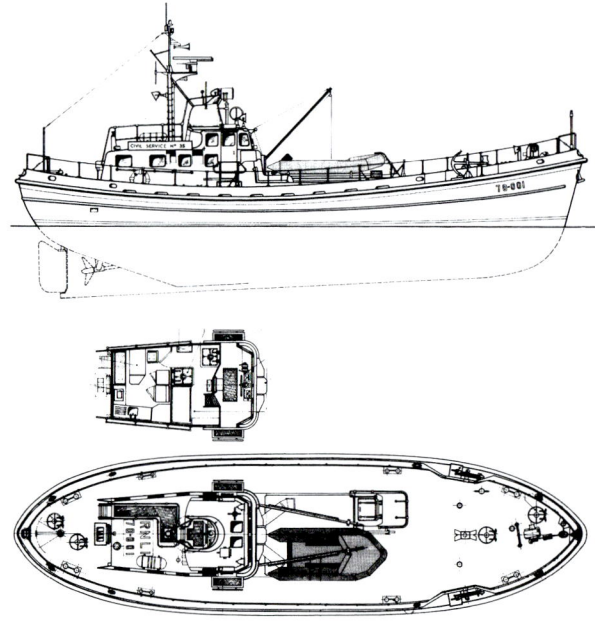

▲ Profile and deck layout of the first 70ft Clyde, ON.987.

MOTOR LIFEBOATS

28 • Clyde cruising 70ft

	Year (Yd No) Builder Place	Name Donor	ON (Op No) Cost Weight	Engines	Stations (launches/lives saved)	Disposal
1	1965 (2271) Yarrow & Co Scotstoun	**Charles H. Barrett (Civil Service No.35)** Civil Service Lifeboat Fund.	987 (70-001) £63,906.15.5 82t	2x230hp Gardner 8L3B 8-cylinder	Trials 2.1966-3.68 (at Ullapool 1966-67) Clovelly 3.1968-9.1975 (179/38) Relief 1975-27.5.1988 (107/58)	Sold 12.1988
2	1966 (2272) Yarrow & Co Scotstoun	**Grace Paterson Ritchie** Legacy of Miss Grace P. Ritchie.	988 (70-002) £65,112.19.9 78t14	2x230hp Gardner 8L3B 8-cylinder	Relief 1966-1975 (54/12) Kirkwall 3.1968-6.1974 (57/43) Kirkwall 8.1975-7.1988 (73/29)	Sold 1.1989
3	1974 (Y44) Bideford Ship Yard North Devon	**City of Bristol** Special Appeal in Bristol, and legacies of Mrs Q. Rimer, Dr S.M. Riddick, Mr S.V. Shrosbree, and Mr H.J. Vagg.	1030 (70-003) £208,462.26 85t4	2x230hp Gardner 8L3B 8-cylinder	Clovelly 9.1975-8.1988 (191/84)	Sold 12.1988

of 11.14 knots, the Clyde had a range of about 650 nautical miles, while at the cruising speed of 10.4 knots, at 1,000rpm, the range was 860 nautical miles. The Clyde was the first RNLI lifeboat design with a flying bridge position, which was located on top of the main superstructure and at which the engine and steering controls duplicated. Three anchors were carried: two standard RNLI pattern anchors, one each in port and starboard recesses, and a stockless anchor housed in the hawsepipe at the stemhead, which was raised by a hydraulic windlass on the foredeck.

ON.987 went into service in 1965 at Clovelly, North Devon, from where she covered St George's Channel, the southern end of the Irish Sea and the mouth of the Bristol Channel; ON.988 performed a similar duty from a base at Kirkwall, in Orkney, covering the treacherous Pentland Firth and surrounding area. The last boat, ON.1030, was built as a relief for the first two, but was sent to Clovelly where she became station lifeboat, leaving ON.987 to serve as the relief vessel. Up to 1975 the second Clyde, ON.988, was commanded by an RNLI inspector or staff coxswain, with a full-time crew, but when she went on station at Kirkwall she was operated as a normal station lifeboat with one full-timer and the rest of the crew made up of volunteers. This boat was involved in the extensive search for the capsized Longhope lifeboat T.G.B. (ON.962) in March 1969, and was tested to the limit on that wild night in the Pentland Firth, when eight volunteers from Longhope tragically lost their lives.

▲ The second of the three Clyde cruising lifeboats, Grace Paterson Ritchie (ON.988), served in Orkney, being stationed at Kirkwall for most of her RNLI career. After RNLI service, she was sold to the National Lifesaving Association of Iceland and renamed Henry H. Halfdanssen. In 2001 she was replaced by a newer lifeboat in Iceland and sold again, this time to a private buyer who brought her back to Scotland.

▲ The last of the Clyde cruising lifeboats to be built, City of Bristol (ON.1030), at Narrow Quay, Bristol for her formal naming ceremony on 1 September 1974. She served from a base at Clovelly in North Devon, covering the Bristol Channel, between 1975 and 1988. She was noticeably different in appearance to the other two boats, with a much enlarged superstructure. (By courtesy of Jeff Morris)

28 • Clyde cruising 70ft

▲ The first 70ft Clyde class lifebot, Charles H. Barrett (Civil Service No.35) (ON.987), on trials. She was funded by the long-established Civil Service Lifeboat Fund and named after the former honorary secretary and treasurer of the Fund. (Beken, by courtesy of the RNLI)

Although the Clydes were capable of remaining at sea for prolonged periods, having a large range and fully-equipped crew quarters, experience showed this to be an impractical and expensive way of operating in UK waters. Despite each boat having a relatively large sea area to cover from the respective operational bases, cruising operations were not appropriate to the kinds of rescues typically performed by RNLI lifeboats. In addition, the Clyde's draught was often too great for many rescue situations, and the boats proved rather costly to maintain and operate.

The boat at Clovelly always had a full-time crew, whose rota usually involved them working two weeks on and two weeks off, with a Staff Coxswain in charge, although at Kirkwall volunteers made up the crews. But in the end, the stations at which they were based used them as though they were ordinary lifeboats, and the eventual replacements were all of standard lifeboat designs. When the boats were sold out of service, they all thrived in private hands, with the second of the class serving in Iceland for a time as a lifeboat before ending up in private ownership in Scotland.

Chapter 5
The quest for speed

The quest for speed

◀ (chapter frontispiece) The 12m Mersey Sealink Endeavour (ON.1125) off Hastings, where she served from 1989 to 2018. (Nicholas Leach)

▲ The prototype 44ft Waveney 44-001 at Padstow in May 1964 during her evaluation tour of the UK. Developed and built in America by the United State Coast Guard, the 44-footer revolutionised British lifeboat design. (Grahame Farr, by courtesy of the RNLI)

▶ The 44ft Waveney Khami (ON.1002), second of the British-built Waveneys, pictured shortly after she entered service at Great Yarmouth and Gorleston, with her wheelhouse and aft cabin painted white. She served at Gorleston until 1980, when she was replaced by another new Waveney.

▼ The 44ft Waveney Thomas Forehead and Mary Rowse II (ON.1028) served at Plymouth for thirteen years and was then transferred to Fowey. On 15 February 1978 she stood by the trawler Elly Gerda, which was in difficulties in severe weather, and later rescued two of her crew after the trawler had run aground on the Rennis Rocks in a violent south-easterly storm with very heavy snow and a very rough sea conditions. For this rescue, the Bronze Medal was awarded to Second Coxswain Patrick John Marshall and Mechanic Cyril Alcock in recognition of their courage, determination and seamanship. (By courtesy of the RNLI)

During the 1960s, the RNLI began to introduce faster all-weather lifeboats, starting with a 44ft steel-hulled self-righting type which was purchased from the United States Coast Guard for trials around Britain. This was a significant step forward for the RNLI on a number of fronts. For the first time, the Institution had acquired a design not conceived by its own designers, and showed faith in radical ideas for a rescue craft, rather than continuing with the tried and trusted technology of post-war Britain. This boat, self-righting by virtue of its watertight cabins, was faster – at about fifteen knots – than conventional displacement-hulled lifeboats then in service, and was in many ways completely different from traditional British lifeboat designs.

The US boat, numbered 44-001 by the RNLI, was taken on an extensive tour round the British Isles, visiting as many lifeboat stations as possible so that crews' opinions of the new design could be gauged. The reaction of lifeboat crews who saw the boat at first hand was so positive that a building programme was soon embarked upon. Given the class name Waveney, the design was the first of the modern generation of 'fast' lifeboats. The British-built Waveneys entered service in 1967, the first at Dun Laoghaire to cover Dublin Bay and the busy approaches to Dublin port, and the second at Great Yarmouth & Gorleston in Norfolk.

The Gorleston boat, Khami (ON.1002), had an outstanding career lasting more than two decades and was involved in several medal-winning services during that time. The first took place on 9 November 1969, when she was launched under the command of Coxswain/Mechanic John Bryan to the Danish motor vessel Karen Bravo, which was listing in gale-force winds and rough seas. The lifeboat undertook a very rough passage until she reached the casualty, which was pitching heavily, with big seas breaking over her. In taking five people off, Coxswain Bryan placed the lifeboat's port bow alongside seven times, each time synchronising the lifeboat's movements with the heavy seas to reduce the distance the men would have to jump, while keeping the lifeboat clear of the ship's thrashing propellers. Once the five had been taken off, Khami and her crew stood by until, about midnight, the two vessels began to make for Gorleston harbour, reaching port in the early hours of 10 November. For outstanding seamanship, Bryan was awarded the Bronze medal and the Thanks of the Institution on Vellum was accorded to the other members of the crew.

The quest for speed

The Waveney proved to be a highly successful design and the twenty-two boats of the class that were built by the RNLI were well-liked at the stations from where they operated. The introduction of the design marked a breakthrough, with, for the first time, the Institution looking overseas for a design of lifeboat and showing a willingness to employ the latest technology. Previously, a more cautious approach had been taken with regard to lifeboat development, with new technology shunned in favour of equipment that was thoroughly tried, tested and proven.

The Waveney proved that cutting-edge technology could be beneficial, that fast lifeboats' sea-keeping qualities were more than good enough for search and rescue work, and, in the interests of greater speed, the RNLI was prepared to forego the heavy iron keels and twin propeller tunnels hitherto seen as integral to motor lifeboats. As a result, RNLI staff began to look at a larger and faster lifeboat in the late 1960s, as speedier craft would be able to better meet the changing demands placed on the lifeboat service by an increasing number of services to pleasure craft. The faster the lifeboat, the quicker a casualty could be reached, thus reducing the chances of a situation deteriorating and making a rescue more difficult.

The result of the RNLI's planning was a new 52ft type, the Arun class, which proved to be one of the finest lifeboat types ever developed.

▲ Rotary Service (ON.1031) was one of only two 50ft Thames class lifeboats to be built. Her hull configuration for operational service was very different from that of the original design, as she underwent significant modifications during the development stages until the design was deemed acceptable. (By courtesy of the RNLI)

◄ The second and third Aruns: the 54ft Arun Edward Bridges (Civil Service & Post Office No.37) (ON.1037, on left) was the first of the five 54ft Aruns that were built, and had the flying bridge forward on the wheelhouse; the second Arun, which was 52ft in length, Sir William Arnold (ON.1025), had a unique wheelhouse and flying bridge arrangement; she served almost a quarter of a century at the Guernsey station of St Peter Port, launching more than 500 times on service during an illustrious career. (By courtesy of the RNLI)

MOTOR LIFEBOATS

The quest for speed

Capable of between eighteen and twenty knots, the Arun represented a new direction for lifeboat design. It had a fully enclosed wheelhouse for rescuers and rescued, a flared bow to protect the deck and wheelhouse from spray and a broad beam for stability, and a flying bridge provided an outside steering position with good visibility. Another advance was the hull material. Although the first three boats were constructed from cold-moulded wood, the fourth boat was built in glass reinforced plastic (GRP), a material which the RNLI had considered but rejected previously; however, further advances in its construction meant it was suitable for lifeboats. Its advantages were its strength and economy of build, as a mould could be used to manufacture identical hulls at a time when wooden- and steel-hulled boats were becoming increasingly expensive. When the Arun was being designed, construction in GRP was always the intention, even though the early boats were of wood.

The Aruns, of which forty-six were built, were fantastic boats. Many outstanding rescues were performed using them, none more so than that undertaken in December 1981 by the St Peter Port lifeboat *Sir William Arnold* (ON.1025), the second Arun to be built. On 13 December she launched to the Ecuadorian motor vessel *Bonita*, which was in distress in the English Channel. The St Peter Port volunteer crew had carefully checked the boat in readiness for what would be a prolonged service in heavy weather before the moorings were slipped, and the Arun set out at full speed into storm force ten winds, gusting to hurricane force

▲ Two Aruns together at Longhope in June 2004: The Queen Mother (ON.1149, on left) was taking over station duties from the older Sir Max Aitken II (ON.1098), which had spent almost five years at the Orkney station, having been originally built for Stornoway. (Nicholas Leach)

▶ The 52ft Arun Davinia and Charles Matthews Hunter (ON.1078) was the twenty-first of the forty-six Aruns built by the RNLI for service around the coasts of the United Kingdom and Ireland. (By courtesy of the RNLI)

The quest for speed

twelve. The sea was extremely rough and, during the passage, the lifeboat broached six times, but full speed was maintained. At 4.30pm she arrived on scene, with the wind still force eleven and the violent storm creating fifteen-metre seas, and stood by as five people were lifted off by helicopter. However, when subsequent attempts to lift the remaining crew to safety failed, the lifeboat had to take over.

Sir William Arnold, under the command of Coxswain Michael Scales, spent three and half hours making a variety of approaches through floating wreckage to rescue twenty-nine people, with one man drowning. During the approaches, the lifeboat was rising level with *Bonita*'s afterdeck on each crest, and falling below the bottom edge of her rudder in the troughs, a distance of fifty feet. The first three men to jump to the lifeboat fell twenty-five feet to the deck and one was badly injured. In confused seas at the stern of the casualty, and despite the risk of severe damage, the lifeboat then rescued survivors using a heaving line. During one violent astern manoeuvre first one engine, then the other, failed. Although both were restarted quickly, the bow of the lifeboat was trapped under *Bonita*'s transom until the lifeboat's engines pulled her clear. Out of an estimated total of fifty runs in to the casualty, ten were made to take off one man.

When no more could be done to help, Coxswain Scales set course for Brixham and the passage, which involved the lifeboat heading into force ten to eleven winds and heavy seas, was an extremely arduous one. Speed was reduced to minimise the risk of further injury being sustained by the survivors. The lifeboat arrived at Brixham, where the crew, now completely exhausted, spent the night before returning home the following day, with only minimal damage to the lifeboat. For this outstanding service the Gold medal for conspicuous gallantry was awarded to Coxswain Scales and Bronze medals went to each of his crew. This extraordinary service was one of many medal-winning rescues undertaken in Arun lifeboats, which proved to be outstanding boats. Indeed, so good were they that many went overseas to continue as lifeboats after their RNLI careers had come to an end, notably in Iceland and China.

The introduction of the Waveney and Arun 'fast' lifeboats in the 1960s and 1970s marked the beginning of the modernisation of the lifeboat fleet, and during the 1980s and 1990s the quest for faster and safer lifeboats continued. In the early 1980s a large rigid-inflatable design was developed, the Medina, but it never entered operational service, while a smaller 33ft type, the Brede, was conceived from a successful commercial GRP hull form. Only twelve Bredes were completed and the design, which was regarded as an intermediate type with operational limitations, was something of an anomaly in the fleet.

▲ Sir William Arnold (ON.1025) returning to St Peter Port following the service to Bonita.

◄ Michael Scales and the St Peter Port lifeboat crew who were involved in the rescue of the motor vessel Bonita in December 1981.

◄◄ The 52ft Arun Murray Lornie (ON.1144), renamed Sigurvin, on station at Siglufjörður in Iceland in 2010. (Nicholas Leach)

▼ The 33ft Brede Leonore Chilcott (ON.1083) approaches the Town Quay at Fowey for her naming ceremony on 26 April 1984; the relief 33ft Brede Merchant Navy (ON.1087) is at moorings in the background. The Bredes were based on a Lochin 33 commercial hull, and only twelve of them were built. (Paul Richards)

MOTOR LIFEBOATS

29 • Waveney fast afloat 44ft

KEY DATA
▶ Introduced 1966
▶ Last built 1985
▶ 22 built

SPECIFICATIONS
▶ Length 44ft 10in
▶ Beam 12ft 8in
▶ Draught 3ft 118in
▶ Crew 6/7

The 44ft Waveney was a ground-breaking lifeboat design that gave the RNLI outstanding service and proved to be popular with the crews at stations where they served. The Waveney was notable for being the RNLI's first design of 'fast' lifeboat, one capable of more than nine knots, and as such represented a radical departure from the traditional designs used hitherto by the RNLI. Based on the United States Coast Guard's (USCG) 44ft steel-hulled lifeboat, it was adapted for service in UK waters after the RNLI had been trialled and tested the design during the 1960s. The 44-footer came to the attention of the RNLI at the International Lifeboat Conference in Edinburgh in 1963, when the USCG delegation described it as being the product of the most comprehensive construction and evaluation project ever undertaken for a USCG rescue craft.

Following this conference, in January 1964 a small RNLI delegation, led by the chairman, Captain the Hon V.M. Wyndham-Quin, visited the United States to inspect the country's rescue craft and in particular the 44ft lifeboats. On returning to London the delegation reported to the RNLI Committee of Management, who decided to acquire one of the 44ft vessels for evaluation. The USCG made a fully equipped boat, the 28th built at the Curtis Bay, Maryland facility, available for evaluation in the UK. After successful sea trials in America, the boat was accepted by the RNLI and shipped from Baltimore to the UK as deck cargo on a large cargo vessel. The boat arrived in London in May 1964 and, numbered 44-001 by the RNLI, became the prototype vessel. She undertook an extensive tour round Britain and Ireland, with the evaluation running until September 1965, by which time the boat had covered nearly 5,000 miles.

During the tour of lifeboat stations, coxswains and crews saw the radical design at first hand, and responded with favourable comments when on board and at sea. Following the success of the trials, the RNLI decided to order six boats based on the US design but incorporating a number of changes. The Brooke Marine yard in Lowestoft was awarded the contract for the boats' construction, and the class was subsequently designated the Waveney after the river close to the yard. The changes made by the RNLI included an additional fuel tank, the construction of a double bottom beneath the machinery compartment, an extended wheelhouse, raised fore and aft cabin tops to improve the self-righting ability, and an additional power take-off on the starboard engine to drive a hydraulic pump unit for the operation of a windlass.

▲ The prototype 44-footer, CG-44300, completed in 1962, during her trials. The design gained almost instant approval from the crews who tested her. (USCG photo, courtesy of William Wilkinson)

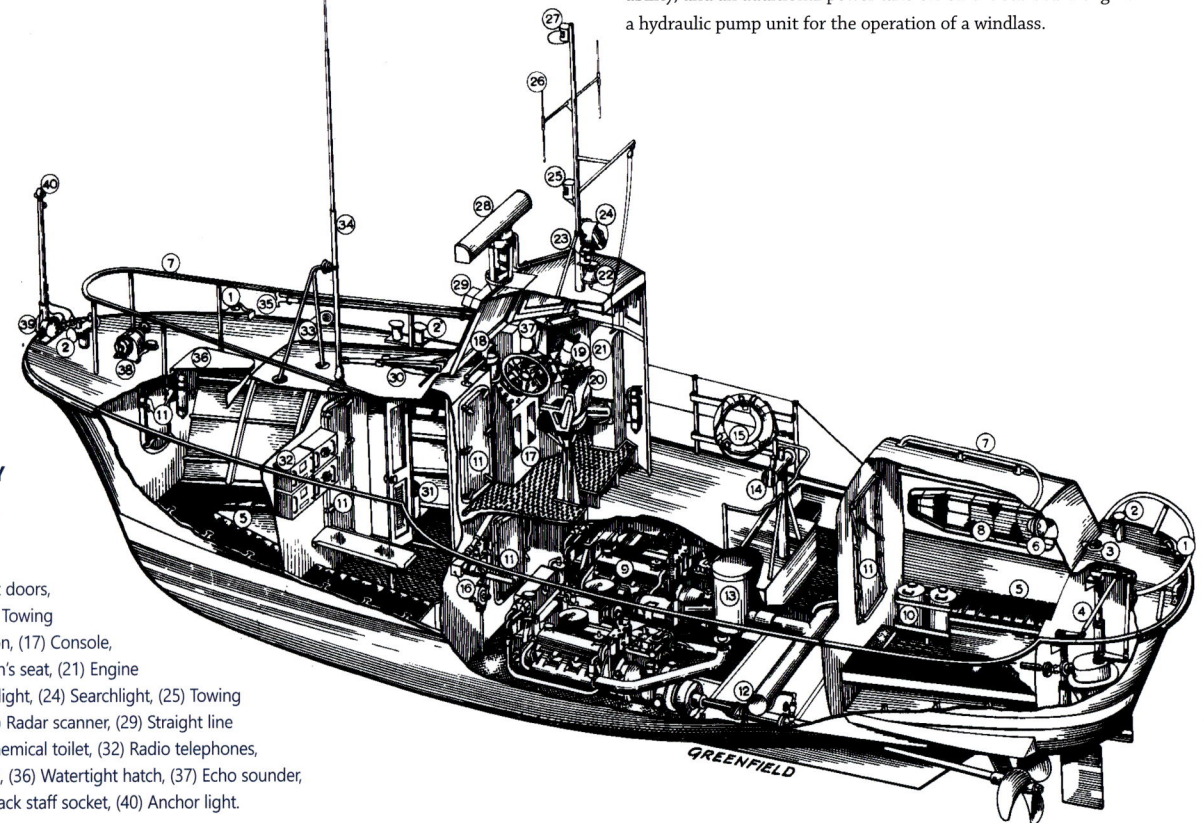

CUTAWAY DRAWING OF 44ft WAVENEY

Key: (1) Fairlead, (2) Bollard, (3) Emergency tiller cap, (4) Steering gear, (5) Locker seat, (6) Stern floodlight, (7) Grab rail, (8) Stokes stretcher, (9) Main engines, (10) 5-gallon foam cans, (11) Quick-acting watertight doors, (12) Exhaust outlet, (13) Engine exhaust silencer, (14) Towing bollard, (15) Breeches buoy, (16) Steering transmission, (17) Console, (18) Compass, (19) Radar display unit, (20) Helmsman's seat, (21) Engine room ventilation trunking, (22) Ship's bell, (23) Stern light, (24) Searchlight, (25) Towing light, (26) UHF dipole aerial, (27) Masthead light, (28) Radar scanner, (29) Straight line windscreen wiper, (30) 60lb Danforth Anchor, (31) Chemical toilet, (32) Radio telephones, (33) Lifting eyeplate, (34) Whip aerial, (35) Boat hook, (36) Watertight hatch, (37) Echo sounder, (38) Hydraulic windlass, (39) Stemhead fairlead and jack staff socket, (40) Anchor light.

MOTOR LIFEBOATS

29 • Waveney fast afloat 44ft

#	Year (Yd No) Builder Place	Name Donor	ON (Op No) Cost Weight	Engines (all diesels)	Stations (launches/lives saved)	Notes Disposal
1	1964 USCG Yard, Curtis Bay	[Not named] USCG Boat No.44328 RNLI General Funds.	— (44-001) — 16t14	2x200hp Cummins V6/ 1973- 2x250hp Mermaid 595/ 1982- 2x203hp Cat D3208	Trials round Britain 1964-67 Relief 1.2.1967-6.3.97 (291/100) Falmouth 8.1978-19.6.79	Display at Chatham Historic Dockyard, Kent
2	1966 (B348) Brooke Marine Lowestoft	John F. Kennedy Legacy of Miss Charlotte M.H. Gibson, Wellington, Somerset, and RNLI Funds.	1001 (44-002) £38,749.00 17t15	2x215hp Cummins V6N215M/ 1983- 2x203hp Caterpillar D3208	Dun Laoghaire 5.1967-29.3.90 (228/155) Relief 29.3.1990-22.8.96 (72/10)	Sold 1997
3	1967 (B349) Brooke Marine Lowestoft	Khami Gift of Mr and Mrs T.G. Bedwell.	1002 (44-003) £38,112.64 17t9	2x215hp Cummins V6N215M/ 1982- 2x203hp Caterpillar D3208	Great Yarmouth & Gorleston 19.8.1967-5.80 (234/71) Relief 6.1980-11.5.97 (240/90)	Sold 5.1999
4	1967 (B350) Brooke Marine Lowestoft	Faithful Forester Ancient Order of Foresters.	1003 (44-004) £37,985.17 17t18	2x215hp Cummins V6N215M/ 1982- 2x203hp Caterpillar D3208	Dover 7.1967-10.1979 (199/138) Holyhead 6.1984-20.9.85 (22/22) Relief 10.1979-27.6.97 (112/40)	Sold 5.1999
5	1967 (B351) Brooke Marine Lowestoft	Margaret Graham An anonymous gift to record the friendship of William Cavenaugh, Hazel Dugan, Theodore and Margaret Harley with the donor.	1004 (44-005) £43,020.19 17t13	2x215hp CumminsV6N215M/ 1982- 2x203hp Caterpillar D3208	Harwich 27.9.1967-3.1980 (173/77) Relief 5.1980-6.1986 (50/14) Amble 9.6.1986-7.1999 (164/6)	Sold 4.8.1999
6	1968 (B352) Brooke Marine Lowestoft	Arthur and Blanche Harris Legacy of Mrs B.A.L. Harris, London.	1005 (44-006) £38,318.59 17t5	2x215hp Cummins V6N215M/ 1979- 2x203hp Caterpillar D3208	Barry Dock 14.3.1968-1974 (108/44) Relief 1974-8.1979 (33/7) Donaghadee 23.8.1979-17.12.1985 (78/43) Relief 1985-93 (55/18) and 1995-6.1996 (9/5) Courtmacsherry Harbour 28.5.1993-9.1995 (17/7)	Sold 5.1999
7	1968 (B353) Brooke Marine Lowestoft	Connel Elizabeth Cargill Legacy of the late W. A. Cargill, Carruth, Bridge of Weir, in memory of his mother.	1006 (44-007) £38,343.59 17t18	2x215hp Cummins V6N215M/ 1982- 2x203hp Caterpillar D3208	Troon 8.1968-25.8.1985 (238/137) Arklow 7.3.1986-6.6.1990 (29/19) Relief 1990-27.9.1997 (33/3)	Sold 5.1999
8	1974 (G&G658) Groves & Guttridge Cowes	Eric Seal (Civil Service No.36) Civil Service Lifeboat Fund.	1026 (44-008) £81,864.31 17t18	2x260hp General Motors 8V-53	Eyemouth 2.1974-3.96 (153/45)	Sold 2000
9	1974 (G&G659) Groves & Guttridge Cowes	Helen Turnbull Legacy of Mr J.B. Turnbull, and Medway Lifeboat Appeal.	1027 (44-009) £73,271.53 17t12	2x260hp General Motors 8V-53	Sheerness 4.4.1974-3.96 (649/297) Achill 28.8.1996-10.10.97 (9/0) Relief 1997-98 (25/7) Sold 28.11.1998	
10	1974 (G&G660) Groves & Guttridge Cowes	Thomas Forehead & Mary Rowse II Legacy of Mr T. Field.	1028 (44-010) £68,736.94 18t2	2x260hp General Motors 8V-53	Plymouth 22.5.1974-31.10.87 (178/90) Fowey 26.1.1988-10.96 (169/35) Relief 10.1996-3.12.97 (4/0)	Sold 1999
11	1974 (G&G661) Groves & Guttridge Cowes	Augustine Courtauld Gift of Mr W. P. Courtauld, and Mayor of Poole's Appeal.	1029 (44-011) £68.736.32 18t1	2x260hp General Motors 8V-53	Poole 11.1974-10.1983 (106/32) Relief 10.1983-85 (8/5) and 1987-90 (9/0) Troon 8.1985-10.1987 (53/38) Arklow 6.1990-2.1997 (78/26)	Sold 21.5.1999
12	1974 (663) Groves & Guttridge Cowes	The White Rose of Yorkshire Gift of Miss Gwynaeth Milburn, Harrogate.	1033 (44-012) £79,018.34 19t2	2x260hp General Motors 8V-53	Whitby 11.1974-12.1988 (239/51) Invergordon 4.1989-5.9196 (66/10) Relief 5.1996-22.3.1997 (7/0)	Sold 11.6.1999
13	1974 (664) Groves & Guttridge Cowes	Thomas James King Proceeds of Jersey Lifeboat Appeal.	1034 (44-013) £79,049.44 18t2	2x260hp General Motors 8V-53	St Helier 8.2.1975-12.1989 (288/155) Relief 1989-93 (20/11) and 1.1996-1.97 (0/0) Dunbar 1.8.1993-1.1996 (21/0)	Sold 8.1998
14	1974 (665) Groves & Guttridge Cowes	St Patrick Proceeds of Irish Lifeboat Appeal.	1035 (44-014) £79,581.98 18t10	2x260hp General Motors 8V-53	Dunmore East 3.1975-10.1996 (252/83)	Sold 21.5.1999

29 • Waveney fast afloat 44ft

	Year (Yd No) Builder Place	Name Donor	ON (Op No) Cost Weight	Engines (all diesels)	Stations (launches/lives saved)	Notes Disposal
15	1975 (666) Groves & Guttridge Cowes	**Lady of Lancashire** An anonymous gift.	1036 (44-015) £85,967.18 18t4	2x260hp General Motors 8V-53	Fleetwood 1.1976-10.1989 (168/94) Dun Laoghaire 3.1990-5.1995 (80/4) Relief 1.1995-5.1996 (0/0)	Sold 11.1996
16	1976 (Y59) Bideford Shipyard North Devon	**Ralph and Joy Swann** Legacy Mrs A. G. Crathorne, and RNLI funds.	1042 (44-016) £128,524.51 19t0	2x250hp Mermaid 595T/ 1981- 2x250hp Caterpillar D3208T	Ramsgate 14.7.1976-2.1990 (292/199) Tobermory 6.8.1990-2.1991 (14/2) Portree 2.5.1991-6.1996 (60/4) Relief 1996-97 (13/1) Achill 10.10.1997-26.1.1998	Sold 6.1998
17	1976 (Y60) Bideford Shipyard North Devon	**The Nelsons of Donaghadee/ 1979- Wavy Line** Wavy Line Grocers Association.	1043 (44-017) £174,688.22 18t10	2x250hp Mermaid 595T/ 1978- 2x250hp Caterpillar D3208T	Donaghadee 10.1976-1978 (1/0) Relief 1978-90 (111/51) and 3.1997-3.98 (0/0) Sunderland 4.1990-3.1997 (113/20)	Sold 11.1997
18	1977 (Y61) Bideford Shipyard North Devon	**The Scout** The Scout Association.	1044 (44-018) £129,079.86 18t18	2x250hp Mermaid 595T/ 1982- 2x250hp Caterpillar D3208T	Hartlepool 2.1977-7.1997 (250/20)	Capsized on service, 28.2.1993, none lost Sold 1997
19	1977 (Y62) Bideford Shipyard North Devon	**Louis Marchesi of Round Table** National Association of Round Tables, Great Britain.	1045 (44-019) £139,823.50 18t14	2x250hp Mermaid 595T/ 1981- 2x250hp Caterpillar D3208T	Newhaven 5.1977-85 (289/134) Relief 8.1985-1986 (0/0) Alderney 10.1986-3.1994 (170/123) Exmouth 8.7.1994-7.1996 (39/5) Relief 12.1996-4.1997 (0/0)	Sold 12.2.1999
20	1980 (FM687) Fairey Marine Cowes	**John Fison** Gift of Mrs D. E. Fison and Mrs Knowles-Franks, legacy of Mrs Sutcliffe.	1060 (44-020) £243,487.34 18t16	2x250hp Caterpillar D3208T	Harwich 11.3.1980-10.1996 (232/97) Relief 1996-22.7.1999 (52/5)	Sold 24.8.1999
21	1980 (FM694) Fairey Marine Cowes	**Barham** Legacies of C. A. S. Stringer, Walton-on-Thames, and Mrs A. G. Miles, Southbourne.	1065 (44-021) £264,914.92 18t9	2x250hp Caterpillar D3208T	Great Yarmouth & Gorleston 5.1980-3.96 (254/71) Relief 4.1996-1999 (26/11)	Sold 1.11.1999
22	1982 (FM710) Fairey Marine Cowes	**The William and Jane** Legacies of Miss Hewson, Mrs Grey, Mr Dunn and others.	1079 (44-022) £319,940 18t1	2x250hp Caterpillar D3208T	Blyth 26.10.1982-12.1995 (136/43) Larne 19.3.1996-11.1996 (23/11)	Sold 7.1999

The hull was built from Corten steel, as in the original USCG design, as Corten had greater resistance to corrosion than other steel. However, the main deck plating and wheelhouse were of aluminium alloy, rather than steel as on the USCG version. These modifications were not carried out retrospectively on 44-001, which remained different from the British-built boats. The design was self-righting by virtue of the inherent buoyancy achieved through the watertight superstructure. To protect the vessel against damage should it be grounded, a double bottom was provided in the forward half-length of the boat, and a keel extended aft. The hull was further divided into seven watertight compartments, framed by a combination of transverse and longitudinal bulkheads. The compartments consisted of cable locker, forward cabin, crew's cabin, engine room, void compartment, after cabin and steering gear compartment.

The first seven Waveneys (including 44-001) were powered by Cummins engines, fitted with a reverse and three-to-one reduction gearbox, and achieved a top speed of thirteen knots. The next seven boats (44-008 to 44-015) were built with General Motors diesels, and the remainder had either Ford Mermaid or Caterpillar diesels, which gave a maximum speed of about sixteen knots. The earlier boats were subsequently re-engined with Caterpillar diesels during the course of their careers.

The RNLI built a total of twenty-one Waveney lifeboats, with the last leaving service in 1999. In America, more than 100 boats of the 44ft design saw service with the USCG, and the design was also used by the Canadian Coastguard, the Norwegian lifeboat service, the Iranian Navy and the lifeboat service in Portugal. A number of the RNLI's Waveneys were sold out of service to foreign lifeboat societies and continued life-saving duties in Australia, New Zealand and Namibia. In America the 44-footers were often called upon to battle surf at dangerous river bars and several capsized on service. In the UK, one of the Waveneys, The Scout (ON.1044), capsized on service, but successfully righted without the loss of any crew.

29 • Waveney fast afloat 44ft

▲ The RNLI's second Waveney, Khami (ON.1002), being lifted into the water at Lowestoft. The hull shape, keel and propellers are clearly shown in this photo. The early boats of the class initially had a white superstructure, but this was changed to the standard orange during the boats' service careers.

▶ Self-righting trials of Faithful Forester (ON.1003) at Brooke Marine, Lowestoft. The Waveney was inherently self-righting due to the hull shape and watertight superstructure, which made it unstable in the capsized position. All of the Waveneys underwent self-righting trials similar to that illustrated.

▲ Arthur and Blanche Harris (ON.1005) on trials shortly after being completed; she was one of the six Waveneys built at Lowestoft by Brooke Marine, and her first station was Barry Dock.

▲ The prototype Waveney 44-001 entering Newhaven harbour during a temporary stint there. Built in the USA, she came to the UK in 1964 and served the majority of her career as a Relief lifeboat. (RNLI)

MOTOR LIFEBOATS　　　155

29 • Waveney fast afloat 44ft

▲ The White Rose of Yorkshire (ON.1033) off Whitby. The 44ft Waveney was the first lifeboat at the station to be kept afloat, replacing a 41ft Watson that had been launched down a slipway into the harbour.

▶ Thomas James King (ON.1034) on exercise off Dunbar. She was originally stationed at St Helier, in the Channel Islands, and was named for that station's Gold medal-winning Coxswain. (By courtesy of the RNLI)

▼ (left) The Scout (ON.1044) at moorings at Hartlepool. The Scout capsized on service on 28 February 1993, but successfully righted without loss of life.

▼ (right) John Fison (ON.1060) on station at Harwich. She was the second Waveney to serve the station, replacing one of the earlier Waveneys, Margaret Graham (ON.1004), in March 1980. (Nicholas Leach)

156 MOTOR LIFEBOATS

30 • Keith Nelson intermediate 40ft

The unique 40ft Keith Nelson, ON.1017, was introduced in the late 1960s as an experimental lifeboat at a time when the RNLI was examining new design ideas and looking to build faster lifeboats. Designed by TT Boat Designs Ltd, of Bembridge, IOW, and moulded of glass reinforced plastic (GRP) by Halmatic Ltd, Havant, for Keith Nelson, Bembridge, the 40ft boat was used to test whether a standard GRP hull could withstand severe weather conditions and to enable the RNLI to assess the material's suitability for future lifeboat construction. ON.1017 was the first RNLI lifeboat to be built of GRP and underwent lengthy sea trials before being sent to selected stations for operational evaluation. The intention was to find a lifeboat as seaworthy as conventional lifeboats but faster and, by using GRP in the construction, built at substantially lower cost and wooden boatbuilding was becoming increasingly expensive.

The internal and deck layout of ON.1017 was designed by the RNLI, in conjunction with Keith Nelson, using a combination of chopped strand and woven rovings. About 440 cubic feet of polyurethane foam in blocks was incorporated to provide reserve buoyancy. The layout from forward consisted of the forepeak, forecabin, wheelhouse, engine room, aft shelter and after peak with the forecabin fitted with two seats and stowage for equipment. The forepeak was filled with foam and enclosed by a watertight bulkhead. The wheelhouse chart room contained the engine control panels and electronic equipment. The radar scanner and VHF and UHF aerials were mounted above the wheelhouse. An RFD six-man life raft was mounted on the aft deck and a towing post was fitted on the bridge deck.

The bulkheads and fuel tanks were moulded in the hull, with fuel carried in four tanks. The deck was a separate GRP moulding bonded to the hull. Fitted with twin Thornycroft six-cylinder four-stroke turbo-charged diesel engines developing 125hp at 2,400rpm, the boat had a maximum speed of nineteen knots and a cruising speed of seventeen. The two-to-one reduction gearboxes were supplied by the Self Changing Gear Co and were of the MRF 500 hydraulic type. With a fuel capacity of 320 gallons, she had a range of 440 nautical miles at her cruising speed.

The only Keith Nelson to be used by the RNLI was given the operational number 40-001 when she was introduced and, as part of her trials, was sent to Sheerness on evaluation with a view to Sheerness becoming a new lifeboat station. She remained at Sheerness from April to November 1969, proving the need for a lifeboat to cover the Medway, and then went to Calshot where she established another new station at the mouth of the Solent, gaining a distinguished service career there. Although ON.1017 was successful and proved that GRP was a suitable material for lifeboat design, one of the drawbacks of the Keith Nelson design was that it was not self-righting. So, by the 1980s, with the RNLI looking to operate a fleet entirely of self-righting lifeboats, it was taken out of service as soon as a suitable replacement, in the form of the 33ft Brede, was available.

KEY DATA
▶ Introduced 1968
▶ 1 built

SPECIFICATIONS
▶ Length 41ft 2in
▶ Beam 12ft
▶ Speed 19 knots

	Year (Yd No) Builder Place	Name Donor	ON (Op No) Cost Weight	Engines	Stations Disposal
1	1968 (1017) Keith Nelson Bembridge	**Ernest William and Elizabeth Ellen Hinde** Legacy of Mrs E. E. Hinde.	1017 (40-001) £24,559 11t15	2x125hp Thornycroft T.400	Sheerness 4.1969-20.11.69 (32/4) Calshot 25.7.1970-3.85 (199/88) Sold 9.1985

▲ The only 40ft Keith Nelson lifeboat used by the RNLI, ON.1017, on trials in 1969, prior to her being given a name; she was formally named at a ceremony at Calshot on 28 July 1972. (RNLI)

▲ Ernest William and Elizabeth Ellen Hinde (ON.1017) on trials prior to becoming an operational lifeboat at Calshot; she could reach speeds of up to nineteen knots. (RNLI)

MOTOR LIFEBOATS

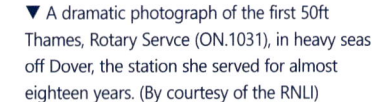

31 • Thames fast afloat 50ft

KEY DATA
- Introduced 1973
- Last built 1974
- 2 built

SPECIFICATIONS
- Length 50ft
- Beam 14ft 6in
- Speed 19 knots
- Crew 5/6

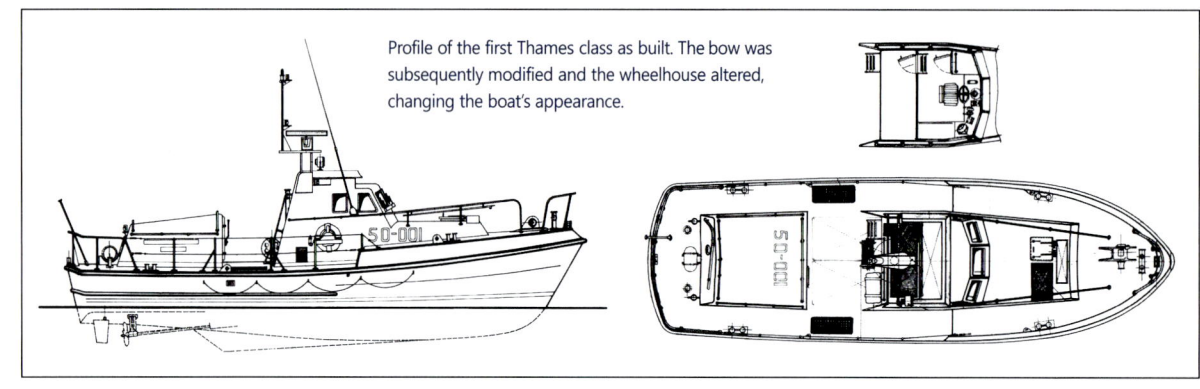

Profile of the first Thames class as built. The bow was subsequently modified and the wheelhouse altered, changing the boat's appearance.

▼ A dramatic photograph of the first 50ft Thames, Rotary Servce (ON.1031), in heavy seas off Dover, the station she served for almost eighteen years. (By courtesy of the RNLI)

The 50ft Thames was one of two designs for a fast lifeboat produced in the early 1970s (the Arun was the other), when the RNLI's Committee of Management realised that, after the successful introduction of the 44ft Waveney, a slightly larger and faster boat was needed. RNLI staff undertook the initial design for the 50ft boat, a detailed design study was carried out by the shipyard of Brooke Marine Ltd of Lowestoft, and a model was tank-tested by the British Hovercraft Corporation. The success of the tests resulted in an order for two boats with Brooke Marine, builder of the first Waveneys, who had already built a version of the 50ft boat which went on to be used as a pilot boat.

The design was based on that of the Waveney, but was 6ft longer and had a fully enclosed wheelhouse and chartroom, with a flying bridge above, while the engine room below the wheelhouse was also much larger than that on the Waveney. The hull plating was of Corten steel and the boat was subdivided into seven compartments by watertight bulkheads. These were: forepeak, anchor cable locker, forecabin, midships cabin, engine-room, after cabin and tiller flat. A double bottom extended from the forepeak to the after engine-room bulkhead. The boat was self-righting due to its inherent buoyancy, which was realised provided that the two watertight doors were closed to both cabins.

The design was designated the Thames class because most of the design work was carried out at the RNLI's London Offices by the Thames. Four further boats were ordered during 1974: ON.1038 to ON.1041, 50-003 to 50-006 inclusive; the first two from Brooke Marine, and the others from Richard Dunston, Hessle, near Hull. However, these were cancelled, never having been allocated stations, as the Arun class, which was being developed at the same time, was deemed more suitable.

The problems with the Thames hull design during their early years of service resulted in the boats being altered several times. During trials, the original bows on both boats were found to be unsuitable, making the boats very wet and sometimes difficult to steer on a true course. As a result, new GRP bows were built and extensively trialled. The new bow reduced wetness and enabled a better wheelhouse layout to be found for the crew. As a result, after the trials, new steel bows were built for both boats, and once these were deemed suitable the boats entered operational service.

The Thames were fitted with Decca Navigation Mk.21 equipment and a Kelvin Hughes Type 17 W radar, together with other standard electronic equipment. The main engines were twin General Motors 8V-7I diesels, each developing 390bhp at 2,300rpm, fitted with Allison hydraulically operated reverse reduction gearboxes. These gave a cruising speed of seventeen knots and a maximum speed of nineteen knots. The fuel capacity of 400 gallons meant that, at full speed, the range was almost 200 nautical miles, which increased to 229 nautical miles at cruising speed. The first Thames, Rotary Service (ON.1031), entered service at Falmouth in December 1974 and stayed in Cornwall for four years before being transferred to Dover, where she proved to be a busy lifeboat.

31 • Thames fast afloat 50ft

	Year (Yd No) Builder Place	Name Donor	ON (Op No) Cost Weight	Engines	Stations (launches/lives saved)	Notes Disposal
1	1973 (B394) Brooke Marine Lowestoft	**Rotary Service** Gift of Rotary International of Gt Britain and Ireland, legacies of Mr Craig, Miss Redgate and Miss Fowkes.	1031 (50-001) £199,041 24t15	2x390hp General Motors 8V71T	Falmouth 1974-1978 (45/17) Dover 3.10.1979-3.1997 (454/200)	Sold 1997
2	1974 (B395) Brooke Marine Lowestoft	**Elizabeth Ann/** 1979- **Helmut Schroder of Dunlossit** Various gifts and legacies/1979- gift of Bruno Schroder and Mrs Mallinckrodt.	1032 (50-002) £200,000 27t4	2x390hp General Motors 8V71T	Relief 1975-1979 (trials only) Islay 2.5.1979-2.1997 (210/60) Crew training (Poole) 1997-1998	Capsized and righted on service 18.11.1979, none lost Sold 1998

◀ Self-righting trials of Rotary Service (ON.1031) at Lowestoft; the boat was self-righting through inherent buoyancy, provided that the two watertight doors were closed. (RNLI)

◀ Two photographs of the first 50ft Thames Rotary Service (ON.1031) with different bows. The upper photo shows her at Falmouth being lifted into the water, and the lower photo shows her at Dover in her final configuration.

▼ The second Thames lifeboat Helmut Schroder of Dunlossit (ON.1032) on engine trials off Port Askaig, Islay, August 1996. (Nicholas Leach)

MOTOR LIFEBOATS

32 • Arun fast afloat 52-54ft

KEY DATA
- Introduced 1971
- Last built 1990
- 46 built

SPECIFICATIONS
- Length 52ft and 54ft (15.86m and 16.50m)
- Breadth 17ft (5.20m)
- Draft 5ft (1.50m)
- Speed 18.2 knots
- Range 220 nautical miles at full speed
- Crew 6 or 7
- Displacement 25.25 tons (prototype), 32.25 tons (steel), 31 tons (GRP)

During the 1960s the RNLI Committee of Management was looking to introduce faster offshore lifeboats into the RNLI fleet. The process had started with the Waveneys in the mid-1960s, but a larger lifeboat was needed. In the late 1960s the RNLI drew up a specification for a twenty-knot, fully self-righting all-weather lifeboat, of about 52ft in length which would lie afloat at moorings, and the design would be suitable for eventual construction in glass-reinforced plastic (GRP), which would be a first for the RNLI. Using GRP for lifeboat construction was the most economic path for the RNLI to take as building in wood and steel had become ever more expensive.

In 1969 the Committee decided to proceed with a design for a 52ft lifeboat, with a speed of between eighteen and twenty knots, which had been produced by Alan McLachlan, of Messrs G. L. Watson, Glasgow. His plans were for a transom stern semi-displacement hull 52ft in length, which had soft bilges and multiple spray rails at the waterline. The deep-V monohedron hull incorporated shallow tunnels to afford some protection for the propellers. The general arrangement and superstructure layout of the boat was developed by the RNLI's technical staff. The design was designated the class name Arun after the river at Littlehampton where the first boat of the new class was built, and she was launched in 1971.

The Arun reached speeds in excess of eighteen knots, as planned, making it twice as fast as earlier classes of lifeboats as a result of the semi-planing hull form. The hull shape and watertight wheelhouse provided the buoyancy necessary for inherent self-righting, and the flying bridge incorporated an upper steering position. The hull of the prototype was of cold moulded timber construction on laminated timber frames, with a double bottom extending practically the full length of the hull. An inner skin was formed to the sides of the boat and the resultant void, together with the double bottom, was filled with expanded foam polyurethane. The decking, longitudinal and transverse bulkheads, inner skin, and bottom were all made from mahogany plywood and transverse bulkheads subdivided the boat into six watertight compartments: forepeak, anchor cable locker, forecabin, engine-room, after cabin and steerage flat.

The prototype Arun had a straight sheerline and the flying bridge was located at the rear of the superstructure. The second boat also had the flying bridge at the rear of the superstructure but, as with all subsequent boats, had a cutaway freeboard to enable easier recovery of people in the water. The third boat was modified so that the flying bridge was sited forward and the Y class inflatable was placed behind it at the rear of the superstructure. The boat was steered from either inside the wheelhouse or from the flying bridge on top of the superstructure.

Inside the wheelhouse were seats, with safety belts and arm rests, for each member of the crew, with specific positions for the coxswain, navigator, radio operator, mechanic and crew members, together with seating provision for a doctor. The two survivors' cabins below

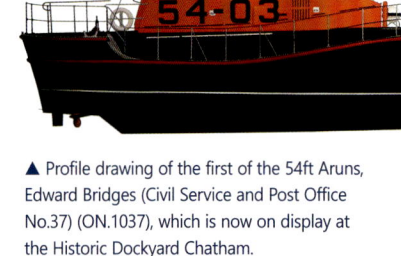

▲ Profile drawing of the first of the 54ft Aruns, Edward Bridges (Civil Service and Post Office No.37) (ON.1037), which is now on display at the Historic Dockyard Chatham.

Cutaway drawing of prototype 52ft Arun ON.1018

Key: (1) Inflatable dinghy, (2) Aft cabin with galley, (3) Flying bridge, (4) Radio/radar operator, (5) Coxswain's seat, (6) Watertight hatch to forward cabin, (7) Navigator's position, (8) Rope stowage, (9) Emergency life raft, (10) Forward cabin, (11) Cable locker, (12) Polyurethane foam buoyancy, (13) Petter generator set, (14) Two 375bhp Caterpillar D336 diesel engines, (15) Fuel tanks port and starboard, each of 259 gallons, (16) Coffer dam entrance to wheelhouse to prevent flooding if boat capsizes.

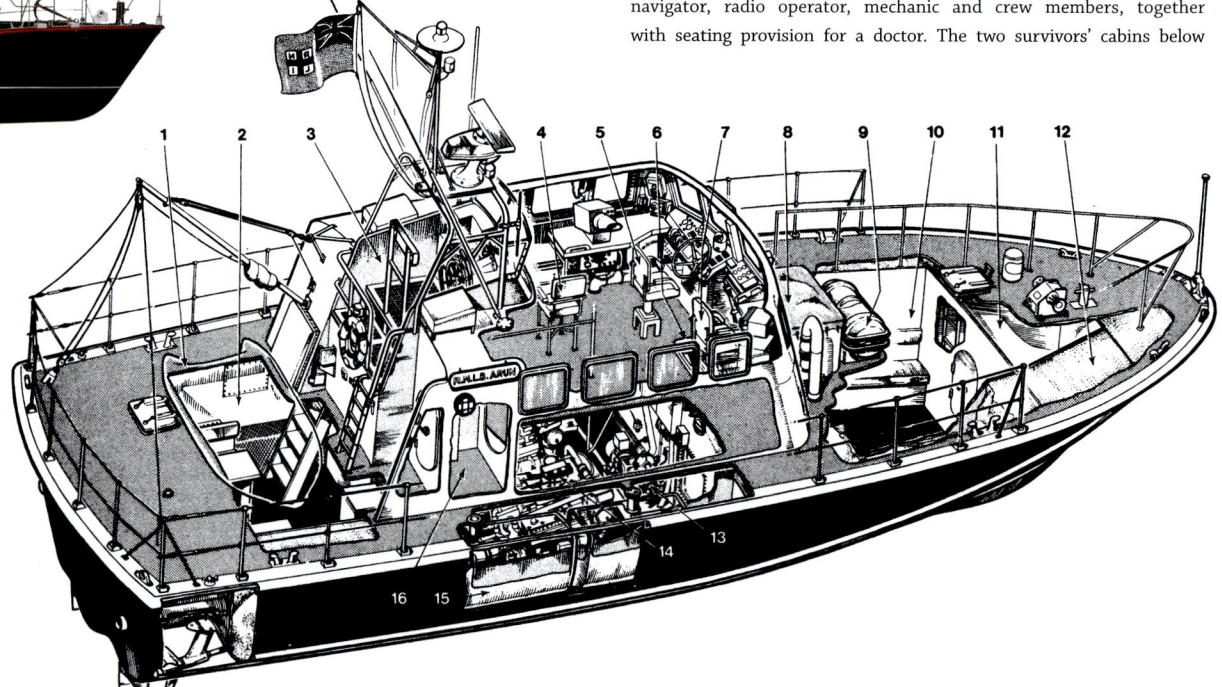

32 • Arun fast afloat 52-54ft

deck contained rescue equipment, including first aid gear, stretchers, emergency rations and blankets. A small Y class inflatable was carried on the wheelhouse roof for rescue work close inshore. The Y boat was originally launched by means of a manual davit, but this was later replaced by a ramp system down which the inflatable was launched over the stern.

The first three boats, ON.1018, ON.1025 and ON.1037, were all constructed in cold-moulded timber but later boats, with the exception of ON.1100, which was the only steel-hulled Arun, were constructed from glass reinforced plastic. Various other changes were made during the build programme: from 1978, ON.1057 (52-10), an aluminium alloy wheelhouse reintroduced; from 1979, ON.1058 (52-11), the wheelhouse layout was redesigned and an open plan was introduced; and from 1988, ON.1149 (52-43), the hull laminate was changed to epacryn resin.

The length of the boats varied slightly: five of the earlier boats, ON.1037 (54-03), ON.1049 (54-04) to ON.1052 (54-07), were 2ft longer, at 54ft in length through having a rounded transom, and indicated by the use of the operational number '54'. It was believed that this would give better handling in following seas and also make the corners of the transom less vulnerable. Subsequent boats had a square transom and were 52ft in length, as were the first two. All GRP-hulled boats were moulded by Halmatic Ltd, Havant, and fitted out by the builder listed. The wooden and steel-hulled Aruns were assembled complete by the builder as listed.

The first boat, ON.1018 (52-01), was powered by twin Caterpillar TA 0336 diesels. The second and third boats, ON.1025 (52-02) ON.1037 (54-03), were fitted with more powerful twin Caterpillar TA 343 diesels, each developing 460bhp at 2,000rpm, through two to one reduction gearboxes. The intention was that they would achieve twenty-two or twenty-three knots, but in practice the Aruns did not reach much more than twenty knots and eighteen was the norm.In addition to standard radio and other electronic equipment, these boats were fitted with Decca Mk.101 Super Radar, Decca Navigator Mk.21, and Decca Automatic Pilot Type 350. The last boat of the class was built in 1990 after a number of modifications had been made throughout the build programme.

Such was the success of the design that other lifeboat societies around the world have built Arun lifeboats. In 1988 a steel-hulled 52ft Arun was built by the Canadian Coast Guard, the success of which led to the building of further boats of the class with aluminium hulls, for service in Canada. The type is also used in Greek waters, with ten hulls moulded by Halmatic for the Greek Coastguard, while the RNLI has sold Aruns out of service to lifeboat SAR organisations in Iceland, Finland, Chile and Australia.

▼ (left) The second 52ft Arun, Sir William Arnold (ON.1025) at St Peter Port, Guernsey. Like the prototype ON.1018, she had a superstructure arrangement which was not repeated on any of the later Aruns. (Brian Green)

▼ (right) The prototype Arun lifeboat Arun (ON.1018) off Barry Dock in March 1997, towards the end of her operational career. (Nicholas Leach)

▼▼ The third Arun Edward Bridges (Civil Service & Post Office No.37) (ON.1037) at moorings in Brixham harbour while she was on station at Torbay. She was withdrawn from service in 1994 and placed on display at Chatham Historic Dockyard. The Arun was one of the most successful classes of lifeboat ever built and in 1982 the RNLI received a Design Council Award, presented by HRH Duke of Edinburgh, for the hull shape and overall design of the boat, the first lifeboat to achieve such recognition.

MOTOR LIFEBOATS

32 • Arun fast afloat 52-54ft

◀ The fourth Arun Tony Vandervell under way during her extensive tour round the UK and Ireland in 1975. She was the first GRP-hulled Arun and her hull, deck and superstructure contained nearly a ton of polyurethane buoyancy foam, six tons of glass fibre and three tons of polyester resin. The hull was built by Halmatic and the building work was completed in eighteen months. (By courtesy of the RNLI)

▼ (left) One of the 54ft Aruns, The Gough-Ritchie (ON.1051), on trials. She served at Port St Mary for more than twenty years. The manually-operated davit at the aft end of the wheelhouse was used to launch the Y class inflatable from the wheelhouse roof. The Gough-Ritchie was sold out of service to the Chilean lifeboat service and was renamed Capitan Eduardo Simpson Roth, being based in Valparaiso. (By courtesy of the RNLI)

▼ (right) Walter and Margaret Couper (ON.1059) served at Campbeltown for twenty years, and was one of the first three 52ft Aruns that saw the adoption of a more standard design. She was sold out of service in May 2001 to the Finland Lifeboat Society. (By courtesy of the RNLI)

162

MOTOR LIFEBOATS

32 • Arun fast afloat 52-54ft

	Year (Yd No) Builder Place	Name Donor	ON (Op No) Cost Weight	Engines (hull material)	Stations (launches/lives saved)	Disposal
1	1971 (22) William Osborne Littlehampton	**Arun** Birds Eye Foods, Miss Alice Johnston, and various other legacies.	1018 (52-01) £99,110.40 25t5	2x375hp Caterpillar D336/ 1992- Caterpillar 3208TA (wood hull)	St Peter Port 1.10.1972-6.11.1973 (25/13) Barry Dock 7.6.1974-5.1997 (331/75)	Sold 1997
2	1973 (93) William Osborne Littlehampton	**Sir William Arnold** Special Local Appeal.	1025 (52-02) £132,094.55 28t13	2x460hp Caterpillar D343 (wood hull)	St Peter Port 6.11.1973-6.1997 (503/224)	Sold 1998
3	1975 (700) William Osborne Littlehampton	**Edward Bridges (Civil Service and Post Office No.37)** Civil Service and Post Office LB Fund.	1037 (54-03) £162,383.47 30t8	2x460hp Caterpillar D343 (wood hull)	Torbay 4.1975-16.4.1994 (456/285)	Display at Chatham Historic Dockyard
4	1976 (1250) Halmatic Ltd/ William Osborne	**Tony Vandervell** The Vandervell Foundation.	1049 (54-04) £143,824.05 31t16	2x460hp Caterpillar D343 (GRP hull)	Weymouth 3.1976-11.6.1999 (598/359)	Sold 1999
5	1976 (WR4665) Halmatic Ltd Havant	**B. P. Forties** British Petroleum Co Ltd and students of Aberdeen University.	1050 (54-05) £158,455.61 31t16	2x460hp Caterpillar D343 (GRP hull)	Aberdeen 6.1976-28.8.1998 (112/11) Sold 1998	
6	1976 (1255) Halmatic Ltd/ William Osborne	**The Gough-Ritchie** Gift of Mrs A. A. Ritchie, Baldine, Isle of Man.	1051 (54-06) £171,269.64 31t12	2x460hp Caterpillar D343 (GRP hull)	Port St Mary 9.1976-5.1998 (162/63)	Sold 10.1998
7	1977 (WR4908) Halmatic Ltd Havant	**City of Bradford IV** City of Bradford Lord Mayor Appeal, and other funds.	1052 (54-07) £163,453.48 32t8	2x460hp Caterpillar D343 (GRP hull)	Humber 3.1977-8.1987 (416/106) Thurso 26.3.1988-3.1989 (12/2) Ballyglass 17.10.1989-8.1990 (9/0) Tobermory 7.2.1991-7.1998 (186/24)	Sold 1999
8	1977 (1565) Halmatic Ltd/ William Osborne	**Joy and John Wade** The Wade Foundation and the Yarmouth IOW Lifeboat Appeal.	1053 (52-08) £186,877.95 32t14	2x460hp Caterpillar D343 (GRP hull)	Yarmouth 19.7.1977-24.1.2001 (677/258) Relief 1-8.2001 (3/0)	Sold 3.2002
9	1978 (WR5172) Halmatic Ltd Havant	**Spirit of Tayside** Broughty Ferry Lifeboat Appeal.	1056 (52-09) £231,729.50 34t0	2x460hp Caterpillar D343 (GRP hull)	Broughty Ferry 6.5.1978-2.1999 (123/1)	Sold 1999
10	1978 (1850) Halmatic Ltd/ William Osborne	**Soldian** Lerwick Lifeboat Appeal and various legacies.	1057 (52-10) £225,452.39 32t2	2x460hp Caterpillar D343 (GRP hull)	Lerwick 8.1978-6.1997 (245/260) Relief 1997-98 and 1999-12.2001 (1/0) Achill 26.1.1998-4.1999 (6/3)	Sold 6.2002
11	1979 (1945) Halmatic Ltd/ William Osborne	**Elizabeth Ann** John Slater Foundation, Sir Kirby Laing Foundation, and Cornish Lifeboat Appeal.	1058 (52-11) £299,737 32t1	2x460hp Caterpillar D343 (GRP hull)	Falmouth 6.1979-1997 (249/52) Relief 2.1997-12.2001 (67/3)	Sold 6.2002
12	1979 (WR5845) Halmatic Ltd Havant	**Walter and Margaret Couper** Legacy of Miss Margaret G. Couper.	1059 (52-12) £302,748 32t0	2x460hp Caterpillar D343 (GRP hull)	Campbeltown 9.1979-5.1999 (274/130) Relief 1999-19.5.2001 (13/1)	Sold 19.5.2001
13	1979 (2020) Halmatic Ltd/ William Osborne	**George and Olive Turner** Legacy Mrs O. B. Turner, the Sir James Knott Trust, and Tyneside LB Appeal.	1061 (52-13) £302,285 31t6	2x460hp Caterpillar D343 (GRP hull)	Tynemouth 2.1980-10.1999 (286/58) Relief 21.10.1999-18.9.2000 (1/0)	Sold 25.9.2000
14	1980 Halmatic Ltd/ W. A. Souter	**Edith Emile** Gift of Mrs Edith E. Currie, Brentwood, Essex.	1062 (52-14) £367,795 31t16	2x460hp Caterpillar D343 (GRP hull)	Relief 1980-1998 (249/36)	Sold 2000

MOTOR LIFEBOATS

32 • Arun fast afloat 52-54ft

	Year (Yd No) Builder Place	Name Donor	ON (Op No) Cost Weight	Engines (hull material)	Stations (launches/lives saved)	Disposal
15	1980 (2150) Halmatic Ltd/ William Osborne	**Hyman Winstone** Gift of Mrs Marie Winstone, Sheffield.	1067 (52-15) £350,000 31t3	2x485hp Caterpillar 3408TA (GRP hull)	Holyhead 7.1980-12.10.1983 (44/30) Ballycotton 4.1985-1998 (216/62) Relief 3-11.1998 (0/0) and 2000-6.7.2002 (43/4) Larne 11.1998-8.2000 (13/0)	Sold 2003
16	1981 (2250) Halmatic Ltd/ William Osborne	**Richard Evans (Civil Service No.38)** Civil Service and Post Office Lifeboat Fund.	1070 (52-16) £272,221 30t17	2x485hp Caterpillar 3408TA (GRP hull)	Portrush 1.3.1981-4.2000 (316/69) Relief 2000-6.2003 (0/0)	Sold 2003, wrecked on passage to Iceland, 12.2003
17	1981 (FM707) Halmatic Ltd/ Fairey Marine	**Sir Max Aitken** The Beaverbrook Foundation.	1071 (52-17) £281,953 31t0	2x485hp Caterpillar 3408TA (GRP hull)	Relief 1981-27.11.2002 (359/117)	Sold 2002
18	1981 (2305) Halmatic Ltd/ William Osborne	**Robert Edgar** Gift of Mrs Esme S. Edgar and Mr Anthony Edgar.	1073 (52-18) £328,860 32t12	2x485hp Caterpillar 3408TA (GRP hull)	St Mary's 6.1981-12.1997 (121/84) Relief 12.1997-26.8.1999 (14/0) Weymouth 9.1999-7.2002 (70/1)	Sold 2002
19	1981 Halmatic Ltd/ W. A. Souter	**Marie Winstone** Gift of Mrs Marie Winstone.	1076 (52-19) £344,094 32t0	2x485hp Caterpillar 3408TA (GRP hull)	Fishguard 25.8.1981-1994 (138/33) Torbay 3.2.1995-2001 (280/63) Relief 2001-6.2002 (3/0)	Sold 2002
20	1982 (2400) Halmatic Ltd/ William Osborne	**Duchess of Kent** United Grand Lodge of Freemasons.	1077 (52-20) £357,299 31t16	2x485hp Caterpillar 3408TA (GRP hull)	Relief 27.4.1982-10.2002 (215/71)	Sold 2003
21	1981 (2450) Halmatic Ltd/ William Osborne	**Davina & Charles Matthews Hunter** Legacy of Miss Lilian Ferguson Hunter, in memory of her parents.	1078 (52-21) £353,209 31t1	2x485hp Caterpillar 3408TA (GRP hull)	Mallaig 16.7.1981-1.2001 (309/44) Relief 2001-6.2003 (36/2)	Sold 8.2003
22	1981 Halmatic Ltd/ W. A. Souter	**Ralph and Bonella Farrant** RNLI General Funds.	1081 (52-22) £350,839 30t14	2x485hp Caterpillar 3408TA (GRP hull)	Relief 26.7.1982-8.1994 (226/106) Fenit 18.8.1994-2.1999 (91/49) Relief 1999-8.2003 (116/24)	Sold 2004
23	1982 (2510) Halmatic Ltd/ William Osborne	**Margaret Frances Love** Legacies of Mr Frank Love and Lady Frances Murphy.	1082 (52-23) £362,214 30t12	2x485hp Caterpillar 3408TA (GRP hull)	Valentia 14.3.1982-11.1996 (192/73) Barry Dock 11.5.1997-8.2003 (129/10)	Sold 2005
24	1983 (FM715) Halmatic Ltd/ Fairey Marine	**Mabel Alice** Gift of Mr David Robinson, in memory of his wife.	1085 (52-24) £345,467 30t12	2x485hp Caterpillar 3408TA (GRP hull)	Penlee 8.5.1983-2.2003 (275/83)	Sold 2004
25	1983 (2590) Halmatic Ltd/ William Osborne	**A. J. R. and L. G. Uridge** Lionel G. Uridge Will Trust and gift of Mrs A. A. Burnley.	1086 (52-25) £369,078 30t15	2x485hp Caterpillar 3408TA (GRP hull)	Relief 15.9.1983-2003 (345/111) Torbay 4.1994-2.1995 (43/26)	Sold 2003
26	1984 (2620) Halmatic Ltd/ William Osborne	**St Brendan** RNLI General Funds.	1092 (52-26) £360,072 30t8	2x485hp Caterpillar 3408TA (GRP hull)	Rosslare Harbour 1.6.1984-9.2001 (147/28)	Written off after damaged in collision when hit at moorings by ferry, 9.9.2001, sold 2003
27	1984 (2650) Halmatic Ltd/ William Osborne	**Charles Brown** Gift of Mr David Robinson.	1093 (52-27) £383,638 31t11	2x485hp Caterpillar 3408TA (GRP hull)	Buckie 5.4.1984-5.2003 (270/172) Relief 5.2003-2004 (13/0)	Sold 2004
28	1984 Halmatic Ltd/ W. A. Souter	**Sir Max Aitken II** Gift of the Beaverbrook Foundation.	1098 (52-28) £377,974 31t0	2x485hp Caterpillar 3408TA (GRP hull)	Stornoway 6.3.1984-2.1999 (238/67) Relief 3.2-6.8.1999 (2/0) Longhope 12.8.1999-6.2004 (20/0)	Sold 11.2005

32 • Arun fast afloat 52-54ft

	Year (Yd No) Builder Place	Name Donor	ON (Op No) Cost Weight	Engines (hull material)	Stations (launches/lives saved)	Disposal
29	1984 (2700) Halmatic Ltd/ William Osborne	**Joseph Rothwell Sykes and Hilda M.** Legacies of Mr J. Sykes, Mrs N. Sykes, and other gifts.	1099 (52-29) £370,000 31t0	2x485hp Caterpillar 3408TA (GRP hull)	Stromness 12.10.1984-10.1998 (89/8) Broughty Ferry 20.1.1999-4.2001 (52/0) Relief 2001-6.02 (2/0)	Sold 2002
30	1986 (FM722) Fairey Marine Cowes	**Snolda** Various oil companies, Local Appeal, and the Miss I. F. Harvey Trust.	1100 (52-030) £391,021 32t5	2x485hp Caterpillar 3408TA (steel hull)	Aith 19.7.1986-5.1998 (79/29) Training 1998-2007 (Numbered TL-01)	Sold 2007
31	1984 Halmatic Ltd/ W. A. Souter	**Newsbuoy** Special Appeal by the Newspaper Society.	1103 (52-31) £400,000 31t5	2x485hp Caterpillar 3408TA (GRP hull)	Relief 23.10.1984-2004 (198/49) Plymouth 1.11.2002-15.2.2003 (25/0)	Sold 2005
32	1985 (2790) Halmatic Ltd/ William Osborne	**Keith Anderson** Gift of Mrs Esme Anderson, London.	1106 (52-32) £390,000 30t15	2x485hp Caterpillar 3408TA (GRP hull)	Newhaven 9.8.1985-10.1999 (521/119) Relief 15.11.1999-10.2000 (0/0) Hartlepool 25.10.2000-8.2003 (56/2)	Sold 2004
33	1985 (2830) Halmatic Ltd/ William Osborne	**City of Belfast** The City of Belfast Appeal.	1107 (52-33) £433,138 31t5	2x485hp Caterpillar 3408TA (GRP hull)	Donaghadee 7.12.1985-4.2003 (323/58) Relief 2003-04 (9/0)	Sold 11.2005
34	1986 Halmatic Ltd/ W. A. Souter	**Margaret Russell Fraser** Bequest Margaret Fraser, Glasgow, and other gifts and legacies.	1108 (52-34) £417,616 31t5	2x485hp Caterpillar 3408TA (GRP hull)	Relief 14.6.1986-2001 (293/152) Calshot 4.4.2002-8.2004 (118/15)	Sold 2005
35	1986 (1013) Halmatic Ltd/ Berthon Bt Co	**City of Dublin** The City of Dublin Appeal.	1113 (52-35) £543,552 31t86	2x485hp Caterpillar 3408TA (GRP hull)	Howth 22.8.1986-3.2002 (260/63) Relief 3.2002-03 (25/0)	Sold 5.2004
36	1987 (3010) Halmatic Ltd/ William Osborne	**Roy and Barbara Harding** RNLI General Funds.	1118 (52-36) £466,448 30t3	2x485hp Caterpillar 3408TA (GRP hull)	Aran Islands 4.7.1987-6.1997 (315/43) Castletownbere 7.4.1998-1.2004 (83/26)	Sold 9.2004
37	1987 (1014) Halmatic Ltd/ Berthon Bt Co	**Kenneth Thelwall** Bequest of Mr Kenneth Thelwall, Walkington, Yorkshire.	1123 (52-37) £574,433 30t6	2x485hp Caterpillar 3408TA (GRP hull)	Humber 13.8.1987-3.1997 (383/68) Relief 1997-1998 (28/10) Holyhead 17.9.1998-12.2003 (101/15)	Sold 2005
38	1987 (0002) Halmatic Ltd/ W. A. Souter	**City of Glasgow III** The City of Glasgow Appeal, and other gifts and legacies.	1134 (52-38) £415,000 30t9	2x485hp Caterpillar 3408TA (GRP hull)	Troon 25.10.1987-25.2.2004 (432/139) Relief 25.2.2004-04 90/0)	Sold 2004
39	1988 (WR8722) Halmatic Ltd Havant	**Mickie Salvesen** Legacy of Mrs Mary Salvesen.	1135 (52-39) £587,133 31t0	2x485hp Caterpillar 3408TA (GRP hull)	Kirkwall 5.7.1988-3.1998 (89/35) Relief 3-8.1998 (1/0) and 2000-2003 (26/9) Aberdeen 28.8.1998-7.2000 (25/0) Barry Dock 8.8.2003-1.2006 (57/0)	Sold 2006
40	1988 (0007) Halmatic Ltd/ W A Souter	**City of Plymouth** City of Plymouth Appeal, and other gifts and legacies.	1136 (52-40) £592,478 29t3	2x485hp Caterpillar 3408TA (GRP hull)	Plymouth 26.1.1988-1.11.2002 (579/115) Relief 11.2002-9.2004 (4/0)	Sold 10.2004
41	1988 (1015) Halmatic Ltd/ Berthon Bt Co	**Ann Lewis Fraser** The Fraser of Allander Foundation.	1143 (52-41) £552,162 30t	2x485hp Caterpillar 3408TA (GRP hull)	Barra Island 7.1988-6.1998 (103/44) Tobermory 5.7.1998-2003 (103/4) Relief 2003-04 (8/0)	Sold 2004
42	1989 Halmatic Ltd/ Robson	**Murray Lornie** Trustees of the Ben Vorlich Trust, Jersey.	1144 (52-42) £553,417 32t	2x500hp Caterpillar 3408TA (GRP hull)	Lochinver 20.7.1989-2004 (144/64) Castletownbere 1-8.2004 (18/0)	Sold 2005

32 • Arun fast afloat 52-54ft

	Year (Yd No) Builder Place	Name Donor	ON (Op No) Cost Weight	Engines (hull material)	Stations (launches/lives saved)	Disposal
43	1989 (WO3170) Halmatic Ltd/ William Osborne	**The Queen Mother** Bequest of Miss Sarah Sinclair Gray, Dunoon, and RNLI funds.	1149 (52-43) £580,514 31t4	2x500hp Caterpillar 3408TA (GRP hull)	Thurso 24.3.1989-4.2004 (168/59) Longhope 6.2004-10.2006 (19/4) Relief 2006-2008 (3/0)	Sold 2009
44	1989 (WO3200) Halmatic Ltd/ William Osborne	**Hibernia** The Irish Government through the Irish Sailors Act 1988.	1150 (52-44) £577,826 29t18	2x500hp Caterpillar 3408TA (GRP hull)	Relief 1989-2007 (315/44)	Sold 2007
45	1990 Halmatic Ltd/ Robson	**Mabel Williams** Bequest of Mabel Williams.	1159 (52-45) £640,001	2x500hp Caterpillar 3408TA (GRP hull)	Ballyglass 29.8.1990-8.1998 (52/19) Relief 8.1998-9.2001 (51/2) Rosslare Harbour 10.9.2001-7.2.2004 (28/19) Calshot 8.2004-2.2007 (115/0)	Sold 2007
46	1990 (WO3269) Halmatic Ltd/ William Osborne	**Duke of Atholl** Bequest of Sir David Robinson.	1160 (52-46) £614,659 29.6 tonnes	2x500hp Caterpillar 3408TA (GRP hull)	Relief 1990-2003 (232/57) Hartlepool 17.8.2003-27.9.2004 (27/0) Relief 2004-2007 (4/0)	Sold 2007

▲ The relief 52ft Arun Duchess of Kent (ON.1077) on duty at Dunbar. She served in the Relief Fleet for twenty years. (Nicholas Leach)

▼ Charles Brown (ON.1093) on exercise off Buckie. She was one of several Aruns sold out of service to the China Rescue & Salvage Bureau. (N. Leach)

Joseph Rothwell Sykes and Hilda M (ON.1099) at Stromness for her naming ceremony on 22 August 1985. She served the Orkney station for fourteen years. (Orkney Photographic Archives)

32 • Arun fast afloat 52-54ft

▲ The only steel-hulled Arun to be built, Snolda, served at Aith for twelve years and, for the last nine years of her career, was used as a training lifeboat, with the number TL-01 on her bow. (Nicholas Leach)

◀ City of Belfast (ON.1107) on exercise off Donaghadee, wearing her original livery, with the operational number shown on the wheelhouse. (By courtesy of the RNLI)

▼ (left) Murray Lornie (ON.1144) on exercise at Castletownbere in 2004. Built for Lochinver, she had an RNLI service career of just sixteen years.

▼ (right) One of the last 52ft Aruns to be built, The Queen Mother (ON.1143), at Longhope, the second of the two Scottish stations she served. She was named on 9 August 1989 by HM Queen Elizabeth the Queen Mother, and was the last Arun in RNLI service. (Nicholas Leach)

MOTOR LIFEBOATS

33 • Brede intermediate 33ft

KEY DATA
- Introduced 1979
- Last built 1985
- 12 built

SPECIFICATIONS
- Length 33ft (10.06m)
- Breadth 12ft (3.66m)
- Waterline length 27ft 6in (8.38m)
- Draft 4ft 3in (1.30m)
- Speed 18 knots
- Displacement 8.5 tons

The 33ft Brede was based on the commercially-designed Lochin 33 angling boat, which had been developed by Lochin Marine, and was built at their yard in Rye, Sussex. The hull was designed by small boat specialist designer Robert Tucker ARINA and, with sufficient power, was capable of reaching speeds of more than thirty knots. Named after the river which flows through Rye where all the boats were built, the Brede was intended to replace a small number of offshore lifeboats where it was believed the cost of providing a new offshore lifeboat could not be justified on operational grounds. The RNLI's Committee of Management determined that a new type was required which could fill a gap in capability between the largest inshore lifeboat, the Atlantic 21 rigid-inflatable, and was faster but with less endurance than the 44ft Waveney.

The RNLI was searching for a sturdy boat with good seakeeping qualities, and turned to a commercial company, Lochin Marine, whose 33ft GRP-hulled design was deemed to meet the requirements. The hull had already been used in pleasure and work boats, and Lochins were liked by fishermen, as well as by pilotage and harbour authorities. For the RNLI, adapting a suitable commercial hull was found to be an economical and highly satisfactory solution. The first Brede was ordered by the RNLI in October 1978, being fitted out by Lochin using a standard layout, and numbered 33–01 by the RNLI. The prototype boat was never given a name and was used for only trials and evaluation purposes beginning in early 1980. This boat was fitted with a large buoyancy block aft to give a self-righting capability, but was the only Brede to be so equipped.

After trials with the first boat, a second boat was ordered incorporating a series of modifications, including an enlarged wheelhouse that provided the self-righting capability, thus enabling the buoyancy block to be dispensed with. The revised wheelhouse also provided increased headroom in the wheelhouse and had rearward sloping forward windows. This improved design provided the basis for the subsequent boats and, during the next three years, a further ten were constructed, which were sent to selected lifeboat stations in England and Scotland where they were kept afloat at moorings, and three were built for the Relief Fleet.

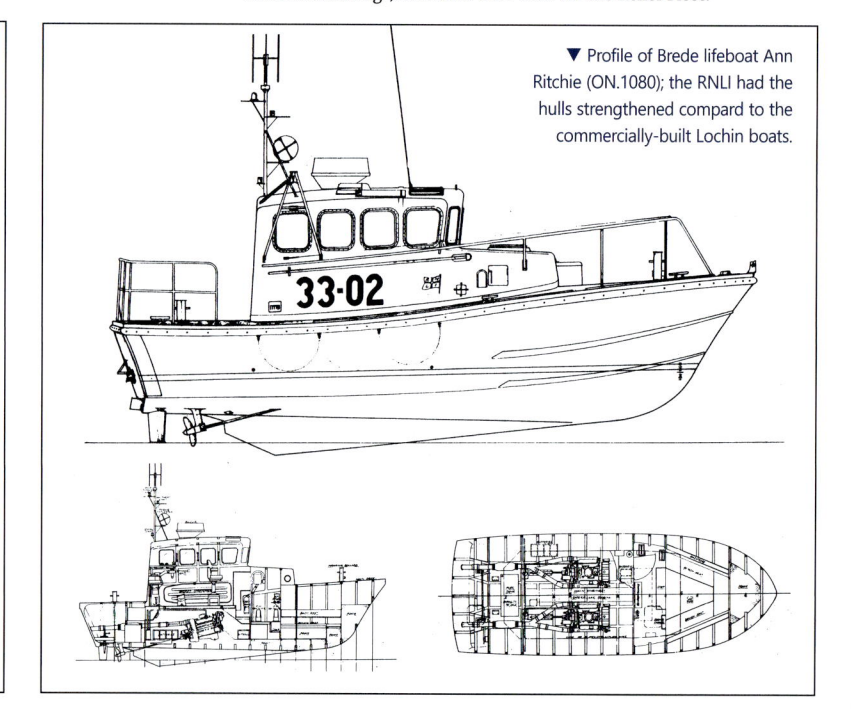

▶ The prototype Brede lifeboat 33-01 during her trials. The large foam block at her stern provided a self-righting capability. This boat was used for trials only, after which it was sold by the RNLI. (By courtesy of the RNLI)

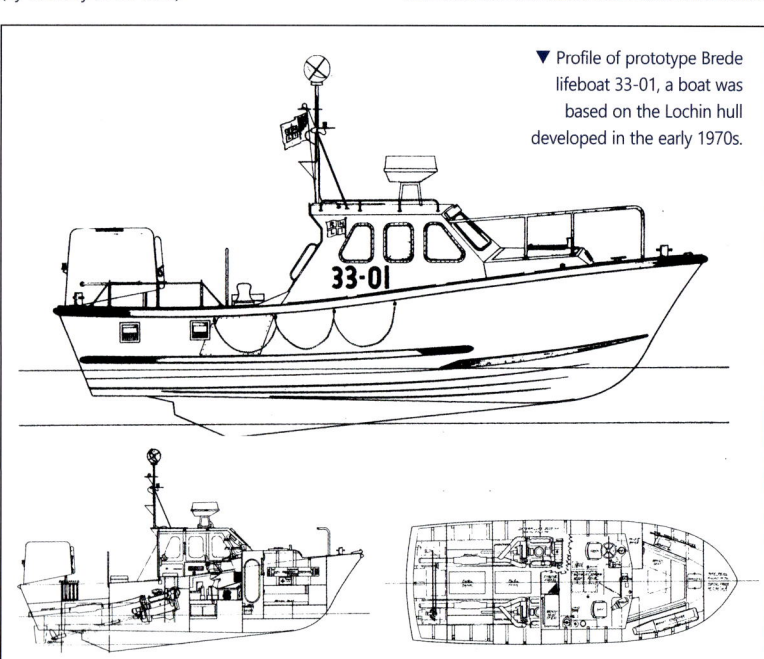

▼ Profile of prototype Brede lifeboat 33-01, a boat was based on the Lochin hull developed in the early 1970s.

▼ Profile of Brede lifeboat Ann Ritchie (ON.1080); the RNLI had the hulls strengthened compard to the commercially-built Lochin boats.

168

MOTOR LIFEBOATS

33 • Brede intermediate 33ft

	Year (Yd No) Builder Place	Name Donor	ON (Op No) Cost Weight	Engines	Stations (launches/lives saved)	Notes Disposal
1	1979 (1066) Lochin Marine Rye, Sussex	[Not named] RNLI General Funds.	1066 (33-01) £107,628 –	2x203hp Caterpillar 3208 NA	Trials only 1980-82 (with well deck aft)	Sold 1982
2	1982 (1080) Lochin Marine Rye, Sussex	Ann Ritchie Gift of Mrs A. A. Ritchie, Isle of Man.	1080 (33-02) £157,169 9t6	2x203hp Caterpillar 3208 NA	Oban 25.10.1982-19.9.1987 (186/20)	Scrapped 1.1988
3	1982 (1083) Lochin Marine Rye, Sussex	Leonore Chilcott Gift of Mr Paul Chilcott, Guernsey.	1083 (33-03) £153,475 8t10	2x203hp Caterpillar 3208 NA	Fowey 16.10.1982-1.1988 (56/19)	Sold 1990
4	1982 (1084) Lochin Marine Rye, Sussex	Philip Vaux Bequest of Mrs Elizabeth Felicity Vaux.	1084 (33-04) £155,939 8t10	2x203hp Caterpillar 3208 NA	Girvan 16.2.1983-4.1989 (57/17)	Sold 1989
5	1983 (1087) Lochin Marine Rye, Sussex	Merchant Navy Merchant Navy Appeal.	1087 (33-05) £152,207 8t10	2x203hp Caterpillar 3208 NA	Relief 18.4.1983-9.1987 (34/10) Oban 19.9.1987-28.3.1989 (73/11)	Sold 1990
6	1983 (1088) Lochin Marine Rye, Sussex	Caroline Finch Legacies of Mr W.H. Finch, Mr H.E. Rohll, Mrs M.G. Shaw and Mr W. J. Orley.	1088 (33-06) £155,645 8t12	2x203hp Caterpillar 3208 NA	Exmouth 4.8.1983-8.7.1994 (178/64)	Sold 1994
7	1983 (1089) Lochin Marine Rye, Sussex	Inner Wheel Inner Wheel Clubs of Great Britain and Ireland.	1089 (33-07) £154,043 8t11	2x203hp Caterpillar 3208 NA	Poole 16.10.1983-5.9.2001 (812/176) Calshot 12.2001-4.4.2002 (3/0)	Sold 2002
8	1984 (1090) Lochin Marine Rye, Sussex	Foresters Future Ancient Order of Foresters, plus other gifts and legacies.	1090 (33-08) £160,984 8t13	2x203hp Caterpillar 3208 NA	Alderney 10.3.1984-1986 (70/74) Relief 10.1986-2.9.2002 (210/35)	Sold 2002
9	1984 (1101) Lochin Marine Rye, Sussex	Enid of Yorkshire Gift of Arnold T. Sanderson, North Ferriby, North Humberside.	1101 (33-09) £177,331 9t6	2x203hp Caterpillar 3208 NA	Relief 22.6.1984-8.9.1997 (113/12)	Sold 1997
10	1984 (1102) Lochin Marine Rye, Sussex	Nottinghamshire The Nottinghamshire Lifeboat Appeal.	1102 (33-10) £179,079 8t11	2x203hp Caterpillar 3208 NA	Invergordon 16.7.1984-7.1988 (21/6) Oban 26.3.1989-7.97 (502/30)	Sold 1997
11	1985 (1104) Lochin Marine Rye, Sussex	Safeway Safeway Food Stores Appeal.	1104 (33-11) £184,775 8t11	2x203hp Caterpillar 3208 NA	Calshot 24.3.1985-12.2001 (259/40)	Sold 2002
12	1985 (1105) Lochin Marine Rye, Sussex	Amateur Swimming Associations Amateur Swimming Associations of England, Scotland and Wales.	1105 (33-12) £186,421 8t11	2x203hp Caterpillar 3208 NA	Relief 30.5.1985-1989 (48/20) Girvan 11.4.1989-29.8.1993 (60/5)	Sold 9.1993

33 • Brede intermediate 33ft

The design's hull was divided into five main watertight compartments, and void spaces were filled with reserve buoyancy materials. The boat was found to have good stability and provided a god working platform whether under way or stopped. The boats built for the RNLI were all were fitted with twin Caterpillar 3208NA naturally-aspirated diesel engines developing 203bhp at 2,800rpm, which were modified to operate after self-righting in the event of capsize. The boats had a speed of approximately twenty knots and, with a fuel capacity of 182 gallons, at the maximum speed of twenty knots, the Bredes had a range of 140 nautical miles. At full speed the boat lifted to head seas and spray was thrown clear of the wheelhouse structured.

The GRP wheelhouse provided seated accommodation for four crew and a stretcher for a casualty. Equipment comprised VHF radio, echo sounder, radar and VHF DF. Forward of the wheelhouse was the survivors' cabin, which was large enough to take eight seated survivors. Blankets, stretcher, first aid gear and emergency rations were carried. A strong towing bollard was fitted and an emergency tiller could be fitted on the port rudder stock if needed.

Although they proved to be capable life-saving craft, the Bredes did not have long operational careers and were replaced by larger all-weather lifeboats, which the RNLI had not been able to justify financially when the Brede design was first developed. A total of eleven Bredes saw service, but of these only three spent more than a decade on operational station duties. The first Brede was in service for less than five years. However, several Bredes were sold for further life-saving service in South Africa, where they were well liked and found to be ideal rescue craft.

▲ The second 33ft Brede Ann Ritchie (ON.1080) was the first to be built with the revised wheelhouse and deck layout. (By courtesy of the RNLI)

▶ The fifth 33ft Brede, Merchant Navy (ON.1087), was built for the Relief Fleet, but served at Oban for two years, although her operational service with the RNLI lasted for just six years. (Nicholas Leach)

▼ Inner Wheel (ON.1089) moored at Poole, the station she served for almost eighteen years. (Nicholas Leach)

MOTOR LIFEBOATS

33 • Brede intermediate 33ft

▲ (left) Caroline Finch in the River Exe; she operated from a berth at Exmouth Docks for just under eleven years. She was sold in 1994 to the South African Lifeboat Service, becoming one of several Bredes to go to South Africa for further sea rescue service. (By courtesy of the RNLI)

▲ (right) The penultimate 33ft Brede to enter service was Safeway (ON.1104), which served at Calshot, at the mouth of the Solent; her seveteen-year career made her one of the longest-serving of the Bredes. (Nicholas Leach)

◀ Foresters Future (ON.1090) was built for service at Alderney, a new station in the Channel Islands, established in March 1984. She was involved in two Bronze medal-winning rescues in 1986 while in service at Alderney. (Nicholas Leach)

▼ Enid of Yorkshire on relief duties at Oban in July 1995. She was named on 22 June 1984 at a ceremony at Bridlington (Nicholas Leach)

MOTOR LIFEBOATS

34 • Medina rigid-inflatable

KEY DATA
- Introduced 1980
- Last built 1982
- 3 built

SPECIFICATIONS
- Overall length 39ft 6in (12.12m)
- Beam 14ft (4.27m)
- Rigid-hull length 34ft 6in (10.56m)
- Rigid-hull beam 11ft 4in (3.45m)
- Crew 4

▲ The prototype Medina ON.1069 during her initial trials, with an open deck configuration and a self-righting air-bag on the roll bar aft, with the radar dome above the steering position.

The Medina class was an experimental rigid-inflatable design, nearly 40ft in length, based on the concept of the smaller Atlantic 21 rigid-inflatable. It was seen as an intermediate lifeboat by the RNLI; intermediate meant, according to the RNLI, a 'fast boat of about 35ft in length, essentially simple but with outstanding seakeeping qualities, which would bridge the gap between present offshore and inshore lifeboats, giving greater flexibility in the provision of effective cover to all parts of the coast'. At some stations the RNLI believed that an intermediate boat could replace a small offshore lifeboat, such as a 35ft 6in Liverpool, doing as good a job but more economically and having the added advantage of greater speed. The Brede was the commercially designed intermediate boat, and the Medina was the one designed by the RNLI's design team at its Cowes Base, working under the leadership of David Stogden, MBE, and built by W. A. Souter's yard at West Cowes.

The Medina was essentially an extension of the ideas embodied in the Atlantic 21 inshore lifeboat, which was also developed at the Cowes Base. However, the Medina was powered by twin inboard diesel engines, rather than twin outboards as found on the Atlantic. The hull was sharply veed forward for easy riding and good seakeeping, and included a bold sheer, with a flat area for the last 9ft which assisted planing and kept the boat upright if it grounded. The hull was cold moulded of four layers of 5mm mahogany with half an inch marine ply deck, and was divided into watertight compartments by five longitudinal wooden box girders with seven transverse watertight bulkheads.

Mounted on the rigid hull was the sponson, which was designed to be completely clear of the water when the boat was under way. The sponson was made by Avon of hypalon/neoprene fabric, and the tubes were 31in in diameter, tapering down to 25in in the bow so they did not obstruct forward vision. They were supported inboard by glass-fibre box seatings and were glued to the hull by laminated reinforcing strips. The tubes were divided into compartments by inner baffles which would ensure the sponson remained largely inflated even if one compartment was damaged.

The prototype was built as an open boat, with self-righting capability provided by an inflatable air-bag fitted to a roll bar at the stern. A basic aluminium forward superstructure housed the steering position, and included a basic shelter large enough to take a stretcher and survivors. A gantry at the after end of the superstructure carried a radar scanner, navigation and blue flashing lights an the VHF aerial. The roll bar carried the deflated buoyancy bag. The deck arrangements were somewhat experimental, and on the second and third boats enclosed wheelhouses were fitted, which gave an inherent self-righting capability as well as the necessary crew protection for a boat capable of more than twenty knots.

The second boat had two different wheelhouses fitted, as the first was found to be too small. The wheelhouse on the third boat was larger still, and incorporated an upper steering position. After bottom damage to the hull of ON.1069, William Osborne's yard designed a stronger hull structure which was used for ON.1091 and this was found to be better.

The first Medina was powered by twin Sabre 212hp diesel engines, with power transmitted through twin Sternpowr type 83 outdrive units. On initial trials the boat reached a speed of more than twenty-six knots, with the engines running at 2,450rpm, on the measured mile. The engines were in a watertight aluminium casing accessed by hatches. The outdrives

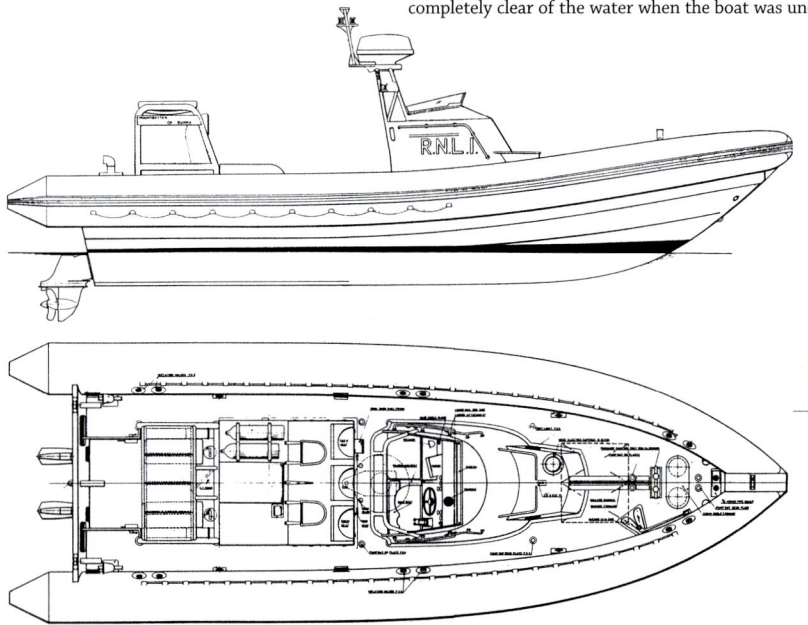

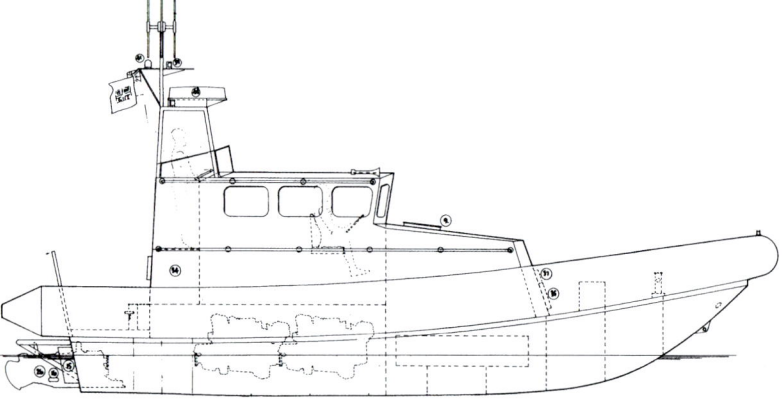

▲ Line drawing of the third Medina, ON.1091, which had a wheelhouse with a small flying bridge at the aft end and waterjet propulsion. Fitting an effective wheelhouse to the rigid-inflatable hull was not straightforward and the second boat, ON.1072, had two different wheelhouses, both built in aluminium.

◀ Line drawing of the first Medina, ON.1069, which had an open deck layout, with a roll bar at the stern; the boat ended up being used largely as a test bed for equipment and machinery.

MOTOR LIFEBOATS

34 • Medina rigid-inflatable

	Year (Yd No) Builder Place	Name Donor	ON Cost Weight	Engines	Stations	Disposal
1	1980 W. A. Souter Cowes	**Mountbatten of Burma** Appeal by Romsey Branch, in honour of Lord Mountbatten.	1069 – –	2x212hp Sabre with twin Sternpower Type 83 outdrives/ 1983- 3x203hp Seadrive outboards (p)	Trials at Brighton 6.1983, Littlehampton (stored) Open boat with steering console, SR via air-bag	Sold 1.10.1989
2	1981 W. A. Souter Cowes	**Countess Mountbatten of Burma** Appeal by Romsey Branch, in honour of Lord Mountbatten.	1072 – –	2x Volvo TAMD 60B and Volvo Type 750 outdrives/ 2x350hp Caterpillar 3208TA & Parker PP140 Jet Unit	Visited Dungeness 7.1985, Redcar 11.1985, Blackpool 5.1986, Dunbar, Appledore Watertight wheelhouse, SR in four secs; larger wheelhouse fitted by William Osborne 1984	Sold 11.8.1989
3	1982 (WO2576) William Osborne Littlehampton	[Not named] RNLI funds.	1091 – –	2x285hp Caterpillar with Castoldi type 06 3208 water jets	Trials, RNLI Depot, Poole (stored) Enclosed wheelhouse	Sold 30.4.1989

could be tilted when the boat took the ground, as the intention was for the boat to be capable of being launched from a slipway or a carriage. The first Medina had a maximum fuel capacity of 156 gallons, and a range at maximum speed of 150 nautical miles. The second boat was fitted with twin Volvo TAMD 60B engines and Volvo Type 750 outdrives.

The first two boats were funded by an appeal, launched in 1979, supported by Lord Louis Mountbatten. Within a few days of the appeal launch, however, Mountbatten was tragically assassinated. As a result, the appeal attracted considerable support, funding two lifeboats rather than one, and they were named after Mountbatten and his wife, although neither were ceremonially christened but did carry name places.

Although the hull shape and basic design concept showed initial promise, problems were experienced finding engines of a suitable power-

▲ (left) The Medinas ON.1072 (on left) and ON.1091 at the RNLI's Depot at Poole in 1988, shortly before they were sold. (Nicholas Leach)

▲ (right) The prototype Medina ON.1069 during her initial trials, with an open deck configuration and a self-righting air-bag on the roll bar aft, with the radar dome above the steering position.

◀ The first Medina, ON.1069, was used as a floating test bed for various types of equipment. Although she was found to be an excellent sea boat during trials, there were problems with the various propulsion systems, which included a three Seeadrive configuration, developing 203hp, which gave a speed of over thirty knots, fitted in 1982.

MOTOR LIFEBOATS

34 • Medina rigid-inflatable

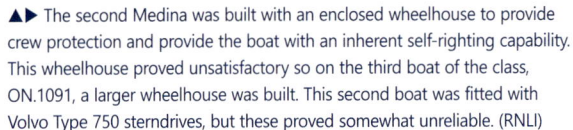

▲▶ The second Medina was built with an enclosed wheelhouse to provide crew protection and provide the boat with an inherent self-righting capability. This wheelhouse proved unsatisfactory so on the third boat of the class, ON.1091, a larger wheelhouse was built. This second boat was fitted with Volvo Type 750 sterndrives, but these proved somewhat unreliable. (RNLI)

▼ ON.1072 undertaking launch and recovery trials at Redcar in November 1985. The launch carriage was purpose-built for the Medina, but was pushed by the station's standard Fowler launching tractor. (David Phillipson)

▶ Koningin Beatrix, the first rigid-inflatable to enter operational service in the Netherlands, measured 12.7m by 4.7m and served at Burghsluis (1986-96) and Urk (1998-2008). Her rigid hull was constricted from aluminium, and she was powered by twin 680hp Perkins diesel engines driving PP140 waterjets to give a speed of thirty-four knots. Since her introduction, the Dutch lifeboat service has built numerous rigid-inflatable craft, including the 10.6m Valentijn type which is launched and recovered from beaches.

to-weight ratio which operated reliably. Several different units and combinations were tried, coupled to both propellers and waterjets. The third boat, ON.1091, which was never named, was fitted with Castoldi Type 06 waterjet units, while the first Medina had three outboard units fitted at one stage, but none of these proved suitable. Further problems were experienced when the hull was damaged during beach launching. The second boat, ON.1072, was used for a series of launch and recovery trials at Redcar and Blackpool in November 1985 using a purpose-designed launching carriage and as part of a trials passage for the boat.

In 1986 the RNLI announced that a fourth Medina hull was to be built, but as the 12m Mersey class proved more suitable as a carriage-launched lifeboat, this additional boat was never completed. Despite exhaustive trials and numerous modifications made over the course of eight years, the RNLI decided that the Medina would not meet its standards and the project was abandoned. By the end of the 1980s the three boats, having spent long periods in storage and never seen operational service, had been sold. The last, ON.1091, went on to have a life-saving career at Stonehaven, being operated by the Maritime Rescue Institute partly as a lifeboat and partly for training in the early years of the twenty-first century.

Although the RNLI abandoned its own Medina project, various overseas lifeboat organisations went on to develop large rigid-inflatables and operate them successfully. In 1983 the Norwegian Society for Sea Rescue built a 36ft 9in rigid-inflatable, which had a speed of 27 knots. In 1984 the Netherlands lifeboat society KZHMRS had a 41ft 3in rigid-inflatable built, named Koningin Beatrix, which had an enclosed wheelhouse and served with distinction, and in 1986 the Canadian Coast Guard had a 46ft 9in rigid-inflatable built. The Dutch went on to become the most successful proponents of the large rigid-inflatable for rescue work. After the two previously independent Dutch lifeboat organisations merged in May 1991, to become the KNRM (Koninklijke Nederlandse Redding Maatschappij), the newly-unified organisation built and developed various rigid-inflatable lifeboats of different sizes, and the country's fleet of offshore lifeboats consists entirely of fast rigid inflatables.

Chapter 6
Into the twenty-first century

Into the twenty-first century

◀ (chapter frontispiece) The 16m Tamar Spirit of Padstow (ON.1283) off the North Cornish coast. The Tamar was a revolutionary design and the first class of lifeboat to be fitted with the SIMS computer system. (Nicholas Leach)

▲ The prototype 47ft Tyne City of London (ON.1074) on trials shortly after being completed. The Tyne was designed for slipway launching and had a steel hull and aluminium wheelhouse. (By courtesy of Ian Booth)

▶ The 47ft Tyne Lady Rank (ON.1114) from Angle on exercise in Milford Haven. She was one of forty Tynes which were built for the RNLI, and gave outstanding service over the course of more than three decades. (Nicholas Leach)

▼ The 12m Mersey Lifetime Care (ON.1148) was the first RNLI lifeboat to be built from fibre composite materials; she served in the Relief Fleet.

Following the introduction of the Waveney and Arun lifeboats for stations where the boats were kept afloat at moorings, two other fast lifeboat types were developed: the 47ft Tyne for slipway launching and the 12m Mersey for carriage launching, and both proved very successful, some achieving three decades of life-saving service. As with the Arun, both new types incorporated some notable technological advances. The Tyne, with propellers protected by partial tunnels and bilge keels, was built of steel with an aluminium alloy deck and wheelhouse. Steel had first been used in steam lifeboats in the 1890s, and again when the Clyde class cruising lifeboat was developed during the 1960s. The 44ft design acquired from the USCG, which became the Waveney, was also steel-hulled. The Tyne was built from the material because it was considered cost-effective and best suited for a boat regularly enduring the stresses of slipway launching and recovery.

The most significant advance with the Mersey was the hull material. While the first ten boats were built from aluminium, subsequent boats were moulded from fibre-reinforced composite (FRC) after the material had been thoroughly trialled and tested in a full-size prototype boat, *Lifetime Care* (ON.1148). This boat, which subsequently served in the Relief Fleet, proved that advanced composite materials were well-suited to lifeboat construction. Not only would FRC withstand the rigours of beach launching, which often involved being dragged over shingle and sand, but boats built from the material were also lighter than those made of aluminium. Another of the advantages of FRC was that a mould could be used from which a production series could be constructed relatively quickly. As the Mersey project called for up to forty boats to be in service within four years, speed of construction was a factor, and this was achieved.

Both the Tyne and the Mersey designs had propellers protected by partial tunnels and extended bilge keels. Tunnels for propeller protection had been incorporated in the first motor lifeboats and used in almost every subsequent motor lifeboat design. But where the displacement-hulled boats, such as the Watsons and Barnetts, had their top speed limited by both hull form and tunnels, the Tyne and Mersey designs overcame this with a semi-planing hull and partial tunnels. The protection of propellers has been a consideration in lifeboat design since engines were first used and, although they reduced the effectiveness of the propeller, tunnels were regarded as the best way to guard the propeller against damage.

While the demand on the RNLI's services increased considerably during the last three decades of the twentieth century, the most significant development was the increase in the speed of lifeboats, with the change from slow displacement to fast semi-planing designs, and the consequent reduction in the time taken to reach casualties. In 1986 a target date of

MOTOR LIFEBOATS

Into the twenty-first century

1993 was set, by when fast lifeboats, capable of fifteen knots or more, would be at every station operating an all-weather lifeboat. In December 1993 that goal was achieved when the 12m Mersey Freddie Cooper (ON.1193) arrived at Aldeburgh to complete the network of fast lifeboats. As faster all-weather lifeboats became the norm, in 1990 the RNLI extended its declared area of coverage from thirty to fifty miles offshore, with the aim of having a lifeboat on scene within four hours of launching. These advances in design meant that rescues fifty miles offshore could be achieved, something that would have been inconceivable to the crews of either the pulling lifeboats or the early motor craft.

But even in the 1990s, when Aruns, Tynes and Merseys made up the all-weather lifeboat fleet, the RNLI did not stand still, and during the decade a new generation of even faster lifeboat was developed. The Trent and Severn types, built to replace the Aruns and Waveneys which were reaching the end of their operational lives, entered service in 1992. The new types had a maximum speed of twenty-five knots, were built of FRC and their twin propellers were protected by extended bilge keels. The Trent, at 14m in length, was the smaller of the two, while the 17m Severn was heavier and its greater radius of action made it ideal for operations at the more remote lifeboat stations on the RNLI's network, such as those on the west coast of both Scotland and Ireland.

▲ Freddie Cooper (ON.1193) arriving at Aldeburgh in November 1993, escorted by the 37ft 6in Rother James Cable (ON.1068).

▼ Freddie Cooper (ON.1193) being launched on exercise at Aldeburgh. She was the last 'fast' lifeboat to go on station, replacing the last of the traditional displacement-hulled lifeboats.

◄ The 37ft 6in Rother Mary Gabriel (ON.1000), on left, and the 12m Mersey Lady of Hilbre (ON.1163) at Hoylake in October 1990 as the latter took over duties from the former. This photograph clearly shows the different hull shape of the displacement and semi-planing lifeboats, and the propeller and rudder arrangements. (Nicholas Leach)

MOTOR LIFEBOATS

Into the twenty-first century

▶ The Lerwick lifeboat crew, with the 17m Severn Michael and Jane Vernon (ON.1221) behind, who were involved in the service to the cargo vessel Green Lily on 19 November 1997; they are, left to right, Ian Leask, Michael Grant, Brian Lawrenson, Peter Thomson, Richie Simpson and Coxswain Hewitt Clark. (By courtesy of the RNLI)

▼ 17m Severn (behind) and 14m Trent prototypes ON.1179 and ON.1180 on show to the national media shortly after the two new designs had been finalised. The production boats were different from the prototypes in a number of ways, notably in the position of the flying bridges, but the hull shape was the same. (By courtesy of the RNLI)

One of the first 17m Severns to be built was allocated to Lerwick, in Shetland. She arrived on station in early June 1997, was formally named Michael and Jane Vernon (ON.1221) at a ceremony on 19 July that year, and four months later, on 19 November, was involved in a truly outstanding rescue. The refrigerated cargo vessel Green Lily was in difficulty in horrendous conditions fifteen miles south-east of the Shetland capital. Tugs tried to help the crippled vessel, but in the heavy weather all tow lines parted. At 1.10pm the lifeboat, with the crew strapped into their seats and Coxswain/Mechanic Hewitt Clark in command, set off into the mountainous seas to assist. Although the Coastguard helicopter reached the stricken cargo vessel, winching operations were not possible due to the casualty's violent motion. When the lifeboat arrived on scene at 1.50pm, Green Lily was just over a mile from the shore. As further attempts to tow her to safety failed, she was slowly but surely being blown ashore.

As the vessel was still rolling too violently for the helicopter to winch the crew off, and huge waves were repeatedly sweeping over her, Coxswain Clark decided he had to go alongside, even though the vessel was only 900 yards offshore in quite shallow water. To gain a lee, the lifeboat had to go to the vessel's port side, between the ship and the rocks, leaving little sea room in which to manoeuvre. With Coxswain Clark and Second Coxswain Richard Simpson on the lifeboat's flying bridge, and the other lifeboatmen on the open deck ready to help survivors aboard, the lifeboat was skilfully taken to within thirty feet of the casualty. Operating at the very limits of her capabilities, she was manoeuvred towards the vessel again and again so that the survivors, when the two vessels were level, could be pulled to safety. Every time the lifeboat went alongside, she was slammed hard against the vessel's side and many times Clark had to pull his boat clear at the very last moment to avoid serious damage.

As Green Lily was getting closer to the shoreline, leaving less and less sea room in which the lifeboat could operate, the tug Maersk Champion managed to grapple her anchor-cable and tow the ship into the wind. The lifeboat crew had rescued five men, but ten more were still on board, but, with the vessel now lying head-to-wind, the helicopter was able to save the remaining ten men while the lifeboat stood by. Sadly, during the helicopter's rescue mission, winchman Bill Deacon, who had been lowered onto the casualty's deck, was swept overboard by an exceptionally large wave. Despite a thorough search until the light faded, he was not found.

Green Lily went aground in the appalling conditions and was subsequently smashed to pieces. Coxswain Clark was unable to get the lifeboat close to her again, with the mass of cargo debris, added to the already violent seas, raising safety concerns for his own crew and boat. For this extraordinary rescue Coxswain Clark was awarded the Gold medal and Bronze medals went to the five crew. Amazingly, despite being pounded alongside the cargo ship, Michael and Jane Vernon suffered only superficial damage and all her equipment functioned perfectly throughout the service, testimony to the Severn's design, the fibre reinforced composite hull and the high standard of her construction, as well as the skill and courage of her crew.

The Severn and Trent building programmes continued until 2005, with a total of forty-six and thirty-eight boats of each class, respectively, being completed. By then, the 16m Tamar class, the next design of twenty-five-knot lifeboat, was almost ready for service. Built to replace the 47ft Tynes and designed to be slipway-launched, the Tamar incorporated some significant technological advances, including an integrated computer system (SIMS) to control all the boat's functions, special load-bearing seats for the crew and a small inflatable boat launched from the stern through a hydraulically powered door. In total, twenty-seven Tamars were built,

Into the twenty-first century

▲ The 16m Tamar City of London III (ON.1294) launching at Sennen Cove, with the keel and bilge keel arrangements clearly visible. The lifeboat house at Sennen was extensively rebuilt to accommodate the Tamar. (Nicholas Leach)

◀ Two Tamars, Mark Mason (ON.1291, from Angle) and Norah Wortley (ON.1306), at St Davids, where the last of the thirteen Tamar boathouses was completed in 2016. (Nicholas Leach)

▼ The first 13m Shannon The Morrell (ON.1309) alongside the 12m Mersey Pride and Spirit (ON.1186) at Dungeness. (Nicholas Leach)

of which thirteen were slipway launched, being operated from stations where impressive new purpose-built lifeboat houses were constructed. The Tamar programme, including the building of thirteen slipway stations, represented an enormous investment by the RNLI.

As the Tamar build programme got under way, another new design, for a carriage-launched boat 13.7m in length, was being developed to replace the 12m Mersey. The prototype of this new design, ON.1285, was fitted out by VT Halmatic at Portchester during 2005; twin 510hp CAT C9 diesels powered two Hamilton waterjets, and the boat thus became the RNLI's first modern all-weather lifeboat to use waterjets for propulsion. As the prototype subsequently proved to be unsuitable, the boat was completely redesigned, and a new hull was developed, which proved to be far superior. Although the first hull was not usable, the experience with waterjets gained by the RNLI's in-house design teams pointed the way ahead, and twin 650hp Scania D13 engines driving twin Hamilton HJ364 waterjets were used in the production Shannons. After more than a decade of development, trials and evaluation, one of the RNLI's best lifeboat designs entered service, and the fleet of Shannons is likely to number upwards of seventy when the build programme is completed.

MOTOR LIFEBOATS 179

35 • 47ft Tyne

KEY DATA
- Introduced 1982
- Last built 1990
- 40 built

SPECIFICATIONS
- Length 47ft (14.3m)
- Beam 15ft (4.6m)
- Draught 4ft 2in (1.27m)
- Crew 6

▼ Line drawing of the prototype Tyne ON.1074; the side decks on the first two Tynes had a step in the sheerline, so a false side deck was fitted.

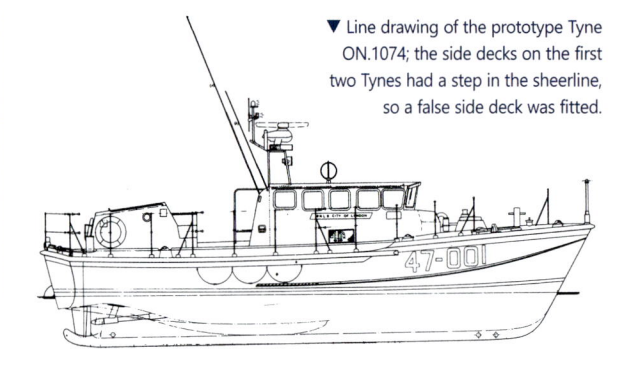

▲ Sir John Fisher (ON.1141) under construction at Marshall Branson boatyard, Amble in March 1989; three Tynes were built at Amble. (Tony Denton)

▼ The prototype 47ft Tyne City of London (ON.1074) on trials; she went on to serve at Selsey. (RNLI)

The 47ft Tyne was designed in the late 1970s as a fast replacement for the nine-knot Watson and Barnett displacement-hulled lifeboats at stations which employed slipway launching. Faster lifeboats had already been introduced into the RNLI's fleet in the shape of the Waveney and Arun, but these could only be kept afloat. A new fast lifeboat design was required for slipway stations. However, the RNLI stipulated that the design had to be within certain parameters so that the boat could fit into existing lifeboat houses. The requirements were for a boat with an overall length not exceeding 47ft 3in, a maximum beam of 15ft and a height from the underside of the keel to the top of the wheelhouse of 13ft. The weight could not exceed twenty-four tons, ensuring that most boathouses in service could take the new design.

The basic lines plan for the hull of the fast slipway lifeboat (FSB), as it was first designated, was provided by the National Maritime Institute. The hull was semi-planing with a shallow draught of 4ft 2in (1.27m), a long straight keel with a shallow conventional sheerline, and a flared bow above the waterline. Protection for the propellers was given by partial tunnels, substantial bilge keels, and a straight wide keel extending to the transom and ending in a hauling shoe, elements all necessary for slipway launching and working in shoal waters. The wheelhouse had a low profile to fit into existing boathouses, with a flying bridge midships, and there was a separate cabin aft of the upper steering position. The hull plating and internal structure was built from corrosion-resistant steel, with aluminium alloy for the deck and superstructures. Other materials, notably wood and glass reinforced plastic, were considered but rejected on grounds of wear resistance and cost. The class name Tyne was chosen to reflect the close connection of P. Denham Christie, chairman of the Boat Committee, with the FSB project. Mr Denham Christie came from Newcastle and served as coxswain of Tynemouth lifeboat from 1953 to 1963.

The first two Tynes, ON.1074 and ON.1075, served as pre-production prototypes and were subjected to a period of evaluation to assess and refine the design, with the changes then incorporated into the production boats. The hull shape of all the boats was essentially the same, but on the first two boats the deck had a step in the sheerline. Aft of this step, the deck had a heavy camber covered by a lightweight false side-deck. This was deemed an unnecessary complication and so, with the third boat, ON.1094, the turtle side decks were changed to flush decks. In addition, the after engine room bulkhead was moved to increase the volume of the aft cabin from this boat onwards, by adding dedicated rope stowage lockers, and the upper steering position, having initially been designed for use during recovery with only a small wheel, was enhanced.

The first two Tynes were fitted with General Motors 8V-71 diesel engines, similar to those installed in the 50ft Thames lifeboats. With engine room space at a premium, engines with a high power-to-size and power-to-weight ratio were needed, something provided by the General Motors diesels. After the 8V-71 model had been installed in the two pre-production prototypes, a newer model, the GM 6V-92, became available and so this was used in the boats from ON.1094. Further changes were made as more Tynes were built, and from The Lady Rank (ON.1114) onwards the main deck was constructed from aluminium rather than steel. This boat was also fitted with a ZF 160 BW gearbox rather than the standard GM gearbox, the Allison Type M20 used in the first ten boats, as it was slightly lighter and offered an improved reduction ratio.

Twin rudders were fitted, which were power assisted and had hand hydraulic controls. Two main fuel tanks, holding 510 gallons of diesel between them, were supplemented by a reserve tank of 102 gallons. This gave the boats a range of 238 nautical miles. Trim planes were incorporated into the stern to enable the running trim to be altered to suit the sea conditions.

During the 1990s a number of the boats were re-engined with twin 565bhp six-cylinder Detroit Diesel Series 92 DDEC diesels in an attempt

35 • 47ft Tyne

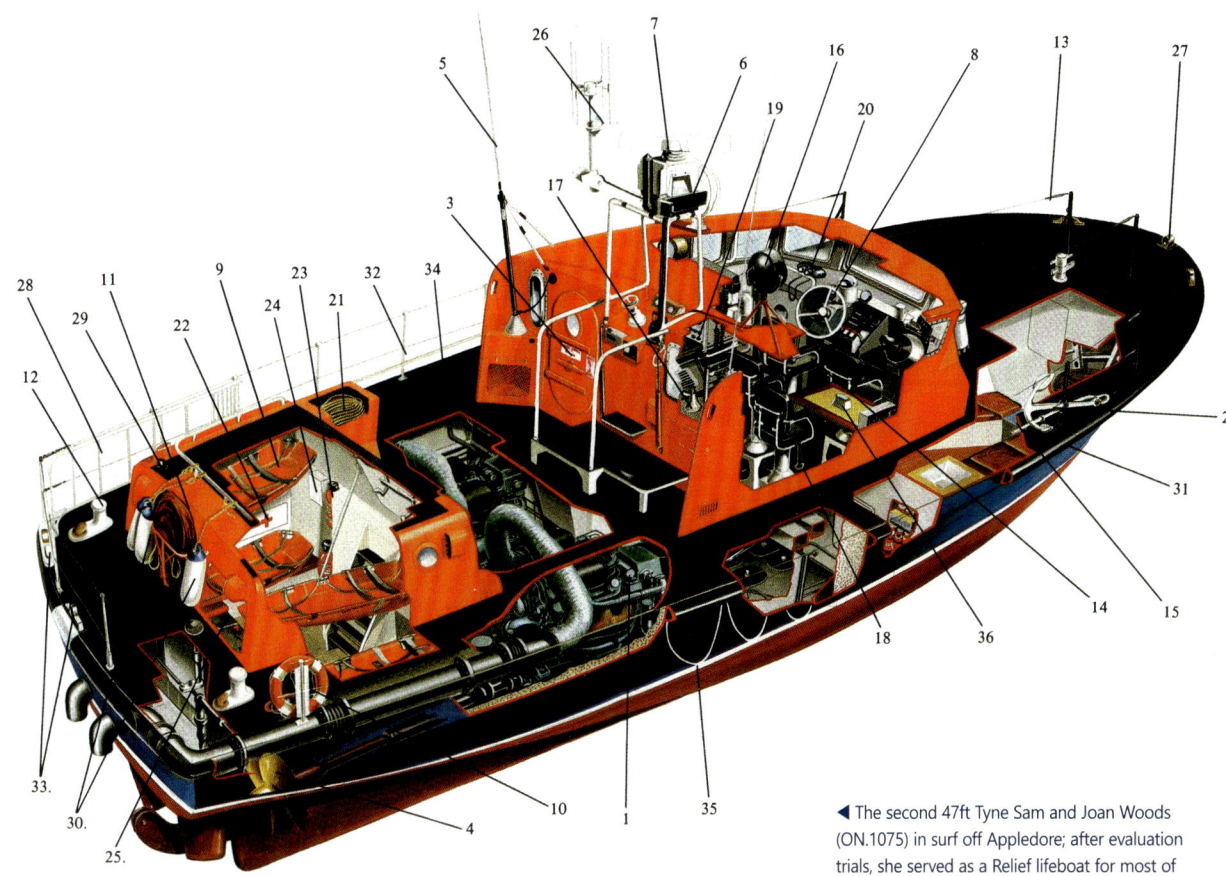

CUTAWAY DRAWING OF 47FT TYNE

◀ KEY • (1) Engine, (2) Anchor, (3) Watertight door, (4) Propeller, (5) Aerial, (6) Navigation lights, (7) Radar, (8) Steering wheel, (9) Stretcher, (10) Breeches buoy, (11) Drogue, (12) Bollard, (13) Jackstay, (14) Helmsman's seat, (15) Toilet, (16) Searchlight, (17) Loudhailer, (18) Seat belts, (19) Radio, (20) Binoculars, (21) Veering line, (22) First aid kit, (23) Fire extinguisher, (24) Mouth-to-mouth resuscitator, (25) Battery, (26) Blue flashing light, (27) Stemhead fairlead fitting, (28) Haul-up cleat, (29) Sternlight, (30) Fenders, (31) Rubber fendering, (32) Stanchion, (33) Fairleads, (34) Non-slip deck paint, (35) Lifeline, (36) Chart and magnifier.

▲ Ethel Anne Measures (ON.1096), the fifth 47ft Tyne to enter service, on trials. (RNLI)

◀ The second 47ft Tyne Sam and Joan Woods (ON.1075) in surf off Appledore; after evaluation trials, she served as a Relief lifeboat for most of her career. (RNLI)

▼ City of Edinburgh (ON.1109) on trials shortly after being completed by Fairey Marine; initially slipway launched at Fraserburgh, she was later operated from moorings. (RNLI)

MOTOR LIFEBOATS 181

35 • 47ft Tyne

to overcome problems with the original engines, which had a tendency to stall and backdrive. The backdriving caused the fuel lift pump seals to blow out, resulting in the engines being disabled. New engines were seen as the solution, so a pair of Detroit Diesel Electronic Control (DDEC) Series 60 engines was fitted to the relief Tyne Mariners Friend (ON.1142) in 1994; this boat was used for extensive trials to assess the engines' suitability.

The Series 60 was an inline-six four-stroke diesel engine that was first produced in 1987 and four different versions were manufactured. The engine was electronically controlled by the proprietary DDEC system, which was the first commercially available engine, having been built for highway use, with such electronic controls. The DDEC system provided engine diagnostics, shutdown timers, progressive shift functions, fault history record keeping, automatic stall preventing and cruise control.

The trials of the engines fitted to Mariners Friend proved the system and showed that the new power units eliminated the tendency to stall and backdrive, while also providing improved fuel management and gave the boats a slightly greater speed. However, problems with the new engine system were experienced in the late 1990s and many of the re-engined boats had to be withdrawn from service while the faults were rectified. During the course of the production lifecycle of the DDEC engine, four different versions were produced, with the DDEC II and III (introduced in 1992) systems being used in the Tynes.

Mariners Friend had the original type DDEC engines, and these were in turn replaced in 1997 by a newer version. In 1994 the RNLI's Executive Committee resolved to have all Tynes re-engined, and replace all the 6V units with new DDEC engines. By early 1997 ten boats had been converted, with two in progress, leaving twenty-six Tynes unconverted. The cost was approximately £90,000 per boat, provided the work was carried our during a scheduled refit. However, the RNLI decided that boats with an estimated lifespan of less than nine years would not be considered as re-engining was deemed not to be cost effective. In the event, the programme was further curtailed and only fifteen boats were fitted with the new engines; of these, eleven had DDEC 2.5 and four had DDEC 3 engines.

Modifications made to the boats while they were in operational service increased their weight by as much as a ton. As a result the self-righting capability was reviewed and it was deemed that an increase in superstructure volume was required to maintain an inherent righting capability. From boat number thirty, David Robinson (ON.1145), the aft cabin height was increased by 125mm. All boats subsequently had this modification carried out while they were undergoing surveys. However, in 2004, during the development of the Tyne's replacement (see table 39), further questions were raised about the boats' self-righting ability.

The RNLI developed a computer model to test self-righting ability, and applied this retrospectively to the Tyne. The computer simulation suggested that, in the unlikely situation that a Tyne was carrying a large number of survivors in particularly challenging sea conditions, it may possibly not self-right as designed. Therefore, it was decided to install a pair of airbags on the aft cabin roof of all Tynes. The programme began in October 2004 and was completed by May 2005, with the work being relatively straightforward as the RNLI has plenty of expertise and experience in the use of air-bags. A rack was fitted on the aft cabin to which the airbags were attached.

Although most Tynes were operated from slipway stations, a number were kept afloat as the design's protected propellers made it suitable for working in shallow waters, being built for stations such as Salcombe, Lowestoft and St Helier, where the lifeboat lies afloat but had to operate over sandbars or rocks. The Tynes gave outstanding service, and their coxswains and crews became attached to the powerful boats, which gained a reputation for having excellent sea-keeping qualities. The last to leave service was Annie Blaker (ON.1153), at Wicklow in Ireland, which was replaced in April 2019, by when the Tynes had given operational service with the RNLI for almost four decades in total.

▲ Self-righting trials of Norman Salvesen (ON.1121) at Amble on 22 May 1988. The self-righting capability of the design came from the watertight wheelhouse and hull, and righting was achieved in about six second. (Tony Denton)

▶ The air-bags deployed on the Padstow Tyne James Burrough (ON.1094). The conversion work was undertaken inside the boathouse, with the inflation cylinders for the airbags being fitted inside the aft cabin. (By courtesy of Padstow RNLI)

▶▶ The airbags deployed on Max Aitken III (ON.1126) while she was at the RNLI Depot, Poole, 8 October 2009. (Peter Edey)

182 MOTOR LIFEBOATS

35 • 47ft Tyne

▲ Phil Mead (ON.1110) was one of the batch of four Tynes which entered service in late 1985 and 1986. She served at Teesmouth for twenty years, and when she was withdrawn in April 2006 the station was closed. (Nicholas Leach)

◄ The fourth St Cybi II (Civil Service No.40) (ON.1095) on trials. After twelve years at Holyhead, she served a further decade in the RNLI's Relief FLeet. (By courtesy of the RNLI)

▼ The sixth 47ft Tyne Ruby and Arthur Reed II (ON.1097) being launched at Cromer (left) and recovered up the slipway (right). She was the last of four Tynes built in 1984-85, ordered after the prototype boats had proved the general design. The rudder, keel and propeller arrangements are evident in the photograph of the boat being hauled up the slipway. (Nicholas Leach)

MOTOR LIFEBOATS

35 • 47ft Tyne

Mariners Friend (ON-1142), which was built for service in the Relief Fleet, was the first of the class to be fitted with the more powerful DDEC diesel engines. She is pictured on Relief duty at Kilmore Quay in 2006, with the self-righting air-bags on the aft cabin visible; this was just before she became station boat at Lough Swilly. (Nicholas Leach)

35 • 47ft Tyne

	Year (Yd No) Builder Place	Name Donor	ON (Op No) Cost Weight	Engines (twn diesels)	Stations (launches/lives saved)	Disposal
1	1982 (FM708) Fairey Marine Cowes	**City of London** City of London Appeal.	1074 (47-001) £430,000 25t5	2x425hp General Motors 8V-71-TI	Selsey 11.1983-2.2006 (415/58)	Sold 2007
2	1982 (FM709) Fairey Marine Cowes	**Sam and Joan Woods** RNLI General Funds.	1075 (47-002) £432,628 24t11	2x425hp General Motors 8V-71-TI	Relief 1984-93 (59/24) & 1996-2006 (94/9) Walton & Frinton 8.1993-5.1996 (67/10)	Sold 2007
3	1984 (FM716) Fairey Marine Cowes	**James Burrough** Gift of Miss H. B. Allen, East Clandon, Surrey.	1094 (47-003) £451,906 24t0	2x425hp General Motors 6V-92-TA	Padstow 12.1984-7.2006 (293/97)	Sold 2007
4	1985 (717/2770) Fairey Marine/ William Osborne	**St Cybi II (Civil Service No.40)** Civil Service Lifeboat Fund.	1095 (47-004) £449,412 24t4	2x425hp General Motors 6V-92-TA	Holyhead 9.1985-12.1997 (267/119) Relief 1997-2006 (106/5)	Sold 2007
5	1985 (FM718) Fairey Marine Cowes	**Ethel Anne Measures** J.F. & E.A. Measures Charity, Mumbles Lifeboat Appeal, various other donors.	1096 (47-005) £447,453 25t5	2x425hp General Motors 6V-92-TA	Mumbles 7.1985-7.2006 (364/70) Relief 2006-07 (3/0)	Sold 2007
6	1985 (FM719) Fairey Marine Cowes	**Ruby and Arthur Reed II** Bequest of Mrs R.M. Reed and Cromer Lifeboat Appeal, and other gifts and legacies.	1097 (47-006) £439,560 25t5	2x425hp General Motors 6V-92-TA	Cromer 12.1985-17.11.1996 (75/29) Relief 1997-98 (28/0) and 2007-08 (0/0) Cromer 4.3.1999-3.2007 (44/9)	Sold 7.2008
7	1985 (FM1058) Fairey Marine Cowes	**City of Edinburgh** The City of Edinburgh Lifeboat Appeal.	1109 (47-007) £454,597 24t0	2x425hp General Motors 6V-92-TA	Fraserburgh 11.1985-5.2002 (180/115) Relief 5.2002-2008 (61/0)	Sold 2008
8	1985 (FM1059) Fairey Marine Cowes	**Phil Mead** Trustees of Phil Mead Charitable Trust, and local appeal.	1110 (47-008) £459,511 25t5	2x425hp General Motors 6V-92-TA	Teesmouth 1.1986-4.2006 (346/42) Relief 4.2006-2008 (10/3)	Sold 2008
9	1986 (FM1060) Fairey Marine Cowes	**William Luckin** Bequest of Mrs Rose Mary Luckin, and RNLI Funds.	1111 (47-009) £456,592 25t5	2x425hp General Motors 6V-92-TA	Arranmore 4.1986-2.2000 (280/46) Lough Swilly 4.2001-6.07 (67/8)	Sold 6.2008
10	1986 (2880) Wright, Derby/ William Osborne	**RFA Sir Galahad** Royal Fleet Aux liaryAppeal, Shropshire Lifeboat Appeal, and Tenby Branch Appeal.	1112 (47-010) £445,000 25t5	2x425hp General Motors 6V-92-TA	Tenby 6.9.1986-4.2006 (364/254) Relief 4.2006-2.2008 (29/0) Angle 26.2.2008-3.2009 (20/0)	Sold 1.2010
11	1987 (2970) Wright, Derby/ William Osborne	**The Lady Rank** The Rank Foundation.	1114 (47-011) £535,803 25t5	2x425hp General Motors 6V-92-TA	Angle 6.1987-2.2008 (271/99) Relief 2.2008-2011 (26/0)	Sold 7.2011
12	1987 (2990) Wright, Derby/ William Osborne	**Good Shepherd** An Ecumenical Appeal to Churches, with various other gifts and legacies.	1115 (47-012) £543,917 25t66	2x425hp General Motors 6V-92-TA	Relief 4.1988-5.2010 (239/74)	Sold 6.2010
13	1987 (1116) Wright, Derby/ Lochin Marine	**Robert and Violet** Anonymous gift.	1116 (47-013) £532,057 24t98	2x425hp GM 6V-92-TA/ 1997– 2x500hp GM 6V-T92-TA DDEC 3	Moelfre 1.1988-5.2013 (394/92) Lough Swilly 5.2013-4.2015 (16/0)	Sold 7.2015
14	1986 (FM1073) Fairey Marine Cowes	**James Bibby** Gift of Mr J.B. Bibby, of Liverpool.	1117 (47-014) £528,430 22t9	2x425hp GM 6V-92-TA/ 1996– 2x500hp GM 6V-T92-TA DDEC 3	Barrow 9.1986-1.2008 (202/14) Relief 2008-2010 (39/0)	Sold 2.2011
15	1987 (FM1106) Fairey Marine Cowes	**Hetty Rampton** Trustees of Miss Hetty Mabel Rampton's Charity.	1120 (47-015) £508,696 25t5	2x425hp General Motors 6V-92-TA	Porthdinllaen 4.1987-8.2012 (316/52) Relief 8.2012-2015 (3/0)	Sold 2016

MOTOR LIFEBOATS

35 • 47ft Tyne

	Year (Yd No) Builder Place	Name Donor	ON (Op No) Cost Weight	Engines (twn diesels)	Stations (launches/lives saved)	Disposal
16	1987 (1121) Wright, Derby/ Harrison, Amble	Norman Salvesen Bequest of Mrs Norman Salvesen.	1121 (47-016) £537,000 25t8	2x425hp GM 6V-92-TA/ 1997– 2x500hp GM 6V-T92-TA DDEC 2.5	Wick 9.1988-2.1997 (120/54) Sennen Cove 12.1998-10.2009 (130/10) Relief 10.2009-2014 (10/0)	Sold 6.2014
17	1987 (0012) Wright, Derby/ W.A. Souter	Owen and Anne Aisher Gift of Sir Owen Aisher, Branksome, Poole.	1122 (47-017) £537,000 26t	2x425hp General Motors 6V-92-TA	Relief Fleet 1988-2012 (315/66)	Sold 6.2013
18	1987 (FM1189) Fairey Marine Cowes	Max Aitken III The Beaverbrook Foundation.	1126 (47-018) £537,000 24t98	2x425hp GM 6V-92-TA/ 1996– 2x500hp GM 6V-T92-TA DDEC 2.5	Bembridge 12.1987-2.2009 (479/141) Relief 2.2009-2012 (30/1)	Sold 6.2013
19	1987 (FM1190) Fairey Marine Cowes	Babs and Agnes Robertson Anonymous gift (Robertson and Baxter Ltd, Glasgow).	1127 (47-019) £537,000 25t2	2x425hp General Motors 6V-92-TA	Peterhead 1.1988-4.2006 (215/33) Relief 4-7.2006 (3/0) Mumbles 7.2006-2.2014 (129/0)	Sold 2014
20	1987 (1130) Wright, Derby/ Lochin Marine	The Baltic Exchange II The Baltic Exchange with other gifts and bequests.	1130 (47-022) £584,362 25t14	2x425hp General Motors 6V-92-TA	Salcombe 8.1988-3.2008 (377/115) Relief 3.2008-09 (23/0)	Sold 2010
21	1987 (0027) Wright, Derby/ W. A. Souter	City of Sheffield The City of Sheffield Lifeboat Appeal.	1131 (47-023) £566,000 25t2	2x425hp GM 6V-92-TA/ 1997– 2x500hp GM 6V-T92-TA DDEC 2.5	Whitby 12.1988-4.1996 (239/88) Relief 4.1996-7.97 and 10.2000-9.01 (25/9) Hartlepool 7.1997-10.2000 (31/8) Poole 5.9.2001-11.2016 (554/1)	Sold 6.2017 for display at Emergency Services Museum, Sheffield
22	1987 (FM1191) Fairey Marine Cowes	Spirit of Lowestoft The Lowestoft Appeal with other gifts and legacies.	1132 (47-020) £520,166 25t04	2x425hp GM 6V-92-TA/ 1997– 2x500hp GM 6V-T92-TA D DEC 3	Lowestoft 11.1987-10.2014 (560/83) Relief 10.2014-2018 (0/0)	Display at Historic Dockyard, Chatham, 2019
23	1987 (FM1192) Fairey Marine Cowes	The Famous Grouse The Famous Grouse Competition Appeal.	1133 (47-021) £537,000 25t37	2x425hp General Motors 6V-92-TA	Relief 12.1987-4.2004 (176/37) Kilmore Quay 4.2004-10.2010 (187/0) Releif 2010-2012 (0/0)	Sold 2013
24	1988 (FM1193) Fairey Marine Cowes	Hilda Jarrett Legacy of Mrs H.J. Jarrett, together wth other bequests and RNLI Funds.	1137 (47-024) £560,000 25t25	2x425hp General Motors 6V-92-TA	Baltimore 3.1988-3.2012 (360/92) Relief 3.2012-2015 (10/0)	Sold 7.2015
25	1988 (FM1194) Fairey Marine Cowes	Lord Saltoun Legacy of Mrs Mary Salvesen.	1138 (47-025) £537,000 25t07	2x425hp GM 6V-92-TA/ 1997– 2x500hp GM 6V-T92-TA DDEC 2.5	Longhope 3.1988-8.1999 (41/9) Relief 8.1999-2.2012 (111/6)	Sold 2012
26	1988 (FM1195) Fairey Marine Cowes	Garside Legacies of Thomas Harold Garside and Dorothy Garside.	1139 (47-026) £537,000 25t38	2x425hp General Motors 6V-92-TA	St Davids 25.5.1988-10.2016 (345/79)	Sold 2018
27	1988 (FM1196) Fairey Marine Cowes	George Gibson Mr G.C. Gibson, OBE, through the Gibson Charitable Trust.	1140 (47-027) £537,000 25t	2x425hp GM 6V-92-TA/ 1997– 2x500hp GM 6V-T92-TA DDEC 2.5	Appledore 6.1988-3.2010 (259/22) Relief 3.2010-11 (13/0)	Sold 2013
28	1989 (1141) Wright, Derby/ Marshall-Branson, Amble	Sir John Fisher The Sir John Fisher Foundation.	1141 (47-028) £560,000 26t43	2x425hp General Motors 6V-92-TA	Relief 1989-1992 (5/0) Workington 8.6.1992-4.2017 (270/50)	Sold 2018
29	1989 (0056) Wright, Derby/ W. A. Souter	Mariners Friend The H.B. Allen Charitable Trust.	1142 (47-029) £550,000 26t35	2x425hp GM 6V-92-TA/ 1994– 2x500hp GM 6V-T92-TA DDEC 2.5	Relief 9.1989-6.2007 (190/49) Lough Swilly 6.2007-10.2012 (46/1) Relief 10.2012-2013 (0/0)	Sold 5.2014

MOTOR LIFEBOATS

35 • 47ft Tyne

	Year (Yd No) Builder Place	Name Donor	ON (Op No) Cost Weight	Engines (twn diesels)	Stations (launches/lives saved)	Disposal
30	1988 (FM1208) Fairey Marine Cowes	**David Robinson** Legacy of the late Sir David Robinson.	1145 (47-030) £550,131 25t10	2x425hp General Motors 6V-92-TA	The Lizard 8.1988-7.2011 (211/89) Relief 7.2011-2016 (16/0)	Sold 4.2017
31	1988 (FM1209) Fairey Marine Cowes	**Voluntary Worker** The Volvo Concessionaires Ltd, Tesco Stores Ltd Promotions, and other gifts.	1146 (47-031) £537,000 25t12	2x425hp GM 6V-92-TA/ 1995– 2x500hp GM 6V-T92-TA DDEC 2.5	Lytham St Annes 12.1988-1.1990 (10/8) Relief 20.1.1990-2005 (181/41) Selsey 2.2006-7.2017 (197/7)	Sold 2018
32	1988 (FM1210) Fairey Marine Cowes	**Sir William Hillary** Legacy of the A.J. Woolfenden, Gawsworth, Cheshire.	1147 (47-032) £537,000 25t9	2x425hp General Motors 6V-92-TA	Douglas 11.1988-7.2018 (336/88)	Sold 2019
33	1989 (FM1237) Fairey Marine Cowes	**Mary Irene Millar** Legacies of the late Mrs Mary Irene Millar, Miss Mary Milne Stewart and Mrs Muriel Johns, together with other gifts.	1151 (47-033) £582,557 25t5	2x425hp General Motors 6V-92-TA	Portpatrick 3.1989-11.2011 (251/70) Relief 11.2011-2013 (0/0)	Sold 12.2013
34	1989 (FM1238) Fairey Marine Cowes	**Moonbeam** Mr and Mrs Roland Sutton, Grampian.	1152 (47-034) £580,150 25t7	2x425hp GM 6V-92-TA/ 1995– 2x500hp GM 6V-T92-TA DDEC 3	Montrose 5.1989-9.2015 (170/7)	Sold 2016
35	1989 (FM1239) Fairey Marine Cowes	**Annie Blaker** Bequest of Annie Lydia Blaker, and RNLI general funds.	1153 (47-035) £575,636 25t77	2x425hp General Motors 6V-92-TA	Wicklow 10.1989-4.2019 (375/38)	Sold 2019
36	1989 (0068) Wright, Foston Derby	**Kenneth Thelwall II** Bequest of Kenneth Thelwall, Walkington, Yorkshire.	1154 (47-036) £615,082 26t24	2x425hp GM 6V-92-TA/ 1997– 2x500hp GM 6V-T92-TA DDEC 2.5	Ramsgate 4.1990-8.94 (92/16) Walton & Frinton 5.1996-5.2011 (288/15)	Sold 9.2011
37	1989 (FM1257) FBM Marine Cowes	**Sarah Emily Harrop** Bequest of Sarah Emily Harrop.	1155 (47-037) £589,183 25t92	2x425hp GM 6V-92-TA/ 1996– 2x500hp GM 6V-T92-TA DDEC 2.5	Lytham St Annes 1.1990-10.98 (91/17) Relief 1998-2006 (133/6) Calshot 2.2007-1.2010 (161/1) Shoreham Harbour 21.4-11.2010 (11/0)	Sold 2010
38	1989 (FM1258) FBM Marine Cowes	**William Street** W.O. Street Foundation; bequests of Major Percy Holley, Francis Balshaw; gift Miss H. Richmond.	1156 (47-038) £592,016 26t58	2x425hp GM 6V-92-TA/ 1997– 2x500hp GM 6V-T92-TA DDEC 2.5	Fleetwood 10.1989-8.2016 (536/37)	Sold 2016
39	1990 (FM1259) FBM Marine Cowes	**Alexander Coutanche** Jersey Lifeboat Appeal and the States of Jersey.	1157 (47-039) £592,669 25t69	2x425hp GM 6V-92-TA/ 1997– 2x500hp GM 6V-T92-TA DDEC 2.5	St Helier 12.1989-6.2009 (401/677) Calshot 1.2010-7.2012 (99/2) Lough Swilly 10.2012-5.2013 (2/0) Relief 2013-2014 (2/0)	Sold 12.2014
40	1990 (1158) Wright, Derby/ Marshall-Branson	**Hermione Lady Colwyn** Shoreham LB Appeal and bequest of Lady Colwyn.	1158 (47-040) £720,020	2x425hp General Motors 6V-92-TA	Shoreham Harbour 9.1990-4.2010 (414/39)	Sold 6.2010

Two Tynes ON.1128 and ON.1129 (designated 47-020 and 47-021) were ordered from Cygnus boatyard, but the orders were cancelled in 1986 and reallocated to Fairey Marine

MOTOR LIFEBOATS

35 • 47ft Tyne

▲ Sir John Fisher (ON.1141) being lifted out of the water at Workington by the unique gantry crane. This method of launching was developed as being the most suitable for the specific conditions at that station. (Nicholas Leach)

▲ Lord Saltoun (ON.1138) on exercise while serving on Relief duty at Baltimore. She was built for Longhope, where she was slipway launched, but was replaced by a 52ft Arun in 1999 at a time when the RNLI were reducing the number of stations where slipway launching was employed. (Nicholas Leach)

▶ Two Tynes at Mumbles: Babs and Agnes Robertson (ON.1127) and Baltic Exchange II (ON.1130); the latter had been on relief duty at the station. (Nicholas Leach)

188   MOTOR LIFEBOATS

35 • 47ft Tyne

◀ Annie Blaker (ON.1153), off the Wicklow coast, was the last Tyne in operational service.

▲ The last 47ft Tyne was Hermione Lady Colwyn (ON.1158), pictured launching at Shoreham Harbour.

▼ Alexander Coutanche (ON.1157) off Jersey; she was one of several Tynes which were kept afloat.

MOTOR LIFEBOATS 189

36 • 12m Mersey

KEY DATA
▶ Introduced 1986
▶ Last built 1993
▶ 38 built

SPECIFICATIONS
▶ Length 38ft (11.62m)
▶ Beam 12ft 6in (3.81m)
▶ Depth 6ft (1.86m)
▶ Draught 2ft 10in (0.875m)
▶ Displacement 14.3 tonnes (maximum)
▶ Fuel capacity: 1,110 litres
▶ Crew 6

The fast carriage lifeboat (FCB) was developed during the 1980s for stations where a carriage launch was practised, and fulfilled the RNLI's stated commitment made in 1983 to have fast lifeboats at all stations by 1990. The FCB had to fit inside existing boathouses and was to be launched using the same method as the Oakley and Rother lifeboats that were to be replaced. These design limitations led to the development of a boat with an overall length of 38ft, a beam of 12ft 6in, and twin engines driving twin propellers, which were protected by semi-tunnels.

The hull configuration, determined after much deliberation and tank testing, was of round bilge semi-displacement form with a soft nose stem, a side spray rail, flowing s-shaped sheerline and radiused raked transom, with partial tunnels to protect the twin screws. The propellers were tucked out of the way, protected by the straight centreline keel and twin bilge keels. The hull was subdivided by four watertight bulkheads into five compartments, which comprised a forepeak cable locker, a survivors' cabin with seating for ten people, machinery space, tank space and an after peak steering gear compartment. The low profile wheelhouse extended over the forward part of the engine room and part of the survivor cabin, which was situated ahead of the engine room.

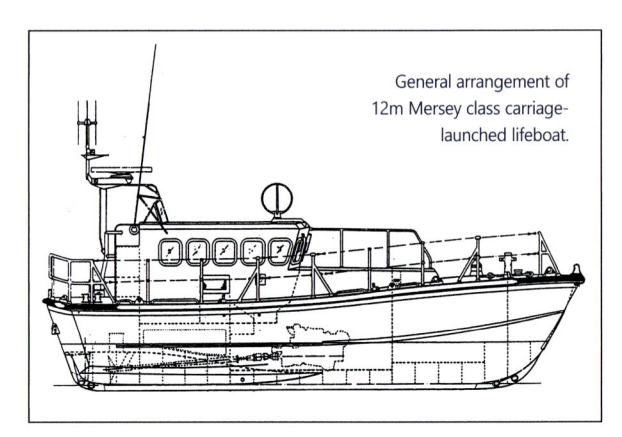

General arrangement of 12m Mersey class carriage-launched lifeboat.

The first FCB, ON.1119, was a full-scale prototype which did not see service and was never formally named before being sold, having been used only for tests and trials. This full-scale boat was used in place of large scale models because of the complications that carriage launching brought to hull design. Following this prototype, the second and third boats, Peggy

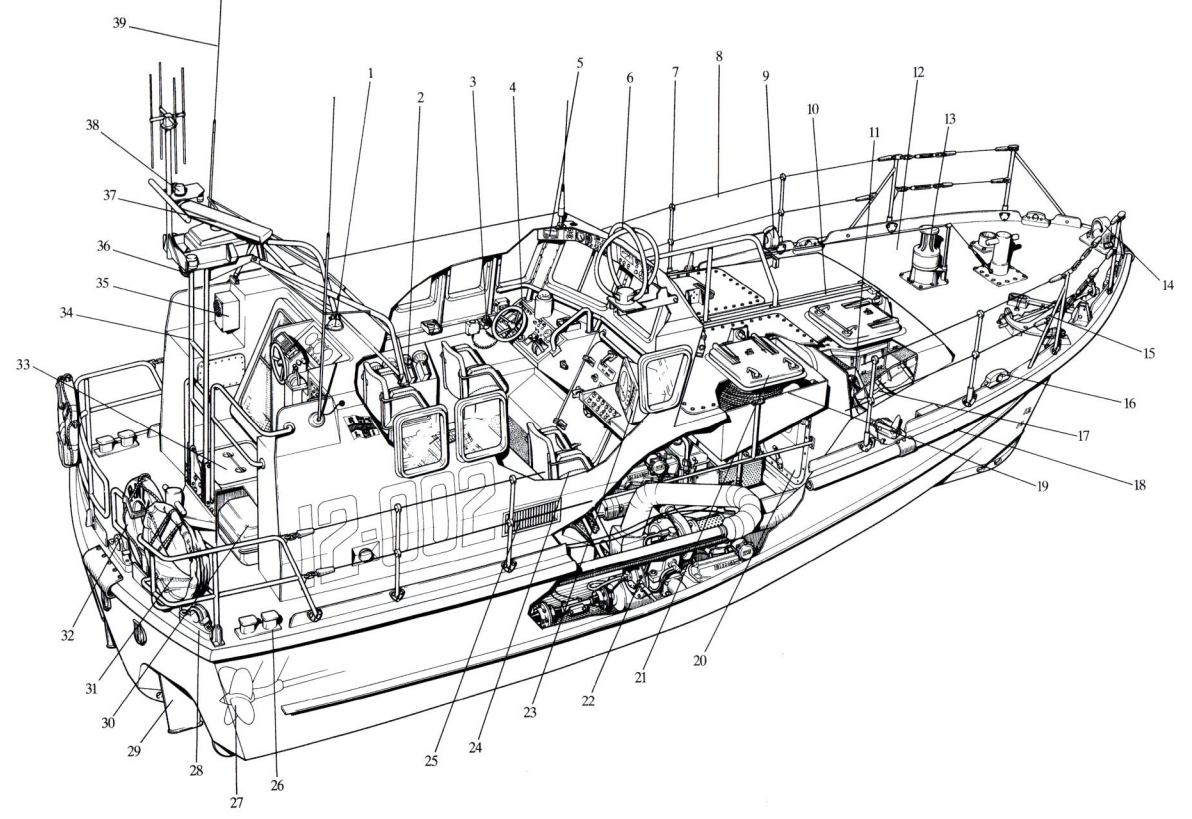

▲ The prototype fast carriage boat, ON.1119, at William Osborne's boatyard at Littlehampton in September 1987; this boat was only used for trials and evaluation purposes. Following the trials, the bow design was changed and the stepped section was removed and the bilge keel arrangements at the stern were altered. (Tony Denton)

CUTAWAY OF 12m MERSEY

(1) Compass, (2) Torches, (3) Intercom, (4) Steering wheel, (5) Echo sounder, (6) DF loop, (7) Stanchion, (8) Guard wires, (9) Loudspeaker, (10) Boathook, (11) Fire extinguisher, (12) Non-slip deck paint, (13) Capstan, (14) Fairlead, (15) Anchor, (16) Starboard fairlead fitting, (17) Stretcher, (18) Fendering, (19) Fend-off, (20) Watertight door, (21) Watertight hatch, (22) Main engine, (23) Radar, (24) Seat, (25) Engine room air-filter, (26) Bollard, (27) Propeller, (28) Stern fairlead, (29) Rudder, (30) Liferaft, (31) Drogue, (32) Breeches buoy, (33) Access hatch, (34) Mast, (35) Capsize valve, (36) Navigation light, (37) Radar scanner, (38) Blue flashing light, (39) Whip aerial.

MOTOR LIFEBOATS

36 • 12m Mersey

◀ Two photographs of ON.1125, one of the two production prototype 12m Merseys, being recovered and launching at Bridlington during trials in February 1988. The propellers and rudders were protected by partial tunnels set into the hull. The tunnels, along with the main and bilge keels, provided protection in shallow water and during beach recovery or slipway operations. (Paul Arro)

◀ Merseys on trials: ON.1148 (on left), the first FRC Mersey, and ON.1125 visting Cowes in July 1988 a few days after the class name Mersey had been announced by the RNLI and ON.1125, to be named Sealink Endeavour, had been allocated to Hastings. She was refitted in late 1988 to bring her up to new lifeboat standards and went to her station in February 1989. (Nicholas Leach)

▼ Lifetime Care (ON.1148) out of the water at the RNLI Depot, Poole, 8 October 1994. She was the first FRC-hulled Mersey and served in the Relief Fleet. (Nicholas Leach)

and Alex Caird (ON.1124) and Sealink Endeavour (ON.1125), were built, initially as production prototypes, and had aluminium hulls. Aluminium was chosen because of its weight-saving properties when compared to steel, as the weight of the boat was crucial if the design was to reach the desired speed and be suitable for launching from a carriage. ON.1125 was developed first and undertook the initial trials of the design, being followed by ON.1124, which incorporated a number of improvements in the fit-out of the hull. The two prototype aluminium hulls and superstructures, built by Aluminium Shipbuilders Ltd at their Portchester yard, were the first all-aluminium lifeboats used by the RNLI.

However, the long-term intention was to produce the FCB hulls from a new material, fibre reinforced composite (FRC); both aluminium and FRC were materials new to RNLI lifeboat design. During 1987 and 1988 FRC was evaluated and thoroughly tested thoroughly tested in a fourth hull, Lifetime Care (ON.1148), which was built from an epoxy resin matrix reinforced with glass and Kevlar fibres. The decision to use FRC was taken to speed up the construction process as the aim was to have forty boats in service within four years. FRC enabled a moulded hull to be built, thus utilising pre-constructed sections and pre-assembled components, resulting in an shorter build time overall.

ON.1148 was ordered in September 1987 and delivered in March 1988, undertaking seakeeping and handling trials. She was run on and off Dungeness beach 243 times and dragged for almost a mile over the shingle, which represented twenty years' launching. An inspection of the bottom revealed that no damage had been caused to the hull, apart from some scuffing of the paint. While trials with the FRC prototype (ON.1148) were ongoing, eight more hulls (ON.1161 to ON.1168) were ordered to be built of aluminium in June 1988, as the intention was always to build the first production boats from aluminium. From Marine Engineer (ON.1169) onwards, however, FRC was used, and FRC proved to be ideal in operational conditions; composites have been used for all subsequent lifeboat designs.

Power came from two Caterpillar 3208T turbo-charged diesel engines mounted amidships, rated at 285hp each and driving through two-to-one

MOTOR LIFEBOATS

36 • 12m Mersey

▲ The first production FRC-hulled 12m Mersey Marine Engineer (ON.1169) on her carriage in the lifeboat house at Bridlington, showing the partial tunnels protecting the propellers and rudders. (Nicholas Leach)

▶ Marine Engineer (ON.1169) being launched from Bridlington for the last time, December 2017, having been replaced by a new 13m Shannon. (Nicholas Leach)

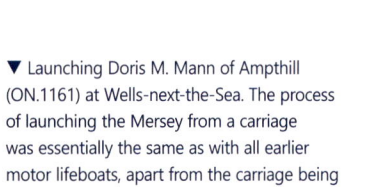

▼ Launching Doris M. Mann of Ampthill (ON.1161) at Wells-next-the-Sea. The process of launching the Mersey from a carriage was essentially the same as with all earlier motor lifeboats, apart from the carriage being redesigned for the larger boat. (Nicholas Leach)

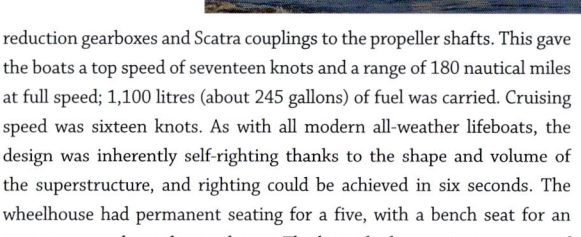

reduction gearboxes and Scatra couplings to the propeller shafts. This gave the boats a top speed of seventeen knots and a range of 180 nautical miles at full speed; 1,100 litres (about 245 gallons) of fuel was carried. Cruising speed was sixteen knots. As with all modern all-weather lifeboats, the design was inherently self-righting thanks to the shape and volume of the superstructure, and righting could be achieved in six seconds. The wheelhouse had permanent seating for a five, with a bench seat for an extra two people, such as a doctor. The boats had a survivor capacity of twenty-one with the self-righting capability retained, and forty-three without remaining self-righting.

The wheelhouse was set well aft and the sheer line of the hull flattened towards the bow. The masts and aerials could be lowered so that she can fit into a boathouse. Two steering positions were incorporated in the design: an elevated upper steering position for 360 degree views and one inside the wheelhouse. Communications and navigation equipment included VHF (very high frequency) and MF (medium frequency) radios, VHF direction finder (DF), global positioning system (GPS) with electronic chart system and radar. The MF DF was removed mid-life, and a Laserplot electronic chart system was added. Medical equipment included oxygen and a resuscitation kit, Entonox for pain relief, large responder bag and two different stretchers. A small inflatable unpowered X boat, which was manually launched and rowed by the crew, was an optional extra, and not every Mersey carried one.

The design was given the class name Mersey in line with the RNLI's policy of naming lifeboat classes after rivers. Mersey was chosen to maintain a link with the Liverpool class, to reaffirm the Institution's links with the Merseyside area and its maritime tradition, and because stations on the approaches to the river received boats of the class. The new design was formally announced by the RNLI to the media on 14 July 1988, when the RNLI's director, Lt Cdr Brian Miles, said: 'This is an historic day for the RNLI. We now have a carriage-launched lifeboat which has twice the speed of those she is designed to replace. The new class represents the final piece of the jigsaw in our plan to complete the introduction of fast lifeboats.' A total of forty Merseys were planned, but the build programme ran to thirty-seven boats, of which ten were aluminium hulled.

36 • 12m Mersey

#	Year (Yd No) Builder Place	Name Donor	ON (Op No) Cost Weight	Engines	Stations (launches/lives saved)	Disposal
1	1986 (2940) Cunningham/ William Osborne	[Not named] —	1119 — —	2x285hp Caterpillar 3208T (aluminium hull)	Experimental prototype Used for trials only	Scrapped and hull sold 1989
2	1987 (WO3130) Aluminium SB/ William Osborne	**Peggy and Alex Caird** Bequest of Miss M. M. Caird, Hull.	1124 (12-001) £574,084 13.85 tonnes	2x285hp Caterpillar 3208T (aluminium hull)	Bridlington 15.12.1988-8.1995 (105/19) Relief 8.1995-2009 (101/8) and 2010-15 (13/0) Bridlington 5.2.2009-20.10.2010 (53/2)	Sold 2015
3	1987 (WO3070) Aluminium SB/ William Osborne	**Sealink Endeavour** Sealink British Ferries Ltd Promotion, bequests Dr W. Murphy, Mrs Dorothy M. Kellett and other gifts.	1125 (12-002) £498,625 14 tonnes	2x285hp Caterpillar 3208T (aluminium hull)	Trials 1987-3.1989 (2/4) Hastings 13.3.1989-2018 (357/37)	
4	1988 (0061) Green Marine/ W. A. Souter	**Lifetime Care** The Volvo Concessionaires Limited promotion.	1148 (12-11) £586,845 13.67 tonnes	2x285hp Caterpillar 3208T (FRC hull)	Relief 10.1989-8.2017 (244/52)	Sold 3.2017
5	1989 (FM1266) FBM Ltd Cowes	**Doris M. Mann of Ampthill** Legacy of Doris M. Mann, Ampthill, Beds.	1161 (12-003) £468,209 14.91 tonnes	2x285hp Caterpillar 3208T (aluminium hull)	Wells 3.7.1990-	
6	1990 (FM1267) FBM Ltd Cowes	**Royal Shipwright** The Worshipful Company of Shipwrights, and others.	1162 (12-004) £434,231 14.46 tonnes	2x285hp Caterpillar 3208T (aluminium hull)	Relief 1990-3.2007 (134/28) Cromer 3.2007-1.2008 (10/0) Relief 1.2008-9.2018 (52/0)	Sold 12.2016
7	1990 (FM1268) FBM Ltd Cowes	**Lady of Hilbre** Mersey Lifeboat Appeal, and other gifts and legacies.	1163 (12-005) £430,556 14 tonnes	2x285hp Caterpillar 3208T (aluminium hull)	Hoylake 10.1990-12.2014 (263/39) Relief 12.2014-	
8	1990 (FM1269) FBM Ltd Cowes	**Andy Pearce** Bequests of Andrew Pearce and Mr Ralph C. Merriott, with other gifts and legacies.	1164 (12-006) £429,494 14 tonnes	2x285hp Caterpillar 3208T (aluminium hull)	Llandudno 23.11.1990-10.2017 (249/50) Relief 2017-18	Sold 2019
9	1990 (WO3317) Aluminium SB/ William Osborne	**Spirit of Derbyshire** Spirit of Derbyshire and Ilfracombe Lifeboat Appeals.	1165 (12-007) £444,498 14.25 tonnes	2x285hp Caterpillar 3208T (aluminium hull)	Ilfracombe 20.7.1990-6.2015 (352/40)	Sold 2015
10	1990 (0084) Aluminium SB/ W. A. Souter	**Lincolnshire Poacher** Lincolnshire Lifeboat Appeal and Van Geest Charitable Trust.	1166 (12-008) £460,212 14.16 tonnes	2x285hp Caterpillar 3208T (aluminium hull)	Skegness 7.8.1990-2.2017 (353/38) Relief 2.2017-	
11	1990 (WO3359) Aluminium SB/ William Osborne	**The Princess Royal (Civil Service No.41)** Civil Service, Post Office and British Telecom Lifeboat Fund.	1167 (12-009) £445,432 14 tonnes	2x285hp Caterpillar 3208T (aluminium hull)	St Ives 23.10.1990-11.2015 (316/17) Relief 2015-2016 (0/0)	Sold 2016
12	1990 (0085) Aluminium SB/ W. A. Souter	**Lilly and Vincent Anthony** Bequest of Miss Amy Anthony.	1168 (12-010) £552,881 14 tonnes	2x285hp Caterpillar 3208T (aluminium hull)	Pwllheli 25.1.1991-	
13	1991 (FM1277) Green Marine/ FBM Ltd	**Marine Engineer** Institute of Marine Engineers, with other gifts and legacies.	1169 (12-12) £672,594 14 tonnes	2x285hp Caterpillar 3208T (FRC hull)	Relief 25.4.1991-8.1995 (22/4) Bridlington 13.8.1995-11.2017 (264/22) Douglas 2.7.2018-	
14	1991 (FM1278) Green Marine/ FBM Ltd	**Keep Fit Association** Keep Fit Association Appeal with other gifts and legacies.	1170 (12-13) £651,481 14 tonnes	2x285hp Caterpillar 3208T (FRC hull)	Filey 2.6.1991-	
15	1991 (FM1279) Green Marine/ FBM Ltd	**Ann and James Ritchie** Bequest of Mrs Ann Ritchie.	1171 (12-14) £577,746 14 tonnes	2x285hp Caterpillar 3208T (FRC hull)	Ramsey 12.7.1991-	
16	1991 (FM1280) Green Marine/ FBM Ltd	**Frank and Lena Clifford of Stourbridge** Legacy of Mr Frank Clifford.	1172 (12-15) £649,376 14 tonnes	2x285hp Caterpillar 3208T (FRC hull)	New Quay 8.4.1992-	

MOTOR LIFEBOATS

36 • 12m Mersey

	Year (Yd No) Builder Place	Name Donor	ON (Op No) Cost Weight	Engines	Stations (launches/lives saved)	Disposal
17	1991 (FM1281) Green Marine/ FBM Ltd	**Grace Darling** Grace Darling Anniversary Appeal, and other gifts.	1173 (12-16) £652,978	2x285hp Caterpillar 3208T (FRC hull)	Seahouses 7.8.1991-	
18	1991 (FM1282) Green Marine/ FBM Ltd	**Kingdom of Fife** Anstruther Lifeboat Appeal, and legacy of Dr Nora Allan.	1174 (12-17) £657,069	2x285hp Caterpillar 3208T (FRC hull)	Anstruther 16.10.1991-	
19	1991 (FM1283) Green Marine/ FBM Ltd	**Fanny Victoria Wilkinson and Frank Stubbs** Legacy of Mr Frank Stubbs.	1175 (12-18) £653,911	2x285hp Caterpillar 3208T (FRC hull)	Scarborough 27.9.1991-12.2016 (263/27) Relief 12.2016-5.2018 (0/0)	Sold 2018
20	1991 (FM1284) Green Marine/ FBM Ltd	**The Four Boys** Land's End Lifeboat Appeal, and money raised by Stoke Poges Appeal.	1176 (12-19) £655,250	2x285hp Caterpillar 3208T (FRC hull)	Sennen Cove 2.1991-12.1998 (90/47) Relief 12.1998-7.99 (1/0) Amble 22.7.1999-12.2016 (273/29)	Sold 2018
21	1991 (FM1285) Green Marine/ FBM Ltd	**Leonard Kent** Legacy of the late Mr Leonard Kent.	1177 (12-20) £629,121	2x285hp Caterpillar 3208T (FRC hull)	Margate 12.1991-	
22	1991 (FM1286) Green Marine/ FBM Ltd	**Margaret Jean** Gift of Peter and Jean Bath, Cambridgeshire.	1178 (12-21) £647,436	2x285hp Caterpillar 3208T (FRC hull)	Relief 2.1992-5.2008 (11/116) Exmouth 5.2008-5.2014 (104/3) Relief 5.2014-	
23	1992 (0101) Green Marine/ W. A. Souter	**Ruby Clery** Bequest of Miss Ruby Alexander Clery, London.	1181 (12-22) £662,663	2x285hp Caterpillar 3208T (FRC hull)	Peel 6.1992-	
24	1992 (FM1322) Green Marine/ FBM Ltd	**Robert Charles Brown** The J. Reginald Corah Foundation Fund, Maud Elkington Charitable Trust.	1182 (12-23) £669,046	2x285hp Caterpillar 3208T (FRC hull)	Swanage 12.6.1992-4.2016 (686/80) Relief 2016-2019	Sold 2019
25	1992 (0102) Green Marine/ W. A. Souter	**Lil Cunningham** Gift of Miss Betty H. I. Cunningham, Derby.	1183 (12-24) £648,092	2x285hp Caterpillar 3208T (FRC hull)	Rhyl 21.6.1992-	
26	1992 (FM1323) Green Marine/ FBM Ltd	**Bingo Lifeline** Bingo Association of Great Britain, bequest of Mrs Anne Mills, and other gifts and legacies.	1184 (12-25) £676,799	2x285hp Caterpillar 3208T (FRC hull)	Relief 29.7.1992-	
27	1992 (WO3546) Green Marine/ William Osborne	**Moira Barrie** Legacy of the late Miss Barrie, Worcestershire.	1185 (12-26) £683,097	2x285hp Caterpillar 3208T (FRC hull)	Barmouth 7.10.1992-4.2019 (153/17)	
28	1992 (0103) Green Marine/ W. A. Souter	**Pride and Spirit** Gift of Mr and Mrs Eric Cass, of Virginia Water, Surrey.	1186 (12-27) £645,034	2x285hp Caterpillar 3208T (FRC hull)	Dungeness 24.9.1992-3.2014 (288/34) Clifden 8.2014-1.2016 (26/1) Relief 14.1.2016-	
29	1992 (WO3555) Green Marine/ William Osborne	**Mary Margaret** Bequests of Denis A. S. Williams and Mary Margaret Williams.	1187 (12-28) £678,261	2x285hp Caterpillar 3208T (FRC hull)	Kilmore Quay 12.1992-4.2004 (211/48) Relief 4.2004-	
30	1992 (FM1324) Green Marine/ FBM Marine	**Eleanor and Bryant Girling** Bequest of Mrs Eleanor B. Girling.	1188 (12-29) £704,230	2x285hp Caterpillar 3208T (FRC hull)	Newcastle 9.1993-	
31	1992 (0104) Green Marine/ W. A. Souter	**Her Majesty The Queen** An Appeal to Police Constabularies in UK with other gifts and legacies.	1189 (12-30) £692,161	2x285hp Caterpillar 3208T (FRC hull)	Relief 25.1.1993-11.96 (27/11) Cromer 7.11.1996-4.3.99 (21/6) Relief 3-12.1999 (4/0) Lytham St Annes 16.12.1999-6.2018 (141/10) Relief 6.2018-	

36 • 12m Mersey

	Year (Yd No) Builder Place	Name Donor	ON (Op No) Cost Weight	Engines	Stations (launches/lives saved)	Disposal
32	1992 (WO3560) Green Marine/ William Osborne	**Doris Bleasdale** Bequest of Miss Doris Bleasdale.	1190 (12-31) £687,473	2x285hp Caterpillar 3208T (FRC hull)	Clogher Head 3.1993-2019 (244/30)	
33	1993 (FM1325) Green Marine/ FBM Ltd	**Joy and Charles Beeby** Legacy of Charles Beeby, Long Itchington, Warwickshire.	1191 (12-32) £683,050	2x285hp Caterpillar 3208T (FRC hull)	Berwick-upon-Tweed 2.1993-	
34	1993 (0105) Green Marine/ W. A. Souter	**Fisherman's Friend** Promotion by Lofthouse of Fleetwood, with other gifts and legacies.	1192 (12-33) £634,460	2x285hp Caterpillar 3208T (FRC hull)	Relief 4.1993-1.2016 (160/21) Clifden 14.1.2016-2019	
35	1993 (FM1326) Green Marine/ FBM Ltd	**Freddie Cooper** Legacy of Mrs Winifred May Cooper.	1193 (12-34) £686,761	2x285hp Caterpillar 3208T (FRC hull)	Aldeburgh 12.1993-	
36	1993 (FM1327) Green Marine/ FBM Ltd	**Inchcape** Funded by local appeal, gifts and legacies; named after Inchcape Rock off Arbroath.	1194 (12-35) £695,463	2x285hp Caterpillar 3208T (FRC hull)	Arbroath 8.1993-	
37	1993 (WO3582) Green Marine/ William Osborne	**Royal Thames** Appeal by Royal Thames Yacht Club local appeal and other gifts and legacies.	1195 (12-36) £691,763	2x285hp Caterpillar 3208T (FRC hull)	Eastbourne 7.1993-6.2012 (959/115) Leverburgh 8.2012-5.2018 (72/0) Relief 5.2018-	
38	1993 (0106) Green Marine/ W. A. Souter	**Silvia Burrell** Legacy of the late Miss Silvia Burrell, of Edinburgh.	1196 (12-37) £690,887	2x285hp Caterpillar 3208T (FRC hull)	Girvan 8.1993-4.2018 (237/19)	Sold 2019

◀ Recovery of Ann and James Ritchie (ON.1171) on the beach at Ramsey, Isle of Man. The beach recovery process involved the boat being hauled out of the water bow first prior to being recarriaged. (Nicholas Leach)

MOTOR LIFEBOATS

36 • 12m Mersey

▲ Lincolnshire Poacher (ON.1166), one of the aluminium-hulled Merseys, at Skegness, where she served for twenty-seven years. (Nicholas Leach)

▶ Launching Lilly and Vincent Anthony (ON.1168) into the harbour at Pwllheli. She was the last aluminium-hulled Mersey to be built and entered service at Pwllheli in January 1991. (Nicholas Leach)

▼ (left) Recovery of Keep Fit Association (ON.1170) at Filey. Skids have been laid on the beach, one of which is adapted to bring the boat level ready to be haled back onto her carriage. This photo clearly shows the tunnel and propeller arrangement. (Nicholas Leach)

▼ (right) Robert Charles Brown (ON.1182), pictured launching at Swanage, was one of five 12m Merseys to be launched from slipways rather than carriages. (Nicholas Leach)

196   MOTOR LIFEBOATS

36 • 12m Mersey

▲ (left) Lil Cunningham (ON.1183) launching on exercise at Rhyl, with the crew standing by to release the securing chains. (Nicholas Leach)

▲ (right) Pride and Spirit (ON.1186) launching on exercise down the steep shingle beach at Dungeness in August 1998. (Nicholas Leach)

◀ Silvia Burrell (ON.1196) on exercise off Girvan harbour; the last Mersey to be built, she was one of very few Merseys to be operated from a mooring. (Nicholas Leach)

▼ Two Merseys together at East Cowes for maintenance work, August 2003: Royal Thames (ON.1195) from Eastbourne (on left) and Doris Bleasdale (ON.1190) from Clogher Head; both were FRC hulled, and were more or less identical. (Peter Edey)

MOTOR LIFEBOATS 197

37 • 17m Severn

KEY DATA
- Introduced 1991
- Last built 2004
- 46 built

SPECIFICATIONS
- Length 17m (55ft 9in)
- Breadth 5.5m (18ft)
- Draught 1.68m (5ft 6in)
- Fuel capacity 5,500 litres (1,200 gallons)
- Displacement 37.5 tonnes (36.9 tons)

▶ The prototype 17m Severn 17-01 (ON.1179) on trials. This lifeboat never entered operational service but became a trials platform and subsequently a training lifeboat number TL-02. The flying bridge on the production boats was moved slightly aft, and the overall length of the superstructure was shortened.

▲ The prototype 17m Severn, ON.1179, at Hartlepool in 1992 during trials, with her superstructure painted yellow.

▼ ON.1179 became a trials platform and later a training lifeboat. She carried two names, firstly Maurice and Joyce Hardy, as here, at the RNLI Depot, Poole, June 1995. (Nicholas Leach)

The Arun and Waveney lifeboats, designed in the 1960s and 1970s, operated from stations where they were kept afloat at moorings and began the transformation of the lifeboat fleet into one consisting of fast self-righting craft which could reach casualties quicker and operate for longer than the traditional wooden-hulled boats. Although both types had been extremely successful, the RNLI believed that, with experience, technical progress and further advances in marine design, lifeboats could be improved, and even faster and more advanced all-weather lifeboats could be built, which would be better equipped and, most significantly, reach speeds up to twenty-five knots. As a result, two new designs were developed by the RNLI's in-house designers in the late 1980s and early 1990s, designated as Fast Afloat Boat 3 (FAB3) and Fast Afloat Boat 4 (FAB4), to replace the Waveneys and Aruns.

The requirements for the new design were agreed after much consultations between the Operations Department, RNLI coast staff and the Technical Department during 1988, with the prerequisites being a maximum speed of at least twenty-five knots, protected propellers giving an ability to take the ground, and easy maintenance. The larger of the two designs, initially designated FAB3, was 17m in length, the length between perpendiculars was 15.5m, the moulded depth was 3.3m and the approximate displacement was 34.5 tonnes.

Following discussions it was decided to investigate the feasibility of a hard chine hull form, in either aluminium or fibre reinforced composite (FRC). To protect the propellers, tunnels were incorporated into the hull, with bilge keels designed so that they could become detached, if necessary, without affecting the hull's structural integrity. However, the introduction of full propeller protection provided by deep tunnels, centre keel and side bilge keels, added thirty per cent to the hydrodynamic resistance and limited the choice of propeller diameter for optimum propulsion characteristics.

Once decisions had been made about the overall hull forms and bilge keels, model tests were undertaken by British Maritime Technology, followed by instrumented seakeeping trials using radio-controlled scale models in open water. The tests were carried out off the Isle of Wight in March 1989 using two models in a variety of sea conditions. The outcome of the trials was the decision to proceed with the hard chine hull form and to modify the integral sprayrail that had been incorporated in the models.

It was also decided to build the hull from fibre-reinforced composite (FRC), which combined strength with relatively light weight. The hull was subdivided by six watertight bulkheads into seven compartments, with a fully effective double bottom in all the spaces except the engine room; two longitudinal bulkheads were fitted along the length of the boat, forming wing tanks and transverse bulkheads between adjacent spaces. This was sufficient to make the fitting of additional foam buoyancy unnecessary. Self-

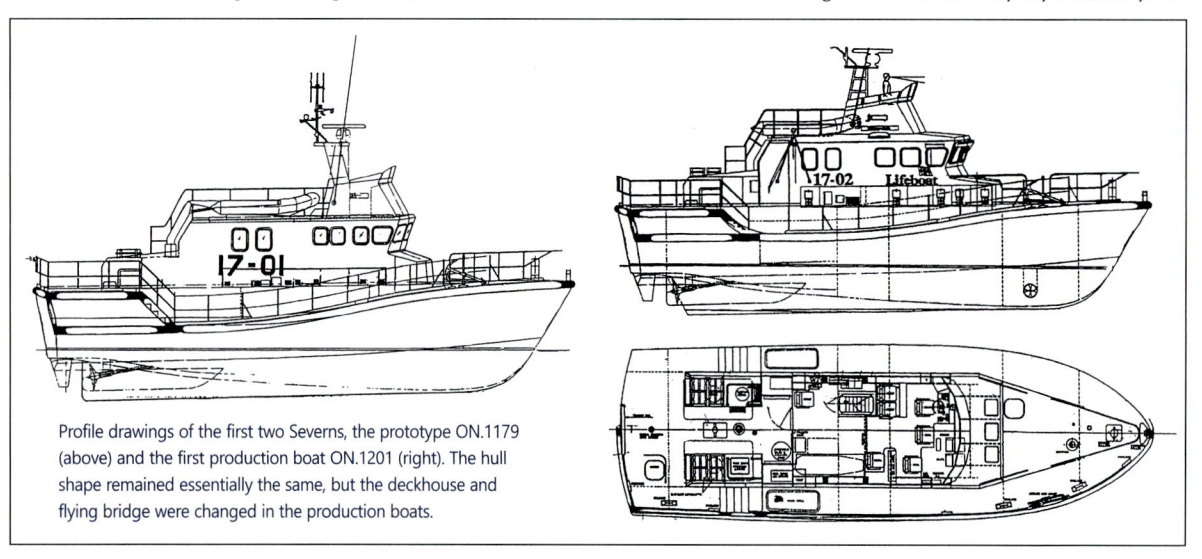

Profile drawings of the first two Severns, the prototype ON.1179 (above) and the first production boat ON.1201 (right). The hull shape remained essentially the same, but the deckhouse and flying bridge were changed in the production boats.

MOTOR LIFEBOATS

37 • 17m Severn

righting was achieved by the watertight wheelhouse, which had sufficient buoyancy to bring the boat upright in the event of a capsize. The deck sheerline was dropped in a way to similar that on the Arun class, reducing the freeboard to ease handling and recovering casualties from the water.

Unlike in previous lifeboat designs, FAB3's engines were positioned aft, which meant good access to the machinery for maintenance; the propellers were driven via U-drive shafting arrangements. This enabled the engines to be removed through large hatches on the aft deck, while providing enough space in the hull for twenty seated survivors in two dedicated survivors' spaces. A separate compartment forward of the engine room formed the fuel tank space and two flexible fuel tanks, each carrying 500 gallons, were incorporated into this space.

The wheelhouse was arranged so that the crew would be self-contained during rescue operations. A transverse watertight bulkhead provided a separate wheelhouse space, and contained permanent seating for six crew and a doctor, with provision for two loaded stretchers. Housed in the forward console in the wheelhouse were the engine controls, the hydraulic steering unit and wheel, tachometers, alarms, compass, helm indicator, trimtab controls, and switches for navigation lights, wipers and horn, as well as autopilot and bow thruster controls. These controls were duplicated on the flying bridge. The fore cabin below deck contained the galley, with hot and cold tapped water, a microwave as well as a toilet.

The prototype Severn and Trent class lifeboats were launched in March and October 1991 respectively and on completion of satisfactory builders' trials were accepted by the RNLI for technical trials and operational evaluation. The RNLI's trials, comprising speed and fuel consumption, steering and manoeuvring, were carried out to verify the required hydrodynamic characteristics. Instrumented trials to monitor seakeeping characteristics, noise and vibration were also undertaken. Both FAB3 and FAB4 circumnavigated Britain and the east coast of Ireland to provide wider experience of the prototypes in different environments and to enable as many different people as possible, from lifeboat stations from all round the coast, to evaluate and comment on the boats.

◀ Severns in build: (left) the hull of David and Elizabeth Acland (ON.1243) at Green Marine, Lymington, with the internal bulkheads evident, 8 July 1998; (right) the hull of Sybil Mullen Glover (ON.1264) arrives at Souter Shipyard, Cowes from Lymington on 23 October 2001. This photo shows the bilge keels, which were designed to come away on heavy impact without damaging the hull. The original keels had failed under way, and so a new keel twice the strength of the original was subsequently fitted. New side keels were fitted to all Severns and no boat of the class went on station without the new keels. (Peter Edey)

◀ In build: an unidentified Severn lifeboat fitting out at Berthon Boat Company, Lymington in October 1994; the hulls and deckhouses were moulded separately by Green Marine, and then joined during the fitting out process at a different boatyard. (Nicholas Leach)

▼ The first two Severns out of the water at the RNLI Depot, Poole on 19 June 1995. On the left is The Will (ON.1201) with the prototype 17-01 (ON.1179) on the right. The original bilge keels, to protect the propellers, can be seen on both these boats. (Nicholas Leach)

MOTOR LIFEBOATS

37 • 17m Severn

During the early technical trials of the Severn class lifeboat it was apparent that, while the boat was capable of exceeding the design performance, particularly in heavy seas, a number of structural issues were apparent. Supporting structures, such as frames and floors, were found to be failing, and the outside skin, particularly in the forward third of the craft, showed signs of stress. An assessment of the loads causing these failures led the RNLI to re-examine the design loads, and the thickness of the shell laminate was increased and the supporting structure was upgraded on the Severn prototype. The operational crew soon found that manoeuvring the boat was difficult, and requested a bow thruster be fitted to assist close quarter manoeuvring. A Vosper Thornycroft thruster unit, with a 50hp hydraulically-driven impeller, was therefore installed in the forward part of the vessel and a fairing added in front of the aperture.

The prototype was powered by twin Caterpillar 3412TA diesel engines, each of 1,050hp at 2,150rpm, which gave the boat a speed of twenty-five knots. In the production boats, the engines were upgraded to 1,250bhp at 2,300rpm. A small Y class inflatable was carried on the wheelhouse roof for inshore work, and was launched and recovered by a lightweight framework and winch. This system was subsequently replaced by a powered davit, mounted on the starboard end of the superstructure. Lifting the inflatable by davit reduced the time and effort needed to launch and recover it.

Operational trials and subsequent coastal evaluation were undertaken to confirm the suitability of the accommodation, machinery and deck arrangements of the vessel in calm water, and the ability to work the boat successfully in all weathers and at night. The RNLI's trials team put to sea in all weathers, initially from the Headquarters base in Poole and subsequently from as many operational stations as is possible. With the exception of the wheelhouse arrangements, very little adverse criticism was received from the trials team or operational crews regarding the vessels, although additional grab rails and minor fixtures and fittings were added from time to time.

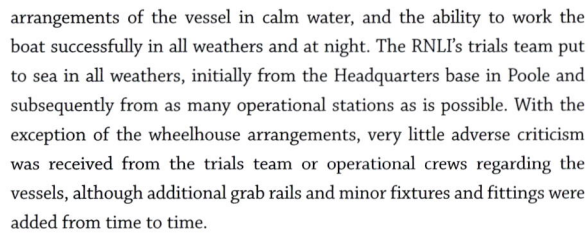

In the production boats, the deckhouse was reduced in size, making a single compartment; the flying bridge was moved aft; modifications were made to the Y boat launch and recovery system; and the number of watertight bulkheads in the hull was reduced by combining the lower survivor space and the forecabin. The wheelhouse configuration had been the subject of lengthy debate and modifications were made to the production boats. These included moving the steering position from the centreline to the port side and repositioning the chart table so that it was located in front of the navigator's position. Additional electronic equipment, such as a laser plotter and autopilot, was also incorporated.

Before entering service, in December 1992 FAB3 was designated the class name Severn, and FAB4 became the Trent, after the rivers that run through the heart of the country from where the RNLI receives a large amount of income. On completion of the operational trials and coastal evaluation both the Severn and the Trent class prototype lifeboats were refitted for the Press Day, when they were presented to the public for the first time and their class names announced.

Following this, contracts were negotiated for the moulding of the hull, deck and superstructure in epoxy resin vacuum-bagged fibre-reinforced laminates and orders for the construction of the hull, deck and superstructures were placed with Green Marine of Lymington. Contracts for the outfitting of the Severn and Trent class lifeboats were then negotiated with a number of south coast boatbuilders, and the build programme got under way. Apart from the prototype, the hull of which was built by Halmatic at Havant, all hulls and superstructures were fabricated in FRC by Green Marine, Lymington, and fitted out by different builders, as listed in the accompanying tables.

The first production boat, ON.1201 (17-02), was originally allocated to Stornoway, in the Outer Hebrides, and was completed during 1995. However, during the trials off Cornwall in January 1996, before she reached her station, the boat sustained damage after falling heavily from the crest of a seven metre wave while she was travelling at seventeen knots. Four of the crews' seat buckled and four crew received minor injuries, the aerial mast was bent and one of the side keels became detached. The lifeboat remained fully operational and watertight, however, with machinery and electronics systems unaffected by the shock.

The subsequent examination revealed some damage to the starboard longitudinal bulkhead and two connecting supports between the bulkhead

▲ One of the first group of Severns to be built, Spirit of Guernsey (ON.1203), departing Gorleston in October 1996 before she went on station at St Peter Port. As pictured, she carries the original livery, with the operational number, 17-04, on her deckhouse while the hydraulic davit for launching the small Y class inflatable has yet to be fitted. (Gary Markham)

▼ The first Severn to go on station, Albert Brown (ON.1202), was declared operational at Harwich in October 1996. (Nicholas Leach)

37 • 17m Severn

and the hull. As a result, there was a delay in placing Severn class boats on station as RNLI technical staff carried out a thorough examination of this first production boat. There was a full assessment of the structural damage, which determined how much strengthening work was required to the affected components. However, once this work had been done, and the modifications had been made, the first Severn, Albert Brown (ON.1202), went on station at Harwich in October 1996. ON.1201, the first production boat, was completely altered and then reallocated to the Relief Fleet, being used for trials initially and she never went to Stornoway.

The Severn class lifeboat soon proved herself on service, and on 19 November 1997 Michael and Jane Vernon (ON.1221), the recently-completed Severn at Lerwick, under the Command of Coxswain Hewitt Clark, helped rescue fifteen crew members from the stranded cargo vessel Green Lily in breaking seas almost 50ft high off the rocky coast of Shetland. Coxswain Clark was subsequently awarded the RNLI's Gold medal in recognition of his incredible seamanship and Bronze Medals for each of her other five crew.

The superiority of the Severn class lifeboat was recognised by the government in August 1999, when Deputy Prime Minister, John Prescott, presented the RNLI with a Millennium Project plaque at a special ceremony on the Thames. By 2000 more than twenty Severns were in service, and over the next few years eight boats a year were completed. Although the RNLI initially envisaged about 100 Severn and Trent class lifeboats would be built, by the time the building programme was completed in 2004, forty-six Severns had been constructed, of which forty-five saw operational service. The last of the Severns, Margaret Joan and Fred Nye (ON.1279), was named and dedicated at the RNLI's then new training facility, the Lifeboat College, in Poole, on 5 May 2005 by Bob Cripps, RNLI Engineering Manager, who was instrumental in the development and production of the Severn.

During the subsequent years the boats were modified in various ways, including having a davit installed for launching the Y class inflatable. A more significant issue, evident following several years of experience of service conditions, was the performance of the Caterpillar engines, which were operating for long periods at almost maximum output, placing considerable strain on them and resulting in a number of failures. As a result, in 2008 the RNLI looked to install new and more reliable engines, and assessed a series of diesel engines built by MTU for fast vessels. The relief lifeboat Margaret Joan and Fred Nye (ON.1279) was the first Severn

▲ Violet, Dorothy and Kathleen (ON.1236) (above left) at Lymington, March 1998, during her fitting out by Berthon Boat Company; and (above) capsize trials of City of London II (ON.1220) at Cowes, October 1996. (Peter Edey)

▼ Lerwick lifeboat Michael and Jane Vernon (ON.1221) on service to the cargo vessel Green Lily, November 1997. (By courtesy of the RNLI)

MOTOR LIFEBOATS

37 • 17m Severn

▶ Barra Island lifeboat Edna Windsor (ON.1230) heading out of Castlebay, in the Outer Hebrides, on exercise; during refits, the aluminium parts of Severns were left unpainted, giving the boats an outward appearance that was rather different to when they first entered service. (Nicholas Leach)

▼ Tom Sanderson (ON.1238) on exercise at Stronoway, in the Outer Hebrides; she was one of two Severns that did not have a hydraulic launch davit for the Y class inflatable installed; the other Severn was Richard Cox Scott (ON.1256) at Falmouth. (Nicholas Leach)

to be fitted with new engines, receiving two 1,500hp MTU 10V2000 M93 ten-cylinder units at Berthon Boat Co in November 2008. After trials, they were removed and refitted at Poole Depot in November 2010. They were replaced by twin 1,600hp MTU 10V2000 M94 V10 diesel units, with twin turbochargers and after-coolers, at Poole in June 2011.

The boat was taken round stations for appraisal by coxswains and station mechanics and, such was the success of the trials, that the RNLI decided in 2010 that these would be the standard engines for the entire Severn Fleet. Several modifications were made to meet the requirements of the RNLI, notably to ensure they would continue to operate in the event of a capsize. Inverting a running diesel engine would normally cause engine oil to enter the cylinders through the crankcase ventilation system, causing uncontrolled combustion. To counter this, modifications were made, including a redesign of the sump and oil pick up. The sumps were deepened and narrowed to improve oil pick up in rough weather, and the sump was fitted with a baffle plate to prevent oil splashing out.

The original Caterpillar 3412 TA diesel engines generated 1,250bhp each. The new engines had a rated power output of 1,600bhp, at a maximum of 2,450rpm. This would have powered the Severn to a top speed of more than thirty-five knots, but that would have been greater than the design speed of the hull so, in practice, the engines were tuned to run at a maximum of 1,300rpm, which delivered approximately eighty per cent of full power and took the boat to its designed hull speed of twenty-five knots. MTU units are manufactured by Tognum Corporation in Friedrichshafen, Germany, which, following a takeover, became Rolls-Royce Power Systems. The re-engining of the Severns was a relatively long-term programme, with almost thirty boats completed by 2019. Electronics upgrades to the radar and navigation systems were also undertaken, with a single workstation with chart functionality replacing the previous chart and navigation systems. The first boats were upgraded in 2016 with the fitting of new radar and navigation systems, VHF radios and direction finding units, together with extensive associated re-wiring.

By the time the re-engining programme was under way, questions were raised about a potential replacement for the Severn. However, extensive research, testing and analysis of the strength and structure of the hulls and superstructures showed that the Severns could have a service life of fifty years. It was also decided that the all-weather lifeboat fleet would eventually consist of three types: the Shannon, the Tamar and the Severn. To fulfil this aim, and in order to ensure that the lifeboats were equipped with the most up-to-date equipment and electronics, boats of the Severn class were rebuilt internally under the Severn Life Extension Programme (SLEP).

The MTU diesels had proved to be very effective main engines, gearbox and drive trains, and coupled to the five-bladed propeller, which replaced the original four-bladed propeller used when the Severn first entered service, was deemed serviceable for many years. This solution to the main drive of the boat was a major factor in the decision to extend the boats' life. Work started at the ALC, Poole in April 2019 on the relief boat The Will (ON.1201), with initially all of the internal fixtures and fittings, wiring and electronics being removed, leaving just the FRC shell.

Every aspect of the boat's fit-out was renewed, with the latest electronics, navigation systems and crew seating being installed, the hydraulic systems were modernised, and a SIMS system similar to that used on the Shannon was fitted, which included engine data loggers to manage the boat's engineering systems; the crew seating was replaced and the configuration modernised. So, apart from the hull, deck and superstructure, everything else about the boat was new. The work was undertaken at the RNLI's All-Weather Lifeboat Centre in Poole, which had a capacity to work on up to six boats a year.

37 • 17m Severn

	Year (Yd No) Builder Place	Name Donor	ON (Oo No) Cost Weight	Engines	Stations (launches/lives saved) Disposal
1	1991 (WO3444) Halmatic Ltd/ William Osborne	**Maurice and Joyce Hardy**/ 1995- unnamed/ 1998- **Peter and Marion Fulton** RNLI general funds.	1179 (17-01) £1,350,000 36t18	2x1,050hp Caterpillar 3412TA	Trials 1992-98 (6/0) Training 1998-9.2004 (8/0) (numbered TL-02) Sold 1.2005
2	1994 (1023) Green Marine/ Berthon Bt Co	**The Will**/ 2019- **Hogg Hardie** The Will Charitable Trust.	1201 (17-02) £1,692,011 41 tonnes	2x1,250hp Caterpillar 3412TA/ 2010- 2x1,500hp MTU 10V2000 M93	Relief 1996-97 (2/4) and 2002- Falmouth 11.3.1997- 17.12.2001 (91/24)
3	1994 (1024) Green Marine/ Berthon Bt Co	**Albert Brown** Bequest of Victoria Maisie Brown, London, in memory of her husband.	1202 (17-03) £1,563,238 41 tonnes	2x1,250hp Caterpillar 3412TA/ 2013- 2x1,600hp MTU 1135/10/L	Harwich 2.10.1996-
4	1994 (MR3845) Green Marine/ Halmatic Ltd	**Spirit of Guernsey** Guernsey Severn Lifeboat Appeal, and various legacies and gifts.	1203 (17-04) £1,652,417 41 tonnes	2x1,250hp Caterpillar 3412TA/ 2014- 2x1,600hp MTU 1135/10/L	St Peter Port 6.6.1997-
5	1996 (MR3861) Green Marine/ Halmatic Ltd	**Pride of the Humber** Humber Lifeboat Appeal; fund-raising by volunteers of the North-East region; and various bequests.	1216 (17-05) £1,464,125 41 tonnes	2x1,250hp Caterpillar 3412TA/ 2011- 2x1,500hp MTU 10V2000 M93	Humber 8.3.1997-
6	1996 (1025) Green Marine/ Berthon Bt Co	**David Kirkaldy** Mr David Kirkaldy.	1217 (17-06) £1,514,578 41 tonnes	2x1,250hp Caterpillar 3412TA/ 2016- 2x1,600hp MTU 1135/10/L	Aran Islands 6.6.1997-
7	1996 (1426) Green Marine/ FBM Ltd, Cowes	**John and Margaret Doig** Bequest of Miss Mary Doig together with other legacies.	1218 (17-07) £1,469,303 41 tonnes	2x1,250hp Caterpillar 3412TA/ 2012- 2x1,600hp MTU 1135/10/L	Valentia 29.11.1996-
8	1996 (1427) Green Marine/ FBM Ltd, Cowes	**Helmut Schroder of Dunlossit II** Mr Bruno Schroder and Mrs George Mallinckrodt.	1219 (17-08) £1,437,168 41 tonnes	2x1,250hp Caterpillar 3412TA/ 2015- 2x1,600hp MTU 1135/10/L	Islay 9.3.1997-
9	1996 (1026) Green Marine/ Berthon Bt Co	**City of London II** City of London Centenary appeal, and other gifts and legacies.	1220 (17-09) £1,595,834 41 tonnes	2x1,250hp Caterpillar 3412TA/ 2013- 2x1,600hp MTU 1135/10/L	Dover 15.3.1997-
10	1997 (1433) Green Marine/ FBM Ltd, Cowes	**Michael and Jane Vernon** The Lerwick Lifeboat Appeal and various legacies and donations.	1221 (17-10) £1,580,000 41 tonnes	2x1,250hp Caterpillar 3412TA/ 2013- 2x1,600hp MTU 1135/10/L	Lerwick 2.6.1997-
11	1997 (1027) Green Marine/ Berthon Bt Co	**The Whiteheads** Bequest of Miss Olive Elsie Whitehead, Newquay, Cornwall.	1229 (17-11) £1,725,000 41 tonnes	2x1,250hp Caterpillar 3412TA	St Mary's (Scilly) 1.12.1997-
12	1997 (1435) Green Marine/ FBM Ltd, Cowes	**Edna Windsor** Bequest from Mrs Edna Windsor.	1230 (17-12) £1,725,000 41 tonnes	2x1,250hp Caterpillar 3412TA	Barra Island 13.6.1998-
13	1997 (1436) Green Marine/ FBM Ltd, Cowes	**Margaret Foster** Legacy of Miss Margaret Ellen Foster, Emsworth, Hampshire.	1231 (17-13) £1,725,000 41 tonnes	2x1,250hp Caterpillar 3412TA/ 2011- 2x1,500hp MTU 10V2000 M93	Kirkwall 26.3.1998-
14	1998 (1028) Green Marine/ Berthon Bt Co	**Charles Lidbury** Bequest of Miss Mary Lidbury, Dulverton, Somerset.	1232 (17-14) £1,725,000 41 tonnes	2x1,250hp Caterpillar 3412TA/ 2017- 2x1,600hp MTU 1135/10/L	Aith 2.5.1998-

▲ The first Severn Peter and Marion Fulton (ON.1179) after her naming ceremony at Poole, 15 April 1998. (Nicholas Leach)

▲ Pride of the Humber (ON.1216) at speed in the Humber estuary. (Nicholas Leach)

▲ Helmut Schroder of Dunlossit II (ON.1219) on exercise off Port Askaig, Islay. (Nicholas Leach)

▲ Penlee's Severn Ivan Ellen (ON.1265) on exercise in Mount's Bay (Nicholas Leach)

MOTOR LIFEBOATS

37 • 17m Severn

▲ Violet, Dorothy and Kathleen (ON.1236) on proving trials. (Peter Edey)

▲ Ernest and Mary Shaw (ON.1241) on exercise at Campbeltown. (Nicholas Leach)

▲ Henry Alston Hewat (ON.1250) on exercise at Mallaig. (Nicholas Leach)

▲ Volunteer Spirit (ON.1254) heading out of Poole harbour. (Nicholas Leach)

	Year (Yd No) Builder Place	Name Donor	ON (Oo No) Cost Weight	Engines	Stations (launches/ lives saved) Disposal
15	1998 (1442) Green Marine/ FBM Ltd, Cowes	**Bryan and Gordon** Legacies from Bryan Clifford Griffiths and Gordon William Griffiths.	1235 (17-15) £1,725,000 41 tonnes	2x1,250hp Caterpillar 3412TA/ 2011- 2x1,500hp MTU 10V2000 M93	Ballyglass 14.8.1998-
16	1998 (1030) Green Marine/ Berthon Bt Co	**Violet, Dorothy and Kathleen** Bequest of Miss Violet Jane Matton, Seaford, East Sussex.	1236 (17-16) £1,725,000 41 tonnes	2x1,250hp Caterpillar 3412TA/ 2014- 2x1,600hp MTU 1135/10/L	Stromness 22.10.1998-
17	1998 (1443) Green Marine/ FBM Ltd, Cowes	**Fraser Flyer (Civil Service No.43)** Civil Service, Post Office & BT Lifeboat Fund, the Ancient Order of Foresters, other gifts and legacies.	1237 (17-17) £1,725,000 41 tonnes	2x1,250hp Caterpillar 3412TA	Relief 4.2.1999-
18	1999 (1031) Green Marine/ Berthon Bt Co	**Tom Sanderson** Legacy of Mr Tom Sanderson, Milnthorpe, Cumbria.	1238 (17-18) £1,700,000 41 tonnes	2x1,250hp Caterpillar 3412TA/ 2015- 2x1,600hp MTU 1135/10/L	Stornoway 1.2.1999-
19	1999 (1448) Green Marine/ FBM Ltd, Cowes	**Ernest and Mary Shaw** Gift of the late Ernest J. Shaw and his widow, Mrs Mary Shaw, Glasgow.	1241 (17-19) £1,796,000 41 tonnes	2x1,250hp Caterpillar 3412TA	Campbeltown 31.5.1999-
20	1999 (1032) Green Marine/ Berthon Bt Co	**Spirit of Northumberland** The Tynemouth Lifeboat Appeal and other gifts and legacies.	1242 (17-20) £1,750,000 41 tonnes	2x1,250hp Caterpillar 3412TA/ 2011- 2x1,600hp MTU 1135/10/L	Tynemouth 21.10.1999-
21	1999 (1449) Green Marine/ FBM Ltd, Cowes	**David and Elizabeth Acland** Combination of seven legacies and a number of gifts.	1243 (17-21) £1,700,000 41 tonnes	2x1,250hp Caterpillar 3412TA/ 2015- 2x1,600hp MTU 1135/10/L	Newhaven 8.11.1999-
22	1999 (1033) Green Marine/ Berthon Bt Co	**Myrtle Maud** Legacy of Myrtle Maud Campbell Orde.	1244 (17-22) £1,750,000 41 tonnes	2x1,250hp Caterpillar 3412TA/ 2015- 2x1,600hp MTU 1135/10/L	Arranmore 27.1.2000-
23	2000 (1455) Green Marine/ FBM Ltd, Cowes	**Katie Hannan** Legacy of Mrs Katrina Hannan, London, together with local appeal.	1247 (17-23) £1,750,000 41 tonnes	2x1,250hp Caterpillar 3412TA	Portrush 15.6.2000-1.2008 (118/22) Wrecked on service 29.1.2008, and scrapped
24	2000 (1035) Green Marine/ Berthon Bt Co	**Bon Accord** Local appeal, donations and legacies, named after City's motto.	1248 (17-24) £1,750,000 41 tonnes	2x1,250hp Caterpillar 3412TA/ 2012- 2x1,600hp MTU 1135/10/L	Aberdeen 20.7.2000-
25	2000 (1456) Green Marine/ FBM Ltd, Cowes	**Eric and Susan Hiscock (Wanderer)** Bequest of Mrs Susan Oakes Hiscock, Yarmouth, IOW.	1249 (17-25) £1,800,000 41 tonnes	2x1,250hp Caterpillar 3412TA/ 2016- 2x1,600hp MTU 1135/10/L	Yarmouth 12.2000-
26	2000 (1036) Green Marine/ Berthon Bt Co	**Henry Alston Hewat** Legacy of Miss Catherine M. Hewat, Glasgow, and Mallaig Lifeboat Appeal.	1,250 (17-26) £1,800,000 41 tonnes	2x1,250hp Caterpillar 3412TA/ 2016- 2x1,600hp MTU 1135/10/L	Mallaig 30.1.2001-
27	2001 (0144) Green Marine/ Souter Sh Yd	**Volunteer Spirit** Fund-raising by branches and guilds during RNLI's 175th anniversary.	1254 (17-27) £1,800,000 41 tonnes	2x1,250hp Caterpillar 3412TA	Relief 8.5.2001-
28	2001 (1037) Green Marine/ Berthon Bt Co	**Alec and Christina Dykes** Bequest of the late Mrs Helen Christina Dykes, of Torbay.	1255 (17-28) £1,800,000 41 tonnes	2x1,250hp Caterpillar 3412TA	Torbay 31.10.2001-

37 • 17m Severn

	Year (Yd No) Builder Place	Name Donor	ON (Oo No) Cost Weight	Engines	Stations (launches/lives saved) Disposal
29	2001 (0145) Green Marine/ Souter Sh Yd	**Richard Cox Scott** Bequest of Mrs Ruth M. Dix Scott, Cornwall, in memory of her husband.	1256 (17-29) £1,800,000 41 tonnes	2x1,250hp Caterpillar 3412TA	Falmouth 18.12.2001-
30	2001 (1038) Green Marine/ Berthon Bt Co	**William Gordon Burr** Legacy of Mrs Norah Burr, of Lightcliffe, Halifax, West Yorkshire.	1257 (17-30) £1,800,000 41 tonnes	2x1,250hp Caterpillar 3412TA/ 2012- 2x1,600hp MTU 1135/10/L	Relief 15.2.2002-4.2008 (62/5) Portrush 4.2008-
31	2002 (051) Green Marine/ DML Devonport	**Roger and Joy Freeman** Legacy of Hilda Freeman, Solihull, with various other legacies.	1260 (17-31) £1,800,000 41 tonnes	2x1,250hp Caterpillar 3412TA/ 2014- 2x1,600hp MTU 1135/10/L	Relief 10.9.2002-
32	2002 (0150) Green Marine/ Souter Sh Yd	**Ernest and Mabel** Gift of Miss Beryl Taylor, Surrey, and otehr gifts and legacies.	1261 (17-32) £1,800,000 41 tonnes	2x1,250hp Caterpillar 3412TA	Weymouth 16.7.2002-
33	2002 (1039) Green Marine/ Berthon Bt Co	**Beth Sell** Legacy of Mrs Mima Elizabeth Sell, with bequests of Mrs Cyril H. Wells, and others.	1262 (17-33) £1,900,000 41 tonnes	2x1,250hp Caterpillar 3412TA	Relief 16.8.2002-
34	2002 (052) Green Marine/ DML Devonport	**Osier** Legacy of Peter Albert George Acke.	1263 (17-34) £1,900,000 41 tonnes	2x1,250hp Caterpillar 3412TA	Relief 11.10.2002-
35	2002 (0151) Green Marine/ Souter Sh Yd	**Sybil Mullen Glover** Legacy of Mrs Daphne Sybil Glover.	1264 (17-35) £1,900,000 41 tonnes	2x1,250hp Caterpillar 3412TA	Plymouth 15.2.2003-
36	2002 (1040) Green Marine/ Berthon Bt Co	**Ivan Ellen** Legacy of Harold Ivan Leech.	1265 (17-36) £1,900,000 41 tonnes	2x1,250hp Caterpillar 3412TA	Penlee 15.3.2003-
37	2003 (054) Green Marine/ DML Devonport	**William Blannin** Legacies of Kenneth Maurice Williams, of Salisbury, with other gifts and legacies.	1268 (17-37) £1,800,000 41 tonnes	2x1,250hp Caterpillar 3412TA/ 2017- 2x1,600hp MTU 1135/10/L	Buckie 27.5.2003-
38	2002 (1041) Green Marine/ Berthon Bt Co	**Daniel L. Gibson** Legacy of John Gibson, Yorkshire.	1269 (17-38) £1,900,000 41 tonnes	2x1,250hp Caterpillar 3412TA/ 2014- 2x1,600hp MTU 1135/10/L	Relief 2002-
39	2002 (055) Green Marine/ DML Devonport	**Elizabeth Fairlie Ramsey** Bequest of Elizabeth Ramsey, of Edinburgh, and J. T. Graham.	1270 (17-39) £1,800,000 41 tonnes	2x1,250hp Caterpillar 3412TA/ 2016- 2x1,600hp MTU 1135/10/L	Tobermory 20.8.2003-
40	2003 (056) Green Marine/ DML Devonport	**Julian and Margaret Leonard** Legacy of Julian and Mrs Margaret Leonard, Saffron Walden and Brighton.	1271 (17-40) £1,800,000 41 tonnes	2x1,250hp Caterpillar 3412TA/ 2013- 1,500hp MTU 10V2000 M93	Lochinver 25.11.2003-
41	2003 (1042) Green Marine/ Berthon Bt Co	**Christopher Pearce** Bequest of Christopher Michael Pearce.	1272 (17-41) £1,900,000 41 tonnes	2x1,250hp Caterpillar 3412TA	Holyhead 21.12.2003-
42	2003 (057) Green Marine/ DML Devonport	**The Taylors** Bequest of Mrs Vera Rita Elizabeth Taylor, Aberdeen.	1273 (17-42) £1,800,000 41 tonnes	2x1,250hp Caterpillar 3412TA/ 2017- 2x1,600hp MTU 1135/10/L	Thurso 7.4.2004-

▲ Richard Cox Scott (ON.1256) on trials prior to going on station at Falmouth. (Peter Edey)

▲ The relief Severn Roger and Joy Freeman (ON.1260) on exercise at Harwich. (Nicholas Leach)

▲ Ernest and Mabel (ON.1261) on exercise in Weymouth Bay. (Nicholas Leach)

▲ Sybil Mullen Glover (ON.1264) on exercise off Plymouth. (Nicholas Leach)

MOTOR LIFEBOATS

37 • 17m Severn

	Year (Yd No) Builder Place	Name Donor	ON (Oo No) Cost Weight	Engines	Stations (launches/ lives saved) Disposal
43	2004 (0160) Green Marine/ Souter Sh Yd	**Donald and Barbara Broadhead** Bequest of Mrs Barbara Broadhead, Newark, together with other gifts.	1276 (17-43) £1,800,000 41 tonnes	2x1,250hp Caterpillar 3412TA/ 2017- 2x1,600hp MTU 1135/10/L	Rosslare Harbour 9.7.2004-
44	2004 (1043) Green Marine/ Berthon Bt Co	**Annette Hutton** Legacy of Annette A. M. Hutton, Blackrock, Co Dublin.	1277 (17-44) £1,800,000 41 tonnes	2x1,250hp Caterpillar 3412TA/ 2012- 2x1,600hp MTU 1135/10/L	Castletownbere 12.8.2004-
45	2004 (0161) Green Marine/ Souter/Berthon	**The Duke of Kent** Six different legacies combined.	1278 (17-45) £1,800,000 41 tonnes	2x1,250hp Caterpillar 3412TA	Relief 25.2.2005-
46	2004 (1044) Green Marine/ Berthon Bt Co	**Margaret Joan and Fred Nye** Legacies of Miss Joan Nye, Miss C. H. G. Willis, Mrs M. Howarth, and others.	1279 (17-46) £1,900,000 41 tonnes	2x1,250hp Caterpillar 3412TA/ 2008- 2x1,500hp MTU 10V2000 M93/ 2010- 2x1,600hp MTU 1135/10/L	Relief 17.11.2004-

▲ Donald and Barbara Broadhead (ON.1276) on exercise at Rosslare Harbour. (Nicholas Leach)

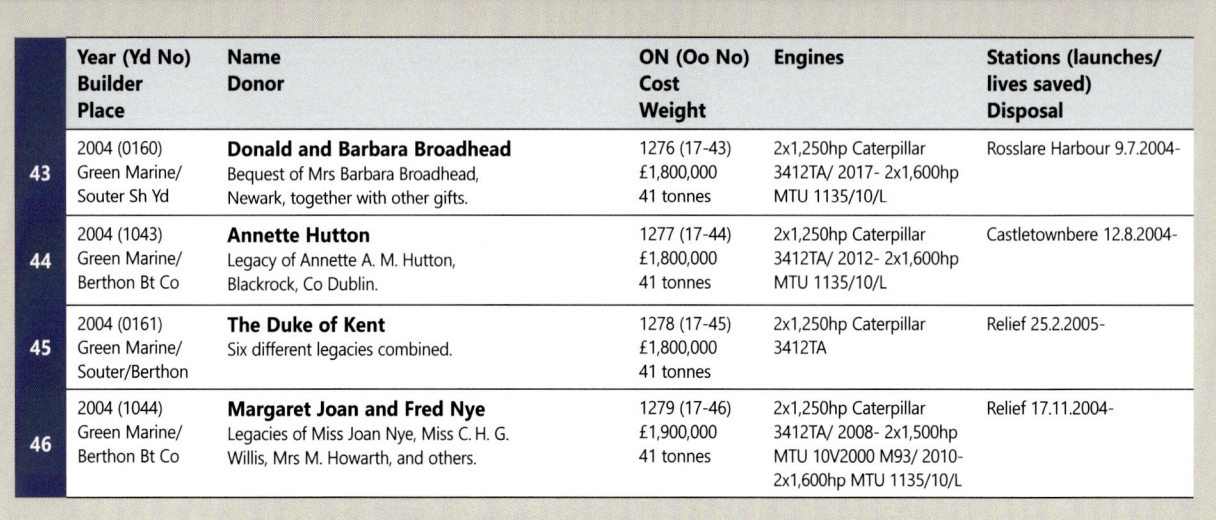

▼ Annette Hutton (ON.1276) on exercise at Castletownbere. (Nicholas Leach)

▲ The Taylors (ON.1273) on exercise in the Pentland Firth. (Nicholas Leach)

▼ Two Severns, ON.1269 and ON.1272, being fitted out at Berthon Boat Company, Lymington. (Nicholas Leach)

MOTOR LIFEBOATS

37 • 17m Severn

The last Severn to be built, Margaret Joan and Fred Nye (ON 1277), served in the Relief Fleet and is pictured on duty at Lochinver. (Nicholas Leach)

38 • 14m Trent

KEY DATA
- Introduced 1991
- Last built 2004
- 38 built

SPECIFICATIONS
- Length 14.26m (46ft 9in)
- Breadth 4.53m (14ft 10in)
- Depth 2.5m (8ft 4in)
- Draught 1.295m (4ft 3in)
- Fuel 4,100 litres (900 gallons)
- Displacement 25.5 tonnes

▼ The prototype 14m Trent 14-01 (ON.1180) on trials in December 1992 (left) and heading down the Manchester Ship Canal (right) for a publicity exercise in September 2006. This lifeboat, which was subsequently named Earl and Countess Mountbatten of Burma (ON.1180), served at Alderney on a temporary basis and then became a Relief lifeboat and was later used for training until being sold out of service in 2019. (RNLI)

The 14m Trent class was developed as at the same time as the 17m Severn, being designated 'Fast Afloat Boat 4' during the trials and testing stages. The two new types, capable of twenty-five knots, were designed to replace the Waveney and Arun fast afloat boats. The Trent's hull was similar to that of the Severn, but was scaled down by a ratio of one to 0.824. It therefore shared many features, including the substantial bilge keels to provide protection for the propellers and allow the boat to take the ground if necessary. However, as it was smaller, it had a shallower draught, 1.083m as opposed to 1.35m on the Severn, thus making the boat more suitable for working closer inshore.

The design was built from fibre reinforced composite (FRC), and the hull, deck and superstructure were of sandwich construction. The structure was of monocoque form, with the density of the foam structure and the outer skin on the production boats being greater than that used in the prototype, to account for greater stresses determined during trials. The initial problems of structural integrity found on the Severn were not experienced on the Trent production boats.

The sheerline was swept down for ease of survivor recovery, as on the Severn, and the hull, subdivided by five bulkheads into six compartments, was of a hard chine design. The six compartments comprised a forepeak cable locker, fore store, forecabin/survivor cabin, tank space, machinery space, and an aft peak steering compartment. The wheelhouse, housing electronic navigation and communication aids, had permanent seating for six crew, with provision for one stretcher in the wheelhouse and another in the fore cabin. The coxswain/helm's seat, with the normal engine controls and steering systems, was set on the port side of the wheelhouse, an unusual departure from traditional lifeboats on which it was located on the centreline. The engine controls and monitoring equipment were duplicated on the flying bridge.

The engine room configuration was also a departure from previous RNLI lifeboats, as the engines were staggered within the hull. One powered the propeller through a U-drive shaft arrangement, and the other via a conventional straight drive. This layout was adopted to provide more space and made machinery maintenance easier, as well as conform to exhaust and ventilation requirements. The prototype was fitted with twin 808bhp MAN D2840LXE marine diesels rated at 2,300rpm, coupled to twin ZF BW 195S type reverse/reduction gearboxes at a ratio of 2.03:1. The flexible fuel tanks were located in a separate compartment forward of the engine room. Approximately 4,100 litres (900 gallons) of fuel was carried, enabling ten hours of running at full speed, as well as giving ten per cent of fuel in hand. Fire-fighting and salvage gear was held on deck.

The prototype was launched in October 1991 and, on completion of satisfactory builder's trials, was accepted by the RNLI for technical trials and operational evaluation. During the trials very little adverse criticism was received from the trials team or operational lifeboat crews. The only request for change, in addition to a modified wheelhouse arrangement, was for the provision of some kind of small inflatable daughter boat. Lack of space prevented this being added, but an inflatable dinghy was provided

38 • 14m Trent

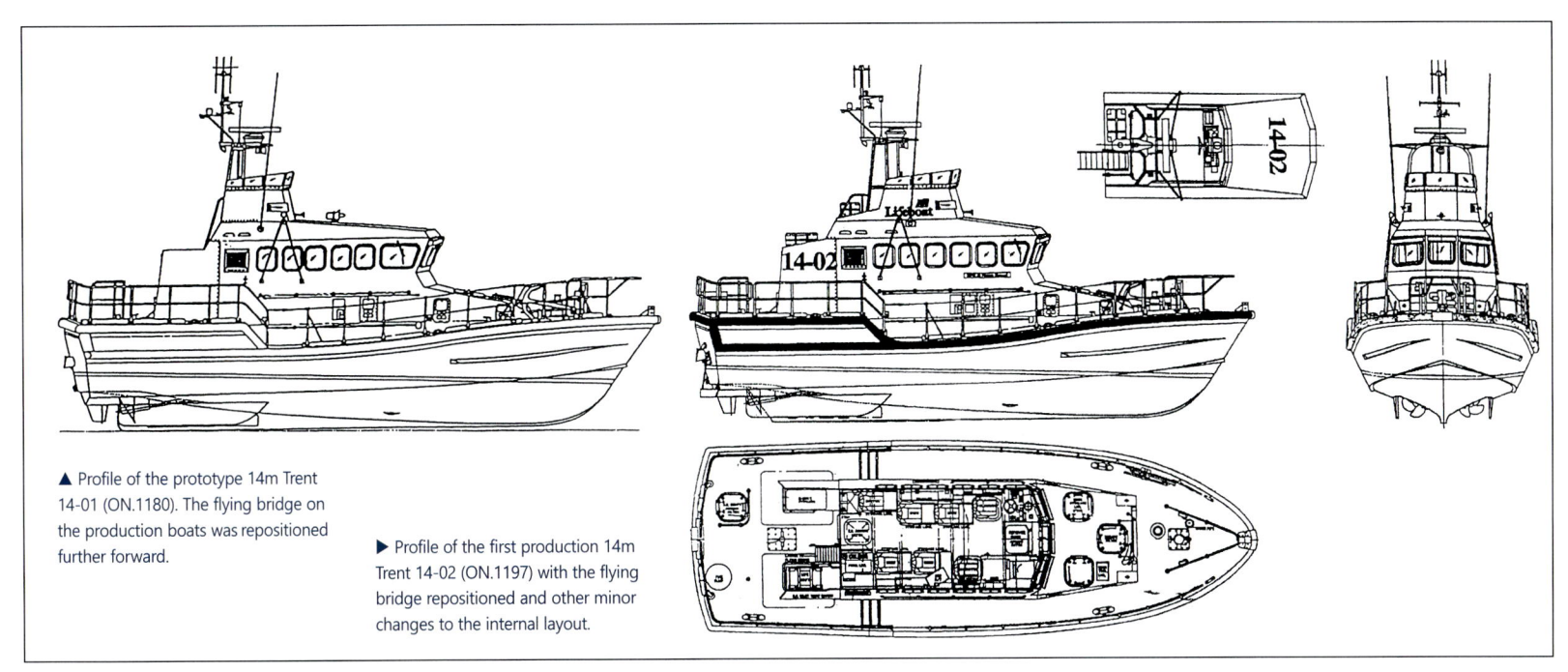

▲ Profile of the prototype 14m Trent 14-01 (ON.1180). The flying bridge on the production boats was repositioned further forward.

▶ Profile of the first production 14m Trent 14-02 (ON.1197) with the flying bridge repositioned and other minor changes to the internal layout.

in a stowage on deck as a compromise, and could be inflated if needed. The other issue was the position of the flying bridge, which was moved forward, to provide a better view over the foredeck, on the production boats.

Following acceptance of the prototype (ON.1180) from the builder's, operational trials and coastal evaluation were undertaken during 1992, and over the course of three months the prototype was taken on extensive coastal evaluation trials around the UK and Ireland, being based, in turn, out of Newhaven, Dover, Lowestoft, Grimsby, Tynemouth, Eyemouth, Kirkwall, Portree, Campbeltown, Portrush, Dun Laoghaire, Dunmore East, Fleetwood, Barry Dock and Fowey. In November 1992 the prototype was refitted ready for the press launch. In December 1992, at the official press launch, the type was designated the class name Trent after the river that runs through the heart of the country, from where the RNLI receives a large proportion of its income. During much of 1993 wheelhouse and machinery modifications and evaluation were undertaken, and orders were placed at Souter Shipyard on the Isle of Wight for the first four boats.

The first production Trent was accepted in July 1994 but the early boats were plagued by a series of teething problems, mainly to the machinery, with excessive vibration causing the main engine flywheel to become loose. Engine manufacturer MAN accepted full responsibility for the faults and made good the repairs without any cost to the RNLI. Once the initial issues had been resolved, however, the Trent class lifeboats have given outstanding service around the coast.

The building programme for the production boats took ten years to complete, lasting from 1994 to 2004. All hulls and superstructures were fabricated in FRC by Green Marine, at their Lymington yard, and then fitted out by the builders listed below. Sadly, one of the boats, Sir Ronald Pechell Bt (ON.1207), broke from her moorings at Torness Power Station in March 2008 and was swept onto rocks, suffering damage so severe that she was subsequently scrapped. By the end of the second decade of the twenty-first century plans for their replacement were being made, and the RNLI announced that most would be replaced by Shannon class boats.

▼ Dublin Bay is covered by two 14m Trents: Anna Livia (ON.1200) from Dun Laoghaire, on right, covers the south side, and Roy Barker III (ON.1258) from Howth, the north side. (Nicholas Leach)

MOTOR LIFEBOATS

38 • 14m Trent

Esme Anderson (ON.1197) off Ramsgate.

Windsor Runner (Civil Service No.42) (ON.1204) off Blyth, in her original livery. (Nicholas Leach)

Douglas Aikman Smith (ON.1206) on exercise in the Cromarty Firth. (Nicholas Leach)

George and Ivy Swanson (ON.1211) on exercise in the Thames Estuary. (Nicholas Leach)

	Year (Yd No) Builder Place	Name Donor	ON (Op No) Cost Weight	Engines	Stations (Launches/lives saved) Disposal
1	1991 (WO3522) Green Marine/ William Osborne	**Earl and Countess Mountbatten of Burma** Funds donated nationwide to the Mountbatten of Burma Appeal.	1180 (14-01) £1,000,000 25t2	2x808hp MAN D2860 LE401	Trials 1991-1994 (1/2) Alderney 7.3.1994-21.7.95 (42/27) Relief 7.1995-2014 (175/30) Training 9.2014-2019 (2/0) Sold 2019
2	1994 (WO3612) Green Marine/ William Osborne	**Esme Anderson** Bequest of Mrs Esme Grace Anderson.	1197 (14-02) £1,368,399 27t10	2x808hp MAN D2860 LE401	Ramsgate 24.8.1994-
3	1994 (0107) Green Marine/ Souter Sh Yd	**Blue Peter VII** Proceeds of BBC TV programme Blue Peter Pieces of Eight Appeal (1993-4).	1198 (14-03) £1,182,622 27t10	2x808hp MAN D2860 LE401	Fishguard 2.9.1994-
4	1994 (WO3617) Green Marine/ William Osborne	**Roy Barker I** Bequest of Frederick Roy Barker, St Lawrence, Jersey, Channel Islands.	1199 (14-04) £1,224,165 27t10	2x808hp MAN D2860 LE401	Alderney 21.7.1995-
5	1994 (0108) Green Marine/ Souter Sh Yd	**Anna Livia** Proceeds of the Dublin Bay Lifeboat Fund, with other gifts and legacies.	1200 (14-05) £1,193,978 27t10	2x808hp MAN D2860 LE401	Dun Laoghaire 29.6.1995-
6	199 (MR3778) Green Marine/ Halmatic Ltd	**Windsor Runner (Civil Service No.42)** Civil Service, Post Office and British Telecom Lifeboat Fund.	1204 (14-06) £1,150,394 27t10	2x808hp MAN D2860 LE401	Blyth 21.12.1995-16.7.2004 (95/15) Relief 16.7.2004-
7	1994 (WO3618) Green Marine/ William Osborne	**Frederick Storey Cockburn** Bequest of Frederick Storey Cockburn.	1205 (14-07) £1,103,695 27t10	2x808hp MAN D2860 LE401	Courtmacsherry Harbour 18.9.1995-
8	1995 (0109) Green Marine/ Souter Sh Yd	**Douglas Aikman Smith** Bequest of Mr Aikman Smith, owner of Shortridge Ltd, Dumfries.	1206 (14-08) £1,045,325 27t10	2x808hp MAN D2860 LE401	Invergordon 4.5.1996-
9	1995 (WO3614) Green Marine/ William Osborne	**Sir Ronald Pechell Bt** Bequest of Dora, Lady Pechell, with a local appeal in Dunbar.	1207 (14-09) £1,082,746 27t10	2x808hp MAN D2860 LE401	Dunbar 17.12.1995-3.2008 (206/171); broke from moorings 23.3.2008 and wreckd; scrapped
10	1995 (0110) Green Marine/ Souter Sh Yd	**Samarbeta** Volvo Cars UK Limited and legacies from Elizabeth Longman and Constance Rogers.	1208 (14-10) £1,034,005 27t10	2x808hp MAN D2860 LE401	Great Yarmouth & Gorleston 25.2.1996-
11	1995 (WO3656) Green Marine/ William Osborne	**Barclaycard Crusader** Barclaycard Profiles points holders, with other legacies and gifts.	1209 (14-11) £1,096,226 27t10	2x808hp MAN D2860 LE401	Eyemouth 31.3.1996-2018 Training 2019-
12	1995 (0111) Green Marine/ Souter Sh Yd	**Forward Birmingham** Forward Birmingham Lifeboat Campaign, with gifts and legacies.	1210 (14-12) £1,116,298 27t10	2x808hp MAN D2860 LE401	Exmouth 6.7.1996-5.2008 (213/18) Relief 5.2008-
13	1995 (WO3657) Green Marine/ William Osborne	**George and Ivy Swanson** Bequest of Mrs Ivy Ethel Swanson, together with various other bequests.	1211 (14-13) £1,149,481 27t10	2x808hp MAN D2860 LE401	Sheerness 16.3.1996-
14	1996 (0112) Green Marine/ Souter Sh Yd	**George and Mary Webb** The Mary Webb Trust.	1212 (14-14) £1,103,008 27t10	2x808hp MAN D2860 LE401	Whitby 10.4.1996-

38 • 14m Trent

	Year (Yd No) Builder Place	Name Donor	ON (Op No) Cost Weight	Engines	Stations (Launches/lives saved) Disposal
15	1996 (WO3658) Green Marine/ William Osborne	**Henry Heys Duckworth** Gift of Mrs Lilian Duckworth, in memory of her husband.	1213 (14-15) £1,104,656 27t10	2x808hp MAN D2860 LE401	Relief 23.2.1996- Barry Dock 23.1-28.7.2006
16	1996 (0113) Green Marine/ Souter Sh Yd	**Stanley Watson Barker** Bequest of Stanley Watson Barker, Dagenham, Essex; and other legacies.	1214 (14-16) £1,115,189 27t10	2x808hp MAN D2860 LE401	Portree 7.6.1996-
17	1996 (WO3659) Green Marine/ William Osborne	**Elizabeth and Ronald** Mrs Elizabeth Mary Manners-Clarke.	1215 (14-17) £1,075,285 27t10	2x808hp MAN D2860 LE401	Dunmore East 7.10.1996-
18	1997 (0114) Green Marine/ Souter Sh Yd	**Maurice and Joyce Hardy** Gift and bequest from Maurice Hardy CBE CEng, Twyford, and USA.	1222 (14-18) £970,411 27t10	2x808hp MAN D2860 LE401	Fowey 10.10.1996-
19	1997 (WO3690) Green Marine/ William Osborne	**Ger Tigchelaar** Mr Frits Oppenheim.	1223 (14-19) £1,175,606 27t10	2x808hp MAN D2860 LE401	Arklow 19.2.1997-
20	1997 (0115) Green Marine/ Souter Sh Yd	**Roy Barker II** Bequest of Frederick Roy Barker, St Lawrence, Jersey, Channel Islands.	1224 (14-20) £1,127,664 27t10	2x808hp MAN D2860 LE401	Wick 13.2.1997-
21	1997 (WO3691) Green Marine/ William Osborne	**MacQuarie** Bequest Lt Cdr Hugh MacQuarie Stone MBE RD, bequest of Mrs Mary Noond.	1225 (14-21) £1,127,868 27t10	2x808hp MAN D2860 LE401	Sunderland 28.3.1997-2.10.2004 (282/16) Relief 10.2004-
22	1997 (0116) Green Marine/ Souter Sh Yd	**Edward Duke of Windsor** Bequest of late Duchess of Windsor, and other legacies.	1226 (14-22) £1,580,000 27t10	2x808hp MAN D2860 LE401	Relief 15.4.1997-
23	1997 (WO3692) Green Marine/ William Osborne	**Mora Edith Macdonald** Bequest of Miss Mora Edith Macdonald, Glasgow.	1227 (14-23) £1,200,000 27t10	2x808hp MAN D2860 LE401	Oban 17.7.1997-
24	1997 (0117) Green Marine/ Souter Sh Yd	**Dora Foster McDougall** Bequest of Mrs Dora Foster McDougall.	1228 (14-24) £1,580,000 27t10	2x808hp MAN D2860 LE401	Relief 12.10.1997-
25	1998 (WO3735) Green Marine/ William Osborne	**Austin Lidbury** Bequest of Miss Mary Lidbury, Dulverton, Somerset.	1233 (14-25) £1,200,000 27t10	2x808hp MAN D2860 LE401	Ballycotton 5.3.1998-
26	1998 (WO3736) Green Marine/ William Osborne	**Gough-Ritchie II** The Ritchie Charitable Trust.	1234 (14-26) £1,190,000 27t10	2x808hp MAN D2860 LE401	Port St Mary 21.5.1998-
27	1999 (WO3764) Green Marine/ William Osborne	**Robert Hywel Jones Williams** Legacy of Robert Hywel Jones Williams.	1239 (14-27) £1,200,000 27t10	2x808hp MAN D2860 LE401	Fenit 28.2.1999-
28	1999 (WO3765) Green Marine/ William Osborne	**Sam and Ada Moody** Bequest of Ada Moody.	1240 (14-28) £1,200,000 27t10	2x808hp MAN D2860 LE401	Achill 28.4.1999-

▲ Henry Heys Duckworth (ON.1213) on relief duty at Great Yarmouth & Gorleston in her original livery, February 1997. (Nicholas Leach)

▲ Stanley Watson Barker (ON.1214) on exercise at Portree. (Nicholas Leach)

▲ Elizabeth and Ronald (ON.1215) heading out on exercise at Dunmore East. (Nicholas Leach)

▲ Gough-Ritchie II (ON.1234) on exercise off the southern tip of the Isle of Man. (Nicholas Leach)

38 • 14m Trent

	Year (Yd No) Builder Place	Name Donor	ON (Op No) Cost Weight	Engines	Stations (Launches/lives saved) Disposal
29	2000 (0138) Green Marine/ Souter Sh Yd	**Inner Wheel II** Inner Wheel Appeal 1997-2000 together with various legacies.	1245 (14-29) £1,200,000 27t10	2x908hp MAN 2840 LE403	Relief 3.4.2000-9.2006 (50/5) Barry Dock 12.9.2006-
30	2000 (0139) Green Marine/ Souter Sh Yd	**Dr John McSparran** Bequest of Miss Margaret McSparran, Co Antrim, in memory of her brother.	1246 (14-30) £1,400,000 27t10	2x808hp MAN D2860 LE401	Larne 3.8.2000-
31	2001 (0142) Green Marine/ Souter Sh Yd	**Elizabeth of Glamis** Broughty Ferry Lifeboat Appeal, and legacies of Dr Ian Campbell Low and Dr Ronald Bonar.	1252 (14-31) £1,200,000 27t10	2x808hp MAN D2860 LE401	Broughty Ferry 14.4.2001-
32	2001 (0143) Green Marine/ Souter Sh Yd	**Corinne Whiteley** Legacy of Mrs Corinne Whiteley, Mansfield.	1253 (14-32) £1,200,000 27t10	2x808hp MAN D2860 LE401	Relief 9.5.2001-
33	2002 (0148) Green Marine/ Souter Sh Yd	**Roy Barker III** Bequest of Frederick Roy Barker, St Lawrence, Jersey, Channel Islands.	1258 (14-33) £1,250,000 27t10	2x808hp MAN D2860 LE401	Howth 16.3.2002-
34	2002 (0149) Green Marine/ Souter Sh Yd	**Willie and May Gall** Bequest of Mrs May Crombie Gall.	1259 (14-34) £1,240,452 27t10	2x808hp MAN D2860 D2840LXE	Fraserburgh 8.5.2002-
35	2002 (0154) Green Marine/ Souter Sh Yd	**John Neville Taylor** Bequest of John Neville Taylor, Westcliffe-on-Sea, Essex	1266 (14-35) £1,300,000 27t10	2x808hp MAN D2860 LE401	Relief 17.11.2002-5.2008 (73/2) Dunbar 8.5.2008-
36	2003 (0155) Green Marine/ Souter Sh Yd	**Saxon** Bequest of Mrs Freda Berwyn Rivers, London, in memory of her husband.	1267 (14-36) £1,300,000 27t10	2x808hp MAN D2860 LE401	Donaghadee 17.4.2003-
37	2004 (0158) Green Marine/ Souter Sh Yd	**Betty Huntbatch** Bequest of Mrs Betty Huntbatch, Brentwood, Essex.	1274 (14-37) £1,300,000 27t10	2x808hp MAN D2860 LE401	Relief 9.2003-9.2004 (5/0) Hartlepool 27.9.2004-
38	2004 (0159) Green Marine/ Souter Sh Yd	**Jim Moffat** The Moffat Charitable Trust and Lifeboats of the Clyde Appeal.	1275 (14-38) £1,300,000 27t10	2x808hp MAN D2860 LE401	Troon 25.2.2004-

▲ Dr John McSparran (ON.1246) on exercise off the Antrim coast. (Nicholas Leach)

▲ Elizabeth of Glamis (ON.1252) on exercise in the River Tay off Broughty Ferry (Nicholas Leach)

▲ Roy Barker III (ON.1258) on exercise at Howth, Dublin Bay. (Nicholas Leach)

▲ Willie and May Gall (ON.1259) at Fraserburgh.

▶ Betty Huntbatch (ON.1275) on exercise off Hartlepool. (Nicholas Leach)

▶▶ Jim Moffat (ON.1275), the last Trent to be built, heads out of Troon harbour. (Nicholas Leach)

212   MOTOR LIFEBOATS

38 • 14m Trent

One of the first Trents to enter service, Blue Peter VII (ON.1198), pictured on exercise off Fishguard more than twenty years after entering service. She was funded by the BBC TV programme Blue Peter's Pieces of Eight Appeal (1993-94), which funded a series of inshore lifeboats as well as the all-weather lifeboat. (Nicholas Leach)

39 • Tamar fast slipway 16m

KEY DATA
- Introduced 2005
- Last built 2013
- 27 built

SPECIFICATIONS
- Length 16m (45ft 11in)
- Breadth 5m (14ft 10in)
- Draught 1.35m (4ft 3in)
- Weight 31.5 tonnes
- Crew 6
- Endurance 10 hours at 25 knots
- Engines Twin 1,015hp Caterpillar 3412TA turbo-charged diesels, each rated at 2,150rpm
- Fuel 4,300 litres carried

▼ The prototype Tamar ON.1251 at St Peter Port in 2003, participating in the celebrations marking the Guernsey station's bicentenary. This boat was different in many respects to the production boat and was used for trials only, being sold in 2006 once the production run began. (Nicholas Leach)

The Tamar class, developed as the Fast Slipway Boat 2 (FSB2), was designed to replace the eighteen-knot Tyne (FSB1) class lifeboats, which had been in service since the 1980s. The RNLI's technical department began work on the design in 1996, carrying out model testing using the Defence Evaluation and Research Agency's (DERA) test tanks in Gosport with the main aim of producing a lifeboat design which was capable of being slipway launched and could achieve speeds up to twenty-five knots. After testing many models for manoeuvring and sea-keeping capabilities, the RNLI selected one on which to base the hull form of FSB2. The FSB2 programme then went out to competitive tender, resulting in a four-phase contract being placed with Plymouth-based Devonport Management Limited (DML), who went on to build all the Tamars.

The first phase of the programme was the development and construction of the experimental boat, ON.1251, during 2000. Having been fitted out, it was launched in September 2001 and used on extensive evaluation trials around the UK and Ireland, which resulted in this experimental boat being converted into a fully-fledged prototype lifeboat during a rebuild in 2003. The prototype was evaluated by the RNLI's operations staff, after which a second vessel was ordered, ON.1280. This pre-production boat was used to resolve problems in the build processes to ensure a minimum of changes would be made to the design during the main construction programme.

The FSB2 had a flat rather than raked keel to enable it to be launched and recovered on a slipway. The propellers were raised up and, as the engines were to be started in the boathouse and be run dry for some time, particular attention was paid to engine exhaust cooling and lubrication.

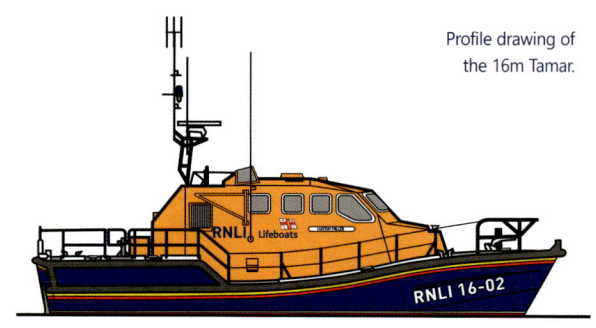

Profile drawing of the 16m Tamar.

Propellers and rudders were protected by a central keel and smaller side keels, which were steel lined, and supported the boat on the slipway, being crucial to the stern-first recovery procedure. In the production boats the deck sheer line was dropped in a similar fashion to the Trent and Severn class to improve casualty recovery, a new exhaust system and more traditional stern exhausts were used, and the internal layout and configuration of the wheelhouse was different.

Construction of the Tamar involved methods similar to those used in the Trent and Severn classes. DML employed the composite boatbuilding company Green Marine of Lymington, builder of Trent and Severn hulls, to manufacture the hull and deck structure for FSB2, and, with weight an important issue, the best material for the hull was deemed to be fibre reinforced plastic (FRP). The hull was made up of a single-skin section below the chine and 100mm thick foam-cored FRC sandwich above, with a longitudinally-stiffened bottom and sandwich construction topsides. The rest of the deck, the bulkheads and the superstructure were made of 25mm foam-cored FRP sandwich construction. Composite hulls provide great strength yet are relatively lightweight structures, and the RNLI had undertaken much research in the use of these advanced composites.

The Tamar was powered by twin 1,015bhp (746bkW) Cat C18 marine diesel engines, running at 2,300rpm, which provided a power-to-weight performance sufficient for the boats to reach the intended top speed of twenty-five knots. The in-line six-cylinder eighteen-litre engine, driving twin fixed-pitch five-bladed propellers, gave good acceleration and fuel economy, as well as low emissions. About 4,600 litres of fuel was carried, giving the boats a range of approximately 250 nautical miles. Displacement of the boat was approximately thirty-two tonnes, and a hydraulically powered bow thruster was fitted to improve manoeuvrability.

A considerable amount of advanced technology was incorporated into the Tamar. The boat was controlled using fly-by-wire technology with a joystick replacing the wheel, and mechanical back-up was provided in the event of system failure. An innovative integrated systems and information management system (sims), developed by Servowatch for the RNLI, was fitted to so that crew could monitor, operate and control many of the lifeboat's systems directly from the safety of their seats via flat screens.

39 • Tamar fast slipway 16m

◀▲ Self-righting trials of the first Tamar lifeboat Peter and Lesley-Jane Nicholson (ON.1280) at DML, November 2004; these photographs give a good indication of the hull shape and keel and propeller configuration. (RNLI)

This meant less time was spent standing up and moving around the lifeboat, thus minimising the chances of crew injury when the lifeboat was operating in rough weather. On a single screen, SIMS provided the crew with access to communications, including VHF and MF radios, direction finder and intercom; navigation, including radar, chart, differential global positioning system, depth of water and speed of boat; and machinery monitoring, including engines, transmission, fuel consumption and bilges.

From an operational point of view, the crew could manage most of the lifeboat's functions remotely while the boat was under way. Using sims also allowed better task-sharing between crew members, as the various functions required to operate the lifeboat could be accessed via screens at any of the six crew positions. A new seat design was also introduced; these specially-designed seats reduced loadings on crew members' spines in rough weather. The two control stations and helm positions were also considerably higher than on a Tyne class lifeboats, providing better 'height of eye', which was useful when searching for a casualty in the water.

The first Tamars were completed during 2005, with the first production boat, Peter and Lesley-Jane Nicholson (ON.1280), being allocated to the Relief Fleet. Three to four boats a year were produced by DML over the course of the next seven years, with a total of twenty-seven boats being built in total. In order for the Tamars to be slipway-launched, the RNLI committed to completely rebuilding those stations where slipways were the only possible launching solution. Some boathouses had been rebuilt prior to the Tamar being completed, but at eleven further stations new boathouses with slipways were constructed as part of a massive investment programme. The last of the new boathouses was built at St Davids.

Shortly after the first of the Tamars were placed into service, there were the usual checks to ensure the boats were operating as designed. However, the slight hull damage to the Barrow boat Grace Dixon (ON.1288), when she suffered a slam in excess of her design load while on passage to her station, was investigated in detail. While a programme to inspect the hulls of all the Tamar fleet was in progress, a detailed examination of the Tamar built for Sennen Cove, City of London III (ON.1294), was carried out at the Babcock yard in Plymouth.

As the Tamars are intended to be kept in service for up to fifty years, the RNLI decided that as a precaution they would upgrade the hull formation, thus reducing the chance of any future structural damage. To do this work from inside the boat would have been extremely costly and time consuming, so a decision was made to carry it out externally by applying a number of layers of additional laminate to the hull bottom, below the chine line, in the area of the tank and survivor spaces. This work was mostly undertaken at the All-Weather Lifeboat Centre at Poole.

▼ The first Tamar lifeboat Peter and Lesley-Jane Nicholson (ON.1280) at Tenby in March 2005. She spent two weeks at the station undergoing launch and recovery trials on the slipway; the Tenby boathouse was the first to be purpose-built for the 16m Tamar. (Nicholas Leach)

MOTOR LIFEBOATS

39 • Tamar fast slipway 16m

▲ Haydn Miller (ON.1281) off Tenby for the station's annual lifeboat day. (Nicholas Leach)

▲ Helen Comrie (ON.1284) on exercise in the Pentland Firth, June 2013. (Nicholas Leach)

▲ Grace Dixon (ON.1288) arriving at Barrow in December 2008. (Nicholas Leach)

▲ Victor Freeman (ON.1293) being launched at Tenby after her naming ceremony. (N. Leach)

	Year (Yd No) / Builder / Place	Name / Donor	ON (Oo No) / Cost / Weight	Engines	Stations / Disposal
1	2000 (050) Green Marine/ DML Devonport	[Un-named]	1251 — 31.5 tonnes	2x1,015bhp Caterpillar C18 6-cylinder	Trials 2000-05 (1/0) Rebuilt 2003 Sold 2006
2	2005 (062) Green Marine/ DML Devonport	Peter and Lesley-Jane Nicholson RNLI funds.	1280 (16-01) £2,000,000 31.5 tonnes	2x1,015bhp Caterpillar C18 6-cylinder	Relief 7.12.2005-
3	2005 (063) Green Marine/ DML Devonport	Haydn Miller Bequest of Haydn Gustav Miller.	1281 (16-02) £2,500,000 31.5 tonnes	2x1,015bhp Caterpillar C18 6-cylinder	Tenby 28.4.2006-
4	2006 (064) Green Marine/ DML Devonport	The Misses Robertson of Kintail Gift from The Robertson Trust, founded by the Misses Robertson of Robertson and Baxter Ltd, Glasgow.	1282 (16-03) £2,500,000 31.5 tonnes	2x1,015bhp Caterpillar C18 6-cylinder	Peterhead 29.4.2006-
5	2006 (065) Green Marine/ DML Devonport	Spirit of Padstow Gift of the late Mrs Mickie Allen.	1283 (16-04) £2,500,000 31.5 tonnes	2x1,015bhp Caterpillar C18 6-cylinder	Padstow 17.7.2006-
6	2006 (066) Green Marine/ DML Devonport	Helen Comrie Bequests of Thomas Leslie M. Comrie and Dr Ben Porges, together with other gifts and legacies.	1284 (16-05) £2,500,000 31.5 tonnes	2x1,015bhp Caterpillar C18 6-cylinder	Longhope 26.10.2006-
7	2007 (067) Green Marine/ DML Devonport	Frank and Anne Wilkinson Bequest of the late Mrs Anne Mary Elizabeth Wilkinson, Huddersfield.	1286 (16-06) £2,500,000 31.5 tonnes	2x1,015bhp Caterpillar C18 6-cylinder	Relief 2007-08 (2/0) Barrow 1-12.2008 (4/0) Relief 2008-
8	2007 (068) Green Marine/ DML Devonport	Lester Bequest of Mr Derek Clifton Lethern, Southfields, London.	1287 (16-07) £2,600,000 31.5 tonnes	2x1,015bhp Caterpillar C18 6-cylinder	Cromer 6.1.2008-
9	2007 (069) Green Marine/ DML Devonport	Grace Dixon Bequest of Grace Dixon, Welton, East Yorkshire.	1288 (16-08) £2,500,000 31.5 tonnes	2x1,015bhp Caterpillar C18 6-cylinder	Barrow 17.12.2008-
10	2008 (070) Green Marine/ DML Devonport	Baltic Exchange III The Baltic Exchange, Marjorie's Settlement Trust, together with other gifts and legacies..	1289 (16-09) £2,500,000 31.5 tonnes	2x1,015bhp Caterpillar C18 6-cylinder	Salcombe 10.3.2008-
11	2008 (071) Green Marine/ DML Devonport	Edward and Barbara Prigmore Legacy of Mrs Barbara Joyce Prigmore, Wellingborough, Northamptonshire.	1290 (16-10) £2,500,000 31.5 tonnes	2x1,015bhp Caterpillar C18 6-cylinder	Relief 6.8.2008-
12	2008 (072) Green Marine/ DML Devonport	Mark Mason Grand Lodge of Mark Master Masons, London; the Tamar Lifeboat Appeal for Angle; and RNLI funds.	1291 (16-11) £2,500,000 31.5 tonnes	2x1,015bhp Caterpillar C18 6-cylinder	Angle 23.3.2009-
13	2009 (073) Green Marine/ DML Devonport	George Sullivan Bequest of the late Major George Langford Sullivan, MBE, and local appeals.	1292 (16-12) £2,500,000 31.5 tonnes	2x1,015bhp Caterpillar C18 6-cylinder	St Helier 14.6.2009-
14	2009 (074) Green Marine/ DML Devonport	Victor Freeman Legacy of Mrs Winifred Adeline Freeman, Bognor Regis, West Sussex, in memory of her son; with other donations and bequests.	1293 (16-13) £2,500,000 31.5 tonnes	2x1,015bhp Caterpillar C18 6-cylinder	Relief 8.7.2009-

39 • Tamar fast slipway 16m

▲ (left) The small Y cass inflatable being launched from the stern of Kiwi (ON.1305) at Moelfre. The Y class is deployed via a hydraulically operated stern door, a set-up unique to the Tamar. (Nicholas Leach)

▲ (right) The first Tamar lifeboat to enter service on the coast was Haydn Miller (ON.1281) at Tenby; she is pictured launching on 25 June 2006 for her naming ceremony. (Nicholas Leach)

▲ Spirit of Padstow (ON-1283), pictured on exercise off the North Cornwall coast, was one of the first Tamars to go on station. (Nicholas Leach)

◀ Norah Wortley (ON.1306) being recovred up the slipway at St Davids. This photo gives a good idea of the considerable size of the boathouses built for the Tamar lifeboats, compared to the older boathouses which had given, in some instances, over a century of use. (Nicholas Leach)

MOTOR LIFEBOATS

39 • Tamar fast slipway 16m

	Year (Yd No) Builder Place	Name Donor	ON (Oo No) Cost Weight	Engines	Stations Disposal
15	2009 (075) Green Marine/ DML Devonport	**City of London II** The City of London Branch.	1294 (16-14) £2,700,000 31.5 tonnes	2x1,015bhp Caterpillar C18 6-cylinder	Sennen Cove 8.1.2010-
16	2010 (076) Green Marine/ DML Devonport	**Enid Collett** Legacy of Enid Marjory Collett, Great Shelford, Cambridgeshire, with other gifts and legacies.	1295 (16-15) £2,700,00031.5 tonnes	2x1,015bhp Caterpillar C18 6-cylinder	Shoreham Harbour 10.12.2010-
17	2010 (077) Green Marine/ DML Devonport	**Mollie Hunt** Legacy of the late Miss Evelyn Mary Hunt, Budleigh Salterton, and other gifts and legacies.	1296 (16-16) £2,700,000 31.5 tonnes	2x1,015bhp Caterpillar C18 6-cylinder	Appledore 29.3.2010-
18	2010 (078) Green Marine/ DML Devonport	**Alfred Albert Williams** Bequest of a couple from Oxfordshire and the Bembridge Lifeboat Appeal.	1297 (16-17) £2,700,000 31.5 tonnes	2x1,015bhp Caterpillar C18 6-cylinder	Bembrdge 20.10.2010-
19	2010 (079) Green Marine/ DML Devonport	**Killarney** Legacy of Mrs Florence Mary Weeks, Surrey.	1298 (16-18) £2,700,000 31.5 tonnes	2x1,015bhp Caterpillar C18 6-cylinder	Kilmore Quay 27.10.2010-
20	2011 (080) SAR Composites/ Babcock	**Irene Muriel Rees** Bequest of Irene Muriel Rees, Cliff Way, Frinton, plus RNLI funds.	1299 (16-19) £2,700,000 31.5 tonnes	2x1,015bhp Caterpillar C18 6-cylinder	Walton and Frinton 9.5.2011-
21	2011 (081) SAR Composites/ Babcock	**Rose** An anonymous donation from a charitable trust and the Lizard Lifeboat Appeal.	1300 (16-20) £2,700,000 31.5 tonnes	2x1,015bhp Caterpillar C18 6-cylinder	Lizard 16.7.2011-
22	2011 (082) SAR Composites/ Babcock	**John Buchanan Barr** Legacy of Catherine Barr, in memory of her husband, Dr John Buchanan Barr MBE.	1301 (16-21) 31.5 tonnes	2x1,015bhp Caterpillar C18 6-cylinder	Portpatrick 13.11.2011-
23	2011 (083) SAR Composites/ Babcock	**Alan Massey** Legacy from Mrs Dorothy May Massey, Watford, together with the generous bequests of Henry and Joan Jermyn, John Noel Harvey Ward and John Heath.	1302 (16-22) 31.5 tonnes	2x1,015bhp Caterpillar C18 6-cylinder	Baltimore 9.3.2012-
24	2012 (084) SAR Composites/ Babcock	**Diamond Jubilee** Legacy of John Alan Jackson, Eastbourne Lifeboat Appeal, legacy of Alice Kendall and various other gifts.	1303 (16-23) 31.5 tonnes	2x1,015bhp Caterpillar C18 6-cylinder	Eastbourne 27.6.2012-
25	2012 (085) SAR Composites/ Babcock	**John D. Spicer** Bequest of the late John Dominic Spicer, from Oxfordshire.	1304 (16-24) 31.5 tonnes	2x1,015bhp Caterpillar C18 6-cylinder	Porthdinllaen 24.8.2012-
26	2012 (086) SAR Composites/ Babcock	**Kiwi** Bequest of the late Reginald James Clark, New Zealand.	1305 (16-25) 31.5 tonnes	2x1,015bhp Caterpillar C18 6-cylinder	Moelfre 9.5.2013-
27	2013 (087) SAR Composites/ Babcock	**Norah Wortley** Bequest of Mrs Diane Mary Symon, of Newton Abbot.	1306 (16-26) 31.5 tonnes	2x1,015bhp Caterpillar C18 6-cylinder	St Davids 19.4.2013-
28	2013 (088) SAR Composites/ Babcock	**Roy Barker IV** Roy Barker Memorial Fund.	1307 (16-27) 31.5 tonnes	2x1,015bhp Caterpillar C18 6-cylinder	Mumbles 8.2.2014-

▲ Enid Collett (ON.1295) launching from the slipway at Shoreham Harbour. (Nicholas Leach)

▲ Irene Muriel Rees (ON.1299) heading away from Walton pier on exercise. (Nicholas Leach)

▲ John Buchanan Barr (ON.1301) on exercise off Portpatrick. (Nicholas Leach)

▲ Kiwi (ON.1305) on show at Moelfre for the station's lifeboat day. (Nicholas Leach)

39 • Tamar fast slipway 16m

Last of the twenty-seven Tamars to be built, Roy Barker IV (ON.1307), pictured crossing Swansea Bay in October 2013, just after she had first arrived at her station, Mumbles. (Nicholas Leach)

40 • Shannon

KEY DATA
- Introduced 2013
- Still in production

SPECIFICATIONS
- Length 13.6m
- Breadth 4.5m
- Draught 1m
- Weight 18 tonnes (maximum)
- Crew 6
- Endurance 250 nautical miles
- Engine Twin 650hp Scania D13 (d), twin Hamilton HJ364 waterjets
- Speed 25 knots maximum
- Fuel 2,740 litres carried

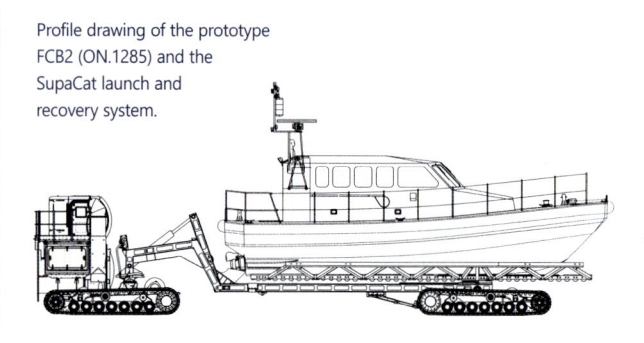

Profile drawing of the prototype FCB2 (ON.1285) and the SupaCat launch and recovery system.

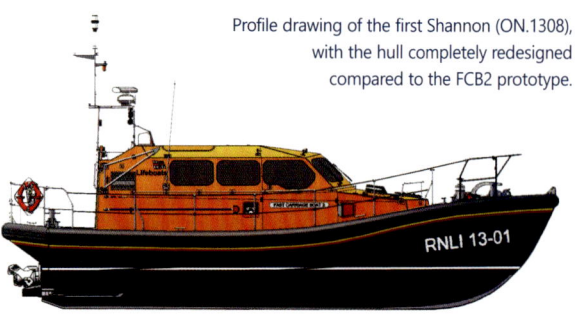

Profile drawing of the first Shannon (ON.1308), with the hull completely redesigned compared to the FCB2 prototype.

▼ The prototype FCB2 ON.1285 at the RNLI's Depot, Poole in October 2005 during the trials and evaluation process. The boat proved the viability of waterjets for beach-launched lifeboats, but the hull design was found not to be suitable for lifeboat operations. (Nicholas Leach)

The Shannon class lifeboat was developed during the early years of the twenty-first century as a replacement for the 12m Mersey carriage-launched lifeboat. Planning for the new twenty-five-knot Fast Carriage Boat (FCB2) began in 2001 when Carmarc Ltd, a UK-based small boat designer, was commissioned by the RNLI to work with the RNLI's Engineering Office to produce a fast 13.6m (44ft) all-weather self-righting lifeboat. The new lifeboat was to be capable of being launched and recovered from beaches, and operate in extreme conditions around the coasts of the United Kingdom and Ireland.

The contract included the design and development of a double-chine hull form, which was configured with waterjet propulsion to achieve the required design speed of twenty-five knots. Once the basic design had been agreed, with input coming from coxswains and crews around the coast, an order was placed for a prototype, which was moulded by Green Marine, Lymington, out of fibre reinforced composite (FRC) in 2004. Green Marine provided extensive knowledge of composite structures to the project, including the 3D modelling and drawing work. The hull consisted of two layers of FRC bonded to a foam core, giving a structure that was strong and rigid, but also light. The wheelhouse and deck were also made of a single composite piece, of sandwich construction, and this was bonded to the hull during the fitting-out stage. The boat was fitted out by VT Halmatic at Portchester during 2005.

Earlier in the FCB2 project, trials were conducted with a waterjet-powered test boat, an Ocean Dynamics Ribworker rigid-inflatable named Odyn, which was used to demonstrate that this form of propulsion was suitable for a beach-launched lifeboat. The results proved that twin waterjets were the best propulsion solution, as they not only ensured the design had a shallow draft, but also provided it with good manoeuvrability.

Once it had been completed, the prototype lifeboat, ON.1285, was taken on a series of trails, including being capsized to prove its self-righting capability. Although not intended to be a fully operationally capable lifeboat during the development stage, with none of the internal spaces cosmetically finished, ON.1285 had many of the basic systems installed, with similar levels of redundancy to those found on operational boats. The trials were also to demonstrate the manoeuvrability and seakeeping of the hull, as well as test the machinery systems. The first impressions of the new boat were positive, from the handling to the layout. The craft managed thirty knots during trials in fine weather, although production boats were expected to achieve about twenty-seven knots.

The upper steering position had a wheel and various other controls, including levers for the waterjets' buckets, one lever for each jet. On the armrest of the coxswain's chair in the wheelhouse was a joystick for steering, with the same steering and jet controls duplicated on the upper steering position. The wheelhouse had six seats, three either side. The survivors' cabin and anchor locker were accessed via steps from the wheelhouse. Under the wheelhouse floor were two fuel tanks built into either side of the hull, and a watertight door led to the engine room.

40 • Shannon

◀ The prototype FCB2, ON.1285, undergoing launch and recovery trials at Wells-next-the-Sea in 2005 using a Talus MB-H tractor with the launch carriage developed by Biglands, which was coupled to a Talus unit. (Nicholas Leach)

◀◀ The waterjet-powered Ribworker rigid-inflatable Odyn during a crew training course out of the RNLI's Depot at Poole in October 2005. This RIB was used to assess the suitability of waterjet propulsion for the FCB2 design, and the boat was subsequently retained by the RNLI for training and familiarisation courses for crews receiving Shannon lifeboats. (Nicholas Leach)

As the lifeboat was to be carriage launched, the RNLI also completely rethought and redesigned the launch and recovery procedure, developing a bespoke system that enabled launching and recovery to be speeded up and undertaken more safely. Two designs of carriage were initially proposed, one made by Clayton Engineering Ltd (Biglands) and the other by SupaCat Ltd of Honiton, Devon. The SupaCat was a completely new concept and featured a powered carriage as well as a new cab for the driver. The Clayton system, meanwhile, was a modification of the well-proven Talus MB-H crawler tractor attached to a newly-designed drive-through carriage.

Preliminary trials with the launch systems were undertaken at Poole using ON.1285 between 4 and 6 October 2005, before the boat and launch rigs were taken to Instow in Devon for beach trials. More launch and recovery trials were held around the end of the year and during 2006, when the prototype boat and rigs were taken to various lifeboat stations, including Dungeness and Wells. As a result of the trials, the SupaCat

▲ The prototype FCB2, ON.1285, being recovered, bow first, at Llandudno in July 2011 during launch and recovery trials with the redesigned SLRS rig. (Tony Denton)

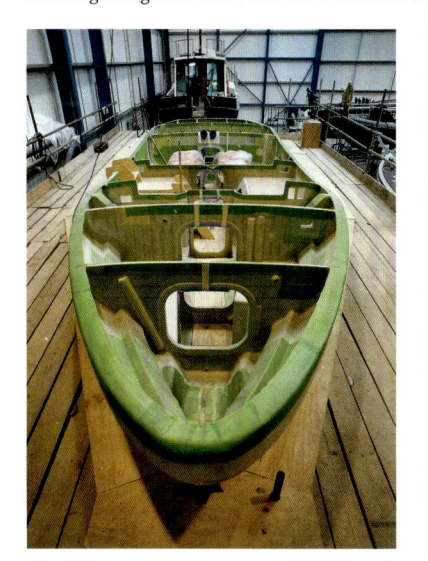

◀ The bare FRC hull of the first Shannon, ON.1308, during its construction at Berthon Boat Company, Lymington. (Peter Edey) ▼

MOTOR LIFEBOATS   221

40 • Shannon

▶ The waterjet arrangement on the prototype FSB2, ON.1285, pictured while the boat was being used for launch and recovery trials and testing at Wells-next-the-Sea. (Nicholas Leach)

▶▶ The waterjets on Patsy Knight (ON.1312), the fifth Shannon to be built, which was stationed at Lowestoft, where she was kept afloat. These two photographs give an indication of some of the differences between the prototype and the production boats. (Peter Edey)

▼ The first Production Shannon, ON.1308, being fitted out at Berthon Boat Company, Lymington in 2011, with the work nearing completion. The first eleven Shannons were fitted out at Lymington by Berthon. (Peter Edey)

design was deemed to be the most suitable, and so it was adapted and refined for operational use. It provided sufficient flexibility to allow the method of launch and recovery to be tailored to the local beach conditions. The launching mechanism featured a single release point at the bow, unlike with the Mersey launch using chains released by four crew members on deck, with this being controlled by the coxswain.

The new system was also more user-friendly and removed the possibility of a foul-up during launch because of incorrect chain release or the launching falls snagging on the propellers or rudders. One of the main requirements when developing the launch and recovery system was to recover FCB2 bow first to the carriage. Mersey recovery involved pulling the lifeboat up the beach until enough space was available astern to position the carriage and tractor and then pull the Mersey backwards onto the carriage. This was time consuming and, on some beaches, recovery had to be delayed until the tide conditions were suitable.

Water jets meant the boat had a shallower draught than the Mersey, so the FCB2 could get closer to the shore before grounding; in rough conditions, coming ashore at speed allowed the boat to clear the danger area of breaking surf for a safe recovery. After FCB2 had been hauled bow first onto the carriage and secured, the hydraulically-powered cradle was rotated through 180 degrees ready for the next launch. One of the benefits of the new system was the reduction in the number of shore helpers required, especially during recovery. To launch, only a tractor driver and head launcher were required.

Supacat produced a pre-production prototype in 2010 and, following trials, rebuilt the prototype to pre-production standards, incorporating a series of upgrades, including a new lightweight composite cab with improved all-round vision, new marine-proofed track system and a new 450hp Scania engine DC12 12.7-litre turbo-charged diesel. The carriage cradle was also redesigned, and in September 2011 this was trialled at various locations, including at Llandudno, where an undulating and deep shingle bank could not be negotiated using existing in-service launch systems; at Dungeness, where the system tackled the steep pebble beach; and at Hoylake, where spring tides mean distances of up three miles of soft mud have to be covered on occasions. The Supacat launch rig was redesignated the Shannon Launch & Recovery System (SLRS), and in 2012 the RNLI ordered six units from Supacat for delivery in 2013 and 2014. Subsequent units have been built by Clayton Engineering in Knighton and SC Innovation, a division of the Supacat Group, in Devon.

Following operational experience the RNLI decided that it would be possible, in certain locations, to dispense with the power drive to the carriage, and SC Innovations developed a 'non-powered carriage' version, which offered considerable cost savings. The tractor unit was capable of operating with both powered and non-powered trailers to eliminate the need for a relief non-powered system.

40 • Shannon

Meanwhile, in 2008, during rough weather trials with the experimental FCB2, ON.1285, it was found that the hull design was not meeting the operational requirements for an RNLI lifeboat, especially when travelling up-sea in steep waves. In such conditions the hull had a tendency to 'slam', making the ride on board unacceptably uncomfortable for the crew. As a result a new hull design had to be developed, with the process being opened to tender, and the FCB2 project was extended by three years.

Seven new designs were submitted for consideration, six from external companies and one from the RNLI's in-house design team. Six scale models were then built and tested by Seaspeed Marine Consulting Ltd. These models, driven by twin waterjets, were self-righting, radio-controlled and fully instrumented for both acceleration and motion in all three planes vertical, transverse and longitudinal, and incorporated a small video camera in the wheelhouse at the coxswain position. To recreate realistic conditions, most of the testing was completed in open water in the Solent and Chichester Harbour, with extreme weather surf zone testing in Poole Bay. Additional testing to back up the open water data was completed by Seaspeed at QinetiQ's ocean basin and ship tank at Haslar, Gosport. QinetiQ, an international defence and security company, donated three days use of the tank to the RNLI.

The key performance criteria for the new hull was to reduce up-sea

▲▼ The first Shannon, ON.1308, being shown off to the national media at Sandbanks, Dorset on 25 September 2012. (Nicholas Leach)

◀ The first Shannon, ON.1308, successfully completing her self-righting trial at Berthon Marina, Lymington on 30 January 2012. Righting was achieved, as with all fast lifeboats, by virtue of the wheelhouse buoyancy making the hull unstable in the upturned position; from being fully inverted, the Shannon came back to the upright in 4.5 seconds. (By courtesy of the RNLI)

MOTOR LIFEBOATS

40 • Shannon

▲ The main building hall at the All-Weather Lifeboat Centre (ALC) at Poole, with Shannon hulls and decks at various stages of completion. The two building halls each have six bays, and the construction process sees the boats being moved from one bay to the next as the fitting-out progresses. A new Shannon is completed approximately every two months. (Nicholas Leach)

▶ The third Shannon to be bult at the ALC in Poole, Frederick William Plaxton (ON.1322) destined for Scarborough, being fitted out in April 2016 in the main building hall. (Nicholas Leach)

▶▶ Two Shannon at the ALC in Poole in contrasting states: on the right is Kenneth James Pierpoint (ON.1321), built for Fleetwood, the second Shannon completed at the ALC, with an unidentified hull and deck assembley alongside ready to be fitted out. (Nicholas Leach)

slamming without comprising down-sea performance. The trials were some of the most extensive ever conducted by the RNLI, with all models performing well. However, the design developed by the RNLI's in-house team of naval architects, led by Peter Eyre, provided the best overall performance, with better seakeeping and around seventy per cent less slam incidents compared to the experimental FCB2. In April 2009 the RNLI announced that the in-house design had been chosen, with the next stage of the development cycle being to optimise the hull form to further improve performance, with fuel economy being an important factor.

The new hull design was narrow at the bow, wide in the aft section, and steeper in the mid region; this shape provided good overall stability while at the same time minimised slamming as the boat travelled through the water. The hull tended to cut through the tops of waves rather than riding on their crest, which reduced the slamming effect, while the shape and angle of the side of the hull also made broaching in heavy seas less likely. The design also reduced both traverse and vertical movements, providing a fast, manoeuvrable and stable working platform.

In 2010 Norco GRP Ltd, a Poole-based company, in association with MouldCAM Ltd, produced the hull moulds for the new design. MouldCAM offered the best solution regarding build accuracy, time and cost, despite being located in Brisbane, Australia. Once the moulds had been completed, they were shipped to the UK, where Norco completed final assembly prior to their delivery to SAR Composites, in Lymington, who were to produce the hulls and deckhouses. The construction process involved the hull and wheelhouse being cooked to seventy degrees centigrade prior to being removed from the moulds.

After the hull moulding had been completed at SAR composites, it was transferred to Berthon Boat Company, also at Lymington, to be fitted out, which included the installation of electrical looms, SIMS equipment, engines and waterjets. The deck/wheelhouse was then delivered to Berthon and, after external painting, was also fitted out. After the initial internal fitting out, hull and deck/wheelhouse were joined together, ready for the completion of what was the prototype of the new FCB2, ON.1308.

Throughout the hull design process, discussions were under way about the best fit-out of the boat, considering the kind of seating to be fitted in the wheelhouse and its positioning, the boat's controls, the electronic System and Information Management System (SIMS) and the engines. The deck layout was determined by the requirement to provide an aft deck space suitable for helicopter winching and towing operations. The interior of the wheelhouse was the subject of much discussion, with decisions made about the best positions for the seats, engine controls, SIMS screens, lights and switches, air-conditioning, chart table and casualty handling.

Perhaps the most notable aspect of the FCB2's design was the propulsion system, as it was the first modern RNLI all-weather lifeboat to be powered

40 • Shannon

by waterjets, rather than propellers. After extensive research into engine options, and discussions with various manufacturers, it was decided to fit Scania thirteen-litre diesel engines. Although they were a new design, trials proved successful with the necessary 650hp being generated, with each engine fed from its own 1,370-litre fuel tank. The Scania engines powered twin Hamilton HJ365 waterjets, and the design speed of twenty-five knots was easily achieved. Waterjets gave the boat outstanding manoeuvrability and far better boat handling than on the Mersey.

In April 2011 the RNLI Trustees announced that the FCB2 design had been given the class name Shannon, the first time an Irish river had been chosen for a lifeboat class. The first Shannon, ON.1308, took to the water for the first time in January 2012 to undertake capsizing and righting trials, which were successfully completed. The boat then returned to the yard for final fitting out and was officially launched on 14 February 2012 ready to undertake sea trials. Throughout 2012 trials continued, during which the boat accrued the equivalent of four years' operational service, enabling crews to experience and comment on the boat's performance.

On 25 September 2012 the first Shannon, ON.1308, was presented to the national media, as the RNLI stated its intention to have its entire fleet capable of twenty-five knots over the course of the next decade. The announcement also stated that about fifty Shannons would be built, but the design subsequently proved to be so good and so versatile that this number was revised upwards, with seventy boats or more planned as of 2019. After ON.1308 had been formally accepted into RNLI service on 3 July 2013, she was named Jock and Annie Slater, after a former RNLI Chairman and his wife, at Poole on 11 July 2013 and entered the Relief Fleet. Orders for the next five Shannons had been placed, and the first operational Shannon to go to the coast for service, The Morrell (ON.1309), arrived at Dungeness for the first time in February 2014, taking up operational duties on 5 March.

The development of the Shannon, regarded as the future of life-saving in the UK and Ireland, was an enormous project for the RNLI, and involved not just designing and developing a new boat, and coming up with a new launch and recovery system, but also, and perhaps the most ambitious aspect of all, building a lifeboat construction facility at the RNLI's Headquarters site in Poole so lifeboat production could be taken in-house

▲ The naming ceremony at the Lifeboat College at Poole on 11 July 2013 of Jock and Annie Slater (ON.1308), the first Shannon. (Nicholas Leach)

▼ Launch and recovery of 13m Shannons at Bridlington (left) and Lytham St Annes (right) using the specially-designed SLRS rig. (Nicholas Leach)

MOTOR LIFEBOATS 225

40 • Shannon

▲ The first Shannon to go to the coast for operational service, The Morrell (ON.1309), arriving at Dungeness on 21 February 2014. (Nicholas Leach)

▶ Recovery of Ella Larsen (ON.1337) at Barmouth using SLRS rig SC-T18. The bow-first recovery facilitated by the launch system designed for Shannon provided for a safer and faster recovery process and was one of the criteria specified in the original design brief. (Nicholas Leach)

▼ Looking up the cradle of the SLRS rig SC-T18 on the beach at Barmouth. The SLRS provided in effect a mobile slipway to transport the Shannon in all beach conditions. The complete system can be shut down and left submerged in water up to nine metres deep, if necessary. (Nicholas Leach)

by the charity. The first twelve Shannons were fitted out by Berthon Boat Company at Lymington, with the FRC hulls moulded by SAR Composites, between 2013 and 2015. While they were being built, construction of the RNLI's new lifeboat building facility at Poole was taking place

The All-Weather Lifeboat Centre (ALC), as it was designated, was officially opened on 21 August 2015 and since then all new Shannons have been built at this facility. The entire build process, from hull moulding to deck and hull assembly to fit out, trials and acceptance, is managed at the ALC. The two build halls have the capacity to produce six new Shannons a year. The idea behind the ALC was to make lifeboat building more economical and more efficient, as building and maintaining lifeboats at the new facility is estimated to yield considerable savings in production costs, and will offset the £24 million cost of constructing the factory. The ALC has two boat halls with flexible bays for manufacturing and maintaining lifeboats; a component manufacturing area; a boat storage area; paint preparation area with built-in extraction system and heat curing facility; and workshops, office facilities, storage areas and a visitor viewing gallery.

In March 2016 the first Shannon to be completed by the new All-Weather Lifeboat Centre at Poole, Cosandra (ON.1319), entered service in the Relief Fleet, and the following month the last of the Shannons built by Berthon Boat Co, Lymington, George Thomas Lacy (ON.1320), was completed and placed on station at Swanage; this was notable because it was the first Shannon to be slipway launched.

The RNLI plan to build at least seventy Shannons in total, and so the design is set to become the most numerous single class of all-weather lifeboat ever to see operational service in the UK and Ireland. This will be facilitated by the All-weather Lifeboat Centre, which has enabled the RNLI to effectively control the lifeboat building process, so, as well as minimising risks within the building supply chain, the new facility gives greater control over quality and costs. By bringing all-weather lifeboat building in house and capitalising on the expertise within the organisation, the RNLI has been able save at least £3 million a year.

40 • Shannon

	Year (Yd No) Builder Place	Name Donor	ON (Op No) Cost Weight	Stations Disposal
1	2005 Green Marine/ VT Halmatic	**Effseabee Too** RNLI funds.	1285	Trials 2005-12 Sold 2013
2	2012 (1046) SAR Composites/ Berthon Bt Co	**Jock and Annie Slater** RNLI general funds.	1308 (13-01) 17.62 tonnes	Trials 2012-13 (1/0) Relief 11.7.2013-3.2019 Wicklow 5.4.2019-
3	2013 (1047) SAR Composites/ Berthon Bt Co	**The Morrell** Legacy of Mrs Barbara Morrell, Bromley, Kent.	1309 (13-02) 18 tonnes	Dungeness 5.3.2014-
4	2014 (1048) SAR Composites/ Berthon Bt Co	**R. and J. Welburn** Legacy of Joan Welburn, East Devon.	1310 (13-03) 18 tonnes	Exmouth 26.5.2014-
5	2014 (1049) SAR Composites/ Berthon Bt Co	**Storm Rider** RNLI's summer and Christmas appeals of 2012.	1311 (13-04) 18 tonnes	Relief 17.5.2014-
6	2014 (1050) SAR Composites/ Berthon Bt Co	**Patsy Knight** Legacy of Patsy Knight, Kessingland.	1312 (13-05) £2,000,000 18 tonnes	Lowestoft 2.10.2014-
7	2014 (1051) SAR Composites/ Berthon Bt Co	**Edmund Hawthorn Micklewood** Legacy of Miss Paulette Micklewood, Oxford.	1313 (13-06) £2,000,000 18 tonnes	Hoylake 9.12.2014-
8	2014 (1052) SAR Composites/ Berthon Bt Co	**Reg** Legacy of Reginald James Pritchard, Haslemere and Bosham.	1314 (13-07) £2,000,000 18 tonnes	Relief 29.1.2015-
9	2015 (1053) SAR Composites/ Berthon Bt Co	**Derek Bullivant** Legacy of Derek Jim Bullivant, Bewdley, Worcestershire.	1315 (13-08) £2,000,000 18 tonnes	Lough Swilly 23.4.2015-
10	2015 (1054) SAR Composites/ Berthon Bt Co	**The Barry and Peggy High Foundation** Gift of Barry High OBE, through the Barry and Peggy High Foundation; legacy of Anthony Mutter; donation from Forster Wood Foundation.	1316 (13-09) £2,100,000 18 tonnes	Ilfracombe 18.6.2015-
11	2015 (1055) SAR Composites/ Berthon Bt Co	**Ian Grant Smith** Bequest of Ruth Grant Smith, who died in 2005, in memory of her husband.	1317 (13-10) £2,100,000 18 tonnes	Montrose 2.9.2015-
12	2015 (1056) SAR Composites/ Berthon Bt Co	**Nora Stachura** Bequest of Nora Strachura, Swindon.	1318 (13-11) £2,100,000 18 tonnes	St Ives 11.2015-
13	2015 (0001) SAR Composites/ ALC, Poole	**Cosandra** Legacy of Alexandra Arsenis, and RNLI Christmas Appeal.	1319 (13-12) £2,100,000 18 tonnes	Relief 11.3.2016-
14	2016 (1057) SAR Composites/ Berthon Bt Co	**George Thomas Lacy** Legacy of the late Mr George Lacy.	1320 (13-13) £2,100,000 18 tonnes	Swanage 20.4.2016-
15	2016 (0002) SAR Composites/ ALC, Poole	**Kenneth James Pierpoint** Legacy of Miss Kathleen Mary Pierpoint, Altrincham, Cheshire.	1321 (13-14) £2,100,000 18 tonnes	Fleetwood 20.7.2016-
16	2016 (0003) SAR Composites/ ALC, Poole	**Frederick William Plaxton** Bequest of Frederick Plaxton, in memory of his father.	1322 (13-15) £2,100,000 18 tonnes	Scarborough 19.12.2016-

▲ Storm Rider (ON.1311) at Poole on show for the RNLI Open Days, August 2015. (Nicholas Leach)

▲ Reg (ON.1314) arriving at Bremerhaven in Germany in May 2015 for the 150th anniversary of the DGzRS, the German lifeboat service. (N. Leach)

▲ The Barry and Peggy High Foundation (ON.1316) arriving at Ilfracombe. (Nicholas Leach)

▲ Kenneth James Pierpoint (ON.1321) at moorings in the River Wyre off Fleetwood. (Nicholas Leach)

40 • Shannon

▲ William F. Yates launching on exercise at Llandudno, March 2018. (Nicholas Leach)

▲ Brianne Aldington (ON.1328) on trials at Barmouth, January 2019. (Nicholas Leach)

▲ Stella and Humfrey Berkeley (ON.1332) arriving at Leverburgh, April 2018. (Nicholas Leach)

▲ Richard and Caroline Colton (ON.1335) beaching at Hastings. (Nicholas Leach)

	Year (Yd No) Builder Place	Name Donor	ON (Op No) Cost Weight	Stations Disposal
17	2016 (0004) SAR Composites/ ALC, Poole	**Elizabeth and Leonard** Legacy of Mrs Elizabeth Foley Brumfield, Hull, and Amble lifeboat appeal.	1323 (13-16) 18 tonnes	Amble 23.12.2016-
18	2016 (0005) SAR Composites/ ALC, Poole	**Joel and April Grunnill** Legacy of Joel Grunnill, of Skegness; gift of April Grunnill, of Skegness.	1324 (13-17) 18 tonnes	Skegness 11.2.2017-
19	2016 (0006) SAR Composites/ ALC, Poole	**William F. Yates** The Gladys Yates estate, in memory of William Frederick Marple Yates, of Widnes, and other gifts and legacies.	1325 (13-18) 18 tonnes	Llandudno 10.10.2017-
20	2017 (0007) SAR Composites/ ALC, Poole	**Dorothy May White** Legacy of the late Mrs Dorothy May White, Birmingham; the Sir John Fisher Foundation; and Workington RNLI's Shannon class appeal.	1326 (13-19) 18 tonnes	Workington 11.4.2017-
21	2017 (0008) SAR Composites/ ALC, Poole	**Denise and Eric** Bequest of Denise and Eric Rowse.	1327 (13-20) 18 tonnes	Selsey 10.7.2017-
22	2017 (0009) SAR Composites/ ALC, Poole	**Brianne Aldington** Bequest of Brian and Catherine Aldington, London.	1328 (13-21) 18 tonnes	Relief 8.9.2017-2019 Clifden 17.8.2019-
23	2017 (0010) SAR Composites/ ALC, Poole	**Antony Patrick Jones** Legacy of Antony Patrick Jones, of Bridlington.	1329 (13-22) 18 tonnes	Bridlington 26.11.2017-
24	2017 (0011) SAR Composites/ ALC, Poole	**Elizabeth and Gertrude Allan** The John and Elizabeth Allan Memorial Trust	1330 (13-23) 18 tonnes	Girvan 20.4.2018-
25	2018 (0012) SAR Composites/ ALC, Poole	**Barbara Anne** Bequest of Miss Barbara Anne Cameron Roberts, of Winchester; a local appeal, and other gifts and donations.	1331 (13-24) 18 tonnes	Lytham St Annes 8.6.2018-
26	2018 (0013) SAR Composites/ ALC, Poole	**Stella and Humfrey Berkeley** Bequest of Humfrey Berkeley, Boston Spa; other contributions from Mrs Muriel Madeleine Mackay, Hugh John Waterman, Miss Isabel May Hogg, and Lord Leverhulme's Charitable Trust.	1332 (13-25) 18 tonnes	Leverburgh 2.5.2018-
27	2018 (0014) SAR Composites/ ALC, Poole	**John Metters** Bequest of John Metters, Nether Hayford, Northamptonshire.	1333 (13-26) 18 tonnes	Relief 4.2018-
28	2018 SAR Composites/ ALC, Poole	**Joanna and Henry Williams** Bequest of Joanna and Henry Williams, Plymouth, Devon.	1334 (13-27) 18 tonnes	Relief 8.2018-
29	2018 SAR Composites/ ALC, Poole	**Richard and Caroline Colton** Bequest of Richard Coulton, Wellingborough, and named after the donor and his wife.	1335 (13-28) 18 tonnes	Hastings 7.11.2018-
30	2018 SAR Composites/ ALC, Poole	**Helen Hastings** Bequest of Helen Hastings, Stocksfield.	1336 (13-29) 18 tonnes	Eyemouth 9.1.2019-
31	2019 SAR Composites/ ALC, Poole	**Ella Larson** The Basil Larsen 1999 Charitable Trust.	1337 (13-30) 18 tonnes	Barmouth 10.4.2019-
32	2019 SAR Composites/ ALC, Poole	**Michael O'Brian** Legacy from Henry Tomkins, Wexford.	1338 (13-31) 18 tonnes	Clogher Head 8.7.2019-

40 • Shannon

Edmund Hawthorn Micklewood (ON.1313) on exercise off the Wirral peninsula. Operating from Hoylake, the Shannon is an ideal vessel to cover the shallow waters of the Mersey and Dee estuaries. (Nicholas Leach)

40 • Shannon

	Year (Yd No) Builder Place	Name Donor	ON (Op No) Cost Weight	Stations Disposal
33	2019 SAR Composites/ ALC, Poole	**Ruth and David Harper** Bequests of David Leslie Arthur and Mrs Eva Mary Cooper.	1339 (13-32) 18 tonnes	Relief 3.5.2019-
34	2019 SAR Composites/ ALC, Poole	**Bridie O'Shea** Gift from a relative in memory of Bridie O'Shea. Richmond, Surrey.	1340 (13-33) 18 tonnes	Relief 2019-
35	2019 SAR Composites/ ALC, Poole	**Anthony Kenneth Heard**	1341 (13-34) 18 tonnes	Rhyl 2019-
36	2019 SAR Composites/ ALC, Poole	**Frank and Brenda Winter**	1342 (13-35) 18 tonnes	Peel
37	2020 SAR Composites/ ALC, Poole	**John and Elizabeth Allan**	1343 (13-36) 18 tonnes	Seahouses
38	2020 SAR Composites/ ALC, Poole	**Agnes A. P. Barr**	1344 (13-37) 18 tonnes	Invergordon
39	2020 SAR Composites/ ALC, Poole	**Judith Copping Joyce**	1345 (13-38)	Sheerness
40	2020 SAR Composites/ ALC, Poole	**Roger Smith**	1346 (13-39)	Pwllheli
41	2020 SAR Composites/ ALC, Poole		1347 (13-40)	Relief
42	2020 SAR Composites/ ALC, Poole		1347 (13-41)	

▲ Helen Hastings (ON1336) arriving on station at Eyemouth, December 2018. (Nicholas Leach)

▲ Ruth and David Harper (ON.1339) at Rhyl being turned on the SLRS carriage. (Nicholas Leach)

▼ Dorothy May White (ON.1326, left) and Denise and Eric (ON.1327, right) being launched at Workington and Selsey respectively. The davit launch system is unique to Workington and dates from the early 1990s, having been designed for a Tyne class lifeboat (see p.188). (Nicholas Leach)

MOTOR LIFEBOATS

Chapter 7

Inshore lifeboats

Inshore Lifeboats

▲ (left) One of the first inflatable inshore lifeboats on trials. The inflatable lifeboat could be launched quickly and easily, and was ideally suited for work inshore, helping people cut off by the tide, stranded on rocks or adrift in small inflatables.

▲ (right) One of the experimental rigid-inflatable ILBs, X-2, on trials at Gorleston in the 1970s. (By courtesy of the RNLI)

▶ RFD PB16 inflatable Alan Thurlow Ashford (D-301) served at Bangor in the 1980s; D-301 was later used as a boarding boat. (By courtesy of RNLI)

▼ D class inshore lifeboat D-186 at Aberystwyth, where she served from 1970 to 1983. The original premise of the ILB has remained the same for more than half a century, and ILBs are the workhorses of the fleet. (By courtesy of the RNLI)

While significant advances were made in offshore lifeboat provision during the 1960s, a new type of lifeboat joined the RNLI's fleet at the same time and, arguably, had an even greater impact than the new 'fast' designs. The inshore rescue boat, later designated the inshore lifeboat (ILB), was introduced to operational service in 1963 and has become an integral part of the lifeboat fleet, as ever more sophisticated ILBs have been developed culminating in the Atlantic 85 and IB1 craft in use today.

The idea for using inflatables for rescue work was first suggested in 1959 by RNLI naval architect Richard Oakley, designer of two lifeboat types named after him, who proposed that an inflatable, made in England by RFD, should be assessed as RFD claimed that it could be used as an acceptable rescue craft. Deputy Chief Inspector Captain Tony Wicksteed tested the boat, and later recalled that he 'soon found that the inflatable unbelievably good and safe, as long as nothing went wrong with the engine'. RNLI HQ staff at the time believed that outboard engines were not reliable enough to be used as the only means of propulsion for a lifeboat, and were initially hesitant about their use.

However, while the early inflatables were rudimentary, with engines of questionable reliability, both boats and power units were soon improved, with more equipment being added, including VHF radio, flexible fuel tanks, flares and anchors, and the engines being developed to become immersion proof. The ILBs, with a speed of twenty knots, were considerably faster than any lifeboat in service during the 1960s, and the benefits this offered in sea rescue were soon evident. Although the design has been improved considerably during the course of the six decades since ILBs first went into service, the basic tenet has remained the same and ILBs are easy to launch, fast, manoeuvrable and ideal for inshore work, and since 1970 have been responsible for undertaking thirty per cent of all lifeboat launches.

To supplement the 16ft inflatable inshore lifeboat, larger and more capable ILBs were also developed, including rigid-hulled craft 18ft in length and twin-engined inflatables, most notably the Atlantic 21 rigid-inflatable. The Atlantic has become one of the most successful designs of lifeboat ever and, since its development at Atlantic College in the late 1960s, has been involved in some outstanding rescues. The idea behind its development was an improvement on the basic inflatable ILB. A boat with greater speed, crew comfort and general capabilities was needed and fitting sponsons to a rigid hull provided an excellent rescue boat.

A larger and faster version, the Atlantic 75, was introduced in the 1990s, and in 2005 the even larger Atlantic 85 entered the RNLI's fleet. Many fine rescues have been undertaken in Atlantic ILBs, none more so than that on 24 August 2004 involving the Porthcawl Atlantic 75 Giles (B-726) to the fishing vessel Gower Pride which, with the skipper and an injured fisherman on board, had suffered engine failure in force eight

Inshore Lifeboats

winds and rough seas. In the atrocious sea conditions, the Atlantic was brought close enough for a towline to be connected to pull the casualty away from the bank. But the tow broke and so a second rope was rigged. At one point, Gower Pride was hit by a large breaking wave on the starboard side and thrown against the lifeboat. The Atlantic was manoeuvred away to avoid being damaged and began the slow tow in the heavy seas. By this time, Mumbles lifeboat Ethel Anne Measures (ON.1096) was on scene and the tow was transferred to the larger lifeboat. The two lifeboats then completed the passage back to station to land the survivors. For her part in this fine rescue, the Porthcawl helm Aileen Jones was awarded the Bronze medal, the first woman in over a century to be awarded a bravery medal.

In addition to the development of new all-weather types, at the start of the twenty-first century the RNLI examined new areas of life-saving and introduced specialised rescue craft in areas that had never hitherto been covered. For places inaccessible by boat and rescue those in difficulty on sand and mud banks, inshore rescue hovercraft were introduced. On several inland waterways the RNLI placed rescue craft, including at four stations in Ireland and four stations to cover the tidal reaches of the Thames using commercially developed jet-powered craft. The RNLI also developed flood rescue teams to assist with flooding incidents, and acquired Arancia inshore rescue boats for use by lifeguards on beaches.

So, as the RNLI approaches its 200th anniversary in 2024, having taken the first tentative steps to introduce motor power to the lifeboat fleet in the early 1900s, the charity continues to develop new ways of saving lives at sea, while at the same time improving lifeboat design and equipment to ensure that its volunteer lifeboat crews have the best and safest tool with which to carry out rescue work over the course of the next 200 years.

◀ The experimental Atlantic type inshore lifeboat B-6 was used for trials at Lymington and Helensburgh during the early 1970s, and was one of several experimental boats assessed during this period. (By courtesy of the RNLI)

▼ The twenty-first century incarnation of the B class rigid-inflatable inshore lifeboat is the Atlantic 85, powered by twin 115hp engines, with a speed of over thirty knots and crewed by four volunteers. Annette Mary Liddington (B-838) was stationed at Beaumaris in 2010 to cover the treacherous Menai Strait. (Nicholas Leach)

◀ Littlehampton's two inshore lifeboats blast their way out of the harbour. Many stations operate the combination of Atlantic and D class inflatable inshore lifeboats, which is ideal for most rescues that are carried out. (Nicholas Leach)

▼ The Arancia inshore rescue boat A-56 in the surf at Perranporth beach, operated by RNLI lifeguards. The Arancia was developed specially for surf conditions and is used by lifeguards throughout the UK and Ireland. (Nathan Williams/RNLI)

MOTOR LIFEBOATS

A class rigid-hulled inshore lifeboats

KEY DATA
- Introduced 1966
- Last built 1984

SPECIFICATIONS
- Hatch 20ft 6in x 7ft 3in
- Dell Quay Dory 17ft 1in x 7ft
- McLachlan 20ft 6in/18ft 6in x 8in
- Boston Whaler 20ft x 7ft 2in

▲ Two photos of the prototype Hatch boat 18-01 on trials in the 1960s. The boat was modified to have two configurations, one with an aft steering position and the other with the helm located forward. She was subsequently renumbered A-1 and was based at Plymouth for much of her relatively short operational career. (RNLI)

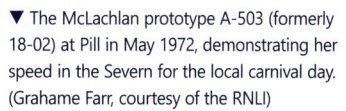

▼ The McLachlan prototype A-503 (formerly 18-02) at Pill in May 1972, demonstrating her speed in the Severn for the local carnival day. (Grahame Farr, courtesy of the RNLI)

During the 1960s, the RNLI assessed various ways of improving the effectiveness of the inflatable inshore lifeboat (ILB), introduced during the early years of the decade and well established by the end of the decade. An inshore boat with greater capabilities, including night operations, was deemed necessary, and to this end a number of designs for rigid-hulled ILBs were looked at, starting with the experimental Hatch boat designed by George Hatch, AMRINA, an RNLI senior draughtsman. The first Hatch boat was built in wood by William Osborne Ltd at Littlehampton and was displayed at the International Boat Show at Earls Court in January 1967. The new craft was intended to serve a dual purpose, operating as both a boarding boat, to take lifeboat crews from the shore to lifeboats at moorings, and as a rescue boat. Experience had shown that boarding boats were quite often needed for rescues when speed was essential, and the Hatch boat, faster than any other lifeboat then in service, fulfilled this need.

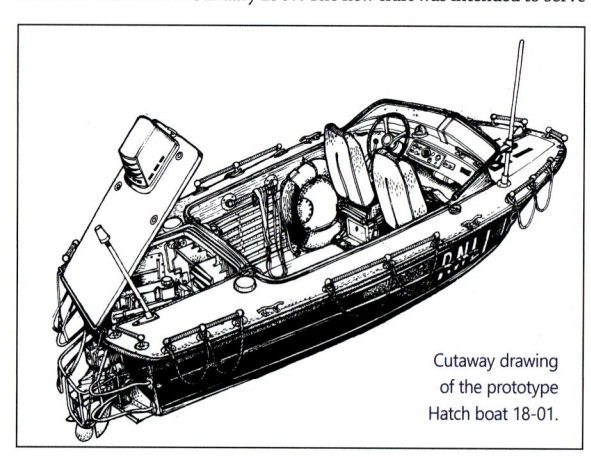

The hull was similar in form to that used by offshore power boats, with a moderately high freeboard and a flared bow, and in calm conditions speeds of up to twenty-six knots were achieved. The boat, to be operated by two crew, measured 20ft 6in overall, with a beam of 6ft 11in and a depth of 3ft 3in. It had wide flush decks fore and aft, handrails and lifelines at the deck edge and a propeller guard, and the hull was divided by bulkheads to give four watertight compartments with a large open cockpit for crew and survivors enabling at least eight people to be taken on board. Foamed polystyrene blocks were built into the wooden hull throughout for buoyancy, and an inboard engine with outboard drive was chosen to utilise the advantages of outboard drives without the vulnerability of an outboard engine. The prototype was fitted with a Volvo Penta AQ110/100 petrol unit rated at 110bhp.

Only two Hatch boats were completed as, during 1968, while the boat was being trialled, the RNLI commissioned another fast rigid-hulled boat for inshore rescue, designed by and named after J.A. McLachlan, MRINA, and which was deemed to be superior. The McLachlan design incorporated several notable features, including a ragged chine hull and seawater ballast stability tanks. The ragged chines were a series of steps which effectively reduced the hull surface in contact with the water and

Cutaway drawing of the prototype Hatch boat 18-01.

A class rigid-hulled inshore lifeboats

thus minimised the pounding found with normal hard-chine boats. Nine chines extended the full length of the hull, each inclined at an angle to the water to cushion the underside and deflect spray. The hull was divided into watertight compartments filled with polyurethane foam, and three water stability ballast tanks were fitted, being positioned forward, centre and aft.

The steering and engine controls were located amidships in a semi-enclosed streamlined bridge structure, which housed the wheel, compass, engine throttles and radio equipment. Draining was achieved through the use of standard RNLI-pattern side scuppers. The high foredeck provided reasonable protection for at least eight survivors, while the crew of two were sheltered by the midships structure with its own breakwater and wind deflector. Twin 60hp inboard petrol engines with outboard drives were mounted in watertight engine compartments in the stern and gave a maximum speed of twenty-two knots. In later boats, stern drive diesel engines were installed in place of the petrol versions.

The first of the McLachlans, 18-02, was ordered in September 1969, and measured 20ft 6in long by 8ft, and was built of mahogany by W.A. Souter at Cowes. She was used for trials at a number of stations. In September 1969 the RNLI ordered further McLachlans with GRP hulls from William Osborne; these and all subsequent boats measured 18ft 6in, 16ft 4in at the waterline, and had a beam of 8ft 3in. They were fitted with twin 90bhp Evinrude inboard diesel engines coupled to outboard drives. The wooden prototype was used as the mould for the GRP-hulled boats.

As well as the McLachlan, the RNLI tested out a commercially designed rigid-hulled boat manufactured by Dell Quay and known as a Dory. The Dory was built of glass reinforced plastic (GRP), with the cavity between hull and deck filled under pressure by rigid polyurethane foam. The hull, strengthened to take the aluminium-built steering console, had two

▲ The first two McLachlans, 18-004 and 18-02 at Pill, a station on the Severn Estuary which was served by two McLachlans between 1971 and 1974. 18-004, later renumbered A-504, was stationed at nearby Weston-super-Mare for most of her career. (Grahame Farr, courtesy of the RNLI)

◀ Dell Quay Dory 17-002, later numbered A-501, on station at Lyme Regis, and named Bob Abbott. (By courtesy of the RNLI)

▼ The first Dell Quay Dory inshore lifeboat 17-01, pictured during trials, was later numbered A-500. The Dory design was found to be suitable for service at specific stations, but was not used on a widespread basis. (Builder's photo)

MOTOR LIFEBOATS

A class rigid-hulled inshore lifeboats

ON	Year Dimensions/type	Stations (launches/lives saved) Notes
A-1 (ex 18-01)	1966 Hatch	Displayed at International LB Conference, St Malo, France, 6.1967; Falmouth 1967-67, Shoreham 1967-67, Plymouth 7.1968-5.72
A-2 (ex 18-03)	1966 Hatch	Poole 1967-69, Torbay 7.1969-10.74
A-500 (ex 17-01)	1968 Dell Quay Dory	Eastney 8.1968-6.69, Ramsgate 7.1969-12.71 (23/16), Poole 2.1972-12.1973 (21/7)
A-501 (ex 17-002)	1969 Dell Quay Dory	Lyme Regis 6.1969-9.73 (51/49), Poole 7.1974-5.75 (26/7)
A-502 (ex 17-003)	1969 Dell Quay Dory	Poole 6.1969-2.1972 (28/19), Ramsgate 2.1972-5.75 (28/7), Poole 8.1975-1.85 (275/38)
A-503 (ex 18-02)	1967 McLachlan (20'6")	Eastney 7.1967-7.70 (7/6), Poole 1971 (8/0), Weston-super-Mare 1971 (5/0), Pill 7.1971-10.72 (25/6)
A-504 (ex 18-004)	1970 McLachlan	Weston-super-Mare 5.1970-12.1983 (171/60)
A-505 (ex 18-005)	1970 McLachlan	Eastney 7.1970-9.71, Oban 5.1972-5.1973 (12/6), Eastney 12.1974-10.75 (30/6), Humber (as Boarding Boat) 1977-87
A-506 (ex 18-006)	1971 McLachlan	Peel 5.1972-6.1976 (3/3), Poole 12.1976-8.79 (1/0), Plymouth 8.1979-8.80 (20/0)
A-507 (ex 18-007)	1971 McLachlan	Weston-super-Mare 12.1972-2.73 (3/0), Peel 5.1973-8.76 (15/8), Ramsgate 1977 (1/0), Plymouth 1977-10.83 (58/12)
A-508 (ex 18-008)	1971 McLachlan	Eastney 9.1971-12.1974 (41/26), Invergordon 7.1976-11.79 (1/0), Falmouth 4.1980-1.1988 (92/19), Sold 1988
A-509	1972 McLachlan	Plymouth 5.1972-10.76 (85/22), Brighton 5.1978-7.78 (2/0), Falmouth 1981-83 (5/10), Sold 1988
A-510	1973 McLachlan	Pill 6.1973-10.1974 (14/10), Ramsgate 6.1975-8.1984 (141/32), Falmouth 1985-86 (3/0), Humber (boarding boat) 6.1986-1.87
A-511	1973 McLachlan	Oban 6.1974-1982 (87/9), Falmouth 4.1984-9.1985 (15/20) Sold 9.1985
A-512	1974 McLachlan	Torbay 3.1975-6.1987 (176/55), Falmouth 1-5.1988 (0/0) Scrapped at Grimsby 5.1988
A-513	1984 Boston Whaler	Poole 1.1985-12.1994 (592/106), capsized on service 23.11.1986, removed from station for repair, returned 10.6.1988

Two of the boats were named: A-501 was named Bob Abbott (1969-73) in memory of Coxswain Robert W. Abbott, from Lyme Regis; A-513 was named Sam and Iris Coles, and was funded by the Mayor of Poole Charity Year local appeal.

▲▲ McLachlan class A-503 at Falmouth in 1973; she was different to the other McLachlan boats, being 20ft 6in in length. (By courtesy of the RNLI)

▲ The 18ft 6in McLachlan design as exemplified by 18-005, pictured on builder's trials. She was later renumbered A-505. (Builder's photo)

eighteen-gallon petrol tanks incorporated into the base with a locker above to store equipment. Two 36hp Penta outboard engines were fitted to give a top speed of twenty-five knots. The draft with engines in use was just eighteen inches, and only eight inches with the engines raised.

Although only a few McLachlans and Dell Quay Dorys were built, they gave good service during the 1970s and 1980s. At Poole, in Dorset, where the lifeboat covers the large natural harbour, the Dell Quay Dory, with its shallow draught, was particularly suitable. As a result, when a new ILB was needed for the station in the 1980s, the Poole crew requested another Dory. As Dell Quay were no longer in business, a standard American-built Boston Whaler Outrage was acquired and, numbered A-513, was fitted out as a lifeboat by the RNLI's Cowes Base to meet the challenges of Poole Harbour. The boat had an overall length of 20ft (6m), a maximum beam of 7ft 2in (2.2m) and a maximum draught (at rest) of just 2ft (0.6m). The console and roll bar were fitted in such a way as to allow the boat to pass under the harbour bridges, even at high water.

Although the Boston Whaler was a one-off, many standard components from the Atlantic 21 were used on the boat. A towing bollard was fitted aft and power was provided by twin 60hp Evinrude outboard engines, giving a maximum speed of thirty knots. The fuel capacity of fifty gallons gave an endurance at full speed of 5.8 hours, and the boat was operated by three crew. She served at Poole for almost a decade, saving over 100 lives.

A class rigid-hulled inshore lifeboats

▲ The 18ft 6in McLachlan A-510 following her arrival at Pill on 22 June 1973; she served the station for less than a year. (Grahame Farr)

◀ The 18ft 6in McLachlan A-512 at Torbay. She was initially fitted with a steering console but this was removed during her career.

▶ McLachlan A-504 on display at Chatham Historic Dockyard.

▲ The 18ft 6in McLachlan A-508 moored at Falmouth in July 1982. (Tony Denton)

▲ The unique 20ft Boston Whaler Outrage lifeboat Sam and Iris Coles (A-513) at Poole. (John Buckby)

MOTOR LIFEBOATS 237

B class rigid-inflatable inshore lifeboats

KEY DATA
- Atlantic 21: 1970-1993 (96 built)
- Atlantic 75: 1993-2003 (97 built)
- Atlantic 85: 2004- (120 built to 2019)

SPECIFICATIONS
- Atlantic 21: 22ft 9in x 7ft 6in, hull 19ft 4in
- Atlantic 75: 24ft x 8ft 8in (7.38m x 2.65m, depth 0.41m)
- Atlantic 85: 8.3m x 2.8m (8.44m x 2.85m, depth 0.53m)

FLEET LISTING
- Space does not permit complete listings of Atlantic inshore lifeboats

▶ B-504 at Littlehampton, where she served for two years, during which time she was named Blue Peter I. She was one of the first Atlantic 21s, and this photo shows the original configuration, without a roll bar at the stern and in-line seating for three crew, rather than the delta pattern, as became standard on Atlantics. (Jeff Morris)

▶ The prototype Atlantic 21 B-1 ('Bravo 1') became B-500 and was tried operationally at Hartlepool and Appledore. The 21ft 4in boat was powered by twin 40hp Mercury outboards. (Grahame Farr, by courtesy of the RNLI)

▶▶ B-511 at Largs in the early 1970s; she was one of the first Atlantics fitted with a roll bar at the stern, above the twin outboard engines.

▼ The experimental boat X1 on trials at Atlantic College in South Wales, summer 1968. (Grahame Farr, by courtesy of the RNLI)

The Atlantic rigid-inflatable is one of the most successful designs of lifeboat ever developed. The type has been modified, enlarged and improved over more than four decades to become an extremely efficient and effective rescue tool that is in widespread service, from the inland waters of the Thames to the west coast of Ireland, and everywhere in between. The Atlantic is the fastest lifeboat in the RNLI's feet, and it is estimated that at least seventy-five per cent of rescues can be undertaken by Atlantics. The twenty-first century incarnation, the Atlantic 85, is fitted with powerful twin engines, has seats for four crew, water ballast tanks, and carries a range of sophisticated electronic equipment.

The Atlantic was developed during the 1960s after the introduction of the 16ft inflatable inshore lifeboat had proved to be a great success. While effective for daylight operation in moderate conditions, the inflatable was found to have limitations and a more sophisticated, capable and larger inshore lifeboat type was needed which could operate in worse weather and at night. The RNLI experimented with various ILB designs during the 1960s, but eventually chose one developed by Rear Admiral Desmond John Hoare at Atlantic College, based at St Donat's Castle in South Wales.

Admiral Hoare, who died in 1988, developed the new design after being dissatisfied with the standard ILB supplied to Atlantic College by the RNLI.

B class rigid-inflatable inshore lifeboats

It was found to be poorly suited to the short, steep seas of the Bristol Channel, where strong currents and a considerable tidal rise and fall meant a faster and more manoeuvrable boat was needed. Under Hoare's guidance, a series of experimental boats were built, which incorporated a rigid floor and deep-vee hull. The sides and bow were enclosed within a continuous buoyancy tube divided into airtight compartments, while the transom, which supported the twin outboard engines, was open to allow any water shipped to escape. The rigid hull supported the weight of the boat and, without the inflatable sponsons in contact with the water, gave the boat good sea-keeping capabilities and a greater speed, with the boats achieving more than thirty knots. The sponsons gave the boat great stability while the upper surface of the rigid hull formed the floor of the boat.

The first experimental boat went to Gorleston for trials and another, with a longer and modified hull, was sent to Lyme Regis. The new design was further refined and developed, with modifications resulting in the construction of three more boats, numbered B-1, B-2 and B-3. These boats were adopted by the RNLI and subsequently classified as the Atlantic 21. The early boats had seating in line for three crew, and carried only rudimentary equipment. The rigid hulls were originally built of plywood and divided into watertight compartments, but, when full-scale production began, hulls were moulded from glass reinforced plastic (GRP) by Halmatic of Havant. The GRP hulls were then taken to Cowes, where the sponson was secured to the hull and the boat fitted out by RNLI staff.

The RNLI's designers added a self-righting capability as the boats were being developed for service. The engines were made inversion-proof so that they would restart in the event of a capsize, and an inflatable air-bag was mounted on a roll bar fitted above the engines at the stern. In the event of the boat being capsized, a crew member activated a gas bottle, which inflated the bag to bring the boat upright in a few seconds. Following experience gained in operational conditions, the seating arrangements were modified and the three seats were arranged in a delta-shape behind the steering console in the centre of the boat; the helmsman steered with one hand on the wheel while adjusting the throttles with the other.

The first boat of the new design went on station at Hartlepool in 1972, to cover Tees Bay, and the advantages of the Atlantic 21 soon became apparent. It offered greater speed, comfort and safety, and an increasing

▲ Atlantic 21s Waveney Forester (B-531), left, and American Ambassador (B-554), above, served at Great Yarmouth & Gorleston and Atlantic College respectively. (By courtesy of the RNLI)

▼ Helene (B-711) was one of the first Atlantic 75s to enter service; she was stationed at Bundoran from 1995 to 2009. (Nicholas Leach)

MOTOR LIFEBOATS

B class rigid-inflatable inshore lifeboats

▲ Atlantic 75 Peggy Keith Learmond (B-739) on exercise off Largs, which is one of the busiest lifeboat stations in Scotland. (Nicholas Leach)

▼ Atlantic 75 Vic and Billie Whiffen (B-776) being launched by davit at Southend-on-Sea; she was stationed there from 2001 to 2015, after which she was transferred to Blyth. A number of Atlantics are launched by davit. (Nicholas Leach)

▶ Relief Atlantic 75 London's Anniversary 175 (B-755) on duty at Blackpool in March 2011. (Nicholas Leach)

▶ The last Atlantic 75 to be built, Miss Sally Anne (Baggy) (B-796), served at Kinsale from December 2003 to August 2018. She was initially kept afloat, so her hull was covered with white anti-fouling paint, but was subsequently operated from a new lifeboat house, built in 2008-09, from which she was launched by davit. (Nicholas Leach)

number of stations operated the boats, which took over from the slower conventional lifeboats. As the pattern of casualties changed during the 1970s and 1980s, requiring faster lifeboats to respond to incidents, offshore lifeboats were replaced by Atlantics at many stations, including Newbiggin, Clacton, Youghal, Redcar, Kirkcudbright, Flamborough and Sheringham. During their first two decades of service, Atlantic 21s launched over 15,000 times, saving nearly 5,000 lives.

In the early 1990s the design was further improved at the RNLI's Inshore Lifeboat Centre (ILC) at Cowes with the development of a larger version. Designated the Atlantic 75, the boat was 38cm longer overall and 20cm broader than the Atlantic 21, and her name was derived from the length of nearly 7.5m. Twin 70hp Evinrude outboard motors, slightly more powerful than on the 21, gave a maximum speed of about thirty-two knots; twin 75hp Yamaha outboards were used later after Evinrude went bankrupt. The boats had a fuel capacity of 182 litres, which gave an endurance of two and a half hours. The hull design was improved to give a more comfortable ride than on the Atlantic 21 for the three-man crew, and up to twenty survivors could be taken on board.

The hulls were built from polyester glass-reinforced fibre, with marine plywood stiffening, and were constructed at Souters Shipyard in West Cowes. Fitting out took place at the ILC. The crew seating arrangements and self-righting roll bar remained much the same as on the 21, albeit slightly enlarged. In total, ninety-six Atlantic 21s and ninety-seven Atlantic 75s were built by the RNLI, although not all entered service in the UK, with a few going to foreign lifeboat societies, including several Atlantic 21s to the Royal South Holland Society for the Rescue of Shipwrecked (KZHMRS). A number of Atlantic 75s were also built for the Koninklijke Nederlandse Redding Maatschappij (KNRM), the unified Dutch lifeboat service, in 2003-04; the design was ideal for service off the Netherlands' North Sea coasts as well as on the country's various inland seas.

Production of the Atlantic 75 ended in 2003, by when the RNLI was developing its replacement, the Fast Inshore Boat 1, a larger and faster rigid-inflatable with space for more equipment. The RNLI developed and tested the new version of the Atlantic during 2004 and 2005, and towards the end of 2005 the first of the new type, which was designated

B class rigid-inflatable inshore lifeboats

Atlantic 85 Donald McLauchlan (B-808) and Atlantic 21 James Burgess (B-589) together at Walmer in December 2006, when the former took over duties from the latter. (Nicholas Leach)

▼ Baron van Lyndon is one of two Atlantic 75s operated from the KNRM's Ouddorp station in the Netherlands. The KNRM operates several Atlantic 75s, all built at the RNLI's ILC. (Nicholas Leach)

▶ Atlantic 85 Sgt Bob Martin (Civil Service No.50) (B-826) and D class inflatable Gladys Maud Burton (D-804) at Poole, where they operate from the purpose-built floating boathouse. (Nicholas Leach)

MOTOR LIFEBOATS

B class rigid-inflatable inshore lifeboats

▲ Capsize and righting training using Atlantic 85 Chelsea Flower Show (B-802) at the RNLI's Lifeboat College in Poole. The purpose-built capsize pool enables the volunteer crews to experience a capsize, and training in using the righting system, which involves inflating the airbag on the roll bar (right). (Nicholas Leach)

▶ Atlantic 85 Douglas, Euan and Kay Richards (B-904), pictured on exercise in Upper Lough Erne, was stationed at Carrybridge in November 2017, and is one of four Atlantics to serve the inland waterways of Ireland. (Nicholas Leach)

▶▶ St Catherine's Atlantic 85 Eric W. Wilson (B-841) on exercise off Jersey. (Nicholas Leach)

▼ Launch of Atlantic 85 Joy Morris MBE (B-831) at St Bees; many Atlantics are launched from drive-on drive carriages using purpose-built waterproofed tractors. (Nicholas Leach)

the Atlantic 85, was ready for service. The Atlantic 85 was 8.3m in length, making it almost a metre longer than the Atlantic 75 and considerably larger than the original Atlantic 21. Seating for four crew members was provided, and more electronic equipment was carried, including GPS, radar to aid operations in poor visibility, intercom for crew communications, night-vision equipment, VHF radio, VHF direction-finding equipment and an electronic chart. Powered by twin 115hp Yamaha four-stroke engines and built from foam-cored carbon composite, the 85 had a top speed of thirty-five knots and was fitted with radar for operations in poor visibility. At every stage of the design project, experienced Atlantic helmsmen were involved, while crew members from every Atlantic lifeboat station played a part in testing the new design, providing feedback to the design team.

The first Atlantic 85, Drayton Manor (B-801), entered service in the Relief Fleet in 2006 following two years of trials. The next two prototypes, Chelsea Flower Show (B-802) and William Hurst (B-803), were also allocated to the Relief Fleet, while the first boat to be placed on operational service at the coast was Lydia MacDonald (B-804), which went to Macduff in Scotland in June 2006. A build programme commenced, and by the end of 2006 five new Atlantic 85s were on station around the coast, having replaced Atlantic 21s at stations which never operated a 75. Since then, approximately eight new Atlantics have been built per year at the RNLI's ILC, and by the end of 2019 more than 120 Atlantic 85s were in service around the coast, making it the most numerous of any lifeboat type.

A mark of the success of the rigid-inflatable design, of which the Atlantic is the original, is its use by SAR organisations around the world. Many have bought them second hand from the RNLI, and Atlantics are used by rescue services in Iceland, Finland and Greece, as well as in the Netherlands, where rigid-inflatables of varying sizes are used extensively. The design has also been used in the commercial small boat world and a plethora of derivatives is available to the private or commercial buyer.

B class rigid-inflatable inshore lifeboats

C class twin-engined inflatable inshore lifeboats

KEY DATA
- Introduced 1972
- Last built 1990
- 24 built

SPECIFICATIONS (C-505 on)
- Length 17ft 6in (5.33m)
- Beam 7ft 1in (2.16m)
- Weight 1,300lbs

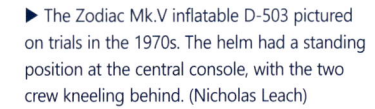

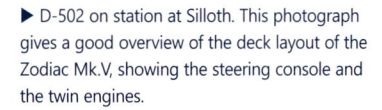

▶ The Zodiac Mk.V inflatable D-503 pictured on trials in the 1970s. The helm had a standing position at the central console, with the two crew kneeling behind. (Nicholas Leach)

▶ D-502 on station at Silloth. This photograph gives a good overview of the deck layout of the Zodiac Mk.V, showing the steering console and the twin engines.

▶▶ Zodiac Mk.V D-506 on station at Portaferry, where she served for six years before being replaced by an Atlantic 21.

During the 1970s the RNLI was looking for a design of inshore lifeboat that was more capable than the standard D class inflatable to enhance inshore cover. The inflatable was ideal for many rescue situations, but a larger inshore lifeboat was needed, so a series of inflatables were trialled and tested, together with various rigid-inflatable and rigid-hulled ILBs. Five inflatables, all based on the 19ft Zodiac Mk.V apart from one supplied by RFD, were acquired for initial evaluation purposes.

Their most notable feature of these boats was the standing console amidships, made from a tubular steel framework for the helmsman. The standing position raised the line of sight, but proved to be very exposed at high speeds; the other two crew would be kneeling behind, with one operating the radio. The boats had twin engines, which gave a speed of about twenty-five knots. Although the Zodiac Mk.V was deemed to be a good sea boat, its design was rather punishing on the crew. By the mid-1970s, the larger Atlantic 21 had been developed, showing great promise

MOTOR LIFEBOATS

C class twin-engined inflatable inshore lifeboats

than the Zodiac inflatable, and this type was deemed more suitable for the kind of rescues undertaken by the 19ft Zodiacs at Minehead and Silloth, the two stations where the boats were deployed.

During the late 1970s further developments with twin-engined inflatables took place after the RNLI had determined that a boat of a size between the Atlantic 21 and D class inflatable was needed. The result was the C class, which was based on the Zodiac Mk.IV inflatable. It measured 17ft 6in in length and was essentially a larger and more powerful version of the standard D class inflatable. The C class boats from C-505 (originally numbered D-505) onwards were of the Mk.IV type, were fitted with twin 40hp outboard engines, and had a top speed of approximately thirty knots. Manned by a crew of three or four, the boats could be righted manually after a capsize using a system specially designed by the RNLI. They also had a buoyancy system which allowed them to continue on service even if the bow was punctured. Similar equipment to the standard D class inflatable was carried, but the C class also had a searchlight.

The design was developed by the RNLI to meet the requirement for a craft operating all year round, day and night, at a time when many D class inflatables were only operational in the daytime and during the summer months. It was also intended for service at stations where, for operational

ON	Year	Type	Name / Donor	Stations (launches/saved) / Disposal
C-500	1972	Zodiac Mk.V	— / Minehead Rotary Club.	Trials 1972-1974, Minehead 1974-1979 (55/26)
C-501	1972	RFD 320	— / —	Trials 1972
C-502	1972	Zodiac Mk.V	**John Gilpin** / Gift from the John Gilpin Trust.	Trials 1973-74, Silloth 1975-9.77 (19/7), Boarding Boat 1977-87
C-503	1973	Zodiac Mk.V	— / —	Trials 1973-77, Silloth 9.1977-6.79 (8/3), Boarding Boat 1981-87
C-504	1973	Zodiac Mk.V	— / —	Relief 1973-86 (used as Boarding Boat at Cowes Depot)
C-505	1978	Zodiac Mk.IV	— / The Ruthven-Stuart family, in memory of Stella Ruthven-Stuart.	St Abbs 3.1979-4.86, Relief 4.1986-88, Red Bay 8.1986-5.87, Clifden 10.1988-2.89, sold locally 11.1990
C-506	1980	Zodiac Mk.IV	— / Legacy of Mrs M. K. Hawken.	Portaferry 5.1980-7.86 (89/29), Relief 7.1986-9.87, Arran (Lamlash) 9.1987-6.88 (6/1), Relief 6.1988-5.91 (9/0), Arranmore (boarding boat) 4.1994-4.97, scrapped 8.1988
C-507	1980	Zodiac Mk.IV	— / Central London Committee.	Mudeford 1981-5.88 (219/104), Relief 1989-2.90 (8/1)
C-508	1980	Zodiac Mk.IV	**Chris Pirson** / In memory of Christopher Pirson.	Relief 1981-12.91 (85/30), Ballyglass (boarding boat) 8.1993-10.96
C-509	1982	Zodiac Mk.IV	**Oats** / Rag Committee of University of Wales.	Aberystwyth 5.1983-6.93 (186/62), Relief 6.1993-95, Tighnabruaich 7.1995-1.96 (5/0), Cardigan 4.1996-4.98 (11/1), scrapped 4.1998
C-510	1982	Zodiac Mk.IV	— / Bournemouth Borough's Sea Angling Festival.	Criccieth 16.9.1983-8.1991 (102/23), Kinghorn 1992-95 (36/1), withdrawn 1995
C-511	1982	Zodiac Mk.IV	— / Clubs with Rugby Football Union.	Newquay 14.12.1983-6.94 (232/81), Relief 1995-1996 (6/0), Boarding Boat 1996-2008
C-512	1982	Zodiac Mk.IV	— / Gift of Miss Diana Phillips, in memory of her parents.	Cullercoats 12.6.1984-4.91 (87/43), Relief 4.1991-11.1995 (32/3)
C-513	1982	Zodiac Mk.IV	**Sebag of Jersey** / Gift of Frederick E. Cohen, in memory of Sebag Cohen.	St Catherine 14.4.1984-10.90 (79/24), Relief 8.1991-7.1995 (29/10), Tighnabruaich 1994-1995 (10/0)
C-514	1984	Zodiac Mk.IV	— / Ind Coope Alloa Brewery Co Ltd and Co-op in Scotland.	Kinghorn 16.6.1984-8.1993 (100/21), Relief 1993-6.95, Red Bay 1996-97, Clifden 10.1997-6.1998 (4/4)
C-515	1985	Zodiac Mk.IV	— / Bequest of Mrs Peggy Patria Clowes, in memory of her husband.	St Bees 9.1985-3.1995 (55/13)
C-516	1986	Zodiac Mk.IV	**Belsize Charitable Trust No.1** / The Belsize Charitable Trust, in memory of Eric David Jackson.	St Ives 2.10.1986-10.95 (182/57)
C-517	1984	Zodiac Mk.IV	— / Lewes & District Lifeboat Appeal.	Rye Harbour 1986-96 (194/48), Relief 1996-97, Boarding Boat 1997-2008
C-518	1984	Zodiac Mk.IV	— / Gift of Mrs Nany Lynda Hopkinson, Windermere.	Cardigan 29.3.1987-6.97 (172/45)
C-519	1984	Zodiac Mk.IV	**Thomas Corbett**	Red Bay 25.6.1987-7.95 (89/15), Relief 11.1995-1.1996 (0/0), Tighnabruaich 1.1996-9.97 (22/3)
C-520	1986	Zodiac Mk.IV	— / —	Relief 2.1988-96 (41/23), Boarding Boat 1996-2008
C-521	1988	Zodiac Mk.IV	**Prince of Arran** / Fred, Olsen Cruise Line, passengers of Black Prince.	Arran (Lamlash) 6.1988-1.98 (90/12), sold 27.1.1998
C-522	1988	Zodiac Mk.IV	— / Bequest of Peter and Steve Laban.	Clifden 7.1989-10.1997 (52/9), Rosslare Harbour (boarding boat) 10-12.1997, publicity 7.1988, sold
C-523	1990	Zodiac Mk.IV	**British Diver IV** / Special Appeal organised by British Sub-Aqua Club.	Criccieth 12.1991-7.93 (65/14), Tighnabruaich 4-9.1994 (11/3), Red Bay 28.7.1995-4.96 (9/0), Cardigan 6.1997-5.98 (28/4), sold 1998

MOTOR LIFEBOATS

C class twin-engined inflatable inshore lifeboats

▶ The first twin-engined inflatable, D-500, at Minehead in 1978; she was one of only three 19ft Zodiac Mk.V inflatables in RNLI service and was stationed at Minehead for five years. (Grahame Farr files, By courtesy of the RNLI)

reasons, the larger Atlantic 21 was not deemed suitable. However, after relatively short careers, the C class inflatables were replaced at most of the stations they served by an Atlantic 21 or the larger Atlantic 75 rigid-inflatable, and in the 1990s the type was phased out of service. A number were used as boarding boats at stations where all-weather lifeboats were kept at exposed moorings and a large twin-engined boat was required, but by the end of the twentieth century all had been replaced and sold out of service.

When they were introduced in the 1970s, the twin-engined inflatables were given the D class prefix to indicate they were fully inflatable, as opposed to rigid (A class) or rigid-inflatable (B class) ILBs, and were numbered D-500, D-501, etc, with the 500 suffix indicating the boats were twin-engined. The standard D class inflatables at the time were numbered D-1 to D-499. However, in May 1984, a review of numbering resulted in the boats being redesignated as the C class to distinguish from their smaller single-engined sisters.

▶ C-512 putting out on service from Newquay in August 1992. She was on relief duty at the Cornish station during 1992, launching ten times and saving one life during her stint. (Nicholas Leach)

▼ (left) D-509 puts out from Aberystwyth. The twin-engined inflatables were originally numbered with a 'D-' prefix, but were redesignated C class in the 1980s, so those ILBs built before 1984 (up to and including C-513) were originally numbered D-5xx, becoming C-5xx subsequently. (Jeff Morris)

▼ (right) C-518 on exercise off Cardigan in 1996. She was one of nineteen Zodiac Mk.IV twin-engined ILBs to see operational service during the 1980s and 1990s. (Nicholas Leach)

246 MOTOR LIFEBOATS

C class twin-engined inflatable inshore lifeboats

◀ C-505 served at Red Bay for less than a year; she is pictured in the surf off the Antrim coast.

▶ C-519 at Red Bay, where she served for more than seven years. Red Bay was served by four C class inflatables before an Atlantic 21 took over in 1996. (By courtesy of Red Bay RNLI)

◀ C-505 on her launching trailer outside the ILB house at Red Bay. She was powered by twin 40hp Mariner outboard engines. (Red Bay RNLI)

▼ C-522 outside the lifeboat house at Clifden on the road-going trailer; this was towed to a number of different launch sites around Connemara by the Land Rover, determined by the location of a casualty. (Nicholas Leach)

MOTOR LIFEBOATS

247

D class inflatable inshore lifeboats

KEY DATA
- Introduced 1963 as IRB, later ILB
- RFD PB16 (1963-1985: 228 built)
- Avon EA16 (1985-2002: 260 built)
- IB1 (251 built since 2001)

SPECIFICATIONS
- RFD PB16: 15ft 6in x 6ft 4in
- Zodiac Mk.II: 15ft 6in x 6ft 4in
- Avon EA16: 16ft 3in x 6ft 7in
- IB1: 4.95m x 2m

▶ The first inshore rescue boat, IRB No.1, outside her boathouse at Aberystwyth. (Jeff Morris)

▶▶ Inshore rescue boat IRB No.32, with her crew wearing little in the way of protective clothing and life-jackets used on offshore lifeboats.

▼ Diagram of the RNLI's early inshore rescue boat from the 1960s, which carried only basic equipment and compared to its twenty-first century successor was rather rudimentary.

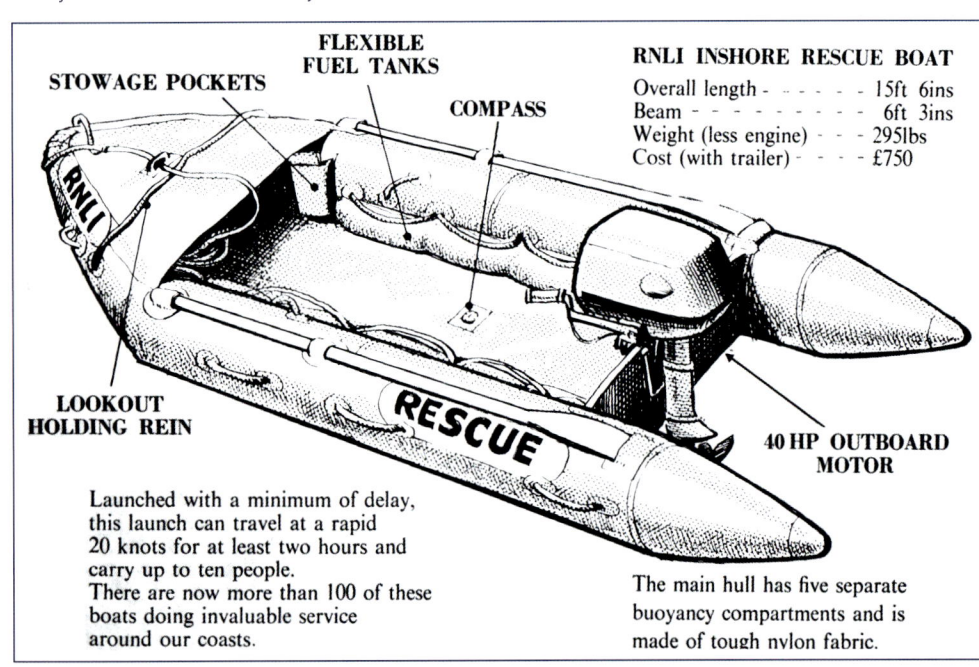

STOWAGE POCKETS — **FLEXIBLE FUEL TANKS** — **COMPASS** — **LOOKOUT HOLDING REIN** — **40 HP OUTBOARD MOTOR**

RNLI INSHORE RESCUE BOAT
Overall length - - - - - 15ft 6ins
Beam - - - - - - - - - 6ft 3ins
Weight (less engine) - - - 295lbs
Cost (with trailer) - - - - £750

Launched with a minimum of delay, this launch can travel at a rapid 20 knots for at least two hours and carry up to ten people.
There are now more than 100 of these boats doing invaluable service around our coasts.

The main hull has five separate buoyancy compartments and is made of tough nylon fabric.

The introduction of the inshore lifeboat (ILB) in the early 1960s was one of the most significant developments in the history of the lifeboat service. In 1960 no small inflatable lifeboats were in operation, but within forty years their numbers had increased to such an extent that they were the most numerous type in the RNLI fleet. The inshore lifeboat, which was initially designated inshore rescue boat (IRB), was introduced as a result of the changing demands being made on lifeboats. During the two decades after Second World War, more and more people used the sea for leisure purposes as incomes and leisure time increased. As a result the leisure industry expanded and the number of inshore incidents to which lifeboats were called increased, with swimmers, dinghies and small motor boats getting into difficulty, often in relatively calm weather. Conventional lifeboats were not well suited to such work, being too slow and required a relatively large number of crew, and so a simple, fast inflatable rescue craft, suited to working inshore, was seen as the best way to undertake these rescue.

The RNLI acquired an inflatable boat in 1962 for trials, and a delegation visited France, where similar boats were in operation, to obtain advice and see the boats in action. The 16ft inflatable craft, made from nylon coated with neoprene/hypalon, were crewed by two or three, powered by a 40hp outboard engine, and could be launched quickly and easily. The advantages of these boats were their speed, which at twenty knots was considerably faster than any lifeboat in service during the 1960s; their ability to go alongside other craft or persons in the water without causing or suffering damage; the short time taken to launch; and their low running costs.

Following the initial testing and trials, the first inshore rescue boats were introduced in the summer of 1963, when eight were sent to the following stations for the season: Aberystwyth, Gorleston, Redcar, Wells, Mudeford, Southwold, West Mersea and Whitstable. Such was their success that in each of the following years an increasing number of stations began to operate the boats. In the first year of operation, the eight IRBs launched thirty-nine times and saved ten lives. The following year, nineteen more IRBs entered service and by 1966 the number on station had risen to seventy-two, of which thirty-two remained in service throughout the year, while the rest operated during the summer months only. Many were co-located at stations which had conventional offshore lifeboats, but many new stations were also established to operate just an ILB.

As the RNLI's inshore fleet expanded, so did the boats became more sophisticated. Modifications were made and the rudimentary inflatable was developed into a reliable and effective rescue craft: an inner tube was fitted to prevent air leaking out of the sponsons; floorboards able to take the strain of high speeds were developed; and foam rubber mattresses

D class inflatable inshore lifeboats

were installed to improve the safety and comfort of the crew. However, despite these improvements, crews still took a pounding, especially in surf conditions, and so an age limit of forty-five was imposed on the volunteer crews. As well as the' design being improved, extra equipment was added as technology advanced. This equipment included VHF radio, first aid kit, flares, compass, a spare propeller and an anchor.

The first boats were supplied to the RNLI by RFD, a company well known for providing life-rafts on board ships. The RFD PB16 type was 15ft 6in in length, had a beam of 6ft 3in, and weighed 550lbs. A handful of 15ft 6in Zodiac Mk.III boats were also used during the 1980s and 1990s, but the RFD PB16 was in more widespread use, having a distinctive appearance, with black tubes and orange patches. Until 1985 the lifeboats were purchased as bare hulls from French (Zodiac) or UK (RFD) manufacturers, being fitted out at the RNLI's Cowes Base on the Isle of Wight. The IRBs were initially just numbered consecutively, but when the 'D class' designation was introduced, along with the term inshore lifeboats (ILBs), in the early 1970s the D-### numbering was also instituted.

While the RFD boats proved to be fine craft, by the early 1980s, with further advances in design and technology, the RNLI developed a new and slightly larger ILB in conjunction with Avon Inflatables. The new type, designated the EA16 type (Evans/Avon) after the long-serving member of the Cowes Base staff Trevor Evans who led the in-house design project, was 16ft 3in in length with a 6ft 7in beam, and weighed 745lbs. It had better seakeeping, stability, manoeuvrability and seakindliness than the commercial inflatables that had been used hitherto, its design set new standards and the EA16 was a major advance in terms of standardisation.

The next development of the ILB came at the start of the twenty-first century when, between 2000 and 2003, the Inshore Boat 1 (IB1) project saw the RNLI's naval architects re-examine the inflatable design to produce a replacement for existing boats. As a result, the ILB was completely re-engineered and a faster craft was developed, incorporating the latest advances in material and equipment technology. It was more consistent in its performance, better equipped and easier to maintain. The IB1 had a 50hp engine with electric startup, giving a speed of twenty-five knots; floor sections and transom fabricated from composite materials, which were as strong and stiff as plywood, the material used hitherto for ILBs, but were lighter and easier to maintain; and the hull was made from hypalon-coated polyester, which gave a more consistent boat shape and performance. A new stowage pod was fitted to allow the anchor to be stowed ready-rigged for deployment, and also provided housing for other equipment. The new design was trialled during 2002 and 2003 and the production version was introduced into service in August 2003. Since then over 200 IB1 inshore lifeboats have been built, and there are no plans to significantly change the design.

▲ RFD PB16 type inflatable Blue Peter III (D-216) at North Berwick. The station was one of four (later five) whose ILB was funded by various appeals made by the Blue Peter TV programme. (By courtesy of the RNLI)

◄◄ Inshore rescue boat No.109 being brought ashore after a service call at Llandudno in the 1970s. (By courtesy of the RNLI)

◄ IRB No.152 being launched at Bournemouth, a summer-only station which was established in 1965 and closed after the 1972 season. (Jeff Morris)

▼ The RFD PB16 inflatable D-177 being launched at Minehead, where inshore lifeboats took over from the slow 35ft 6in Liverpool lifeboat B.H.M.H. Funded by Minehead Rotary Club, D-177 served the station for thirteen years. (Jeff Morris)

MOTOR LIFEBOATS

D class inflatable inshore lifeboats

▲ The Avon EA16 inflatable Michel Philippe Wolvers (D-326) at Larne in Northern Ireland in 1995. This was the first ILB to serve at the station, which was opened in 1994. (Nicholas Leach)

▼ The Avon EA16 Kensington Rescuer (D-362) off Sheerness, where she served for eight years. The crew are wearing standard ILB kit, which then consisted of Typhoon drysuit and Beaufort lifejacket.

▼ The Avon EA16 inflatable Kip and Kath (D-472) on exercise at Burry Port. The EA16 was the first standard design of D class inflatable introduced after a series of commercial types had been used.

▲▲ The Avon EA16 inflatable Rose Elizabeth Lawrence (D-321) at Amble.

▲ Relief D class inflatable D-418, which was built in 1991, at North Berwick.

250 MOTOR LIFEBOATS

D class inflatable inshore lifeboats

▲ The Avon EA16 inflatable Walter Grove (D-531) breaking through the surf off Port Eynon beach. She served at Horton & Port Eynon for ten years from 1998.

▶ Rosemary Palmer (D-569), which served at Amble, was one of the last Avon EA16 inflatables to be built; the last, D-576, was stationed at Teddington on the Thames.

▼ (left) Joan and Ted Wiseman 50 (D-605) on exercise off Eastbourne. She was one of the first of the new IB1 inflatable inshore lifeboats to be placed on operational service.

▼ (right) The IB1 inflatable Henry Philip (D-617) at Bude. The D class inflatable is well suited to surf conditions, such as those found off North Cornwall's beaches.

MOTOR LIFEBOATS

D class inflatable inshore lifeboats

▲ Basil Eric Brooks (D-732) is one of two D class inflatables on station at Blackpool, and these are complemented by an Atlantic 85. (Nicholas Leach)

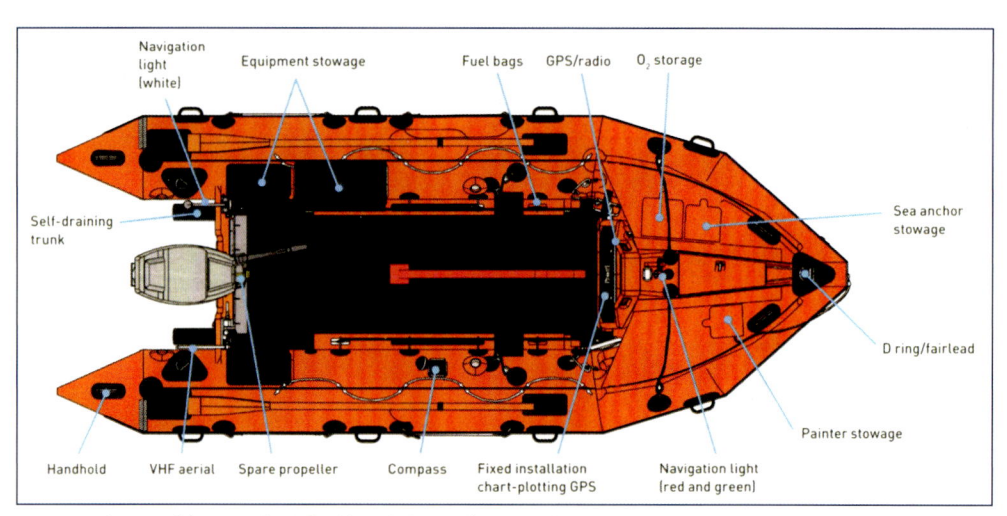

▲ An RNLI diagram of the IB1 D class inflatable, with the significant parts labelled; the IB1 is powered by a 50hp Mariner outboard, has a displacement of 300kg, and a fuel capacity of sixty-eight litres, which gives an endurance of three hours at maximum speed.

▲ Copeland Bell (D-707) at Port Isaac, one of relatively few stations which operate only a D class inflatable. (Nicholas Leach)

▶ Craig Steadman (D-814) in the surf at Barmouth after her naming on 1 October 2017. (Nicholas Leach)

▼ Windsor Spirit (D-721) being launched at Bridlington using the Tooltrak tracked vehicle TT04; launching ILBs across beaches, with vehicles similar to this, is a widespread practice at the RNLI's station. (Nicholas Leach)

252 MOTOR LIFEBOATS

D class inflatable inshore lifeboats

Stanley Whiteley Chadwick (D-790) breaking through the surf off the beach at Mablethorpe, the station she has served since December 2015. Mablethorpe is one of many stations where the D class inflatable is co-located with an Atlantic B class rigid-inflatable. (Nicholas Leach)

E class Fast response lifeboats

KEY DATA
- Introduced Mk.1 2002, Mk.2 2011
- 9 built in total (6 Mk.1, 3 Mk.2)

SPECIFICATIONS (Mk.1)
- Length 9m, beam 2.94m, depth 0.67m
- Weight 3.86 tonnes fully fuelled
- Crew 3
- Engines 2 x 240hp Steyr 246 marine diesels, 4,100rpm, Hamilton waterjets
- Speed 33 knots
- Fuel capacity 520 litres
- Range 4 hours at maximum speed

SPECIFICATIONS (Mk.2)
- Length 10.5m, beam 2.9m without collar; 3.5m with collar, depth 0.7m
- E-07: 5.9 tonnes; E-08 and E-09: 5.4 tonnes
- Crew 4
- Engines 2 x 435hp Volvo D6 435 marine diesels, 3,300rpm, Hamilton waterjets
- Speed 40 knots
- Fuel capacity 500 litres
- Range 3 hours at maximum speed

▶ Three of the first four E class lifeboats, E-001, E-002 and E-004, passing the Tower of London on 2 January 2002, the day the RNLI's lifeboat service on the Thames commenced. (Nicholas Leach)

▼ E-002, as built, on the Thames for the first time, January 2002. She was subsequently named Olive Laura Deare and was further adapted for Thames service by the RNLI. (Nicholas Leach)

In January 2001 the RNLI announced that it would be operating lifeboats on the tidal stretches of the River Thames in response to a request from the Maritime and Coastguard Agency (MCA) to provide an SAR service. The criteria required a lifeboat to operate at any point on the Thames between Canvey Island and Teddington Lock. The RNLI determined that, in order to achieve the criteria, a fast, highly manoeuvrable vessel was required. As no lifeboat in the fleet was capable of achieving the required speed, and timescales were tight, a suitable vessel was sourced directly from commercial manufacturers, and six fast rescue craft, with hulls built from lightweight aluminium alloy, were purchased. The planing hull was fitted with a collar fabricated from a polyurethane-coated closed cell foam. The vessels were designated E class lifeboats.

The E class, formally introduced in January 2002 for exclusive use at the three Thames lifeboat stations of Gravesend, Tower Pier and Chiswick, were based on a 9m fast response craft design from Tiger Marine Ltd, a company based at Trearddur Bay in Anglesey. Six boats were acquired to ensure a back-ups were available for the three stations. Built at FBM Babcock Naval Shipyard, Rosyth, the Tiger Marine boats, with a speed of more than thirty-three knots, enabled incidents to be reached within fifteen minutes, which was the MCA requirement for the service.

The Tiger Marine-designed boats were powered by twin Steyr/Bukh turbo diesel engines, each delivering 230hp at 4,000 to 4,400rpm via drive-shafts, connected to Hamilton 241 water jet units. The craft had an open transom and a large working deck for easy survivor recovery. Aerials, warning sirens, navigation lights and a righting bag were located on an A-frame mounted aft. The electronics fitted included a VHF radio, Metropolitan Police radio, echo sounder, radar and chart plotter, GPS satellite navigation, and mobile phones. Self-righting in the event of a capsize with an air-bag fitted on the A-frame, the boats carried a full inventory of lifesaving and safety equipment, including searchlights and bilge pumps. They were designed to operate at full speed with an endurance of four hours, crewed by three, and with the capacity to take up to twenty survivors.

The individual boats were not permanently assigned to any station, but were operated in a pool between the three stations, and cycled through to build up operational hours. Maintenance was initially undertaken partly by RNLI staff and partly by the Metropolitan Police boatyard at Wapping, about ten miles from Chiswick, under contract. This yard was also used as the storage depot for the boats when they were not in use. Tower, Chiswick and Gravesend have operated with a mix of full-time and volunteer crew living at the stations during shifts to ensure twenty-four-hour operations.

MOTOR LIFEBOATS

E class Fast response lifeboats

◀ E class lifeboats E-001, E-002 and E-004 at Tower Bridge on 2 January 2002. (Nicholas Leach)

▼ E class Mk.1 lifeboats Public Servant (Civil Service No.44) (E-001) and Olive Laura Deare (E-002), off Gravesend in 2006, after being modified by the RNLI. (Nicholas Leach)

During the boats' initial year in service, problems with the design were soon evident, so the RNLI undertook a rectification and modification programme to improve the boats' operational effectiveness and make them more reliable. The RNLI's Technical Office undertook a detailed survey to determine what improvements were needed and also gathered a 'wish list' from the crews. The programme highlighted the unreliability of the electrics and the need for a better fuel system and tanks. Improvements were also required to the bilge system, the deck hatches and the seating console configuration. The roll-cage and radar platform needed upgrading to provide navigation and emergency lights and an improved radar installation, and better deck access was also required. The design review took place at the Inshore Lifeboat Centre in Cowes and involved technical and engineering staff from the RNLI's head office, the ILC and the coast, together with representatives from the stations on the Thames.

The work to modify the boats was undertaken during 2003 and 2004. Along with better engine instrumentation, an intercom/radio set-up was fitted, which allowed communications between crew and external agencies, together with radar/plotter, two VHF radios, a Metropolitan Police radio, navigation/blue flashing/deck flood lights and an electric bilge pump. E-002, the first boat to be modified, was redelivered to the Thames in July 2003. After a number of areas were highlighted for further improvements by the crews operating the boats, these were introduced on E-001 and subsequent boats as they were refitted. E-001 was launched in November 2003 having been modified and delivered to the Thames a month later, with the other boats following during 2004. The modifications enabled improved maintenance regimes, which led to greater reliability. With the boats operating on a full-time basis, they were heavily used, attending incidents most days.

When originally put into service, the boats were estimated to have a life of seven years. So in 2007 a project team was set up to investigate the options for a replacement E class boat. Gravesend had been supplied with an Atlantic 85 in November 2008, due to the coastal nature of its location,

ON	Name Donor	Year Builder	Stations Disposal
E-001	**Public Servant (Civil Service No.44)** CISPOTEL Lifeboat Fund.	2001 Tiger Marine	Thames (Tower/Chiswick/Gravesend 1.2002-09; Tower/Chiswick 2009-12)
E-002	**Olivia Laura Deare** Bequest of Olivia Deare, Gravesend.	2001 Tiger Marine	Thames (Tower/Chiswick/Gravesend 1.2002-09; Tower/Chiswick 2009-12)
E-003	**Chelsea Pensioner** Bequest of Dr Patricia Mary Martyn Baguley, Cockermouth.	2001 Tiger Marine	Thames (Tower/Chiswick/Gravesend 1.2002-09; Tower/Chiswick 2009-15)
E-004	**Ray and Audrey Lusty** Legacy of Raymond and Audrey Lusty, Farnham.	2001 Tiger Marine	Thames (Tower/Chiswick/Gravesend 1.2002-09; Tower/Chiswick 2009-12)
E-005	**The Legacy** Bequest of Lieut Philip F. S. King.	2001 Tiger Marine	Thames (Tower/Chiswick/Gravesend 1.2002-09; Tower/Chiswick 2009-18)
E-006	**Joan and Ken Bellamy** Bequest of Joan and Ken Bellamy.	2001 Tiger Marine	Thames (Tower/Chiswick/Gravesend 1.2002-09; Tower/Chiswick 2009-)
E-07	**Hurley Burly** Gift of Mrs Kay Hurley MBE.	2011 MST, Liverpool	Thames (Tower/Chiswick) 24.6.2012-
E-08	**Dougie and Donna B** Bequest of Mrs Rosemary Battams.	2012 MST, Liverpool	Thames (Tower/Chiswick) 23.5.2012-
E-09	**Brawn Challenge** The Brawn Lifeboat Challenge.	2012 MST, Liverpool	Thames (Tower/Chiswick) 7.2012-

MOTOR LIFEBOATS

E class Fast response lifeboats

▲ The first E class Mk.2 lifeboat Hurley Burly (E-07) on the Thames after her naming ceremony in October 2011. She was funded by Mrs Kay Hurley MBE. (Nicholas Leach)

▼ E class Mk.2 lifeboats Brawn Challenge (E-09) and Dougie and Donna B (E-08) on the Thames off Chiswick. (Nicholas Leach)

and so the E class boats were then operated only from Tower and Chiswick stations. As the original E class lifeboats had not fully met the operational requirements, mainly in terms of speed, this needed addressing in a new design; there were also through-life human factors and legislative considerations that had to be considered in the replacement boats.

Having carried out an extensive vendor assessment, a suitable concept design was identified, which was developed by the contractor and the E class Project Team to ensure the specific RNLI requirements are met.

The replacement boat was required to have a top speed of forty knots; be operable by two crew, but with seating capacity for four; have a minimum of three hours endurance at full speed; be capable of a one-tonne bollard pull; be capable of carrying twenty survivors including one stretcher-borne; give easy access for survivor recovery and crew to be able to reboard unassisted from the water.

The first concept design for the Mk.2 boats was based upon a 10m hull with twin inboard diesels, twin waterjets and a solid collar. As with the majority of the RNLI's inshore lifeboat fleet, the hull was constructed from a composite that had significant benefits in terms of good durability and reduced maintenance costs when compared to an aluminium hull. In addition, there was sufficient margin on the top speed to allow for some added weight through the life of the boat (approximately fifteen years) such that if new equipment needs to be carried, the operational requirements can still be met. The console arrangement for the Mk.2 boats put the crew at the centre of the design with regard to ergonomics and comfort. However, the significant improvements came at a price and consequently the replacement lifeboats were significantly more expensive than the original boats due to the increased capability, reliability and technology specified for the replacement boats.

The Mk.2 hull and deck structure were constructed by MST (Marine Specialised Technology), a commercial firm based in Liverpool, with the collar being shaped into a teardrop form. Aside from improving the aesthetics of the craft, the rounded shape is intended to aid man overboard recovery, while the sloping underside and absence of sharp corners was aimed at preventing casualties from becoming snagged during recovery operations. The only exception to this is in the bow area, whereby the collar has been flattened off to enable 'bow pushing' to be carried out without damaging the collar. The internal design of the collar was also engineered to minimise weight, while retaining the required level of buoyancy and robustness. The collar was attached following further user input to ensure the fittings are in the optimum location.

The fit-out involved engine and water jet installations, the fuel tanks being put in place and various items such as the forward deck hatches being installed. The command console, engine box and engine hatches were built from an advanced composite sandwich construction utilising closed cell foam, glass, carbon laminate and epoxy resin. Input from the console user group resulted in a redesign of the crew seats. Power came from two 435hp Volvo D6 435 marine diesel engines, each of 3,300rpm, with propulsion from Hamilton waterjets giving a speed of forty knots.

Three Mk.2 boats were built: the first entered service in 2011, being mainly based at Tower, and was followed by two others in 2012, which were operated from Chiswick. Following the introduction of the Mk.2 boats, four of the six Mk.I boats were retired from service, and E-005 and E-006 were rebuilt at Diverse Marine, Cowes, into one boat, The Legacy (E-005), which returned to service on 26 October 2018.

E class Fast response lifeboats

▲ The E class Mk.2 lifeboat Brawn Challenge (E-09) on patrol off Chiswick. The deck layout and teardrop-shaped collar are clearly shown in this photograph. (Nicholas Leach)

◀◀ Hurley Burly (E-07) moored at Tower lifeboat station, where she is based, being kept afloat alongside Lifeboat Pier. Tower is the RNLI's busiest lifeboat station. (Nicholas Leach)

◀ One of the original E class Mk.1 lifeboats, Olive Laura Deare (E-002), has been preserved and was placed on display as part of the RNLI Historic Lifeboat Collection at Chatham Historic Dockyard in 2013. (Nicholas Leach)

MOTOR LIFEBOATS

H class Inshore rescue lifeboats

KEY DATA
▶ Introduced 2002
▶ 7 built in total

SPECIFICATIONS
▶ Length 7.75m
▶ Crew 3/4, seats for 6-8
▶ Weight 2,500kg (fuly loaded)
▶ Endurance 3 hours
▶ Maximum speed 30 knots

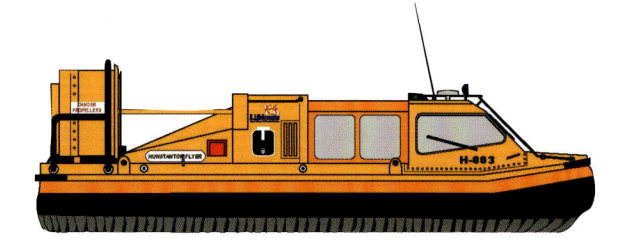

▶ Profile drawing of the RNLI's inshore rescue hovercraft, which were introduced in 2002.

▶▶ The first hovercraft, Molly Raynor (H-001), at the RNLI's Depot in Poole in May 2004, undertaking crew training and familiarisation. (Nicholas Leach)

The inshore rescue hovercraft was introduced to meet the demand for a rescue craft capable of crossing terrain such as tidal marshes and mudflats that dry out at low tide and which can be inaccessible by boat. The RNLI began assessing whether hovercraft could be used as effective rescue tools in 2001. During the trials, it was specified that the hovercraft must operate safely in different terrains and volunteer crews had to be able to master 'flying' it.

The commercially available Griffon 470TD craft, built by Griffon Hovercraft of Southampton, was trialled. The hull was constructed of marine grade aluminium, while the topsides and fan ducts were moulded fibre reinforced composites. The 470TD had two propeller-fans over the stern, driven by twin 85hp 1.9-litre Volkswagen intercooled and turbo-charged diesel engines. The craft, capable of speeds in excess of thirty knots, had seating for between six and eight people, including the pilot, or could carry a total of 470kg (1,036lbs) of payload. The craft had a range of three hours at full speed, and a 'get home' capability of operating on only one engine if necessary.

During the evaluation trials in Poole harbour, the hovercraft showed that it could withstand damage, was easy to prepare for launch, worked well over sand and mud, and crew training was comparable to that undertaken by inshore lifeboat crews. The craft was tested over a variety of terrains, including grasses, mud banks and different beach conditions. Limitations included its carrying capacity, a maximum of 470kg; an inability to work on porous surfaces; and a weather restriction to wind speeds of less than twenty-five knots and wave heights less than 0.6m (2ft).

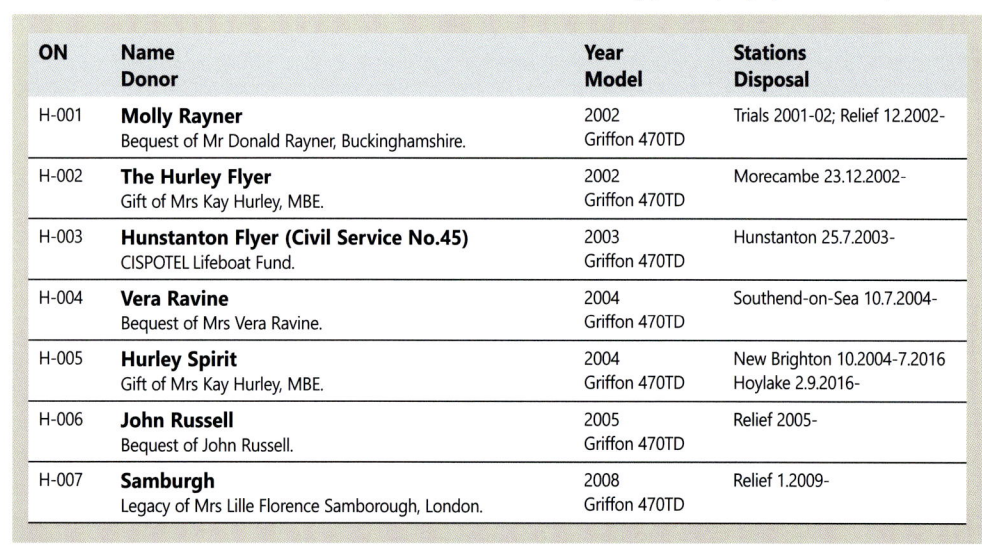

Following the trials at Poole, and as part of the hovercraft pilot scheme, the craft was taken to five lifeboat stations, selected because they had handled incidents in which a hovercraft might have been of use and because extensive sand or mudflats in the stations' areas of operation inhibited the ability of existing water-borne lifeboats. Trials were held at Hunstanton, which covers the sandbanks of the Wash; Morecambe, which covers the treacherous Morecambe Bay; Flint and West Kirby, which deal with incidents on the rivers Dee and Mersey respectively; and Southend-on-Sea, where mudflats of the Thames Estuary can cause problems.

Once all the tests had been completed, a report was submitted to the RNLI's executive committee in November 2001, which subsequently led to the decision to introduce hovercraft to the RNLI's fleet, to be co-located at existing lifeboat stations. Morecambe became the first station to have a hovercraft, with The Hurley Flyer (H-002) arriving in December 2002 and being declared operational soon thereafter. Three further hovercraft were ordered from Griffon and, by the end of 2004, Hunstanton, Southend-on-Sea, and New Brighton were all operating the craft. Subsequently the craft at New Brighton was transferred to Hoylake.

At some of the stations to which the craft were sent, notably Hunstanton, Southend and Morecambe, purpose-built new buildings were erected to house them, and various different methods of getting the craft under way were employed. At New Brighton and Morecambe an Iveco truck was supplied to transport the craft by road to a launch site, with Morecambe later getting a MAN truck; a small tractor was supplied to Southend to enable the craft to be lowered down and hauled up a small slipway.

ON	Name Donor	Year Model	Stations Disposal
H-001	**Molly Rayner** Bequest of Mr Donald Rayner, Buckinghamshire.	2002 Griffon 470TD	Trials 2001-02; Relief 12.2002-
H-002	**The Hurley Flyer** Gift of Mrs Kay Hurley, MBE.	2002 Griffon 470TD	Morecambe 23.12.2002-
H-003	**Hunstanton Flyer (Civil Service No.45)** CISPOTEL Lifeboat Fund.	2003 Griffon 470TD	Hunstanton 25.7.2003-
H-004	**Vera Ravine** Bequest of Mrs Vera Ravine.	2004 Griffon 470TD	Southend-on-Sea 10.7.2004-
H-005	**Hurley Spirit** Gift of Mrs Kay Hurley, MBE.	2004 Griffon 470TD	New Brighton 10.2004-7.2016 Hoylake 2.9.2016-
H-006	**John Russell** Bequest of John Russell.	2005 Griffon 470TD	Relief 2005-
H-007	**Samburgh** Legacy of Mrs Lille Florence Samborough, London.	2008 Griffon 470TD	Relief 1.2009-

MOTOR LIFEBOATS

H class Inshore rescue lifeboats

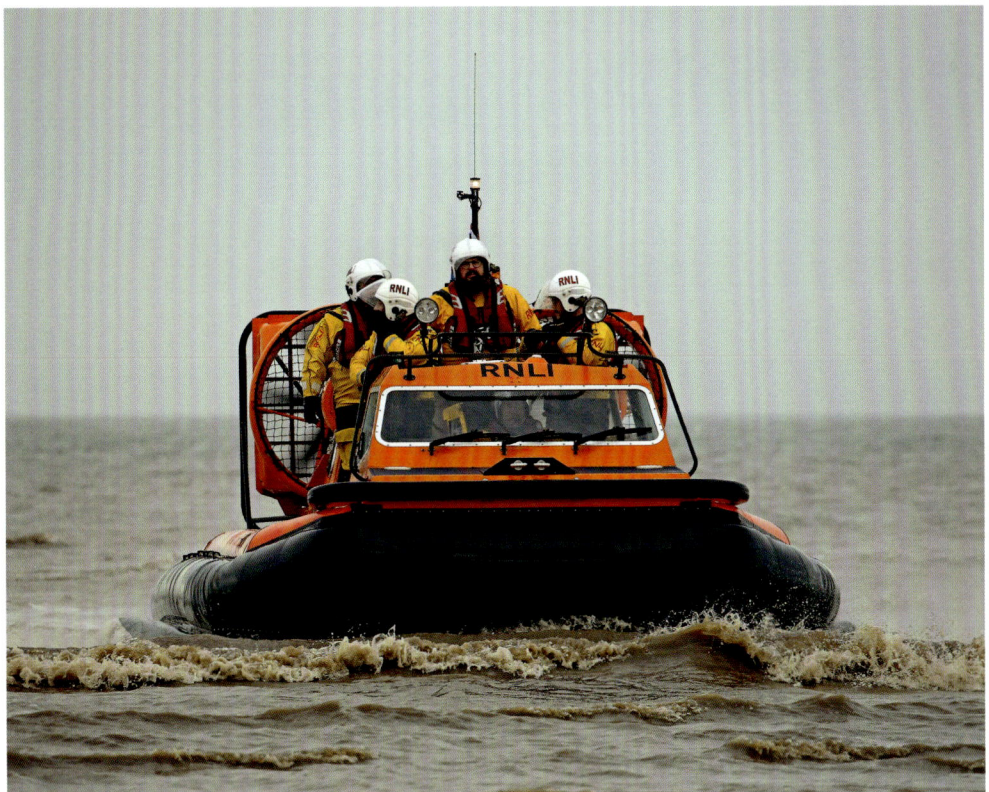

◀ The first hovercraft to become operational was The Hurley Flyer (H-002), which was sent to Morecambe in December 2002 and cost £122,000. She is pictured at Fleetwood during that station's open day. (Nicholas Leach)

◀ Hunstanton Flyer (Civil Service No.45) (H-003) on exercise on the beach at Hunstanton. She covers the dangerous sands of the Wash and has proved to be an important asset to the station. (Nicholas Leach)

▲ The relief hovercraft Samburgh (H-007) and Hurley Spirit (H-005) at New Brighton, on the banks of the Mersey estuary, during a changeover. The hovercraft covering the Mersey was moved to Hoylake in 2016. (Nicholas Leach)

▼ Vera Ravine (H-004) on the slipway at Southend-on-Sea. The small tractor is used to lower the craft down the slipway and into the Thames Estuary, and also recover it. (Nicholas Leach)

MOTOR LIFEBOATS

Appendix Lifeboats on display

There are a significant number of lifeboats on display around the United Kingdom, including many pulling and sailing craft which are not included in the main body of this book but which have been included here so as to provide a comprehensive listing of where old lifeboats can be seen. The most significant collection of former lifeboats can be found at the Historic Dockyard Chatham, which contains examples of many significant designs of motor lifeboats. Another noteworthy collection is that at the Mo Museum in Sheringham, which houses all the lifeboats that served the Norfolk station between 1904 and 2007, and includes the only Atlantic 75 ILB currently preserved. Preserving and maintaining old lifeboats is a difficult, time-consuming and usually expensive business, but as well as those lifeboats listed here, which are mostly in collections ashore, many others are maintained in private hands and in as near to original condition as possible, kept afloat and used as pleasure boats.

▲ The 35ft 6in Liverpool motor Lucy Lavers (ON.832) has been completely restored and is based at Wells, from where she operates trips.

▼ The 37ft Oakley Sir James Knott (ON.975) at Kirkleatham Old Hall Museum, Redcar.

Arreton Barns (Isle of Wight)
1887 • Queen Victoria (ON.112) • 34' self-righter
1922 • Langham (ON.676) • 40' SR motor

Ballycotton
1930 • Mary Stanford (ON.733) • 51' Barnett

Barrow (New Dock Museum)
1951 • Herbert Leigh (ON.900) • 46'9" Watson motor

Caister
1953 • W. Ross MacArthur of Glasgow (ON.906) • 35'6" Liverpool motor

Cardiff (Nantgarw)
1956 • Watkin Williams (ON.922) • 42' Watson motor

Cemaes
1907 • Charles Henry Ashley (ON.583) • 38' Watson

Historic Dockyard Chatham
1897 • St Paul (ON.406) • 38' N&S
1909 • Lizzie Porter (ON.597) • 35' self-righter
1924 • B. A. S. P. (ON.687) • 45' Watson motor
1938 • Helen Blake (ON.809) • 28' Harbour
1948 • Susan Ashley (ON.856) • 41' Watson motor
1950 • St Cybi (Civil Service No.9) (ON.884) • 52' Barnett
1951 • North Foreland (Civil Serv No.11) (ON.888) • 46'9" Watson motor
1954 • Grace Darling (ON.927) • 35'6" Liverpool motor
1957 • J. G. Gravesof Sheffield (ON.942) • 37' Oakley
1963 • The Will and Fanny Kirby (ON.972) • 37' Oakley
1964 • 44-001 • 44' Waveney
1974 • Edward Bridges (Civil Ser & Post Off No.37) (ON.1037) • 54' Arun
1987 • Spirit of Lowestoft (ON.1132) • 47' Tyne
2001 • Olive Laura Deare (E-002) • E class

Cowes (Classic Boat Museum)
1939 • Jesse Lumb (ON.822) • 46' Watson motor

Cromer (Henry Blogg Museum)
1935 • H. F. Bailey (ON.777) • 46' Watson motor

Donaghadee
1950 • Sir Samuel Kelly (ON.885) • 46'9" Watson motor

Flamborough
1953 • Friendly Forester (ON.915) • 35'6" Liverpool motor

Gorleston (old boathouse)
1923 • John and Mary Meiklam of Gladswood (ON.670) • 46'6" Norfolk & Suffolk motor

Guernsey (outside Peninsula Hotel)
1949 • J. B. Couper of Glasgow (ON.872) • 35'6" Liverpool motor

Harwich (The Green)
1967 • Valentine Wyndham-Quin (ON.985) • 37' Oakley

Hastings
1921 • Priscilla Macbean (ON.655) • 35' SR motor
1931 • Cyril and Lilian Bishop (ON.740) • 35'6" SR motor

Irvine (Scottish Maritime Museum)
1898 • Jane Anne (ON.417) • 37' self-righter
1962 • T. G. B. (ON.962) • 47' Watson motor

London (Park School, Avron Road)
1964 • William Henry and Mary King (ON.980) • 37' Oakley

Longhope
1933 • Thomas McCunn (ON.759) • 45'6" Watson motor

Lynmouth
1911 • Docea Chapman (ON.623) • 34' SR Rubie

Lytham
1901 • Chapman (ON.461) • 35ft Liverpool

Moelfre (Sea Watch Centre)
1970 • Birds Eye (ON.996) • 37' Oakley

Newbiggin
1965 • Mary Joicey (ON.984) • 37' Oakley

Peterhead
1939 • Julia Park Barry of Glasgow (ON.819) • 46'9" Watson motor

Polperro
1902 • Ryder (ON.489) • 35' self-righter

Poole (Old Lifeboat House)
1939 • Thomas Kirk Wright (ON.811) • 32' Surf

Redcar
1802 • Zetland • 31' North Country

Redcar (Kirkleatham Old Hall Museum)
1963 • Sir James Knott (ON.975) • 37' Oakley

Seaham
1950 • George Elmy (ON.873) • 35'6" Liverpool motor

Sheffield (National Emergency Services Museum)
1988 • City of Sheffield (ON.1131) • 47' Tyne

Sheringham (Mo Museum)
1904 • J. C. Madge (ON.536) • 41' Liverpool
1936 • Foresters' Centenary (ON.786) • 35'6" Liverpool motor
1960 • Manchester Unity of Oddfellows (ON.960) • 37' Oakley
1994 • Manchester Unity of Oddfellows (B-702) • Atlantic 75

Sheringham (Town Quay)
1894 • Henry Ramey Upcher • 34'8" non-self-righter

Southampton (Hythe Marina)
1966 • Ruby and Arthur Reed (ON.990) • 48'6" Oakley

Southwold
1893 • Alfred Corry (ON.353) • 44' N&S

South Shields
1833 • Tyne • 32' North Country

Swansea (Landore)
1906 • John and Naomi Beattie (ON.562) • 35' SR
1947 • William Gammon — Man & Dist XXX (ON.849) • 46'9" Watson motor

Walton-on-the-Naze
1900 • James Stevens No.14 (ON.432) • 43' Norfolk & Suffolk

Wells-next-the-Sea
1939 • Lucy Lavers (ON.832) • 35'6" Liverpool motor (kept afloat)
1965 • Ernest Tom Neathercoat (ON.982) • 37' Oakley

Whitby
1918 • Robert and Ellen Robson (ON.669) • 34' SR Rubie

NB Pulling and sailing lifeboats have been included in this list

MOTOR LIFEBOATS

Appendix Lifeboats on display

▲ Cyril and Lilian Bishop (ON.740), a 35ft 6in self-righting motor lifeboat, has been restored cosmetically for display in Hastings, where she served for almost twenty years; she went to Dunkirk in 1940 along with several other lifeboats. (Nicholas Leach)

▲ The 35ft 6in Liverpool motor Foresters' Centenary (ON.786) on display at the Mo Museum, Sheringham; built in 1936, she was on station for twenty-five years and is one of four lifeboats at the museum which served Sheringham. (Nicholas Leach)

▲ The 46ft Watson motor Julia Park Barry of Glasgow (ON.819) on display at Peterhead.

▲ The 41ft Watson motor Susan Ashley (ON.856), at the Historic Dockyard Chatham, forms part of the Lifeboat Collection, which contains many examples of historic motor lifeboats. (Nicholas Leach)

▲ The 46ft 9in Watson motor Herbert Leigh (ON.900) outside the Dock Museum in Barrow-in-Furness; she served at Barrow from 1951 to 1982, and has been at the Museum since 1989. (Nicholas Leach)

MOTOR LIFEBOATS

Index

[Not named – Brede] (1066) 33/1
[Not named – Medina] (1091) 34/3
[Not named – Mersey] (1119) 36/1
[Not named – Severn] (1179) 37/1
[Not named – Tamar] (1251) 39/1
[Charles Henry Ashley] (843) 17/27
[Herbert John] (796) 13/18
[Millie Walton] (842) 17/26
[W and B] (839) 19/1
44-001 29/1
684 RM (684) 5/13
A. E. D. (717) 10/2
A. J. R. and L. G. Uridge (1086) 32/25
A. M. T. (963) 23/13
Abdy Beauclerk (751) 14/1
Agnes Cross (663) 2/2
Aguila Wren (892) 19/18
Alan Massey (1302) 39/23
Albert Brown (1202) 37/3
Alec and Christina Dykes (1255) 37/28
Alexander Coutanche (1157) 35/39
Alexander Tulloch (622) 3/8
Alfred Albert Williams (1297) 39/18
Alfred and Clara Heath (672) 4/9
Alfred and Patience Gottwald (946) 22/8
Alice Upjohn (1048) 25/9
Always Ready (766) 13/5
Amateur Swimming Associations (1105) 33/12
Amelia (979) 24/12
Andy Pearce (1164) 36/8
Ann and James Ritchie (1171) 36/15
Ann Isabella Pyemont (798) 13/20
Ann Letitia Russell (813) 15/7
Ann Lewis Fraser (1143) 32/41
Ann Ritchie (1080) 33/2
Anna Livia (1200) 38/5
Anne Allen (760) 13/2
Annette Hutton (1277) 37/44
Annie Blaker (1153) 35/35
Annie Blanche Smith (830) 17/22
Annie Ronald and Isabella Forrest (792) 13/14
Anthony Kenneth Heard (1341) 40/35
Anthony Robert Marshall (869) 19/7
Antony Patrick Jones (1329) 40/23
Archibald and Alexander M. Paterson (924) 21/10
Arthur and Blanche Harris (1005) 29/6
Arun (1018) 32/1
Augustine Courtauld (1029) 29/11
Augustus and Laura (810) 16/3
Austin Lidbury (1233) 38/25
B. A. S. P. (687) 5/16
B. H. M. H. (882) 19/16
B. P. Forties (1050) 32/5
Babs and Agnes Robertson (1127) 35/19
Baltic Exchange (964) 23/14
Baltic Exchange II (1130) 35/20
Baltic Exchange III (1289) 39/10
Barbara Anne (1331) 40/25

Barclaycard Crusader (1209) 38/11
Barham (1065) 29/21
Barry & Peggy High Foundation (1316) 40/10
Bassett-Green (891) 19/17
Beryl Tollemache (859) 14/5
Beth Sell (1262) 37/33
Betty Huntbatch (1274) 38/37
Bingo Lifeline (1184) 36/26
Birds Eye (996) 24/25
Blue Peter VII (1198) 38/3
Bon Accord (1248) 37/24
Brianne Aldington (1328) 40/22
Brothers (671) 5/9
Bryan and Gordon (1235) 37/15
C. and S. (690) 5/19
C. D. E. C. (712) 9/10
Calouste Gulbenkian (961) 24/3
Canadian Pacific (714) 9/12
Canadian Pacific (803) 17/10
Caroline Finch (1088) 33/6
Caroline Oates Aver and William Maine (831) 13/25
Caroline Parsons (763) 12/18
Catherine (732) 9/17
Catherine Harriet Eaton (767) 12/19
Cecil and Lilian Philpott (730) 9/16
Cecil Paine (850) 19/2
Charles Brown (1093) 32/27
Charles Cooper Henderson (761) 14/2
Charles Dibdin (Civil Service No.2) (762) 14/3
Charles Dibdin (Civil Service No.32) (948) 22/9
Charles Fred Grantham (977) 24/10
Charles H. Barratt (Civil Service No.35) (987) 28/1
Charles Henry (1015) 26/4
Charles Henry Ashley (866) 20/7
Charles Lidbury (1232) 37/14
Charlotte Elizabeth (774) 9/22
Charterhouse (563) 4/1
Chieftain (864) 19/6
Christopher Pearce (1272) 37/41
City of Belfast (1107) 32/33
City of Birmingham (1012) 27/6
City of Bradford I (680) 5/12
City of Bradford II (709) 9/7
City of Bradford III (911) 20/19
City of Bradford IV (1052) 32/7
City of Bristol (1030) 28/3
City of Dublin (1113) 32/35
City of Edinburgh (1109) 35/7
City of Edinburgh (802) 17/9
City of Glasgow (362) (steam) p.11
City of Glasgow (446) (steam) p.11
City of Glasgow (720) 10/5
City of Glasgow II (899) 21/6
City of Glasgow III (1134) 32/38
City of Leeds (881) 12/27
City of London (1074) 35/1
City of London II (1220) 37/9

City of London III (1294) 39/15
City of Nottingham (726) 12/1
City of Plymouth (1136) 32/40
City of Sheffield (1131) 35/21
Civil Service No.35 (987) 28/1
Civil Service No.4 (756) 12/16
Civil Service No.5 (753) 9/20
Civil Service No.6 (784) 17/3
Clara and Emily Barwell (893) 19/19
Clarissa Langdon (793) 13/15
Claude Cecil Staniforth (943) 21/15
Connel Elizabeth Cargill (1006) 29/7
Constance Calverley (902) 19/22
Corinne Whiteley (1253) 38/32
Cosandra (1319) 40/13
Countess Mountbatten of Burma (1072) 34/2
Crawford and Constance Conybeare (829) 17/21
Cunard (728) 9/14
Cuttle (833) 13/27
Cyril and Lilian Bishop (740) 12/6
Daniel L. Gibson (1269) 37/38
David and Elizabeth Acland (1243) 37/21
David and Elizabeth King & E. B. (1010) 27/4
David Kirkaldy (1217) 37/6
David Robinson (1145) 35/30
Davina and Charles Matthews Hunter (1078) 32/21
Davys Family (1064) 25/13
Deneys Reitz (919) 20/20
Denise and Eric (1327) 40/21
Derek Bullivant (1315) 40/9
Diamond Jubilee (1303) 39/24
Diana White (999) 25/2
Doctors (983) 24/16
Donald and Barbara Broadhead (1276) 37/43
Dora Foster McDougall (1228) 38/24
Doris Bleasdale (1190) 36/32
Doris M. Mann of Ampthill (1161) 36/5
Dorothy and Philip Constant (967) 22/7
Dorothy May White (1326) 40/20
Douglas Aikman Smith (1206) 38/8
Douglas Currie (1021) 27/11
Douglas Hyde (896) 20/14
Dr John McSparran (1246) 38/30
Duchess of Kent (1077) 32/20
Duchess of Kent (908) 20/17
Duke of Atholl (1160) 32/46
Duke of Connaught (649) 5/3
Duke of Connaught (668) 5/8
Duke of Cornwall (Civ Ser No.33) (952) 21/19
Duke of Kent (1055) 25/11
Duke of Kent (1278) 37/45
Duke of Montrose (934) 22/5
Duke of Northumberland (231) (steam) p.11
Duke of York (769) 15/2
Dunleary (Civil Service No.7) (658) 5/6
Dunleary II (814) 17/13
Dunnet Head (Civil Service No.31) (920) 23/1
E. C. J. R. (879) 12/25

E. M. E. D. (705) 8/3
E. M. M. Gordon Cubbin (936) 21/12
Earl and Countess Howe (968) 26/1
Earl and Countess Mountbatten of Burma (1180) 38/1
Edgar, George, Orlando and Eva Child (861) 19/3
Edian Courtauld (910) 20/18
Edith Clauson-Thue (895) 19/21
Edith Emilie (1062) 32/14
Edmund and Mary Robinson (812) 15/6
Edmund Hawthorn Micklewood (1313) 40/7
Edna Windsor (1230) 37/12
Edward and Barbara Prigmore (1290) 39/11
Edward and Isabella Irwin (778) 17/2
Edward and Mary Lester (991) 24/20
Edward Bridges (Civil Service & Post Office No.37) (1037) 32/3
Edward Duke of Windsor (1226) 38/22
Edward Z. Dresden (707) 9/5
Edward, Prince of Wales (678) 5/10
Effseabee Too (1285) 40/1
Eleanor and Bryant Girling (1188) 36/30
Elizabeth and Albina Whitley (772) 13/11
Elizabeth and Gertrude Allan (1330) 40/24
Elizabeth and Leonard (1323) 40/17
Elizabeth and Ronald (1215) 38/17
Elizabeth Ann (1032) 31/2
Elizabeth Ann (1058) 32/11
Elizabeth Elson (713) 9/11
Elizabeth Fairlie Ramsey (1270) 37/39
Elizabeth Newton (679) 5/11
Elizabeth of Glamis (1252) 38/31
Elizabeth Rippon (865) 20/6
Elizabeth Wills Allen (791) 13/13
Ella Larsen (1337) 40/31
Elliot Galer (602) 3/4
Elliott Gill (918) 19/31
Elsie (648) 5/2
Emma Constance (693) 7/2
Enid Collett (1295) 39/16
Enid of Yorkshire (1101) 33/9
Eric and Susan Hiscock (Wanderer) (1249) 37/25
Eric Seal (Civil Service No.36) (1026) 29/8
Ernest and Mabel (1261) 37/32
Ernest and Mary Shaw (1241) 37/19
Ernest Tom Neathercoat (982) 24/15
Ernest William and Elizabeth Ellen Hinde (1017) 30/1
Esme Anderson (1197) 38/2
Ethel Anne Measures (1096) 35/5
Ethel Day Cardwell (647) 4/7
Ethel Mary (949) 21/18
Euphrosyne Kendal (912) 21/7
Fairlight (973) 24/6
Faithful Forester (1003) 29/4
Famous Grouse (1133) 35/23
Fanny Victoria Wilkinson and Frank Stubbs (1175) 36/19

Field Marshall and Mrs Smuts (846) 17/28
Fifi and Charles (765) 13/4
Fisherman's Friend (1192) 36/34
Foresters' Centenary (786) 13/12
Foresters Future (1090) 33/8
Forward Birmingham (1210) 38/12
Four Boys (1176) 36/20
Francis W. Wotherspoon of Paisley (951) 23/5
Frank and Anne Wilkinson (1286) 39/7
Frank and Lena Clifford of Stourbridge (1172) 36/16
Frank and William Oates (795) 13/17
Frank Penfold Marshall (992) 24/21
Frank Spiller Locke (939) 21/14
Fraser Flyer (Civil Service No.43) (1237) 37/17
Freddie Cooper (1193) 36/35
Frederick and Emma (659) 5/7
Frederick Angus (757) 12/17
Frederick Edward Crick (970) 23/17
Frederick H. Pilley (657) 1/7
Frederick Kitchen (621) 3/7
Frederick Storey Cockburn (1205) 38/7
Frederick William Plaxton (1322) 40/16
Friendly Forester (915) 19/28
G. W. (724) 3/15
Garside (1139) 35/26
General Farrell (614) 4/4
George and Caroline Ermen (877) 19/15
George and Elizabeth Gow (827) 13/24
George and Ivy Swanson (1211) 38/13
George and Mary Webb (1212) 38/14
George and Olive Turner (1061) 32/13
George and Sarah Strachan (749) 9/19
George Elmy (873) 19/11
George Gibson (1140) 35/27
George Shee (734) 10/8
George Sullivan (1292) 39/13
George Thomas Lacy (1320) 40/14
George Urie Scott (1007) 27/1
Ger Tigchelaar (1223) 38/19
Gertrude (847) 17/29
Glencoe, Glasgow (857) 15/11
Good Hope (821) 17/18
Good Shepherd (1115) 35/12
Gordon Warren (835) 16/7
Gough-Ritchie (1051) 32/6
Gough-Ritchie II (1234) 38/26
Grace Darling (1173) 36/17
Grace Darling (927) 19/32
Grace Dixon (1288) 39/9
Grace Paterson Ritchie (988) 28/2
Greater London (Civil Service No.3) (704) 8/2
Greater London II (Civ Ser No.30) (921) 20/21
Guide of Dunkirk (826) 12/22
Guy and Clare Hunter (926) 20/23
H. C. J. (708) 9/6
H. F. Bailey (670) 2/3
H. F. Bailey (694) 5/21
H. F. Bailey (777) 17/1
H. F Bailey II (714) 9/12

262   MOTOR LIFEBOATS

Index

Hampshire Rose (1024) 25/6
Har-Lil (993) 24/22
Harold Salvesen (1022) 25/4
Harriot Dixon (770) 13/9
Haydn Miller (1281) 39/3
Hearts of Oak (684) 5/13
Helen Blake (809) 18/1
Helen Comrie (1284) 39/6
Helen Hastings (1336) 40/30
Helen Peele (478) (steam) p.11
Helen Smitton (603) 3/5
Helen Sutton (799) 13/21
Helen Turnbull (1027) 29/9
Helen Wycherley (959) 23/11
Helena Harris - Man & Dist XXXI (903) 19/23
Helmut Schroder of Dunlossit (1032) 31/2
Helmut Schroder of Dunlossit II (1219) 37/8
Henry Alston Hewat (1250) 37/26
Henry Blogg (840) 17/24
Henry Comber Brown (925) 20/22
Henry Frederick Swan (646) 4/6
Henry Heys Duckworth (1213) 38/15
Henry Vernon (613) 4/3
Her Majesty the Queen (1189) 36/31
Herbert John (825) 13/23
Herbert Joy (683) 6/2
Herbert Joy II (742) 12/8
Herbert Leigh (900) 20/15
Hermione Lady Colwyn (1158) 35/40
Hetty Rampton (1120) 35/15
Hibernia (1150) 32/44
Hilda Jarrett (1137) 35/24
Hilton Briggs (889) 21/3
Horace Clarkson (1047) 25/8
Howard D (797) 13/19
Howard Marryat (932) 20/28
Hugh William, Viscount Gough (1020) 27/10
Hyman Winstone (1067) 32/15
Ian and Anne Butler () T/
Ian Grant Smith (1317) 40/11
Inbhear Mor (807) 15/4
Inchcape (1194) 36/36
Inner Wheel (1089) 33/7
Inner Wheel II (1245) 38/29
Irene Muriel Rees (1299) 39/20
Isa and Penryn Milsted (917) 19/30
Isaac and Mary Bolton (880) 12/26
Ivan Ellen (1265) 37/36
J. and W. (722) 3/13
J. B. Couper of Glasgow (872) 19/10
J. B. Proudfoot (694) 5/21
J. G. Gravesof Sheffield (942) 24/1
J. H. W. (738) 12/4
J. Reginald Corah (1023) 25/5
J. W. Archer (685) 5/14
J. W. Archer (933) 22/4
J.J.K.S.W. (702) 10/1
Jack Shayler and the Lees (1009) 27/3
James and Barbara Aitken (909) 22/2
James and Catherine Macfarlane (979) 24/12

James and Catherine Macfarlane (989) 26/2
James and Margaret Boyd (913) 21/8
James and Mariska Joicey (1008) 27/2
James and Ruby Jackson (876) 19/14
James Ball Ritchie (995) 24/24
James Bibby (1117) 35/14
James Burrough (1094) 35/3
James Cable (1068) 25/14
James Macfee (711) 9/9
James Stevens No.3 (420) (steam) p.11
James Stevens No.4 (421) (steam) p.11
Jane Hay (974) 24/7
Jane Holland (673) 4/10
Jean Charcot (844) 17a/2
Jeanie (957) 23/9
Jeanie Speirs (788) 17/5
Jesse Lumb (822) 17/19
Jim Moffat (1275) 38/38
Joanna and Henry Williams (1334) 40/28
Jock and Annie Slater (1308) 40/2
Joel and April Grunnill (1324) 40/18
John A Hay (561) 1/1
John and Charles Kennedy (790) 17/7
John and Frances Macfarlane (956) 21/20
John and Lucy Cordingley (868) 20/9
John and Margaret Doig (1218) 37/7
John and Mary Meiklam of Gladswood (663) 2/2
John and Mary Meiklam of Gladswood (670) 2/3
John and Sarah Eliza Stych (743) 12/9
John and William Mudie (752) 12/15
John Buchanan Barr (1301) 39/22
John D. Spicer (1304) 39/25
John F. Kennedy (1001) 29/2
John Fison (1060) 29/20
John Gellatly Hyndman (923) 21/9
John Metters (1333) 40/27
John Neville Taylor (1266) 38/35
John Pyemont (824) 15/9
John R Webb (684) 5/13
John R. Webb (729) 9/15
John Russell (699) 9/2
John Ryburn (565) 3/2
John Ryburn (837) 16/9
John Taylor Cardwell (642) 4/5
Jose Neville (834) 13/28
Joseph Adlam (654) 5/5
Joseph Braithwaite (773) 13/12
Joseph Hiram Chadwick (898) 21/5
Joseph Rothwell Sykes and Hilda M (1099) 32/29
Joseph Soar (Civil Service No.34) (971) 23/18
Joy and Charles Beeby (1191) 36/33
Joy and John Wade (1053) 32/8
Julia Park Barry of Glasgow (819) 17/16
Julian and Margaret Leonard (1271) 37/40
K .T. J. S. (698) 9/1
K. B. M. (681) 3/11
K. E. C. F. (700) 9/3

Kate Greatorex (816) 16/5
Katherine and Virgoe Buckland (905) 19/25
Kathleen Mary (950) 23/4
Katie Hannan (1247) 37/23
Keep Fit Association (1170) 36/14
Keith Anderson (1106) 32/32
Kenneth James Pierpoint (1321) 40/15
Kenneth Thelwall (1123) 32/37
Kenneth Thelwall II (1154) 35/36
Khami (1002) 29/3
Killarney (1298) 39/19
Kingdom of Fife (1174) 36/18
Kiwi (1305) 39/26
L. P. and St Helen (703) 6/3
Lady Harrison (745) 12/11
Lady Jane and Martha Ryland (731) 10/6
Lady Kylsant (721) 3/12
Lady MacRobert (1019) 27/9
Lady Murphy (997) 24/26
Lady of Hilbre (1163) 36/7
Lady of Lancashire (1036) 29/15
Lady Rank (1114) 35/11
Lady Rothes (641) 1/6
Lady Scott (Civil Service No.4) (867) 20/8
Langham (676) 4/13
Laura Moncur (958) 23/10
Laurana Sarah Blunt (744) 12/10
Lawrence Ardern, Stockport (817) 16/6
Leonard Kent (1177) 36/21
Leonore Chilcott (1083) 33/3
Lester (1287) 39/8
Lifetime Care (1148) 36/4
Lil Cunningham (1183) 36/25
Lilla Marras, Douglas and Will (928) 20/24
Lilly and Vincent Anthony (1168) 36/12
Lilly Wainwright (976) 24/9
Lily Glen - Glasgow (739) 12/5
Lincolnshire Poacher (1166) 36/10
Lloyd's (754) 10/10
Lloyd's II (986) 24/19
Lord Saltoun (1138) 35/25
Lord Southborough (Civil Service No.1) (688) 5/17
Louis Marchesi of Round Table (1045) 29/19
Louisa Anne Hawker (965) 23/15
Louisa Polden (737) 12/3
Louise Stephens (820) 17/17
Lucy Lavers (832) 13/26
M. O. Y. E. (695) 5/22
M. T. C. (878) 12/24
Mabel Alice (1085) 32/24
Mabel E. Holland (937) 22/6
Mabel Marion Thompson (818) 17/15
Mabel Williams (1159) 32/45
MacQuarie (1225) 38/21
Manchester and Salford (689) 5/18
Manchester and Salford XXIX (841) 17/25
Manchester Unity of Oddfellows (960) 24/2
Margaret (947) 23/3
Margaret Dawson (782) 13/11

Margaret Foster (1231) 37/13
Margaret Frances Love (1082) 32/23
Margaret Graham (1004) 29/5
Margaret Harker Smith (667) 4/8
Margaret Jean (1178) 36/22
Margaret Joan and Fred Nye (1279) 37/46
Margaret Russell Fraser (1108) 32/34
Maria (560) 3/1
Maria Noble (916) 19/29
Marie Winstone (1076) 32/19
Marine Engineer (1169) 36/13
Mariners Friend (1142) 35/29
Mark Mason (1291) 39/12
Mary Ann Blunt (748) 12/14
Mary Ann Hepworth (808) 15/5
Mary Gabriel (1000) 25/3
Mary Irene Millar (1151) 35/33
Mary Joicey (984) 24/17
Mary Margaret (1187) 36/29
Mary Pullman (981) 24/14
Mary Scott (691) 2/4
Mary Stanford (733) 10/7
Matthew Simpson (823) 15/8
Maurice and Joyce Hardy (1179) 37/1
Maurice and Joyce Hardy (1222) 38/18
Max Aitken III (1126) 35/18
Merchant Navy (1087) 33/5
Michael and Jane Vernon (1221) 37/10
Michael and Lily Davis (901) 20/16
Michael O'Brian (1338) 40/32
Michael Stephens (838) 17/23
Mickie Salvesen (1135) 32/39
Milburn (692) 5/20
Millie Walton (840) 17/24
Millie Walton (848) 17/30
Minister Anseele (845) 17a/1
Misses Robertson of Kintail (1282) 39/4
Moira Barrie (1185) 36/27
Mollie Hunt (1296) 39/17
Mona (775) 9/23
Moonbeam (1152) 35/34
Mora Edith Macdonald (1227) 38/23
Morison Watson (741) 12/7
Morrell (1309) 40/3
Mountbatten of Burma (1069) 34/1
Murray Lornie (1144) 32/42
Myrtle Maud (1244) 37/22
N. T. (701) 9/4
Nellie and Charlie (764) 13/3
Nelsons of Donaghadee (1043) 29/17
Newbons (674) 4/11
Newsbuoy (1103) 32/31
Nora Stachura (1318) 40/12
Norah Wortley (1306) 39/27
Norman B. Corlett (883) 21/1
Norman Nasmyth (836) 16/8
Norman Salvesen (1121) 35/16
North Foreland (Civ Serv No.11) (888) 20/13
Nottinghamshire (1102) 33/10
Oldham (750) 13/1

Oldham IV (894) 19/20
Osier (1263) 37/34
Osman Gabriel (998) 25/1
Owen and Ann Aisher (1122) 35/17
Patsy Knight (1312) 40/6
Peggy and Alex Caird (1124) 36/2
Pentland (Civil Service No.31) (940) 23/2
Peter and Lesley-Jane Nicholson (1280) 39/2
Peter and Marion Fulton (1179) 37/1
Peter and Sarah Blake (755) 10/11
Phil Mead (1110) 35/8
Philip Vaux (1084) 33/4
Pride and Spirit (1186) 36/28
Pride of the Humber (1216) 37/5
Prince David (677) 3/10
Princess Alexandra of Kent (945) 21/17
Princess Marina (1016) 26/5
Princess Mary (715) 7/4
Princess of Wales (1063) 25/12
Princess Royal (Civil Service No.7) (828) 17/20
Princess Royal (Civil Service No.41) (1167) 36/11
Priscilla Macbean (655) 6/1
Prudential (697) 8/1
Queen (404) (steam) p.11
Queen Mother (1149) 32/43
Queen Victoria (719) 10/4
R. A. Colby Cubbin No.1 (929) 20/25
R. A. Colby Cubbin No.2 (930) 20/26
R. A. Colby Cubbin No.3 (935) 21/11
R. and J. Welburn (1310) 40/4
R. Hope Roberts (1011) 27/5
R. L. P. (858) 15/12
R. P. L. (897) 17/6
Rachel and Mary Evans (806) 15/3
Ralph and Bonella Farrant (1081) 32/22
Ralph and Joy Swann (1042) 29/16
Ramsay-Dyce (944) 21/16
Rankin (776) 10/12
Reg (1314) 40/8
RFA Sir Galahad (1112) 35/10
Richard and Caroline Colton (1335) 40/29
Richard Ashley (875) 19/13
Richard Cox Scott (1256) 37/29
Richard Evans (Civ Serv No.39) (1070) 32/16
Richard Silver Oliver (794) 13/16
Richard Vernon and Mary Garforth of Leeds (931) 20/27
Robert (955) 23/8
Robert and Dorothy Hardcastle (966) 24/4
Robert and Marcella Beck (696) 7/3
Robert and Phemia Brown (904) 19/24
Robert and Violet (1116) 35/13
Robert Charles Brown (1182) 36/24
Robert Edgar (1073) 32/18
Robert Hywel Jones Williams (1239) 38/27
Robert Lindsay (874) 19/12
Robert Patton - The Always Ready (766) 13/5
Robert Theophilus Garden (609) 4/2
Roger and Joy Freeman (1260) 37/31

Index

Rosa Woodd and Phyllis Lunn (758) 15/1
Rosabella (779) 16/1
Rose (1300) 39/21
Rotary Service (1031) 31/1
Rowland Watts (938) 21/13
Roy and Barbara Harding (1118) 32/36
Roy Barker I (1199) 38/4
Roy Barker II (1224) 38/20
Roy Barker III (1258) 38/33
Roy Barker IV (1307) 39/28
Royal British Legion Jubilee (1013) 27/7
Royal Shipwright (1162) 36/6
Royal Silver Jubilee 1910-1935 (780) 16/2
Royal Thames (978) 24/11
Royal Thames (1195) 36/37
Ruby and Arthur Reed (990) 26/3
Ruby and Arthur Reed II (1097) 35/6
Ruby Clery (1181) 36/23
Ruth and David Harper (1339) 40/33
S. G. E. (787) 17/4
S. G. E. (804) 17/11
Safeway (1104) 33/11
Sam and Ada Moody (1240) 38/28
Sam and Joan Woods (1075) 35/2
Samarbeta (1208) 38/10
Samuel and Marie Parkhouse (805) 17/12
Samuel Oakes (651) 3/9
Sarah Ann Austin (800) 13/22
Sarah Emily Harrop (1155) 35/37
Sarah Jane and James Season (953) 23/6
Sarah Tilson (854) 20/4

Sarah Townsend Porritt (886) 20/11
Sarah Ward and William David Crossweller (716) 9/13
Saxon (1267) 38/36
Scout (1044) 29/18
Sealink Endeavour (1125) 36/3
Shamrock (649) 5/3
Shoreline (1054) 25/10
Silver Jubilee (Civil Service No.38) (1046) 25/7
Silvia Burrell (1196) 36/38
Sir Arthur Rose (801) 17/8
Sir David Richmond of Glasgow (723) 3/14
Sir Fitzroy Clayton (628) 1/5
Sir Godfrey Baring (887) 20/12
Sir Heath Harrison (785) 12/21
Sir James Knott (975) 24/8
Sir John Fisher (1141) 35/28
Sir Max Aitken (1071) 32/17
Sir Max Aitken II (1098) 32/28
Sir Ronald Pechell Bt (1207) 38/9
Sir Samuel Kelly (885) 20/10
Sir William Arnold (1025) 32/2
Sir William Hillary (725) 11/1
Sir William Hillary (1147) 35/32
Snolda (1100) 32/30
Soldian (1057) 32/10
Solomon Browne (954) 23/7
Southern Africa (860) 10/13
Spirit of Derbyshire (1165) 36/9
Spirit of Guernsey (1203) 37/4
Spirit of Lowestoft (1132) 35/22

Spirit of Northumberland (1242) 37/20
Spirit of Padstow (1283) 39/5
Spirit of Tayside (1056) 32/9
St Albans (863) 19/5
St Andrew (Civil Service No.10) (897) 15/13
St Brendan (1092) 32/26
St Cybi (Civil Service No.9) (884) 21/2
St Cybi II (Civil Service No.40) (1095) 35/4
St Patrick (1035) 29/14
Stanhope Smart (747) 12/13
Stanley Watson Barker (1214) 38/16
Stella and Humfrey Berkeley (1332) 40/26
Storm Rider (1311) 40/5
Susan Ashley (856) 15/10
Swn-Y-Mor (Civil Service No.6) (784) 17/3
Sybil Mullen Glover (1264) 37/35
T. B. B. H. (686) 5/15
T. G. B. (962) 23/12
Taylors (The) (1273) 37/42
Thomas and Annie Wade Richards (768) 12/20
Thomas Corbett (862) 19/4
Thomas Forehead and Mary Rowse (890) 21/4
Thomas Forehead and Mary Rowse II (1028) 29/10
Thomas James King (1034) 29/13
Thomas Kirk Wright (811) 16/4
Thomas Markby (706) 4/14
Thomas McCunn (759) 9/21
Three Sisters (1014) 27/8

Three Sisters (771) 13/10
Tillie Morrison, Sheffield (851) 12/23
Tillie Morrison, Sheffield II (914) 19/27
Tom Sanderson (1238) 37/18
Tony Vandervell (1049) 32/4
Tynesider (852) 20/2
V. C. S. (675) 4/12
Valentine Wyndham-Quin (985) 24/18
Victor Freeman (1293) 39/14
Vincent Nesfield (994) 24/23
Violet Armstrong (815) 17/14
Violet, Dorothy and Kathleen (1236) 37/16
Viscountess Wakefield (783) 14/4
Voluntary Worker (1146) 35/31
Volunteer Spirit (1254) 37/27
W. and S. (736) 9/18
W. M. Tilson (855) 20/5
W. R. A. (781) 13/10
W. Ross MacArthur of Glasgow (906) 19/26
Walter and Margaret Couper (1059) 32/12
Watkin Williams (922) 22/3
Wavy Line (1043) 29/17
Westmorland (727) 12/2
White Rose of Yorkshire (1033) 29/12
White Star (710) 9/8
Whiteheads (The) (1229) 37/11
Will (The) (1201) 37/2
Will and Fanny Kirby (972) 24/5
William and Clara Ryland (735) 10/9
William and Harriot (718) 10/3
William and Jane (1079) 29/22

William and Kate Johnston (682) 7/1
William and Laura (595) 3/3
William and Laura (870) 19/8
William and Mary Durham (941) 22/6
William Blannin (1268) 37/37
William Cantrell Ashley (871) 19/9
William Evans (653) 5/4
William F. Yates (1325) 40/19
William Gammon - Manchester and District XXX (849) 20/1
William Gordon Burr (1257) 37/30
William Henry and Mary King (980) 24/13
William Luckin (1111) 35/9
William MacPherson (620) 3/6
William Maynard (746) 12/12
William Myers and Sarah Jane Myers (969) 23/16
William Street (1156) 35/38
William Taylor of Oldham (907) 22/1
Willie and May Gall (1259) 38/34
Windsor Runner (Civ Serv No.42) (1204) 38/6
Winston Churchill (Civ Serv No.8) (853) 20/3

- The official number (ON) is in brackets
- The index entries refer to the list number and the boat's number within the list.
- Some lifeboats have 'The' in their name, but as this is somewhat inconsistent it has been omitted most index entries

Bibliography

Barnett, James R. (1933): *Modern Motor Lifeboats* (Blackie, Glasgow).

— (1936): Recent Developments in the Motor Lifeboats of the RNLI (*International Lifeboat Conference Report*, 1936, pp.146-153).

— (1940): Fifty Years of Lifeboat Design (in *The Lifeboat*, Apr 1940, pp.233-235).

— (1950): *Modern Motor Lifeboats* (Blackie, Glasgow).

Cameron, Ian (2002): Riders of the Storm (Weidenfeld & Nicolson, London).

Denton, Tony and Leonard, Richie (2019): *Lifeboat Enthusiasts Handbook 2019* (Lifeboat Enthusiasts' Society).

Dutton, Lt Cdr W.L.G. (1975): Review of the Royal National Lifeboat Institution's Lifeboats in the Twentieth Century.

Fry, Eric (1975): *Lifeboat Design and Development* (David & Charles, London).

Kirton, Tim (1987): The Watsons: Variations on a theme (LBES Newsletter, No.87, pp.8-13).

Hudson, F.D., Hicks, I.A. and Cripps, R.M. (1993): The design and development of modern lifeboats (*Institute of Mechanical Engineers*, Vol 207).

Leach, Nicholas (2001): *The Waveney Lifeboats: An illustrated history of the RNLI 44ft Waveney lifeboats 1967-1999* (Bernard McCall, Portishead).

— (2001): *A Saviour of Souls: William and Kate Johnston, the story of a legendary prototype lifeboat* (Norfolk & Suffolk Research Group).

— (2003): *Oakley Lifeboats: An Illustrated History of the RNLI's Oakley and Rother Lifeboats* (Tempus Publishing Ltd, Stroud).

— (2005): *RNLI Motor Lifeboats* (Landmark Publishing Limited, Ashbourne).

— (2011): *Arun Lifeboats: An Illustrated History of the Arun Lifeboats 1971-2009* (Kelsey Publishing Ltd, Cudham, Kent).

— (2018): *The Lifeboat Service in Wales, station by station* (Foxglove Publishing, Lichfield).

— (2019): *Clyde Rescue Cruisers: The RNLI's rescue cruisers, their and history* (Foxglove Publishing, Lichfield).

RNLI (1902): Sketch of the progress made in the Construction of Coast Lifeboat in Great Britain 1785-1900 (in *The Lifeboat*, Vol.XVIII, 1.2.1902, pp.289-293).

Swann, Cdr F.R.H. (1973): Lifeboat Development (in *Yachting World*, Jan 1973).

— (1973): Technical Developments in the Lifeboat Service (in *The Lifeboat*, Vol.XLII, No.443, pp.446-452).

Welford, S.E. (1974): Is it Right to Right? The development of the self-righting lifeboat (in *Naval Architect*, July, p.93).